·2026·

SPECIAL INFORMATION
SERVICE COMPANY

KOREAN NATIONAL POLICE UNIVERSITY

경찰대학
기출문제

영 어

2025~2016

10
개년

연차별 동형
기출문제

영어

2026
경찰
대학
기출문제

10 총·정·리
2025~2016학년도
개년

인쇄일 2025년 3월 1일 10판 1쇄 인쇄
발행일 2025년 3월 5일 10판 1쇄 발행
등 록 제17-269호
판 권 시스컴2025

발행처 시스컴 출판사
발행인 송인식
지은이 경찰대학입시연구회

ISBN 979-11-6941-648-1 13740
정 가 23,000원

주소 서울시 금천구 가산디지털1로 225, 514호(가산포휴) | **홈페이지** www.nadoogong.com
E-mail siscombooks@naver.com | **전화** 02)866-9311 | **Fax** 02)866-9312

발간 이후 발견된 정오사항은 나두공 홈페이지 도서정오표에서 알려드립니다.(나두공 홈페이지 → 자격증 → 도서정오표)
이 책의 무단 복제, 복사, 전재 행위는 저작권법에 저촉됩니다. 파본은 구입처에서 교환하실 수 있습니다.

머리말

경찰대학은 국가치안부문에 종사하는 경찰간부가 될 자에게 학술을 연마하게 하고 심신을 단련시키기 위하여 설립된 국립대학입니다. 경찰대학을 졸업하면 초급 간부인 경위로 임관하여 국가 수호의 주도적인 역할을 하게 됩니다. 즉, 경찰대학에는 졸업과 동시에 취업이 보장된다는 이점이 있기 때문에 해마다 응시 인원이 증가하고 있어 경찰대학의 높은 인기를 실감할 수 있습니다.

그렇다면 경찰대학에 입학하려면 무엇이 가장 중요할까요?

당연한 말이지만 바로 1차 필기시험입니다. 왜냐하면 1차 시험에서 6배수 안에 들어야 그 다음 사정에 응시할 수 있는 기회가 주어지기 때문입니다. 1차 시험을 잘 보기 위해서는 무엇보다도 기출문제를 꼼꼼하게 파악하고 풀어보는 것이 중요합니다. 그래야 실제 시험에서 긴장하지 않고 실수를 최소화할 수 있기 때문입니다. 기출문제 풀이는 모든 시험의 필수적인 요소라고 할 수 있습니다.

이에 본서는 경찰대학 입시에 필수적인 과년도 최신 기출문제를 실어 연도별로 기출문제를 풀어볼 수 있도록 구성하였으며, 정답 및 해설에서 알기 쉽고 자세하게 풀이하였습니다.

본서는 여러분의 합격을 응원합니다!

경찰대학 입학 전형

모집 정원

50명(남녀통합선발)(일반전형 44명, 특별전형 6명)
※학과는 법학과/행정학과 각 25명 정원이며 2학년 진학 시 결정
※일반/특별전형 미충원 시 다른 전형 정원으로 전환함

지원 자격

- 1984. 1. 1부터 2009. 12. 31까지 출생한 대한민국 국적을 가진 자
  ※군복무 기간 1년 미만은 1세, 1년 이상~2년 미만은 2세, 2년 이상은 3세 연장
- 고등학교 졸업자, 2026. 2월 졸업예정자 또는 법령에 따라 이와 같은 수준 이상의 학력이 있다고 인정된 자
  ※인문·자연계열 구분 없이 응시 가능
  ※검정고시 응시자는 2025년 12월 31일 이전에 합격한 사람에 한함

결격 사유

-「경찰공무원법」제8조 제2항의 결격사유에 해당하는 자
  ※「국적법」제11조의2 제1항의 복수국적자는 입학 전까지 외국 국적 포기 절차가 완료되어야 함
- 경찰대학 학생모집 시험규칙으로 정한 신체기준(신체 조건과 체력 조건을 말한다)에 미달하는 자
- 위에서 지원 자격으로 제시된 학력, 연령, 국적에 해당하지 않는 자

1차 시험 방법

과 목		국 어	영 어	수 학
문 항 수		45문항	45문항	25문항
시험시간		60분	60분	80분
출제형태		객관식(5지 택일 형태) ※수학은 단답형 주관식 5문항 포함		
배점	전체	100점	100점	100점
	문항	2점, 3점	2점, 3점	3점, 4점, 5점
출제범위		독서, 문학	영어 I, 영어 II	수학 I, 수학 II

전형 절차

구 분		내 용	장 소
인터넷 원서접수 (11일간)		▪ 대학 홈페이지에 접속하여 원서접수 (대행업체 홈페이지와 링크)	인터넷
1차 시험	시험	▪ 지구(14개) : 서울 · 부산 · 대구 · 인천 · 광주 · 대전 · 경기 · 강 원 · 충북 · 전북 · 경남 · 울산 · 제주 · 충남 ※ 지정장소는 원서접수 후 홈페이지 공지 ▪ 수험표, 컴퓨터용 사인펜, 수정테이프, 신분증(주민등록증, 학생증, 운전면허증, 여권 등 사진 대조 가능) 휴대	응시지구 지방경찰청 지정장소
	시험문제 이의제기	홈페이지 1차 시험 이의 제기 코너에서 이의 접수	인터넷
	합격자 발표	▪ 대학 홈페이지 발표 ▪ 원서접수 홈페이지 성적 개별 확인	인터넷
2차 시험	구비서류 제출	미제출자 불합격 처리	인편 또는 등기우편
	자기소개서 제출	제출 기간 내 원서 접수 대행업체 "자기소개서 업로드"에 작 성 완료한 자기소개서 제출(파일 업로드)	인터넷
	신체검사서 제출	경찰공무원 채용 신체검사(약물검사 포함) 가능한 국 · 공립 병원 또는 종합병원에서 개별 수검(검사비용 등 수험생 부담) ※ 미제출자 불합격 처리	인편 또는 등기우편
	체력 · 적성검사, 면접시험	세부 일정은 1차 시험 후 홈페이지 공지 ※ 식비는 수험생 부담	경찰대학
최종 합격자 발표		대학 홈페이지 발표	인터넷
합격자 등록		원서접수 홈페이지에서 입학등록 및 입학등록표 출력	인터넷
1차 추가합격자 발표		원서접수 홈페이지 개별 확인	인터넷
1차 추가합격자 등록		원서접수 홈페이지에서 입학등록 및 입학등록표 출력 ※ 이후 등록포기자 발생 시 개별 통지	인터넷
청람교육 입교		본인이 직접 입교 후 합숙 예정 ※ 미입교 및 퇴교자 발생 시 추가합격 개별 통지	경찰대학

신체 및 체력조건

– 신체조건(남 · 여 공통)

구 분	내 용
체격	국 · 공립병원 또는 종합병원에서 실시한 경찰공무원 채용시험 신체검사 및 약물검사의 결과 건강상태가 양호하고, 직무에 적합한 신체를 가져야 함
시력	시력(교정시력 포함)은 좌 · 우 각각 0.8 이상이어야 함
색각	색각 이상(약도 색약은 제외)이 아니어야 함
청력	정상(좌우 각각 40데시벨(db) 이하의 소리를 들을 수 있는 경우를 말함)이어야 함
혈압	고혈압 또는 저혈압이 아니어야 함 • 고혈압 : 수축기 혈압이 145mmHg을 초과하거나 확장기 혈압이 90mmHg 초과 • 저혈압 : 수축기 혈압이 90mmHg 미만이거나 확장기 혈압이 60mmHg 미만
사시 (斜視)	복시(複視 : 겹보임)가 없어야 함(다만, 안과 전문의가 직무수행에 지장이 없다고 진단한 경우는 제외)
문신	내용 및 노출여부에 따라 경찰공무원의 명예를 훼손할 수 있다고 판단되는 문신이 없어야 함

– 순환식 체력검사 기준

채용기준	4분 40초 이하

• 합격 기록: 5분 10초 이하

• 불합격 기록: 5분 10초 초과

채용기준	4.2kg 조끼 착용

• 4.2kg 조끼 미착용 후 평가 실시

• 순환식 체력검사 불합격 시 당일에 한해 2회 추가기회 부여

• 경찰대학 입학생들은 졸업(임용) 전 채용기준으로「순환식 체력검사」를 통과하여야 함

• 채용기준: 4.2kg 조끼를 착용하고 신체저항성 기구 32kg으로 중량 강화하여 4분 40초 이하 수행

최종 사정(1,000점 만점) 방법

- 1차 시험 성적(20%) : 환산 성적 200점 만점 → 최종사정 환산 성적=(3과목 합계점수)×200/300
- 체력검사 성적(5%) : 환산 성적 50점 만점 → 최종사정 환산 성적=20점+[(평가 원점수)×3/5]
- 면접시험 성적(10%) : 환산 성적 100점 만점 → 최종사정 환산 성적=50점+[(평가 원점수)÷2]

항 목	점수(100)	비고
적성	40	■ 평가원점수 100점 만점 기준 60점 미만 불합격
창의성·논리성	30	※ 적성 면접 평가 40점 만점 기준으로 4할(16점) 미만자는 전체 평가 원점수 60점 이상이어도 불합격
집단토론	30	■ 생활태도 평가의 감점상한은 최대 10점으로 하고, 감점하
생활태도	감점제	는 사유는 면접시험 안내 시 별도로 설명

- 학교생활기록부 성적(15%) : 교과 성적 135점, 출석 성적 15점 만점(고등학교 1학년 1학기~3학년 1학기)

<table>
<tr><td rowspan="3">교과성적
산출방법</td><td colspan="10">■ 이수단위와 석차등급(9등급)이 기재된 전 과목 반영
■ 산출공식 = 135점 - (5 - 환산평균) × 5
  - 환산평균 = (환산총점) ÷ (이수단위 합계)
  - 환산총점 = (과목별 단위 수 × 석차등급 환산점수)의 합계
  - 학교생활기록부 석차등급 환산점수</td></tr>
<tr><td>석차등급</td><td>1등급</td><td>2등급</td><td>3등급</td><td>4등급</td><td>5등급</td><td>6등급</td><td>7등급</td><td>8등급</td><td>9등급</td></tr>
<tr><td>점 수</td><td>5점</td><td>4.5점</td><td>4점</td><td>3.5점</td><td>3점</td><td>2.5점</td><td>2점</td><td>1.5점</td><td>1점</td></tr>
<tr><td></td><td colspan="10">※ 예체능 교과(우수, 보통, 미흡 3등급 평가) 제외</td></tr>
<tr><td rowspan="4">출석성적
산출방법</td><td colspan="10">1·2학년 및 3학년 1학기까지 결석일수를 5개 등급으로 구분</td></tr>
<tr><td>결석일수</td><td colspan="2">1일 미만</td><td colspan="2">1~2일</td><td colspan="2">3~5일</td><td colspan="2">6~9일</td><td>10일 이상</td></tr>
<tr><td>점 수</td><td colspan="2">15점</td><td colspan="2">14점</td><td colspan="2">13점</td><td colspan="2">12점</td><td>11점</td></tr>
<tr><td colspan="10">- 무단지각, 조퇴, 결과는 합산하여 3회를 결석 1일로 계산
- 질병 및 기타 인정사항으로 인한 결석, 지각, 조퇴, 결과는 결석일수 계산에서 제외
  ※ 학교생활기록부 출결사항에서 사고(무단)의 경우만 산정</td></tr>
<tr><td>학생부
비적용
대상자</td><td colspan="10">대학수학능력시험 성적에 따라 유사한 성적군의 학교생활기록부 성적과 비교하여 산출한 비교내신 반영
- 고등학교 졸업학력 검정고시 출신인 사람
- 고등학교에서 조기졸업을 하였거나 상급학교 조기입학 자격을 갖춘 사람
- 외국 소재 고등학교에서 과정의 1개 학기 이상을 이수하여 고등학교 1학년 1학기부터 3학년 1학기까지 1개 학기 이상의 학교생활기록부가 없는 사람
- 그 밖에 위에 나열한 사람에 준하는 사유로 고등학교 1학년 1학기부터 3학년 1학기까지 1개 학기 이상의 학교생활기록이 없는 사람
- 석차등급(9등급제)을 적용받지 않은 사람</td></tr>
</table>

- 대학수학능력시험 성적(50%) : 국어·수학·영어 및 탐구 2과목 필수(계열 구분없이 사회·과학탐구 영역 중 2과목 선택), 한국사 필수

영 역	합계	국어·수학	영어	탐구	한국사
점 수	500점	각 140점	등급별 환산점수	80점	수능 환산 점수에서 등급별 감점

※ 탐구영역에서 제2외국어·직업탐구는 제외(사회탐구·과학탐구 대체 불가)

※ 한국사 : 수능 환산점수에서 등급에 따라 감점 적용

등급	1	2	3	4	5	6	7	8	9
반영점수	0	-0.5	-1			불합격			

▌구비 서류

1차 시험	■ 대상 : 응시자 전원 ■ 홈페이지에서 대행업체 웹사이트 접속하여 응시원서 접수(수수료 : 25,000원) ■ 인터넷에 게시된 양식에 따라 응시원서 작성 ■ 컬러사진 3.5cm×4.5cm(온라인 응시원서 작성 시 첨부파일로 첨부)
2차 시험	■ 대상 : 1차 시험 합격자 ■ 신원진술서 2부 ■ 개인정보제공동의서 2부 ■ 기본증명서(상세) 1부 ■ 가족관계증명서(상세) 1부 ■ 고등학교 학교생활기록부 2부 　(비적용 대상자는 졸업증서나 검정고시 합격증 사본 등을 제출하되 원본은 면접시험 시 지참) ■ 고등학교 개인별 출결 현황 1부(해당자만) 　※3학년 기간 중 결석, 지각, 조퇴, 결과 기록이 있는 경우 발생한 학기의 증명을 위해 제출

▌응시자 유의사항

– 응시자는 경찰대학 홈페이지의 입학안내 게시사항을 확인하고 안내에 따라야 함
– 다음에 해당하는 응시자는 불합격(합격 및 입학 취소) 처리됨
　1. 제출기간 내 구비서류 미제출자
　2. 1차 시험 또는 2차 시험에 결시한 자
　3. 원서 접수 후 지원자격에 부합하지 않은 사실이 확인된 자
　4. 부정행위, 서류의 허위 기재, 위조, 변조, 기타 부정한 방법으로 지원한 자
　5. 신체검사, 체력검사, 면접시험 등 기준 미달자
　6. 국내 또는 외국 소재 고등학교 졸업(예정)자로서 최종 합격한 자 중 2022학년도 학기 개시일 이전 졸업 증명서를 제출하지 않은 자
　7. 사회적 물의 야기 등으로 경찰대학 대학운영위원회에서 합격취소 결정한 자
– 제출한 서류는 반환하지 않음

 모집 요강은 추후 변동될 수 있으므로 반드시 경찰대학 홈페이지에서 확인하시기 바랍니다.

순환식 체력검사

구분	합격		불합격
기록	5분 10초 이하		5분 10초 초과
	채용기준	4분 40초 이하	

※ 4.2kg 조끼 미착용 후 평가 실시	채용기준	4.2kg 조끼 착용

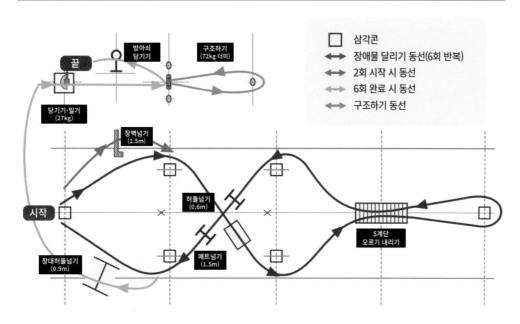

수행방법	① [파란선] 매트넘기, 5계단오르내리기, 허들넘기로 구성된 장애물 달리기* 1회 　　*장애물 달리기: 매트넘기 1회, 5계단오르내리기 2회(왕복), 허들넘기 2회 ② [주황선] 장애물 달리기 2회 시작 시 1.5m 높이 장벽 넘기 ③ [파란선] 장애물 달리기 추가 5회 반복 수행 ④ [노란선] 장대허들(0.9m) 넘기 왕복 3회 ⑤ [노란선] 신체저항성 기구(27kg) 당기기·밀기 각 3회 총 6회

채용기준	32kg

⑥ [초록선] 72kg 더미 끌고 반환점 돌아오기(10.7m)
⑦ [노란선] 38권총 방아쇠 당기기(주손·반대손 각 16, 15회)

※ 순환식 체력검사 불합격 시 당일에 한해 2회 추가기회 부여

※ 경찰대학 입학생들은 졸업(임용) 전 채용기준으로 「순환식 체력검사」를 통과하여야 함

- 채용기준: 4.2kg 조끼를 착용하고 신체저항성 기구 32kg으로 중량 강화하여 4분 40초 이하 수행

경찰대학 Q&A

Q1 경찰대학의 학과에는 무엇이 있나요?

법학과, 행정학과 총 2개의 학과가 있습니다.

Q2 학과별로 모집하나요?

학과 구분 없이 50명을 모집하며, 2학년 진학 시 학생의 희망에 따라 각 학과별 25명씩 학과를 선택합니다. 특정 학과 지원자가 많을 경우 1학년 성적에 의하여 강제로 나눌 수 있습니다.

Q3 특성화 고등학교, 검정고시 합격자도 지원할 수 있나요?

특성화 고등학교, 검정고시 합격자 모두 아무 제한 없이 지원할 수 있습니다. 다만, 경찰대학에서 요구하는 대학수학능력시험의 영역을 응시해야 합니다.

Q4 편입학제도가 있나요? 타 대학 수시합격자도 지원할 수 있나요?

2023학년도부터 편입학제도가 실시됩니다.(일반 대학생 25명, 재직경찰관 25명)
※ 경찰대학은 특별법에 의해 설립된 대학으로 복수지원 금지규정에 해당되지 않습니다.

Q5 외국어 특기, 경시대회 입상, 학생회 활동, 봉사활동, 무도 단증 등에 대한 가산점이 있나요?

어떤 종류에 대해서도 가산점을 부여하지 않고 있으며, 아울러 차별이나 감점도 없습니다.

Q6 아버지, 친척 등이 전과자인데, 응시에 제한을 받나요?

연좌제는 법으로 금지되고 있으므로 부모, 형제, 친척의 전과 등으로 인해 본인에게 영향은 없습니다.

Q7 1차 시험은 어디에서 보나요?

1차 시험은 수험생 응시지구의 관할 지방경찰청이 지정하는 장소에서 실시되며 보통 해당 지방경찰청 소재지 내 지정학교에서 시행됩니다. 장소는 원서접수 후 홈페이지에 별도로 공지합니다.

Q8 1차 시험은 어떤 과목을 보나요?

1차 시험 과목은 국어, 영어, 수학입니다. 각각 100점 만점 기준 고득점자 순으로 모집정원(50명)의 6배수를 선발합니다. 커트라인 동점자는 모두 합격처리합니다.

Q9 1차 시험의 시험시간, 출제형태, 난이도 등은 어떻게 되나요?

1차 시험의 시험시간은 국어 60분(45문항), 수학 80분(25문항), 영어 60분(45문항)이고, 객관식(5지 택일 형)이며 수학 과목만 단답형 주관식 5문항이 포함되어 있습니다. 말하기, 듣기 평가는 제외됩니다. 문제의 난이도는 응시자의 수준을 고려하여 출제하므로 일반적인 시험보다 어렵다고 느끼는 학생들이 있으며, 문제 형식은 가급적 수능시험 형태를 유지하는 것을 기본으로 합니다.

Q10 수학능력시험은 최종에 어떤 방법으로 반영하나요?

국어, 수학, 영어 및 탐구 2과목(계열 구분없이 사회·과학탐구 영역 중 2과목) 표준점수를 총 500점 만점으로 반영합니다. 국어, 수학은 각 140점 만점으로 반영하고, 영어는 등급별 환산점수로, 탐구는 80점 만점으로 반영합니다. 최종사정 1,000점 만점 중 500점을 반영하므로 50% 반영하는 것입니다.

Q11 내신은 어떤 방법으로 산출 하나요?

내신성적 산출은 학교생활기록부에 기재된 과목별 석차등급(1~9등급)을 반영하여 산출하게 되며 1학년 1학기부터 3학년 1학기까지 5학기를 적용하고 학기별 배점비율은 동일합니다.

Q12 수능시험만 잘 봐도 합격이 가능한가요?

최종합격생 선발 시, 대학수학능력시험 성적은 50%가 반영되므로 수능만 잘 본다고 해서 반드시 합격하는 것은 아닙니다.

이 책의 구성과 특징

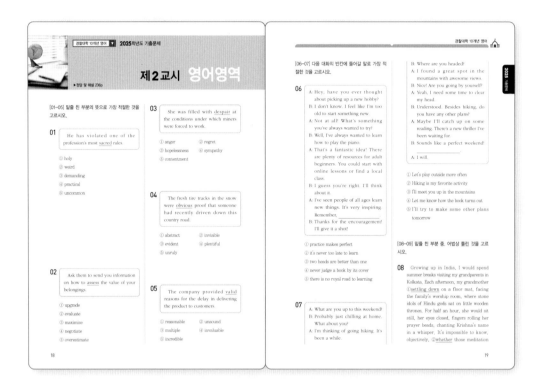

경찰대학 연도별 최신 10개년 기출문제

■ 경찰대학 1차 시험 영어영역의 기출문제를 2025학년도부터 2016학년도까지 연도별로 정리하여 수록함으로써 연도별 기출 경향과 출제 방향을 파악할 수 있도록 구성하였습니다.

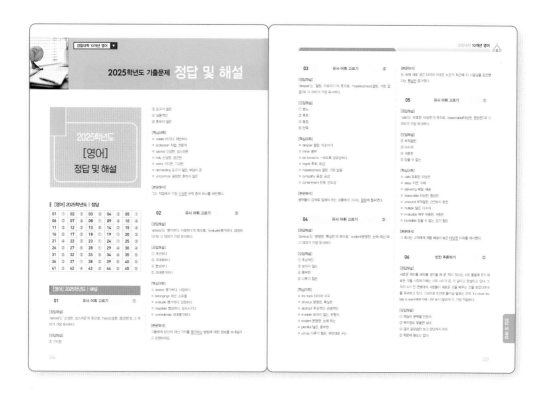

정답 및 해설

- **정답해설** : 각 문항별로 자세하고 알기 쉽게 풀이하여 수험생들이 쉽게 이해할 수 있도록 구성하였습니다.

- **오답해설** : 정답을 아는 것에서 나아가 오답이 오답인 이유를 명백히 이해할 수 있도록 오답에 대한 해설도 함께 수록하였습니다.

- **핵심어휘** : 본문에 제시된 주요 어휘를 정리하여 단어를 쉽게 익힐 수 있도록 구성하였습니다.

- **본문해석** : 본문 해석을 함께 수록하여 문제를 좀 더 쉽게 이해할 수 있도록 구성하였습니다.

목차

기출문제

정답 및 해설

경찰대학 스터디 플랜

날 짜	연 도	과 목	내 용	학습시간
Day 1~3	2025학년도	• 영어영역 기출문제		
Day 4~6	2024학년도	• 영어영역 기출문제		
Day 7~9	2023학년도	• 영어영역 기출문제		
Day 10~12	2022학년도	• 영어영역 기출문제		
Day 13~15	2021학년도	• 영어영역 기출문제		
Day 16~18	2020학년도	• 영어영역 기출문제		
Day 19~21	2019학년도	• 영어영역 기출문제		
Day 22~24	2018학년도	• 영어영역 기출문제		
Day 25~27	2017학년도	• 영어영역 기출문제		
Day 28~30	2016학년도	• 영어영역 기출문제		

2026
경찰대학 10개년 영어

제2교시 영어영역

[01-05] 밑줄 친 부분의 뜻으로 가장 적절한 것을 고르시오.

01
> He has violated one of the profession's most sacred rules.

① holy
② weird
③ demanding
④ practical
⑤ uncommon

02
> Ask them to send you information on how to assess the value of your belongings.

① upgrade
② evaluate
③ maximize
④ negotiate
⑤ overestimate

03
> She was filled with despair at the conditions under which miners were forced to work.

① anger
② regret
③ hopelessness
④ sympathy
⑤ contentment

04
> The fresh tire tracks in the snow were obvious proof that someone had recently driven down this country road.

① abstract
② invisible
③ evident
④ plentiful
⑤ unruly

05
> The company provided valid reasons for the delay in delivering the product to customers.

① reasonable
② unsound
③ multiple
④ invaluable
⑤ incredible

[06-07] 다음 대화의 빈칸에 들어갈 말로 가장 적절한 것을 고르시오.

06

A: Hey, have you ever thought about picking up a new hobby?

B: I don't know. I feel like I'm too old to start something new.

A: Not at all! What's something you've always wanted to try?

B: Well, I've always wanted to learn how to play the piano.

A: That's a fantastic idea! There are plenty of resources for adult beginners. You could start with online lessons or find a local class.

B: I guess you're right. I'll think about it.

A: I've seen people of all ages learn new things. It's very inspiring. Remember, _____.

B: Thanks for the encouragement! I'll give it a shot!

① practice makes perfect

② it's never too late to learn

③ two heads are better than one

④ never judge a book by its cover

⑤ there is no royal road to learning

07

A: What are you up to this weekend?

B: Probably just chilling at home. What about you?

A: I'm thinking of going hiking. It's been a while.

B: Where are you headed?

A: I found a great spot in the mountains with awesome views.

B: Nice! Are you going by yourself?

A: Yeah, I need some time to clear my head.

B: Understood. Besides hiking, do you have any other plans?

A: Maybe I'll catch up on some reading. There's a new thriller I've been waiting for.

B: Sounds like a perfect weekend! _____.

A: I will.

① Let's play outside more often

② Hiking is my favorite activity

③ I'll meet you up in the mountains

④ Let me know how the book turns out

⑤ I'll try to make some other plans tomorrow

[08-09] 밑줄 친 부분 중, 어법상 틀린 것을 고르시오.

08
Growing up in India, I would spend summer breaks visiting my grandparents in Kolkata. Each afternoon, my grandmother ①settling down on a floor mat, facing the family's worship room, where stone idols of Hindu gods sat on little wooden thrones. For half an hour, she would sit still, her eyes closed, fingers rolling her prayer beads, chanting Krishna's name in a whisper. It's impossible to know, objectively, ②whether those meditation

sessions helped my grandmother achieve some sort of communion with a higher power, but a growing body of scientific evidence suggests she benefited from it in multiple ways. The practice was ③likely an effective approach for her to manage her stress. It may have also helped slow down aging-related cognitive decline. It also probably enhanced her ability to cope with pain. ④Defined most broadly as the exercise of focusing one's attention on the current moment, meditation in some form has been practiced for millennia by religious traditions around the world —most rooted in a quest for spiritual enlightenment. Today, the popularity of meditation ⑤has grown in parallel with awareness about the importance of mental health and stress relief.

* throne: 왕좌

09 Anger is clearly related to aggression but they are not one and the same. It is possible to be aggressive without being angry and it is ① equally possible to be angry without becoming aggressive. However, the two (the emotion of anger and the behaviour of aggression) are linked and are biologically based, with obvious survival value. Anger always results in a much increased burst of energy and, ② although biologically based, is seen by some psychologists as largely socially constructed. That is, some people might be temperamentally more prone to anger than others, but the extent ③ to which they express this is probably socially

determined. In our culture, for example, boys are encouraged to express their anger more openly than girls and a far greater proportion of men than women are made ④ take anger management courses. These are ⑤ learned differences, not differences of biology. [3점]

[10~11] (A), (B), (C)의 각 네모 안에서 문맥에 맞는 낱말로 가장 적절한 것을 고르시오.

10 As a result of the political and social changes of recent decades, cultural pluralism is now generally recognized as an organizing principle of this society. In (A) addition / contrast to the idea of the melting pot, which promised to erase ethnic and group differences, children now learn that variety is the spice of life. They learn that America has provided a shelter for many different groups and has allowed them to (B) maintain / reform their cultural heritage or to assimilate, or—as is often the case—to do both; the choice is theirs, not the state's. They learn that cultural pluralism is one of the norms of a free society; that differences among groups are a national resource rather than a problem to be solved. Indeed, the unique feature of the United States is that its common culture has been formed by the interaction of its subsidiary cultures. It is a culture that has been influenced over time by immigrants, American Indians, Africans (slave and free), and by their descendants. American music, art, literature, language, food, clothing, sports, holidays, and customs all show the effects of the blending of (C) similar / diverse cultures in one nation. Paradoxical though it may seem, the United States has a common culture that is multicultural.

* subsidiary: 부차적인

	(A)		(B)		(C)
①	addition	…	maintain	…	similar
②	addition	…	addition	…	similar
③	contrast	…	maintain	…	similar
④	contrast	…	maintain	…	diverse
⑤	contrast	…	reform	…	diverse

11 Popular understanding of the interrelationship between knowledge and power is frequently expressed through the phrase "Knowledge is power." Foucault, in his genealogical studies, (A) confirms / reverses the logic of this expression. He contends that it is not the acquisition of knowledge that gives one power. Instead, knowledge is already always deeply invested with power in such a way that it must be said that "power is knowledge." Thus, in Foucault's analysis, knowledge is never separate from power but is instead a specific means for (B) exercising / resisting power. In this way, power is not simply something embodied within an individual or a social structure and expressed by brute coercion or punishment. Power appears in its most potent form when successfully translated into systems of "knowledge" and thus removed from reflection under the veil of obvious truths. The (C) inseparability / separability of power and knowledge is so thoroughgoing, according to Foucault, that he often conjoins the two into the term power/knowledge.

* coercion: 강제

	(A)		(B)		(C)
①	confirms	…	exercising	…	inseparability
②	confirms	…	resisting	…	inseparability
③	reverses	…	exercising	…	inseparability
④	reverses	…	resisting	…	separability
⑤	reverses	…	exercising	…	separability

[12-13] 밑줄 친 부분 중, 문맥상 낱말의 쓰임이 적절하지 않은 것을 고르시오.

12 Every economics textbook will tell you that competition between rival firms leads to innovation in their products and services. But when you look at innovation from the long-zoom perspective, competition turns out to be less ① central to the history of good ideas than we generally think. Analyzing innovation on the scale of individuals and organizations—as the standard textbooks do—② broadens our view. It creates a picture of innovation that overstates the role of proprietary research and "survival of the fittest" competition. The long-zoom approach lets us see that openness and connectivity may, in the end, be more ③ valuable to innovation than purely competitive mechanisms. Those patterns of innovation deserve recognition—in part because it's

2025 기출문제

21

intrinsically important to understand why good ideas emerge historically, and in part because by ④ embracing these patterns we can build environments that do a better job of nurturing good ideas, whether those environments are schools, governments, or social movements. We can think more creatively if we open our minds to the many ⑤ connected environments that make creativity possible. [3점]

* proprietary: 독점의

13 The great American author Edgar Allan Poe, who needs no ① lengthy introduction, is one of the writers who invented the modern short story. A modern short story is different from earlier forms of tales and fables not only in that it sets the story on a modern realistic background but also in the way its form ② concentrates on a single dramatic event. In Poe's case, this single event very often has to do with some ③ abnormal act typically involving death and murder. It was Poe's innovation to narrate such disturbing event from the viewpoint of the murderer himself, so that the reader of Poe's short story has to hear the vivid voice of the ④ aggressor who takes great care to give a detailed account of how he committed the act. The ⑤ disadvantage of such mode of storytelling is that it allows the writer to explore that mysterious thing, the human mind, in a most intimate and extreme fashion.

14 Virgil에 관한 다음 글의 내용과 일치하지 <u>않는</u> 것은?

Virgil's masterful poetry earned him a legacy as the greatest poet in the Latin language. Throughout the Middle Ages and the Renaissance, his fame only grew. Before the invention of the printing press, when classical texts, transmitted by the hands of scribes, were scarce, Virgil's poetry was available to the literate classes, among whom he was regarded as the most significant writer of the ancient time. He inspired poets across languages, including Dante in Italian, Milton in English, and an anonymous French poet who reworked the *Aeneid* into the medieval romance *Le Roman d'Eneas*. In what became a Christian culture, Virgil was viewed as a pagan prophet because several lines in his works were interpreted as predictions of the coming of Christ. Among writers of the Renaissance, Virgil was appreciated for his vivid portrayals of human emotion. Modern critics, on the other hand, have been less kind. Virgil's poetry is often judged in relation to that of his Greek predecessors, especially the *Iliad* and the *Odyssey*, epics attributed to Homer that also portray the Trojan War. Most contemporary scholars hold that Virgil's poetry pales in comparison to Homer's.

* pagan: 이교도의

① His skillful poems in Latin made him a noted poet.

② His reputation fell into a decline during the Renaissance.

③ He influenced the poems of different languages.

④ His poetry clearly expressed human emotion.

⑤ His poetry was valued less than Homer's by modern critics.

15 Alice James에 관한 다음 글의 내용과 일치하는 것은?

Alice James is always classified as some famous person's sister or brother. Both of her brothers, Henry James the novelist and William James the philosopher, are important figures in their fields. Her family itself was a famous and respected household in Cambridge, MA. Yet Alice, the youngest daughter, was something of a problem, ever since she had her first mental breakdown at sixteen. She also suffered from numerous health problems. The brothers, in the meantime, were becoming more and more successful in their public career. Alice James died at the age of forty-four, yet she left behind a most interesting record of her thoughts during the last three years of her life. She was, however, too weak even to write. Her close friend

K. P. Loring wrote down her words for her. Loring also printed a copy of her diary for Alice's brothers and herself. The challenge in reading her journal is to appreciate the mixture of anger, self-pity, and, of course, the pain the writer feels. One should also remember that hers was a uniquely feminine experience, as women in those times were very often considered to be a "case" or "problem" to be studied and treated by male doctors.

① She came from a lower-class family in Cambridge.

② She was the oldest child in her family.

③ Her brothers failed to gain a reputation.

④ She left a dictated writing of her thoughts.

⑤ Her journal was full of her pity for other women.

16 다음 글의 내용과 일치하는 것은?

The American transition to analytic philosophy was mediated by several important figures, institutions, and events. One such figure was Morris Cohen (1880-1947). Born in Russia, he was educated at City College of New York. With a 1905 Harvard Ph.D., he taught at City from 1912 to 1938, and at the University of Chicago from 1938 to 1941. Known for his interest in logic and the philosophy of science, he was a committed naturalist who recognized no non-scientific methods capable of attaining knowledge in philosophy. One of his students was the Czechoslovakian-born Ernest Nagel, who, after earning his B.A. at City, got his Ph.D. in 1931 from Columbia University. With the exception of a year at Rockefeller University in the 1960s, he spent his career at Columbia University teaching and writing about the philosophy of science and explaining the centrality of logic to philosophy.

① Cohen was born in Czechoslovakia.

② Cohen taught at City College of New York until 1941.

③ Cohen was known for his interest only in logic.

④ Nagel earned his Ph.D. from Harvard University in 1931.

⑤ Nagel spent most of his career at Columbia University.

[17-21] 다음 글의 빈칸에 들어갈 말로 가장 적절한 것을 고르시오.

17 In terms of education, history has not always received a good press. Advising his son in 1656, Francis Osborne was far from enthusiastic about the subject. His experience of hearing contradictory reports about the Civil Wars of his own time (contemporary history), led him to be doubtful about the _____ of records of less recent events. Such historical records, he concluded, were likely to present a 'false, or at best but a contingent beliefe'; and as such they hardly warranted serious study. Osborne's anxiety about his son potentially wasting his time by studying history that is unreliable, implies an understanding of history as being ideally of a certain kind —the kind that yields certain, 'factual' knowledge about the past. Now, although that model was already under challenge in Osborne's day, it has persisted to some extent up to our own time.

* contingent: 부수적인

① continuity

② reliability

③ rediscovery

④ conciseness

⑤ predictability

18 Every intelligence has to _____.
A human brain, which is genetically primed to categorize things, still needs to see a dozen examples as a child before it can distinguish between cats and dogs. That's even more true for artificial minds. Even the best-programmed computer has to play at least a thousand games of chess before it gets good. Part of the AI breakthrough lies in the incredible amount of collected data about our world, which provides the schooling that AIs need. Massive databases, self-tracking, web cookies, online footprints, terabytes of storage, decades of search results, and the entire digital universe became the teachers making AI smart. Andrew Ng explains it this way: "AI is akin to building a rocket ship. You need a huge engine and a lot of fuel. The rocket engine is the learning algorithms but the fuel is the huge amounts of data we can feed to these algorithms."

① be taught

② exceed itself

③ think by itself

④ be governed by rules

⑤ calculate all possibilities

19 Etymology is the study of the root or origin of a word: it derives from the Greek root *etymos*, meaning 'true'. The importance and the implications of etymology are considerable. Generally speaking, there are two contradictory processes at work in the relation between etymology and meaning. The first is a gradual erosion of the original link: words tend to move steadily away from their original meanings. Contrary to this is a desire to revive the link, to get words 'to make sense' with their past. People _____, and even invent them if they do not exist. Some words do indeed have such striking origins. Few of us ever forget (once we are told) that the *sandwich* derives from the Earl of Sandwich, a compulsive gambler who, in order not to leave the gaming table during a twenty-four-hour bout, sustained himself in part with slices of cold beef between slices of toast. Thus was born the *sandwich*, first recorded in 1762. [3점]

* erosion: 침식

① prefer memorable or logical origins for words

② pay little attention to the implications of etymology

③ consider the original meanings of words unimportant

④ are unaware of the contradictory processes of etymology

⑤ dislike any association between use and meaning of words

20 Our intuition is that in chess experts, the parsing of board games becomes a reflex. Indeed, research proves that a single glance is enough for any grand master to evaluate a chessboard and to remember its configuration in full detail, because he automatically parses it into meaningful chunks. Furthermore, a recent experiment indicates that this segmenting process is truly unconscious: a simplified game can be flashed for 20 milliseconds, sandwiched between masks that make it invisible, and still influence a chess master's decision. The experiment works only on expert chess players, and only if they are solving a meaningful problem, such as determining if the king is under check or not. It implies that the visual system takes into account the identity of the pieces (rook or knight) and their locations, then quickly binds together this information into a meaningful chunk ("black king under check"). These sophisticated operations _____. [3점]

* parsing: 분석

① happen only when the master's consciousness is working

② unfold consciously with meaningful awareness

③ occur entirely outside conscious awareness

④ succeed through careful analysis and repetition

⑤ prove that multisensory information can be bound together

21 The industrial (and associated agricultural) revolution which occurred in Europe during the eighteenth and nineteenth centuries not only changed the nature of work, but also dramatically transformed the organization of society, gender and kinship relationships, and _____. In particular, the composition of, and link between, the rural and the urban was completely overturned as a result of the large−scale migration of potential industrial workers from the countryside to the cities where the factories of the emerging manufacturing bourgeoisie were located. The scope of the demographic change that occurred at this time is underlined by research showing that at the beginning of the nineteenth century only 15 British towns had populations of more than 20,000 but by its end there were 185. Indeed, it has been estimated that in 1800 only 2.2 percent of the population of Europe lived in cities of more than 100,000−today that geopolitical space is predominantly urbanized and highly industrialized.

* kinship: 친족 ** demographic: 인구학의

① the geographical features of some nations

② the system of the manufacturing industry

③ the concept of social justice and equality

④ the dominant form of human settlement

⑤ the definition of the working class

22 다음 글의 빈칸 (A), (B)에 들어갈 말로 가장 적절한 것은?

Are you the type of person who sees the proverbial glass as half full or as half empty? People with more optimistic attitudes—who see the glass as half full—tend to be more resilient than others to the effects of stress, including stress associated with physical disorders. _____(A)_____, investigators link optimism to lower levels of emotional distress among heart disease and cancer patients and to lower levels of reported pain among cancer patients. Optimism in pregnant women even predicts better birth outcomes, as measured, for instance, by higher infant birth weights. Optimism in coronary artery bypass surgery patients is also associated with fewer serious postoperative complications. _____(B)_____, people with more pessimistic attitudes tend to report greater emotional distress in the form of depression and social anxiety.

* resilient: 탄력 있는

	(A)		(B)
①	For instance	⋯⋯	Hence
②	For example	⋯⋯	On the other hand
③	In addition	⋯⋯	Nevertheless
④	However	⋯⋯	Therefore
⑤	In fact	⋯⋯	As a result

[23~26] 다음 글의 제목으로 가장 적절한 것을 고르시오.

23　One of the most daring deep-space missions NASA has ever planned is turning out to be one of the least publicized. The target is a large asteroid named 1992KD, which orbits the sun millions of km from Earth. But that destination is almost incidental to the performance of the spacecraft that will make the trip. Though it looks little different from countless other unmanned spaceships NASA has launched, the ship will be navigated by an electronic brain that has been likened to HAL, the independent-minded computer in the film *2001 Space Odyssey*, and will move through space under power of a system that has long been the stuff of technological fantasies: an ion propulsion engine. If all goes as planned, Deep Space 1, scheduled for launch later this month, will be the forerunner of a new generation of spacecraft. While flight planners hope the ship will make some interesting observations about the target asteroid, including its composition and the structure of its surface, DS1's prime assignment is to validate a host of new technologies NASA had always considered too risky to try on a high-profile mission. [3점]

* asteroid: 소행성 ** propulsion: 추진

① A Smart New Kind of Spacecraft

② The Launch of Unmanned Rockets

③ Failure of DS1's Risky Technologies

④ Performance of Computerized Engine System

⑤ New Mission to Navigate a Larger Asteroid

24 Cattle are sensitive creatures. They have evolved a suite of sensory adaptations to detect predators at long distances. They have a keen sense of smell and hearing at least as good as a dog's or cat's. People often say that elephants never forget, but neither do cattle. Cattle can recognize pictures of herd mates as well as humans they know. Charles Darwin argued that both humans and animals possess a similarity in the expression of emotions. We can, of course, discern basic emotions, like pleasure and fear. But what endears dogs to us is their apparent capacity for what we take as their version of love— the longing in their eyes to be with their people and their overall willingness to please. How do you know cattle love you? Pretty much the same way you do with dogs. My bull, Ricky Bobby, happily lies down next to me and puts his horned head in my lap. He loves for me to brush him, and he'll even roll over for a belly rub.

① Cattle Can Be Our New Pets

② Pets Express Emotional Change

③ How to Domesticate Wild Animals

④ Ways to Drive the Cattle Home Safe

⑤ Darwin's Discovery of Animal Behaviors

25 Because of the goals of protecting life and property and maintaining order, and because the police are open for business 24 hours a day in all kinds of weather, it is inevitable that the police are called upon to look after people who cannot or will not properly care for themselves. This includes young children, elderly citizens, the mentally ill, and the homeless. Police assistance to these people can only go so far, of course—police cannot raise other people's children, cure the mentally ill, or build houses for all the homeless people in this country. However, police can and often do provide or arrange for temporary shelter and transportation for those in need. They also make referrals and provide information so that people can take advantage of programs and services available to them. During times when the economy is struggling, when social programs are underfunded, and when many citizens turn a cold shoulder to those less fortunate, police assistance is often the only option for those who cannot properly care for themselves.

① Police Always on the Lookout for Potential Problems

② A Key Objective of the Police: To Prevent Serious Crimes

③ Police Are Here for Those Who Cannot Care for Themselves!

④ Who Is in Charge of Resolving Various Kinds of Conflicts?

⑤ Patrol as the Backbone of the Police Service

26 Although there had been a long tradition of religious and morally enlightening dramas (termed respectively the miracle and morality plays) the first public playhouse in England was built only in 1576. This proved the catalyst for what Gamini Salgado has rightly called 'the greatest efflorescence of dramatic writing England has ever seen'. The conditions of the Elizabethan stage, though difficult to reconstruct with total accuracy now, were generally primitive. To compensate for these inadequacies, a whole new linguistic medium was created. On a bare stage with minimal properties and effects with which to build up a sense of theatrical illusion, the great dramatists, Shakespeare especially, created an extraordinary diversity of experience and range of characters exclusively through the medium of individuated language, worlds of words in which their creations could philosophize, agonize, laugh, suffer and die. [3점]

* catalyst: 촉매 ** efflorescence: 전성기

① Technological Advancements of Elizabethan Theaters

② The Elizabethan Stage and Its Linguistic Innovation

③ Shakespeare's Effective Use of the Primitive Stage

④ The Decline of Religious Drama in England

⑤ The Rise of Medieval Morality Plays

27 다음 글의 주장으로 가장 적절한 것은?

Behind every anhedonic choice that keeps you stuck is the belief that you (or your life) will fall apart if you challenge the rules. This is a powerful myth! It can keep you absolutely paralyzed! The only way to rid yourself of it is to put your psychological strengths to the test. Few people realize how strong they really are until they stop putting up with the problems in their lives and take some steps toward change. It won't be easy. You may get knocked down a few times, but you won't fall apart. On the contrary, the more you assert your ability to take control over your life, the stronger you'll become. Developing psychological strengths is just like developing physical abilities. The more you exercise, the stronger you become.

* anhedonic: 쾌락을 추구하지 않는

① Do not feel you always have to have a realistic plan.

② Identify the conditions that help you become a success.

③ Choose one of your bigger dreams and make it a reality.

④ Set attainable goals and enjoy each small step of progress.

⑤ Stop thinking of yourself as fragile and be mentally strong.

28 다음 글의 주제로 가장 적절한 것은?

No clear-cut category can encompass all jazz. Each performer's idiom is a style unto itself; if it were not so, the music would hardly be jazz. Jazz, like almost all other music, comprises three artistic activities: creating, performing, and listening. In traditional Western European music, these three activities are not always performed by the same individual, although they quite often are. In jazz, however, it is necessary for the performer to combine all three at the same time. Musical creation is an active part of any jazz performance and depends on the performers' understanding of the developing creation, an understanding gained only by their ability to listen well. They must react instantaneously to what they hear from their fellow performers, and their own contribution must be consistent with the unfolding themes and moods. Every act of musical creation in jazz is, therefore, as individual as the performer creating it.

① traits of jazz reflecting performers' individuality

② how to compose jazz for a great performance

③ similarities between jazz and Western music

④ celebrated figures in the modern jazz scene

⑤ influences of traditional music on jazz

[29–30] 다음 글에서 전체 흐름과 관계 <u>없는</u> 문장을 고르시오.

29 Computer-aided instruction is changing the very nature of the educational process at the college level. An increasingly large number of students want a college education, yet they work during the day and may not have a university nearby that offers evening instruction. A solution to this problem is called *distance learning*, meaning that students can enroll in college courses yet not be physically present at the college. ① Course lectures offered at the college are recorded and made available for viewing by students on their personal computers, at whatever time the students have available. ② Thus a course can be offered without regard to time or space because computer technology delivers the course to the student. ③ Some universities are now offering entire degree programs to students through this technology. ④ Hence, distance learning cannot be a good option for students who keep delaying things or those who aren't able to stick to deadlines. ⑤ A student can earn a degree from a university without ever having physically attended the university.

30 It is common knowledge that Descartes was a Cartesian Dualist. (Perhaps it's nothing more than common sense!) ① As everyone knows, he held that there are two worlds, one of mental objects and one of material things, including animals and human bodies. ② The mental objects are 'states of consciousness' (e.g. pains, visual experiences, beliefs and desires, fear and joy); the material objects are more or less complex bits of 'clockwork'. ③ The items in the 'inner world' are understood through the exercise of a special faculty called 'introspection'; objects in the 'outer world' are perceived by the five senses. ④ Like most items of 'common knowledge', the importance of reading is often taken for granted without critical examination. ⑤ Mental states and states of the body are logically independent but causally interrelated: causal interaction is, as it were, the glue bonding mind to body in each individual person.

[31~33] 글의 흐름으로 보아, 주어진 문장이 들어가기에 가장 적절한 곳을 고르시오.

31

But AI promises to transform all areas of human experience.

Humanity has experienced technological change throughout history. Only rarely, however, has technology fundamentally transformed the social and political structure of our societies. (①) More frequently, the preexisting frameworks through which we order our social world adapt and absorb new technology, evolving and innovating within recognizable categories. (②) The car replaced the horse without forcing a total shift in social structure. (③) The rifle replaced the musket, but the general paradigm of conventional military activity remained largely unaltered. (④) Only very rarely have we encountered a technology that challenged our prevailing modes of explaining and ordering the world. (⑤) And the core of its transformations will ultimately occur at the philosophical level, transforming how humans understand reality and our role within it.

32

Seeking refuge, the pair transformed themselves into fish, tied together for safety, and leapt into the river Euphrates.

The constellation Pisces is most often imagined as a pair of fish that are joined together by a rope. This image has been recorded in ancient Egypt of the 2nd millennium BCE and later Babylonian texts. Why these two fish happen to be tied together is not recorded by these earliest sources but later Greek and Roman myths offer some explanations. (①) When the gods were facing the terrible monster Typhon, it is said that Aphrodite and Eros were far away from the battle. (②) Being gods of love and lust, these two had little they could do in the face of such a world-crushing threat. (③) This is the moment that was captured in the form of this constellation. (④) An alternative version has the two fish of Pisces rescuing the gods who rode away on their backs. (⑤) As a reward for their help the fish were placed in the night sky.

33

A principal vehicle of this enterprise was educational reform and specifically the building of a university system dedicated to the ideals of science, reason, and humanism.

Writing just after the end of World War I, an acute observer of the French philosophical scene judged that "philosophical research had never been more abundant, more serious, and more intense among us than in the last thirty years." (①) This flowering was due to the place of philosophy in the new educational system set up by the Third Republic in the wake of the demoralizing defeat in the Franco-Prussian War. (②) The French had been humiliated by the capture of Napoleon III at Sedan and wasted by the long siege of Paris. (③) They had also been terrified by what most of the bourgeoisie saw as seventy-three days of anarchy under the radical socialism of the Commune. (④) Much of the new Republic's effort at spiritual restoration was driven by a rejection of the traditional values of institutional religion, which it aimed to replace with an enlightened worldview. (⑤) Albert Thibaudet highlighted the importance of this reform when he labeled the Third Republic "the republic of professors." [3점]

* siege: 포위 ** anarchy: 무정부

[34-36] 주어진 글 다음에 이어질 글의 순서로 가장 적절한 것을 고르시오.

34

"National forests need more roads like farmers need more drought." We heard somebody say this who was trying to persuade an audience that more roads would be bad for our national forests.

(A) An argument attempts to prove or support a conclusion. When you attempt to persuade someone, you attempt to win him or her to your point of view; trying to persuade and trying to argue are logically distinct enterprises. True, when you want to persuade somebody of something, you might use an argument.

(B) But not all arguments attempt to persuade, and many attempts to persuade do not involve arguments. In fact, giving an argument is often one of the least effective methods of persuading people—which, of course, is why so few advertisers bother with arguments. People notoriously are persuaded by the weakest of arguments and sometimes are undisturbed by even quite good arguments.

(C) The remark, however, is not an argument; it's just a statement that portrays road building in the forests in a bad light. Now, some writers define an argument as an attempt to persuade somebody of something. This is not correct. [3점]

① (A)-(C)-(B) ② (B)-(A)-(C)
③ (B)-(C)-(A) ④ (C)-(A)-(B)
⑤ (C)-(B)-(A)

35

Good critical thinking is a cognitive skill. In general, developing a skill requires three conditions—learning the theory, deliberate practice, and adopting the right attitudes.

(A) However, your attitudes make a big difference as to whether your practice is effective and sustainable. If you hate playing the piano, forcing you to practice is not productive in the long run.

(B) However, knowing the theory is not the same as being able to apply it. You might know in theory that you should balance the bike when you are cycling, but it does not mean you can actually do it. This is where practice comes in, because it translates your theoretical knowledge into actual ability.

(C) By theory we mean the rules and facts we have to know in order to possess the skill. For example, one cannot be a good basketball player without knowing the rules of the game—for example, kicking the basketball is not allowed. Likewise, thinking critically requires knowing a certain amount of logic.

① (A)-(C)-(B) ② (B)-(A)-(C)
③ (B)-(C)-(A) ④ (C)-(A)-(B)
⑤ (C)-(B)-(A)

36

In regard to problem solving, imagery can be used to help solve problems that one could not easily solve using verbal reasoning.

(A) She then realizes that after driving to Washington, traveling to Chicago and then to Buffalo before returning to New York City will save her many hours of driving.

(B) For example, a salesperson who lives in New York City has to drive to three cities, Washington, DC; Buffalo; and Chicago. If she plans to travel to the cities in that order and then return to New York City, she might not be traveling the shortest route.

(C) Hence, she might image a map of the United States and make several virtual trips in her mind's eye. She realizes if she travels to Buffalo after visiting Washington and then after visiting Buffalo travels to Chicago and back to New York, she would be partially retracing her path.

① (A)-(C)-(B) ② (B)-(A)-(C)
③ (B)-(C)-(A) ④ (C)-(A)-(B)
⑤ (C)-(B)-(A)

[37-38] 다음 글의 내용을 한 문장으로 요약하고자 한다. 빈칸 (A), (B)에 들어갈 말로 가장 적절한 것은?

37

To be really smart, an online group needs to obey one final rule and a rather counterintuitive one. The members can't have too much contact with one another. To work best, the members of a collective group ought to be able to think and work independently. This rule came to light in 1958, when social scientists tested different techniques of brainstorming. They posed a thought-provoking question: If humans had an extra thumb on each hand, what benefits and problems would emerge? Then they had two different types of groups brainstorm answers. In one group, the members worked face-to-face; in the other group, the members each worked independently, then pooled their answers at the end. You might expect the people working face-to-face to be more productive, but that wasn't the case. The team with independently working members produced almost twice as many ideas. Traditional brainstorming simply doesn't work as well as thinking alone, then pooling results.

↓

In brainstorming, group members who have direct contact produce __(A)__ ideas than those who work physically separately from one another, which is against our __(B)__ .

	(A)		(B)
①	fewer	......	intuition
②	fewer	......	benefit
③	more	......	conclusion
④	more	......	intuition
⑤	smarter	......	benefit

38

Soon after the first computers appeared, their blunders became the subjects of jokes. The tiniest errors in programming could wipe out clients' bank accounts, or send out bills for outlandish amounts, or trap the computers in cyclical loops that kept repeating the same mistakes. This maddening lack of common sense led most of their users to conclude that machines could never become intelligent. Today, of course, computers do better. Some programs can beat people at chess. Others can diagnose heart attacks. But no machine yet can make a bed, or read a book, or babysit. What makes our computers unable to do the sorts of things that most people can do? Do they need more

memory, speed, or complexity? Do they use the wrong kinds of instruction-sets? Or do machines lack some magical attribute that only a human brain can possess? I will argue that none of those are responsible for the deficiencies of today's machines; instead, all those limitations come from the out-of-date ways in which programmers have chosen to program them.

* blunder: 큰 실수

↓

Although early computers had significant errors, modern machines __(A)__ at tasks like chess and medical diagnosis but struggle with basic human activities due to outdated programming rather than inherent technological __(B)__ .

	(A)		(B)
①	fail	......	problems
②	excel	......	limitations
③	malfunction	......	problems
④	succeed	......	advances
⑤	stare	......	limitations

[39~40] 다음 글을 읽고, 물음에 답하시오.

Pompeii was destroyed by the catastrophic eruption of Mount Vesuvius in 79 A.D., entombing residents under layers of volcanic ash. But there is more to this story of an ancient Roman city's doom. Research published in the journal *Frontiers in Earth Science* offers proof that Pompeii was simultaneously wrecked by a massive earthquake. The discovery establishes a new timeline for the city's collapse and shows that fresh approaches to research can (a) reveal additional secrets from well-studied archaeological sites. Researchers have always had an idea that seismic activity contributed to the city's destruction. The ancient writer Pliny the Younger reported that the eruption of Vesuvius had been accompanied by violent shaking. But, until now, no evidence had been discovered to (b) support this historical account. A team of researchers led by Domenico Sparice from Italy decided to investigate this (c) gap in the record. Dr. Sparice said that excavations of Pompeii to date had not included experts in the field of archaeoseismology, which deals with the effects of earthquakes on ancient buildings. Contributions from (d) specialists in this area were key to the discovery, he said. "The effects of seismicity have been speculated by past scholars, but no factual evidence has been reported before our study," Dr. Sparice said, adding that the finding was "very exciting." The team focused on the Insula of the Chaste Lovers. This area encompasses several buildings, including a bakery and a house where painters were evidently interrupted by the eruption, leaving their paintings (e) colored. After excavation and careful analysis, the researchers concluded that walls in the insula had collapsed because of an earthquake.

* seismic: 지진의 ** excavation: 발굴

39 윗글의 제목으로 가장 적절한 것은?

① Who Found Pompeii Covered with Volcanic Ashes
② Mt. Vesuvius's Influence on the Scenery of Pompeii
③ The Eruption of Mt. Vesuvius Triggered by Earthquake
④ Seismic Timeline by Archaeological Discovery in Pompeii
⑤ The Eruption of Mt. Vesuvius Wasn't Pompeii's Only Killer

40 밑줄 친 (a)~(e) 중, 문맥상 낱말의 쓰임이 적절하지 <u>않은</u> 것은? [3점]

① (a)　　　　② (b)
③ (c)　　　　④ (d)
⑤ (e)

[41-42] 다음 글을 읽고, 물음에 답하시오.

Personality is one of those parts of the human condition that is obvious in everyday life. Each of us is unique and it is the study of personality that stresses this uniqueness, whereas much of the remainder of psychology emphasises similarities between people. Some parts of personality appear to be built in and others appear to be learned. Certainly, personality is also influenced by culture, either through environmental necessity or through beliefs, values, opinions and judgements.

Whichever way that personality is looked at or theorised about, it is clear that it does not exist in a vacuum. A person may be made up of an id, an ego and a superego, or of an actualising self, or of a series of learned social behaviours, or of a set of traits. Whichever of these it might be occurs within a context or a series of situations or experiences, no two of which are the same. So the best way to look at personality in general, or at someone's personality in particular, is through the eyes of _____. People cannot exist without their environment, each influencing the other. It is therefore best to make sense of personality as it exists in its particular environment. Personality cannot exist in isolation.

41 윗글의 제목으로 가장 적절한 것은?

① How Does Personality Develop as One Grows Older?
② Gender Differences in Personality and Social Behaviour
③ Understanding Personality: Uniqueness, Culture, and Context
④ Personality, One Factor That Determines Your Social Behaviours
⑤ What Are the Similarities between Personality and Characteristics?

42 윗글의 빈칸에 들어갈 말로 가장 적절한 것은? [3점]

① emotion　② creativity
③ usefulness　④ interaction
⑤ productivity

[43-45] 다음 글을 읽고, 물음에 답하시오.

(A)
Sophia leaned against the brick wall of North High, tracing the graffiti with her fingers. The final bell had rung, and students were leaving quickly. She looked around for her older sister Sara but couldn't find her. With a sigh, (a) she started walking home. Next week was the school talent show, and she had signed up to sing. She loved singing but had never sung in front of a big audience before.

(B)

Sophia's eyes widened. "Really? That'd be amazing!" They spent the next hour planning and practicing. When they finally said goodbye, Sophia felt more confident because Janet helped her a lot. As she walked home, the evening sun made the town look golden. She realized that unexpected moments and new friends could make everything better. The talent show was no longer something to be scared of but a chance for (b) her to shine.

(C)

As Sophia walked, she was lost in thought and didn't notice Janet, the senior class president, until she was right in front of her. Janet and Sara knew each other, but Sophia had never talked to her before. "Hey, Sophia," Janet said with a big smile. "Hi, Janet. What's up?" (c) she replied, feeling surprised. "I heard you signed up for the talent show," Janet said. "What are you going to sing?" Sophia felt nervous. "I'm not sure yet," (d) she said. "I'm still deciding." Janet smiled again. "Want to grab a coffee and talk about it?"

(D)

They walked to a local cafe and talked about school and music. Janet was easy to talk to, and Sophia felt more relaxed with (e) her. "What kind of music do you like?" Janet asked. "I love classic rock," Sophia said. "So, I'm thinking about doing an acoustic version of classic

rock." Janet's eyes lit up. "That sounds perfect. I play a bit of guitar; maybe I could play with you?"

43 주어진 글 (A)에 이어질 내용을 순서에 맞게 배열한 것으로 가장 적절한 것은?

① (B)-(D)-(C) ② (C)-(B)-(D)

③ (C)-(D)-(B) ④ (D)-(B)-(C)

⑤ (D)-(C)-(B)

44 밑줄 친 (a)~(e) 중, 가리키는 대상이 나머지 넷과 다른 것은?

① (a) ② (b)

③ (c) ④ (d)

⑤ (e)

45 윗글에 관한 내용으로 적절하지 않은 것은?

① Sophia signed up to sing in the school talent show.

② Sophia felt more confident after practicing with Janet.

③ Sophia's sister and Janet knew each other.

④ Sophia was thinking about singing a classic rock song.

⑤ Sophia taught Janet how to play the guitar.

2026

경찰대학
10개년 영어

2024학년도 기출문제

영어영역

제2교시 영어영역

[01~05] 밑줄 친 부분의 뜻으로 가장 적절한 것을 고르시오.

01

No art can conquer the people alone — the people are conquered by an ideal of life advocated by authority.

① opposed

② championed

③ disregarded

④ undermined

⑤ overwhelmed

02

We rarely begin with completely open minds, which would allow us to discuss a topic in a completely impartial way.

① fair

② harmless

③ meaningful

④ timely

⑤ creative

03

We read through the minutes of the last meeting.

① hours   ② records

③ moment   ④ duration

⑤ melody

04

The youngest police officer's duties were confined to taking statements from the crowd.

① limited   ② enlarged

③ classified   ④ promoted

⑤ conformed

05

It goes without saying that the difficulties of color photography are multiplied when movement is added to the composition, and when the image is projected.

① Arguably   ② Probably

③ Fortunately   ④ Agreeably

⑤ Obviously

[06~07] 다음 대화의 빈칸에 들어갈 말로 가장 적절한 것을 고르시오.

06

A: Have you finished your assignment?
B: No, not yet. I plan to do it tonight.
A: Tonight? Aren't you going to the football game?
B: Oh, the game! I completely forgot about it. I've been looking forward to this game.
A: I know. I guess you have a big decision to make.
B: Right. Should I go to the game or just stay home and do the assignment?
A: _____
B: I know. Still, I don't know what to do.
A: Don't worry. I know you'll make the right decision.

① You should've practiced harder.
② I need to stay home tomorrow.
③ Well, it's up to you.
④ I have a profound question.
⑤ We watched the football game yesterday.

07

A: What are you doing?
B: My car doesn't start. I'm trying to find out what's wrong.
A: Oh, no. Do you know about cars? Did you find something?

B: I think the battery is dead. I was out of town for a few weeks, and during that time, nobody had used my car.
A: Did you call your insurance company?
B: For what?
A: Normally, car insurance companies offer battery recharging services. They'll come to you and recharge the battery instantly. It's very convenient.
B: Oh, I didn't know that. _____ I'll call right away.
A: You're welcome.

① This runs great!
② Take your time.
③ What is the registration number?
④ I didn't do anything wrong.
⑤ Thanks for the tip.

[08~09] 밑줄 친 부분 중, 어법상 틀린 것을 고르시오.

08 No one had yet attempted to survey the consequences of the fifteenth-century communications shift from script to print. While recognizing that it would take more than one book to remedy this situation, I also felt that a preliminary effort, however inadequate, was better than none, and began a decade of study — devoted primarily to ① become acquainted with the special literature on early printing and the history of the book. Between 1968 and 1971 some preliminary articles were published to draw reactions from scholars and to take advantage of ② informed criticism. My full-scale work, *The Printing Press as an Agent of Change*, ③ appeared in 1979. It has been abridged for the general reader in the present version. Illustrations have been added, but footnotes ④ have been dropped from this abridgment. The unabridged version should be consulted by any reader ⑤ seeking full identification of all citations and references.

*preliminary: 예비의 **abridge: 단축하다

09 There is no neutral position from which to evaluate the benefits and burdens of new technologies. ① Consider the mass-produced Ford Model T at the beginning of the twentieth century or self-driving cars in the twenty-first century. With cars, we weigh benefits of autonomous mobility and ② swiftly transport against human congestion and earth-devastating pollution. And so it is with photography. Since its inception, skeptics worried that widespread and uncontrolled photography would destabilize communities and governments by spreading lies and ③ invading privacy. This anxiety arose in the early years of the Kodak camera, ④ when its popularity combined with the spread of yellow journalism to produce invasive and misleading photographs. These concerns persist today with ubiquitous digital camera phones, deep-fake videos, and the viral internet. Then and now, arguments about how cameras work and the power of photographic expression ⑤ concern personal lives, international politics, and public justice. [3점]

*inception: 시작

[10~12] (A), (B), (C)의 각 네모 안에서 문맥에 맞는 낱말로 가장 적절한 것을 고르시오.

10 Thanks to its broad popularity, sports could be a powerful tool for raising awareness about the climate crisis among people across the world, regardless of their geographical location and social background. Simply put, the industry could (A) restrain / share important messages about the environment to billions of individuals that are involved in sports either as spectators, practitioners, or facilitators. Such strategy of increasing awareness and educating has shown good results in the past. Research found that fans are (B) receptive / resistant to ecological initiatives organised at sporting events, some even to the extent that they are willing to change their lifestyle habits regarding sustainability. This study precisely concluded that "the norms related to sport events have a significant relationship with (C) negative / positive perceptions of the efforts undertaken by sport organisations while also influencing at-home environmental behavioural intentions."

2024 기출문제

	(A)	(B)	(C)
①	restrain	receptive	negative
②	restrain	resistant	positive
③	share	resistant	positive
④	share	receptive	positive
⑤	share	resistant	negative

11 Whenever a scholar needed a technical term to refer to a concept that English didn't have name for, they would import one from Greek or Latin. If Greek or Latin didn't have name for the concept either — a situation that became increasingly (A) frequent / rare as scientific knowledge rapidly expanded beyond the dreams of the ancients — they would make up a name for the concept out of Latin and/or Greek roots, rather than from English roots. This practice continues to this day. As a result, many (B) abandoned / borrowed Latin terms, and newly formed words from Latin roots as well as affixes that had never been used in Cicero's time, entered English in this period. Many such words fell out of use almost immediately, but many others were (C) picked up / taken out by contemporaries and are still with us today.

	(A)	(B)	(C)
①	frequent	abandoned	picked up
②	frequent	abandoned	taken out
③	frequent	borrowed	picked up
④	rare	abandoned	taken out
⑤	rare	borrowed	picked up

12 The two centuries prior to the time of Plato and Aristotle had been a period of economic liberalization, and with this came an enormous rise in commercial activity including international trade. Moreover, tremendous economic disturbance and social instability accompanied the rapid commercial (A) expansion / reduction, and this greatly influenced Plato and Aristotle's economic thinking. They believed that the instability resulted from the pursuit of financial gain, which, as the fable of Midas made clear, brought with it dreadful consequences. Just as Midas had (B) destroyed / liberated himself in the pursuit of gold, so too had the pursuit of wealth endangered Greek society. It was partly in response to this threat that Plato and Aristotle undertook to examine what life would look like in the ideal state, and their analysis was built around the question of what, in such a state, would constitute "the good life"? It was clear to them that economic growth had undesirable effects, and they stressed the need for an economic system that generated a relatively (C) dynamic / stationary level of economic activity. [3점]

	(A)	(B)	(C)
①	expansion	destroyed	dynamic
②	expansion	liberated	dynamic
③	expansion	destroyed	stationary
④	reduction	destroyed	dynamic
⑤	reduction	liberated	stationary

[13~14] 밑줄 친 부분 중, 문맥상 낱말의 쓰임이 적절하지 않은 것을 고르시오.

13 Because all evidence of the past can only be found in the present, creating a story about the past inevitably implies ① interpreting this evidence in terms of processes with a certain history of its own. We do so because we experience both the surrounding environment and our own persons to be such processes. As a result, all historical accounts are reconstructions of some sort, and thus likely to ② change over time. This also means that the study of history cannot offer absolute certainties, but only ③ precision of a reality that once was. In other words, true historical accounts do not exist. This may sound as if there is endless leeway in the ways the past is viewed. In my opinion, that is not the case. Just as in any other field of science, the major test for historical reconstructions is whether, and to what extent, they ④ accommodate the existing data in a concise and precise manner. Yet there can be no way around the fact that all historical reconstructions consist of a ⑤ selected number of existing data placed within a context devised by the historian.

[3점]

*leeway: 여지

14 The battle against single-use plastic bags may not be won, but it's definitely under way. Restrictions on their use are in place in almost a dozen US states and in many other countries around the world. And in many cases, these efforts have been ① successful at eliminating new sales of thin plastic bags that float up into trees, block waterways, leech microplastics into soil and water, and harm marine life. But this environmental success story of sorts ② masks another problem. Many of us are ③ drowning in reusable bags that retailers sell cheaply or give away to customers as an apparently greener alternative to single-use plastic. Campaigners say these bag hoards are ④ solving fresh environmental problems, with reusable bags having a much higher carbon footprint than thin plastic bags. According to one eye-popping estimate, a cotton bag should be used at least 7,100 times to make it a truly environmentally friendly alternative to a ⑤ conventional plastic bag. The answer to what's the greenest replacement for a single-use plastic bag isn't straightforward, but the advice boils down to this: Reuse whatever bags you have at home, as many times as you can.

*leech: 달라붙어 떨어지지 않다 **hoard: 축적

15 다음 글의 내용과 일치하는 것은?

The son of a minister in Basel, Switzerland, Jacob Burckhardt originally intended to follow his father's footsteps and become a Protestant minister. However, while studying theology in Basel, he came to the conclusion that Christianity was a myth. Turning instead to the study of history and art history, he spent four years studying with Leopold Ranke in Berlin. Burckhardt's relationship with Ranke is the subject of contrary points of view among historians. Some argue that Burckhardt retained a high regard for Ranke throughout his life, despite their differences, which were fundamental. While Ranke saw the power of the state as guardian of order and stability, Burckhardt regarded power as tied to evil. Ranke, the Protestant scholar, confidently sought the hand of a generous God in the events of the past; but Burckhardt, skeptical and withdrawn, saw in history an unending struggle between hostile forces. These differences led other historians to argue that we should not be misled by Burckhardt's references to Ranke as 'my great master'. Rather, Burckhardt came to reject both Ranke's personal ambition and his intellectual approach.

*theology: 신학

① Jacob Burckhardt never wanted to become a minister.

② Jacob Burckhardt studied art history in Basel.

③ Jacob Burckhardt's relationship with Ranke is uncontroversial.

④ Jacob Burckhardt thought power and evil went hand in hand.

⑤ Jacob Burckhardt embraced Ranke's intellectual approach.

[16~17] 다음 글의 내용과 일치하지 <u>않는</u> 것을 고르시오.

16 During a certain stage of sleep, which can be identified by rapid eye movements and characteristic brain wave patterns, we engage in dreaming. Everybody dreams, but unless we concentrate on remembering what we just dreamed, the images fade almost immediately once we wake up. Dreams are often bizarre because they are formed without outside stimulation and are based instead on our own internal associations, memories, and emotional inputs. Often, we can trace our associations to the symbols and metaphors that occur in dreams. Sometimes we are able to decode what it is that the dream sequence and images were expressing. The existence of "lucid dreams" has been established in research studies. People who can have lucid dreams are able to influence their own dreams, recognize that they are having a dream, and are able to wake themselves up if they wish.

① While people are dreaming, their eyes can move.

② Not everyone remembers what they dreamed.

③ Dreams are related with our mind and thought.

④ Dreams can be figurative and be interpreted.

⑤ People are unable to affect their own dreams.

17 Noise from inland wind farms, part of a growing industry located largely in the central midwestern United States and in the Canadian provinces of Ontario and Quebec, is the subject of scientific controversy. It is believed by many scientists to subject nearby residents to insomnia and headaches as well as the muscle aches, anxiety, and depression that result from sleep loss, from low-frequency noise, and possibly from changes in air pressure caused by operation of the turbines. Whether these symptoms are the result of actual wind turbine activity, of weather sensitivity, or of stress reactions brought on by noise annoyance is not entirely clear. Because the definition of noise annoyance includes emotional reactions as well as physical symptoms, studies are showing conflicting results: each side of the controversy can cite extensive evidence, but neither side is convinced by the other's interpretation of research design or findings.

*insomnia: 불면증

① Noise from inland wind farms is a scientifically controversial topic.

② Residents near inland wind farms probably experience both mental and physical illness.

③ Scientists have not successfully identified the major cause of the symptoms that residents near inland wind farms suffer.

④ Noise annoyance is defined only within emotional reactions.

⑤ The results of the research on the noise from inland wind farms are still inconclusive.

[18~22] 다음 글의 빈칸에 들어갈 말로 가장 적절한 것을 고르시오.

18 Different cultural groups think, feel, and act differently. There is no scientific standards for considering one group as essentially superior or inferior to another. Studying differences in culture among groups and societies presupposes a position of cultural relativism. It does not imply normalcy for oneself, nor for one's society. It, however, calls for judgment when dealing with groups or societies different from one's own. Information about the nature of cultural differences between societies, their roots, and their consequences should _____. Negotiation is more likely to succeed when the parties concerned understand the reasons for the differences in viewpoints.

[3점]

① construct our cultural identity

② precede judgment and action

③ form presupposed goals

④ be reevaluated objectively

⑤ explain the fundamental principles

19 Scientific superstructures resemble historical truths, or theological notions of God. They are provisionally useful as being the best we have for the moment, but they are _____. Our acceptance of them remains provisional, our commitment something less than wholehearted, while we continue to search for something better to displace them. In whatever area of human aspiration, the ultimate goal — the 'truth' or 'god' or 'reality' — remains forever elusive, out of reach, beyond us; but our belief that it's there provides the necessary motivation for our continuing search.

① to become the proof of aspiration

② to transform our lifestyle

③ not to motivate your life

④ to display the absolute truth

⑤ not to be relied upon for ever

20 It is estimated that for every human being alive today, there are as many as two hundred million individual insects. Just the total weight of all the ants in the world, all nine thousand different kinds, is twelve times greater than the weight of all the humans on the planet. Despite their amazing numbers and the fact that they are found virtually everywhere, insects and other arthropods are still very alien to us, as if they were beings from another planet. They move on six or more legs, stare with unblinking eyes, breathe without noses, and have hard skinless bodies made up of rings and plates, yet there is something _____ about them, too. Arthropods have to do all the things people do to survive, such as find food, defend themselves from their enemies, and reproduce. They also rely on their finely tuned senses to see, touch, hear, smell, and taste the world around them.

*arthropod: 절지동물

① surprisingly suspicious

② minutely categorized

③ steadily progressive

④ humanly productive

⑤ strangely familiar

21 The fact remains that meditation has been practiced for centuries. Critics agree that, whatever the reason, it does seem to work. It is possible that psychological benefits may exist, even if physiological changes are not well established. Furthermore, studies have not controlled possible differences between persons who choose to practice meditation and those who do not. It is possible that such subject differences exist and that they influence the results of the meditation more than the technique itself. What we can conclude here is that _____. People will continue to meditate, often with beneficial results. Therapists will continue to use it to treat conditions of hypertension, alcohol abuse, drug abuse, insomnia, and many other psychiatric disorders. Similarly, behavioral scientists will continue to study meditation and its effects until more definitive findings are available. Yet there will always be those who refuse to accept objective, scientific evidence as the standard of acceptance and belief. [3점]

*meditation: 명상 **physiological: 생리학의

① the meditation waters are muddy

② its critics should try to practice meditation

③ meditation can relieve various physical pains

④ the definition of meditation is now unclouded

⑤ scientists should examine the methods of meditation

22 Ecological people interact with nature, in contrast with logical people who act upon nature and mythological people who are acted upon by nature. They engage in dialogue with nature. Dikes in Holland are made with layers of mud and rocks and woven willow mats. When the fury of the North Atlantic strikes these dikes they absorb the force with the flexibility of willow branches by moving in tune with the waves. This ecological solution stands in contrast to the logical solution of most European port cities that have built sea walls of steel-reinforced concrete to stop the waves. Acting against nature, these firm walls are eventually smashed apart and need to be rebuilt unlike the Dutch dikes that _____. The mythological solution is to passively accept the edict of nature by neither building firm walls nor flexible dikes. Following the mythological solution, one third of Holland would be under water. [3점]

*dike: 제방 **edict: 칙령, 명령

① silently remain as objective observers

② constantly change with dramatic shifts

③ flexibly move with the natural rhythms

④ actively respond to the ecological mysteries

⑤ simply disregard the order of natural worlds

[23~24] 다음 글의 제목으로 가장 적절한 것을 고르시오.

23 Claims are *not*, as you might think, the opposite of facts. Nor does a claim 'become' a fact once we know it is true. A claim is always a claim, but the truth of some claims is established. And a claim does not necessarily involve some personal advantage or bias. Although in everyday speech we often use the word 'claim' to try to distinguish between statements whose truth is suspect or that are biased and those statements (called 'facts') whose truth is established and that are unbiased, these distinctions are dangerously misleading. All the statements that we think of as 'facts' are, actually, claims; they are so widely and clearly accepted as true that they *seem* different from claims that are not accepted. Put simply, claims are those statements that express beliefs or views about the way the world is or the way the world should be. Whether they are true or not is, of course, important, but it does not determine whether or not they are claims.

① Can We Separate Facts from Claims?

② Landmarks of the Truthful Claims

③ Facts, Everlasting Promises!

④ What Is the Opposite of Facts and Claims?

⑤ A Journey from Suspicion to Determination

24 Don't be afraid to try or to fail. It teaches you strength and how to overcome your personal challenges. Life's trials are not unique to you; they happen to everyone in differing degrees and help develop your mental tolerance and a strong character giving you the tools to help others to avoid the dangers. When you do not achieve the conclusion that you aimed for in a project or task, you often look on it as a defeat. This thought process can keep you stuck in a position of stalemate and prevent real progress because you give up. Never look at this experience as something bad, trying and failing is progress in every sense of the word. It can prove to be the vehicle that really launches you forward with renewed energy and a desire to try again.

*stalemate: 교착상태

① A Stay at the Bottom of Fate

② Welcome Hardships, Kicks of Life

③ Giving Up Is Part of Life's Trials

④ How to Apply Knowledge to Reality

⑤ Be Open-minded to New Experiences

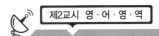

[25~26] 다음 글의 요지로 가장 적절한 것을 고르시오.

25 We are regularly confronted by the need to make choices in our use of language. For most of the time, no doubt, coping with variance does not constitute anything of a problem and may indeed be unconscious: we are dealing with family and friends on everyday affairs; and what is more, we are usually talking to them, not writing. It is in ordinary talk to ordinary people on ordinary matters that we are most at home, linguistically and otherwise. And fortunately, this is the situation that accounts for the overwhelming majority of our needs in the use of English.

① The vast majority of us make careless mistakes in ordinary talk.

② We should not confront family and friends about their everyday affairs.

③ A linguistically diverse group of people must try harder to live in harmony.

④ Making unconscious choices does not constitute using language creatively.

⑤ Our everyday use of English does not usually require coping with variance.

26 As we observe the "objective" world, we view it through our own lenses or filters. Our everyday environment is like water to a fish—it's just there; we don't take note of it. Most of the time, we're not particularly conscious of what we consider normal activities, since we already have a place for them on our mental map; they fall into familiar categories. We have a tendency, as linguists have shown, to generalize from what we know to what we don't know— and either to distort or to delete (edit out) anything that doesn't make sense, given that view. All snow may look alike to Floridians; their experience does not provide a "map" for differentiation, so differences in the type of snow are ignored. Swedes or Aleuts, on the other hand, have the worldview, including the language, to distinguish among many different kinds of snow. Deleting or distorting that information would cause them real inconvenience.

① We should keep the objective filters of our perception.

② We see the world through a lens of subjectivity.

③ Our expectations shape our dream.

④ Our reason should avoid distorted information.

⑤ We must take a neutral position in generalizing what we know.

27 다음 글의 주제로 가장 적절한 것은?

Celtic Studies is a field long connected with the study of mythology. In the western European context the Celtic-speaking peoples have been amongst those most often held up as the recipients of a rich body of 'tradition'. From early descriptions of the Gauls through to modern accounts of Scottish Highland culture we find a reappearing emphasis on oral culture and a concern with the supernatural in daily life. In modern scholarship Celtic languages developed a strong connection to the discipline of comparative Indo-European philology and, in turn, to theories of comparative mythology that are its by-products. Aside from these external perspectives, a primary stimulus of interest for mythologists is the very strong sense of the mythic present within Celtic literature itself; reference to gods, to heroes with supernatural qualities, and to events of the distant past. For these reasons, studies of Celtic religion, folklore and literature have very often been made subject to mythological models of interpretation.

*philology: 문헌학

① the repeated theme in describing supernatural qualities in gods

② the importance of Scottish Highland culture in classic literature

③ the characteristics of Celtic Studies and its connection to mythology

④ the novel perspectives on how to understand Celtic-speaking peoples

⑤ the rich body of tradition present in comparative Indo-European philology

[28~29] 다음 글에서 전체 흐름과 관계 없는 문장을 고르시오.

28 Camouflage, also known as cryptic coloration, is the one-size-fits-all defense in the world of animals. Animals as small as insects and as large as the boldly patterned giraffe —towering at a height of 18 feet (6 m) —depend on their cryptic colorations to help them blend in. ① Colors and patterns may camouflage an animal not only by helping it blend in, but also by breaking up its shape. ② That way, a predator does not recognize it at first. ③ An animal's coloring can hide the roundness of its body, making it look flat. ④ Our planet continues to be damaged as its inhabitants are indifferent to environmental issues. ⑤ Colors and patterns also can help hide an animal's shadow.

*cryptic: 숨은, 비밀의

29 The structuring of time can have many functions, some of which are more or less important in different cultures. But everywhere, one of the main functions is to set the schedule of the culture and, thereby, coordinate the activities of individuals in the culture. Other functions may be to relate the group's activities to some natural phenomena or to some supernatural phenomena. ① The structure may be used to order events in the past or in the future, or to measure the duration of events, or to measure how close or far they are from each other or from the present. ② Above all, the structure provides a means of orientation and gives form to the occurrence of events in the lives of individuals, as well as in the culture. ③ It provides a continuous and coherent framework in which to mark periodically repeating events and in which to place special events. ④ Mathematical ideas as fundamental as order, units, and cycles are the very building blocks. ⑤ As such, the structure imposed on time extends well beyond itself, reflecting and affecting much in a culture.

[30~34] 글의 흐름으로 보아, 주어진 문장이 들어가기에 가장 적절한 곳을 고르시오.

30

> Odysseus got most of these aboard again, though he had to abandon his dead and seriously wounded.

According to the Odyssey, a poem that shows Odysseus in a different light, he first sailed for Thrace after leaving Troy. There he attacked and burned the city-port of Ismarus. (①) A priest of Apollo, whose life he undertook to spare, gratefully gave him several jars of sweet wine, half of which his men drank at a picnic on the beach. (②) Some Thracians who lived inland saw flames rising from Ismarus, and charged vengefully down on the drunken sailors. (③) A fierce north-easterly storm then drove his ships across the Aegean Sea towards Cythera, an island at the southernmost point of Greece. (④) Taking advantage of a sudden calm, he made his men use their oars and tried to round Cythera, bearing north-west for Ithaca, but the storm sprang up more fiercely than before, and blew nine days. (⑤) When at last it dropped, Odysseus found himself within sight of Syrinx, the Lotus-eaters' Island off the North African coast. [3점]

*vengeful: 복수심에 불타는 **oar: 노

31

Of course, grills are but one component of the growing interest in outdoor kitchens.

For consumers who desire more flexibility, an increasing number of companies are offering hybrid gas grills outfitted with pans or pullout drawers to accommodate charcoal and/or wood. (①) In addition, some barbecues can be customized with carts containing refrigeration or even an oven, allowing one to grill and bake at the same time. (②) And those who like their meat smoked on occasion can opt for accessories such as smoking trays and smoker boxes, or simply invest in a separate smoker. (③) In addition, because grilling is a day- and nighttime activity, many of today's barbecues incorporate surface lighting, as well as LEDs on the control panel to ensure temperature settings are visible after dark. (④) However, as these spaces continue to expand in functionality, taking on features that allow for year-round enjoyment, so too will the development of grill technology. (⑤) After all, as Russ Faulk noted, "Everything tastes better off a grill."

*incorporate: 포함하다

32

If an epidemic is particularly fierce or prolonged (like the Black Death), a great number of people who were weak will die, leaving the resistant survivors to repopulate their communities.

When an epidemic hits a population, there will be individuals in that population who have genetic mutations that make them more naturally resistant to infection. (①) Upon facing exposure to the pathogen, they will be more likely to survive than their normal, nonmutant counterparts. (②) After many generations of such "weeding out," the new surviving population will have a much higher frequency of individuals with the mutation than did the original, pre-epidemic population. (③) As a result, they will be more genetically prepared if that epidemic were to ever hit again. (④) Therefore, an epidemic can act as a selective pressure that triggers a change in the genetic profile of a population over time. (⑤) In other words, it can promote human evolution.

*epidemic: 전염병 **pathogen: 병원균

33

The only reason we know even this bare outline is that the tale was passed on by word of mouth until a visitor from the Mediterranean world wrote it down.

Over two thousand years ago, someone on the cold and windswept shores of the Atlantic Ocean sat down before a blazing fire and told a story. (①) Long ago, this person said, there were two gods who were brothers, twins born together from a great mother goddess of the sea. (②) When these brothers grew up, they left the ocean behind and came to dwell among the people who lived near the sea. (③) There was much more to the story, but that is all that survives. (④) In time, that document found its way to a Greek historian named Timaeus from the island of Sicily, who lived just after the age of Alexander the Great. (⑤) He recorded the story as part of his impressive history of the world from legendary times until his own day.

34

In France, many words of the conquering Frankish Germans were incorporated into the vocabulary.

In the fifth century, Germanic expansion brought about the fall of the Roman Empire. Subsequently, without the Roman army to defend them, many lands passed under the control of Germanic tribes. (①) The movements of the West Germanic tribes are particularly important to the story of English. (②) By the end of the fifth century, West Germanic speakers had taken control of much of France and England. (③) These words included the name of the land itself: called *Gallia* (*Gaul*) under the Romans, it now came to be called *Francia* (*France*) 'land of the Franks'. (④) Still, Latin remained the language of France. (⑤) It is perhaps surprising that the conquerors adopted the language of the conquered people, but the high prestige of Latin as the language of a great empire and civilization may have contributed to its survival.

[35~38] 주어진 글 다음에 이어질 글의 순서로 가장 적절한 것을 고르시오.

35

> Petroleum is the "blood" of industry. But as it is buried deep in the earth, how can we find it? Sometimes, considerable labor, materials, and money are spent without exactly identifying the distribution range of petroleum.

(A) Therefore, when explorers detect a great amount of such bacteria in a place, they know there is probably petroleum. On the basis of the quantity of bacteria detected in the sample, they can also predict the quantity of petroleum and gas in reserve.

(B) Here, bacteria can be said to have a mysterious bond with petroleum. Petroleum is composed of various organic compounds, of which the majority is a carbon and hydrogen compound called hydrocarbon.

(C) Although petroleum is buried deep, there are always some hydrocarbons coming up to the earth's surface through the gaps in rock formations. Gas components in petroleum can also leak to the surface. Some bacteria feed on petroleum.

① (A)−(C)−(B) ② (B)−(A)−(C)
③ (B)−(C)−(A) ④ (C)−(A)−(B)
⑤ (C)−(B)−(A)

36

> Pearl Harbor transformed the nature of Hollywood's social concern, and criticism of government information services in the first half of 1942 led the President to create one unified body, the Office of War Information (OWI), from three existing agencies.

(A) It also encouraged Hollywood to publicise the efforts of the Allies and of resistance groups in Norway, Yugoslavia and elsewhere in occupied Europe. By late 1942 the manual began to have an impact on studio production.

(B) Lowell Mellett, a close friend of and adviser to the President, became head of the Bureau of Motion Pictures, part of the OWI's domestic branch. In the same month, June 1942, the administration issued a *Government Information Manual for the Motion Picture Industry*, a document written by Mellett's appointee Nelson Poynter and his staff.

(C) The manual has been seen as 'the clearest possible statement of New Deal, liberal views on how Hollywood should fight the war'. It stressed that the 'people's war' was not just a fight of self−defense but also a fight for democracy. [3점]

① (A)—(C)—(B)   ② (B)—(A)—(C)

③ (B)—(C)—(A)   ④ (C)—(A)—(B)

⑤ (C)—(B)—(A)

37

The reproducibility of published results is the backbone of scientific research. Objectivity is crucial for science and requires that observations, experiments and theories be checked independently of their authors before being accepted for publication.

(A) Unfortunately, this is not the case today, as most peer-reviewed journals belong to a few major publishers, who keep scientific articles behind pay-walls. Since all over the world the majority of research programs are supported by public funds financed by taxpayers, not only researchers, but everyone from everywhere should have access to scientific publications.

(B) Consequently, the set of all scientific publications is the common heritage that researchers have collectively built over centuries, and are constantly developing. Given the constructive and universal nature of science, any researcher should have access, as early

and easily as possible, to all scientific publications.

(C) Indeed, a result to be recognized as scientific must be presented and explained in an article which has been reviewed and accepted by peers, i.e., researchers able to understand, verify and, if necessary, correct it. It is only after successful peer review that a new result can be published and belongs to scientific knowledge.

① (A)—(C)—(B)   ② (B)—(A)—(C)

③ (B)—(C)—(A)   ④ (C)—(A)—(B)

⑤ (C)—(B)—(A)

38

The psychological answers to the question of why we should be bothered with history may seem too obvious to labour.

(A) But, if only because they seem so obvious, these answers can easily be taken for granted, and it's only when we are deprived of our pasts that we realise their importance—if not our actual dependence on them. That is why the examples of deprivation and abnormality recorded by Oliver Sacks and others are so instructive.

(B) From them we can see that a malfunctioning memory, or a complete loss of memory, has crucial implications for our sense of personal identity and therefore our ability to live in society with other people. Our personal histories provide support for our selves and our sanity.

(C) After all, it has become a platitude of history's defenders that the subject is needed as an essential part of education to provide a sense of national identity; and, at the personal level, we are all well enough aware that we have memories that have something to do with who we are, and where we are, and even where we hope to go. [3점]

*sanity: 제정신 **platitude: 상투어

① (A)−(C)−(B)   ② (B)−(A)−(C)
③ (B)−(C)−(A)   ④ (C)−(A)−(B)
⑤ (C)−(B)−(A)

[39~40] 다음 글의 내용을 한 문장으로 요약할 때, 빈칸 (A), (B)에 들어갈 말로 가장 적절한 것을 고르시오.

39

Though it sounds so simple and obvious, people screw this up all the time. When you train, many different factors influence each other and cause the resultant adaptations of the body. The experiences of trainees in gyms around the world for the last century, when combined with research over the last few decades, has enabled us to establish a fairly clear order of importance as to what will and won't give you the most from your training efforts. When you see seemingly conflicting advice —which exercises to do, how heavy to go, how many sets to perform, whether to train to failure, lifting explosively or slowly to 'feel the burn' etc. —you need to decide how important these factors are relative to your goals, and how they will affect the other aspects of your training. By looking at these variables through the lens of a pyramid of importance, you'll save yourself unnecessary confusion. As the classic saying goes, if you want to "fill your cup to the brim" when it comes to your training potential, get your big rocks in place before your pebbles, and your pebbles in place before your sand.

*brim: 가장자리 **pebble: 자갈

↓

As considering __(A)__ factors in training is crucial for maximizing results, a pyramid of importance can help __(B)__ the key elements over seemingly conflicting advice.

	(A)		(B)
①	various	……	prioritize
②	limited	……	prioritize
③	unique	……	generate
④	diverse	……	generate
⑤	powerful	……	characterize

40

Theory and practice are often at odds. Yet there is something particularly strange in the way in which the received theory and the presumed practice of toleration in contemporary societies seem to go their separate ways. Theoretical statements on toleration assume at the same time its necessity in democratic societies, and its impossibility as a coherent ideal. In her introduction to a comprehensive collection on tolerance and intolerance in modern life, Susan Mendus appropriately makes the point that the commitment that liberal societies have to toleration 'may be more difficult and yet more urgent than is usually recognised'.

In contrast with the urgency insisted on by the theory, the practice can appear contented: liberal democratic societies seem to have accepted the need for the recognition and accommodation of difference without registering its depth. So much so that 'practical' people often just dismiss such toleration as an excess of permissiveness. The success of 'zero tolerance' as a slogan for a less forgiving society bears witness to the spread of such a mood in public opinion.

*coherent: 통일성 있는.

↓

Theoretically, tolerance is regarded __(A)__ in democratic societies, but in reality, some people frequently overlook it as a(n) __(B)__ of permissiveness.

	(A)		(B)
①	fundamental	……	overflow
②	fundamental	……	lack
③	radical	……	balance
④	customary	……	luxury
⑤	customary	……	shortage

[41~42] 다음 글을 읽고, 물음에 답하시오.

Why do we gesture? Many would say that it brings emphasis, energy and ornamentation to speech (which is assumed to be the core of what is taking place); in short, gesture is an "add-on." However, evidence is against this. The lay view of gesture is that one "talks with one's hands." You can't find a word so you resort to gesture. Marianne Gullberg debunks this ancient idea. As she simply puts it, rather than gesture starting when words stop, gesture stops as well. The reasons we gesture are more profound. Language is _____. While gestures enhance the material carriers of meaning, the core is gesture and speech together. They are bound more tightly than saying the gesture is an "add-on" or "ornament" implies. They are united as a matter of thought itself. Even if, for some reason, the hands are restrained and a gesture is not externalized, the imagery it embodies can still be present, hidden but integrated with speech (it may surface in some other part of the body, the feet for example).

*debunk: (정체를) 폭로하다

41 윗글의 제목으로 가장 적절한 것은?

① The Hidden Power of Language

② Dissociation Between Gesture and Thought

③ Essential Principles of Gestures

④ Can We Measure the Depth of Our Thought?

⑤ Gestures: More Than Supplements

42 윗글의 빈칸에 들어갈 말로 가장 적절한 것은? [3점]

① inseparable from imagery

② emphasized by underlying meaning

③ different from superficial embodiment

④ dependent upon linguistic decoration

⑤ constructed by externalization

[43~45] 다음 글을 읽고, 물음에 답하시오.

(A)

"Dad, are you keeping an eye on the time?" Tom asked. He thought they had to go to the gate now, but (a) his dad seemed careless about the time. "Yes, I am, Tom. Don't worry. We're not going to be late," Dad said, but he had been saying that for at least twenty minutes. Dad was trying to find a duty-free shop with one special brand of watches. When they got there, the place was packed with a multitude of people. It seemed as though everyone in the airport wanted something from this duty-free shop.

(B)

However, Dad did not even look at his son. He was talking with a salesman while examining a few watches in front of him. The salesman was very patient and considerate. Finally, Dad chose one, and the salesman said, "I'll wrap this for you then." Dad paid quickly and received the package from (b) him. Finally, the transaction was over. Dad turned to his son and said, "Let's roll." Before even Dad finished his words, Tom was already running.

(C)

They dashed along the passageway like 100-meter racers, and the bag of the package was flying, chasing after them. In the distance, (c) the son saw the gate closing and shouted, "Wait, we are here!" "Wait, please!" the father yelled too, right after his son. The attendant saw them, and they made it by the skin of their teeth. Sitting in his seat, Dad said, "See, I was right!" Tom didn't know what to say, but (d) he simply sighed with relief.

(D)

In the shop, there were many small booths selling different goods, and Dad was again walking around to look for the watch booth. "The plane leaves at four thirty, and the boarding begins thirty minutes earlier, which means we have to be at the gate by four," Tom was calculating in his mind and looked at (e) his watch. It was almost four. They should have been at the gate already. It would take at least ten minutes to reach the gate from where they were. Tom looked at his dad and made a long face.

43 주어진 글 (A)에 이어질 내용을 순서에 맞게 배열한 것으로 가장 적절한 것은?

① (B)−(D)−(C) ② (C)−(B)−(D)

③ (C)−(D)−(B) ④ (D)−(B)−(C)

⑤ (D)−(C)−(B)

44 밑줄 친 (a)~(e) 중에서 가리키는 대상이 나머지 넷과 다른 것은?

① (a) ② (b)

③ (c) ④ (d)

⑤ (e)

45 윗글에 관한 내용으로 적절하지 않은 것은?

① Tom was concerned about his dad's attitude toward time.

② The duty−free shop Tom visited was very crowded.

③ The salesperson provided a patient and considerate service.

④ Tom and his dad successfully went on board.

⑤ Tom was delighted with his dad's shopping.

2026

경찰대학
📡 10개년 영어

제2교시 영어영역

▶정답 및 해설 279p

[01~05] 밑줄 친 단어의 뜻으로 가장 적절한 것을 고르시오.

01
When I was a trainee doctor, one of my first patients was an old man with a persistent cough.

① fatal

② occasional

③ irregular

④ chronic

⑤ infectious

02
During the televised court case, the witness statements contradicted each other.

① agreed

② opposed

③ confirmed

④ duplicated

⑤ appreciated

03
As many as two billion people might not exist now if it hadn't been for the advent of agribusiness.

① emergence　　② transformation

③ collapse　　④ manipulation

⑤ supplement

04
Promotion in the first year is only given in exceptional circumstances.

① adverse　　② suspicious

③ customary　　④ profitable

⑤ unusual

05
When a nurse holds a bias toward her patients, she may provide substandard care.

① sophisticated　　② considerate

③ temporary　　④ conventional

⑤ insufficient

[06~07] 다음 대화의 빈칸에 들어갈 말로 가장 적절한 것을 고르시오.

06

A: Hey, Mom. Do you know where my favorite red shirt is?

B: Did you check the top drawer in your room?

A: Yes. But it wasn't there.

B: Take a look inside the dryer, then.

A: Oh, here it is. But it's still wet.

B: _____.

A: Oh, no! The school bus is going to be here any minute.

B: Well, you're just going to have to wear a different shirt then.

① You can buy a new shirt instead

② Then you can wear it right away

③ Just put it in the washing machine

④ I hope you find your favorite shirt soon

⑤ It's going to take at least twenty more minutes

07

A: Congratulations on getting the Medal of Honor, Sergeant Park.

B: I don't know if I deserve it, Commissioner.

A: Of course you do. What you did to save that young man's life was very brave.

B: _____.

A: That's very modest of you. It's people like you that make our department proud.

B: Thank you. I'm just glad the young man is doing well.

A: Thanks to you, our city's streets are a little safer and warmer.

B: I will cherish this moment forever.

① I've never been afraid of anything

② I've always considered myself to be a hero

③ I'm sure anyone else would have done the same

④ I'm not sure if you're the right person for this medal

⑤ I think arresting criminals should come before everything

[08~09] 밑줄 친 부분 중, 어법상 틀린 것을 고르시오.

08 The most common theory points to the fact that men are stronger than women, and that they have used their greater physical power to force women into submission. A more subtle version of this claim argues that their strength allows men to monopolise tasks that demand hard manual labour, such as ploughing and harvesting. This gives them control of food production, which in turn ① translate into political power. However, the statement that 'men are stronger than women' is true only on average, and only with regard to certain types of strength. Women are generally more resistant to hunger, disease and fatigue than men. There are also many women who can run faster and ② lift heavier weights than many men. Furthermore, and most problematically for this theory, women have, throughout history, ③ been excluded mainly from jobs that require little physical effort such as the priesthood, law and politics, while ④ engaging in hard manual labour in the fields, in crafts and in the household. If social power ⑤ were divided in direct relation to physical strength, women should have got far more of it. [3점]

09 Hugs play a role in physical intimacy and health. Researchers examined the interplay between exposure to illness, social support, and daily hugs. In the name of science (and possibly a hundred bucks), 404 healthy adults agreed to inhale nasal drops that exposed ① them to the common cold. First, the researchers drew blood samples to confirm ② that the volunteers were not immune. Then they surveyed the participants over fourteen consecutive days, ③ asked about hugs received. Finally, they exposed volunteers to the cold virus and ④ monitored symptoms, such as mucus production, in quarantine for five days. Those who got daily hugs ⑤ were 32 percent less likely to get sick. Hugs don't make you impervious to a cold, it turns out. But the huggers who did get sick didn't get as sick. They had less severe symptoms and got better faster.

[10~12] (A), (B), (C)의 각 네모 안에서 문맥에 맞는 낱말로 가장 적절한 것을 고르시오.

10

Are hybrid cars really environmentally friendly? It depends on how they're used. They're great for city drivers, when a hybrid can rely almost fully on its electric motor, which is quiet, doesn't create any emissions, will turn off completely when the car is stationary and, crucially, gives (A) poor / superb fuel economy. Drive out onto the highway, though, and the hybrid will have to fall back on its petrol engine because the electric motor simply doesn't have the power to drive the car at (B) higher / lower speeds, nor the energy to run for long distances. In such cases the hybrid will act just like a comparable conventional petrol-powered car, offering similar fuel economy and the same emissions. You should also take into account that the manufacturing of batteries for a hybrid car requires a lot of energy. Then, after they have reached the end of their life—which may be after just a few years—more energy is required to decommission and recycle them. This and the development impact actually make hybrid cars (C) less / more environmentally friendly than the manufacturers would like you to believe.

	(A)	(B)	(C)
①	poor	lower	less
②	poor	lower	more
③	poor	higher	less
④	superb	higher	more
⑤	superb	higher	less

11

Given the diversity of American society, it has been impossible to insulate the schools from pressures that result from differences and tensions among groups. When people differ about basic values, sooner or later those (A) agreements / disagreements turn up in battles about how schools are organized or what the schools should teach. Sometimes these battles remove a terrible injustice, like racial segregation. Sometimes, however, interest groups (B) retain / politicize the curriculum and attempt to impose their views on teachers, school officials, and textbook publishers. Across the country, even now, interest groups are pressuring local school boards to remove myths and fables and other imaginative literature from children's readers and to inject the teaching of creationism in biology. When groups cross the line into extremism, advancing their own agenda without regard to reason or

to others, they threaten public education itself, making it difficult to teach any issues honestly and making the entire curriculum (C) invulnerable / vulnerable to political campaigns.

	(A)	(B)	(C)
①	agreements	retain	invulnerable
②	agreements	politicize	vulnerable
③	disagreements	retain	invulnerable
④	disagreements	politicize	vulnerable
⑤	disagreements	retain	vulnerable

12

As the largest predatory fish on Earth, great white sharks are already impressive, armed with up to 300 sharp teeth and weighing up to 5,000 pounds. Now, new research adds more intrigue to the oceanic beasts, suggesting that the animals can change color—perhaps as a (A) camouflage / cluster strategy to sneak up on prey. In new experiments off South Africa, researchers dragged a seal decoy behind a boat to (B) dispel / entice several sharks to leap out of the water near a specially designed color board with white, gray, and black panels. The team photographed the sharks each time they jumped, repeating the experiment throughout the day. One

65

shark, easily (C) concealable / identifiable because of a mark on its jaw, appeared as both dark gray and much lighter gray at different times of day. The scientists verified this using computer software to correct for variables such as weather, light levels, and camera settings.

	(A)	(B)	(C)
①	camouflage	dispel	identifiable
②	camouflage	entice	identifiable
③	camouflage	entice	concealable
④	cluster	entice	concealable
⑤	cluster	dispel	identifiable

[13~14] 밑줄 친 부분 중, 문맥상 낱말의 쓰임이 적절하지 않은 것을 고르시오.

13 Left to their own devices, most children won't hesitate to, say, lick a doorknob or wipe snot with their sleeve. But is there any truth to the idea that their ① distaste for getting dirty can be beneficial to their health? That theory dates to the 1800s, when European doctors realized that farmers suffered fewer allergies than city slickers. However, it didn't gain widespread attention until 1989, when British epidemiologist David Strachan discovered that youngsters with older siblings were less susceptible than other kids to hay fever and eczema. Strachan suggested that early childhood infections "transmitted by unhygienic contact" helped ② foster a robust immune system. His theory, called the hygiene hypothesis, provides a ③ convenient explanation for why allergies and asthma, as well as autoimmune disorders like multiple sclerosis and Crohn's disease, have increased 300 percent or more in the U.S. since the 1950s. Maybe Western societies have become too clean for their own good, and parents too ④ fearful of a little dirt. "Whatever it is that's happening in the modern world, it's causing the immune system to be ⑤ active when it doesn't need to be," says microbiologist Graham Rook of University College London. [3점]

14 Age is much more than the number of birthdays you've ① clocked. Stress, sleep, and diet all influence how our organs cope with the wear and tear of everyday life. Factors like these might make you age faster or slower than people born on the same day. That means your biological age could be quite different from your chronological age—the number of years you've been alive. Your biological age is likely a better ② reflection of your physical health and even your own mortality than your chronological age. But calculating it isn't nearly as ③ straightforward. Scientists have spent the last decade developing tools called aging clocks that assess markers in your body to ④ veil your biological age. The big idea behind aging clocks is that they'll essentially indicate how much your organs have ⑤ degraded, and thus predict how many healthy years you have left.

2023 기출문제

15 Porcelain Tower에 관한 다음 글의 내용과 일치하는 것은?

In early 15th-century China, the Yongle Emperor of the Ming dynasty ordered the construction of a towering monument to honor his mother. The Porcelain Tower was a grand pagoda built in the city of Nanjing—the imperial capital at the time—as part of the grand Bao'en Buddhist Temple complex. The tower was constructed from white porcelain bricks, which would have glistened in the sunlight, and adorned with vibrant glazed designs of animals, lowers and landscapes in greens, yellows and browns. Historians studying the remnants suggest that the glazed porcelain bricks were made by highly skilled workers, but sadly the methods used to make them have been lost to history. Some of the largest bricks were more than 50 centimeters thick and weighed as much as 150 kilograms each, with the colored glazes staying bright for centuries. Nowadays, workers trying to replicate these porcelain slabs struggle to make anything larger than five centimeters thick and their colors fade after just a decade.

① Its bricks were all the same size.

② It stood in a temple of a rural area.

③ It was built to honor the Emperor's mother.

④ It was decorated with the shapes of the sun.

⑤ Its porcelain slabs have been successfully replicated today.

16 Nadine Gordimer에 관한 다음 글의 내용과 일치하는 것은?

The South African novelist Nadine Gordimer was awarded the Nobel Prize for Literature in 1991 not only for her excellent literary skills but also for her consistent and courageous criticism of apartheid, which was a system of strictly segregating the blacks from the whites in all spheres of life. Her attack on apartheid was not primarily a political gesture. As a novelist, she was more interested in the human aspect of apartheid and racism. She knew, for one thing, that she herself, as a white middle-class intellectual living in South Africa, benefited from the system. She also knew that the whites responsible for keeping up the racist system suffered in their own ways from it. Her novels and short stories, therefore, concentrate on the moral dilemmas imposed on the individuals by the social relations of South Africa. Although as an intellectual she is capable of making unambiguous political statements on delicate social issues, as a novelist she is more interested in the less clear aspects of humans living in a society based on inequality and injustice.

① Her novels neglected the ethical problems faced by the whites.

② Her fight against apartheid was mainly driven by political ambition.

③ Her growth as a writer was attributed to her middle-class black parents.

④ She was acknowledged for her strong stance against racial discrimination.

⑤ She was praised for her ability to avoid delicate issues on South African politics.

[17~23] 다음 글의 빈칸에 들어갈 말로 가장 적절한 것을 고르시오.

17

Imagine you jump into a river to save a drowning child. This would probably seem to most people a good thing to do. For Kant, however, it is only a good thing to do if you jumped into the river to save the drowning child because you knew it was your moral duty to do so. If you jumped into the river to save the child because you thought it might make you look good, would impress your friends and get you on television or even because you cared for the child, then, from a Kantian perspective, it

is no longer a moral act. For Kant, it is not essential that you actually save the drowning child. What counts is the will or intention to save them. Where the consequentialist, obviously, would be primarily focused on the outcome, Kant is concerned with choice and _____. [3점]

① repression   ② decision

③ intuition   ④ satisfaction

⑤ motivation

18

The ability to record information is one of the lines of demarcation between primitive and advanced societies. Basic counting and measurement of length and weight were among the oldest conceptual tools of early civilizations. By the third millennium B.C. the idea of recorded information had advanced significantly in the Indus Valley, Egypt, and Mesopotamia. Accuracy increased, as did the use of measurement in everyday life. The evolution of script in Mesopotamia provided a precise method of keeping track of production and business transactions. Written language enabled early civilizations to measure reality, record it, and retrieve it later. Together, measuring and recording _____ the creation of data. They are the earliest foundations of datafication.

① complicated   ② reversed

③ imitated   ④ hindered

⑤ facilitated

① subjective opinion

② racy headlines

③ boring truth

④ online etiquette

⑤ exaggerated ads

19

The news is not what it used to be. These days most consumers get most of their bulletins online. Since online publishing is cheap, a profusion of new sources have sprung up. Websites run by established newspapers compete with newer, online-only outlets and professional (or amateur) blogs, not to mention the mix of articles, digital chain-letters and comments curated by the algorithms of social-media sites such as Facebook and Twitter. Established media have struggled. Much of the advertising that used to pay journalists' salaries has gone to Facebook and Google, the two big technology firms that dominate the market for online advertising. Print circulation has collapsed. Local papers have been particularly hard hit, with many going bust. Social-media algorithms prioritise attention-grabbing clickbait over _____, which helps propel nonsense around the world. Collins, a dictionary-publisher, declared "fake news" its 2017 neologism of the year.

20

Since the 1990s, businesses and police have teamed up to pump classical music onto crime-ridden streets, parking lots, and malls. Why? Because there's evidence that a little bit of Bach may deter crime. In 2005, the London Underground started piping classical music at certain Tube stations, and within a year, robberies and vandalism were sliced by a third. Light-rail stations in Portland, Oregon—and other transit hubs like New York's Port Authority bus terminal—have also reported drops in vagrancy thanks to the crime-stopping powers of Baroque maestros like Vivaldi. The logic? For one, classical music can be calming. But more importantly, the people who loiter and vandalize—often teenagers— usually don't enjoy orchestral music. And if an environment's soundscape annoys you, then chances are you won't _____. Apparently, this works on animals too. At Gloucestershire Airport in Staverton, England, airport chiefs learned the best way to scare away

2023 기출문제

birds was to drive a van blaring Tina Turner's biggest hits. [3점]

*vagrancy: 방랑, 부랑죄

① get emotionally stable

② want to loaf around there

③ be in the mood for classical music

④ commit a serious crime on the spot

⑤ pay attention to the music any more

① felt the need to free themselves to succeed

② were burdened with expectations from their elders

③ internalized the social values of their environment

④ learned how to avoid oppressive norms and conventions

⑤ had the desire to develop and realize their own potential

21

African American psychologists Kenneth and Mamie Phipps Clark used sets of toy babies—some with white skin, some with brown—to understand how black children living under segregation in the 1940s developed their sense of self. Black kids presented with both options preferred the pale doll; some even cried when asked which looked like them. The Clarks took this as evidence that youths _____ : They saw themselves as inferior because of their skin color. The tests impressed attorneys in the famous *Brown v. Board of Education* lawsuit, where Kenneth testified that segregation led to self-hatred. The Supreme Court's 1954 ruling on that case finally integrated schools and spurred a growing movement for civil rights.

22

Astrology contends that which constellation the planets are in at the moment of your birth profoundly influences your future. A few thousand years ago, the idea developed that the motions of the planets determined the fates of kings, dynasties, and empires. Astrologers studied the motions of the planets and asked themselves what had happened the last time that, say, Venus was rising in the Constellation of the Goat; perhaps something similar would happen this time as well. It was a subtle and risky business. Astrologers came to be employed only by the State. In many countries it was a capital offense for anyone but the official astrologer to read the signs in the skies: a good way to overthrow a regime was to predict its downfall. Chinese court astrologers who made inaccurate predictions were executed. Others simply doctored the records so that afterward _____ . Astrology developed into a strange combination of observations, mathematics and careful record-keeping with fuzzy thinking and fraud. [3점]

① a more cautious position would be adopted

② they were in perfect conformity with events

③ people would pay close attention to the stars

④ descendants could learn from their ancestors

⑤ observations of the planets could be encouraged

23

Why don't teens talk to their parents? "Basically, they don't think their parents will understand," says a noted psychologist. "When they are constantly reprimanded or instructed, they may feel that a parent doesn't care how they feel. Silence for a teenager is a weapon. It's their way of saying, "You can't control me anymore." But that doesn't mean you need to spend the next few years in suspended animation. It does mean you have to establish an atmosphere of trust, understanding and flexibility. Here is how: _____ . If your daughter tells you her best friend said her new outfit was awful, refrain from saying, "Why should you care what Jennifer says?" Teenagers care very much what their peers think, and the wise parent accepts that as normal. Try instead, "That must have made you feel terrible. It hurts when people we care about say mean things."

① Resist the temptation to control and keep silent

② Acknowledge and legitimize a teenager's feelings

③ Encourage teens to accept criticism from others

④ Maintain family rituals as a way of staying in touch

⑤ Take adolescent mood swings and silences personally

[24~26] 다음 글의 제목으로 가장 적절한 것을 고르시오.

24

It wasn't unusual in Victorian London to see children digging through junkyards, looking for anything they could resell: scraps of metal, rags, bones—which could be used to make buttons and soap—and even dead cats, which they sold to furriers. But the most prized find? Coal dust. Brickmakers, who mixed it with clay to make blocks, paid a pretty penny for it. It's not that coal dust was scarce. In fact, because of open-hearth fires, ash was everywhere, and would have clogged the city's streets were it not for the dustmen who lugged it from dustbins to the city's outskirts. The scene resembled a regular Dickensian recycling operation: women, men, and children working thigh-deep in dust. Their bosses got filthy rich, but as London's dust supply outstripped demand, profits declined. By the late 19th century, prospects had already tarnished for these once "Golden Dustmen."

① When Victorians Got Rich on Dust
② A Foolproof Recipe for Brickmaking
③ How Bad Is Working in a Coal Mine?
④ Child Labor During the Industrial Revolution
⑤ Air Pollution: Why London Struggled to Breathe

25

The company formerly known as Facebook is so convinced that the metaverse is the future of the internet that last year it changed its name to Meta. Meta and its boss Mark Zuckerberg think that eventually many of us will work, play, and shop in the metaverse. Or at least our avatars will. While for many people this all sounds fanciful, a growing number of companies are buying up space in the metaverse so that they can set up shop there. These firms include the likes of Adidas, Burberry, Gucci, Tommy Hilfiger, Nike, Samsung, Louis Vuitton, and even banks HSBC and JP Morgan. The question for such businesses, though, is what location they pick. There are now some 50 or so different providers of worlds within the metaverse, with the most popular ones including The Sandbox, Decentraland, Voxels, and Somnium Space, plus Meta's own Horizon Worlds. Retailers and other investors are having to gamble on which of these will go on to become the dominant force in the metaverse, gaining the most visits from our avatars. And which other worlds may fade away into obscurity. Further, within the winning ecosystems, firms have to try to pick what will be the most popular areas.

① Setting up Shop in the Metaverse

② Opening Electronic Bank Branches

③ Building Virtual Eco-friendly Environments

④ Climbing the Social Ladder in the Metaverse

⑤ Dominating the Shopping Space with Avatars

26

A new study tests the common belief that the angrier people appear after a service failure, the more compensation they'll get—and shows that often the reverse is true. The effect of intense anger on service reps, the researchers found, varies according to a cultural trait known as *power distance*, or PD: a person's level of acceptance of power differences and hierarchy. Across four experiments involving simulated service interactions, participants with high PD—those who accepted power differences as natural or inevitable—gave more compensation to mildly angry customers than to intensely angry ones, while participants with low PD did just the opposite. Why? The high-PD subjects saw displays of intense anger as inappropriate and punished them, while the low-PD subjects saw the displays as threatening and rewarded them. But when the perception of threat was mitigated (participants were told that customers couldn't harm them), low-PD people, too, gave more compensation to mildly angry customers.

① Does Time Really Fly When You're Having Fun?

② Does the Squeaky Wheel Get the Most Oil?

③ Can a Rolling Stone Gather Any Moss?

④ Can Too Many Chefs Spoil the Broth?

⑤ Can a Stitch in Time Save Nine?

[27~28] 다음 글의 주제로 가장 적절한 것을 고르시오.

27

After the go-go 1990s and 2000s, the pace of economic integration stalled in the 2010s, as firms struggled with the aftershocks of a financial crisis, a populist revolt against open borders and President Donald Trump's trade war. The flow of goods and capital stagnated. Many bosses postponed big decisions on investing abroad: just-in-time gave way to wait-and-see. No one knew if globalisation faced a blip or extinction. Now the waiting is over, as the pandemic and war in Ukraine have triggered a once-in-a-generation reimagining of global capitalism in boardrooms and governments. Everywhere you look, supply chains are being transformed, from the $9 trillion in inventories, stockpiled as insurance against shortages and inflation, to the fight for workers as global firms shift from China into Vietnam. This new kind of globalisation prioritises doing business with people you can rely on, in countries your government is friendly with. It could descend into protectionism, big government and worsening inflation.

① the era of globalisation ushered in by new businesses

② the promotion of globalisation through cost efficiency

③ the switch to a security-first model of globalisation

④ the disruption of globalisation caused by war

⑤ the threat of globalisation to workers' rights

28

Members of the Lost Generation viewed the idea of the "American Dream" as a grand deception. This becomes a prominent theme in F. S. Fitzgerald's *The Great Gatsby* as the story's narrator Nick Carraway comes to realize that Gatsby's vast fortune had been paid for with great

misery. To Fitzgerald, the traditional vision of the American Dream—that hard work led to success—had become corrupted. To the Lost Generation, "living the dream" was no longer about simply building a self-sufficient life, but about getting stunningly rich by any means necessary. The term "American Dream" refers to the belief that everyone has the right and freedom to seek prosperity and happiness, regardless of where or into what social class they were born. A key element of the American Dream is the assumption that through hard work, perseverance, and risk-taking, anyone can rise "from rags to riches," to attain their own version of success in becoming financially prosperous and socially upwardly mobile. Since the 1920s, the American Dream has been questioned and often criticized by researchers and social scientists as being a misplaced belief that contradicts reality in the modern United States.

① the repentance of self-reliance through hard work

② the fallacy of the great American Dream

③ the revision of the American Dream

④ the criticism of material success in America

⑤ the realization of the Lost Generation's ideals

[29~30] 다음 글의 요지로 가장 적절한 것을 고르시오.

29

Caitlin Mooney is 24 years old and passionate about technology that dates to the age of Sputnik. Mooney, a recent New Jersey Institute of Technology graduate in computer science, is a fan of technologies that were hot a half-century ago, including computer mainframes and software called COBOL that powers them. That stuff won't win any cool points in Silicon Valley, but it is essential technology at big banks, insurance companies, government agencies and other large institutions. During Mooney's job hunt, potential employers saw her expertise and wanted to talk about more senior positions than she was seeking. "They would get really excited," Mooney said. She's now trying to decide between multiple job offers. The resilience of decades-old computing technologies and the people who specialize in them shows that new technologies are often built on lots of old tech.

① Old technology can still be of great use.
② Keep up with the changing times in the tech world.
③ The best job is one that makes full use of your abilities.
④ Silicon Valley is always in the market for new technology.
⑤ The future of digital technology lies within academic institutions.

30

It's tempting to assume that past successes are a sign of good judgment, and in some cases they may be. The multigenerational success of some German midsize companies and the sheer longevity of Warren Buffett's investment performance are frequently cited examples. But success can have other parents. Luck, the characteristic that Napoleon famously required of his generals, is often the unacknowledged architect of success. Those in sports can attest to the importance of luck as well as skill. Grant Simmer, navigator and designer in four America's Cup yachting victories, has acknowledged the help of luck in the form of mistakes made by his competitors. Sometimes, what looks like sustained success may conceal trickery. Before the Enron scandal broke, in 2001, CEO Jeff Skilling was hailed as a highly successful leader. Toshiba's well-regarded boss, Hisao Tanaka, resigned in disgrace in 2015 after a $1.2 billion profit overstatement covering seven years was unearthed. [3점]

① A watched pot never boils.

② All that glitters is not gold.

③ Time and tide wait for no man.

④ Birds of a feather flock together.

⑤ Don't put all your eggs in one basket.

[31~32] 다음 글에서 전체 흐름과 관계 <u>없는</u> 문장을 고르시오.

31 For centuries, natives of the New Hebrides islands considered a head full of lice a sign of good health. "Observation over the centuries had taught them that people in good health usually had lice and sick people very often did not. The observation itself was accurate and sound," writes Darrell Huff in *How to Lie with Statistics*. ① But the correlation didn't mean lice are the key to good health—it's the other way around. ② Healthy people had lice because their body was just the right temperature, a perfect home for bugs. ③ Thus the proliferation of lice was a key determinant in promoting health in the human body. ④ But when people ran a high fever, their flesh became hot, sending the lice scattering. ⑤ Lice didn't cause good health—they preyed on it.

32 Cryptocurrencies have been around since 2009, and in all this time they have never come to play a major role in real-world transactions—El Salvador's much-hyped attempt to make bitcoin its national currency has become a disaster. ① Suppose, for example, that you use a digital payments app like Venmo, which has amply demonstrated its usefulness for real-world transactions. ② So how did cryptocurrencies come to be worth almost $3 trillion at their peak? ③ Why was nothing done to rein in "stablecoins," which were supposedly pegged to the U.S. dollar but were clearly subject to all the risks of unregulated banking, and are now experiencing a cascading series of collapses reminiscent of the wave of bank failures that helped make the Great Depression great? ④ My answer is that while the crypto industry has never managed to come up with products that are of much use in the real economy, it has been spectacularly successful at marketing itself, creating an image of being both cutting edge and respectable. ⑤ It has done so, in particular, by cultivating prominent people and institutions. [3점]

*cryptocurrency: 암호화폐

[33~34] 글의 흐름으로 보아, 주어진 문장이 들어가기에 가장 적절한 곳을 고르시오.

33

> But newly analyzed fossils including wing bones, presented today in the journal *Royal Society Open Science*, have changed the story.

In ancient Flores, an island in eastern Indonesia, "hobbit"-size humans shared the landscape with an immense bird. (①) At more than five feet tall, the Ice Age stork *Leptoptilos robustus* would have towered over the three-foot-tall Homo floresiensis, who lived more than 60,000 years ago. (②) Paleontologists previously thought the big bird was a flightless species that had adapted to live in an isolated island ecosystem. (③) Despite the stork's size, its 12-foot wingspan likely would have allowed it to soar overhead. (④) This new realization prompted paleontologists to revise what they previously thought about the anatomy and behavior of *L. robustus*. (⑤) Rather than a hunter of small prey, the new study suggests the bird was probably a scavenger like other prehistoric, flying storks that are known to have relied on dead animals for their meals.

*paleontologist: 고생물학자

34

> Lead ions—while still toxic in other ways—also helped produce nitric oxide, a free radical that killed bacteria before they could infect the eyes.

Egyptians famously rimmed their eyes with black makeup. The makeover wasn't just for humans—cows led into ritual slaughter also got the face paint, as shown in art from 2500 B.C.E. (①) Manuscripts from the era claimed that the eyeliner protected wearers from eye infections, but modern-day scientists were skeptical. (②) After all, the most common formula contained lead. (③) But in 2009, a team of chemists led by a researcher from the University of Pierre and Marie Curie in Paris analyzed samples scraped from tombs and found the ancients were onto something. (④) Further, some of the compounds in the eyeliner aren't native to Egypt, leading researchers to believe that the makeup wasn't just used because it was on hand—it was deliberately manufactured. (⑤) The study's authors dubbed the eyeliner the first large-scale chemical manufacturing process known to us.

35 다음 글의 내용을 한 문장으로 요약할 때, 빈칸 (A), (B)에 들어갈 말로 가장 적절한 것은?

Ancient Greek democracy allowed the public to participate directly in the affairs of government, choosing policies and making governing decisions. In this sense, the people were the state. In contrast, the Roman Empire laid out the concept of republicanism, which emphasized the separation of powers within a state and the representation of the public through elected officials. Thus, while Greece gives us the idea of popular sovereignty, it is from Rome that we derive the notion of legislative bodies like a senate. In their earliest forms, neither Greek democracy nor Roman republicanism would be defined as liberal democracies by today's standards. Both emphasized certain democratic elements but restricted them in fundamental ways. As political rights and institutions have expanded over the centuries, republicanism and democracy have become intertwined to produce the modern liberal democratic regime we know today.

Although the forms of government in ancient Greece and Rome were (A) , together they provided the (B) for modern democracy.

	(A)		(B)
①	primitive	......	deficiencies
②	interchangeable	......	inspiration
③	ideal	......	riddles
④	dissimilar	......	foundation
⑤	groundbreaking	......	groundwork

36 다음 글의 빈칸 (A), (B)에 들어갈 말로 가장 적절한 것은?

How we look at purpose is often connected to perceived importance. (A) , we say that the purpose of the bee is to pollinate the flower if we see the flower as the object of primary concern; but if we are, say, beekeepers, we would be more likely to say that the purpose of the bee is to produce honey to feed the hive. Here purpose can be seen to be relative to a larger context—carrying seeds for flowers, or producing honey for the hive—and is connected with exploiting or using something for certain ends. (B) , in nature it is often not quite clear who is using who. Is the small bird that eats ticks from the hide of the rhinoceros using the rhino as a large all-you-can-eat buffet, or is the rhino using the bird as a means of ridding itself of annoying ticks? They both need each other. So purpose is relative, then, and relates to something's or someone's relative importance.

	(A)		(B)
①	For instance	······	Otherwise
②	In contrast	······	Moreover
③	For instance	······	Yet
④	In contrast	······	Thus
⑤	Furthermore	······	However

[37~38] 주어진 글 다음에 이어질 글의 순서로 가장 적절한 것을 고르시오.

37

The women's movement since the sixties has developed in a way that exactly mirrors traditional male attitudes. It is as if we have a pattern burned into our brains and we can't move outside it. I've been thinking recently about why on the whole the women's movement has not fulfilled its potential.

(A) In today's Japan there are very few women in public life, much fewer than anywhere in the West, and when they are, it's nearly always in cultural things. So, all the great explosion of energy has ended up with a very narrow section of the female population doing better than it did before.

(B) They have good jobs, usually in cultural things like television and radio, newspapers, and so on. This is also true in countries where women have an extremely bad time, like Japan.

(C) It burst on the scene with enormous energy all over Europe and in America. Yet the energy dissipated, and what has actually been achieved is this: that in all the European countries and America and Canada middle-class women who were probably young in the sixties and are now middle-aged have done rather well.

① (A)-(C)-(B)　　② (B)-(A)-(C)
③ (B)-(C)-(A)　　④ (C)-(A)-(B)
⑤ (C)-(B)-(A)

38

Ever more scholars see cultures as a kind of mental infection or parasite, with humans as its unwitting host. Organic parasites, such as viruses, live inside the body of their hosts.

(A) The human dies, but the idea spreads. According to this approach, cultures are not conspiracies made up by some people in order to take advantage of others. Rather, cultures are mental parasites that emerge accidentally, and thereafter take advantage of all people infected by them.

(B) In just this fashion, cultural ideas live inside the minds of humans. They multiply and spread from one host to another, occasionally weakening the hosts and sometimes even killing them. A cultural idea can compel a human to dedicate his or her life to spreading that idea, even at the price of death.

(C) These parasites multiply and spread from one host to the other, feeding off their hosts, weakening them, and sometimes even killing them. As long as the hosts live long enough to pass along the parasite, it cares little about the conditions of its host. [3점]

① (A)–(C)–(B)   ② (B)–(A)–(C)

③ (B)–(C)–(A)   ④ (C)–(A)–(B)

⑤ (C)–(B)–(A)

[39~40] 다음 글을 읽고, 물음에 답하시오.

To many Americans, Cinco de Mayo is a day for eating Mexican food and drinking liberally. But the real history is far more _____.

It started in the 1860s. France wanted to expand its empire into Mexico, and Napoleon III ordered his troops to head toward Mexico City to overthrow Mexico's democratically elected President Benito Juárez, while Abraham Lincoln was preoccupied with the Civil War. The hyperorganized French forces were widely expected to triumph, leading to a new Mexican monarchy that would side with the Confederacy.

But then, on May 5, 1862, the Mexican forces defeated the French in the Battle of Puebla. That surprise victory brought together Latinos who had come north during the gold rush, leading to spontaneous celebrations, says David E. Hayes-Bautista, author of *El Cinco de Mayo: An American Tradition*. (The first took place in Tuolumne County in California.) Soon they started a network of organizations to support the fight against slavery both in Mexico and the U.S.

But in the 1930s, though, as the Civil War became a more distant memory, Cinco de Mayo's significance as a civil rights holiday started to fall by the wayside. By the 1980s and 1990s the number of Hispanic consumers had risen dramatically, and marketers—especially within the spirits industry—seized the moment. They made the holiday ubiquitous by turning it into a general celebration of Mexican-American culture, and the parties rage on today.

39 윗글의 빈칸에 들어갈 말로 가장 적절한 것은? [3점]

① geographically driven

② politically charged

③ conspiracy ridden

④ culturally distorted

⑤ economically balanced

40 윗글의 제목으로 가장 적절한 것은?

① The Surprising Evolution of Cinco de Mayo

② The Political Significance of Mexican Cuisine

③ Revisiting the History of Mexican Immigration

④ All Against Slavery: Struggles of the Confederacy

⑤ The Restoration of Civil Rights Through Cinco de Mayo

[41~42] 다음 글을 읽고, 물음에 답하시오.

Have you ever looked at the nighttime horizon and gasped at the sight of a spectacularly large moonrise? Typically, if you glance up at the sky hours later, the moon will seem to have shrunk. Dubbed the moon illusion, this phenomenon has been witnessed for thousands of years, a visual trickery that takes place all in the mind. And, even after so long, scientists still disagree on what exactly is happening in our brains. To test it, you can snap a picture of the rising moon on the horizon and compare it to an image taken later that night. The size will remain consistent, even if your eyes deceive in the moment. _____(A)_____,

during a supermoon, when the date of the full moon coincides with the point closest to Earth in the lunar orbit and the moon appears roughly 7 percent bigger, the naked eye can barely see the increase—even if you convince yourself otherwise.

One common explanation for the illusion is that when the moon is near the horizon, trees or buildings juxtaposed against the sky fool your brain into perceiving the moon as closer to Earth, and therefore extra big. _____(B)_____, astronauts in orbit also witness the moon illusion without foreground objects, so this doesn't quite solve the problem. While other hypotheses abound, the moon illusion still holds some intrigue for scientists—and anyone who takes the time to sit back and savor this lunar mystery.

*juxtapose: 나란히 놓다

41 윗글의 제목으로 가장 적절한 것은?

① Traveling to the Moon Made Easy

② Lunar Eclipse During Supermoons

③ The Breathtaking View from Outer Space

④ The Optical Illusion of the Size of the Moon

⑤ The Shrinking Universe: A Cause for Worry?

42 윗글의 빈칸 (A), (B)에 들어갈 말로 가장 적절한 것은?

	(A)		(B)
①	Similarly	......	Moreover
②	For example	......	On one hand
③	Similarly	......	However
④	For example	......	Likewise
⑤	On the contrary	......	Therefore

[43~45] 다음 글을 읽고, 물음에 답하시오.

(A)

It was 1948, and Eleanor Abbott was bored. The retired schoolteacher was stuck in a San Diego hospital surrounded by young children who, like her, were suffering from polio. The kids were lonely and sad, and Abbott, with nothing else to do, decided that a cheerful board game could be the perfect antidote. So she supposedly grabbed a piece of butcher paper and started sketching plans.

(B)

While Milton Bradley kept that origin story under wraps for decades, the game's connection to the disease didn't stop there. It's possible that polio helped make *Candy Land* famous. In the early 1950s, a polio epidemic swept the country. The best way to stay healthy was to avoid people. Public swimming pools, playgrounds, and bowling alleys were shuttered. Moviegoers were encouraged to sit far from each other at the theater. Wary parents wouldn't even let their kids outside to play. Healthy or sick, everybody needed entertainment to help pass the time. That, coupled with the fact that postwar Americans had more money and leisure time than ever, provided ideal conditions for making a child's board game popular. Plus, it was about candy!

(C)

Today, polio has practically been eradicated from the globe. *Candy Land*, however, keeps on giving. It's sold more than 40 million copies and was inducted into the National Toy Hall of Fame in 2005. But Abbott kept a humble low profile for the rest of her life. According to Nicolas Ricketts of The Strong—a museum in Rochester, New York, devoted to the history and exploration of play—when Abbott received her first royalty check, she gave much of the money right back to the children she met in the ward. How sweet!

(D)

The end result was perfect for young children. No counting. No reading. Players simply needed to grasp colors and follow instructions on the cards to travel around the board, stopping at various delicious-sounding locations along the way. She shared it with the children in the polio ward, and they loved it. One year later, Milton Bradley bought the game—and it became a surprise hit: *Candy Land*.

43 주어진 글 (A)에 이어질 내용을 순서에 맞게 배열한 것으로 가장 적절한 것은? [3점]

① (B)–(D)–(C)

② (C)–(B)–(D)

③ (C)–(D)–(B)

④ (D)–(B)–(C)

⑤ (D)–(C)–(B)

44 윗글의 제목으로 가장 적절한 것은?

① How to Play *Candy Land* with Kids

② The Bittersweet History of *Candy Land*

③ Using *Candy Land* as an Educational Tool

④ *Candy Land*: Boosting Children's Confidence

⑤ The Decline of the Popularity of *Candy Land*

45 윗글의 내용과 일치하지 <u>않는</u> 것은?

① *Candy Land* requires basic arithmetic skills.

② America was struck with an epidemic in the 1950s.

③ Eleanor Abbott made *Candy Land* while hospitalized.

④ Eleanor Abbott shared her first royalty check with others.

⑤ At first, Milton Bradley did not reveal the origin story of *Candy Land*.

He who learns but does not think, is lost!

He who thinks but does not learn is in great danger.

배우기만 하고 생각하지 않으면 얻는 것이 없고,

생각만 하고 배우지 않으면 위태롭다.

2026
경찰대학
10개년 영어

2022학년도 기출문제

영어영역

[01~05] 밑줄 친 단어의 뜻으로 가장 적절한 것을 고르시오.

01

> Tracking stray dogs may soon be easier thanks to the ubiquitous microchip.

① vociferous   ② equivocal

③ omnipresent   ④ inexorable

⑤ complimentary

02

> Through public education, political advocacy, and protests, we also sought to protect open spaces and forests from unscrupulous developers.

① prudent   ② abnormal

③ industrious   ④ indifferent

⑤ dishonest

03

> Individuals who took such action risked being ostracized by their fellow workers.

① bewildered   ② rectified

③ inundated   ④ permeated

⑤ excluded

04

> Stuttering was an embarrassing nemesis that Timothy struggled with throughout his childhood.

① adversary   ② catalyst

③ convention   ④ prodigy

⑤ zenith

05

> As I exchanged banal congratulations with the climbers filing past, inwardly I was frantic with worry.

① affectionate   ② aversive

③ ordinary   ④ apprehensive

⑤ exaggerated

[06~07] 다음 대화의 빈칸에 들어갈 말로 가장 적절한 것을 고르시오.

06

A : Hey, you know what? Last night, I saw the International Space Station with my own eyes!

B : Really? That's amazing! Is it really possible to see the ISS from Earth?

A : Yes. It looked like a bright star moving across the sky.

B : _____?

A : It moved very quickly, so I could easily tell the difference between it and the stars around it. You can check the location of the ISS on the NASA website if you want to see it.

B : That sounds really neat. I'll try that.

① Would you explain the difference between the ISS and the NASA

② Can you see the star in the center of the clouds

③ What was the purpose of watching the ISS

④ How did you know that it was the ISS

⑤ How far is it from Earth

07

A : What are you doing?

B : I'm looking through a blog about some interesting things.

A : What is so interesting?

B : According to this blog, a monster called Nessie lives in a lake in Scotland.

A : Oh, that's quite interesting, but you'd better not believe it. These kinds of things are not proven.

B : _____.

A : The photos could have been modified. I think it is important to approach things with reasonable suspicion rather than just believing everything that you see.

B : Okay, I'll try to keep that in mind.

① Scientists believed its existence, really

② However, that seems to be my mistake

③ The monster disturbs the order of nature

④ There are lots of photos of Nessie, though

⑤ Yes, they are completely proven to be authentic

08 밑줄 친 부분 중, 어법상 틀린 것은?

Mental illness in many ways remains a mystery to us. Some scientists think that it is hereditary. Others think it is caused by a chemical imbalance in the body. Other factors ① considering are a person's environment or perhaps an injury to the brain. Experts have differing opinions as to ② what causes mental illness and different ideas on how to treat it. One method is to place mentally ill people in hospitals and even prisons ③ to separate them from society. Another method is to give medications under the supervision of a psychiatrist to modify behavior. Mentally ill persons under medication often ④ live in supervised housing. Another method of treatment pioneered by Sigmund Freud is psychoanalysis, ⑤ whereby the patient receives many hours of counseling and talk therapy at a psychiatrist's office. The above treatments are often combined.

[09~11] (A), (B), (C)의 각 네모 안에서 문맥에 맞는 낱말로 가장 적절한 것을 고르시오.

09

Some people get (A) nervous/relaxed living placidly and safely. They run as surely toward danger as most people run away from it. They bungee jump, or skid down gravel roads on mountain bikes, or hang by their fingertips from minuscule cracks in the face of cliff, or even quit secure jobs in order to take a chance on some risky venture. They are risk-takers, and scientists have long wondered why they deliberately (B) court/evade loss, injury, or even death. Answers to that question involve a complex interplay of psychological and physiological factors. The key ingredient in the body's physiological response to danger is adrenaline. The body produces this chemical in the center of the adrenal glands atop the kidneys. When a physically or mentally stressful situation (C) arises/disappears, a flood of adrenaline into the blood stream prepares the body to act swiftly and forcefully to protect itself.

	(A)	(B)	(C)
①	nervous	court	arises
②	nervous	evade	disappears
③	relaxed	court	arises
④	relaxed	court	disappears
⑤	relaxed	evade	arises

10

(A) Fleeing/Hunting has been perfected to a fine art, inspiring mythic levels of speed, endurance, and agility in prey species. Plain animals, such as antelopes, gazelles, and zebras, have also learned to measure their attackers' talents against their own. Knowing that lions, leopards, and cheetahs are capable of only short bursts of speed, the hoofed residents rarely (B) idle/panic at the sight of a cat as long as they have running room and a head start. The important thing is to keep an eye out so the predator doesn't "steal the bases" and get close enough for a deadly sprint. Against hunting dogs and wolves, however, prey animals know they can't depend on their endurance alone. Canines are not as fast as cats, but they can run for a long time, long enough to (C) exhaust/invigorate weak, old, or sick prey.

	(A)	(B)	(C)
①	Fleeing	idle	exhaust
②	Fleeing	panic	invigorate
③	Fleeing	panic	exhaust
④	Hunting	panic	invigorate
⑤	Hunting	idle	invigorate

11

If you're thinking your way through a melodic and harmonic combination and you're struggling a little, often the best combinations of these two elements work in (A) contrary/parallel motion. In other words, as your melody rises up, try to make the bass note of the chord progression you're accompanying it with fall. Equally, when your melody line falls, bring the bass notes (and their chords) upwards. This doesn't have to be true for every single melody note and every single chord but, as a rule, (B) implanting/separating the movement between these two parts and imagining a mirror between them—so that movement in one direction prompts movement the other way in the other part—often works well. The reason for this is that the listener likes to hear one part as a melody and the other part as (C) discord/harmony, so that a single line can be identified as carrying 'the tune'. Somehow, this is often easier for the brain if the supporting line is as different as possible from the part playing the melody. [3점]

	(A)	(B)	(C)
①	contrary	separating	harmony
②	contrary	implanting	discord
③	contrary	implanting	harmony
④	parallel	implanting	discord
⑤	parallel	separating	harmony

2022 기출문제

[12~13] 밑줄 친 부분 중, 문맥상 낱말의 쓰임이
적절하지 않은 것을 고르시오.

12 Running a farm in the Middle West today is likely to be a very expensive operation. This is particularly true in the Corn Belt, where the corn that ① fattens the bulk of the country's livestock is grown. The heart of the Corn Belt is in Iowa, Illinois, and Indiana. The soil is extremely ② futile, the rainfall is abundant, and there is a long, warm growing season. All this makes the land extremely valuable. When one adds to the cost of the land the cost of livestock, seed, machinery, fuel, and fertilizer, farming becomes a very expensive operation. Therefore many farmers are ③ tenants and much of the land is owned by banks, insurance companies, or wealthy business people. These owners rent the land out to farmers, who generally provide machinery and labor. Some farms operate on contract to milling companies. The companies buy up farms, put in managers to run them, provide the machinery to farm them, and take the ④ produce for their own use. Machinery is often equipped with electric lighting to ⑤ permit round-the-clock operation.

13 Digital information plays a part in the increasing uncertainty of knowledge. First, the infinitude of information now accessible through the Internet ① dwarfs any attempt to master a subject—it is simply no longer possible to know what is to be known in any area. The response is to focus on ever narrower or more esoteric disciplines or interests, or to admit that all that can be done is to ② sample the field. Second, the stature of knowledge is challenged, because the quality of what can be accessed is often ③ unknown. In the printed book, the signs of quality—publisher, author affiliation, and so on—are usually clearly marked. But the quality of information on the Internet is not always so obvious, sometimes deliberately ④ unveiled, sometimes simplistic but loud. Even the encyclopedic is not guaranteed : Wikipedia bills itself as 'the free encyclopedia that anyone can edit'. Despite the theory that correct material will usually overcome incorrect, there is nevertheless a caveat that knowledge is always ⑤ relative.

14 Songbird House에 관한 다음 글의 내용과 일치하는 것은?

Songbird House opened July 23, 2012 and is located in an historic house built in 1904. While our focus is coffee and tea, you will love our house-made pastries and breakfast sandwiches. We are proud to have a low staff turn-over so that we all personally get to know our customers and in turn, our customers are assured of consistent quality. Sixty percent of the faces we welcome are our regulars, but we have fun meeting a beautiful variety of people from all walks of life every day. No matter who you are, who you love, or where you are in life. Come on in! Business people, students, creatives, nursing mothers—I want you to feel comfortable. Songbird is an extension of your living room.

① Songbird House was a well-known historical site in 1904.

② Breakfast is not offered in Songbird House.

③ New staff members are frequently employed.

④ More than half of the customers visit this cafe regularly.

⑤ Songbird House is a company which renovates living rooms.

15 cobra lily에 관한 다음 글의 내용과 일치하지 않는 것은?

The cobra lily is a unique and eye-catching plant thanks to its dramatic leaves that resemble the heads of cobra snakes. Its curling leaves rise from the base of the plant and round out into hooded foliage. Along with its almost startling appearance, these carnivorous plants feed on insects as well as small vertebrates. Native to North America, the cobra lily is often found growing in distinct groupings in boggy areas that are devoid of nutrition. Their hooded leaves secrete an aroma that attracts insects and then allows the plant to gather fuel from trapping and digesting their prey. Once inside, it's difficult for insects to escape, and the plant will also secrete digestive enzymes to help break down the animal matter. Unlike many other pitcher plants, however, cobra lily plants are not able to collect rainwater to trap prey.

① Its leaves take after the heads of cobra snakes.

② It is eaten by small animals with a backbone.

③ It is often found in marshlands.

④ It attracts insects by secreting a pleasant smell.

⑤ It does not trap prey by gathering rainwater.

[16~17] 다음 글의 제목으로 가장 적절한 것을 고르시오.

16

Its unmistakable smell permeates Seoul subway carriages during the rush hour, and admirers claim it is the healthiest food on the planet. Once valued as a source of vitamin C before the arrival of refrigerators, kimchi now crops up on menus far from its birthplace on the Korean peninsula. The spicy, garlicky cabbage dish is to be found as a pizza topping and taco filling in the UK, Australia and the US. Kimjang, the traditionally communal act of making kimchi, was recently awarded world cultural heritage status by UNESCO. But despite its growing popularity in restaurants from Los Angeles to London, Korea's national dish is in crisis in its country of origin. To kimchi's basic ingredients of napa cabbage, garlic, seasoning and copious amounts of chilli power, we can now add a trade war with China and fears of lasting damage to Korean cultural identity.

① Kimchi : Soaring in Popularity

② How does Kimchi Impact Health?

③ Korea Wins a Trade War Against China

④ Kimjang : Put Forward for UNESCO Award

⑤ Popularity and Crisis of Korea's National Dish

17

Innovative solutions—to prevent, monitor and clean (PMC) marine litter—are necessary to restore healthy oceans and maintain their well-being over time. And again, little is known about how many of these solutions have been developed and implemented, and to what extent they have been effective as information is scattered across platforms and not easily accessible. In a global analysis by Bellou and colleagues, also in *Nature Sustainability*, the researchers identify 177 PMC solutions and find that 106 of them address monitoring; 33 address prevention (mostly via wastewater treatment); only 30 address cleaning. They also find an inconsistent use of litter size terms across the various developers, which required a harmonization effort to assess the type of litter addressed—results show that 137 of the solutions targeted macrolitter. Overall, only few solutions reached technical readiness and no solution was validated for efficiency and environmental impacts. [3점]

① Saving Marine Animals : Target the Microlitter

② A Passive Journey to the Marine Discovery

③ Oceanic Threats to Human Race

④ Want to Heal the Ocean? More Work Needed

⑤ Questioning the Utility of Sea Wastes Recycling

[18~19] 다음 글의 주제로 가장 적절한 것을 고르시오.

18

After observing the "care" given the aged in the United States, I can only conclude that personalization in that culture involves not only the acquisition of certain symbols and statuses, but also the achievement of a series of successes. By that token, an individual who fails or who has lost the capacity to succeed is considered less a person, because he or she has withdrawn from the success mechanism. Old people in the United States, because they have withdrawn or have been displaced from the occupational system, are deprived of the ability to succeed or fail; they are seen as scarcely persons at all—unless they can still symbolize their past success by continued consumption capability. In this way an individual's retention of consumption capability, even after he or she has withdrawn from the success machinery, is taken as an adequate substitute for success, because, through this consumption, an indispensable service is rendered to the economy.

① various strategies of personalization
② a typical misconception about old people
③ problems of aged care in the United States
④ one aspect of personalization in the United States

⑤ contribution of consumption to the United States economy

19

It is simply unclear just how technologies can be inevitable, at least from an ethical perspective, and how they can be autonomous. Some individuals elect to use a given technology; others do not. For any technology, it could be the case that all individuals elect not to use it. A competitor could arise, or moral argument may appear and convince a critical number of people no longer to use a technology. That technology then ceases to be implemented because of individuals' decisions. The technology, or at least its implementation, is thus not inevitable. Insofar as it depends upon individuals' electing to maintain it, it is not autonomous. An effort to fashion an ethics of technology based upon technologies' inevitability and autonomy would not reflect the way that people make choices, much less ethical decisions, nor reflect the entire relationship between individuals and technologies.

① technical critiques against autonomy
② the impact of ethics on the innovative technology
③ how to understand and utilize an ethical technology

2022 기출문제

④ reasons why people have to publicize their favorite technology

⑤ the destiny of a technology determined by individual choices

[20~22] 다음 글의 요지로 가장 적절한 것을 고르시오.

20

The flood of people—foreign-born and native-born, white and black—fit no single profile. A minority were professionals : businessmen and teachers, doctors and lawyers, priests, ministers, and rabbis. Most were working people who filled the factories, built the homes, scrubbed the floors, and nursed the babies of the well-to-do. These new residents brought more than brawn to the cities, though. They brought their religions, their politics, their institutions, and their art. They jammed the streets on the feast days of their village saints and they emptied them on the Day of Atonement. They opened tiny storefront churches and substantial fraternal lodges. They rushed to vaudeville theaters, where Jewish entertainers honed their craft, and to the ghetto dancehalls, where ragtime bands pushed the boundaries of American music. And they elbowed their way into the cities' public life.

① American frontiers overcame unexpected troubles.

② The perilous damage was begot by the new people.

③ Diverse immigrants engendered the political renaissance.

④ Minor cultures are transformed so as to fit into American public life.

⑤ The immigrants released their own cultures into the American mainstream.

21

The power of apologies as a display of caring lies at the heart of the veritable avalanche of them that we are now seeing in the public sphere. Government, for instance, can demonstrate that they care about a group that was wronged, such as when the United States apologized in 1997 to African-American men who were denied treatment for syphilis as part of a medical experiment. Offering an apology to another country is an effective way to lay the ground work for future cooperation. In the late 1990s, the Czech Republic remained the only European nation with which Germany had not reached a settlement providing restitution for Nazi persecution during World War II. Germany refused to pay Czech victims until the Czechs formally apologized for their postwar expulsion of ethnic

Germans from the Sudetenland. In the interest of receiving both reparations and Germany's support for inclusion in NATO, the Czech government offered the apology in 1997. Germany responded by setting up a philanthropic fund for the benefit of the Czechs, and both NATO and the European Union have invited the Czech republic to join their ranks. [3점]

① Germany did not pay Czech victims until the Czechs expressed apologies for their postwar behavior.

② Apologies help people repair schisms between the rich and the poor countries.

③ Apologies restore equilibrium in domestic and international relations.

④ Apologies are often manipulated to suggest that people let bygones be bygones.

⑤ The United States apologized to African-American men who were denied treatment for syphilis.

22

Nothing is more jarring to the nervous system than repeated interruptions when you're in the midst of concentrating on an important problem. One of the worst mistakes is to get into the habit of taking every phone call no matter what you're doing. A good way to handle the telephone is to concentrate your calls in one time segment, say between nine and ten in the morning or four and five in the afternoon. During that time you take all calls, and call people back who called you. You aren't being rude to refuse a call because you are busy. You are being wise. If you are a victim of the telephone, telephone screening can change your work life.

① Consciously project ease and enjoyment.

② Beware of any lingering fears of success.

③ Become aware of your natural optimum work cycles.

④ Think of success as a process, not a final destination.

⑤ Insulate yourself as much as possible from interruption.

[23~30] 다음 글의 빈칸에 들어갈 말로 가장 적절한 것을 고르시오.

23

You can buy a television at the store so you can watch television at home, but the television you buy isn't the television you watch, and the television you watch isn't the television you buy. Expressed that way, it seems confusing, but in daily life it isn't confusing at all, because we never have to think too hard about what television is, and we use the word *television* to talk about all the various different parts of the bundle : industry, content, and appliance. Language lets us work at the right level of _____; if we had to think about every detail of every system in our lives all the time, we'd faint from overexposure. This bundling of object and industry, of product and service and business model, isn't unique to television. People who collect and preserve rare first editions of books, and people who buy mass-market romance novels, wreck the spines, and give them away the next week, can all legitimately lay claim to the label book lover.

① consistency   ② literacy

③ ambiguity   ④ discretion

⑤ popularity

24

The situations into which the product of mechanical reproduction can be brought may not touch the actual work of art, yet the quality of its presence is always depreciated. This holds not only for the art work but also, for instance, for a landscape which passes in review before the spectator in a movie. In the case of the art object, a most sensitive nucleus—namely, its authenticity—is interfered with whereas no natural object is vulnerable on that score. The authenticity of a thing is the essence of all that is transmissible from its beginning, ranging from its substantive duration to its testimony to the history which it has experienced. Since the historical testimony rests on the authenticity, the former, too, is jeopardized by reproduction when substantive duration ceases to matter. And what is really jeopardized when the historical testimony is affected is the _____ of the object. [3점]

① authority   ② negativity

③ promotion   ④ performance

⑤ limitation

25

Remember those electrons that are orbiting the nucleus of an atom. Well those electrons contain energy; however, this energy is not always stable. The stability depends on the number of electrons that are within an atom. Atoms are more stable when their electrons orbit in pairs. An atom with an odd number of electrons must have an unpaired electron. When oxygen has one unpaired electron it is known as superoxide. Atoms and molecules such as superoxide that have unpaired electrons are called free radicals. The unpaired electron in free radicals makes the atom or molecule unstable. Electrons in atoms "hate" not existing in pairs. An atom with an unpaired electron wants to become stable again, so it quickly seeks out _____ to "steal" from another atom or molecule. The instability of free radicals is what poses a threat to macromolecules such as DNA, RNA, proteins, and fatty acids.

① other cells   ② powerful energy

③ a stable nucleus   ④ another electron

⑤ nutritious proteins

26

Underlying the issues about the role of self-esteem in language learning are the fundamental concepts of attribution and self-efficacy. Attribution theory focuses on how people explain the causes of their own success and failures. Bernard Weiner describes attribution theory in terms of four explanations for success and/or failure in achieving a personal objective : ability, effort, perceived difficulty of a task, and luck. Two of those four factors are internal to the learner : ability and effort; and two are attributable to external circumstances outside of the learners : task difficulty and luck. According to Weiner, learners tend to explain, that is, to attribute, their success on a task on these four dimensions. Depending on the individual, a number of causal determinants might be cited. Thus, failure to get a high grade on a final exam in a language class might for some be judged to be a consequence of their poor ability or effort, and by others to difficulty of exam, and perhaps others to _____.

① just plain old bad luck

② previous learning experiences

③ excessive self-esteem in language learning

④ using inappropriate teaching methods

⑤ the lack of self-efficacy

27

Black and Hispanic New Yorkers represent 51% of the city's population, yet account for 62% of Covid-19 deaths. They have twice the rate of death compared with whites, when adjusted for age. This disparity likely is the result of several factors. Co-morbid conditions, such as hypertension and diabetes, are strongly associated with death from Covid-19 and are more common in black and Hispanic communities. But what causes high rates of poorly controlled hypertension and diabetes? Lack of appropriate health care. People who cannot easily find good health care for reasons of money, time, location, or trust may be more likely to stay at home undiagnosed and spread the virus— as well as experience potentially fatal delays in diagnosis and treatment. The explanation is the same for New York City as for Italy, New Orleans and probably Iran : _____ in health and health care.

① doctors are reluctant to carry out their roles

② minorities develop an appropriate policy

③ the virus exploits weaknesses

④ we have understood the urgency

⑤ treatments for the variants of Covid−19 require education

28

The sociocultural approach begins by attacking the heart of the problem : What is creativity? To explain creativity, we _____, and this turns out to be surprisingly difficult. All of the social sciences face the task of defining concepts that seem everyday and familiar. Psychologists argue over the definitions of intelligence, emotion, and memory; sociologists argue over the definitions of group, social movement, and institution. But defining creativity may be one of the most difficult tasks facing the social sciences, because everybody wants to believe he's creative. People typically use "creativity" as a complimentary term of praise. It turns out that what gets called creative has varied according to the historical and cultural period. Psychologists have sometimes wondered if we'll ever reach a consensus about creativity, and even whether it is a useful subject for scientific study at all. [3점]

① should establish a set of rules

② first need to agree on what it is

③ must do an extensive research on the word

④ examine the psychological implication of the term

⑤ mostly concentrate on the essence of its meaning

29

Every new tool shapes the way we think, as well as what we think about. The printed word helped make our cognition linear and abstract, along with vastly enlarging our stores of knowledge. Newspapers shrank the world; then the telegraph shrank it even more dramatically. With every innovation, cultural prophets bickered over whether we were facing a technological apocalypse or a utopia. Depending on which Victorian-age pundit you asked, the telegraph was either going usher in an era of world peace or drown us in a Sargasso of idiotic trivia. Neither prediction was quite right, of course, yet neither was quite wrong. The one thing that both apocalyptics and utopians understand and agree upon is that every new technology pushes us toward new forms of behavior while nudging us away from older, familiar ones. Living with new technologies means understanding _____. [3점]

① why they were ignored in the past

② how the telegraph functions properly

③ what innovations should be made in the future

④ what causes technological innovations

⑤ how they bias everyday life

30

A moral argument is often stopped in its tracks when someone refuses to consider a position by saying that '_____'. The implication is that anybody's judgement is as good as anyone else's, and that no one has a right to tell others what to do. The fact that I do not like bananas may be a fact about me, but it has no bearing on what you may enjoy. Similarly, it is implied, if I disapprove of something, that may tell you about me, but it has no relevance to what you should do. The confusion in all this is displayed by the idea that we have no 'right' to tell others what to do. We seem at the same moment to be denying that moral claims can tie everyone down, and asserting that there is at least one moral claim that we should all respect, namely that we ought not to impose our views on others. [3점]

① action speaks louder than words

② I can't agree with you more

③ that is just your opinion

④ we are on the same boat

⑤ never judge a book by its cover

31 다음 글의 빈칸 (A), (B)에 들어갈 말로 가장 적절한 것은?

The nature of the initial attachments we make in life is crucial to our later development and social and emotional experiences. These attachments have a strong influence on any later attachments that we might make. So,   (A) , if an initial attachment has been ambivalent, flicking about between feeling secure and feeling insecure, then such might also be a person's commitment to a group. A person might join an interest group reluctantly, become enthusiastic for a time but constantly be on the alert for social slights or loss of status perceived as brought about by other members of the group. This would lead to a tendency to withdraw.   (B) , a person whose initial attachments were secure might well be attracted in a straightforward way to joining groups and to be reasonably steadfast in membership.

	(A)	(B)
①	for example	In comparison
②	for example	Hence
③	in fact	Nevertheless
④	in addition	Therefore
⑤	in addition	On the other hand

[32~33] 다음 글에서 전체 흐름과 관계 <u>없는</u> 문장을 고르시오.

32   It is time for a deeper probe in a different setting, entered at a different angle, to a greater depth, and exploring a deeper causation. Why have the creative arts so dominated the human mind, everywhere and throughout history? We will not find the answer in the finest art galleries and symphony halls. ① The innovations of jazz and rock, arising more directly from human experience, will probably give us a better idea of where to excavate. ② Nevertheless, Hollywood composers began experimenting in the vocabularies of jazz and the structuring model of rock. ③ Because the creative arts entail a universal, genetic trait, the answer to the question lies in evolutionary biology. ④ Bear in mind that Homo sapiens has been around about 100,000 years but literate culture has existed for less than a tenth of that time. ⑤ So the mystery of why there are universal creative arts comes down to the question of what human beings were doing during the first nine-tenths of their existence. [3점]

33   To keep from breaking glass, all movement near and on the glass must be parallel (don't put any pressure on the glass when scraping), and always use a pull-type scraper. ① That way if you slip, all the force is away from the glass and it won't break. ② To remove glazing points, hook the sharp edge of the pull-type scraper into their soft metal points and pull them out along with the putty. ③ The glass manufacture corporations have begun to move their factories to some of East Asian countries to reduce the production cost. ④ Double−check to make sure all of the glazing points are removed, and that old putty beside and under the edge of the glass is loose. ⑤ If not, you need another round of heat.

[34~35] 주어진 글 다음에 이어질 글의 순서로 가장 적절한 것을 고르시오.

34

> Psychologists and behaviour ecologists think that the ability to learn should be favoured over the genetic transmission of fixed trait when the environment in which an animal lives changes often, but not too often.

(A) In such a case, the environment is stable enough to favour learning, but not so stable as to favour genetic transmission. David Stephens, while agreeing with the above, has challenged the assumptions about environmental stability saying that various types of stability need to be separated.

(B) Information is best passed on by genetic transmission when the environment rarely changes, because such a means of transmission avoids the cost of learning and the environment the offspring

encounters is similar to that of their parents. However, if the environment is constantly changing, there is nothing worth learning as what is learnt is completely irrelevant in the next situation.

(C) Past experience, thus, is of no predictive value. Therefore, genetic transmission of a fixed response, rather than a learned response, is favoured. Somewhere, in between an environment that never changes and one that always does, learning is favoured over genetic transmission of a fixed response as it is worth paying the cost of learning. [3점]

① (A) − (C) − (B)　② (B) − (A) − (C)
③ (B) − (C) − (A)　④ (C) − (A) − (B)
⑤ (C) − (B) − (A)

35

> One of the more recent theories of creativity is *psychoeconomics*. This may not sound like it applies directly to education, but actually it does help to clarify what needs to be done in the classroom and why there are problems designing education that supports creativity.

(A) Consider, for example, the idea of educational objectives. Educators have only so much time in the school day, and just so many resources, and there is a great deal of accountability in today's schools, at least in the United States.

(B) Additionally, creative thinking is original, so by definition an educator will not know what the result will be if he or she presents an open-ended task that in fact does allow creative thinking. The problem, then, is that the benefits are uncertain and it is difficult to justify the costs (i.e., the investment of time).

(C) This all means that the curriculum must have a clear payoff. Creativity does not. It is often dependent on a student's intrinsic motivation and the self-expression of an individual student.

① (A) − (C) − (B)　　② (B) − (A) − (C)

③ (B) − (C) − (A)　　④ (C) − (A) − (B)

⑤ (C) − (B) − (A)

36 글의 흐름으로 보아, 주어진 문장이 들어가기에 가장 적절한 곳은?

> However, some businesses (for example, small retailers) do not usually find it practical to match each sale to a particular cost of sales figure as the accounting period progresses.

The cost of sales (or cost of goods sold) figure for a period can be identified in different ways. (①) In some businesses, the cost of sales is identified at the time a sale has been made. (②) Sales are closely matched with the cost of those sales and so identifying the cost of sales figure for inclusion in the income statement is not a problem. (③) Many large retailers (for example, supermarkets) have point-of-sale (checkout) devices that not only record each sale but also simultaneously pick up the cost of the goods that are the subject of the particular sale. (④) Other businesses that sell a relatively small number of high-value items also tend to match sales revenue with the cost of the goods sold at the time of the sale. (⑤) They find it easier to identify the cost of sales figure at the end of the accounting period.

[37~38] 다음 글을 읽고, 물음에 답하시오.

On June 23, 1970, I had just been mustered out of the Army after completing my one-year tour of duty in Vietnam. I was a 23-year-old Army veteran on a plane from Oakland, Calif., returning home to Dallas, Texas.

I had been warned about the hostility many of our fellow countrymen felt toward returning Nam vets at that time. There were no hometown parades for us when we came home from that unpopular war. Like tens of thousands of others, I was just trying to get home without incident.

I sat, in uniform, in a window seat, chain-smoking and avoiding eye contact with my fellow passengers. No one was sitting in the seat next to me, which added to my isolation. A young girl, not more than 10 years old, suddenly appeared in the aisle. She smiled and, without a word, timidly handed me a magazine. I accepted her offering, her quiet "welcome home." All I could say was, "Thank you." I do not know where she sat down or who she was with because right after accepting the magazine from her, I turned to the window and wept. Her small gesture of compassion was the first I had experienced in a long time.

That young girl undoubtedly has no memory of what happened years ago. I like to think of her as having grown up, continuing to touch others and teaching her children to do the same. I know she might have been told to give me the "gift" by her mother. Her father might still have been in Vietnam at that point or maybe he had not survived the war. It doesn't matter why she gave me the magazine. The important thing is she did.

Since then, I have followed her example and tried, in different ways for different people, to do the same for them. Like me on that long ago plane ride, they will never know why a stranger took the time to extend a hand. But I know that my attempts since then are all because of that little girl. Her offer of a magazine to a tired, scared andlonely soldier has echoed throughout my life.

37 윗글의 제목으로 가장 적절한 것은?

① Can We Beat the Combat?

② A Small Act of Kindness Matters

③ The Triumph of a Courageous Soldier

④ Pain in the Mind of War Veterans

⑤ In Search of the Little Girl

38 윗글의 내용과 일치하는 것은?

① The narrator has to return to Vietnam in a month.

② The narrator had been one of the military personnel.

③ The narrator was emotionally hurt by the young girl.

④ The young girl had been a good friend of the narrator.

⑤ The young girl followed the narrator's footsteps in her life.

[39~40] 다음 글을 읽고, 물음에 답하시오.

The twentysomething age group is often referred to as the period of emerging adulthood. Some say that being 30 is now equivalent to being age 21 a generation ago. The term *quarterlife crisis* was coined to describe the problems and issues facing twentysomethings. According to recent college graduates, the quarterlife crisis is a "response to overwhelming instability, constant change, too many choices, and a panicked sense of helplessness." Indecision and apprehension are common companions during this period. On leaving the protective spheres of family and college, twentysomethings encounter disorientation and confusion regarding identity, career choices, living arrangements, establishing independence, discovering and harnessing a life passion, and creating new social networks. Having little experience at making major life decisions and accepting responsibility for them places twentysomethings in a transition zone of trying to find guideposts on what to do, where to go, and who to be. It is a time of _____, making premature resolutions, and sometimes paralysis due to indecision.

39 윗글의 제목으로 가장 적절한 것은?

① Twentysomethings in Their Heyday

② The Hot—blooded Youth of the Twenties

③ Challenges : What the Emerging Adult Faces

④ Infinite Possibilities of Twentysomethings

⑤ A Mind of Steel in the Twenties

40 윗글의 빈칸에 들어갈 말로 가장 적절한 것은?

① body and soul   ② cause and effect

③ pride and joy   ④ pros and cons

⑤ trial and error

[41~42] 다음 글을 읽고, 물음에 답하시오.

The response to mother figure is called filial imprinting. The range of objects which can elicit approach and attachment in young birds (a) are very large. Stimuli for imprinting may be visual, auditory or olfactory. There seems to be no limit to the range of visual stimuli. Movements help to catch attention like flashing lights. A stationary object will attract young birds (b) provided it is contrasting with its background.

Auditory stimuli are found to be attractive to many young birds. For example, in mallard ducklings, sound is very important to induce following the mother figure. Wood-ducks nest in holes in trees. The call of the mother from the water outside the nest hole induces the young ones (c) to approach the mother in spite of the fact that they have not seen her properly.

An example of odor stimuli is provided by the 5 to 14 day old baby shrews. These baby shrews become imprinted on the odor of the individual mother that is nursing them. Young shrews form a caravan early in life, having learned the odor of their mother, (d) which they will follow. When 5 or 6 day old shrews are provided with a substitute mother of another species, the odor of this caretaker mother becomes imprinted upon them.

Later, when the shrews are 15 days old, they are returned back to their real mother. It was seen that these siblings do not follow her and do not form the caravan like chain on any siblings that (e) were left with the real mother. However, they followed a piece of cloth impregnated with the odor of their caretaker mother, a response that demonstrates that young shrews become imprinted with the

_____.

41 밑줄 친 (a)~(e) 중에서 어법상 틀린 것은?

① (a) ② (b)

③ (c) ④ (d)

⑤ (e)

42 윗글의 빈칸에 들어갈 말로 가장 적절한 것은? [3점]

① time spent in following their caretaker mother

② odor of whoever nurses them when they are young

③ call of their caretaker mother before they leave their nest

④ amount of visual attention paid to their real mother

⑤ care of their real mother when they grow up

[43~45] 다음 글을 읽고, 물음에 답하시오.

(A) "Are you carrying any fruit or handguns?"

"Sure, I've got three kilos of kiwis in the trunk, and she has a .44 magnum in her purse."

No, that's not what I say to the border guard. It's best not to joke with these guys. They don't have much of a sense of humor, and they like to tear cars apart. Border guards make me nervous. I feel better as soon as I'm beyond those expressionless eyes and frozen faces.

(B) The rain slashes sideways, driving me back inside under an awning I try to use for cover. The ferry is starting to sway. Margaret tells a story of a ferry ride she once took from Sicily to Malta when she got seasick from diesel fumes and waves. Some kids are running toy cars up and down the plastic seats. Through rain mottle windows the mountaintops are obscured in mist. Soon we're pulling into the dock on the far side. Cars file off the ferry, and we heard the last nine miles to the hot springs. Admission is $4.00 Canadian.

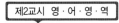

(C) It winds along Kootenai Lake for fifty miles with only about three spots for cars to pass the whole way. We're the last car to board. Nautical looking workers in navy blue direct us to a parking space on the lower deck. We climb steep stairs to the passenger level. The wind and rain gain intensity as the ferry pulls away from the dock and heads across the lake. I step outside on the deck, but only for a minute.

(D) But a trip to Ainsworth is worth facing a hundred border guards. Ainsworth Hot Springs. I've been wanting to go for years now. Everyone I know has been there. It's gotten to the point where I feel deprived whenever anyone starts talking about Ainsworth. So off my friend Margaret and I go on a cold, rainy November Tuesday—not a bad day for hot spring. A few miles into Canada the road changes.

(E) There aren't any locker; each of us gets a plastic bag to put our clothes in, which we check with a clerk who gives out velcro wristbands with claim numbers on them. Mine is 38. Rain dots my body as I head out to the pool. The big pool is warm—a good place to get psyched-up for the hotter pool above and the caves. The caves! That's what makes Ainsworth so unique. We paddle back into the mountainside following the hot water to its source. Dim lights reveal an incredible scene.

43 주어진 글 (A)에 이어질 내용을 순서에 맞게 배열한 것으로 가장 적절한 것은?

① (B) − (D) − (C) − (E)

② (B) − (D) − (E) − (C)

③ (D) − (C) − (B) − (E)

④ (D) − (C) − (E) − (B)

⑤ (E) − (C) − (D) − (B)

44 윗글에 나타난 Ainsworth에 대한 화자의 심경 변화로 가장 적절한 것은?

① relieved → tensed

② determined → excited

③ frightened → amazed

④ regretful → committed

⑤ dejected → uninterested

45 윗글의 내용과 일치하지 <u>않는</u> 것은?

① The narrator did not have a casual talk with the border guard.

② Ainsworth was nine miles away from the Canadian border.

③ The travelers faced heavy rain and wind on the ferry.

④ Margaret went to the trip with the narrator.

⑤ The cave was the point that made Ainsworth distinctive from other hot springs.

2026
경찰대학
10개년 영어

2021 학년도 기출문제

영어영역

제2교시 영어영역

[01~05] 밑줄 친 단어의 뜻으로 가장 적절한 것을 고르시오.

01

The news of the rock star's <u>tawdry</u> affair sent shockwaves across his fans all over the world.

① legal   ② immoral

③ passionate   ④ unexpected

⑤ weird

02

Joanne moved to a house in the suburbs because she was easily <u>irked</u> by her apartment neighbors.

① ousted   ② tricked

③ annoyed   ④ disappointed

⑤ persuaded

03

After the philanthropist passed away, close relatives revealed that he was <u>parsimonious</u> when it came to his own lifestyle.

① apathetic   ② stingy

③ distant   ④ objective

⑤ considerate

04

Mr. Brown's favorite pastime was to sit on his porch on <u>languid</u> summer afternoons.

① tardy   ② humid

③ peaceful   ④ capricious

⑤ charming

05

Marley's cheesecakes are very popular among New Yorkers, and their recipe has been <u>arcane</u> for generations.

① identical   ② improved

③ inherited   ④ secretive

⑤ diversified

[06~07] 다음 대화의 빈칸에 들어갈 말로 가장 적절한 것을 고르시오.

06

A : Excuse me. Do you know the way to Dan's Department Store?

B : Sure. But it's a good half-hour walk from here.

A : That's pretty far. Is there another way besides walking?

B : You can also take the M11 Bus two blocks from here.

A : _____

B : The Houston Street Stop. Dan's isn't far from there.

A : I'll ask someone for directions when I get off. Thanks a lot.

B : No problem. Good luck.

① How long will it take by bus?

② What if I decided to walk?

③ Where do I get off?

④ Can you lead the way to Dan's?

⑤ Do you know what time they open?

07

A : Congratulations, Cadet Lee.

B : Thank you, Sergeant Louis.

A : After the graduation ceremony today, you will officially be a police officer in the Tonawanda Police Department.

B : Yeah. I can't believe it myself.

A : You deserve it. You've worked really hard.

B : Thank you. Do you have any parting words of wisdom?

A : _____

B : I won't. I will always work for the citizens of our city.

A : I'm sure you will make us proud.

① Take advantage of the perks of being an officer of the law.

② If you work hard, you will make a great police officer.

③ Always be suspicious since anyone can be a criminal.

④ Just let me know if this line of work isn't for you.

⑤ Never forget our motto, "to serve and to protect."

[08~09] 밑줄 친 부분 중, 어법상 틀린 것을 고르시오.

08   Doctors are known for using complicated words that make them sound either extremely intelligent or really out of touch with ① which most people can understand. The medical word for hiccups, singultus, is a perfect example of ② when physicians sound ridiculous. Hiccups are caused when the diaphragm becomes irritated and pushes air rapidly up in such a way that it makes an irregular sound. Some things that irritate the diaphragm and cause

2021 기출문제

hiccups ③ are distension of the stomach from food, alcohol, or air, sudden changes in gastric temperature, or use of alcohol and/or tobacco in excess. Hiccups also can be caused by excitement or stress. While most cases of the hiccups last only ④ a few minutes, some cases of the hiccups can last for days or weeks. This is very unusual, though, and it's usually a sign of ⑤ another medical problem.

09 Tim Richardson's mom, Doris Bohannon, says he's been riding bikes since he ① had been three years old and wrenching since not long after that. And she should know. She's ② the one who taught him how to fix bikes—by bringing home trashed bikes from the dump for her kids ③ to tinker with. "Mom's the mechanic in the family," says Richardson, who grew up in Odd, West Virginia, population 832. "④ Being in a rural area, you either learned how to fix your bike yourself, or you didn't ride." That ethos has carried over to his bike shop, Shenandoah Bicycle Company, in Harrisonburg, Virginia, ⑤ where customers are encouraged to figure out their own bike dilemmas.

[10~11] (A), (B), (C)의 각 네모 안에서 문맥에 맞는 낱말로 가장 적절한 것을 고르시오.

10

Anyone who's crossed a parking lot in August knows that blacktop soaks up a lot of (A) heat/moisture. It turns out, rethinking the color of the surfaces around us could help cool the planet. Roofs and pavements cover 60 percent of urban areas. Scientists calculate that lightening their color worldwide could have the same effect on global warming as keeping 48.5 billion tons of CO_2 out of the atmosphere. That's roughly the equivalent of taking every car in the world off the road for 18 years. This elegantly simple solution works because of increased albedo—the degree to which (B) abrasive/reflective surfaces bounce back the sun's energy. Closer to home, color-consciousness does more than fight climate change. Choosing roofing material that (C) absorbs/repels less heat can mean substantial energy savings. Studies show a "cool roof" can cut air-conditioning bills by 20 percent or more.

	(A)	(B)	(C)
①	moisture	reflective	absorbs
②	moisture	abrasive	repels
③	heat	reflective	absorbs
④	heat	reflective	repels
⑤	heat	abrasive	absorbs

11

Seven billion people have seven billion agendas, and thinking about the big picture is a relatively rare (A) frugality/luxury. A single mother struggling to raise two children in a Mumbai slum is focused on the next meal; (B) refugees/vacationers in a boat in the middle of the Mediterranean scan the horizon for any sign of land; and a dying man in an overcrowded London hospital gathers all his remaining strength to take in one more breath. They all have far more (C) trivial/urgent problems than global warming or the crisis of liberal democracy.

	(A)	(B)	(C)
①	frugality	refugees	trivial
②	frugality	vacationers	trivial
③	luxury	refugees	trivial
④	luxury	vacationers	urgent
⑤	luxury	refugees	urgent

[12~13] 밑줄 친 부분 중, 문맥상 낱말의 쓰임이 적절하지 않은 것을 고르시오.

12
Ocean plastic is estimated to kill millions of marine animals every year. Nearly 700 species, including ① endangered ones, are known to have been affected by it. Some are harmed ② visibly—strangled by abandoned fishing nets or discarded six-pack rings. Many more are probably harmed invisibly. Marine species of all ③ sizes, from zooplankton to whales, now eat microplastics, the bits smaller than one-fifth of an inch across. On Hawaii's Big Island, on a beach that seemingly should have been ④ tainted—no paved road leads to it—I walked ankle-deep through microplastics. They crunched like Rice Krispies under my feet. After that, I could understand why some people see ocean plastic as a looming ⑤ catastrophe, worth mentioning in the same breath as climate change.

13
A factor that's important in coping with a crisis, and that differs from person to person, is something that psychologists call "ego strength." That includes self-confidence, but it's much ① broader. Ego strength means having a sense of yourself, having a sense of purpose, and ② accepting yourself for who you are, as a proud independent person not dependent on other people for ③ approval or for your survival. Ego strength includes being able to ④ tolerate strong emotions, to keep focused under stress, to express yourself freely, to perceive reality accurately, and to make sound decisions. Those linked qualities are essential for exploring new solutions and ⑤ reinforcing the paralyzing fear that often arises in a crisis. [3점]

2021 기출문제

111

14 San Marcos Café에 관한 다음 글의 내용과 일치하는 것은?

Expect quite a greeting when you visit San Marcos Café. A mismatched flock of peacocks and peahens, wild turkeys and roosters all cavort around the front and back of the restaurant. The poultry are not allowed in the dining area, but there was one very famous leghorn rooster named Buddy about 15 years ago who served long tenure as unofficial maitre d' of the restaurant. Dressed in black tie, Buddy cheerfully greeted guests at the door and crowed through the breakfast hour. Wandering chickens notwithstanding, San Marcos Café is a real find. A cozy, charming ranchhouse decorated in country-kitchen style, it serves one of the best cinnamon rolls.

① Various poultry can be spotted around the café.

② A few roosters are allowed to enter the dining area.

③ A rooster served as waiter starting 10 years ago.

④ Buddy's costume consisted of a red tie.

⑤ They no longer serve cinnamon rolls.

15 Thomas Eisner에 관한 다음 글의 내용과 일치하지 <u>않는</u> 것은?

Thomas Eisner, an ecologist and evolutionary biologist at Cornell University, died last week at age 81 of complications from Parkinson's disease. In hundreds of journal articles on topics ranging from spider webs to bombardier beetles, Eisner explored how insects and arthropods defend themselves, capture prey, and attract mates in sometimes complex ways. With Cornell collaborator Jerrold Meinwald, he helped found the field of chemical ecology—the study of how animals and plants use chemicals to communicate. An outspoken conservationist, Eisner promoted the idea of allowing companies to "bioprospect" in the rainforest for useful chemicals in order to raise money to protect biodiversity. Eisner was also a pianist, a popular science writer, and—with his wife, Maria—a nature photographer whose images of larval hooks, beetle hairs, and other minute wonders graced many pages and covers of *Science*.

① He died at age 81 from Parkinson's disease complications.

② He was interested in how insects catch their prey.

③ His wife founded the field of chemical ecology.

④ His agendas included protecting rainforest biodiversity.

⑤ His works of photography appeared in *Science*.

④ The Butterfly Effect of a Faltering European Economy

⑤ Economic Outlook for the Average Joe: Cloudy with Rain

[16~17] 다음 글의 제목으로 가장 적절한 것을 고르시오.

16

Since 1967, median household income in the United States, adjusted for inflation, has stagnated for the bottom 60 percent of the population, even as wealth and income for the richest Americans have soared. Changes in Europe, although less stark, point in the same direction. Corporate profits are at their highest levels since the 1960s, yet corporations are increasingly choosing to save those profits rather than invest them, further hurting productivity and wages. And recently, these changes have been accompanied by a hollowing out of democracy and its replacement with technocratic rule by globalized elites. [3점]

① Inflation: A Huge Hurdle for the Economy

② Public Demand for Corporate Transparency

③ If a Technocrat Sneezes, Do Banks Catch a Cold?

17

I am lying here in my private sick bay on the east side of town between Second and Third avenues, watching starlings from the vantage point of bed. Three Democrats are in bed with me: Harry Truman (in a stale copy of the *Times*), Adlai Stevenson (in *Harper's*), and Dean Acheson (in a book called *A Democrat Looks at His Party*). I take Democrats to bed with me for lack of a dachshund, although as a matter of fact on occasions like this I am almost certain to be visited by the ghost of Fred, my dash-hound everlasting, dead these many years. In life, Fred always attended the sick, climbing right into bed with the patient like some lecherous old physician, and making a bad situation worse. All this dark morning, I have reluctantly entertained him upon the rumpled blanket, felt his oppressive weight, and heard his fraudulent report. He was an uncomfortable bedmate when alive; death has worked little improvement—I still feel crowded, still wonder why I put up with his natural rudeness and his pretensions.

① Books Versus Pets: Who Makes a Better Companion?

② Reminiscing About a Bedfellow on a Dark Morning

③ A Message of Hope from My Beloved Dash−hound

④ Unexpected Arrival of a Dog: A New Beginning

⑤ The Truth Behind the Politics of Medical Care

[18~19] 다음 글의 주제로 가장 적절한 것을 고르시오.

18

The inherent fragility of the economic system does not mean that it cannot be made safer. A lot can be done, has been done, and can still be done. But in designing reforms, it's important to choose the objective carefully. The goal should not be to eliminate the risk of the failure of individual banks or large institutions. Failure has its merits. It's important for creating the right incentives, spurring innovation, and promoting efficiency. Rather, policymakers should strive to enhance the resilience of the broader financial system. Even when the system is under extreme stress, it needs to remain able

to perform its basic functions of providing payment, clearing, and settlement services; offering credit; and transferring risk. In other words, policymakers should try to build a system in which an idiosyncratic event does not turn into a systemic crisis. This means seeking not only to reduce the probability of financial distress but also to increase the probability that the real economy remains insulated from it. [3점]

① drafting economic policies based on statistics

② building an economy based on idiosyncratic events

③ putting the needs of people ahead of corporations

④ predicting potential problems in the economic system

⑤ reforming an economic system to withstand distress

19

After language had evolved as the principal communication system of modern humans, people were left with the question of who to communicate with through music. Music is, after all, a derivative of 'Hmmmmm,' which itself evolved as a means of communication, so the communicative function could not easily be dropped; there remained a compulsion among modern humans to communicate with music, as there still is today. How could this be fulfilled? Communication with other humans was now far better achieved by language than by music, other than for prelinguistic infants. But in the minds of modern humans there was now another type of entity with whom they could and should communicate: supernatural beings. So the human propensity to communicate through music came to focus on the supernatural— whether by beating the shaman's drum or through the compositions of Bach.

① effects of music on our views on the supernatural

② functional diversity of music compared to language

③ music as a means to communicate with the supernatural

④ advantages of language as a medium of communication

⑤ influence of music on the development of language

[20~22] 다음 글의 요지로 가장 적절한 것을 고르시오.

20

The EU, with its 512 million citizens, has, until recently, led the charge into a zero-emission green economy. The People's Republic of China, with its nearly 1.4 billion people, has roared onto the field in recent years with its plan to transition into a postcarbon era. And now the United States, with its 325 million citizens, is poised to join the herd. Without all three elephants marching in sync, sharing best practices, establishing common codes, regulations, standards, and incentives, and reaching out together to bring the rest of humanity into the fold, the race to a zero-carbon civilization in less than twenty years will be lost.

① Population problems need to be addressed before racing to a postcarbon era.

② With all three elephants marching in sync, no competitor will win the race.

③ China's participation is an optimistic sign for the zero-emission economy.

④ Cooperation among the key members is essential for a zero-carbon world.

⑤ A zero-carbon civilization is destined to backfire within twenty years.

21

Traditionally, research has treated goal pursuit as a solitary endeavor. But everyday experiences show that our relationships can either foster or impede our progress. If you want to wake up earlier each morning, you're better off with a spouse who shuts off his bedside lamp at 10 p.m. If you want to become a vegetarian, your spouse's feelings on tofu versus steak will probably have an impact.

Now researchers are examining that influence. A Washington University study found that being married to a spouse who is highly conscientious—that is, organized and reliable—predicts future job satisfaction and higher income. Research by Wilhelm Hofmann at the University of Cologne in Germany indicates that high relationship satisfaction positively affects feelings of control over goal pursuit. Hofmann posits that the stability of happy relationships makes it easier to focus. According to Hofmann, "When people's everyday life feels stable and predictable, they feel more in control of their ability to pursue their goals."

① The chances of achieving your goals hinge on your spouse.

② Psychological stability is the main indicator of your wellbeing.

③ Setting a realistic goal is heavily influenced by your partner.

④ Personal feelings are directly related to pursuing your goals.

⑤ The conscientiousness of your spouse leads to a successful marriage.

22

In the U.S., windmills have been estimated to kill at least 45,000 birds and bats each year. That sounds like a lot of birds and bats. To place that number in perspective, consider that pet cats that are allowed to wander in and out of their owners' houses have been measured to kill an average of more than 300 birds per year per cat. If the U.S. population of outdoor cats is estimated at about 100 million, then cats can be calculated to kill at least 30 billion birds per year in the U.S., compared to the mere 45,000 birds and bats killed per year by windmills. That windmill toll is equivalent to the work of just 150 cats.

① Policies on birds and bats should be based on statistics.

② Cat owners are advised not to let their cats roam free outdoors.

③ Windmills need to be regulated to meet environmental standards.

④ Windmills do not threaten avian wildlife as much as outdoor cats.

⑤ The outdoor cat population must be curbed for ecological balance.

[23~30] 다음 글의 빈칸에 들어갈 말로 가장 적절한 것을 고르시오.

23

We tend to think of statistical sampling as some sort of _____ bedrock, like the principles of geometry or the laws of gravity. But the concept is less than a century old, and it was developed to solve a particular problem at a particular moment in time under specific technological constraints. Those constraints no longer exist to the same extent. Reaching for a random sample in the age of big data is like clutching at a horse whip in the era of the motor car. We can still use sampling in certain contexts, but it need not—and will not—be the predominant way we analyze large datasets. Increasingly, we will aim to go for it all.

① impertinent   ② immutable

③ immature   ④ imminent

⑤ impartial

24

The human fetus, until recently, was a largely invisible and voiceless member of society. Technological innovations over the past few decades have given the fetus greater physical reality and new claims to legal rights while at the same time offering women more grounds for preventing, redefining, and even terminating pregnancy. Conflicts associated with expanded technological options for contraception and abortion offer one vantage point on these issues. Another set of disputes concerns the gradual uncoupling of biological reproduction from social parenting through technological means such as artificial insemination, *in vitro* fertilization, and embryo implantation. Intersecting with the reconfigurations of the family through adoption and divorce, these unconventional reproductive pathways have begun to _____ the accepted meanings of "mother," "father," "child," and "family." [3점]

① undermine   ② duplicate

③ summarize   ④ consolidate

⑤ simplify

25

When we look in the mirror, we see some of the "instruments" necessary for choice. Our eyes, nose, ears, and mouth gather information from our environment, while our arms and legs enable us to act on it. We depend on these capabilities to effectively negotiate between hunger and satiation, safety and vulnerability, even between life and death. Yet our ability to choose involves more than simply _____. Your knee may twitch if hit in the right place by a doctor's rubber mallet, but no one would consider this reflex to be a choice. To be able to truly choose, we must evaluate all available options and select the best one, making the mind as vital to choice as the body.

① reacting to sensory information

② giving into your utmost desires

③ selecting what is most beneficial

④ searching for instant gratification

⑤ suppressing your natural instincts

and business software, gain an edge from the experience that comes with a founder's age. According to research by a tech entrepreneur, the average age of successful start-up founders in these and other high growth industries was 40. It goes to show that if you have the financial resources, the right network and, most important, a great idea, _____. [3점]

① inner success is the reward

② age is nothing but a number

③ it all comes down to who you know

④ the last piece of the puzzle is capital

⑤ youth will always find a way to prevail

26

There is no question that starting a business is easier when you are younger. The fewer nonwork responsibilities you have, the more likely you are to pour your blood, sweat and tears into a new venture. But that does not mean you should leave school or your job to start a company just because you are young. Venture capitalists often favor fresh meat. Michael Moritz of Sequoia Capital, one of Silicon Valley's biggest VC firms, has gushed about how entrepreneurs in their mid to late 20s "see no boundaries, see no limits, see no obstacle that they cannot hurdle." Still, start-ups in some industries, such as biotech

27

Professor Wilhelm Roentgen of the Bavarian University of Wurzburg first made the discovery of x-rays public in December 1895. The notion of a new kind of ray, unrefractable and indifferent to electromagnetic fields, befuddled the scientific world and precipitated feverish research into their nature and implications for the long-standing theories of light and matter. _____. The notion of a "dark light" that could penetrate flesh as easily as glass and produce photographic images of the skeleton was intoxicating. Overnight, the mysterious rays became popular icons constantly encountered in advertisements, prose, songs, and cartoons. More than one thousand articles and fifty books were published on the subject in 1896 alone.

① Popular culture was equally mesmerized
② Advertisers and politicians followed suit
③ This discovery was challenged by many
④ The financial sector was taken aback
⑤ Rarely did it reflect the public craze

28

For a threat to be effectual, its utterer must have the means to carry it out and want the addressee to act otherwise than would be the case without the prompting of the utterance. Then, once a speaker is seen by the target to be in such a position of power, any utterance forecasting _____, even if not framed explicitly as involving the utterer's own behavior, can be reasonably understood as a threat. This is how we make sense of remarks that contain no overtly threatening material. For example, when a Mafia boss in a movie says, "Tonight you sleep with the fishes," it is not taken as an invitation to sleep over at the speaker's house in the room with the aquarium, but as a chilling message of imminent doom. [3점]

① a cordial invitation to an aquarium
② explicit withdrawal of a future action
③ the maintenance of the present status
④ an unspoken agreement of cooperation
⑤ negative consequences to the addressee

29

The volume of Neanderthal brains ranged from 1,200 to 1,750 cc, about the same (1,200 to 1,700 cc) range as that of early and present specimens of modern *Homo sapiens*. This doesn't mean that they were as clever as modern human beings, since brain size _____. People who live in colder climates tend to have larger brains, and Neanderthals lived in Eurasia during a cold period. Neanderthal skeletal bones also show that they were massive. They had short, stocky bodies; males probably weighed about 145 pounds and stood less than five feet seven inches tall. Brain volume also is correlated with heavier massive muscles and body weight in closely related species. Heinz Stephan, a German neuroanatomist, has been studying the sizes of the brains and their various parts in many species over the past forty years. His detailed measurements show that bigger muscles require bigger brains, independent of intelligence. [3점]

① inevitably determines intelligence and body weight

② is a compensation for muscle loss and malnutrition

③ is also related to muscularity and climatic conditions

④ indicates the habitat and the surrounding environment

⑤ has long been noted as a vessel of intellect for mankind

30

The world of business is one area in which _____.
Many people now work alone at home. With access to a large central computer, employees such as secretaries, insurance agents, and accountants do their jobs at display terminals in their own homes. They no longer have to actually see the people they're dealing with. In addition, employees are often paid in an impersonal way. Workers' salaries are automatically credited to their bank accounts, eliminating the need for paychecks. Fewer people stand in line with their coworkers to receive their pay or cash their checks. Finally, personal banking is becoming a detached process. Customers interact with machines rather than people to deposit or withdraw money from their accounts. Even some bank loans

are approved or rejected, not in an interview with a loan officer, but by a computer program.

① technology is isolating us

② employees are being overworked

③ artificial intelligence benefits humans

④ managing finances is the top priority

⑤ human resources are evenly allocated

31 다음 글의 빈칸 (A), (B)에 들어갈 말로 가장 적절한 것은?

Many people, including many scientists, tend to confuse the mind with the brain, but they are really very different things. The brain is a material network of neurons, synapses, and biochemicals. The mind is a flow of subjective experiences, such as pain, pleasure, anger and love. Biologists assume that the brain somehow produces the mind, and that biochemical reactions in billions of neurons somehow produce experiences such as pain and love.   (A)   , so far we have absolutely no explanation for how the mind emerges from the brain. How come when billions of neurons are firing electrical signals in a particular pattern, I feel pain, and when the neurons fire in a different pattern, I feel love? We haven't got a clue. _____(B)_____, even if the mind indeed emerges from the brain, at least for now studying the mind is a different undertaking than studying the brain.

	(A)		(B)
①	In addition	‥‥‥	For example
②	However	‥‥‥	Hence
③	In addition	‥‥‥	Hence
④	However	‥‥‥	Nevertheless
⑤	Therefore	‥‥‥	For example

[32~33] 다음 글에서 전체 흐름과 관계 없는 문장을 고르시오.

32 The Internet of Things (IoT) can revolutionize the business and consumer landscape by bridging digital and material worlds. ① Any industry reliant on making, moving or selling objects that were previously not connected to the internet stands to benefit. ② Many industries, however, do not have the infrastructure with 5G broadband connection that can mobilize their IoT. ③ The specific benefits IoT can bring to a business depend on how the technology is used. ④ For example, sensors can be used to reduce waste by optimizing lighting or heating based on occupancy levels, or reduce spoilage of products in transit by monitoring temperatures. ⑤ IoT can also generate revenue and increase productivity, such as acoustic offshore oilfield sensors that analyze activity through pipelines to maximize output and help identify new resource pools.

33 Students of criminology, as well as the average citizen, are often unaware that criminalization of drugs is a twentieth-century American creation. Earlier, what we now construe as "drugs" were not dealt with differently than the vast array of other substances that arguably hold some potential for damaging (or enhancing) health. ① What we now think of as "hard drugs" were once readily available as medicines and even food additives. ② Coca-Cola once lived up to the advertisement jingle dubbing it the "real thing" by including cocaine as a stimulating ingredient, later replaced by caffeine. ③ The past 40 years have witnessed a "drug war" based on the idea that law enforcement should aggressively seek to eliminate specified drugs. ④ Our contemporary view of drugs was launched when Congress passed the Harrison Act in 1914, effectively criminalizing the sale and possession of opiates. ⑤ Legislation criminalizing marijuana was in place in 16 states by 1930, and in all states by 1937.

[3점]

34 글의 흐름으로 보아, 주어진 문장이 들어가기에 가장 적절한 곳은?

> When the researchers opened the boxes, they found that nearly all the caterpillars, with or without vision, had changed their body colors to match the sticks in their box.

Peppered moths are masters of camouflage. (①) In the larval stage, they can change the color of their skin to blend into their settings— even without seeing those surroundings, a new study found. (②) After raising more than 300 peppered moth larvae, U.K. researchers obscured the vision of some with black paint. (③) The larvae were placed in boxes containing white, green, brown, or black sticks, and given time to adapt. (④) The researchers then moved the caterpillars into new boxes containing sticks of two different colors, and about 80 percent of the insects chose to rest on sticks that matched their body color. (⑤) The researchers say their findings provide strong evidence that peppered moth larvae are capable of dermal photoreception—seeing with their skin.

[35~36] 주어진 글 다음에 이어질 글의 순서로 가장 적절한 것을 고르시오.

35

> Urban America was electrified between 1900 and the onset of the Great Depression in 1929, and rural America followed suit between 1936 and 1949. The electrification of factories made way for the era of mass-produced goods, with the automobile as the kingpin.

(A) Without electricity, Henry Ford would not have had available electric power tools to bring the work to the workers and manufacture an affordable automobile for millions of Americans. The mass production of the gasoline-powered Model T car altered the temporal and spatial orientation of society.

(B) Concrete highways were laid out over vast stretches of America, culminating in the US Interstate Highway System—the largest public works project in world history—creating a seamless coast-to-coast road system. The interstate highways were the impetus for a mass exodus of millions of families from urban areas to the newly emerging suburbs popping up off the highway exits.

(C) Millions of people began to trade in their horses and buggies for automobiles. To meet the increased demand for fuel, the nascent oil industry revved up exploration and drilling, built oil pipelines across the country, and set up thousands of gasoline stations to power the millions of automobiles coming off the assembly lines. [3점]

① (A) – (C) – (B) ② (B) – (A) – (C)

③ (B) – (C) – (A) ④ (C) – (A) – (B)

⑤ (C) – (B) – (A)

36

Not everyone is aware of the way their emotions impact others in their lives. Even when emotions are appropriate, their intensity may lead to problems. Some feelings, of course, are inappropriate.

(A) Such messages tend to confuse the recipient of that emotion and can lead to problems. When people express emotions, they may facilitate relationships or derail them. Understanding the impact of emotional expression is the core of psychotherapy.

(B) When they are congruent, the emotion fits with the message that is being sent. Some people may indicate one emotion with their words and another with their tone of voice. Sometimes this is referred to as the difference between verbal and nonverbal behavior.

(C) Whether or not an emotion is considered appropriate is related to the context in which it is displayed as well as the people involved.

Emotions may also be either congruent or incongruent.

① (A) – (C) – (B) ② (B) – (A) – (C)

③ (B) – (C) – (A) ④ (C) – (A) – (B)

⑤ (C) – (B) – (A)

[37~38] 다음 글을 읽고, 물음에 답하시오.

One morning, when I awoke, the temperature was barely five degrees and the wind was blowing fiercely. Daddy and the other cowboys went about their chores regardless, but my mama held me back. "Why don't you and I make a chocolate cake today?" she said.

Mama told me the ingredients I needed to find and began spooning flour and sugar into a bowl. "How do you know how much to use?" I asked. I'd never seen her look at a recipe to cook anything.

"It's about finding the right balance. You'll make mistakes at first, but that's how you learn," she said.

Soon the house was filled with the sweet aroma of rich, velvety chocolate. The heat from the oven was warm and welcoming.

"You know what comes next?" Mama asked me.

"Eating!" I said.

Mama laughed. "First comes cleaning up," she said, filling the sink with hot soapy water. Hmm, even fun jobs required hard work. "The joy of cooking isn't about the eating. It's about seeing the smiles on people's faces."

I didn't quite see how a smile could beat a piece of chocolate cake until I was a few years older. I was 15, and Daddy, my brother and I were pitching in at a friend's ranch, an annual custom called neighboring up. Around midday, I heard an old man, sweat running down his face, say, "We better get paid well today." *Wow, we're getting cash money,* I thought. Then I looked up to see car after car coming down the driveway, people bringing platters of fried chicken, breaded pork chops, salads of all kinds, cakes and pies. The cowboys were grinning from ear to ear. To this day, I remember how good that food tasted after a morning of hard work. That afternoon, the cowboys worked twice as hard, laughing and cutting up. I thought about what Mama had said about why she liked to cook. To be able to give folks that much pleasure, well, that seemed pretty special.

37 윗글의 제목으로 가장 적절한 것은?

① Old Habits Die Hard

② You Are What You Eat

③ Are You a Good Neighbor?

④ Wide Variety of Cowboy Cuisine

⑤ A Lesson on the Joy of Cooking

38 윗글의 내용과 일치하는 것은?

① When Mama cooked, she followed the recipe faithfully.

② Mama said the most important thing about cooking was the taste.

③ The neighboring up custom was practiced every month.

④ What the old man meant by payment was the food.

⑤ The cowboys were not happy about working in the afternoon.

[39~40] 다음 글을 읽고, 물음에 답하시오.

It is sometimes proposed that direct brain-computer interfaces, particularly implants, could enable humans to exploit the fortes of digital computing—perfect recall, speedy and accurate arithmetic calculation, and high-bandwidth data transmission—enabling the resulting hybrid system to radically outperform the unaugmented brain. But although the possibility of direct connections between human brains and computers has been demonstrated, it seems unlikely that such interfaces will be widely used as enhancements any time soon.

To begin with, there are significant risks of medical complications—including infections, electrode displacement, hemorrhage, and cognitive decline—when implanting electrodes in the brain. Perhaps the most vivid illustration to date of the benefits that can be obtained through brain stimulation is the treatment of patients with Parkinson's disease. The Parkinson's implant is relatively simple: it does not really communicate with the brain but simply supplies a stimulating electric current to the subthalamic nucleus. A demonstration video shows a subject slumped in a chair, completely immobilized by the disease, then suddenly springing to life when the current is switched on: the subject now moves his arms, stands up and walks across the room, turns around and performs a pirouette. Yet even behind this especially simple and almost miraculously successful procedure, there lurk negatives. One study of Parkinson patients who had received deep brain implants showed reductions in verbal fluency, selective attention, color naming, and verbal memory compared with controls. Treated subjects also reported more cognitive complaints. Such risks and side effects might be tolerable if the procedure is used to alleviate severe disability. But in order for healthy subjects to volunteer themselves for neurosurgery, there would have to be some very _____ of normal functionality to be gained.

39 윗글의 제목으로 가장 적절한 것은?

① Full Functionality Gained Via Brain-Computer Interface

② A Breakthrough in Parkinson's Disease Treatment

③ How Best to Augment Brain Power with Implants

④ Direct Brain-Computer Interfaces: Pros and Cons

⑤ Hopes for Success Dwindle Away in Neuroscience

40 윗글의 빈칸에 들어갈 말로 가장 적절한 것은?

① substantial enhancement

② universal application

③ complicated achievements

④ complete deprivation

⑤ authoritative establishments

[41~42] 다음 글을 읽고, 물음에 답하시오.

For centuries, it was believed that disabled people like me were living under a curse that was inflicted by God. Well, I suppose it's possible that I've (A) upset/pleased someone up there, but I prefer to think that everything can be explained another way; by the laws of nature. If you believe in science, like I do, you believe that there are certain laws that are always obeyed. If you like, you can say the laws are the work of God, but that is more a definition of God than a proof of his existence. In about 300 BCE, a philosopher called Aristarchus was fascinated by eclipses, especially eclipses of the Moon. He was (B) brave/obedient enough to question whether they really were caused by gods. Aristarchus was a true scientific pioneer. He studied the heavens carefully and reached a bold conclusion: he realised the eclipse was really the shadow of the Earth passing over the Moon, and not a (C) natural/divine event. Liberated by this discovery, he was able to work out what was really going on above his head, and draw diagrams that showed the true relationship of the Sun, the Earth and the Moon. From there he reached even more remarkable conclusions. He deduced that the Earth was not the centre of the universe, as everyone had thought, but that it instead orbits the Sun. In fact, understanding this arrangement explains all eclipses. When the Moon casts its shadow on the Earth, that's a solar eclipse. And when the Earth shades the Moon, that's a lunar eclipse. But Aristarchus took it even further. He suggested that stars were not chinks in the floor of heaven, as his contemporaries believed, but that stars were other suns, like ours, only a very long way away. What a stunning realisation it must have been. The universe is a machine governed by principles or laws—laws that _____.

41 (A), (B), (C)의 각 네모 안에서 문맥에 맞는 낱말로 가장 적절한 것은?

	(A)	(B)	(C)
①	upset	obedient	natural
②	upset	obedient	divine
③	upset	brave	divine
④	pleased	obedient	natural
⑤	pleased	brave	divine

42 윗글의 빈칸에 들어갈 말로 가장 적절한 것은? [3점]

① decipher God's secret codes

② reveal the existence of God

③ transcend human scientific capacity

④ can be understood by the human mind

⑤ strengthen the bond between God and nature

[43~45] 다음 글을 읽고 물음에 답하시오.

I actually knew about Stravinsky very early on in my life. I was about twelve. I was taking piano lessons from Denise, a nice, frizzy-haired, thirty-something bachelorette who would come to our apartment to teach me *Für Elise*, Bach's variations, and, to keep me interested, the theme from *Star Wars*. Despite the minor point that I showed no musical talent whatsoever, I somehow decided I needed to take it to the next level. I needed to become a composer.

So one week, I spent hours every afternoon plonking around on the piano in our foyer, scribbling down notes, erasing, scribbling some more. Finally, on Friday, Denise came, and I played my opus for her. It sounded like a combination of a traffic jam on Madison Avenue, a fax machine, and weasels in heat.

"Good for you, A.J.," she said. "You're experimenting in atonal compositions."

"Yes, I'm very interested in atonal compositions." Of course, I had no idea what atonal compositions were; in fact, I was trying desperately to write tonal compositions. It's just that (A) <u>my ear was 100 percent tin.</u>

"It reminds me of Stravinsky," she said.

"Ah, yes, Stravinsky," I replied, nodding my head. Denise was being exceedingly nice. She didn't want to discourage me, but the only way it could have reminded her of Stravinsky is if Stravinsky had accidentally sat on the keyboard.

That's how I first learned of the Russian master. Then, in college, I expanded my knowledge of Stravinsky by four words: *The Rites of Spring*. An atonal composer who wrote *The Rites of Spring*. So that's about where I stood.

From the *Britannica*, I learned two important things. First, it's *The Rite of Spring*. Only one rite. So I'd been sounding like a jackass all these years when I made the occasional allusion to Stravinsky. Second, *The Rite of Spring* was enough to cause an "opening-night riot" when it debuted at the Théâtre de Champs Elysées on May 29, 1913.

Stravinsky's score—with its "scandalous dissonances and rhythmic brutality"—caused an uproar among the chic Paris audience. The commotion was so loud, the ballet dancers couldn't hear the orchestra in the nearby pit. But the dancers kept dancing anyway, urged on by the choreographer, who stood on a chair in the wings, shouting and miming the rhythm.

I love this. I can't believe that less than a century ago, a ballet with some discordant notes could cause an actual riot. Nowadays, audience members at the ballet rarely riot. They are often too busy falling asleep. Or if they are really upset, they leave after the first act to get a nice pasta dinner somewhere.

43 윗글에 나타난 필자의 태도로 가장 적절한 것은?

① optimistic and jubilant

② objective and impartial

③ amusing and candid

④ annoyed and critical

⑤ calm and reserved

44 밑줄 친 (A)가 의미하는 바로 가장 적절한 것은?

① I lacked the keyboard dexterity expected of a composer.

② I suffered from a strong blow to my ear by Denise.

③ I had a knack for composing atonal and tonal music.

④ I could not hear the differences between musical notes.

⑤ My composition skills were overshadowed by my playing.

45 'I'에 관한 윗글의 내용과 일치하지 <u>않는</u> 것은?

① My piano teacher was unmarried and in her thirties.

② I once learned the *Star Wars* theme on the piano.

③ I gained a comprehensive understanding of Stravinsky in college.

④ The *Britannica* helped me realize my misunderstanding about Stravinsky.

⑤ I was surprised that discordant notes caused a riot.

2026
경찰대학 10개년 영어

2020학년도 기출문제

영어영역

제2교시 영어영역

▶정답 및 해설 341p

[01~06] 밑줄 친 단어의 뜻으로 가장 적절한 것을 고르시오.

01

Procrastination becomes a major problem in your work life when important tasks or responsibilities are left undone or are completed in a slipshod manner because inadequate time was left to complete the task properly.

① hastiness   ② postponement

③ spontaneity   ④ concern

⑤ exaggeration

02

A worldwide financial crisis began in the last half of 1997, when the currencies of several Asian economies plummeted in value.

① boomed suddenly

② bounced back

③ got stuck

④ made a difference

⑤ dropped sharply

03

If you can't weave quotations deftly into the fabric of your prose, abjure them altogether and paraphrase instead.

① abandon   ② compose

③ revise   ④ brainstorm

⑤ elaborate

04

The increasing power of the personal computer is making it possible to develop applications that are smarter and more responsive to the user. Anyone who has used a spelling or a grammar checker has experienced this type of application at a very rudimentary level.

① basic   ② deep

③ optimal   ④ conscious

⑤ abstract

05

One reason to think that written languages will look more or less like they do now is the fact that so far they have proved extremely <u>tenacious</u>. The Chinese system has changed little in more than 3,000 years, and Modern Greek is written with an alphabet that has been used for almost as long.

① arbitrary   ② reliable

③ useful   ④ graphic

⑤ persistent

06

Lacking a clear formula for making decisions, we get reactive and fall back on familiar, comfortable ways to decide what to do. As a result, we <u>haphazardly</u> select approaches that don't support our goals.

① covertly   ② invariably

③ explicitly   ④ randomly

⑤ precisely

[07~09] 밑줄 친 부분 중, 어법상 **틀린** 것을 고르시오.

07 As with the question of the date ① <u>at which</u> European antiquarianism was superseded by archaeology, it is not easy to suggest a specific date when the writings of 'early travellers' and the collecting of Egyptian antiquities ② <u>became transformed</u> into something approaching the modern discipline of Egyptology. Most histories of Egyptian archaeology, however, see the Napoleonic expedition at the beginning of the 19th century as the first systematic attempt to record and describe the standing remains of pharaonic Egypt. The importance of the *Description del'Egyptek*, which was the multi-volume publication that ③ <u>resulted from</u> the expedition, lay not only in its high standards of accuracy but also in the fact that ④ <u>they</u> constituted a continuous and internally consistent appraisal by a group of scholars, thus ⑤ <u>providing</u> the first real assessment of ancient Egypt in its entirety.

*antiquarianism : 골동품 연구

08 Fire destroys about 350 ① <u>million</u> ha (1,350 mi^2) of forest every year. Some fires are set by humans to cover up illegal logging or land clearing. Others are started by natural causes. The greatest fire hazard in the world is in sub-Saharan Africa, which accounts for about ② <u>half</u> the global total. Uncontrolled fires tend to be ③ <u>worst</u>

in countries with corrupt or ineffective governments and high levels of poverty, civil unrest, and internal refugees. ④ As global climate change brings drought and insect infestations to many parts of the world, there's a worry ⑤ which forest fires may increase catastrophically.

09 If contemporary experience ① has taught us anything, surely it is the need for a president to hit the ground running. The difference between Reagan's quick start and Clinton's stumble put one on the path toward ② a succession of legislative triumphs and the other on the road to a debacle in health care and a loss of Congress. Had Clinton not been as agile as he was in recovering in late 1993 and then again in 1995, he ③ would be a one-term president. As it was, he never became the transformational figure he had hoped. In most institutions, the power of a leader grows over time. A CEO, a university president, the head of a union, acquire stature through the quality of their long-term performance. The presidency is ④ just the opposite: power tends to evaporate quickly. It's not that a president must rival Franklin Roosevelt in his First Hundred Days, but his first months in office are usually the widest window of opportunity he will have, ⑤ even if he serves two full terms. That's why he has to move fast.

[10~11] 다음 글의 밑줄 친 부분 중, 문맥상 낱말의 쓰임이 가장 적절하지 않은 것을 고르시오.

10 The book, "Superforecasting: Arts and Science of Prediction," opens with a discussion of Archie Cochrane, a Scottish doctor born in 1909, who did more than perhaps anyone else to transform medicine from a black art into a ① fully fledged science. His insight—deeply controversial half a century ago—was that a doctor's qualifications, eminence and confidence are ② irrelevant and that the only test of a treatment's effectiveness was whether it could be shown, statistically and rigorously, to work. Mr. Tetlock, the author of the book, hopes to bring about a similar rigor to how people ③ analyze forecasts of the future. That will be an ④ easy struggle. Prediction, like medicine in the early 20th century, is still mostly based on ⑤ eminence rather than evidence. [3점]

11 Polling is like Internet dating. There is a little wiggle room in the ① veracity of information provided. We know that people ② shade the truth, particularly when the question asked are embarrassing or sensitive. Respondents may overstate their income. They may not ③ deny that they do not vote. They may hesitate to express views that are unpopular or socially unacceptable. For all these reasons, even the most carefully designed poll is dependent on the ④ integrity of the respondents' answers. Election polls depend crucially on ⑤ <u>sorting</u> those who will vote on Election Day from those who will not. Individuals often say they are going to vote because they think that is what pollsters want to hear. Studies that have compared self-reported voting behavior to election records consistently find that one-quarter to one-third of respondents say they voted when in fact they did not.

of the same species, sharing the same DNA pool. They will happily mate and their puppies will grow up to pair off with other dogs and produce more puppies.

	(A)	(B)	(C)
①	fertile	sterile	similar
②	fertile	fertile	similar
③	fertile	sterile	separate
④	sterile	fertile	separate
⑤	sterile	fertile	similar

[12~13] (A), (B), (C)의 각 네모 안에서 문맥에 맞는 낱말로 가장 적절한 것을 고르시오.

12

Biologists classify organisms into species. Animals are said to belong to the same species if they tend to mate with each other, giving birth to (A) fertile/sterile offspring. Horses and donkeys have a recent common ancestor and share many physical traits. But they show little sexual interest in one another. They will mate if induced to do so — but their offspring are (B) fertile/sterile. Mutations in donkey DNA can therefore never cross over to horses, or vice versa. The two types of animals are consequently considered two distinct species, moving along (C) separate/similar evolutionary paths. By contrast, a bulldog and a spaniel may look very different, but they are members

13

Big data has its drawbacks. The flood of information — some of it useful, some not — can (A) overwhelm/maximize one's ability to quickly and efficiently process data and take appropriate action. If we fail to create and utilize methodologies and tools for effectively using big data, we may continue to (B) evolve/drown in it. In the context of national security, lacking adequate big data tools could have profound, even deadly, consequences. However, there are steps that we can take now — steps that are already being taken in many cases — to ensure that we successfully (C) harness/renounce the power of big data. [3점]

	(A)	(B)	(C)
①	overwhelm	drown	harness
②	overwhelm	evolve	renounce
③	overwhelm	drown	renounce
④	maximize	evolve	harness
⑤	maximize	drown	renounce

[14~15] 다음 글에서 전체 흐름과 관계 <u>없는</u> 문장을 고르시오.

14 America is not actually a "melting pot" in the sense that people from different backgrounds somehow all become the same. America has always included a great diversity of ideas, attitudes, and behaviors. ① For example, the constitutional separation of church and state, a fundamental principle present since early days in the United States, guarantees that people of all religion have the same freedoms and rights for worship and religious behavior. ② People of diverse religious backgrounds are not expected to "melt" together into one religion. ③ Conflicts simply occur among people, whether of the same or different background. ④ Other laws guarantee the equal rights of all people regardless of skin color, gender, and age. ⑤ The United States does not even have an official national language — and many government and other publications in various geographical areas are offered in a variety of languages as well. In short, America as a nation has always recognized the realities and benefits of diversity.

15 No one questions that machines displace individual workers from certain jobs and that in the short run this often creates difficult problems. ① For example, the use of diesel engines and electric power by railroads has made obsolete the position of fireman — the employee who shoveled coal into the locomotive boiler that produced the steam for the train's steam engine — but because of union support, railroads had to fill this position for many years after steam power ceased being used by trains. ② However, such problems are temporary. ③ Ultimately, advances in machine technology tend to reduce costs and prices or to hold them down, and by enabling people to buy more goods, they create new employment opportunities. ④ Machines reduce the need for human skills. ⑤ If some industries employ fewer workers, others employ more. At the same time, new products are introduced and new industries are established. [3점]

[16~23] 다음 글의 빈칸에 들어갈 말로 가장 적절한 것을 고르시오.

16

It is a principle in many legal systems that a competent adult has a right to refuse any, even lifesaving, treatment. This principle applies to the treatment of physical illness. It does not apply however in many countries to those with mental illness. Take the case of England, where it is the Mental Health Act that governs the _____ treatment of patients with mental disorder.

① alternative　　② compulsory

③ adjunctive　　④ incremental

⑤ preventive

17

A social-conflict analysis begins by pointing out that sports are closely linked to social inequality. Some sports — including tennis, swimming, golf, and skiing — are expensive, so participation is largely limited to the well-to-do. Football, baseball, and basketball, however, are accessible to people of all income levels. In short, the games people play are not simply a matter of choice but also reflect social _____.

① bonds　　② needs

③ trends　　④ standing

⑤ preference

18

What should the effect of success on motivation be? Should it necessarily increase motivation? The argument earlier suggests that if learners realize that successful performance in some activity leads toward their goal, then expectancies are likely to rise. This would appear to say that success will tend to increase motivation, but matters are not that simple. This argument considers potential motivation and ignores motivational arousal. Motivational arousal is based on a person's assumption of how much effort is needed to perform an activity correctly. Studies indicate that motivational arousal is greatest for tasks that are assumed to be of moderate difficulty. If success rate is considered very high or very low, motivational arousal is _____. In other words, we try hardest for things we consider challenging but not nearly impossible.

① weakened　　② mobilized

③ fluctuated　　④ stabilized

⑤ alternated

19

For historians of Africa identity can be a tricky intellectual issue. Africans are, like people everywhere, compilations of numerous identities, some of which are personally or collectively claimed, others of which are imposed by outsiders. If people are asked who the most famous living African is, the usual answer is 'Nelson Mandela.' But as we write this in the aftermath of the 2006 World Cup, there is a good case for saying that the most famous living African is Zinédene Zidane. Let's consider this one individual. Who, or what, is Zidane? He's a Frenchman, born and raised in Marseilles. But he's also a North African, whose parents emigrated from Algeria; and a Berber, with family roots in the Kabyle mountains and reportedly fiercely proud of his ancestral village. He also describes himself as a Muslim. And he is, of course, a footballer. Whichever of these labels Zidane himself chooses to use would depend both on where he is and how he's thinking at the time. Identity, in other words, is as _____ as it is multifaceted.

[3점]

① unique   ② ethnic

③ political   ④ indigenous

⑤ fluid

20

Picasso's oeuvre includes more than 1,800 paintings, 1,200 sculptures, 2,800 ceramics, and 12,000 drawings, not to mention prints, rugs, and tapestries — only a fraction of which have garnered acclaim. In poetry, when we recite Maya Angelou's classic poem "Still I Rise," we tend to forget that she wrote 165 others; we remember her moving memoir *I Know Why the Caged Bird Sings* and pay less attention to her other 6 autobiographies. In science, Einstein wrote papers on general and special relativity that transformed physics, but many of his 248 publications had minimal impact. If you want to be original, "the most important possible thing you could do," says Ira Glass, the producer of *This American Life* and the podcast *Serial*, "is _____."

*oeuvre : 일생의 작품

① do a lot of work

② reject the default

③ take radical risks

④ gain new insights

⑤ explore better options

21

Lightner Witmer received his doctorate in psychology in 1892 in Germany under Wilhelm Wundt, who many view as the founder of experimental psychology. He also studied under James McKeen Cattell, another pioneer of experimental psychology. At the time Witmer received his doctorate, psychology was essentially an academic discipline, a field of research. It had almost none of the applied functions that characterize the field today. In short, in the late 1800s, _____.

① the field of experimental psychology was not popular

② psychologists didn't practice psychology, but studied it

③ Lightner Witmer was a leading psychologist in Germany

④ it took much effort to receive a doctoral degree in psychology

⑤ Wilhelm Wundt set the stage for the birth of clinical psychology

22

When Adam Smith lectured at the University of Glasgow in the 1760s, he introduced the study of demand by posing a puzzle. Common sense, he said, suggests that the price of a commodity must somehow depend on what that good is worth to consumers — on the amount of *utility* that the commodity offers. Yet, Smith pointed out, some cases suggest that _____. Smith cited diamonds and water as examples. He noted that water has enormous value to most consumers; indeed, its availability can be a matter of life and death. Yet water generally either is free or sells at a very low price, whereas diamonds sell for very high prices even though few people would consider them necessities.

① a good's price may depend on its availability

② a good's price may be intertwined with its value

③ a good's utility may have little influence on its price

④ a good's utility may depend on its supply and demand

⑤ a good's quantity demanded may not depend on its price

23

While to-do lists serve as a useful collection of our best intentions, they also tyrannize us with trivial, unimportant stuff that we feel obligated to get done — because it's on our list. Which is why most of us have a love-hate relationship with our to-do lists. If allowed, they set our priorities the same way an inbox can dictate our day. Most inboxes overflow with unimportant e-mails masquerading as priorities. Tackling these tasks in the order we receive them is behaving as if the squeaky wheel immediately deserves the grease. But, as Australian prime minister Bob Hawke duly noted, "The things which are most important _____."

[3점]

① can easily lead you astray

② don't always scream the loudest

③ sometimes undermine our success

④ are just first things we thought of

⑤ must be at the mercy of things which matter least

24 다음 글의 빈칸에 공통으로 들어갈 말로 가장 적절한 것은?

A blockchain is used in bitcoin to prevent the double-spend problem. Before bitcoin, the issue with a digital currency was that someone could spend the same unit of digital currency in multiple places at the same time. A blockchain solves this problem by providing a shared ledger, which ensures that everyone knows and agrees on how much of the digital currency has transacted among users at any point in time. It is thought that blockchains might provide an effective tool in detecting and preventing corrupt or fraudulent activities. This thinking is premised on the _____ of a blockchain. The _____ prevents any one party from altering past entries, as one might be able to do with paper or digital records.

① availability

② innovation

③ multiplicity

④ flexibility

⑤ immutability

25 다음 글의 빈칸 (A), (B)에 들어갈 말로 가장 적절한 것은?

Former Congresswoman Patricia Schroeder pinpointed one of the most important reasons for women to enter the workforce when she argued that the primary reason they do so in such unprecedented numbers is that they have to maintain their families. Many family women work because they must work. For others, although families have become smaller, wants have become larger. _____(A)_____, for these family women, work is not an actual necessity but it is a social need: It is the only way the family can meet its desires. _____(B)_____, for black and other minority females, work has been a necessity for much longer than for white females. Women in the workforce as a percentage of total women of working age rose from 32 percent in 1972 to over 70 percent in the early 2000s. Analysts who study such trends say that the percentage of working women with children is expected to continue to grow even through some very high-income women may choose to stop working and stay home with their children.

[3점]

	(A)	(B)
①	Therefore	......	However
②	Otherwise	......	In addition
③	Thus	......	Nevertheless
④	Moreover	......	Therefore
⑤	For example	......	On the other hand

[26~27] 다음 글을 읽고 물음에 답하시오.

Convinced that human actions derived their emotional energy from the 'heart', which could only be addressed and activated by judiciously selected symbols, Gandhi evolved a powerful cluster of culturally (1) evocative symbols including the spinning wheel, the cow, and the 'Gandhi cap' (a white cotton cap popularized by him). The spinning wheel, for example, which Gandhi asked everyone to ply, served several symbolic purposes. It was a way of gently (2) rebelling against modern technological civilization and (3) denouncing the dignity of India's rural way of life. (a) It united the cities and the villages and the Westernized elite and the masses, and was an 'emblem of their fellowship.' The spinning wheel also established the dignity of manual labor and those engaged in (b) it and (4) challenged the traditional Indian culture which despised both. (c) It symbolized social compassion, for those who did not need the proceeds of (d) its products were urged to give away those products to the needy, an infinitely superior moral act to the (5) patronizing donation of money. And (e) it also forced the individual to be alone with himself and observe silence for at least some time. Gandhi not only evolved countless symbols of this kind but also became one himself.

*ply : 연장을 부지런히 쓰다
**proceeds : 수입, 매상

26 밑줄 친 (1)~(5) 중에서 문맥상 낱말의 쓰임이 가장 적절하지 <u>않은</u> 것은? [3점]

① (1) ② (2)
③ (3) ④ (4)
⑤ (5)

27 밑줄 친 (a)~(e) 중에서 의미하는 바가 나머지 넷과 <u>다른</u> 것은?

① (a) ② (b)
③ (c) ④ (d)
⑤ (e)

28 다음 글에 나타난 Annemarie의 심경 변화로 가장 적절한 것은?

The train started again. The door at the end of their car opened and two German soldiers appeared. Annemarie tensed. Not here, on the train, too? They were everywhere. Together the soldiers strolled through the car, glancing at passengers, stopping here and there to ask a question. One of them had something stuck in his teeth; he probed with his tongue and distorted his own face. Annemarie watched with a kind of frightened fascination as the pair approached. One of the soldiers looked down with a bored expression on his face. "Where are you going?" he asked. "Gilleleje," Mama replied calmly. "My brother lives there. We are going to visit him." The soldier turned away and Annemarie relaxed. Then, without warning, he turned back. "Are you visiting your brother for the New Year?" he asked suddenly. Mama stared at him with a puzzled look. "New Year?" she asked "It is only October." "And guess what!" Kirsti exclaimed suddenly, in a loud voice, looking at the soldier. Annemarie's heart sank and she looked at her mother. Mama's eyes were frightened. "Shhh, Kirsti," Mama said. "Don't chatter so." But Kirsti paid no attention to Mama, as usual. She looked cheerfully at the soldier, and Annemarie knew what she was about to say: This is our friend Ellen and it's her New Year! But she didn't. Instead, Kirsti pointed at her feet. "I'm going to visit my Uncle Henrik," she chirped, "and I'm wearing my brand-new shiny black shoes!" The soldier chuckled and moved on. Annemarie gazed through the window again.

The trees, the Baltic Sea, and the cloudy October sky passed in a blur as they continued north along the coast.

① hopeful → disappointed

② terrified → relieved

③ excited → offended

④ surprised → upset

⑤ miserable → ashamed

29 다음 글의 내용과 일치하지 <u>않는</u> 것은?

Millions of years ago, a dozen or so genetic changes took place in the ancestor of all of today's felids, which have locked them into eating meat ever since. All cats require a large amount of animal protein in their diet — protein from plants lacks certain amino acids such as taurine that cats need but other mammals (including ourselves) do not. Cats can't make their own prostaglandins — hormones essential to reproduction — and so need to get these from meat. Compared to other mammals, all cats need large amounts of several vitamins, such as niacin, thiamine and retinol, which are more easily extracted from meat than from plants. And because they don't need to tell the difference between ripe and unripe fruit, they've lost

the ability to taste sugars. They have adapted their 'sweet' taste buds for distinguishing between different flavors in meat — which is why pet cats sometimes walk away from food that seems fine to their owners. This knowledge has only come to light in the past 40 years, benefiting not only pet cats but also the captive breeding of endangered felids such as the clouded leopard.

*felids : 고양이과 동물

① 고양이의 조상은 수백만 년 전에 유전적 변이를 겪었다.

② 고양이는 많은 양의 동물성 단백질을 필요로 한다.

③ 고양이는 번식에 필수적인 호르몬을 만들 수 없다.

④ 고양이는 설탕 맛을 느끼지 못한다.

⑤ 고양이는 고기의 다른 맛을 구별하지 못한다.

30 Philip에 관한 다음 글의 내용과 일치하지 <u>않</u>는 것은?

As soon as he came to the throne, Philip began transforming the Macedonian military into a more successful image of what he had seen at Thebes. Philip further lengthened the already longer spears used by the Thebans, creating the Macedonian sarissa, a spear of about eighteen feet in length, double that of the traditional Greek hoplite spear. He retained the Theban wedge formation but also added heavy cavalry to the line, thus incorporating the Macedonians' strongest element into the phalanx. The results spoke for themselves, as over the next twenty years, Philip systematically conquered all of mainland Greece, with the exception of Sparta, which he chose to leave alone. Philip's final great victory was at the Battle of Chaeronea (338 B.C.), in which the Macedonian armies defeated the combined forces of Athens and Thebes. Philip's conquest of the entire mainland was the end of an era, as for the first time, the entire territory was united under the rule of a king.

*phalanx : (고대 그리스의) 방진(方陣)

① 창의 길이를 약 18피트로 늘렸다.

② 기병을 전선에 추가하였다.

③ Sparta를 정복했다.

④ Athens와 Thebes의 연합군을 격퇴했다.

⑤ 그리스 본토를 통합했다.

31 The Code of Hammurabi에 관한 다음 글의 내용과 일치하지 <u>않는</u> 것은?

The Babylonian emperor Hammurabi, who ruled Mesopotamia from about 1792 to about 1750 B.C., is best known for the code of laws that bears his name, one of the earliest law codes yet discovered. His main concern was to maintain order in his empire through authority, which answered the needs of his people. To that effect, he gave his subjects a complex law code. Its 282 decrees, collectively termed the Code of Hammurabi, were inscribed on stone stelae or columns and erected in many places. One was discovered in Persian Susa in the nineteenth century and is now in the Louvre in Paris.

The code dealt primarily civil affairs such as marriage and inheritance, family relations, property rights, and business practices. Criminal offenses were punished with varying degrees of severity, depending on the social status of the offender and the victim. There were clear distinctions between the rights of the upper classes and those of commoners. Payments are generally allowed as restitution for damage done to commoners by nobles. A commoner who causes damage to a noble, however, might have to pay with his head. Trial by ordeal, retribution by retaliatory action, and capital punishment were common practices. But judges distinguished between intentional and unintentional injuries, and monetary fines were normally used as punishment where no malicious intent was manifested. The "eye for an eye" morality often associated with Hammurabi's code was relatively restricted in application and applied only to crimes committed by and against social equals.

① 법전이 새겨진 비석이 19세기에 발견되었다.

② 법전은 형법을 주로 다루었다.

③ 신분에 따라 동일 범죄에 대한 처벌이 달랐다.

④ 사형제도가 포함되었다.

⑤ 재판관들은 상해의 고의성 여부를 구별하였다.

32 다음 글의 제목으로 가장 적절한 것은?

People can actually do two or more things at once, such as walk and talk, or chew gum and read a map; but, like computers, what we can't do is focus on two things at once. Our attention bounces back and forth. This is fine for computers, but it has serious repercussions in humans. Two airliners are cleared to land on the same runway. A patient is given the wrong medicine. A toddler is left unattended in the bathtub. What all these potential tragedies share is that people are trying to do too many things at once and forget to do something they should do. When you try to do two things at once, you either can't or won't do either well. If you think multitasking is an effective way to get more done, you've got it backward. It's an effective way to get less done.

① Fallacy of Multitasking

② The ABCs of Multitasking

③ Multitasking: Why and How

④ Coping Strategies for Multitasking Demands

⑤ Simple Truth behind Great Results: Multitasking

33 다음 글의 주제로 가장 적절한 것은?

Divorce statistics are often used as a measure of family disorganization, and the present high divorce rate is cited as proof that the U.S. family is in serious trouble. However, higher divorce rates today than in the past are not entirely the result of more family unhappiness. In earlier generations, many couples avoided divorce even though their married life was unhappy. They avoided it because it meant social ostracism or, in the case of women, poverty because there were few opportunities for them to earn a good living. As the possibilities for divorced people increased and it became easier to get divorces, more unhappy couples have chosen this route.

① uses of divorce statistics

② collection of divorce statistics

③ reasons why people get divorced

④ cautious interpretation of divorce statistics

⑤ coping with divorce and family breakdown

34 다음 글의 요지로 가장 적절한 것은?

When infant mortality rates are high, as they are in much of the developing world, parents tend to have high numbers of children to ensure that some will survive to adulthood. There has never been a sustained drop in birth rates that was not first preceded by a sustained drop in infant mortality. One of the most important distinctions in our demographically divided world is the high infant mortality rates in the less-developed countries. Better nutrition, improved health care, simple oral rehydration therapy, and immunization against infectious diseases have brought about dramatic reductions in infant mortality rates, which have been accompanied in most regions by falling birth rates. It has been estimated that saving 5 million children each year from easily preventable communicable diseases would avoid 20 or 30 million extra births.

① Infant mortality rates affect birth rates.

② Infant mortality around the world is declining very rapidly.

③ Disparities of wealth are reflected in infant mortality rates.

④ A primary cause of infant mortality is poor quality of water.

⑤ Good prenatal care has been linked to reduced infant mortality.

[35~36] 글의 흐름으로 보아 주어진 문장이 들어가기에 가장 적절한 곳을 고르시오.

35

> Yet, despite its ubiquity, astronomers have no real idea what constitutes dark matter.

Dark matter is measurable; it is just not visible. (①) It is invisible because it is 'dark.' (②) Astronomers infer the presence of dark matter because it explains how galaxies manage to hold themselves together, how gravitational lenses work and the observed temperature distribution of hot gas seen in galaxy clusters. (③) The conclusion is that over 80 per cent of the mass of the Universe is in a form we simply can't see. (④) It may include subatomic particles such as heavy neutrinos or other hypothetical particles like axions. (⑤) Some of it may be locked up in objects that simply elude detection. Currently, astronomers believe most dark matter consists of new elementary particles called weakly interacting massive particles (WIMPs), which apparently do not interact with electromagnetic radiation or atoms. They are therefore invisible to conventional means of detection. [3점]

36

> Burned-out workers sometimes depersonalize the people they need to help, thinking about them as objects or things rather than as feeling human beings.

Burnout is a special kind of psychological consequence of stress that afflicts some employees who experience high levels of work stress day in and day out for an extended period of time. It is especially likely to occur when employees are responsible for helping, protecting, or taking care of other people. Nurses, doctors, social workers, teachers, lawyers, and police officers are at risk for developing burnout due to the nature of their jobs. (①) Three key signs of burnout are feelings of low personal accomplishment, emotional exhaustion, and depersonalization. (②) Burned-out workers often feel that they are not helping others or accomplishing as much as they should be. (③) Emotionally they are worn out from the constant stress of dealing with people who are sometimes in desperate need of assistance. (④) A burned-out social worker, for example, may think about a foster child in need of a new one as a case number rather than as a very scared 12-year-old. (⑤) This psychological consequence may lead to a behavioral consequence when the burned-out social worker treats the child in a cold and distant manner.

[37~38] 주어진 글 다음에 이어질 글의 순서로 가장 적절한 것을 고르시오.

37

> Historically, rational analytic approaches are often seen as providing superior outcomes compared with intuition, although this decision-making process is much slower.

(A) These types of tasks are common in human resource management, strategic, aesthetic, and investment decisions. In short, intuition is most effective when experts are performing judgmental and holistic tasks.

(B) Hence, some talk about a speed versus effectiveness trade-off in decision making. Intuitions, however, can yield better outcomes than rational models depending on the level of the experience of the decision maker and the nature of the task at hand.

(C) Put simply, individuals who have a lot of experience (i.e., experts) in a particular area are primed to be more effective with intuition than rational decision making depending on the type of task they face. Experts, in general, are most effective in their use of intuitive decision making when the task at hand is one where there is more than one right answer or where the task cannot easily be subdivided into smaller chunks.

① (A) − (B) − (C)   ② (B) − (A) − (C)
③ (B) − (C) − (A)   ④ (C) − (B) − (A)
⑤ (C) − (A) − (B)

38

> Today, we are all aware that the ability of airline cabin crew, pilots, flight attendants, and so on to communicate effectively with each other and with passengers is vital to prevent crises.

(A) Because of this, and other dangerous incidents that resulted from poor communication, Federal Aviation Administration made assertiveness and sensitivity training for all airline crew members mandatory to ensure they have the ability to communicate effectively.

(B) Federal Aviation Administration investigators determined that the crash resulted in part because the copilot failed to tell the pilot about problems with engine power readings that were caused by ice on the engine sensors.

(C) A tragic example that demonstrated the way effective communication is so important on an airliner occurred when an Air Florida 737 plane crashed into a bridge over the Potomac River after taking off from National Airport in Washington, D.C.

① (A) − (C) − (B) ② (B) − (C) − (A)

③ (B) − (A) − (C) ④ (C) − (A) − (B)

⑤ (C) − (B) − (A)

[39~40] 다음 글을 읽고 물음에 답하시오.

From childhood on, social interactions, whether within the family or with other groups, provide the context within which the majority of food experiences occur, and hence by which learning of food likes is (a) facilitated. The pleasure associated with such interactions — the festivity of a meal shared with friends, for example — may represent just as positive a conditioning stimulus for a new food flavor as sweetness. Thus, it may be that our estimation of the food at a restaurant has as much to do with the (b) social environment as it does with the chef's skills. In children, pairing foods with the presence of friends, a liked celebrity, or attention by adults all increase liking for those foods, no doubt reflecting the positive value of each of these groups to the child. This process is strongly evident in the (c) relative impact of different social interactions on the food preferences of children. Surprisingly, despite the enormous opportunities in a family for exposing children to the foods eaten by the parents, parental preferences are (d) strong predictors of child food preferences; in fact, they are no better predictors than the preferences of other adults. This suggests that the extent to which these sets of preferences are related has more to do with the wider culture than with any specific food habits within the family. A child's food likes and dislikes are much more likely to be associated with those of peers, especially specific friends, than those of its parents. The ultimate impact of social facilitation of food choice is that the liking eventually becomes (e) internalized. That is, foods chosen because others do so become liked for their own sensory properties.

39 윗글의 제목으로 가장 적절한 것은?

① Cravings for Sweets

② Yum!: Innate Reponses to Food

③ Conditioning Stimulus for New Flavors

④ Judicious Food Choice for Child Rearing

⑤ How is Food Preference Socially Constructed?

40 밑줄 친 (a)~(e) 중에서 문맥상 낱말의 쓰임이 가장 적절하지 않은 것은? [3점]

① (a) ② (b)

③ (c) ④ (d)

⑤ (e)

[41~42] 다음 글을 읽고 물음에 답하시오.

(A) Meerkats might not be the biggest animals on the African plains, nor appear to boast any particularly formidable weapons, like the rhino's horn, or impressive skills, like the cheetah's speed.

(B) Some of these subterranean networks can play host to up to 50 or so individuals, though an average colony is about half this size, with two or three families living together communally. A type of mongoose, they are equipped with sharp, curved claws used for digging and self-defence, as well as acute vision, which comes in very handy for spotting danger. In fact, when they do venture out of their burrows to search for food, there will always be at least one meerkat that stands sentry — often on a rock or in a bush — primarily looking to the skies for their number-one enemy: birds of prey.

(C) As soon as any threat is detected, the lookout will give a shrill warning bark and the others will immediately make a dash for a nearby bolthole or other cover. It's thought that meerkats have dozens of different calls to signify a range of threats. As well as hunting together over a territorial range, meerkats also share childcare duties. Typically, only the colony's alpha pair will mate, but all the others pitch in to babysit, rooming and feeding the pups,

as well as demonstrating valuable life skills, like where to find food, play-fighting and which parts of a scorpion to eat.

(D) Nevertheless, through a combination of hardy biology, smart tricks and a unique community spirit, these mammals have adapted perfectly to their harsh environment. They escape the most extreme temperatures of southern Africa — as well as the vast majority of predators who'd like to make a meal of them — by living in underground burrows.

*sentry: 보초, 감시자

41 주어진 글 (A)에 이어질 내용을 순서에 맞게 배열한 것으로 가장 적절한 것은?

① (B) – (C) – (D) ② (C) – (D) – (B)
③ (C) – (B) – (D) ④ (D) – (C) – (B)
⑤ (D) – (B) – (C)

42 윗글의 내용과 일치하지 <u>않는</u> 것은?

① 미어캣은 몽구스의 한 종류이다.
② 미어캣은 일반적으로 독립적인 생활을 한다.
③ 미어캣은 땅을 파거나 자기방어를 위한 뾰족한 발톱이 있다.
④ 미어캣은 우두머리만 짝짓기를 한다.
⑤ 미어캣은 위협이 있을 경우 보초가 즉시 동료에게 알린다.

[43~45] 다음 글을 읽고 물음에 답하시오.

[가] Two researchers reported that after college students listened to a Mozart piano sonata they scored higher on a spacial reasoning test. Soon after this observation made the news, doting parents were playing Mozart for their babies around the clock. Obviously, they hoped that, like the college students, their babies would become smarter. However, parents should be suspicious of any practice that claims to offer such magical benefits.

[나] What does the evidence suggest? A few studies have found small increases in spatial intelligence following exposure to Mozart's music. However, most researchers have been unable to _____(A)_____ the effect.

[다] A major _____(B)_____ with the "Mozart effect" is that the original experiment was done with adults; it tells us nothing about infants. Also, the study didn't test other styles of music. Why not use the music of Bach or Schubert for that matter? An even more important question is, Does the Mozart effect actually exist?

[라] Why do some studies support the effect and others disconfirm it? Most studies have compared students who heard music to students who rested in silence. However, two psychologists found that listening to a narrated story also improves test scores. This is especially true for students who like listening to stories.

Thus, students who scored higher after listening to Mozart were just more alert or in a better mood.

43 주어진 글 [가]에 이어질 내용을 순서에 맞게 배열한 것으로 가장 적절한 것은? [3점]

① [나] – [라] – [다] ② [다] – [나] – [라]

③ [다] – [라] – [나] ④ [라] – [나] – [다]

⑤ [라] – [다] – [나]

44 윗글의 제목으로 가장 적절한 것은?

① Mozart Effect: Nothing Magical

② Mozart: The Making of a Prodigy

③ Why is Classical Music Good for Babies?

④ Mozart's Sonatas: The Highest Musical Fidelity

⑤ Mozart's Music and Its Pedagogical Implications

45 윗글의 빈 칸 (A), (B)에 들어갈 말로 가장 적절한 것은?

	(A)		(B)
①	support	……	concern
②	duplicate	……	benefit
③	duplicate	……	problem
④	disconfirm	……	benefit
⑤	disconfirm	……	problem

A discovery is said to be an accident meeting a prepared mind.

발견은 준비된 사람이 맞닥뜨린 우연이다.

– 알버트 센트 디외르디(Albert Szent-Gyorgyi)

2026
경찰대학

10개년 영어

2019학년도 기출문제

영어영역

제2교시 영어영역

[01~03] 밑줄 친 단어의 뜻으로 가장 적절한 것을 고르시오.

01

Nothing could be firmer than the tone of this letter, in spite of its <u>pensive</u> gentleness.

① overt　　　　② excessive

③ pervasive　　④ thoughtful

⑤ optimistic

02

The doctor asserted that his lifelong research on the human genome was by no means <u>exhaustive</u>.

① rewarding　　② revolutionary

③ lenient　　　④ independent

⑤ thorough

03

This <u>conundrum</u> was like no other that the police officers had faced before.

① instrument　　② robbery

③ criminal　　　④ puzzle

⑤ demonstration

[04~05] 다음 대화의 빈칸에 들어갈 말로 가장 적절한 것을 고르시오.

04

A : How did the meeting go yesterday?

B : It couldn't have been worse.

A : What happened?

B : I said something I shouldn't have and now Jack won't talk to me.

A : _____.

B : Now I need to gather every ounce of courage to do so.

① It's never too late to apologize

② You can't please everyone all the time

③ Sometimes a quarrel is good for the team

④ Just like everything else, time heals all wounds

⑤ That's why you have to think before you speak

05

> A : Detective Mills, I think this is the guy we are looking for.
> B : Do his prints match the ones from the scene of the crime, Officer Flaherty?
> A : The results haven't come in yet, but two witnesses say they saw someone with his descriptions.
> B : That won't be enough for an arrest warrant.
> A : But, I'm sure this is the perpetrator.
> B : _____.
> A : Okay. Then we'll just have to wait for the results from the lab.

① I'll ask for a warrant right away

② We move on evidence, not feelings

③ I think we already have all the proof we need

④ Let's concentrate on the statements of the witnesses

⑤ Our main duty is to ensure the safety of the civilians

[06~07] 밑줄 친 부분 중, 어법상 틀린 것을 고르시오.

06 A recurrent issue for courts is whose viewpoint to adopt in deciding how much should be disclosed to patients about ① their medical treatment. The majority of states favor the experts, holding that physicians are responsible for disclosing only as much as ② would be considered reasonable by a "reasonable medical practitioner" in the same community and the same specialty. This approach is grounded in the so-called therapeutic privilege, ③ which recognizes the physician's preeminent right to withhold any information that might harm the patient. The less deferential minority rule holds that the adequacy of disclosure should be judged from the standpoint of the "reasonable patient," not from ④ those of the "reasonable physician." Although these general rules are well settled, questions about the adequacy of disclosure still ⑤ arise.

07 Raku is a popular low-temperature, fast-firing process that yields exciting, ① chance surface effects on ceramic ware. From a simple white crackle glaze to a surprising spectrum of color, from humble tea bowls to sculptural forms abstract or figurative, the range of possibility and innovation ② that resides in raku practice keeps it always young and vibrant. The modern Western practice of this ancient process, as well as ③ its purpose, differs from its Eastern roots, but the results of raku are still infinite in their variety, energy, and beauty. Japanese and Western raku offer the ceramist the possibility ④ of experiencing the final results of the firing in a relatively short time, and it is this very quality that makes the practice of raku ⑤ so satisfied. [3점]

[08~09] (A), (B), (C)에 들어갈 말로 가장 적절한 것을 고르시오.

08

Crabs, birds, and manta rays regularly try to crush sea horses for dinner, but a sea horse has some unusual protective armor. Its tail can be (A) [compressed / expanded] to half its normal size without lasting damage, researchers at the University of California, San Diego, recently found. The tail's (B) [resilience / rigidity] comes from its structure: approximately 36 square segments, each made of four bony plates. The plates connect to the spinal column's vertebrae with collagen and can glide past one another, keeping the spine (C) [safe / vulnerable]. Ultimately, the researchers would like to build a robotic arm out of 3-D-printed plates that mimic the seahorse's flexible and tough tail and use it for underwater excursions or to detonate bombs.

	(A)	(B)	(C)
①	compressed	resilience	vulnerable
②	compressed	rigidity	safe
③	compressed	resilience	safe
④	expanded	rigidity	safe
⑤	expanded	resilience	vulnerable

09

Studies of priming effects have yielded discoveries that (A) [confirm / threaten] our self-image as conscious and autonomous authors of our judgments and our choices. For instance, most of us think of voting as a deliberate act that reflects our values and our assessments of policies and is not influenced by (B) [consensus / irrelevancies]. Our vote should not be affected by the location of the polling station, for example, but it is. A study of voting patterns in precincts of Arizona in 2000 showed that the support for propositions to increase the funding of schools was significantly greater when the polling station was in a school than when it was in a nearby location. A separate experiment showed that exposing people to images of classrooms and school lockers also (C) [increased / minimized] the tendency of participants to support a school initiative. The effect of the images was larger than the difference between parents and other voters.

[3점]

	(A)	(B)	(C)
①	confirm	consensus	minimized
②	confirm	consensus	increased
③	confirm	irrelevancies	minimized
④	threaten	irrelevancies	increased
⑤	threaten	irrelevancies	minimized

10 Think of a "discovery" as an act that moves the arrival of information from a later point in time to an earlier time. The discovery's value does not ① <u>equal</u> the value of the information discovered but rather the value of having the information available earlier than it otherwise would have been. A scientist or a mathematician may show great skill by being the first to find a solution that has ② <u>eluded</u> many others; yet if the problem would soon have been solved anyway, then the work probably has not much ③ <u>benefited</u> the world. There *are* cases in which having a solution even slightly sooner is immensely valuable, but this is most plausible when the solution is immediately put to use, either being ④ <u>deployed</u> for some practical end or serving as a foundation to further theoretical work. And in the latter case, where a solution is immediately used only in the sense of serving as a building block for further theorizing, there is great value in obtaining a solution slightly ⑤ <u>later</u> only if the further work it enables is itself both important and urgent.

11 We are committed to reason. If we are asking a question, evaluating possible answers, and trying to persuade others of the value of those answers, then we are reasoning, and therefore have tacitly signed on to the ① <u>validity</u> of reason. We are also committed to whatever conclusions follow from the careful application of reason, such as the theorems of mathematics and logic. Though we cannot logically ② <u>prove</u> anything about the physical world, we are entitled to have confidence in certain beliefs about it. The application of reason and observation to discover ③ <u>steadfast</u> generalizations about the world is what we call science. The progress of science, with its dazzling success at explaining and manipulating the world, shows that knowledge of the universe is ④ <u>possible</u>, albeit always probabilistic and subject to revision. Science is thus a paradigm for how we ought to gain knowledge — not the particular methods or institutions of science but its value system, namely to seek to explain the world, to evaluate candidate explanations ⑤ <u>objectively</u>, and to be cognizant of the tentativeness and uncertainty of our understanding at any time.

12 On a boat off Costa Rica, a biologist uses pliers from a Swiss army knife to try to extract a plastic straw from a sea turtle's nostril. The turtle ① <u>writhes</u> in agony, bleeding profusely. For eight painful minutes the YouTube video ticks on; it has ② <u>logged</u> more than 20 million views, even though it's so hard to watch. At the end the increasingly desperate biologists finally manage to ③ <u>dislodge</u> a four-inch-long straw from the creature's nose. Raw scenes like this, which lay ④ <u>bare</u> the toll of plastic on wildlife, have become familiar: The dead albatross, its stomach bursting with refuse. The turtle stuck in a six-pack ring, its shell ⑤ <u>unscathed</u> from years of straining against the tough plastic. The seal snared in a discarded fishing net. Who is to blame? Take a good look in the mirror. [3점]

13 다음 글의 제목으로 가장 적절한 것은?

Do we live on a rare earth? One so exceptional that it is pretty much alone in hosting a rich diversity of life, with almost all other planets being home to simple microbes at best? Or are we in a universe teeming with living things as complex as those here, meaning that we exist as part of a vast, cosmic zoo? Debate on this rages on, but we say it is time to accept that the latter is very likely. To date we know of at least 3,700 exoplanets and there are likely to be trillions of other potentially habitable exoplanets and exomoons in our galaxy and beyond. We do not know how commonly life arises on them, but many scientists think that it may well emerge from the chemical and physical properties of any suitable planet.

① Earth, the Extraordinary Home

② The Intergalactic Superhighway

③ Are Microbes Our True Ancestors?

④ The Cosmic Zoo: The Big Hoax

⑤ Is Anybody Out There?

14 Frank O'Connor에 관한 다음 글의 내용과 일치하는 것은?

Frank O'Connor was born in Cork, Ireland, of a family too poor to give him a university education. During Ireland's struggle for independence he was briefly a member of the Irish Republican Army. Then he worked as a librarian in Cork and Dublin and for a time was director of the Abbey Theatre before he was established as a writer of short stories. From 1931 on he published regularly in American magazines and taught for some years at Harvard and Northwestern Universities. His declared objective was to find the natural rhythms and stresses of the storyteller's voice in shaping his material. He was indeed a prolific historian of Irish manners and the Irish character.

① He is an Irish playwright holding a Harvard degree.

② He was a member of the stage crew at the Abbey Theatre.

③ His writing career in the US took off in the early 1930s.

④ He tried to blur the rhythms of the storyteller's voice.

⑤ His stories are concerned with early American manners.

15 baiji에 관한 다음 글의 내용과 일치하지 <u>않는</u> 것은?

The baiji is a functionally extinct species of freshwater dolphin formerly found only in the Yangtze River in China. It is also called the Chinese river dolphin. It is not to be confused with the Chinese white dolphin. The baiji population declined drastically in decades as China industrialized and made heavy use of the river for fishing, transportation, and hydroelectricity. The baiji could be the first dolphin species in history that humans have driven to extinction. Efforts were made to conserve the species, but a late 2006 expedition failed to find any baiji in the river. In August 2007, a Chinese man reportedly videotaped a large white animal swimming in the Yangtze, believed to be a baiji. The World Wildlife Fund is calling for the preservation of any possible baiji habitat, in case the species is located and can be revived.

① Its sole habitat was the Yangtze River.

② It should not be mistaken for the Chinese white dolphin.

③ Industrialization played a role in its decline in population.

④ It did not turn up during the 2006 expedition.

⑤ The World Wildlife Fund has given up all hope in reviving the species.

2019 기출문제

16 다음 글의 목적으로 가장 적절한 것은?

Please let me take this opportunity to introduce myself and to welcome you to the neighborhood. My wife, Monica, and I live at #19, just up the road from your new home. We have lived on Meadow Street for the past twenty years. Most likely because I'm older than everyone else around here, I am often addressed as the unofficial "mayor" of the neighborhood.

I have been asked by several of our neighbors to communicate their wishes about a problem that has arisen since you moved in. We all love music, and most of us have had, or will have, teenagers. We would, though, appreciate it if you would ask your teens to turn down the volume.

We all look forward to meeting and greeting you properly after you have the chance to settle in.

① to solicit donations for needy neighbors

② to invite a neighbor to a block party

③ to offer best wishes to a leaving family

④ to request an exchange for a better stereo

⑤ to complain about a neighbor's loud music

17 다음 글의 요지로 가장 적절한 것은?

Laughter is one clue to compatibility. It tells you how much you will enjoy each other's company over the long term. If your laughter together is good and healthy, and not at the expense of others, then you have a healthy relationship to the world. Laughter is the child of surprise. If you can make each other laugh, you can always surprise each other. If you can always surprise each other, you can always keep the world around you new. Beware of a relationship in which there is no laughter. Even the most intimate relationships based only on seriousness have a tendency to turn dour. Over time, sharing a common serious viewpoint on the world tends to turn you against those who do not share the same viewpoint, and your relationship can become based on being critical together.

① A key to a healthy relationship is laughing together.

② "No action, talk only" is the seed of relationship failures.

③ Serious talk leads to endless criticism of one another.

④ The element of surprise brings laughter into your relationship.

⑤ Laugh a lot, and you will end up with new relationships.

[18~24] 다음 글의 빈칸에 들어갈 말로 가장 적절한 것을 고르시오.

18

Good reductionism consists not of replacing one field of knowledge with another but of connecting or unifying them. The building blocks used by one field are put under a microscope by another. A geographer might explain why the coastline of Africa fits into the coastline of the Americas by saying that the landmasses were once adjacent but sat on different plates, which drifted apart. The question of why the plates move gets passed on to the geologists, who appeal to an upwelling of magma that pushes them apart. As for how the magma got so hot, they call in the physicists to explain the reactions in the Earth's core and mantle. None of the scientists is _____.

① innocent   ② dispensable

③ meticulous   ④ qualified

⑤ connected

19

Even small differences in annual economic growth rates, if sustained for decades or centuries, eventually lead to huge differences in the levels of economic well-being. The per capita gross national product of the United States, for example, grew at an annual rate of around 1.7 percent per year during the period 1820 to 1998. This led to a twenty-five-fold increase in living standards, with per capita incomes rising from around $1,200 per person in 1820 to around $30,000 today (in 1990 dollars). The key for the United States to become the world's richest major economy was not spectacularly fast growth, such as China's recent achievement of 8 percent growth per year. The key was _____, the fact that the United States maintained that income growth rate for almost two centuries.

① velocity   ② originality

③ transparency   ④ liquidity

⑤ consistency

20

Believing-for-a-reason _____. I may believe that my neighbor has few friends because no one ever visits him. I may never have made this reasoning explicit, either to myself or to anyone else. Still, if asked the question "Why do you think he has few friends?" I can reply, without any introspection or self-observation: "Because no one ever visits him." That a subject is in the relevant state does not necessarily manifest itself in conscious review of the reasoning but does necessarily include the ability to express it both in the form of a demonstration and an expressive self-explanation, i.e., a rational explanation of one's own belief that one can just give. [3점]

① often results from the state of mutual contradictions

② need not be the result of any conscious process at all

③ may lie in the subject's ability to review a conclusion

④ seldom denies the existence of premise and conclusion

⑤ ought to be constantly mediated by connecting principles

21

We know that blind evolutionary processes can produce human-level general intelligence, since they have already done so at least once. Evolutionary processes with foresight — that is, genetic programs designed and guided by an intelligent human programmer — should be able to achieve a similar outcome with far greater efficiency. This observation has been used by some philosophers and scientists to argue that human-level AI is not only theoretically possible but feasible within this century. The idea is that we can estimate the relative capabilities of evolution and human engineering to produce intelligence, and find that human engineering is already vastly superior to evolution in some areas and is likely to become superior in the remaining areas before too long. The fact that evolution produced intelligence therefore indicates that human engineering will _____.

① compete against superintelligence

② lag far behind evolutionary processes

③ disguise itself as human−level AI

④ soon be able to do the same

⑤ repeat similar mistakes

22

The number of electric cars in the world passed the 2 million mark last year and the International Energy Agency estimates there will be 140 million electric cars globally by 2030 if countries meet Paris climate agreement targets. This electric vehicle boom could leave 11 million tons of spent lithium-ion batteries in need of recycling between now and 2030. However, in the EU as few as 5% of lithium-ion batteries are recycled. _____.
Not only do the batteries carry a risk of giving off toxic gases if damaged, but core ingredients such as lithium and cobalt are finite and extraction can lead to water pollution and depletion among other environmental consequences.

① This has an environmental cost

② It is prohibited to take further steps

③ It has identified the cause

④ This ratifies the Paris climate agreement

⑤ This supports current energy policies

23

The electromagnetic field is everywhere, and every single electron that exists in the universe not only belongs to it, but also is exactly identical to any other electron, anywhere and anywhen. Interchange two of them, and the universe won't notice. Because of that, because of the quantum field they are an expression of, electrons cannot be described as one would describe a macroscopic object. They belong to the field. They are part of it, like a drop of water in the vast ocean, or a gust of wind in the night air, a drop or a gust you cannot localize. As long as one does not look, drops and gusts are just like the ocean itself, like the wind. Mingled into an entity much vaster than themselves, _____.

[3점]

① they provide vectors to the core of the universe

② they create a ripple effect in the quantum field

③ they have no identity of their own

④ they fail to achieve their full potential

⑤ they serve as catalysts for many reactions

2019 기출문제

24

Cost of production concepts are not very useful to the understanding of the economics of agriculture, just as cost of production of pizza is not very useful to understanding the pizza industry. A more appropriate comparison, given the nature of joint production in agriculture, is the relation of cost of production of pizza to the structural understanding of the restaurant industry. Too great a reliance on cost of production is a danger because of the inherent weaknesses of analyses that follow, the resources devoted to cost of production which would be better used elsewhere, and the limited focus of issues which can result from its emphasis. Cost of production seems, on the surface, to be a useful and basic element to economic analysis. Further, noneconomists relate well to the concept of cost of production, while supply functions, input demand functions, length-of-run and other important issues are less obvious concepts. As a result, cost of production often becomes considered as _____.

① an instrumental source of agricultural investment decision

② an end rather than a tool with limited analytic capability

③ one of the weakest indices of long-term market growth

④ a test of inter-industry collaboration assessment

⑤ an obscure measurement of market assets

[25~26] 다음 글의 주제로 가장 적절한 것을 고르시오.

25

In the U.S. the proportion of infants who were nursed at all by their mothers, and the age at which those nursed infants were weaned, decreased through much of the 20th century. For example, by the 1970s only 5% of American children were being nursed at the age of six months. In contrast, among hunter-gatherers not in contact with farmers and without access to farmed foods, infants are nursed far beyond six months, because the only suitable infant food available to them is mother's milk: they have no access to cow's milk, baby formula, or soft food replacements. The age of weaning averaged over seven hunter-gatherer groups is about three years old, an age at which children finally become capable of fully nourishing themselves by chewing enough firm food.

① relationship between the age of weaning and available food

② necessity of early weaning in hunter-gatherer societies

③ controversy over the role of weaning in children's health

④ agricultural motivations for early weaning in children

⑤ demographic contrasts between farmers and hunter-gatherers

③ the critical need for governmental intervention in China

④ the unwarranted concern about China's bond market

⑤ the doomed future of China's accumulating debt

[27~28] 다음 글의 빈칸 (A), (B)에 들어갈 말로 가장 적절한 것을 고르시오.

26

Never has China's bond market had such a stormy spring. It has already set a record for defaults in the second quarter. The cost of credit for firms has shot up. Even the state-owned companies that invest in infrastructure, previously sacrosanct, are seen as risks. What has gone wrong? The answer is nothing at all. Defaults are progress for China, which needs to clear a backlog of accumulated debt. This year's casualties amount to a mere 0.1% of the bond market. But that is still an improvement on the recent past, when investors assumed that the government would rescue any big firm in trouble. [3점]

① the hidden pitfalls of China's economy

② the risky investments on China's infrastructure

27

Deficiencies of innate ability may be compensated for through persistent hard work and concentration. One might say that work substitutes for talent, or better yet that it ___(A)___ talent. He who firmly determines to improve his capacity will do so, provided that education does not begin too late, during a period when the plasticity of nerve cells is greatly reduced. Do not forget that reading and thinking about masterpieces allows one to assimilate much of the skill that created them, providing of course that one extends beyond conclusions to the author's insights, guiding principles, and even style. What we refer to as a great and special talent usually implies superiority that is expeditious rather than qualitative. In scientific undertakings, however, the slow prove to be as useful as the fast because scientists like artists are judged by the quality of what they produce, not by the __(B)__ of production.

	(A)	(B)
①	creates	......	power
②	creates	......	speed
③	suppresses	......	quantity
④	suppresses	......	speed
⑤	encourages	......	power

28

Professions embody expertise, prestige, autonomy, dignity, and formal learning, values that often are incompatible with politics. The historic struggles of public professions to purge themselves of politics — for example, the city manager *versus* party hacks; the librarian *versus* ignorant censors; the environmental scientist *versus* political ideologues — all reflect this __(A)__. Nor do professionals like bureaucracy, which they often view as an impediment to the free exercise of their specializations. Certain kinds of specialized professionals, such as scientists and engineers, working for the federal government express much less satisfaction with their work

than federal executives. Put bluntly, professionals who choose the public service often must overcome their __(B)__ for its two major features: politics and bureaucracy.

[3점]

	(A)	(B)
①	resistance	......	antipathy
②	congruence	......	affinity
③	resistance	......	affinity
④	congruence	......	antipathy
⑤	incompatibility	......	aspiration

[29~30] 주어진 글 다음에 이어질 글의 순서로 가장 적절한 것을 고르시오.

29

For most of Western history, curiosity has been regarded as at best a distraction, at worst a poison, corrosive to the soul and to society. There's a reason for this. Curiosity is unruly.

(A) In short, curiosity is deviant. Pursuing it is liable to bring you into conflict with authority at some point, as everyone from Galileo to Charles Darwin to Steve Jobs could have attested. A society that values order above all else will seek to suppress curiosity.

(B) It doesn't like rules, or, at least, it assumes that all rules are provisional, subject to the laceration of a smart question nobody has yet thought to ask. It disdains the approved pathways, preferring diversions, unplanned excursions, impulsive left turns.

(C) But a society that believes in progress, innovation, and creativity will cultivate it, recognizing that the inquiring minds of its people constitute its most valuable asset. By the time of the Enlightenment, European societies started to see that their future lay with the curious and encouraged probing questions rather than stamping on them.

① (A) – (C) – (B)　　② (B) – (A) – (C)

③ (B) – (C) – (A)　　④ (C) – (A) – (B)

⑤ (C) – (B) – (A)

30

Most existing drones need to be flown by an experienced operator. Indeed, the law often requires this. Drones also need technical support and maintenance.

(A) The drone may fly autonomously, according to a preprogrammed schedule, find its way automatically to a point it is ordered to visit, or be piloted remotely by an operative

of the company that supplies the system, from a control centre anywhere on the planet.

(B) This is a term being applied to the offerings of several firms that aspire to sell the advantages of drones without the associated worries. The box in question is a base station that houses the drone, recharges it and transfers the data it has collected to the customer.

(C) And the people operating them would be well advised to have an understanding of the legal and safety implications of what they are up to. Hence the appeal of the "drone-in-a-box."

① (A) – (C) – (B)　　② (B) – (A) – (C)

③ (B) – (C) – (A)　　④ (C) – (A) – (B)

⑤ (C) – (B) – (A)

31 다음 글에서 전체 흐름과 관계 없는 문장은?

Many animals cooperate effectively, and a few even give loans. The most famous lenders in nature are vampire bats. These bats congregate in their thousands inside caves and every night fly out to look for prey. When they find a sleeping bird or careless mammal, they make a small incision in its skin, and suck its blood. ① But not all vampire bats find a victim every night. ② In order to cope with the uncertainty of their life, the vampires loan blood to each other. ③ Vampires, however, don't give loans in order to alleviate their evolutionary pressure. ④ A vampire that fails to find prey will come home and ask a more fortunate friend to regurgitate some stolen blood. ⑤ Vampires remember very well to whom they loaned blood, so at a later date if the friend returns home hungry, he will approach his debtor, who will reciprocate the favour.

32 글의 흐름으로 보아 주어진 문장이 들어가기에 가장 적절한 곳은? [3점]

> When you see grass as *green*, the green is no more a property of grass than rustish is a property of water.

Imagine that you are a piece of iron. So there you are, sitting around doing nothing, as usual, when along comes a drop of water. What will be your perception of the water? Yes, of course, a bar of iron doesn't have a brain, and it wouldn't have any perception at all. But let's ignore that inconvenient fact and imagine what it would be like if a bar of iron could perceive the water. From the standpoint of a piece of iron, water is above all *rustish*. (①) Now return to your perspective as a human. (②) You know that rustishness is not really a property of water itself but of how it reacts with iron. (③) The same is true of human perception. (④) Green is the experience that results when the light bouncing off grass reacts with the neurons in your brain. (⑤) Greenness is in us—just as rust is in the piece of iron.

33 다음 글에 나타난 "I"의 심경 변화로 가장 적절한 것은?

> I left for Brussels by train in April 1939. Leaving my parents behind when I was only nine years old was deeply distressing. As I reached the border between Germany and Belgium, the train stopped for a brief time and German customs officials came on board. They demanded to see any jewelry or other valuables I might have. I had been forewarned of this request by a young woman who was traveling with me. I had therefore hidden in my pocket a small gold ring with my initials on it, which I had been given as a present on my seventh birthday. My anxiety in the presence of Nazi officers reached almost unbearable heights as they boarded the train, and I feared that they would discover the ring. Fortunately, they paid little attention to me and allowed me to go undisturbed. As

their footsteps grew fainter, a quiet sigh escaped my lips.

① nervous → relieved

② joyous → discouraged

③ indifferent → outraged

④ irritated → terrified

⑤ surprised → disappointed

[34~35] 다음 글을 읽고 물음에 답하시오.

People who learn to extract the key ideas from new material and organize them into a mental model and connect that model to _____ show an advantage in learning complex mastery. A mental model is a mental representation of some external reality. Think of a baseball batter waiting for a pitch. He has less than an instant to decipher whether it's a curveball, a changeup, or something else. How does he do it? There are a few subtle signals that help: the way the pitcher winds up, the way he throws, the spin of the ball's seams. A great batter winnows out all the extraneous perceptual distractions, seeing only these variations in pitches, and through practice he forms distinct mental models based on a different set of cues for each kind of pitch. He connects these models to what he knows about batting stance, strike zone, and swinging so as to stay on top of the ball. These he connects to mental models of player positions: if he's got guys on first and second, maybe he'll sacrifice to move the runners ahead. Because he has culled out all but the most important elements for identifying and responding to each kind of pitch, constructed mental models out of that learning, and connected those models to his mastery of the other essential elements of this complex game, an expert player has a better chance of scoring runs than a less experienced one who cannot make sense of the vast and changeable information he faces every time he steps up to the plate.

34 위 글의 제목으로 가장 적절한 것은?

① Split-Second Decisions Made Easy

② When Baseball Players Go Wild

③ Baseball 101: Choose the Right Bat

④ The Anatomy of a Baseball Pitcher

⑤ How Far Can a Batter Hit the Ball?

35 위 글의 빈칸에 들어갈 말로 가장 적절한 것은? [3점]

① future course of events

② athletic endowment

③ prior knowledge

④ de facto principles

⑤ controlled motivation

[36~37] 다음 글을 읽고 물음에 답하시오.

In the region of western New York State in which I was brought up, as indeed in a huge part of the English – speaking regions of the world, the form *doesn't* (a) scarcely exists in vernacular speech. Where I come from, almost everyone says *It don't matter and He don't need that.*

Naturally, my high school English teacher, Mrs. Breck, took strong exception to this usage, and she relentlessly (b) waged her own little war upon it. I well remember sitting in class one day when her campaign was in full swing. Having heard my classmate Norman say, for the seven hundredth time that day, something like "He don't know that," she decided to strike: "He *doesn't* know that, Norman." "Yeah, that's right," replied Norman, "he *don't.*" "Not *don't*, Norman," reiterated Mrs. Breck, her face turning an interesting colour, "say 'He DOESN'T know that.'" "But... but..." A look of (c) contentment appeared on Norman's face. "But it don't *sound* right!"

This little episode encapsulates very neatly the (d) contrast between the very special position of one particular form of English, which we call standard English, and all the other varieties of English that there are, which we may collectively term non-standard English. The great majority of English-speakers grow up learning and speaking the (e) local vernacular form of English, which is almost always significantly different from standard English, and is sometimes spectacularly different.

36 위 글의 제목으로 가장 적절한 것은?

① Good Old Days: Reflections on My English Teacher

② Avoid Dialect Extinction for Diversity's Sake

③ Sounding Right: A Dilemma for Policy-Makers

④ Standard vs. Non-standard English: Don't It Matter?

⑤ Vernacular vs. Prestige English: End the War

37 위 글의 밑줄 친 부분 중, 문맥상 낱말의 쓰임이 적절하지 <u>않은</u> 것은?

① (a)　　　　② (b)

③ (c)　　　　④ (d)

⑤ (e)

[38~39] 다음 글을 읽고 물음에 답하시오.

That music can increase cooperation and helpfulness by inducing good moods has been demonstrated experimentally. Rona Fried and Leonard Berkowitz undertook a study with their students at the University of Wisconsin. They divided them into four groups and induced different moods in three of them by playing them different pieces of music. Two selections from Mendelssohn's 'Songs Without Words' were chosen to instill a soothing mood in one group; Duke Ellington's 'One O'Clock Jump' was played to create feelings of excitement in another; and John Coltrane's 'Meditations' was used to instill negative emotions, of sadness and despondency, in the third group. The fourth, control group simply sat in silence for the seven-minute duration of the musical recordings. The students had to complete a mood questionnaire both before and after listening to the music, and this confirmed that the music had made a significant difference to their feelings.

Just before they were dismissed, the experimenter asked for volunteers to help with another, quite unrelated experiment which would require anywhere between fifteen minutes and two hours of their time. They were requested to complete a form to specify whether they were prepared to help, and if so for what amount of time. This, of course, was the test of helpfulness — the experimenter wanted to discover whether the four groups varied in their willingness to help according to the type of music to which they had been listening.

This _____. Those who had listened to the Mendelssohn pieces turned out to be the most helpful, as measured by their willingness to help with the second experiment and the length of time they were prepared to offer. On both measures, the students who had listened to Coltrane's music, leading to adverse moods, were the least willing to be helpful.

38 위 글의 요지로 가장 적절한 것은?

① Cooperative groups tended to prefer Mendelssohn's music.

② Classical music instilled soothing moods in people.

③ Cooperation and helpfulness were affected by musical talents.

④ Types of music influenced people's willingness to help.

⑤ Excited moods led people to offer more assistance.

39 위 글의 빈칸에 들어갈 말로 가장 적절한 것은?

① had been tested before

② proved to be the case

③ was challenged by many

④ contradicted earlier findings

⑤ needed further support

[40~42] 다음 글을 읽고 물음에 답하시오.

According to most definitions of intelligence, a million years ago humans were already the most intelligent animals around, as well as the world's champion toolmakers, yet they remained insignificant creatures with little impact on the surrounding ecosystem. They were obviously lacking some key feature other than intelligence and toolmaking.

Perhaps humankind eventually came to dominate the planet not because of some elusive third key ingredient, but due simply to the evolution of even higher intelligence and even better toolmaking abilities? It doesn't seem so, because when we examine the historical record, we don't see a direct correlation between the intelligence and toolmaking abilities of individual humans and the power of our species as a whole. Twenty thousand years ago, the average Sapiens probably had higher intelligence and better toolmaking skills than the average Sapiens of today. Modern schools and employers may test our aptitudes from time to time but, no matter how badly we do, the welfare state always guarantees our basic needs. In the Stone Age natural selection tested you every single moment of every single day, and if you flunked any of its numerous tests you (A) were pushing up the daisies in no time. Yet despite the superior toolmaking abilities of our Stone Age ancestors, and despite their sharper minds and far more acute senses, 20,000 years ago humankind was much weaker than it is today.

Over those 20,000 years humankind moved from hunting mammoth with stone-tipped spears to exploring the solar system with spaceships not thanks to the evolution of more dexterous hands or bigger brains. Instead, the crucial factor in our conquest of the world was our ability to connect many humans to one another. Humans nowadays completely dominate the planet not because the individual human is far smarter and more nimble-fingered than the individual chimp or wolf, but because *Homo sapiens* is the only species on earth capable of cooperating flexibly in large numbers. Intelligence and toolmaking were obviously very important as well. But if humans had not learned to cooperate flexibly in large numbers, our crafty brains and deft hands would still be   (B)   .

40 위 글의 밑줄 친 (A)가 의미하는 바로 가장 적절한 것은?

① might prosper eternally

② would die soon

③ sharpened tools slowly

④ could pick flowers quickly

⑤ became a farmer eventually

41 위 글의 빈칸 (B)에 들어갈 말로 가장 적절한 것은? [3점]

① developing far more acute senses

② significantly impacting the ecosystem

③ overcoming numerous hurdles in the wild

④ searching for easy prey in groups

⑤ splitting flint stones rather than uranium atoms

42 위 글의 내용을 한 문장으로 나타낼 때, 빈칸 (C)와 (D)에 들어갈 말로 가장 적절한 것은?

It is not higher intelligence or better (C) , but largescale, flexible cooperation abilities which played a key role in Homo sapiens' (D) of the world.

     (C)   (D)

① dexterity ⋯⋯ domination

② dexterity ⋯⋯ exploration

③ evolution ⋯⋯ cultivation

④ welfare ⋯⋯ domination

⑤ welfare ⋯⋯ exploration

[43~45] 다음 글을 읽고 물음에 답하시오.

(A) Do you know a childlike view of the world can frequently put adult life in perspective? The innocent view of children can help adults to not be so weighed down by their problems. Nancy Craver, director of a day-care center, relates the following story of how a child's perspective helped (a) her turn a big problem into a small one. It was the center's annual multicultural dinner, created as a chance for parents, children, and staff to celebrate both their diversity and their ability to work well together.

(B) As (b) she instinctively reached out her arms, she not only caught the little one but also caught her laughter and excitement. Immediately, those first terrible images melted away. Swinging (c) her around, Nancy was reminded by the child's enthusiasm that this was a celebration. Her laughter and play did not fix things, but it did change Nancy's perspective. And the evening continued better for her and for those around her.

(C) The previous year's celebration had been quite challenging for Nancy, as she had just been hired as the new director. This year (d) she planned things out early so that she could relax and participate in the dinner — or so she thought. At first just minor things went wrong. Then, someone dropped the slide

171

projector that was to be used for an after-dinner presentation. When the dinner itself was over, the woman who had been hired to take the children to another place to play did not show up. The kids became restless and began running about.

(D) In the midst of all this commotion, an elderly man insisted on someone moving the car that was blocking his in the parking lot. With her tension — and temperature — rising, Nancy went to help him get out of the lot. Just as (e) she started back into the building, one of the young children came charging down the stairs and threw herself at her. The images that flashed across Nancy's mind as the child was flying through the air included an injured child, shocked parents, and people saying, "You see, she cannot control or even protect our children!"

43 주어진 글 (A)에 이어질 내용을 순서에 맞게 배열한 것으로 가장 적절한 것은?

① (B) – (D) – (C)　② (C) – (B) – (D)

③ (C) – (D) – (B)　④ (D) – (B) – (C)

⑤ (D) – (C) – (B)

44 밑줄 친 (a)∼(e) 중에서 가리키는 대상이 나머지와 다른 것은?

① (a)　　　　② (b)

③ (c)　　　　④ (d)

⑤ (e)

45 위 글의 Nancy에 관한 내용과 일치하지 않는 것은?

① She was in charge of a day-care center.

② She caught a child in mid-air.

③ She became the director three years ago.

④ She planned for this year's dinner in advance.

⑤ She helped out with a parking problem.

2026
경찰대학
10개년 영어

2018학년도 기출문제

영어영역

[01~05] 밑줄 친 단어의 뜻으로 가장 적절한 것을 고르시오.

01

The students in the movement were deceived into thinking they were in the vanguard of a revolution.

① turmoil
② forefront
③ protection
④ opposition
⑤ preparation

02

The government concluded that the manufacturers colluded to sell their products to minors.

① collaborated
② proposed
③ pretended
④ intended
⑤ intervened

03

His penchant for the finer things in life led to the demise of his family fortune.

① obsession
② aptitude
③ reproach
④ inclination
⑤ extravagance

04

Rawls's sternest critics often tried to cabin him as "relevant only for American or at most Anglo-American audiences."

① confine
② rebuke
③ introduce
④ safeguard
⑤ exemplify

05

Questions about the pending lawsuit were met with circumlocutory replies by the pharmaceutical company representative.

① unequivocal
② succinct
③ unfounded
④ roundabout
⑤ conciliatory

[06~08] 밑줄 친 부분 중, 어법상 **틀린** 것을 고르시오.

06　I was greeted immediately by a member of the White House's legislative staff and led into the Gold Room, ① where most of the incoming House and Senate members had already gathered. At sixteen hundred hours on the dot, President Bush ② announced and walked to the podium, looking vigorous and fit, with that jaunty, determined walk ③ that suggests he's on a schedule and wants to keep detours to a minimum. For ten or so minutes he spoke to the room, ④ making a few jokes, calling for the country to come together, before inviting us to ⑤ the other end of the White House for refreshments and a picture with him and the First Lady.

07　San Francisco Giants pitcher Ryan Vogelsong and his wife, Nicole, watched the Fourth of July fireworks from their apartment's rooftop deck, which ① offers breathtaking views of landmarks such as the Bay Bridge, Alcatraz Island and Coit Tower. It was also there ② where they toasted with champagne his selection to the National League's All-Star team, the improbable high point—at least so far—of an itinerant career. The *San Francisco Chronicle* recently named him ③ as a candidate for the Cy Young Award. It ④ has been that kind of fairy-tale season for Vogelsong, 34, who has an 8-1 record and

a 2.23 ERA for the defending World Series champs. Though his accomplishments this year overshadow anything Vogelsong has done before in baseball, they would not ⑤ be possible without the toils of an odyssey that has included stops in 10 minor league cities, plus San Francisco, Pittsburgh, Japan and Venezuela.

08　The absence of comparisons from the state of nature is crucial to Rousseau. By insisting that creatures who lived apart from sustained relationships could not yet ① have evolved the mind it takes to rank persons, Rousseau draws two great conclusions. First, natural inequalities—greater physical strength, better singing voice, or higher intelligence—come to matter only when a quality we happen to possess ② wins us respect, praise, worth, or value in the eyes of others. The second conclusion is ③ that natural man—and natural man alone—is honest. In society we are always concerned with ④ what others think of us; we are motivated to do what will win us honor and the respect of others. It gets to the point where my sense of myself is derived from the impressions other people ⑤ have me.

2018 기출문제

[09~10] (A), (B), (C)에 들어갈 말로 가장 적절한 것을 고르시오.

09

The realization that the universe consists of atoms and void and nothing else, that the world was not made for us by a providential creator, that we are not the center of the universe, that our emotional lives are no more (A) [distinct / indistinct] than our physical lives from those of all other creatures, that our souls are as material and as mortal as our bodies—all these things are not the cause for (B) [despair / hope]. On the contrary, grasping the way things really are is the crucial step toward the possibility of happiness. It is possible for human beings to live happy lives, but not because they think that they are the center of the universe. Unappeasable desire and the fear of death are the principal (C) [paths / obstacles] to human happiness, but they can be surmounted through the exercise of reason.

	(A)	(B)	(C)
①	distinct	despair	paths
②	distinct	despair	obstacles
③	distinct	hope	obstacles
④	indistinct	hope	obstacles
⑤	indistinct	despair	paths

10

Music therapy as an explicit set of practices first developed in the West during the twentieth century—especially during the First World War, when doctors and nurses witnessed the effect that music had on the psychological, physiological, cognitive and emotional states of the wounded. The first major academic study of music's (A) [aesthetic / medicinal] properties was published in 1948, partly as a response to the continued use of music therapy in military hospitals and in factories during the Second World War. Music therapy is now (B) [rarely / widely] used for those with mental and/or physical disabilities or illnesses. One of its most significant functions is to relax patients who are preparing for, undergoing or recovering from surgery, notably dental, burns and coronary treatments. It is now well attested that music with slow, steady tempos, legato passages, gentle rhythms, predictable change, and simple sustained melodies is (C) [detrimental / conducive] to relaxation.

	(A)	(B)	(C)
①	aesthetic	rarely	detrimental
②	aesthetic	widely	detrimental
③	medicinal	widely	detrimental
④	medicinal	widely	conducive
⑤	medicinal	rarely	conducive

[11~13] 밑줄 친 부분 중, 문맥상 낱말의 쓰임이 적절하지 않은 것을 고르시오.

11 The spiritual dimension is a complex, and controversial area, and is often overlooked within holistic approaches, although it is increasingly being identified as a ① <u>vital</u> element which can have a large influence on the physical, mental and emotional aspects of work. Unfortunately the majority of studies that explore spirituality and resilience treat spirituality as a single entity which is ② <u>easily</u> measured and controlled. Spirituality is in reality a complex, ③ <u>multi-dimensional</u> phenomenon. Hence research which ④ <u>excludes</u> a broad interpretation of spirituality is important in order to expand our understanding. There are some who interpret spirituality using just a religious definition. This ⑤ <u>narrow</u> religious interpretation of spirituality, often seen in America and the UK as a Christian interpretation, is not appropriate for the government agencies that pride themselves on their anti-discriminatory practices.

12 According to one theory, within certain limits the more similar the communicators are, the more effective their communication will be. One limiting condition is that if the similarities between people are so ① <u>pervasive</u> that they have the same attitudes and beliefs about every subject, there is no need for communication. For example, the conversation might be ② <u>lively</u> at a party in which every person was in agreement about every subject from movies to politics. On the other hand, people who are ③ <u>dissimilar</u> in almost every respect lack a common ground, a base from which to share experiences and exchange ideas. According to this theory, the ideal situation is one in which people have many similarities but are dissimilar enough in their attitudes about the subject at hand to interact and perhaps to influence one another's attitudes. Similarity clearly ④ <u>prevails</u>, however. After all, the goal of attitude influence is to change the other person's attitude so that it more closely ⑤ <u>resembles</u> your own.

13 The fourth industrial revolution will affect the scale of conflict as well as its character. The distinctions between war and peace and who is a combatant and noncombatant are becoming uncomfortably ① <u>clarified</u>. Similarly, the battlefield is increasingly both local and global. Organizations such as ISIS operate ② <u>principally</u> in defined areas in the Middle East but they also recruit fighters from more than a hundred countries, largely through social media, while related terrorist attacks can occur anywhere on the planet. Modern conflicts are increasingly ③ <u>hybrid</u> in nature, combining traditional battlefield techniques with elements that were previously mostly associated with armed non-state actors.

However, with technologies ④ <u>fusing</u> in increasingly unpredictable ways and with state and armed non-state actors learning from each other, the potential magnitude of change is not yet widely ⑤ <u>appreciated</u>.

[3점]

14 ger에 관한 다음 글의 내용과 일치하는 것은?

The large, white felt tent, known as a *ger* and seen all over Mongolia, is probably the most identifiable symbol of the country. (The word "yurt" is a Turkic word introduced to the west by the Russians. If you don't want to offend the nationalistic sensibilities of the Mongolians, use the word "ger.") Most Mongolians still live in gers, even in the suburbs of Ulaan Baatar. And it's not hard to understand why: wood and bricks are scarce and expensive, especially out on the steppes, and animal hides are cheap and readily available. Nomadic people obviously have to be flexible and mobile and gers can be moved easily — depending on the size, a ger can be assembled in one to three hours. If the opportunity arises, an invitation to visit or stay in a ger is one that should not be missed.

① Most Mongolians prefer to call it a "yurt."

② You can only find it in urban areas of Ulaan Baatar.

③ It is made of wood and bricks.

④ It can be built in three hours or less.

⑤ It is not recommended for the modern traveler.

15 Yellowstone National Park에 관한 다음 글의 내용과 일치하지 <u>않는</u> 것은?

Yellowstone National Park was created in 1872 to protect its geyser basins. But the 2-million-acre park put the government in the wildlife business, and unfortunately scientific wildlife management did not begin until more than half a century later. No detailed records exist of the area's animal population and feeding behavior at the time the park was established. Early rangers fed elk and bison as one would feed cattle and began killing wolves. By 1926, following a federal directive, the last wolves had been eliminated. Then elk overpopulated the park, eating through grass, brush, and any part of a tree they could reach. So in 1934 the rangers began shooting them, too; records show that in 1962 alone, 4,619 were killed. In 1967 public distaste forced the Park Service to stop the shooting. But the park did not recover.

① The wildlife began to be managed scientifically in the 1900s.

② The exact animal population in 1872 is not known.

③ Elks flourished after the elimination of their natural predator.

④ A total of 4,619 elks were killed in 1962.

⑤ Public opinion halted the shooting of wolves.

[16~21] 다음 글의 빈칸에 들어갈 말로 가장 적절한 것을 고르시오.

16

A good rocket launch site has a few important characteristics. An unpopulated patch of land near an ocean is preferable, so no one gets showered with wayward bits of flaming metal. It's also nice if it's on the equator—like all spheres rotating on an axis, the Earth spins fastest in the middle, which provides rocket boosters with extra oomph. In other words, the best sites tend to be in remote, tropical locations. That such places are also often among the world's poorest gives many launches a _____ feel: billions of dollars in futuristic machinery rising up over rainforests and shantytowns. [3점]

① majestic ② fleeting
③ catastrophic ④ universal
⑤ counterintuitive

17

_____. It is not uncommon to find analysts failing to distinguish between facts and inferences or operating on the assumption that an inference was a fact. It is not unusual to hear an analyst state that his conclusions followed "logically" from the evidence, even though generalizations arrived at inductively are not subject to logical proof. That different types of inquiry are subject to different types of "proof" is an alien concept to many researchers. And the common misuse of *infer* and *imply* reflects not only a lack of knowledge of terminology but also an unfamiliarity with underlying concepts of logic as well. [3점]

① Terminological confusion further aggravates flawed logic
② Logical thinking is a precursor to scientific research
③ Examples of the inability to reason well abound
④ Generalizations are subject to rigorous testing
⑤ Inductive logic prevails in academia

179

18

The doublespeak flows in the government, whether people in government are talking to the public or to each other. The Bureau of Land Management issued a press release in 1986 which began, "In a move to add administrative procedures regarding compliance with statutory requirements, the Department of the Interior's Bureau of Land Management (BLM) today published a rulemaking concerning federal coal leasee qualifications." This doublespeak simply means that the BLM intends to crack down on coal leases. An official in the Department of Commerce who had requested an increase in salary was told that "Because of the fluctuational predisposition of your position's productive capacity as juxtaposed to government standards, it would be monetarily injudicious to advocate an increment." In other words, _____ .

① the pink slip

② all petitions suspended

③ no pay raise

④ no new openings

⑤ an early retirement

19

_____ . We've found a hormone that can rejuvenate the muscles of elderly mice. Osteocalcin —a hormone secreted by bone— boosts the ability of muscles to burn fuel and generate energy, researchers at Columbia University discovered. When the team injected the hormone into old mice, the animals were able to run just as far as their younger counterparts, despite being up to a year older—a long time in mouse years. Old mice that did not receive the hormone ran about half as far. Osteocalcin levels decline with age in both mice and humans, and the team now plans to test whether the hormone can improve muscle function in people too. [3점]

① Wind back the clock

② A stitch in time saves nine

③ Time waits for no man

④ Give the elderly their due

⑤ Speed up the sands of time

20

Like the iron cage of capitalism in which human needs are sacrificed to the exigencies of production, there is a sense in which science in the modern world has also become _____: Within the domain of institutionalized science and academic scholarship, creativity and innovation must be accommodated to the specialized criteria of achievement that govern the various professional disciplines.

① a torchlight shining on intellectual avenues

② emancipated from bureaucratic demands

③ a fortress impregnable to any attack

④ vulnerable to moral issues at hand

⑤ the prison house of the mind

21

During the late nineteenth and early twentieth century, the Frenchman Joseph Pujol was famous for his ability to fart _____ by drawing air into his anus. He put on a stage show, calling himself Le Pétomane, which is French for "The Fartiste." Dressed formally, he would open with a rumble of cannon-fire farting. Various routines followed, most spectacularly an imitation of the 1906 San Francisco earthquake. He could rectally project a jet of

water a distance of 15 feet (4.5 m) and to close, he sang a rhyme about a farm, punctuated with farts that sounded like different animal noises.

① at will   ② silently

③ intermittently   ④ to no avail

⑤ inadvertently

[22~23] 빈칸 (A)와 (B)에 들어갈 말로 가장 적절한 것을 고르시오.

22

For most of your past life experiences, you would probably agree that you need to reconstruct the memories. For example, if someone asked you how you celebrated your birthday three years ago, you'd likely count backwards and try to reconstruct the context. __(A)__, there are some circumstances in which people believe that their memories remain completely faithful to the original events. These types of memories — which are called flashbulb memories — arise when people experience emotionally charged events: People's memories are so vivid that they seem almost to be photographs of the original incident. The first research on flashbulb memories focused on people's recollections of public events. __(B)__ , the researchers asked participants if they had specific memories of how they first learned about the assassination of President John F. Kennedy. All but one of the 80 participants reported vivid recollections.

	(A)		(B)
①	As a result	·····	Consequently
②	As a result	·····	For example
③	Moreover	·····	However
④	Moreover	·····	Consequently
⑤	However	·····	For example

23

In order to promote social engagements among my students, I began encouraging them to bring food and drinks, as well as mats and cushions, to class. With these items, the classroom space is __(A)__ in terms of form and function as it gains a "social" aspect. During the reflection exercises, I observed how some students brought not just mats and cushions, but also pillows and stuffed toys as though they were attending a slumber party! When mats and cushions are not in use, students are seated in chairs strategically arranged around the tables, eating and drinking, as they discuss or review each other's

drafts. As food and drinks are vital to any sociocultural discourse, they help enhance the social atmosphere, __(B)__ communal bonds, and heighten the students' shared identity.

	(A)		(B)
①	altered	·····	cement
②	preserved	·····	dissolve
③	altered	·····	weaken
④	preserved	·····	solidify
⑤	modified	·····	loosen

[24~25] 다음 글의 제목으로 가장 적절한 것을 고르시오.

24

The center of mining and armor technology was Augsburg, in Germany, and that was no coincidence. Augsburg was near one of Europe's major deposits of iron ore, and the demand for metal from feudal states building forces of armored knights soon created a booming mining industry and an equally flourishing armorer business. To the annoyance of their customers throughout feudal Europe, the Germans charged sky-high prices, aware that those customers had no alternative: German armor was the best in the world, and if a customer didn't like the prices, he could sally forth on his next war with sticks and stones. Underwritten by these lavish profits, the German armorers could afford an extensive research and development effort. It resulted in stronger armor, for example, steel helmets with movable visors that covered the entire head.

① Farewell to Arms and Armors

② Past and Future of Armor Business

③ Stones vs. Steel: The Obvious Choice

④ Germany, the Hub of Armor Technology

⑤ High Quality and Low Prices: A Double-Edged Sword

25

Hate to haggle? You're not alone. A national survey found that just 48 percent of shoppers tried bargaining for a better deal on everyday goods and services in the past three years, down from 61 percent in 2007. But if you're chicken, you lose. Eighty-nine percent of those who haggled were rewarded at least once. Successful furniture hagglers saved $300 on average, as did those who questioned a health-related charge. Those who challenged their cell-phone plans saved $80. Clearly, people who don't haggle are leaving money on the table. [3점]

① Can't Hurt to Ask

② ABCs of Haggling Better

③ Furniture Haggling Made Easy

④ Shopping Around: Reap the Rewards

⑤ Does Haggling Actually Inflate Prices?

[26~27] 다음 글의 주제로 가장 적절한 것을 고르시오.

26

Catholicism held that the only God-given vocation was priesthood, but Protestants thought that people could be called to any of the secular crafts and trades. The belief that they were serving God encouraged them to work with religious fervor, leading them to produce more goods and make more money. Weber believed that the Protestant faith led inevitably to a capitalist economic society because it gave believers the chance to view the pursuit of profit as evidence of devotion, rather than of morally suspect motives such as greed and ambition. The idea of predestination also meant that believers need not worry about social inequalities and poverty, because material wealth was a sign of spiritual wealth.

① role of religion in creating social equality

2018 기출문제

② reasons for the rise of the Protestant faith

③ influence of Protestantism on economic ideals

④ importance of morality in economic activities

⑤ differences between Protestants and Catholics

① economic motivations behind the invention of the mirror

② outstanding achievements of German chemists

③ development of commercial glass mirror technology

④ human desires hidden in commercial glass mirrors

⑤ commonalities of ancient mirror technology in Europe

27

Whether out of curiosity, vanity, or a motive as yet unexplored, people throughout the ages have wanted to see their own reflection. As early as 2500 B.C. the Egyptians had mirrors of highly polished metal, usually of bronze, occasionally of silver or gold. The first commercial glass mirrors were made in Venice in 1564; these were made of blown glass that was flattened and coated with an amalgam of mercury and tin. The Venetians proceeded to supply Europe with mirrors for centuries. It wasn't until 1840 that a German chemist named Justus Liebig came up with the method of silvering that we use today. By this technique, silver-ammonia compounds are subjected to the chemical action of a reducing agent, such as invert sugar, Rochelle salt, or formaldehyde, and the resulting metallic silver is spread evenly over the back of a smooth pane of plate glass.

28 다음 글의 목적으로 가장 적절한 것은?

What could be more comforting than seeing your dog or cat curled up in blissful sleep? Both species spend almost half their day engaged in some form of sleep. But not all find it restful: older animals, those with muscular or joint issues, or very active dogs will often pace or relocate frequently. If your companion fits into one of these categories, he might benefit from a therapeutic bed. These specialized products offer support and comfort unlike regular beds or an impromptu sleeping spot. Regardless of age and health, a good bed promotes muscular-skeletal health and offers additional rejuvenating and healing benefits.

① to prevent domestic animal abuse

② to promote specialized pet furniture

③ to explain the benefits of good sleep

④ to inform pet owners of furniture hazards

⑤ to warn pet owners of poor pet sleep habits

② Catch the happiness virus in your local community.

③ Do not force your happy ways on your neighbors.

④ Exercise self-contentment to achieve mental well-being.

⑤ Find happiness by helping the needy around you.

29 다음 글의 요지로 가장 적절한 것은? [3점]

You cannot buy happiness. You cannot go to the nearest grocery store and order a pound of happiness as you would a pound of butter. But, since happiness comes from within, you can secure a measure of happiness by your own acts. You can find that feeling of contentment by helping your less fortunate fellowmen. You can help those who, because of ill-fate, will not have a happy Christmas unless we share with them. During this season of peace and good will, let us not force those in need to look at happiness through our eyes. Rather, let us help them to see and find happiness through their own eyes. Let us not fail the less fortunate of the community.

① Measure your true happiness level by acts of good will.

30 다음 글에 나타난 "I"의 심경으로 가장 적절한 것은?

Taking a deep breath, I began sprinting again, counting my strokes, telling myself that I wouldn't look up again until I'd swum one thousand strokes. Slowly I gained a foot, then a few hundred yards. Now I realized why the English Channel was the Mount Everest of swimming: though everyone's goal is to get to the top, the summit is where the air grows thinner, where everything becomes challenging. *Don't look up for five hundred strokes. Go as fast as you can go. Push it. Pull your arms with everything you have. Kick. Yes. Kick those legs. Pull deeper. Faster. Come on. Pull.*

① frustrated but resilient

② determined and persistent

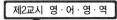
③ daunted and disappointed

④ surprised but exhilarated

⑤ overwhelmed and discouraged

[31~32] 다음 글에서 전체 흐름과 관계 <u>없는</u> 문장을 고르시오.

31 As a rule, physicians should not be considered altruistic when acting in their patients' best interests because they do not have the choices in acting that we ordinarily associate with altruism. Doctors have professional duties to patients that they cannot discharge as a matter of choice. To be sure, becoming a doctor and thereby entering into a professional relationship with patients is an optional act. ① Once a doctor enters into this relationship, however, he or she cannot choose obligations. ② A doctor can choose not to treat a particular patient in a particular situation if doing so would compromise personal and professional integrity. ③ Thus there arises a potential conflict for a physician who sees patients as individuals needing therapeutic treatments. ④ But the doctor must ensure that the patient's care is transferred to another physician. ⑤ Once one becomes a physician, one promises to promote the best medical interests of one's patients. This is not optional, but obligatory. [3점]

32 Unlike other climate issues, the science of sea level rise is fairly simple. ① Ocean levels are increasing mostly because of what heat does to water, in all its various states. ② To combat the rise in ocean levels, it is of utmost importance to understand the molecular structure of water. ③ As global temperature rises, most of the extra heat in the atmosphere — about 90 percent — sinks into the ocean. ④ As the water warms, it expands like mercury in a thermometer. ⑤ This thermal expansion accounts for one-third of sea level rise. The other two-thirds comes from melting mountain glaciers and ice sheets in Greenland and Antarctica.

33 다음 글의 내용을 한 문장으로 나타낼 때, 빈칸 (A)와 (B)에 들어갈 말로 가장 적절한 것은?

In some cases, researchers simply observe animals in nature as a function of different times of day, different seasons of the year, changes in diet, and so forth. These procedures raise no ethical problems. In other studies, however, animals have been subjected to brain damage, electrode implantation, injections of drugs or hormones, and other procedures that are clearly not for their own benefit. Anyone with a conscience (including scientists) is bothered by this fact. Nevertheless, experimentation with animals has been critical to the medical research that led to methods for the prevention or treatment of polio, diabetes, measles, smallpox, massive burns, heart disease, and other serious conditions. Most Nobel prizes in physiology or medicine have been awarded for research conducted on nonhuman animals. The hope of finding methods to treat or prevent AIDS, Alzheimer's disease, stroke, and many other disorders depends largely on animal research. In many areas of medicine and biological psychology, research would progress slowly or not at all without animals.

⬇

Though some __(A)__ studies conducted on animals, unlike simple observational research, raise ethical issues, they are __(B)__ in making progress in various medical fields.

	(A)		(B)
①	experimental	……	instrumental
②	statistical	……	successful
③	field	……	critical
④	developmental	……	plausible
⑤	laboratory	……	negligible

34 글의 흐름으로 보아, 주어진 문장이 들어가기에 가장 적절한 곳은?

> It preserves, and sometimes further simplifies, the relevant information.

Generally speaking, a model is a simplified representation of reality created to serve a purpose. (①) It is simplified based on some assumptions about what is and is not important for the specific purpose, or sometimes based on constraints on information or tractability. (②) For example, a map is a model of the physical world. (③) It abstracts away a tremendous amount of information that the mapmaker deemed irrelevant for its purpose. (④) For example, a road map keeps and highlights the roads, their basic topology, their relationships to places one would want to travel, and other relevant information. (⑤) Various professions have well-known model types: an architectural blueprint, an engineering prototype, and so on. Each of these abstracts away details that are not relevant to their main purpose and keeps those that are.

[35~36] 주어진 글 다음에 이어질 글의 순서로 가장 적절한 것을 고르시오.

35

Common law is otherwise known as case law, which is the law developed by the judges in their judgments (or rulings) on particular cases. The judges are guided by the theory and rules of precedent, which means they are bound by previous rulings that set "precedents."

(A) Equally, judges must sometimes interpret laws that Parliament has passed. One such example involved the Abortion Act 1967. A secretary declined to type a referral letter for a termination, claiming that the right to conscientiously object to participation in an abortion protected her refusal.

(B) This essentially means that they must take into account similar cases decided in the past, particularly those decided in the highest courts. This area of judge-made law is important because there will be situations where Parliament has not enacted a law and it falls to the judges to plug the gap.

(C) The judges looked at the word "participation" and decided that the secretary was not covered, as she was not sufficiently involved in the procedure. [3점]

① (A) − (C) − (B) ② (B) − (A) − (C)
③ (B) − (C) − (A) ④ (C) − (A) − (B)
⑤ (C) − (B) − (A)

36

As robotics starts to spread, the degree to which countries can succeed in the robot era will depend in part on culture—on how readily people accept robots into their lives.

(A) As a result, Japanese culture tends to be more accepting of robot companions as actual companions than is Western culture, which views robots as soulless machines.

(B) The ancient Shinto religion, practiced by 80 percent of Japanese, includes a belief in animism, which holds that both objects and human beings have spirits.

(C) Western and Eastern cultures are highly differentiated in how they view robots. Not only does Japan have an economic need and the technological know-how for robots, but it also has a cultural predisposition.

① (A) − (C) − (B) ② (B) − (A) − (C)
③ (B) − (C) − (A) ④ (C) − (A) − (B)
⑤ (C) − (B) − (A)

[37~38] 다음 글을 읽고 물음에 답하시오.

We've come back to the United States, but Julie's mind is still in Italy. She's yearning for some more of that pizza. She decides to make it herself, with me as her sous chef.

I chop my eggplant and zucchini. We're both quiet, focused on our chores. Next up, the onion chopping. I peel my onion, take it to the sink, turn on the faucet, and start slicing it under the flow.

"What are you doing?"

"I'm cutting the onion underwater."

"Why?"

"It says in the *Britannica* it stops you from crying."

This was an Heloise-style hint from the *Britannica*—one of those rare useful ones—and I was quite excited to be putting it into practice.

"Nope, too dangerous."

"But it's in the *Britannica*."

"Nope, I'm the executive chef. You're the sous chef."

Here I'm confronted with an unfortunate situation: the *Britannica* versus my wife. Two big sources of authority. Which do I choose? Well, the *Britannica* is pretty trustworthy. However, as far as I know, it can't carry my child or ignore me for several days or throw out the T-shirts that it hates.

So I decide Julie wins this one. _____.

37 윗글의 제목으로 가장 적절한 것은?

① Peel Onions Underwater to Avoid Tears

② Battle of Genders Ending in a Draw

③ Aftermath of an Italian Cooking Tip

④ Real Boss in My Home

⑤ Sous Chefs in the *Britannica*

38 윗글의 빈칸에 들어가기에 가장 적절한 것은?

① Which attests to how strong working women are

② I might have to call the *Britannica* for corrections

③ The onion will be cut without water and I will cry

④ I will ignore her for the next few days

⑤ But I'll be the executive chef tomorrow

[39~40] 다음 글을 읽고 물음에 답하시오.

We have long known that ravens are no birdbrains. They have been spotted caching food for later, gathering string to pull up hanging food and even trying to deceive one another. A study published today in *Science* adds an especially impressive twist: Ravens can _____ that they never encounter in nature.

The new study was led by cognitive zoologists in Sweden, who replicated a series of experiments previously used to (a) testing apes' planning abilities, this time using ravens. The ravens were first taught to use a stone to knock a food pellet out of a puzzle box. The next day, without the box present, the birds were (b) offered a choice between the stone tool and "distracter" objects — toys too light or bulky to use as tools. The box (c) would then be brought back 15 minutes after the selection. Despite the delay, the ravens chose the correct tool nearly 80 percent of the time, and successfully used the tools they selected 86 percent of the time. The birds performed almost (d) as well when they had to give an experimenter a bottle cap in exchange for a piece of food. The birds almost always selected the bottle cap over distracters, even though they would have (e) to wait 15 minutes to barter with it. The preference for soon-to-be-useful items persisted when the ravens had to pass up a smaller treat in favor of either the tool or the bartering token — and even when they could use each item only after a 17-hour delay.

39 윗글의 밑줄 친 부분 중 어법상 틀린 것은?

① (a)   ② (b)
③ (c)   ④ (d)
⑤ (e)

40 윗글의 빈칸에 들어가기에 가장 적절한 것은?
[3점]

① preserve tools for emergencies
② work in groups for situations
③ predict events yet to happen
④ trick potential competitors
⑤ plan for future needs

[41~42] 다음 글을 읽고 물음에 답하시오.

I had decided to go and I would go, and I had to be there by my mother's birthday. This was extremely important. I believed that if there was any chance to bring my mother back home it would happen on her birthday. If I had said this aloud to my father or to my grandparents, they would have said that I might as well try to catch a fish in the air, so I did not say it aloud. But I believed it. (A) My father says I lean on broken reeds and will get a face full of swamp mud one day.

When at last Gram and Gramps Hiddle and I set out that first day of the trip, I prayed for the first thirty minutes solid. I prayed that we would not be in an accident (I was terrified of cars and buses) and that we would get there by my mother's birthday — seven days away — and that we would bring her home. Over and over, I prayed the same thing. I prayed to trees. This was easier than praying directly to God. There was nearly always a tree nearby. As we pulled onto the Ohio Turnpike, which is the flattest, straightest piece of road in God's whole creation, Gram interrupted my prayers. "Salamanca —" (B)

I should explain right off that my real name is Salamanca Tree Hiddle. Salamanca, my parents thought, was the name of the Indian tribe to which my great-great-grandmother belonged. (C) My parents were mistaken. The name of the tribe was Seneca, but since my parents did not discover their error until after I was born and they were, by then, used to my name, it remained Salamanca. (D) My middle name, Tree, comes from your basic tree, a thing of such beauty to my mother that she made it part of my name. She wanted to be more specific and use Sugar Maple Tree, her very favorite, but Salamanca Sugar Maple Tree Hiddle was a bit much even for her. (E) My mother used to call me Salamanca, but after she left, only my grandparents Hiddle called me Salamanca (when they were not calling me chickabiddy). To most other people, I was Sal, and to a few boys who thought they were especially amusing, I was Salamander.

41 윗글의 'I'에 관한 내용과 일치하지 않는 것은?

① The purpose of her trip was to bring her mother home.

② Her grandparents accompanied her on the trip.

③ She found it easier to pray to trees than to God.

④ Her parents had a misunderstanding when they named her.

⑤ Most people called her Salamanca or Salamander.

42 다음 문장이 들어가기에 가장 적절한 곳은?

> Sometimes I am as ornery and stubborn as an old donkey.

① (A)　　　　② (B)

③ (C)　　　　④ (D)

⑤ (E)

[43~45] 다음 글을 읽고 물음에 답하시오.

On disembarking at Amsterdam's Schipol Airport, I am struck, only a few steps inside the terminal, by the appearance of a sign hanging from the ceiling, which shows the way to the arrivals hall, the exit and the transfer desks. It is a bright-yellow sign, one meter high and two meters across, simple in design, a plastic fascia in an illuminated aluminum box suspended on steel struts from a ceiling webbed with cables and air-conditioning ducts. Despite its simplicity, even its mundanity, the sign delights me, a delight for which the adjective *exotic*, though unusual,

2018 기출문제

seems apt. The exoticism is located in particular areas: in the double *a* of *Aankomst*, in the neighborliness of the *u* and the *i* in *Uitgang*, in the use of English subtitles, in the word for "desk," *balies*, and in the choice of practical, modernist fonts, Frutiger or Univers.

If the sign provokes in me genuine pleasure, it is in part because it offers the first conclusive evidence of my having arrived elsewhere. It is a symbol of being abroad. Although it may not seem distinctive to the casual eye, such a sign would never exist in precisely this form in my own country. There it would be less yellow, the typeface would be softer and more nostalgic, there would — out of greater indifference to the _____ of foreigners — be no subtitles, and the language would contain no double *as*, a repetition in which I sense, confusedly, the presence of another history and mind-set.

That a sign could be different in different places is evidence of a simple but pleasing idea: countries are diverse, and practices variable across borders. Yet difference alone would not be enough to elicit pleasure, or not for long. The difference has to seem like an improvement on what my own country is capable of. If I call the Schipol sign exotic, it is because it succeeds in suggesting, vaguely but intensely, that the country that made it and that lies beyond the *uitgang* may in critical ways prove more congenial than my own to my temperament and concerns. The sign is a promise of happiness.

43 윗글의 제목으로 가장 적절한 것은?

① At Once Exotic and Nostalgic

② Too Esoteric a Sign Kills Curiosity

③ Sweet Bewilderment: Am I Elsewhere?

④ Various Languages on the Same Platter

⑤ Across the Border: The Pioneering Traveler

44 윗글의 빈칸에 들어가기에 가장 적절한 것은?

① talent ② excitement

③ confusion ④ intimacy

⑤ number

45 Schipol Airport의 표지판에 관한 윗글의 내용과 일치하지 <u>않는</u> 것은? [3점]

① Its length is twice its height.

② It is written in two languages.

③ Its simplicity is the main reason for its exoticism.

④ It gives proof of arriving in another country.

⑤ The writer could not find a sign like it back home.

2026

경찰대학

10개년 영어

2017학년도 기출문제

영어영역

[01~05] 밑줄 친 단어의 뜻으로 가장 적절한 것을 고르시오.

01

It was time to devise a new plan of action as the attorneys <u>categorically</u> rejected our offer.

① unequivocally ② typically
③ impolitely ④ reluctantly
⑤ maliciously

02

After emerging victorious in his long-fought bout against cancer, the media tycoon tried to turn over a new leaf by denouncing his <u>opulent</u> way of life.

① immoral ② proud
③ luxurious ④ unhealthy
⑤ incompetent

03

Sanctions against the country are expected to be among the most <u>contentious</u> issues.

① controversial ② complex
③ elusive ④ secretive
⑤ fruitless

04

That the days of capitalism were <u>numbered</u>, and that the capitalist era must now give way to socialism: these were assumptions widely held by intellectuals on both sides of the Atlantic.

① limited ② prolonged
③ preserved ④ accelerated
⑤ overlapped

05

Many politicians viewed that nation's economic hegemony as <u>presumptuous</u>.

① attentive and alert
② accurate and precise
③ assiduous and diligent
④ achievable and pragmatic
⑤ arrogant and disrespectful

[06~08] 밑줄 친 부분 중, 어법상 틀린 것을 고르시오.

06 An important interruption in the usual flow of energy apparently occurred millions of years ago when the growth of land plants and marine organisms ① exceeded the ability of decomposers to recycle them. The ② accumulating layers of energy—rich organic material were gradually turned into coal and oil by the pressure of the overlying earth. The energy stored in their molecular structure we can now ③ release by burning. And our modern civilization depends on immense amounts of energy from such fossil fuels ④ recovering from the earth. By burning fossil fuels, we are finally passing most of the stored energy on to the environment as heat. We are also passing back to the atmosphere — in a relatively very short time — large amounts of carbon dioxide that ⑤ had been removed from it slowly over millions of years.

07 The earth has many resources of great importance to human life. Some are ① readily renewable, some are renewable only at great cost, and some are not renewable at all. The earth comprises a great variety of minerals, whose properties depend on the history of how they were formed as well as on the elements ② which they are composed. Their abundance ranges from rare to almost unlimited. But the difficulty of ③ extracting them from the environment is as important an issue as their abundance. A wide variety of minerals ④ are sources for essential industrial materials, such as iron, aluminum, magnesium, and copper. Many of the best sources are being depleted, making it more and more difficult and expensive ⑤ to obtain those minerals.

08 On the European continent, Kant rejected the utilitarian defense of liberalism but put forward a compatible case for the autonomy that comes only to the person ① free to choose his own conception of the good life. J.S. Mill himself took inspiration from other German liberals, ② being noted in the frontispiece to *On Liberty* the work of a contemporary, Wilhelm von Humboldt. But this moment of convergence of German and Anglo—American liberalism was soon ③ to pass. With Hegel, and then Marx, German intellectual thought centrally explored the deficiencies in the ethic of individualism ④ held to characterize liberal societies. The transmission of ideas from Kant to Hegel to Marx is so dramatic as ⑤ to rival the initial flow of thought from Plato to Aristotle to Augustine. [3점]

[09~10] (A), (B), (C)에 들어갈 말로 가장 적절한 것을 고르시오.

09

Many of us take broadband Internet for granted, but nearly 1 in 5 Americans lacks access to it, says the Federal Communications Commission (FCC). In rural areas, telecom companies balk at the cost of wiring far-flung homes, while low-income families can find the fees (A) [prohibitive/affordable]. Closing the broadband gap is about more than being able to stream the latest TV dramas. High-speed Internet is a critical tool of modern life, (B) [constraining/enabling] kids to learn digitally and adults to work via the cloud. The FCC recently approved a small broadband subsidy, but the real solution may lie in (C) [increased/decreased] competition for a notoriously consolidated industry. [3점]

	(A)	(B)	(C)
①	prohibitive	enabling	increased
②	prohibitive	enabling	decreased
③	prohibitive	constraining	decreased
④	affordable	constraining	increased
⑤	affordable	enabling	decreased

10

As evolutionary scholar Henry Plotkin says, gaining knowledge of the world across countless generations of organisms, evolution conserves knowledge selectively relative to criteria of need, and that collective knowledge is then held within the gene pool of species. Such collective knowledge is doled out to individuals, who come into the world with (A) [innate/acquired] ideas and predispositions to learn only certain things in specific ways. In other words, whether you're hunting on the savannah or choosing between millions of videos on YouTube, your brain is programmed to (B) [adopt/ignore] almost everything and home in only on what is most important or interesting. Otherwise, you'd be pointing your spear at every tree and rock or, just as annoyingly, you'd be lost in an infinite trail of video links, hoping in vain to find something worthwhile. With an understanding of the (C) [discriminating/integrating] nature of our genes, we can begin to construct the basis for stories that grab our attention and stay in our memory.

	(A)	(B)	(C)
①	acquired	ignore	integrating
②	acquired	ignore	discriminating
③	innate	ignore	discriminating
④	innate	adopt	integrating
⑤	innate	adopt	discriminating

[11~13] 다음 글의 밑줄 친 부분 중, 문맥상 낱말의 쓰임이 적절하지 <u>않은</u> 것을 고르시오.

11 Sea level rise along any given stretch of coast depends on how far away it is from the globe's two big ice buckets: Greenland and Antarctica. While it's easy to think the closest countries will see the biggest rise as the ice melts, it's not so ① <u>simple</u>. Greenland and Antarctica's massive ice sheets ② <u>exert</u> a strong gravitational pull on the waters around them, but as they melt, the attraction weakens, causing nearby sea levels to fall. In addition, without the burden of weight from the ice, the land uplifts, ③ <u>rising</u> slightly more above the water. The effect diminishes with distance, so it's actually the places farther away from the melting ice that will see the biggest ④ <u>drop</u> in sea level. Ocean currents help push the meltwater around the globe. "It's really an amazing and somewhat ⑤ <u>counterintuitive</u> result, but that's the reality," says Jerry Mitrovica, a geophysicist at Harvard University. [3점]

12 Four little heads pop up simultaneously in a pool of blue−black water surrounded by ice as far as the eye can see. They seem to hesitate, reluctant to leave the watery world through which they swim as ① <u>effortlessly</u> as fish. They are Adelie penguins, and the ice ② <u>endangers</u> their existence. The birds leap about excitedly in tight circles, going in and out of the water, perfectly at ease in this ③ <u>frigid</u> sea that surrounds the shores of Antarctica. Their food is tied, literally, to the frozen ocean. Within layers of sea ice, microscopic algae bloom in profusion as sunlight floods in from above. When the sea ice melts with the beginning of summer, the ice algae escape into the water, where they are ④ <u>grazed</u> on by dense swarms of krill — a type of shrimplike crustacean. The krill, ⑤ <u>in turn</u>, are the Adelie penguins' primary food source.

13 The human genome contains an ① <u>enormous</u> amount of information to guide the construction of a complex organism. In a growing number of cases, particular genes can be tied to aspects of cognition, language, and personality. When psychological traits vary, much of the variation comes from ② <u>differences</u> in genes: identical twins are more similar than fraternal twins, and biological siblings are more similar than adoptive siblings, whether ③ <u>raised</u> together or apart. A person's temperament and personality emerge early in life and remain fairly ④ unpredictable throughout the lifespan. And both personality and intelligence show few or no effects of children's particular home environments within their culture: children reared in the same family are similar mainly because of their ⑤ shared genes. Furthermore, neuroscience is showing that the brain's basic architecture develops under genetic control. [3점]

14 Walter Reed에 관한 다음 글의 내용과 일치 하는 것은?

Walter Reed, medical doctor, was a U.S. Army physician who in 1901 found that yellow fever is transmitted by a particular mosquito species. He was born in Virginia and completed the M.D. degree in 1869 at the University of Virginia. Reed obtained his second M.D. in 1870 at New York University's Bellevue Hospital Medical College. Reed joined the U.S. Army as a medical doctor. Then, he got married in 1876. The couple had a son and a daughter, and they adopted a Native American girl later. He also served as the curator of the Army Medical Museum, which later became the National Museum of Health and Medicine. He was stationed to Cuba to study yellow fever, which killed thousands of soldiers. With the help

of other doctors, Reed confirmed that the disease is transmitted by mosquitoes. This finding saved countless lives. To commemorate his achievements, many U.S. hospitals were named after Reed.

① yellow fever의 백신을 개발했다.

② medical doctor 학위를 두 번 취득했다.

③ 두 아이의 아버지가 된 후에 중국 아이를 입 양했다.

④ 버지니아 의대 박물관 curator를 역임했다.

⑤ 쿠바에 자신의 이름을 딴 병원을 설립했다.

15 Lewis와 Clark의 탐사에 관한 다음 글의 내용 과 일치하는 것은?

In 1803, the U.S. government purchased the entire area of Louisiana from France. The territory stretched from the Mississippi River to the middle of the Rocky Mountains, but no one was really sure where the Mississippi River started or where exactly the Rocky Mountains were located. President Thomas Jefferson commissioned an expedition in this area. It comprised a selected group of U.S. Army volunteers under the command of Captain Meriwether Lewis and Second Lieutenant William Clark. Their perilous journey lasted from

May 1804 to September 1806. Their primary objective was to explore and to map the newly acquired territory, and to find a practical route across the western half of the continent. Lewis and Clark departed with forty-three men and supplies for two years. They became acquainted with a sixteen-year-old Native American woman named Sacajawea, which means Bird Woman. With her help, Lewis and Clark obtained horses from the Indians and passed the Indian territory without much trouble.

① 미국은 영국으로부터 Louisiana 지역을 매입했다.
② 탐사는 이미 알려진 Mississippi 강의 시작점에서 출발했다.
③ 탐사 대원들은 육군의 추천을 통해 선발됐다.
④ 모든 탐사를 마치기까지 4년 이상의 기간이 걸렸다.
⑤ 탐사 중에 원주민 여성의 도움을 받았다.

brown on the top side with an off-white underbelly and has very small scales invisible to the naked eye embedded in its skin. At birth, it has an eye on each side of the head. After six months, one eye migrates to the other side. Halibut is often boiled, deep-fried or grilled while fresh. Smoking is more difficult with halibut meat than it is with salmon, due to its ultra-low fat content. Currently, the Atlantic population is so depleted through overfishing that it may be declared an endangered species.

① 북대서양과 북태평양에 서식하는 넙치과 생선이다.
② 육안으로 볼 수 없는 비늘을 가지고 있다.
③ 부화 후 6개월까지는 눈이 머리 양쪽에 있다.
④ 지방 함유량이 낮기 때문에, 연어보다 훈제하기가 어렵다.
⑤ 태평양 지역에서 멸종위기 종으로 공표되었다.

16 halibut에 관한 다음 글의 내용과 일치하지 <u>않</u>는 것은?

Halibut is a common name principally applied to the two flatfish from the family of right-eye flounders in the North Atlantic and the North Pacific. Halibut is dark

17 alien species에 관한 다음 글의 내용과 일치하지 <u>않</u>는 것은?

Ecologists generally define an alien species as one that people, inadvertently or deliberately, carried to its new location. "Only a small percentage of alien species cause problems in their new habitats," says a professor of ecology and evolutionary biology. Yet appearances can deceive, ecologists caution, and many of these exotics may be considered acceptable only because no one has documented their harmful effects. What is more, non-native species can appear innocuous for decades, then turn invasive. Faced with such uncertainty, many ecologists argue for strong steps to be taken. Their approach is to remove exotics from natural ecosystems. But a number of experts question the scientific wisdom of trying to roll back ecosystems to a time when they were more natural. Even many ecologists who would like to rid ecosystems of all exotics admit that this goal is impractical. Further, Professor Rosenzweig at the University of Arizona challenges the prevailing view that invasive alien species reduce biodiversity. The exotics increase the number of species in the environment. Even if alien species cause extinctions, the extinction phase will eventually end, and new species may then begin to evolve, he explains.

① 새 환경에서 거의 문제를 일으키지 않는다고 생각하는 것은 잘못된 관측일 수 있다.

② 새 환경에서 수 십 년간 무해했으나, 그 이후 환경을 해치는 경우도 있다.

③ alien species가 제거된 생태계를 선호하는 생태학자들이 있다.

④ Rosenzweig 교수는 alien species가 생태 다양성을 저해한다는 견해를 반박한다.

⑤ 다른 species의 멸종을 초래하기 시작하면 그 현상은 멈추지 않는다.

[18~23] 다음 글의 빈칸에 들어갈 말로 가장 적절한 것을 고르시오.

18

Judges read statutes and the Constitution for help in devising or refining a rule of conduct that may have a significant impact on the welfare of the community. The community is not always willing to allow its choices to be controlled by what people who lived two centuries ago wrote into the Constitution. The procedure for amending the Constitution is, however, so cumbersome that the judges are under great pressure to use the interpretive process to keep the original document _____.

① obsolete   ② translated

③ concise   ④ flexible

⑤ judgmental

19

I go to the Grand Canyon, for instance. I take great pleasure in the views, and I write to you, my good friend, a postcard with the simple message "Wish you were here." What do I mean by this familiar saying? I mean that my pleasure in seeing the Grand Canyon would be greater if I could share it with you. I sense that, as good as it is to be at the Grand Canyon even by myself, it would be that much better if I could share the experience with you. In other words, my postcard is saying that friends share a common good in the special sense that our pleasure in seeing the Grand Canyon together _____ my pleasure and your pleasure in seeing the canyon on separate days.

① can be divided into

② is more than the sum of

③ equals the combined amount of

④ can last in memory longer than

⑤ does not have to take into consideration

20

The coyote is a long, slim, sick and sorry-looking skeleton, with a gray wolf-skin stretched over it, a tolerably bushy tail that forever sags down, a furtive and evil eye, and a long, sharp face, with slightly lifted lip and exposed teeth. He has a general slinking expression all over.

The coyote is a living, breathing _____. He is always hungry. He is always poor, out of luck, and friendless. The meanest creatures despise him, and even the fleas would desert him in a blink of an eye. [3점]

① epitome of wrath

② analogy of sadism

③ allegory of want

④ symbol of efficiency

⑤ metaphor of dominance

21

When I was young I was very impressed by how food producers could fill jars with whole walnuts. Somehow they could crack the shells while leaving the nuts intact. Most of the times I tried it, I ended up with mixed pieces of shell and nut, managing to get the nut out whole only once every ten times or so. Later, however, I learned that although the manufacturers had a better success rate than I did, they often ended up with mixed shell and nut pieces, too. But I also learned that they did something else: they _____. On those occasions when they were successful, they'd take the whole nuts and stick them in a jar labeled "Whole Walnuts." And on the other occasions, they'd separate the nut pieces from the shell and stick them in a jar labeled "Walnut Pieces."

① selected their results

② bred special kinds of nuts

③ used brand new equipment

④ mixed up their nuts for sale

⑤ learned the lesson the hard way

22

In Hobbes's special vocabulary, "natural rights" are what we have already in the state of nature: a right to do anything that protects our vital motions. Hobbes derives the first law of nature from the fear of death in the state of nature. He derives the second law from the first: I should be willing to surrender my natural right to wage war against you, to the extent that you are reciprocally willing to surrender your natural right to wage war against me. _____. Each individually seeks "some Good to himself" in agreeing to surrender the rights of war, and this Good is "nothing else but the security of a man's person." [3점]

① This mutual disarming is in each person's self-interest

② This shared indifference promotes the peace of the society

③ This reciprocal surrender of rights means fostering animosity

④ This social compromise is conducive to reinforcing the law of nature

⑤ This restraint of waging wars does do good to the weaker of the parties

23

Social learning in the form of stimulus or local enhancement plays an indispensable role in human development, as it does in the cognitive development of many social species. In some cases, however, human beings learn from one another in a qualitatively different way. Human beings sometimes engage in what we call cultural learning. In cultural learning, learners do not just direct their attention to the location of another individual's activity; rather, _____. It is learning in which the learner is attempting to learn not from another, but through another.

① they rely on their own insight to understand others

② they extensively enhance the overall cultural flexibility

③ they attempt to see a situation the way the other sees it

④ they learn to second-guess the hidden agenda of others

⑤ they empower themselves to engage in autonomous learning

24 빈칸 (A)와 (B)에 들어갈 말로 가장 적절한 것은?

One basic criterion for comparing countries is their levels of economic development. The most common tool that economists use to measure economic development is gross domestic product (GDP). GDP provides a basic benchmark for the average per capita income in a country. __(A)__, GDP statistics can be quite misleading. For one thing, people may earn far more in some countries than they do in others, but those raw figures do not take into account the relative costs of living in those countries. __(B)__, as exchange rates between national currencies rise or fall, countries can look richer or poorer than they are.

	(A)	(B)
①	In contrast	However
②	In contrast	For example
③	Moreover	Therefore
④	However	Moreover
⑤	However	In contrast

[25~26] 다음 글의 제목으로 가장 적절한 것을 고르시오.

25

When you're carrying extra pounds, the extra expenses add up, starting with health care. In a 2013 Duke study, researchers tracked health care spending by body mass index (BMI) levels. The average annual cost for a person with a low BMI of 19 was $2,541. With a BMI of 25 — considered overweight — it was $2,893. At a BMI of 33, what's deemed obese, the costs topped $3,439. "The risk of illness starts increasing already from the lower end of 'normal weight,'" says lead researcher Truls Ostbye. The add-ons don't end at the doctor's office. A 2010 McKinsey study estimated that obese Americans spend an aggregate of $30 billion extra on clothes. It is also estimated that a 40-year-old obese man will pay twice as much for life insurance.

① Increasing Costs of Health Care

② Lose Weight, Lower Risk of Illness

③ The Price You Pay for Extra Pounds

④ Do Obese People Spend More on Clothes?

⑤ BMI: Not an Accurate Indicator of Weight

26

Climbing the automobile ladder was hard work, and staying on top was even harder. Each year, employing the practice of perceived obsolescence, Chevrolet would roll out an entirely redesigned, and usually larger, model. A car that had been the height of fashion yesterday would look small, embarrassing, and worn-out tomorrow. As you would imagine, all of this provoked a good deal of anxiety from the bottom to the top of American society. Then in 1959, seemingly out of nowhere, simple full-page newspaper ads began to appear with an unadorned image of the Volkswagen Beetle and the headline "Think Small." The ad didn't say much more, except that the car was modest and efficient — it even called the Beetle a "flivver," contemporary slang for a piece of junk. People found the ads shockingly honest and hilarious, allowing them to publicly express an unnamed anxiety that marketers had been instilling in them for years. Will I make it to the top of the ladder? Who Cares? [3점]

① Hard Economic Times: Think Small

② At the Top of the Automobile Ladder

③ New Ad: Step Down From Your Ladders

④ Does Your Car Represent Your Social Status?

⑤ International Automobile Warfare: Size Matters

[27~28] 다음 글의 주제로 가장 적절한 것을 고르시오.

27

The emotional reaction of disgust is often associated with the obdurate refusal of young children to consume certain vegetables. While such disgust may seem absurd to parents determined to supply their children with nutritious foods, scientists interested in hygienic behavior have a rational explanation. This theory contends that people have developed disgust as a protective mechanism against unfamiliar and possibly harmful objects. A recent study shows that disgust not only deters the ingestion of dangerous substances, but also dissuades people from entering potentially contagious situations. For instance, subjects of the study declared crowded railcars to be more disgusting than empty ones and lice more disgusting than wasps.

① the role of disgust in keeping people safe

② the advantages of getting proper nutrition

③ the difference between danger and contagion

④ the importance of avoiding harmful substances

⑤ the necessity of practicing good hygienic behavior

28

Success as a scientist is not simply a function of the quality of the ideas we hold in our heads, or of the data we hold in our hands, but also of the language we use to describe them. We all understand that "publish or perish" is real and dominates our professional lives. But "publish or perish" is about surviving, not succeeding. You don't succeed as a scientist by getting papers published. You succeed as a scientist by getting them cited. Having your work matter, matters. Success is defined not by the number of pages you have in print but by their influence. You succeed when your peers understand your work and use it to motivate their own.

① the enduring belief of 'the more writing, the better'

② the importance of influencing others in scientific writing

③ the necessity for pursuing research in unexplored areas

④ the favorable peer reviews needed for journal acceptance

⑤ the working ethics and strict quality control in publications

29 다음 글의 요지로 가장 적절한 것은?

You don't have to go vegan, pledge allegiance to an exercise cult or become a full-time meditator to get the longevity benefits of healthy habits. The latest science is showing quite the opposite, in fact: that extending healthy life is attainable for many of us with just a few small changes that aren't especially hard to do — and won't make you miserable. Researchers have learned that logging hours at the gym cannot counteract the negative effects of sitting for long periods, for instance — but something as simple as fidgeting can. They've also discovered that cutting down on how much you eat doesn't have to be excruciating — and it can improve your chance for a longer life.

① Living a healthy lifestyle is easier said than done.

② Key changes in your diet can help you live longer.

③ Exercising is important for people with sedentary lifestyles.

④ Physical and mental well—being can be achieved with hard work.

⑤ Achieving longevity is not as difficult as one might imagine.

30 다음 글에 나타난 David의 심경으로 가장 적절한 것은?

When the elevator began its descent, a broad smile began to form on David's face. The spinning and nausea were gone. The pressure on his chest vanished. He was doing it. He was leaving the job and saying farewell to a nightmare. He found the spine to walk away that gloomy morning. He was standing in the empty elevator, watching with a wide grin as the floor numbers went down in bright red digital numbers. The elevator rocked gently as it fell through the center of the building. When it stopped, David got off and darted to the descending escalators. Somebody called out, "Hey, David, where are you going?" David smiled and waved in the general direction of the voice, as if everything was under control. He went outside, and the air that had seemed so wet and dreary earlier now held the promise of a new beginning.

① sad and agitated

② relieved and hopeful

③ bored and indifferent

④ nervous and confused

⑤ empty and abandoned

[31~32] 다음 글에서 전체 흐름과 관계없는 문장을 고르시오.

31 Pasta's ethnic roots have been long debated. ① Many theories have been put forward, some notably far-fetched. ② An enduring myth, based on the writings of the 13th-century explorer Marco Polo, that pasta was brought to Italy from China, rose from a misinterpretation of a famous passage in Polo's *Travels*. ③ In it, Polo mentions a tree from which something like pasta was made. ④ It was probably the sago palm, which produces a starchy food that resembles, but is not pasta. ⑤ This tree, native to Asia, provided undeniable evidence that Pasta originated in China.

32 Another difference in the concept of justice lies in various societies' ideas of what laws are. In the West, people consider "laws" quite different from "customs." There is also a great contrast between "sins" (breaking religious laws) and "crimes" (breaking laws of the government). ① In many non-Western cultures, however, there is little separation of customs, laws, and religious beliefs; in other cultures, these three may be quite separate from one another, but still very much different from those in the West. ② For these reasons, an action may be considered a crime in one country but be socially acceptable in others. ③ For instance, although a thief is viewed as a criminal in much of the world, in a small village where there is considerable communal living and sharing of objects, the word thief may have little meaning. ④ In small villages, everyone, in a sense, becomes a judge; in such societies, social disapproval of people's activities can serve both as powerful punishment for and as strong deterrent to crime. ⑤ Someone who has taken something without asking is simply considered an impolite person. [3점]

33 글의 흐름으로 보아, 주어진 문장이 들어가기에 가장 적절한 곳은? [3점]

Humans also automatically adjust their behavior to blend with the people around them.

When you interact with other people, you are quite likely to find yourself mimicking them in certain ways. (①) You may, for example, unconsciously match your friends' speech patterns and accents. (②) Social psychologists labeled this type of mimicry the chameleon effect. (③) Chameleons automatically change their color to blend in with their environment. (④) It is speculated that this form of mimicry functions as a type of "social glue." (⑤) By producing identical motor gestures, people make themselves more similar to the other individuals around them.

34 다음 글의 내용을 한 문장으로 나타낼 때, 빈칸 (A)와 (B)에 들어갈 말로 가장 적절한 것은?

Just thinking that a particular brand's products are especially effective may have a kind of placebo effect, researchers have found. In a series of studies, participants received nearly identical tools for skill tests in golf and math. The only difference: Half of the putters bore Nike labels, while half of the earplug sets given to test takers were said to have been made by 3M. Those who thought they were using a Nike putter indeed needed fewer putts, on average, to sink a ball, and participants who thought they had 3M earplugs during the math test answered more questions correctly. It was also found that those with the lowest initial confidence in their abilities seemed to gain the most from the subtle upgrade.

Studies showed that, on average, the performance of participants on tests was __(A)__ when they believed they were using more __(B)__ brands.

2017 기출문제

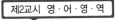

	(A)	(B)
①	enhanced	generic
②	enhanced	athletic
③	enhanced	prominent
④	diminished	popular
⑤	diminished	ordinary

35 주어진 글 다음에 이어질 글의 순서로 가장 적절한 것은?

> From all the meals you've shared with family and friends, you are probably aware that people have very different taste preferences.

[A] The group of individuals who have considerably more than an average number of taste buds are called supertasters. The variations in the density of taste buds on different people's tongues appear to be genetic. Women are much more likely than men to be supertasters.

[B] In fact, the foods mothers eat change the flavor of amniotic fluid, so some food preferences may be shaped in utero. However, people also show remarkable differences in the numbers of taste buds they possess.

[C] Some people love spicy food, for example, whereas others shudder at the thought of a hot pepper. Some preferences are explained by differences in the flavors people experience quite early in life.

*in utero : 자궁 내에

① [A] − [C] − [B] ② [B] − [A] − [C]

③ [B] − [C] − [A] ④ [C] − [A] − [B]

⑤ [C] − [B] − [A]

[36~37] 다음 글을 읽고 물음에 답하시오.

So effective was the mass conversion to the new engineering values that even when the depression hit in 1929, Americans continued to defend the technological vision. (A) They chose instead to vent their anger and fear against greedy businessmen who, in their mind, had undermined and thwarted the lofty aims and goals of the nation's new heroes — the engineers. (B) Quite a few Americans agreed with the earlier criticism of economist and social theorist Thorstein Veblen. He contended in 1921 that only by entrusting the nation's economy to the professional engineers — whose noble standards stood above pecuniary and parochial concerns — could the economy be saved and the country transformed into a new Eden. (C) Internal bickering among its leaders led to a splintering of the movement into warring factions. (D) Then too, Hitler's meteoric rise to power and the Third Reich's fanatical obsession with technological efficiency gave many social thinkers second thoughts about the Technocrats' call for a technological dictatorship in the United States. (E) The technological world view suffered an even more critical setback in 1945 when U.S. airplanes dropped atomic bombs on Japanese cities: the entire world was abruptly forced to look at the dark side of the techno-utopian vision. The postwar generation was the first to live with the constant reminder of modern technology's awesome power to destroy as well as create the future.

36 윗글의 흐름으로 보아, 주어진 문장이 들어가기에 가장 적절한 곳은?

> But the success of technocracy was to be short-lived.

① (A) ② (B)

③ (C) ④ (D)

⑤ (E)

37 윗글의 주제로 가장 적절한 것을 고르시오.

① the technocratic vision and its downfall

② the brief honeymoon for democracy and technology

③ the inevitable arrival of the technological world view

④ the belligerent approach of Technocrats for a better society

⑤ the imbalance between the bright and dark sides of technocracy

[38~39] 다음 글을 읽고 물음에 답하시오.

Even before there is a nation or other organized community to take over from the victims of aggression and their families the responsibility for catching and punishing aggressors, customs evolve that alleviate some of the problems of revenge practices. Among these is the principle of retribution, that is, exact retaliation for a wrong — an eye for an eye. Rather than being bloodthirsty, which is the modern connotation of the word, retribution reduces the likelihood of overreactions (your life for my eye) that are likely to engender feuds. Another   (A)   principle is "composition" (blood money), whereby the victim or the victim's family is required, or at least encouraged, to accept payment in compensation for an injury, discharging the injurer's liability. A transfer of money or goods is less costly to society as a whole than an act of violence, which besides inflicting a net social loss rather than merely transferring wealth from one person to another may provoke further violence. Another   (B)   institution is bilateral kinship. Icelanders reckoned kinship through both the father and the mother (many societies reckon it only through the father and some only through the mother). This not only increased the credibility of revenge as a deterrent to aggression by strengthening the family; it made it more likely that a disputant would have kin on both sides of the dispute. The *Iliad* hints at the further

2017 기출문제

possibility that pity and empathy might limit the savagery of revenge.

38 윗글의 빈칸 (A)와 (B)에 공통으로 들어갈 말로 가장 적절한 것은? [3점]

① modifying ② penalizing

③ conflicting ④ moderating

⑤ captivating

39 윗글의 내용과 일치하는 것은?

① 국가가 가해자를 처벌할 책임을 맡기 전 보복은 주로 폭력으로 이루어졌다.

② '눈에는 눈' 원칙은 피해자의 과잉대응 가능성을 줄였다.

③ 피해자에 대한 물질적인 보상은 공동체가 담당했다.

④ 부모는 가족 구성원의 폭력에 대한 책임을 질 필요가 없었다.

⑤ 연민이나 공감은 보복의 가능성을 줄이는 데 도움이 되지 않았다.

[40~42] 다음 글을 읽고 물음에 답하시오.

[A] Many states have laws requiring individuals to wear a helmet while riding a motorcycle. These laws are frequently challenged, on the grounds that their sole purpose is to protect cyclists from injuring themselves.

[B] In college I had a motorcycle-riding friend who steadfastly refused to wear a helmet. He had been ridiculed so often by the rest of us for his foolishness that (a) he developed a rather eloquent defense that went something like this: "Look, I'm tired of this bourgeois life; I'm out for a little adventure, that's why I ride a bike in the first place. I want it to be dangerous; the thrill is the risk. And the more I risk, the bigger the thrill."

[C] It would seem from the episode that the helmet–free motorcyclist is engaged in other–regarding conduct after all. It is not that the public cares much about what happens to the motorcyclist; we care about the costs to the rest of us that flow from daredevil behavior. Not everyone's lifestyle is equal in terms of the burden or tax (b) he places on public resources. My reckless pal seems a particularly extreme example of an egoist asking the public to support his choice, not just leave (c) him alone.

[D] Was my friend's decision to ride without a helmet a decision that affected only himself? Stones or other objects might fly up from the road, causing (d) him to swerve into others. Even were he to injure only himself, that injury might involve head trauma that could have been avoided by wearing a helmet. My friend would then expect not to be left alone but to be ministered to by ambulance drivers, medics, and EMTs. Valuable time and money would be expended to subsidize his thrill seeking. The medics might not get to another victim in time because they were busy working to stuff brain tissue back inside (e) his cracked skull. Hospital space and resources would also be taxed, doctors called upon, and medical and auto insurance rates pushed upward for all of us.

40 윗글의 [A]에 이어질 내용을 순서에 맞게 배열한 것으로 가장 적절한 것은?

① [B] – [C] – [D] ② [B] – [D] – [C]

③ [C] – [B] – [D] ④ [C] – [D] – [B]

⑤ [D] – [C] – [B]

41 윗글의 주제로 가장 적절한 것은?

① the psyche of a helmetless biker

② a recipe for an accident-free society

③ lifestyles of risk and non-risk takers

④ personal freedom at the expense of others

⑤ a controversial regulation for traffic violators

42 밑줄 친 (a)~(e) 중에서 지칭하는 대상이 나머지와 다른 것은?

① (a) ② (b)

③ (c) ④ (d)

⑤ (e)

[43~45] 다음 글을 읽고 물음에 답하시오.

I have always had an interest in the art of magic. By the time I was ten, I could make handkerchiefs vanish and shuffle a deck of cards thoroughly without altering their order. In my early teens I joined one of the world's best-known magic societies in London. By my early twenties I had been invited to the U.S. to perform several times at prestigious shows.

My love for the world of fascinating tricks and illusion had started with a chance encounter. When I was eight I was asked to complete a school project on the history of chess. Being a diligent young student, I decided to pay a visit to my local library to find books on the topic. I was directed to the wrong shelf and came across some books on magic. I was curious, and started to read all about the secrets that magicians use to achieve the impossible. I have no idea what might have happened if I had been directed to the correct shelf and found the chess books.

Many people have reported how

chance meetings and unplanned encounters with strangers frequently led to a significant shift in career directions. Each one of us could tell stories of how crucial, unplanned events have had a major career impact and how untold thousands of minor unplanned events have had at least a small impact. Influential unplanned events _____; they are everyday occurrences. Serendipity is not serendipitous. Serendipity is ubiquitous.

Take Joseph Pulitzer as an example. He was born in Hungary. As a young man Pulitzer suffered from both poor health and extremely bad eyesight. When he was seventeen, he came to America for a better life. However, he could not find a job there. Pulitzer spent a great deal of time playing chess in his local library. On one such visit he happened to meet an editor of a local newspaper. This unexpected meeting resulted in Pulitzer being offered a job as a junior reporter. He was quite successful in his newspaper career, and became an editor, and eventually owner of two of the best-known newspapers of his day.

43 윗글의 제목으로 가장 적절할 것은?

① Diligence Always Pays Off

② Chances Are It's a Great Chance

③ Joseph Pulitzer: Untold Anecdotes

④ Prestige and Your Career Choices

⑤ Magical Moments Long Remembered

44 윗글의 빈칸에 들어가기에 가장 적절한 것은?

① are preconceived

② are not welcome

③ are not uncommon

④ can predict the future

⑤ can lose their influence

45 윗글에서 Joseph Pulitzer에 관한 내용과 일치하지 않는 것은?

① Hungary에서 출생했다.

② 시력이 나빠서 고생했다.

③ 열일곱 살 때 미국에 갔다.

④ 프로 chess 기사가 됐다.

⑤ 두 개의 신문사를 소유했다.

2026
경찰대학

10개년 영어

2016학년도 기출문제
영어영역

제2교시 영어영역

[01~05] 밑줄 친 단어의 뜻으로 가장 적절한 것을 고르시오.

01

Who would have guessed that the movie star's fame would be ephemeral?

① fleeting
② residual
③ perpetual
④ legendary
⑤ credulous

02

Karen tried to cajole his friend into driving her to the mall, but to no avail.

① coax
② bully
③ slander
④ provoke
⑤ hypnotize

03

She is extremely fastidious about keeping the premises spotless, almost to a fault.

① perilous
② insidious
③ insolvent
④ vindictive
⑤ meticulous

04

Dreams help people work through the day's emotional quandaries. It is like having a built-in therapist.

① bonds
② dilemmas
③ failures
④ ecstasies
⑤ irritations

05

He's going to promote me to Clare's level, and he's telling me discreetly so she won't get jealous.

① rashly
② mildly
③ enviously
④ cautiously
⑤ impartially

[06~08] 밑줄 친 부분 중 어법상 **틀린** 것을 고르시오.

06

I once lived in a coastal village of Papua New Guinea. Children there did not live with their own parents but moved from house to house ① as they wished. Ten-year-olds could ② be seen carrying babies or tending cooking fires. By fourteen they were doing adult work with confidence and pride. As the newest and most interesting thing in the village. I had a dozen or so kids ③ sleeping on my veranda. When tropical diarrhea struck in the small hours of the night, I had to pick my way out through a carpet of small brown bodies. It occurred to me ④ what this would be an easy place to be a parent, since the work and pleasure of parenting was shared by the whole village. In fact, any adult ⑤ who was present was a parent.

07 Born into great wealth but plunged into poverty as a teen, I grew up knowing more about the perils of losing success than the secrets of ① attaining it. Although my parents recovered after ② being stripped of everything in midlife, they never regained a prosperous mindset. And I absorbed their fears ③ more fully than their successes. Those fears fueled my desire to be financially successful and ④ was, in part, what drove me to make a living out of teaching people how to achieve. I grew up to be a motivational speaker who inspired thousands of business executives and professional athletes ⑤ to achieve their goals using valuable principles of success.

08 There are numerous myths and legends associated with gems. Some tell of cursed stones; ① others of stones with special powers of healing, or that protect or give good luck to the wearer. Some of ② the largest known diamonds have legends associated with them that have been told and retold over centuries, and ③

many now lost are surrounded by tales of intrigue and murder. Some mines ④ are thought to be cursed — probably rumors spread by the mine owners to keep unwanted prospectors away. In Myanmar, for instance, where all gemstones belonged to the monarch, the belief that anyone who took a stone from a mine would be cursed ⑤ may have deliberately cultivated to curb losses of a valuable national asset.
[3점]

09 (A), (B), (C)에 들어갈 말로 가장 적절한 것은?

Last summer, a 26-year-old woman in California called 911 to report an emergency. Had she placed her emergency call on a landline, first responders would have been able to (A) [pinpoint/overlook] her location in a matter of seconds. But because the current 911 system has gone largely unchanged since it was designed in the 1960s, police were forced to use (B) [precise/ imprecise] information provided by her wireless carrier to determine where she might be. When an emergency call is made on a mobile device, telecommunicat-ions companies use (C) [triangulation/ circulation] — comparing the signal strength and time the signal takes to reach a number of cell towers — to approximate the phone's position. This technique placed the woman within a one-block radius, and it took over 20 minutes to find her.

	(A)		(B)		(C)
①	pinpoint	–	imprecise	–	triangulation
②	pinpoint	–	imprecise	–	circulation
③	overlook	–	precise	–	circulation
④	overlook	–	precise	–	triangulation
⑤	overlook	–	imprecise	–	circulation

[10~12] 다음 글의 밑줄 친 부분 중, 문맥상 낱말의 쓰임이 적절하지 <u>않은</u> 것을 고르시오.

10 In all history, nothing is so surprising or so difficult to account for as the sudden rise of civilization in Greece. Much of what makes civilization had already existed for thousands of years in Egypt and in Mesopotamia, and had ① spread thence to neighbouring countries. But certain elements had been ② lacking until the Greeks supplied them. What they achieved in art and literature is familiar to everybody, but what they did in the purely intellectual realm is even more ③ ordinary. They invented mathematics and science and philosophy; they first wrote history as ④ opposed to mere annals; they speculated freely about the nature of the world and the ends of life, without being ⑤ bound in the fetters of any inherited orthodoxy. [3점]

11 For ordinary citizens the electric lights that dispelled the gloom of the city at night offered the most dramatic evidence that times had changed. Gaslight — ① illuminating gas produced from coal — had been in use since the early nineteenth century, but its 12 candlepower lamps lighted the city's public spaces only ② dimly. The first commercial use of electricity was for ③ better city lighting. Charles F. Brush's electric arc lamps, installed in Wanamaker's department store in Philadelphia in 1878, threw a brilliant light and soon ④ established gaslight on city streets and public buildings across the country. ⑤ Electric lighting then entered the American home, thanks to Thomas Edison's invention of a serviceable incandescent bulb in 1879. Edison's motto — "Let there be light!" — truly described the experience of the modern city.

12 What else, besides love, gets passed on during a kiss? Dutch researchers tracked how kissing affected the ① oral bacteria of 21 couples. They asked one person in each pair to ② consume a probiotic yogurt drink with specific bacterial strains to track the spread of germs. Then that person was asked to ③ share a ten-second kiss with his or her partner. The average kiss ④ extinguished as many as 80 million bacteria. Although this doesn't sound very hygienic, experts say exposure to someone else's bacteria could actually help ⑤ strengthen your immunity.

13 밑줄 친 ①~⑤ 중에서 의미하는 바가 나머지와 <u>다른</u> 것은?

It's really not that hard to build a flying car — the first working model got up in 1947. The real challenge turns out to be building ① <u>a flying car</u> that makes sense. Elon Musk, CEO of both Tesla and SpaceX, keeps getting asked why he can't mate his two companies and give birth to ② <u>a rocket car</u>. He answered in a series of recent tweets, including: "③ <u>Airborne auto</u> pros: travel in 3D fast. Cons: risk of car falling on head much greater than ④ <u>one moving in two vectors</u>." And Peter Thiel, the famous investor, goes around saying, "We wanted ⑤ <u>real sky cars</u>; instead we got junk."

14 Temple Grandin에 관한 다음 글의 내용과 일치하는 것은?

What do neurologists, cattle and fast-food restaurants have in common? They all owe a great deal to one woman, a renowned animal scientist born with autism, Temple Grandin. Though she did not utter a word until her fourth birthday, she splashed onto the stage of public awareness in 1995, thanks to the famed neurologist Oliver Sacks. But as with many psychological disorders, autism is a spectrum,

and Temple is on one edge. Living on this edge has allowed her to be an extraordinary source of inspiration for autistic children. She is also a source of hope for another mammal: the cow. Using her unique window into the minds of animals, she has developed housing for cattle that improves their quality of life by reducing stress. And though the fast-food industry continues to use cattle in its patties, it has come to appreciate the ethics and compassion of a Grandin burger.

① 자폐증을 갖고 태어난 동물 과학자다.
② 1995년 한 사회 비평가에 의해서 알려지게 되었다.
③ 모든 어린이들에게 영감의 원천이었다.
④ 소의 스트레스를 줄이는 사료를 개발했다.
⑤ Grandin 버거의 비윤리성을 비난했다.

15 filefish에 관한 다음 글의 내용과 일치하는 것은?

Now you see it, now you don't. The slender filefish has a neat way to avoid its predators. It has evolved the ability to become almost invisible. Justine Allen of Brown University was amazed by how fast the fish camouflaged themselves when she saw them in the Caribbean. It took them just two seconds to match the colors of the sea fans, or gorgonians, they swam past. How does it work? To see an object for what it is, you need to be able to perceive its edges, which mark it out as being separate from the background. Allen found that the filefish changes its coloration to create "false edges." For example, it can make a dark, longitudinal stripe appear on its body that looks like a real edge. The eye sees this false edge, and so can miss the true outline of the fish.

① 천적을 피하는 기술이 없다.
② 눈에 안 띄게 하는 능력을 상실했다.
③ 2초 만에 몸의 색을 바꿀 수 있다.
④ 몸의 크기를 늘려서 가짜 윤곽을 만든다.
⑤ 몸에 가로 줄무늬를 만든다.

16 다음 글의 내용과 일치하지 <u>않는</u> 것은?

A source of confusion and misunderstanding that leads to disappointment is the often complex and ambiguous language in insurance contracts. Much of the billions of dollars of damage wrought by Hurricane Katrina on the Gulf Coast of Mississippi occurred when Katrina's huge storm surge damaged or destroyed thousands of homes and businesses. Homeowners, infuriated when they realized that their policies covered wind ─ not water ─ damage, teamed with their state governments to sue insurance carriers. They argued that, even if their insurance did not cover water damage, it still should pay because Katrina's screaming winds drove a wall of water that damaged their property. The homeowners lost the suit, but the insurance industry lost much credibility and people became more concerned that their coverage was much less than it appeared to be on paper.

① 보험 계약서 상의 언어로 인해 오해가 일어나기도 한다.
② Hurricane Katrina로 수십억 달러의 피해가 발생했다.
③ 주택소유자들은 보험회사를 상대로 소송했다.
④ 주택소유자들은 물로 인한 피해도 보상하라고 요구했다.
⑤ 주택소유자들은 보험회사를 상대로 한 소송에서 승소했다.

17 Candace Hill에 관한 다음 글의 내용과 일치하지 <u>않는</u> 것은?

Eleven seconds is the benchmark that separates the women from the girls in the 100 meters. Last Saturday, at the Brooks PR Invitational in Seattle, 16-year-old Candace Hill joined the elite group with a scorching win in 10.98 seconds, becoming the first U.S. high school girl to break the 11-second barrier, smashing the American junior and world youth records. Candace, who finished her second year at Rockdale County High in Georgia last month, is a five-time national champion, and already held Georgia state records in the 100- and 200-meter dash. Her record-setting race would have earned third place at this year's NCAA championships and tied for 10th best in the world this season.

① Seattle에서 개최된 대회에 참가했다.
② 11초 벽을 깬 최초의 미국 여고생이다.
③ 지난달에 고등학교 2학년을 마쳤다.
④ Georgia주 200미터 경주 기록 보유자이다.
⑤ 올해 NCAA 대회에서 3등을 차지했다.

[18~23] 다음 글을 읽고, 빈칸에 들어갈 말로 가장 적절한 것을 고르시오.

18

People's relationship with animals is fraught with _____. They express love and appreciation for them and have enacted laws to forbid cruelty to them. The United States is a pet-keeping society, with more dogs, cats, parrots, hamsters, and other pets combined than people and a $60-billion-a-year industry for their care. Millions of Americans are engaged with wildlife in some way, and some of their happiest moments are spent in unspoiled settings. And yet at the same time, they exploit animals on a massive scale, with billions of creatures killed or abused every year for food, clothing, research, and other purposes.

① gratitude
② hostility
③ protectiveness
④ responsibilities
⑤ contradictions

19

We are such social animals that we are completely preoccupied with what others think about us. The social pressure to conform involves being valued by the group because, after all, most success is really defined by what others think. This preoccupation is all too evident in our modern celebrity culture, and especially with the rise of social networking, where normal individuals spend considerable amounts of time and effort _____. Over 1.7 billion people on this planet use social networking on the Internet to share and seek validation from others. When Rachel Berry, a character in a hit musical series about a performing-arts school, said "Nowadays being anonymous is worse than being poor," she was simply echoing our modern obsession with fame and our desire to be liked by many people—even if they are mostly anonymous or casual acquaintances.

① in pursuit of recognition from others

② to extend their domain of friendship

③ despite massive criticism by experts

④ prompting misgivings among the public

⑤ beyond the limits imposed by authorities

20

Let us unite profound knowledge of the art with the happiest talent for inventing lovely melodies, and then link both with the greatest possible originality, in order to obtain the most faithful picture of Mozart's musical genius. Nowhere in his work does one ever find an idea one had heard before: Even his accompaniments are always novel. One is, as it were, incessantly pulled along from one notion to another, without rest, so that admiration of the latest constantly swallows up admiration for what has gone before, and even by straining all one's forces one is scarcely able to absorb all the beauties that present themselves to the soul. If any fault had to be found with Mozart, it could surely be only this: That such _____ almost tires the

soul and the effect of the whole is sometimes obscured thereby. But happy is the artist whose only fault lies in an all too great perfection.

① plethora of faith

② desolation of spirit

③ command of words

④ redundancy of melodies

⑤ abundance of beauty

21

A picture may be worth a thousand words, but for centuries words ruled the legal domain. Rhetoric, the art of using language, has always been the trademark of lawyers, and trials, especially in Common Law, have been widely understood as battles by words. Alas, all glory is doomed to pass and the second half of the nineteenth century saw a new mode of persuasion rising to dominance, driven by a new class of machine-made testimonies that threatened to turn words into an inferior mode of communicating facts. Ever alert and never involved, machines such as microscopes, telescopes, high-speed cameras and x-ray tubes purported to communicate richer, better, and truer evidence, often inaccessible otherwise to human beings. The emblem for this new type of mechanical objectivity was _____. "Let nature speak for itself," became the watchword, and nature's language seemed to be that of photographs and mechanically generated curves. [3점]

① visual evidence
② verbal testimony
③ legal terminology
④ linguistic eloquence
⑤ subjective expression

22

A study in the *Journal of Consumer Psychology* explored the power of repetition by comparing all No. 1 songs on *Billboard's* Hot 100 list from 1958 to 2012 with tracks that never broke past No. 90. Researchers observed that the simpler and more repetitive a song's lyrics were, the better its chance of reaching the top spot. Such songs also climbed the chart faster than less repetitive ones. This finding supports the theory of processing fluency, which suggests that the easier a message is to digest, _____. Musicians aren't the only ones in on the secret: Similar strategies are used in advertising, through slogans that saturate commercials, and even in comedy; stand-ups often loop to the same punch line throughout a set. [3점]

① the more effort the brain has to exert
② the more positively people will react to it
③ the higher the likelihood of tuning out the message
④ the less the chances of people singing after the song
⑤ the less likely people will decode the hidden message

23

In modern Western society, religion's original explanatory role _____. The origins of the universe as we know it are now attributed to the Big Bang and the subsequent operation of the laws of physics. Modern language diversity is no longer explained by origin myths, such as the Tower of Babel or the snapping of the lianas holding the New Guinea ironwood tree, but is instead considered as adequately explained by observed historical processes of language change. Explanations of sunrises, sunsets, and tides are now left to astronomers, and explanations of winds and rain are left to meteorologists. Bird songs are explained by ethology, and the origin of each plant and animal species, including the human species, is left to evolutionary biologists to interpret.

① provides the basis for scientific theories

② has increasingly become usurped by science

③ has risen to give the best account of nature

④ evokes controversy on the adequacy of science

⑤ is reinforced by creationists and evolutionists alike

24 빈칸 (A)와 (B)에 들어갈 말로 가장 적절한 것은? [3점]

The use of tobacco illustrates what happened to what was almost an element of religion in Maya eyes when it became part of Spanish or, for that matter, all Western culture. Tobacco among the Maya had a very important role in religious life; it was an important element in the prevention and cure of disease, and in some parts was deified. Its pleasure-giving qualities seem in Maya eyes to have been quite   (A)   to its other functions. Yet when tobacco was taken over by the Spaniards it was only as a commodity which gave pleasure to the individual; all the Maya ritualistic and community associations were shed. This process was in line with Spanish   (B)   of those cultural elements of the conquered natives which they absorbed. Maize was no longer the beloved and sacred staff of life; it became for the conqueror

an item of tribute and commercial transactions. Cacao suffered the same degradation.

	(A)		(B)
①	relevant	–	authorization
②	relevant	–	enlightenment
③	identical	–	destruction
④	subordinate	–	inquisition
⑤	subordinate	–	secularization

[25~26] 다음 글의 제목으로 가장 적절한 것을 고르시오.

25

The earliest Robin Hood ballad was printed in 1450, and it does not portray the dashing hero that we have come to know in popular culture. He was a yeoman, rough and cruel at times. The legend was more than likely based on a robber who kept the money he stole from the rich and occasionally helped the poor. He did not want to set up an ideal society in the forest. He and his men sought mainly to rectify social injustices and to live well. Robin Hood became so popular by the seventeenth century that people named places and ships after him. By the nineteenth century, many stories and songs had brought about major changes in the Robin Hood legend. His yeoman origins disappeared, and he increasingly became the heroic outlaw of Sherwood Forest who defended the rights of the poor.

① Robin Hood as a Robber

② Origins of Medieval Yeomen

③ Earlier Struggles of Robin Hood

④ Ideal Society in Sherwood Forest

⑤ Transformations in the Robin Hood Character

26

In one study a hundred men and women wore devices that took readings of their blood pressure whenever they interacted with someone. When they were with family or enjoyable friends, their blood pressure fell; these interactions were pleasant and soothing. When they were with someone who was troublesome, there was a rise. But the biggest jump came while they were with people they felt ambivalent about: an overbearing parent, a volatile romantic partner, or a competitive friend. A mercurial boss looms as the archetype, but this dynamic operates in all our relationships.

① High Blood Pressure: The Silent Assassin

② Uneasy Relationships: Your Body Doesn't Lie

③ Don't Be Bossed Around by Your Biorhythm

④ Can Health Monitoring Devices Save Your Life?

⑤ How Can You Deal with Uncomfortable Interactions?

[27~28] 다음 글의 주제로 가장 적절한 것을 고르시오.

27

Music that was exciting to the contemporaries of Bach and Beethoven is still exciting, although we do not share their culture. The early Beatles' songs are still exciting although the Beatles have unfortunately broken up. Similarly, some Venda songs that must have been composed hundreds of years ago still excite me. Many of us are thrilled by Koto music from Japan, sitar music from India, Chopi xylophone music, and so on. I do not say that we receive music in exactly the same way as the players, but our own experiences suggest that there are some possibilities of cross-cultural communication. I am convinced that the explanation for this is to be found in the fact that at the level of deep structures in music there are elements that are common to the human psyche, although they may not appear in the surface structures.

① the potential of music to enrich culture

② the gradual divergence of music from culture

③ the ability of music to nourish the human psyche

④ the advantages of cross-cultural transmission of music

⑤ the universality of music that transcends time and culture

① the success stories of a realistic role model

② the source of frustration in emulating a role model

③ the importance of selecting a reachable role model

④ the necessity for having an inspiring person around

⑤ the positive effects of imitating a person of high status

28

We often see stories of inspiring people and wonderful successes. Some of us put their pictures on our walls or clip notable quotes from them. But what does that do for us if the inspiring person has done things we will never or could never do? For many of us, the choice of a role model invites comparison, and if our abilities and outcomes do not measure up, the role model serves not as an inspiration but as a source of frustration and defeat. Choose as your role model someone who has accomplished something you can accomplish and something you want to accomplish. There is tremendous value in using co-workers or family members who you admire rather than famous athletes, leaders, or historical figures, who have experienced great successes but whose experience has less in common with yours.

29 다음 글의 요지로 가장 적절한 것은? [3점]

Recently I was reading about the endangered grizzly bears on the coast of British Columbia. The authors emphasized how the cubs were keen observers of their mothers' skills in searching for and consuming food. What the cubs learned by the mothers' modeling was a matter of life and death; without that knowledge the cubs probably would not survive. The same principle applies to us. How can we believe that when we live life like a rat race, our children somehow will not? That as we mindlessly acquire and consume, our children will somehow know moderation and meaning in their relationship to things? If I regularly cheat on little things — like not returning the extra change I receive at the counter, or pocketing found money without trying to find its owner—I am teaching that behavior to children.

① Parents are spending more time reading books on wildlife.

② Mindful consumption lies at the center of being good parents.

③ Good parenting begins and ends with setting a good example.

④ Teaching good behavior to children outweighs earning money.

⑤ Children's behavior is subconsciously mirrored by their parents.

30 다음 글에 나타난 Dave의 심경으로 가장 적절한 것은?

Dave was never quite sure how it happened. He only knew that he awoke as he was being hurled from his bed and, mingled with the startled awakening, there was a terrific explosion. For a moment or more he lay absent-mindedly on the deck of his room, struggling to regain his senses. Then slowly he realized the steady throb of the engines, to which he had grown so accustomed in the week since boarding the ship, had abruptly ceased. What happened? He got up and, feeling his way to the light switch, gave it a turn with a trembling hand. Nothing happened, and he tried it again. The lights did not come on.

① distracted and angry

② confused and nervous

③ overjoyed and proud

④ indifferent and bored

⑤ irritated and stimulated

[31~32] 다음 글에서 전체 흐름과 관계 없는 문장을 고르시오.

31 On the face of it, industrialized agriculture promised to be a most welcome solution to the timeless problem of world hunger. ① But some so-called solutions, as writer and farmer Wendell Berry observed, led to ramifying sets of new problems. ② And during the past several decades, it has become increasingly clear that industrial agriculture has indeed created a host of new problems impacting the health of people and the planet. ③ So corporations and governments, recognizing the opportunity presented by the new technologies, fostered the rapid spread of industrialized agriculture. ④ The use of fertilizers and pesticides, for example, has led to higher rates of cancer and the contamination of soil, streams, and groundwater. ⑤ Monoculture farming has led to the loss of biodiversity, undermining the productivity and stability of ecosystems.

32 From the artfully styled grain bowls to the popular slow-simmered bone broth, the message is clear: The beauty-and-wellness set has become obsessed with nutrition. ① Today, eating virtuously isn't just a means to stay trim; it's a crucial step in fortifying the body for an increasingly fit, and busy, life. ② But in this multitasking age, where lunch comes with a side of email, everyone's got a lot on their plate except, too often, a square meal. ③ This lack of proper nutrition from local foods is only worsened by a sedentary lifestyle. ④ Answering the call across the country is a wave of enterprising young chefs and tech pioneers who are marrying wholesome meals with door-to-door convenience. ⑤ If last year was dominated by the juice cleanse, this is shaping up to be the year of the designer meal delivery.

[3점]

33 글의 흐름으로 보아, 주어진 문장이 들어가기에 가장 적절한 곳은?

> At one point, he clapped me on the back and said: "Son, make sure you talk with everyone here tonight and see that each one feels better about himself when he leaves than he did when he walked in the door."

One of my daughters was married recently, and I spent the evening celebrating with 200 people of all ages. (①) They ranged from my 3-year-old granddaughters to my 85-year-old uncle, who fought in World War II and ran successful law and accounting practices for 5 decades. (②) The advice made me consider what it means to be mentally sharp. (③) Although our ability to learn and remember gradually declines throughout adulthood, there's mounting evidence that our skill at making sense of important information and experiences increases. (④) This is what's known as wisdom, and it's something that scientists are just beginning to study. (⑤) Its classic elements include sound judgment, psychological insight, long and diverse life experience, emotional control, empathetic understanding, and, of course, knowledge.

34 다음 글의 내용을 한 문장으로 나타낼 때, 빈칸 (A)와 (B)에 들어갈 말로 가장 적절한 것은?

> Average life expectancy has risen steadily for decades and except for cancers caused by smoking and exposure to the sun, cancer death rates have dropped or remained relatively stable. Yet surveys have repeatedly shown that people have never been more fretful about their health. "People just seem to see the apocalypse everywhere they turn," said Bruce Ames, who was among the first to point out that natural pesticides are at least 10,000 times

more common than those made by man. "There are some important risks, of course. But everyone should just relax a bit and have some fun." At times that seems hard to do. Provocative warnings about too much cholesterol, not enough vitamin A and what can happen to people who do not exercise enough have become part of the tapestry of American life. To some, cancer seems hidden in every meal.

Although Americans have become ___(A)___ than ever, they seem to be experiencing high levels of ___(B)___ about their health.

     (A)   (B)
① healthier   –   anxiety
② trendier   –   anxiety
③ healthier   –   hope
④ trendier   –   concern
⑤ slimmer   –   concern

35 주어진 글 다음에 이어질 글의 순서로 가장 적절한 것은?

Many people don't want to be travelers. They would rather be tourists, flitting over the surface of other people's lives while never really leaving their own.

[A] To be a real traveler, however, you must be willing to give yourself over to the moment and take yourself out of the center of your universe. You must believe totally in the lives of the people and the places where you find yourself.

[B] Become part of the fabric of their everyday lives. You will realize that the possibilities of life in this world are endless, and that beneath our differences of language and culture we all share the same dream of loving and being loved, of having a life with more joy than sorrow.

[C] They try to bring their world with them wherever they go, or try to recreate the world they left. They do not want to risk the security of their own understanding and see how small and limited their experiences really are.

① [A] – [C] – [B]   ② [B] – [A] – [C]
③ [B] – [C] – [A]   ④ [C] – [A] – [B]
⑤ [C] – [B] – [A]

[36~37] 다음 글을 읽고 물음에 답하시오.

Since 2008 Zsófia Virányi and her colleagues at the Wolf Science Center in Austria have been raising dogs and wolves to figure out what makes a dog a dog—and a wolf a wolf. "You can leave a piece of meat on a table and tell one of our dogs, 'No!' and he will not take it," Virányi says. "But the wolves ignore you. They'll look you in the eye and grab the meat." And when this happens, she wonders yet again how the wolf ever became (A) the domesticated dog. "You can't have an animal — a large carnivore — living with you and behaving like that," she says. "You want an animal that's like a dog: one that accepts 'No!'"

Dogs' understanding of the absolute no may be connected to the structure of (B) their packs, which are not egalitarian like those of the wolves but dictatorial, the center's researchers have discovered. Wolves can eat together, Virányi notes. Even if a dominant wolf flashes its teeth and growls at a subordinate, (C) the lower-ranked member does not move away. The same is not true in dog packs, however. "Subordinate dogs will rarely eat at the same time as the dominant one," she observes. "They don't even try." Their studies also suggest that rather than expecting to cooperate on tasks with humans, dogs simply want to be told what to do.

How the independent-minded, egalitarian wolf changed into (D) the obedient, waiting-for-orders pet and what role ancient humans played in achieving this feat baffle Virányi. She is not alone in her bafflement. Although researchers have successfully determined the time, location and ancestry of nearly every other domesticated species, from sheep to cattle to chickens to guinea pigs, they continue to debate these questions for (E) our best friend, *Canis familiaris*.

36 위 글의 밑줄 친 부분 중 그 의미하는 바가 나머지와 다른 하나는?

① (A)　　　　② (B)
③ (C)　　　　④ (D)
⑤ (E)

37 위 글의 내용과 일치하지 않는 것은?

① Virányi는 개와 늑대를 키우며 그들의 본질에 대해 연구한다.
② 늑대는 고기를 먹지 말라는 사람의 명령을 무시하고 먹는다.
③ 무리 중 강한 늑대가 약한 늑대에게 으르렁대면 약한 늑대는 먹이로부터 물러난다.
④ 무리 중 약한 개와 강한 개가 먹이를 동시에 먹는 일은 없다.
⑤ 양, 소, 닭이 가축화된 시간이나 장소는 알려져 있다.

[38~39] 다음 글을 읽고 물음에 답하시오.

Why do people try to make their expectations ＿＿＿＿＿ their best possible guess of the future, using all available information? The simplest explanation is that it is costly for people not to do so. Joe Commuter has a strong incentive to make his expectation of the time it takes him to drive to work as accurate as possible. If he underpredicts his driving time, he will often be late to work and risk being fired. If he overpredicts, he will, on average, get to work too early and will have given up sleep or leisure time unnecessarily. Accurate expectations are desirable, and the incentives are strong for people to try to make them equal to optimal forecasts by using all available information.

The same principle applies to businesses. Suppose that an appliance manufacturer knows that interest-rate movements are important to the sales of appliances. If the company makes poor forecasts of interest rates, it will earn less profit, because it might produce either too many appliances or too few. The incentives are strong for the company to acquire all available information to help it forecast interest rates and use the information to make the best possible guess of future interest-rate movements. The incentives for equating expectations with optimal forecasts are especially strong in financial markets. In these markets, people with better forecasts of the future get rich.

38 위 글의 제목으로 가장 적절한 것은?

① Set Your Goals As High As Possible

② Reap the Rewards of Optimal Predictions

③ Maximize Profit by Manipulating Interest Rates

④ The Gap Between Theory and Practice in Business

⑤ How Does Commuting Distance Affect Productivity?

39 위 글의 빈칸에 들어갈 말로 가장 적절한 것은? [3점]

① match ② exceed

③ negate ④ transform

⑤ underestimate

[40~42] 다음 글을 읽고 물음에 답하시오.

Motivation gains refer to circumstances that increase the effort expended by group members in a collective task. Motivational gains in which the less capable member works harder is known as the Köhler effect. In some investigations, athletes curled a bar attached to a pulley system until exhaustion. They did this first individually and then in groups of two. Motivation gains happened when the athlete pairs had moderately different abilities. __(A)__, motivation gains did not emerge when athletes had equal or very unequal abilities. It was the weaker member of the group who was responsible for the motivation gain. The psychological mechanisms underlying the Köhler effect are social comparison (particularly when someone thinks that their teammate is more capable) and the feeling that one's effort is indispensible to the group. Group members are willing to exert effort on a collective task when they expect their efforts to be instrumental in obtaining outcomes that they value personally. Moreover, in particular, the weakest member of a team is more likely to work harder when everyone is given feedback about people's performance in a timely fashion.

A more common observation in groups is motivation losses, also known as social loafing. A French agricultural engineer named Max Ringelmann was interested in the relative efficiency of farm labor supplied by horses, oxen, machines, and men. In particular, he was curious about their relative abilities to pull a load horizontally, such as in a tug-of-war. In one of his experiments, groups of 14 men pulled a load, and the amount of force they generated was measured. The force that each man could pull independently was also measured. There was a steady decline in the average pull-per-member as the size of the rope-pulling team increased. One person pulling on a rope alone exerted an average of 63 kilograms of force. (B) , in groups of three, the per-person force dropped to 53 kilograms, and in groups of eight, it plummeted to only 31 kilograms—less than half of the effort exerted by people working alone. This revealed a fundamental principle of teamwork: People in groups often do not work as hard as they do when alone.

40 위 글의 제목으로 적절한 것은?

① Mechanisms of a Tug of War

② Motivational Effects in Teamwork

③ How to Measure Work Efficiency

④ Boosting Motivation in Individual Tasks

⑤ Psychology Behind the Ringelmann Effect

41 위 글의 내용과 일치하지 <u>않는</u> 것은? [3점]

① The Köhler effect occurs when the less capable person works harder in a group.

② Motivation gains are likely to happen when working with people of the same ability.

③ The weakest member tends to work harder when timely feedback is provided.

④ Max Ringelmann studied the efficiency of labor between different groups.

⑤ Max Ringelmann found that people tend to expend less effort when working collectively.

42 위 글의 빈칸 (A)와 (B)에 들어갈 말로 가장 적절한 것은?

	(A)		(B)
①	Likewise	–	However
②	Instead	–	Meanwhile
③	Conversely	–	However
④	Conversely	–	As a result
⑤	Likewise	–	Meanwhile

[43~45] 다음 글을 읽고 물음에 답하시오.

Sheldon Cohen, a psychologist at Carnegie Mellon University, has intentionally given colds to hundreds of people. Under carefully controlled conditions, he systematically exposes volunteers to a rhinovirus that causes the common cold. About a third of people exposed to the virus develop the full panoply of symptoms, while the rest walk away with nary a sniffle.

On the first day, Cohen's experimental volunteers are quarantined for twenty-four hours before they are exposed, to be sure they have not picked up a cold elsewhere. For the next five days the volunteers are housed in a special unit with other volunteers, all of whom are kept at least three feet from one another, lest they reinfect someone. During those five days their nasal secretions are tested for technical indicators of colds (like the total weight of their mucus) as well as the presence of the specific rhinovirus, and their blood samples are tested for antibodies.

We know that low levels of vitamin C, smoking and sleeping poorly all increase the likelihood of infection. The question is, can a stressful relationship be added to that list? Cohen's answer: definitely. Cohen assigns precise numerical values to the factors that make one person come down with a cold while another stays healthy. Those with an ongoing personal conflict were 2.5 times as likely as the others to get a cold, putting rocky relationships in the same causal range

as vitamin C deficiency and poor sleep. Conflicts that lasted a month or longer boosted susceptibility, but an occasional argument presented no health hazard. While perpetual arguments are bad for our health, isolating ourselves is worse. Compared to those with a rich web of social connections, those with the fewest close relationships were 4.2 times more likely to come down with the cold.

The more we socialize, the less susceptible to colds we become. This idea seems counterintuitive: Don't we increase the likelihood of being exposed to a cold virus the more people we interact with? Sure. But vibrant social connections boost our good moods and limit our negative ones, suppressing cortisol and enhancing immune function under stress. Relationships themselves seem to _____ the risk of exposure to the very cold virus they pose.

43 위 글의 제목으로 가장 적절한 것은?

① The Nature of Antibiotic Metabolism in the Human Body

② Rhinovirus Exposure: A Methodology of Utmost Precision

③ The More Social Interactions, the More Severe the Cold

④ Uncommon Findings from the Common Cold Experiment

⑤ New Health Hazards Discovered in Cyberspace

2016 기출문제

44 빈칸에 들어가기에 가장 적절한 것은? [3점]

① be modified by

② push them to

③ be weakened by

④ protect us from

⑤ gradually increase

45 Cohen의 실험과 일치하는 것은?

① 첫날 피험자를 감기 바이러스에 노출시킨다.

② 총 5일 동안 진행된다.

③ 피험자간 신체적 접촉을 허용한다.

④ 코 분비물을 검사한다.

⑤ 혈액 샘플 검사는 생략한다.

KOREAN NATIONAL POLICE UNIVERSITY

경찰대학 기출문제

영 어

2025~2016

10 개년
연차별 동형
기출문제

정답 및 해설

빠른 정답찾기 🔍

2025 학년도

01 ①	02 ②	03 ③	04 ③	05 ①	06 ②	07 ④	08 ①	09 ④	10 ④
11 ③	12 ②	13 ⑤	14 ②	15 ④	16 ⑤	17 ②	18 ①	19 ①	20 ③
21 ④	22 ②	23 ①	24 ①	25 ③	26 ②	27 ⑤	28 ①	29 ④	30 ④
31 ⑤	32 ③	33 ⑤	34 ④	35 ④	36 ③	37 ①	38 ②	39 ④	40 ⑤
41 ③	42 ④	43 ③	44 ⑤	45 ⑤					

2024 학년도

01 ②	02 ①	03 ②	04 ①	05 ⑤	06 ③	07 ⑤	08 ①	09 ②	10 ④
11 ③	12 ③	13 ③	14 ④	15 ④	16 ⑤	17 ④	18 ②	19 ⑤	20 ⑤
21 ①	22 ③	23 ①	24 ②	25 ⑤	26 ⑤	27 ②	28 ④	29 ④	30 ③
31 ④	32 ②	33 ④	34 ⑤	35 ③	36 ③	37 ⑤	38 ④	39 ①	40 ①
41 ⑤	42 ①	43 ④	44 ②	45 ⑤					

2023 학년도

01 ④	02 ②	03 ①	04 ⑤	05 ⑤	06 ⑤	07 ③	08 ①	09 ③	10 ⑤
11 ④	12 ②	13 ①	14 ④	15 ③	16 ④	17 ⑤	18 ⑤	19 ③	20 ②
21 ③	22 ②	23 ②	24 ①	25 ①	26 ②	27 ③	28 ②	29 ①	30 ②
31 ③	32 ①	33 ③	34 ④	35 ④	36 ③	37 ⑤	38 ⑤	39 ②	40 ①
41 ④	42 ③	43 ④	44 ②	45 ①					

2022 학년도

01 ③	02 ⑤	03 ⑤	04 ①	05 ③	06 ④	07 ④	08 ①	09 ①	10 ③
11 ①	12 ②	13 ④	14 ④	15 ②	16 ④	17 ④	18 ④	19 ⑤	20 ⑤
21 ③	22 ⑤	23 ③	24 ①	25 ④	26 ①	27 ③	28 ②	29 ⑤	30 ③
31 ①	32 ③	33 ③	34 ③	35 ①	36 ⑤	37 ②	38 ②	39 ③	40 ⑤
41 ①	42 ②	43 ③	44 ②	45 ②					

2021 학년도

01 ②	02 ③	03 ②	04 ③	05 ④	06 ③	07 ⑤	08 ①	09 ①	10 ③
11 ⑤	12 ④	13 ⑤	14 ①	15 ③	16 ⑤	17 ②	18 ⑤	19 ⑤	20 ④
21 ①	22 ④	23 ②	24 ①	25 ⑤	26 ②	27 ①	28 ⑤	29 ③	30 ①
31 ②	32 ②	33 ③	34 ④	35 ①	36 ⑤	37 ⑤	38 ④	39 ④	40 ①
41 ③	42 ④	43 ③	44 ④	45 ③					

빠른 정답찾기

2020 학년도

01 ②	02 ⑤	03 ①	04 ①	05 ⑤	06 ④	07 ④	08 ⑤	09 ③	10 ④
11 ③	12 ③	13 ①	14 ③	15 ④	16 ②	17 ④	18 ①	19 ⑤	20 ①
21 ②	22 ③	23 ②	24 ⑤	25 ①	26 ③	27 ②	28 ②	29 ⑤	30 ③
31 ②	32 ①	33 ④	34 ①	35 ③	36 ④	37 ③	38 ⑤	39 ⑤	40 ④
41 ⑤	42 ②	43 ②	44 ①	45 ③					

2019 학년도

01 ④	02 ⑤	03 ④	04 ①	05 ②	06 ④	07 ⑤	08 ③	09 ④	10 ⑤
11 ③	12 ⑤	13 ⑤	14 ③	15 ⑤	16 ⑤	17 ①	18 ②	19 ⑤	20 ②
21 ④	22 ①	23 ③	24 ②	25 ①	26 ④	27 ②	28 ①	29 ②	30 ⑤
31 ③	32 ④	33 ①	34 ①	35 ③	36 ④	37 ③	38 ④	39 ②	40 ①
41 ⑤	42 ①	43 ③	44 ③	45 ③					

2018 학년도

01 ②	02 ①	03 ④	04 ①	05 ④	06 ②	07 ⑤	08 ⑤	09 ②	10 ④
11 ④	12 ②	13 ①	14 ④	15 ⑤	16 ⑤	17 ③	18 ③	19 ①	20 ⑤
21 ①	22 ⑤	23 ①	24 ④	25 ①	26 ③	27 ③	28 ②	29 ⑤	30 ②
31 ③	32 ②	33 ①	34 ④	35 ②	36 ⑤	37 ④	38 ③	39 ①	40 ⑤
41 ⑤	42 ①	43 ③	44 ③	45 ③					

2017 학년도

01 ①	02 ③	03 ①	04 ①	05 ⑤	06 ④	07 ②	08 ②	09 ①	10 ③
11 ④	12 ②	13 ④	14 ②	15 ⑤	16 ⑤	17 ⑤	18 ④	19 ②	20 ③
21 ①	22 ①	23 ③	24 ④	25 ③	26 ③	27 ①	28 ②	29 ⑤	30 ②
31 ⑤	32 ④	33 ④	34 ④	35 ④	36 ③	37 ①	38 ④	39 ②	40 ②
41 ④	42 ②	43 ②	44 ③	45 ④					

2016 학년도

01 ①	02 ①	03 ⑤	04 ②	05 ④	06 ④	07 ④	08 ⑤	09 ①	10 ③
11 ④	12 ④	13 ④	14 ①	15 ③	16 ⑤	17 ⑤	18 ⑤	19 ①	20 ⑤
21 ①	22 ②	23 ②	24 ⑤	25 ⑤	26 ②	27 ⑤	28 ③	29 ③	30 ②
31 ③	32 ③	33 ②	34 ①	35 ④	36 ③	37 ③	38 ②	39 ①	40 ②
41 ②	42 ③	43 ④	44 ④	45 ④					

2025학년도 기출문제 정답 및 해설

2025학년도

[영어]

정답 및 해설

▌[영어] 2025학년도 | 정답

01	①	02	②	03	③	04	③	05	①
06	②	07	④	08	①	09	④	10	④
11	③	12	②	13	⑤	14	②	15	④
16	⑤	17	②	18	①	19	①	20	③
21	④	22	②	23	①	24	①	25	③
26	②	27	⑤	28	①	29	④	30	④
31	⑤	32	①	33	⑤	34	④	35	⑤
36	①	37	①	38	②	39	⑤	40	⑤
41	③	42	④	43	③	44	⑤	45	⑤

[영어] 2025학년도 | 해설

01   유사 어휘 고르기   ①

[정답해설]

'sacred'는 '신성한, 성스러운'의 뜻으로, 'holy(신성한, 경건한)'와 그 의미가 가장 유사하다.

[오답해설]

② 기이한

③ 요구가 많은

④ 실용적인

⑤ 흔하지 않은

[핵심어휘]

▫ violate 어기다, 위반하다

▫ profession 직업, 전문직

▫ sacred 신성한, 성스러운

▫ holy 신성한, 경건한

▫ weird 기이한, 기괴한

▫ demanding 요구가 많은, 부담이 큰

▫ uncommon 굉장한, 흔하지 않은

[본문해석]

그는 직업에서 가장 신성한 규칙 중의 하나를 위반했다.

02   유사 어휘 고르기   ②

[정답해설]

'assess'는 '평가하다, 사정하다'의 뜻으로, 'evaluate(평가하다, 감정하다)'와 그 의미가 가장 유사하다.

[오답해설]

① 개선하다

③ 극대화하다

④ 협상하다

⑤ 과대평가하다

[핵심어휘]

▫ assess 평가하다, 사정하다

▫ belongings 재산, 소유물

▫ evaluate 평가하다, 감정하다

▫ negotiate 협상하다, 성사시키다

▫ overestimate 과대평가하다

[본문해석]

그들에게 당신의 재산 가치를 평가하는 방법에 대한 정보를 보내달라고 요청하세요.

03 　　　　유사 어휘 고르기　　　　③

[정답해설]

'despair'는 '절망, 자포자기'의 뜻으로, 'hopelessness(절망, 가망 없음)'와 그 의미가 가장 유사하다.

[오답해설]

① 분노

② 후회

④ 동정

⑤ 만족

[핵심어휘]

▫ despair 절망, 자포자기

▫ miner 광부

▫ be forced to ~하도록 강요당하다

▫ regret 후회, 유감

▫ hopelessness 절망, 가망 없음

▫ sympathy 동정, 공감

▫ contentment 만족, 안도감

[본문해석]

광부들이 강제로 일해야 하는 상황에서 그녀는 절망에 휩싸였다.

04 　　　　유사 어휘 고르기　　　　③

[정답해설]

'obvious'는 '분명한, 확실한'의 뜻으로, 'evident(분명한, 눈에 띄는)'와 그 의미가 가장 유사하다.

[오답해설]

① 추상적인

② 보이지 않는

④ 풍부한

⑤ 다루기 힘든

[핵심어휘]

▫ tire track 타이어 자국

▫ obvious 분명한, 확실한

▫ abstract 추상적인, 관념적인

▫ invisible 보이지 않는, 무형의

▫ evident 분명한, 눈에 띄는

▫ plentiful 많은, 풍부한

▫ unruly 다루기 힘든, 제멋대로 구는

[본문해석]

눈 속에 새로 생긴 타이어 자국은 누군가 최근에 이 시골길을 운전했다는 확실한 증거였다.

05 　　　　유사 어휘 고르기　　　　①

[정답해설]

'valid'는 '유효한, 타당한'의 뜻으로, 'reasonable(타당한, 합당한)'과 그 의미가 가장 유사하다.

[오답해설]

② 부적절한

③ 다수의

④ 귀중한

⑤ 믿을 수 없는

[핵심어휘]

▫ valid 유효한, 타당한

▫ delay 지연, 지체

▫ delivering 배달, 배송

▫ reasonable 타당한, 합당한

▫ unsound 부적절한, 건전하지 못한

▫ multiple 많은, 다수의

▫ invaluable 매우 유용한, 귀중한

▫ incredible 믿을 수 없는, 믿기 힘든

[본문해석]

그 회사는 고객에게 제품 배송이 늦은 타당한 이유를 제시했다.

06 　　　　빈칸 추론하기　　　　②

[정답해설]

새로운 취미를 배워볼 생각을 해 본 적이 있냐는 A의 물음에 B가 새로운 것을 시작하기에는 너무 나이가 든 거 같다고 망설이고 있다. 그러자 A가 전 연령대의 사람들이 새로운 것을 배우는 것을 보았다며 B를 독려하고 있다. 그러므로 빈칸에 들어갈 말로는 ②의 'it's never too late to learn(배우기에 너무 늦지 않았어)'이 가장 적절하다.

[오답해설]

① 연습이 완벽을 만든다

③ 백지장도 맞들면 낫다

④ 결코 겉모습만 보고 판단하지 마라

⑤ 학문에 왕도는 없다

[핵심어휘]

- pick up 알게 되다, 익히게 되다
- plenty of 많은, 풍부한
- inspire 고무하다, 영감을 주다
- encouragement 격려, 고무
- give it a shot 한번 시도해 봐, 한번 해 봐
- royal road 왕도, 지름길

[본문해석]

A: 새로운 취미를 배워볼 생각을 해본 적이 있니?

B: 모르겠어. 새로운 것을 시작하기에는 너무 나이가 든 거 같아.

A: 전혀! 항상 해보고 싶었던 것이 뭐야?

B: 음, 나는 항상 피아노를 배우고 싶었어.

A: 좋은 생각이네! 성인 초보자를 위한 자료가 많이 있어. 온라인 수업으로 시작하거나 현지 수업에서 찾을 수 있지.

B: 네 말이 맞는 거 같아. 생각해볼게.

A: 전 연령대의 사람들이 새로운 것을 배우는 것을 봤어. 그건 매우 고무적이야. 명심해. 배우기에 너무 늦지 않았어.

B: 격려해 줘서 고마워! 한 번 해볼게!

07 빈칸 추론하기 ④

[정답해설]

주말 계획에 대해 이야기하던 중에 B가 하이킹 외에 다른 계획도 있냐고 물었고, A가 기다려온 신작 스릴러를 읽으려고 한다고 답하였다. 그러므로 빈칸에 들어갈 말로는 ④의 'Let me know how the book turns out(책의 결과가 어떻게 되었는지 알려줘)'이 가장 적절하다.

[오답해설]

① 밖에서 더 자주 놀자

② 하이킹은 내가 가장 좋아하는 활동이야

③ 산에서 만나자

⑤ 내일 다른 계획을 세워볼게

[핵심어휘]

- be up to ~하고 있다
- chill 느긋한 시간을 보내다
- It's been a while. 오랜만이야, 간만이야
- awesome 굉장한, 기막히게 좋은
- clear one's head 머리를 식히다
- catch up on ~을 따라잡다, 만회하다
- turn out (일·진행·결과가 특정 방식으로) 되다[되어 가다]

[본문해석]

A: 이번 주말에 뭐 할 거니?

B: 아마 집에서 그냥 쉬고 있을 걸. 너는?

A: 하이킹을 갈까 생각 중이야. 오랜만에.

B: 어디로 갈 건데?

A: 산에서 기막히게 멋진 경치를 볼 수 있는 좋은 곳을 찾았어.

B: 멋지다! 혼자 가니?

A: 응, 머리 식힐 시간이 필요해.

B: 이해해. 하이킹 외에 다른 계획도 있니?

A: 책을 좀 읽을까 해. 기다려온 신작 스릴러가 있어.

B: 완벽한 주말이 되겠구나! 책의 결과가 어떻게 되었는지 알려줘.

A: 알았어.

08 어법상 틀린 것 고르기 ①

[정답해설]

settling down → settled down

settling down은 앞의 my grandparents를 주어로 하는 본동사이므로, 분사가 아닌 동사의 형태로 써야 한다. 앞 문장에서 조동사 'would'가 과거 시제이므로 시제의 흐름상 settling down은 settled down으로 고쳐 써야 옳다.

[핵심어휘]

- summer break 여름방학
- worship room 예배실
- stone idol 석상
- throne 왕좌, 왕위
- prayer beads 묵주, 염주
- chant 찬송하다, 기도문을 읊조리다
- in a whisper 속삭이며, 귓속말로
- meditation session 명상 시간
- communion 영적 교감[교섭]
- a higher power (전지전능한) 하느님, 신
- a body of evidence 일련의 증거
- aging-related 노화와 관련된
- cognitive decline 인지력 감퇴
- enhance 높이다, 향상시키다
- cope with ~에 대처[대항]하다
- millennia 천년 간의, 천년 왕국의
- quest 탐구, 탐색
- enlightenment 깨달음, 교화, 계몽
- in parallel with ~와 병행하여
- awareness 인식, 의식
- relief 완화, 경감

[본문해석]

인도에서 성장한 나는 여름 방학에 콜카타에 있는 조부모님 댁을 방문하곤 했다. 매일 오후 할머니는 가족 예배실을 마주본 채 바닥 매트에 앉아 있었는데, 그곳에는 작은 나무 왕좌에 앉아 있는 힌두교 신들의 석상들이 있었다. 30분 동안 할머니는 가만히 앉아 눈을 감고 손가락으로 묵주를 굴리며 크리슈나의 이름을 속삭이듯 찬송했다. 이러한 명상의 시간이 할머니가 신과 교감하는 데 도움이 되었는지 객관적으로 알 수는 없지만, 일련의 과학적 증거에 따르면 할머니는 여러 방식으로 명상을 통해 도움을 받았으리라 생각된다. 이러한 습관은 할머니가 스트레스를 관리하는 효과적인 방법이었을 것이다. 또한 노화와 관련된 인지력 감퇴를 늦추는 데도 도움이 되었을 것이다. 통증에 대처하는 능력도 역시 향상되었을 것이다. 현 순간에 주의를 집중하는 운동으로 가장 폭넓게 정의되는 명상은 영적 깨달음을 추구하는 데 뿌리를 둔 전 세계의 종교적 전통에 의해 수천 년 동안 어떤 형태로든 수행되어 왔다. 오늘날 명상의 인기는 정신 건강과 스트레스 완화의 중요성에 대한 인식과 함께 높아지고 있다.

09 어법상 틀린 것 고르기 ④

[정답해설]

take → to take

make(사역동사) + 목적어 + 동사원형 구문이 수동태가 되면 be made + to 부정사가 된다. 그러므로 'are made take'는 'are made to take'가 되어야 하므로 'take'를 'to take'로 고쳐 써야 옳다.

[핵심어휘]

- aggression 공격, 공격성
- not one 하나가 아닌, 별개의
- aggressive 공격적인
- equally 동일하게, 마찬가지로
- biologically 생물학적으로
- obvious 분명한, 명백한
- burst 폭발, 터뜨림
- psychologist 심리학자
- construct 형성하다, 구성하다
- temperamentally 기질적으로, 성질상
- prone to ~을 잘 하는, ~의 경향이 있는
- extent 정도, 크기
- proportion 부분, 비율
- anger management 분노 조절

[본문해석]

분노는 분명히 공격성과 관련이 있지만 그것들은 별개이며 동일하지 않다. 화를 내지 않고 공격적인 것이 가능하며 마찬가지로 공격적이지 않고 화를 내는 것도 가능하다. 그러나 이 두 가지(분노의 감정과 공격적인 행동)는 연결되어 있으며 분명한 존재 가치가 있는 생물학적 기초에 기반을 두고 있다. 분노는 항상 에너지 폭발을 훨씬 더 많이 초래하며, 생물학적인 기반을 두고 있음에도 불구하고 일부 심리학자들은 대개 사회적으로 형성된 것으로 보고 있다. 즉, 어떤 사람들은 다른 사람들보다 기질적으로 화를 더 잘 낼 수도 있지만, 이를 표현하는 정도는 아마도 사회적으로 결정된다는 것이다. 예를 들어, 우리 문화에서 사내아이들이 여자아이들보다 더 공개적으로 분노를 표현해도 무방하며, 여자들보다 남자들이 훨씬 더 많은 비율로 분노 조절 학습을 받도록 하고 있다. 이것은 생물학적 차이가 아니라 학습에 의한 차이이다.

10 문맥에 맞는 낱말 고르기 ④

[정답해설]

(A) contrast / (B) maintain / (C) diverse

(A) 앞 문장에서는 인종과 집단의 차이를 없애는 용광로라는 개념에 대해 설명하고 있고, 뒤의 문장에서는 삶에 즐거움을 주는 다양성이란 상반된 개념에 대해 설명하고 있다. 그러므로 빈칸에 들어갈 말로는 'contrast(대조)'가 적절하다.

(B) 다양한 집단이 모여 사는 미국은 그 집단이 자신의 문화유산을 보존거나 아니면 새로운 문화에 동화되는 것을 선택할 수 있다고 설명하고 있다. 그러므로 빈칸에 들어갈 말로는 'maintain(유지하다)'이 적절하다.

(C) 미국은 여러 문화가 혼합된 다문화적인 공통 문화가 존재한다고 설명하고 있다. 그러므로 빈칸에 들어갈 말로는 'diverse(다양한)'가 적절하다.

[핵심어휘]

- decade 10년
- cultural pluralism 문화적 다원성, 문화 다원주의
- recognize 알아보다, 인정하다
- in contrast to ~와 대조적으로, ~와 달리
- melting pot 용광로, 도가니
- erase 지우다, 없애다
- ethnic 민족의, 종족의
- spice of life 삶의 즐거움, 흥미
- shelter 피난처, 안식처
- maintain 지탱하다, 유지하다
- reform 개혁하다, 개선하다
- heritage 유산
- assimilate 동화되다, 흡수하다

정답 및 해설

- as is often the case 흔히 있는 일이지만
- norm 표준, 규범, 기준
- unique 독특한, 고유의
- subsidiary 부수적인, 부차적인
- immigrant 이민자
- slave and free 노예와 해방
- descendant 자손, 후손
- blending 혼합, 혼성
- diverse 다양한, 가지각색의
- paradoxical 역설적인, 모순적인
- multicultural 다문화의, 여러 문화가 공존하는

[본문해석]

최근 수십 년 간의 정치적, 사회적 변화의 결과로 문화 다원주의는 이제 일반적으로 이 사회의 조직 원리로 인정되고 있다. 인종과 집단의 차이를 없애겠다고 약속했던 용광로 개념과 (A) 대조적으로, 이제 아이들은 다양성이 삶의 즐거움이란 것을 안다. 그들은 미국이 다양한 집단에게 안식처를 제공하고 문화유산을 (B) 유지하거나 동화할 수 있도록 해주었으며, 흔히 있는 일이지만 둘 다 할 수도 있다는 것을 안다. 선택은 국가가 아닌 그들의 몫이다. 그들은 문화 다원주의가 자유 사회의 규범 중 하나이며, 집단 간의 차이는 해결해야 할 문제가 아니라 국가적 자원이라는 것을 안다. 실제로 미국의 독특한 특징은 그것의 공통 문화가 부차적인 문화의 상호작용에 의해 형성되었다는 것이다. 이민자, 아메리칸 인디언, 아프리카인(노예와 해방), 그리고 그 후손들에 의해 시간이 흘러 영향을 받은 문화이다. 미국의 음악, 예술, 문학, 언어, 음식, 의복, 스포츠, 휴일, 관습은 모두 한 국가에서 (C) 다양한 문화가 혼합된 효과를 보여준다. 모순처럼 보일 수도 있지만, 미국에는 다문화적인 공통 문화가 존재한다.

11 문맥에 맞는 낱말 고르기 ③

[정답해설]

(A) reverses / (B) exercising / (C) inseparability

(A) "지식은 권력이다"라는 문구가 지식과 권력의 관계를 나타내는 통속적인 표현인데, Foucault는 "권력은 지식이다"라는 문구를 통해 권력을 부여하는 것은 지식이 아니라고 주장하고 있다. 그러므로 빈칸에 들어갈 말로는 'reverses(뒤집다)'가 적절하다.

(B) Foucault의 분석에 따르면 "권력은 지식이다"라고 말해야만 할 정도로 지식은 이미 큰 권력을 부여받았다고 서술하고 있다. 즉, 지식은 권력을 수행하기 위한 구체적인 수단이 되므로, 빈칸에 들어갈 말로는 'exercising(행사하는)'이 적절하다.

(C) 지식은 결코 권력과 분리된 것이 아니라 권력을 행사하기 위한 구체적인 수단이며, 이 둘의 관계는 권력/지식이라는 용어로 표현될 정도로 철저하게 결합되어 있다고 서술하고 있다. 그러므로 빈칸에 들어갈 말로는 'inseparability(불가분성)'가 적절하다.

[핵심어휘]

- interrelationship 연관성, 상호관계
- phrase 구절, 관용구
- genealogical 족보의, 계보의
- confirm 확인하다, 확신하다
- reverse 뒤바꾸다, 뒤집다
- contend 주장하다, 다투다
- acquisition 습득, 획득
- invest with ~을 부여하다
- analysis 분석
- embody 상징하다, 포함하다
- brute 야만적인, 비인간적인
- coercion 강제, 강압
- potent 센, 강한, 강력한
- translate into ~으로 번역하다
- reflection 반사, 반영
- inseparability 불리할 수 없음, 불가분성
- separability 나눌 수 있음, 분리성
- thoroughgoing 철저한, 철두철미한
- conjoin 결합하다, 묶다

[본문해석]

지식과 권력 사이의 상호관계에 대한 통속적인 이해는 흔히 "지식은 권력이다"라는 문구를 통해 표현된다. Foucault는 계보학 연구에서 이 표현의 논리를 (A) 뒤집는다. 그는 사람에게 권력을 부여하는 것은 지식의 습득이 아니라고 주장한다. 대신에 "권력은 지식이다"라고 말해야만 할 정도로 지식은 이미 항상 큰 권력을 부여받았다. 따라서 Foucault의 분석에 따르면, 지식은 결코 권력과 분리된 것이 아니라 권력을 (B) 행사하기 위한 구체적인 수단이다. 이렇듯이 권력은 단순히 한 개인이나 사회 구조 안에서 구현되고 비인간적인 강제나 처벌로 표현되는 것이 아니다. 권력은 "지식"의 체계로 성공적으로 번역되고 그에 따라 명백한 진실의 베일 하에 반성에서 벗어날 때 가장 강력한 형태로 나타난다. Foucault에 따르면 권력과 지식의 (C) 불가분성은 너무나 철저해서 그는 종종 이 둘을 권력/지식이라는 용어로 묶는다.

12	문맥상 부적절한 낱말 고르기	②

[정답해설]

broadens → narrows 또는 diminishes

제시문은 기업 간의 경쟁이 제품과 서비스에 혁신을 가져다준다는 일반적인 생각과 달리, 장기적인 관점에서 보면 개방성과 연결성이 순수한 경쟁 메커니즘보다 혁신에 더 가치가 있다는 내용이다. 그러므로 표준 교과서처럼 개인과 조직의 규모에서 혁신을 분석하는 것은 우리의 관점을 좁게 한다고 볼 수 있다. 따라서 ②의 'broadens(넓히다)'는 'narrows(좁히다)' 또는 'diminishes(축소하다)'로 고쳐 써야 옳다.

[핵심어휘]

▫ long-zoom perspective 장기적인 관점
▫ broaden 넓히다, 확장하다
▫ overstate 과장하다, 허풍 떨다
▫ proprietary 독점의, 전매의
▫ survival of the fittest 적자생존
▫ connectivity 연결(성)
▫ purely 순전히, 전적으로
▫ recognition 인정, 인식
▫ intrinsically 본질적으로
▫ emerge 나타나다, 출현하다
▫ embrace 받아들이다, 수용하다
▫ nurture 양육하다, 육성하다

[본문해석]

모든 경제 교과서는 경쟁 기업 간의 경쟁이 제품과 서비스의 혁신으로 이어진다고 말한다. 하지만 장기적 관점에서 혁신을 살펴보면, 경쟁은 우리가 일반적으로 생각하는 것보다 좋은 아이디어의 역사에서 그다지 중심적인 역할을 하지 못하는 것으로 나타났다. 표준 교과서처럼 개인과 조직의 규모에서 혁신을 분석하면 우리의 관점은 넓어진다(→ 좁아진다). 그것은 독점적 연구와 "적자생존"이란 경쟁의 역할을 과장하는 혁신의 그림을 만들어낸다. 장기적인 접근에서 보면 개방성과 연결성이 결국 순수한 경쟁 메커니즘보다 혁신에 더 가치가 있음을 알 수 있다. 이러한 혁신의 패턴은 부분적으로 좋은 아이디어가 역사적으로 나타나는 이유를 이해하는 것이 본질적으로 중요하기 때문에, 그리고 부분적으로 이러한 패턴을 수용함으로써 학교든, 정부든, 사회 운동이든 간에 좋은 아이디어를 더 잘 육성할 수 있는 환경을 구축할 수 있기 때문에 인정받을 만하다. 창의성을 가능하게 하는 많은 관련 환경에 마음을 열면 더 창의적으로 생각할 수 있다.

13	문맥상 부적절한 낱말 고르기	⑤

[정답해설]

disadvantage → advantage

Edgar Allan Poe가 창시한 현대 단편 소설의 스토리텔링 방식은 작가가 가장 친밀하고 극단적인 방식으로 신비로운 인간의 마음을 탐구할 수 있도록 한다는 것이다. 즉, 이것은 단점이 아닌 장점에 해당하므로, ⑤의 'disadvantage(단점)'는 'advantage(장점)'로 고쳐 써야 옳다.

[핵심어휘]

▫ lengthy 너무 긴, 장황한
▫ fable 우화, 꾸며낸 이야기
▫ realistic 현실적인, 사실적인
▫ concentrate on ~에 집중하다
▫ have to do with ~와 관계가 있다
▫ abnormal 비정상적인
▫ involving 관련된, 연루된
▫ murder 살인, 살해
▫ narrate 이야기 하다, 서술하다
▫ disturbing 충격적인, 불안감을 주는
▫ vivid 생생한, 활발한
▫ aggressor 공격자, 침략자
▫ give account of ~을 설명하다, 이야기 하다
▫ disadvantage 약점, 단점
▫ intimate 친한, 친밀한
▫ extreme 극도의, 심각한

[본문해석]

장황한 소개가 필요 없는 미국의 위대한 작가 Edgar Allan Poe는 현대 단편 소설을 창시한 작가 중 한 명이다. 현대 단편 소설은 이야기를 현대의 사실적인 배경 위에 설정할 뿐만 아니라 그 형식이 하나의 극적인 사건에 집중한다는 점에서 이전의 이야기나 우화의 형식과는 다르다. Poe의 경우, 이 단일 사건은 전형적으로 죽음과 살인에 연루된 비정상적인 행위와 매우 자주 관련이 있다. Poe의 혁신은 살인자 자신의 관점에서 그러한 충격적인 사건을 서술하는 것이었으므로, Poe의 단편 소설을 읽는 독자는 그가 어떻게 범행을 저질렀는지 상세히 설명하기 위해 세심한 주의를 기울이는 공격자의 생생한 목소리를 들어야만 했다. 이러한 스토리텔링 방식의 단점(→ 장점)은 작가가 가장 친밀하고 극단적인 방식으로 신비로운 것, 즉 인간의 마음을 탐구할 수 있도록 한다는 것이다.

14   내용과 불일치 문장 고르기   ②

[정답해설]

글의 서두에서 Virgil의 거장다운 시는 그에게 가장 위대한 라틴어 시인이라는 유산을 남겼고, 중세와 르네상스 시대에 걸쳐 그의 명성이 더욱 높아갔다고 서술되어 있다. 그러므로 르네상스 시대 동안 그의 명성이 쇠퇴했다는 ②의 설명은 제시문의 내용과 일치하지 않는다.

[오답해설]

① 라틴어로 된 그의 능숙한 시들은 그를 유명한 시인으로 만들었다.
→ Virgil의 거장다운 시는 그에게 가장 위대한 라틴어 시인이라는 유산을 남김

③ 그는 다양한 언어로 된 시에 영향을 미쳤다. → 이탈리아어로 단테, 영어로 밀턴, Aeneid를 중세 로망스 Le Roman d'Eneas로 재작업한 무명의 프랑스 시인을 포함하여 언어별로 시인들에게 영감을 줌

④ 그의 시는 인간의 감정을 명확하게 표현했다. → 르네상스 시대의 작가들 사이에서 Virgil은 인간의 감정을 생생하게 묘사한 것으로 평가받음

⑤ 그의 시는 현대 비평가들로부터 Homer의 시보다 좋게 평가받지 못했다. → 대부분의 현대 학자들은 Vigril의 시가 Homer의 시에 비하면 무색할 정도라고 생각함

[핵심어휘]

- masterful 거장다운, 훌륭한
- poetry 시, 시가, 운문
- legacy 유산
- printing press 인쇄기
- transmit 전송하다, 전달하다
- scribe (인쇄술이 발명되기 전의) 필경사
- scarce 부족한, 드문
- literate 글을 쓰고 읽을 수 있는, 문학상의
- significant 의미심장한, 중요한
- anonymous 익명의, 무명의
- rework 고치다, 다시 하다
- pagan 이교도, 비기독교도
- prophet 선지자, 예언자
- prediction 예측, 예견
- appreciate 인정하다, 평가하다
- vivid 생생한, 활발한
- portrayal 묘사, 형용
- predecessor 전임자, 선임자
- epic 서사시, 서사문학
- contemporary 동시대의, 현대의
- hold that ~라 생각[주장]하다
- pale in comparison to ~앞에서 무색해지다, ~에 비해 못하다
- reputation 명성, 평판
- decline 쇠퇴, 하락

[본문해석]

Virgil의 거장다운 시는 그에게 가장 위대한 라틴어 시인이라는 유산을 남겼다. 중세와 르네상스 시대에 걸쳐, 그의 명성은 더욱 높아갔다. 인쇄기가 발명되기 전, 필경사들의 손으로 전달되는 고전 텍스트가 부족했던 시기에 Virgil의 시는 문학 계층이 이용했고, 그들 중에서도 그는 고대의 가장 중요한 작가로 여겨졌다. 그는 이탈리아어로 단테, 영어로 밀턴, Aeneid를 중세 로망스 Le Roman d'Eneas로 재작업한 무명의 프랑스 시인을 포함하여 언어별로 시인들에게 영감을 주었다. 기독교 문화 시대에, Virgil은 작품의 여러 대사가 그리스도의 도래를 예언하는 것으로 해석되어 이교도 예언자로 여겨졌다. 르네상스 시대의 작가들 사이에서 Virgil은 인간의 감정을 생생하게 묘사한 것으로 평가받았다. 반면 현대 비평가들은 그리 호의적이지 않았다. Virgil의 시는 특히 트로이 전쟁을 묘사한 Homer의 서사시인 일리아드와 오디세이 등, 그리스 전임자들의 시와 연관지어 자주 평가된다. 대부분의 현대 학자들은 Vigril의 시가 Homer의 시에 비하면 무색할 정도라고 생각한다.

15   내용과 일치하는 문장 고르기   ④

[정답해설]

제시문에 따르면 Alice는 몸이 너무 약해서 글을 쓸 수조차 없었고, 그녀의 절친한 친구인 Loring이 Alice를 위해 그녀의 말을 글로 적었다고 서술되어 있다. 그러므로 그녀는 자신의 생각을 받아 적은 글을 남겼다는 ④의 설명은 제시문의 내용과 일치한다.

[오답해설]

① 그녀는 케임브리지의 하층민 가정 출신이다. → 그녀의 가족은 매사추세츠 주 케임브리지에서 유명한 존경받는 가정임

② 그녀는 식구 중 맏이였다. → 그녀는 두 오빠를 둔 막내딸임

③ 그녀의 오빠들은 명성을 얻지 못했다. → 그녀의 오빠들인 Henry James는 소설가로, William James는 철학자로 중요한 인물들이며 공적인 경력에서 점점 더 성공을 거두고 있음

⑤ 그녀의 일기장은 다른 여성들에 대한 연민으로 가득했다. → 그녀의 일기는 다른 여성들에 대한 연민이 아니라 자기 연민으로 채워져 있음

[핵심어휘]

- be classified as ~로서 분류되다
- figure 인물
- mental breakdown 신경쇠약, 정신분열
- numerous 많은, 다수의
- in the meantime 그 동안에, 그 사이에
- public career 공인으로서의 경력
- journal 저널, 일기
- appreciate 이해하다, 인식하다
- self-pity 자기 연민
- uniquely 특별히, 독특하게

- feminine 여성
- reputation 명성, 평판
- dictate 받아쓰게 하다, 구술하다

[본문해석]

Alice James는 항상 유명인의 여동생 또는 동생으로 분류된다. 그녀의 두 오빠들인 소설가 Henry James와 철학자 William James는 그들의 분야에서 중요한 인물들이다. 그녀의 가족은 본래 매사추세츠 주 케임브리지에서 유명하고 존경받는 가정이었다. 하지만 막내딸인 Alice는 16살에 첫 정신분열을 일으킨 이후로 문제가 있었다. 그녀는 또한 많은 건강 문제를 겪었다. 그 사이에 오빠들은 공적인 경력에서 점점 더 성공을 거두고 있었다. Alice James는 마흔네 살의 나이에 세상을 떠났지만, 그녀는 인생의 마지막 3년 동안 자신의 생각에 대한 가장 흥미로운 기록을 남겼다. 그러나 그녀는 몸이 너무 약해서 글을 쓸 수조차 없었다. 그녀의 절친한 친구인 K. P. Loring은 Alice를 위해 그녀의 말을 글로 적었다. Loring은 또한 Alice의 오빠들과 자신을 위해 그녀의 일기를 인쇄했다. 그녀의 일기를 읽는 데 있어 어려움은 분노, 자기연민, 그리고 물론 필자가 느끼는 고통의 혼합을 이해하는 것이었다. 또한 당시 여성들은 남성 의사들이 연구하고 치료해야 할 "사례" 또는 "문제"로 간주되는 경우가 많았기 때문에 그녀의 일기는 독특한 여성적 경험이었다는 점도 기억해야 한다.

16 내용과 일치하는 문장 고르기 ⑤

[정답해설]

제시문의 마지막 문장에서 Nagel은 1960년대 록펠러 대학에서의 1년을 제외하고, 컬럼비아 대학에서 과학 철학을 가르치고 글을 쓰며 철학에 대한 논리학의 중심적 역할을 설명하는 데 경력을 보냈다고 서술되어 있다. 그러므로 Nagel이 컬럼비아 대학에서 경력의 대부분을 보냈다는 ⑤의 설명은 제시문의 내용과 일치한다.

[오답해설]

① Cohen은 체코슬로바키아에서 태어났다. → Cohen은 러시아에서 태어남
② Cohen은 1941년까지 뉴욕 시립 대학에서 가르쳤다. → 1912년부터 1938년까지는 시립 대학에서, 1938년부터 1941년까지는 시카고 대학교에서 가르침
③ Cohen은 오직 논리학에 대한 주목으로 유명했다. → 논리학과 과학 철학에 대한 주목으로 유명함
④ Nagel은 1931년에 하버드 대학에서 박사 학위를 받았다. → Nagel은 1931년에 컬럼비아 대학에서 박사 학위를 받음

[핵심어휘]

- transition 이행, 전환
- analytic philosophy 분석철학

- mediate 영향을 주다, 가능하게 하다
- committed 헌신적인, 열정적인
- naturalist 자연주의자, 동물물 연구가
- with the exception of ~은 제외하고
- centrality 중심적 역할[위치]

[본문해석]

미국의 분석철학으로의 전환은 몇몇 중요한 인물, 기관, 사건들에 의해 가능하게 되었다. 그 중 한 명은 Morris Cohen(1880–1947)이었다. 러시아에서 태어난 그는 뉴욕 시립 대학에서 교육을 받았다. 1905년 하버드에서 박사 학위를 받은 그는 1912년부터 1938년까지 시립 대학에서, 그리고 1938년부터 1941년까지 시카고 대학교에서 가르쳤다. 논리학과 과학 철학에 대한 주목으로 유명해진 그는 철학에서 지식을 얻을 수 있는 비과학적 방법을 인정하지 않는 헌신적인 자연주의자였다. 그의 제자 중 한 명은 체코슬로바키아 태생의 Ernest Nagel이며, 시립 대학에서 학사 학위를 받은 후 1931년 컬럼비아 대학에서 박사 학위를 받았다. 1960년대 록펠러 대학에서의 1년을 제외하고, 그는 컬럼비아 대학에서 과학 철학을 가르치고 글을 쓰며 철학에 대한 논리학의 중심적 역할을 설명하는 데 경력을 보냈다.

17 빈칸 추론하기 ②

[정답해설]

제시문에서 남북전쟁에 대한 상반된 보도를 접했던 Osborne은 역사 기록이 반드시 믿을 만한 사실이 아닐 수도 있음을 경험했고, 그의 아들이 신뢰할 수 없는 역사를 공부하는데 시간을 낭비할 수도 있다고 염려하고 있다. 그러므로 빈칸에 들어갈 말은 ②의 'reliability(신뢰성)'이다.

[오답해설]

① 연속성
③ 재발견
④ 간결함
⑤ 예측 가능성

[핵심어휘]

- in terms of ~면에서
- enthusiastic 열렬한, 열광적인
- contradictory 모순된, 상반된
- contemporary history 현대사
- at best 기껏, 잘해야
- contingent 부수적인, 일시적인
- warrant 정당[타당]하게 만들다
- anxiety 불안, 걱정
- unreliable 믿을 수 없는, 신뢰할 수 없는

- factual 사실에 기반을 둔, 사실을 담은
- yield 산출하다, 생산하다
- continuity 지속성, 연속성
- reliability 신뢰성, 신빙성
- rediscovery 재발견
- conciseness 간결, 간략
- predictability 예언[예보]할 수 있음, 예측 가능성

[본문해석]
교육 측면에서, 역사가 항상 언론의 호평을 받는 것은 아니다. 1656년 아들에게 조언을 건넨 Francis Osborne은 그 주제에 대해 결코 열정적이지 않았다. 자신의 시대(현대사)에 남북전쟁에 대한 상반된 보도를 접한 그의 경험으로 인해 최근 일이 아닌 사건에 대한 기록의 신뢰성에 그는 의문을 품었다. 그는 이러한 역사 기록은 "거짓, 잘해야 일시적인 믿음"을 제시할 가능성이 높기 때문에 진지한 연구가 거의 불필요하다고 여겼다. 아들이 신뢰할 수 없는 역사를 공부하는데 시간을 낭비할 수도 있다는 Osborne의 불안감은 역사를 이상적으로 과거에 대한 확실한 '사실적' 지식을 산출하는 특정 종류로 이해하고 있음을 의미한다. 지금 Osborne의 시대에 이미 이 모델이 도전을 받고 있었지만, 우리 시대까지 어느 정도 지속되어 왔다.

| 18 | 빈칸 추론하기 | ① |

[정답해설]
인간이 어릴 때부터의 학습을 통해 고양이와 개를 구별할 수 있는 것처럼 인공지능도 무엇을 잘 하려면 학습이 필요하며, 또한 AI가 비약적으로 발전한 것도 AI가 필요로 하는 학습을 제공하는 엄청난 양의 데이터가 있기 때문이라고 서술하고 있다. 그러므로 빈칸에는 ①의 'be taught(학습하다)'가 들어갈 말로 가장 적절하다.

[오답해설]
② 스스로를 능가하다
③ 스스로 생각하다
④ 규칙에 의해 지배되다
⑤ 모든 가능성을 계산하다

[핵심어휘]
- genetically 유전적으로, 유전상으로
- prime 대비시키다, 준비시키다
- categorize 분류하다, 범주에 넣다
- artificial minds 인공지능
- breakthrough 돌파구, 비약적 발전
- incredible 믿을 수 없는, 엄청난, 대단한
- massive 방대한, 엄청나게 큰
- self-tracking 자기 추적의

- online footprint 온라인 발자국
- be akin to ~과 같은, ~과 흡사한
- huge 거대한, 엄청난

[본문해석]
모든 지능은 학습해야 한다. 유전적으로 사물을 분류할 준비가 되어 있는 인간의 뇌도 고양이와 개를 구별할 수 있기까지 어릴 때 열두 가지의 예시를 봐야 한다. 심지어 인공지능의 경우는 더욱 그렇다. 가장 잘 프로그래밍 된 컴퓨터도 체스 게임을 잘 하려면 적어도 천 번은 실행해야 한다. AI의 비약적 발전의 일부는 AI가 필요로 하는 학습을 제공하는 우리 세계에 대한 엄청난 양의 수집 데이터에 있다. 방대한 데이터베이스, 자가 추적, 웹 쿠키, 온라인 발자국, 테라바이트의 저장 공간, 수십 년에 걸친 검색 결과, 그리고 전 디지털 세계가 AI를 똑똑하게 만드는 선생님이 되었다. Andrew Ng는 그것을 이렇게 설명한다. "AI는 로켓 우주선을 만드는 것과 비슷합니다. 거대한 엔진과 많은 연료가 필요합니다. 로켓 엔진이 학습 알고리즘인 반면 연료는 이러한 알고리즘에 공급할 수 있는 엄청난 양의 데이터입니다."

| 19 | 빈칸 추론하기 | ① |

[정답해설]
상습 도박꾼인 샌드위치 백작에서 유래된 샌드위치란 단어는 한 번 들으면 잊어버리는 사람이 거의 없다며, 어원과 의미 사이의 두 번째 작용에 대해 설명하고 있다. 그러므로 빈칸에 들어갈 말로는 ①의 'prefer memorable or logical origins for words(기억에 남거나 논리적인 어원의 단어들을 선호하다)'이다.

[오답해설]
② 어원의 의미에 거의 주의를 기울이지 않다
③ 단어의 원래 의미를 중요하지 않게 여기다
④ 어원의 상반된 과정을 알지 못하다
⑤ 단어의 사용과 의미 사이의 연관성을 싫어하다

[핵심어휘]
- etymology 어원, 어원학
- derive from ~에서 유래하다, 파생하다
- considerable 상당한, 많은
- implication 영향[결과]
- erosion 부식, 침식
- make sense 의미가 통하다, 이해가 되다
- earl 백작
- compulsive 강박적인, 상습적인
- bout 한바탕, 한차례
- sustain oneself 자신의 생명[생활]을 유지하다
- association 연계, 연관

[본문해석]

어원학은 단어의 뿌리 또는 기원을 연구하는 학문으로, '참'이라는 뜻의 그리스어 어원 etymos에서 유래했다. 어원의 중요성과 영향력은 상당하다. 일반적으로 말하면, 두 가지 상반된 과정이 어원과 의미 사이의 관계에서 작용하고 있다. 첫 번째는 어원과의 연결이 점진적으로 침식되는 것이다. 즉, 단어는 어원의 의미에서 꾸준히 멀어지는 경향이 있다. 이와 반대로 연결을 되살리고 단어가 과거의 단어들과 '의미가 통하기'를 바란다. 사람들은 <u>기억에 남거나 논리적인 어원의 단어들을 선호</u>하며, 심지어 단어가 존재하지 않는다면 창조하기도 한다. 어떤 단어는 실제로 이러한 뚜렷한 기원을 가지고 있다. 샌드위치가 24시간 동안 게임 테이블을 떠나지 않기 위해 토스트 조각 사이에 차가운 소고기 조각을 곁들여 자신을 지탱했던 상습 도박꾼인 샌드위치 백작에서 유래했다는 사실을 (한 번 들으면) 잊어버리는 사람은 거의 없다. 이렇게 샌드위치는 1762년에 처음 기록되어 탄생했다.

20	빈칸 추론하기	③

[정답해설]

제시문에 따르면 체스 선수들의 게임 분석은 반사적으로 이루어지며, 한 눈에 체스판을 검토하고 그 배열을 완벽히 기억하는 등의 세분화 과정이 거의 무의식적으로 일어난다고 설명하고 있다. 그러므로 빈칸에 들어갈 말은 ③의 'occur entirely outside conscious awareness(완전히 의식 밖에서 일어난다)'이다.

[오답해설]

① 마스터의 의식이 작동할 때만 일어난다
② 의미 있는 인식을 의식적으로 전개한다
④ 신중한 분석과 반복을 통해 성공한다
⑤ 다중 감각 정보가 서로 결합될 수 있음을 입증한다

[핵심어휘]

- intuition 직관, 직감
- parsing 어구의 해부, 구문 분석
- reflex 반사 작용(운동)
- glance 힐끗 봄, 일견
- grand master 최고 수준의 체스 선수
- configuration 배열, 환경 설정
- chunk 덩어리, 상당히 많은 양
- segmenting process 세분화 과정
- take into account ~을 고려하다, 계산에 넣다
- piece (체스 · 장기) 말, 알
- sophisticated 세련된, 정교한
- consciousness 의식, 생각
- unfold 펴다, 펼치다
- repetition 반복, 되풀이

- multisensory 여러 감각의, 다중 감각의

[본문해석]

체스 선수들 사이에서 보드 게임 분석이 반사적으로 이루어진다는 것이 우리 생각이다. 실제 연구에 따르면 최고 수준의 체스 선수는 체스판을 의미 있는 덩어리로 자동 분석하기 때문에 한 눈에 체스판을 검토하고 그 배열을 완벽히 기억한다. 또한 최근의 실험은 이러한 세분화 과정이 정말 무의식적이라는 사실을 보여준다. 즉, 간이 경기를 20밀리초 동안 반짝 보여주고 마스크 사이에 끼워 넣어 보이지 않게 해도 여전히 체스 마스터의 결정에 영향을 미칠 수 있다. 이 실험은 전문적인 체스 선수들에게만 적용되며, 왕이 장군인지 멍군인지를 결정하는 것과 같은 의미 있는 문제를 해결하는 경우에만 해당된다. 이는 시각 체계가 말들(루크 또는 나이트)의 신원과 위치를 고려하여 이 정보를 의미 있는 덩어리("장군을 받은 블랙 킹")와 빠르게 결합시키는 것을 의미한다. 이러한 정교한 작업은 <u>완전히 의식 밖에서 일어난다</u>.

21	빈칸 추론하기	④

[정답해설]

유럽에서 일어난 산업 혁명으로 인해 잠재적인 대규모 산업 노동자들이 도시로 이주하면서 2만 명 이상의 도시가 폭증하고 그 지역이 대부분 도시화되고 고도로 산업화되었다고 설명하고 있다. 그러므로 빈칸에 들어갈 말은 ④의 'the dominant form of human settlement(인간 정착지의 지배적인 형태)'이다.

[오답해설]

① 일부 국가의 지리적 특징
② 제조업 시스템
③ 사회 정의와 평등의 개념
⑤ 노동 계급의 정의

[핵심어휘]

- agricultural 농업의
- transform 변형시키다, 완전히 바꿔 놓다
- gender 성, 성별
- kinship 친족
- composition 구성, 구조
- rural 시골의, 농촌의
- urban 도시의
- overturn 뒤집다, 전복하다
- migration 이주, 이동
- emerging 신흥의, 최근에 생겨난
- bourgeoisie 중산층, 부르주아
- scope 범위, 영역
- demographic 인구학의

정답 및 해설

- underline 밑줄을 긋다, 강조하다
- estimate 평가하다, 추정하다
- geopolitical 지정학의, 지정학적인
- predominantly 대개, 대부분
- urbanized 도시화된
- geographical 지리학적인, 지리학상의
- dominant 우세한, 지배적인

[본문해석]

18세기와 19세기 동안 유럽에서 일어난 산업(및 관련 농업) 혁명은 일의 성격을 변화시켰을 뿐만 아니라 사회 조직, 성별 및 친족 관계, 그리고 인간 정착지의 지배적인 형태도 극적으로 변화시켰다. 특히 농촌 지역에서 신흥 제조업 중산층 공장이 위치한 도시로 잠재적 산업 노동자들이 대규모로 이주하면서 농촌과 도시의 구성과 연결 관계가 완전히 뒤집혔다. 이 시기에 발생한 인구 변화의 범위는 19세기 초에는 인구가 2만 명 이상인 영국 도시가 15개에 불과했지만, 19세기 말에는 185개에 달했다는 연구 결과를 통해 강조된다. 실제로 1800년 당시 유럽 인구의 2.2%만이 10만 명 이상의 도시에 살고 있었으며, 오늘날 그 지정학적 공간이 대부분 도시화되고 고도로 산업화된 것으로 추정되었다.

| **22** | 빈칸 추론하기 | ② |

[정답해설]

(A) 심장병 환자들과 암 환자들의 정서적 고통과 통증 완화, 임산부들의 더 나은 출산결과, 관상동맥 우회 수술 환자의 수술 후 합병증 경감 등을 예로 들어 낙관주의가 미치는 영향에 대해 설명하고 있다. 그러므로 빈칸에 들어갈 말로는 'For instance' 또는 'For example' 등이 적절하다.

(B) 앞에서 낙관적인 태도를 지닌 사람들의 긍정적 영향에 대해 설명한 것과 반대로, 비관적인 태도를 가진 사람들의 부정적 영향에 대해 설명하고 있다. 그러므로 'On the other hand(반면에)'가 빈칸에 들어갈 말로 가장 적절하다.

[핵심어휘]

- proverbial 속담에도 나오는, 유명한
- resilient 회복력 있는, 탄력 있는
- disorder 장애, 이상
- investigator 수사관, 조사관
- emotional distress 정신적[정서적] 고통
- pregnant 임신한
- infant 유아, 젖먹이
- birth outcome 출산결과
- coronary artery bypass surgery 관상동맥 우회 수술
- postoperative complication 수술 후 합병증

- depression 우울증, 우울함

[본문해석]

당신은 속담에 나오는 유리잔을 반이 가득 찬 것으로 보는 사람인가, 아니면 반이 비어 있는 것으로 보는 사람인가? 유리잔을 반이 가득 찬 것으로 보는 사람들은 더 낙관적인 태도를 지닌 사람들로 신체장애와 관련된 스트레스를 포함한 스트레스의 영향에 대해 다른 사람들보다 더 회복력이 좋다. (A) 예를 들면, 조사원들은 낙관주의를 심장병과 암 환자들의 정서적 고통 수준을 낮추고 암 환자들의 보고된 통증 수준을 낮추는 것과 결부시킨다. 임산부의 낙관주의는 심지어 더 나은 출산결과, 예를 들면 유아의 출생 당시 체중이 더 높게 측정될 것으로 예측한다. 관상동맥 우회 수술 환자의 낙관주의는 또한 심각한 수술 후 합병증을 줄이는 것과도 관련이 있다. (B) 반면에, 비관적인 태도를 가진 사람들은 우울증과 사회적 불안의 형태로 더 큰 정서적 고통을 보고하는 경향이 있다.

| **23** | 글의 제목 유추하기 | ① |

[정답해설]

제시문은 전자두뇌와 이온 추진 엔진을 탑재했다며, 이달 말 발사 예정인 차세대 우주선인 딥 스페이스 1호의 성능에 대해 소개하고 있다. 그러므로 제시문의 제목으로는 ①의 'A Smart New Kind of Spacecraft(스마트한 새로운 종류의 우주선)'가 가장 적절하다.

[오답해설]

② 무인 로켓의 발사
③ DS1의 위험한 기술 실패
④ 컴퓨터 엔진 시스템의 성능
⑤ 더 큰 소행성으로 항해하는 새로운 임무

[핵심어휘]

- daring 대담한, 위험한
- publicized 알려진, 공개된
- asteroid 소행성
- orbit 궤도를 돌다, 공전하다
- destination 목적지, 도착지
- incidental 부수적인, 부차적인
- launch 진수하다, 발사하다
- unmanned 무인의
- independent-minded 자립심[독립심]이 강한
- liken 비기다, 비유하다
- stuff 것, 물건, 대상
- propulsion 추진, 추진력
- forerunner 선구자, 선인
- prime assignment 주된 임무

□ validate 인증하다, 승인하다

□ a host of 많은, 다수의

□ high-profile 세간의 이목을 끄는, 눈에 띄는

[본문해석]

NASA가 계획한 가장 대담한 심우주 임무 중 하나가 가장 비공개된 임무 중 하나로 밝혀졌다. 목표물은 지구에서 수백만 킬로미터 떨어진 태양 주위를 공전하는 1992KD이라 명명된 대형 소행성이다. 하지만 이 목적지는 이번 여행을 떠날 우주선의 성능에 거의 부수적인 것이다. NASA가 발사한 수많은 무인 우주선과 거의 다르지 않아 보이지만, 이 우주선은 2001년 영화 '스페이스 오디세이'의 독자적인 컴퓨터인 HAL에 비유된 전자두뇌에 의해 항해되며, 오랫동안 기술적 환상의 대상이었던 이온 추진 엔진이라는 시스템의 힘으로 우주를 항해하게 될 것이다. 모든 것이 계획대로 진행된다면, 이달 말 발사 예정인 딥스페이스 1호는 차세대 우주선의 선구자가 될 것이다. 비행 계획자들은 이 우주선이 목표 소행성의 구성 요소와 표면 구조 등 흥미로운 관측을 할 수 있기를 희망하지만, DS1의 주요 임무는 NASA가 항상 너무 위험해서 세간의 이목을 끄는 임무를 수행하기가 어렵다고 생각했던 다수의 신기술을 검증하는 것이다.

24　　글의 제목 유추하기　　①

[정답해설]

제시문에 따르면 개가 사람에게 귀여움을 받는 능력을 갖고 있는 것처럼 소도 똑같은 능력이 있다고 설명하고 있다. 그러므로 제시문의 제목으로는 ①의 'Cattle Can Be Our New Pets(소는 우리의 새로운 반려동물이 될 수 있다)'가 가장 적절하다.

[오답해설]

② 감정 변화를 표현하는 반려동물
③ 야생 동물을 길들이는 방법
④ 소를 집에 안전하게 몰고 가는 방법
⑤ 다윈의 동물 행동 발견

[핵심어휘]

□ evolve 발달하다, 진화하다

□ a suite of 한 벌의, 한 묶음의

□ sensory 감각의

□ adaptation 각색, 적응

□ detect 감지하다, 탐지하다

□ predator 포식자, 포식 동물

□ herd 떼, 무리

□ discern 알아차리다, 식별[구별]하다

□ endear 사랑[귀염]받게 하다

□ apparent 분명한, 명백한

□ bull 황소

□ horned 뿔이 있는, 뿔 모양의

□ belly 배, 복부

□ rub 비비다, 문지르다

□ domesticate 길들이다, 사육하다

[본문해석]

소는 민감한 생물이다. 소는 먼 거리에서 포식자를 감지하기 위해 감각적으로 적응하도록 진화해 왔다. 소는 적어도 개나 고양이만큼 후각과 청각이 예민하다. 사람들은 코끼리가 절대 잊어버리지 않는다고 말하지만 소도 마찬가지이다. 소는 그들이 아는 사람들뿐만 아니라 무리 동료의 사진도 인식할 수 있다. 찰스 다윈은 인간과 동물 모두 감정 표현에 유사점을 가지고 있다고 주장했다. 물론 우리는 쾌락과 두려움과 같은 기본적인 감정을 구별할 수 있다. 하지만 개가 귀여움을 받는 것은 사람들과 함께 있고 싶은 간절한 눈빛과 전체적인 기쁨의 의지, 즉 우리가 사랑이란 형태로 받아들이는 그들의 명백한 능력 때문이다. 소가 당신을 좋아한다는 것을 어떻게 알 수 있을까? 개와 함께 하는 것과 똑같다. 나의 황소 Ricky Bobby는 내 옆에서 행복하게 누워 뿔 달린 머리를 내 무릎 위에 올려놓는다. 그는 내가 쓰다듬는 것을 좋아하고 심지어 배를 문지르기 위해 몸을 굴리기도 한다.

25　　글의 제목 유추하기　　③

[정답해설]

글의 서두에서 자신을 제대로 돌볼 수 없거나 돌보지 못할 사람들을 보살펴 줄 것을 경찰이 요청받는 것은 당연한 일이라고 서술하고 있다. 또한 마지막 문장에서 경찰의 지원이 자신을 제대로 돌볼 수 없는 사람들을 위한 유일한 선택인 경우가 많다고 서술하고 있다. 그러므로 제시문의 제목으로는 ③의 'Police Are Here for Those Who Cannot Care for Themselves!(스스로를 돌볼 수 없는 사람들을 위해 여기 경찰이 왔다!)'가 가장 적절하다.

[오답해설]

① 경찰은 항상 잠재적인 문제를 주시한다
② 경찰의 핵심 목표: 강력 범죄 예방
④ 다양한 종류의 갈등 해결을 담당하는 사람은 누구인가?
⑤ 경찰 업무의 중추인 순찰하기

[핵심어휘]

□ property 재산, 부동산

□ inevitable 불가피한, 당연한

□ assistance 도움, 원조

□ temporary 일시적인, 임시의

□ shelter 피난처, 쉼터

□ transportation 수송, 운송

- ￮ referral 소개, 추천
- ￮ underfunded 자금 부족을 겪는, 재정이 부족한
- ￮ fortunate 다행인, 운 좋은
- ￮ turn a cold shoulder to ~에게 냉대하다
- ￮ conflict 갈등, 충돌
- ￮ patrol 순찰을 돌다
- ￮ backbone 중추, 근간

[본문해석]

경찰은 생명과 재산을 보호하고 질서를 유지한다는 목표 때문에, 그리고 온갖 날씨에도 24시간 근무를 위해 개방해야 하기 때문에 자신을 제대로 돌볼 수 없거나 돌보지 못할 사람들을 보살펴 줄 것을 경찰이 요청받는 것은 당연한 일이다. 이에는 어린 아이들, 노인, 정신질환자, 노숙자 등이 포함된다. 이 사람들에 대한 경찰의 지원은 오직 여기까지이다. 물론 경찰이 다른 사람의 자녀를 키우거나 정신질환자를 치료하거나 이 나라의 모든 노숙자를 위한 집을 지을 수는 없다. 그러나 경찰은 도움이 필요한 사람들을 위해 임시 쉼터와 교통편을 제공하거나 마련할 수도 있고 보통 그렇게 한다. 또한 사람들이 이용할 수 있는 프로그램과 서비스를 활용하도록 추천하고 정보를 제공한다. 경제가 어려울 때, 사회 프로그램 재정이 부족할 때, 많은 시민이 불우한 사람들에게 냉담한 태도를 보일 때, 경찰의 지원이 자신을 제대로 돌볼 수 없는 사람들을 위한 유일한 선택인 경우가 많다.

26 글의 제목 유추하기 ②

[정답해설]

엘리자베스 시대의 무대는 원초적이었기 때문에 셰익스피어가 오로지 개인화된 언어 매체만을 사용하는 특별한 캐릭터를 창조한 것처럼, 이러한 부족함을 보완하기 위해 완전히 새로운 언어 매체가 창조되었다고 설명하고 있다. 그러므로 제시문의 제목으로는 ②의 'The Elizabethan Stage and Its Linguistic Innovation(엘리자베스 시대의 무대와 언어 혁신)'이 가장 적절하다.

[오답해설]

① 엘리자베스 시대의 극장 기술의 발전
③ 셰익스피어의 원시 무대의 효과적 활용
④ 영국의 종교 드라마의 쇠퇴
⑤ 중세 도덕극의 부흥

[핵심어휘]

- ￮ morally 도덕적으로, 도의적으로
- ￮ enlightening 계몽적인, 교화적인
- ￮ respectively 각자, 각각
- ￮ miracle play 기적극(그리스도·성도·순교자의 사적·기적을 다룬 중세의 연극)
- ￮ morality play 도덕극(15~16세기에 유행하던 도덕적 교훈을 가르치는 것을 목적으로 한 연극)
- ￮ playhouse 극장
- ￮ catalyst 촉매, 기폭제
- ￮ efflorescence 전성기, 개화
- ￮ accuracy 정확성, 정확도
- ￮ primitive 원시적인, 원초적인
- ￮ inadequacy 불충분함, 부족함
- ￮ linguistic 언어의, 언어학의
- ￮ bare 벌거벗은, 맨
- ￮ properties 속성, 특성
- ￮ theatrical 연극의, 공연의
- ￮ illusion 환상, 환각
- ￮ diversity 다양성, 포괄성
- ￮ exclusively 배타적으로, 오로지
- ￮ philosophize 철학적인 이야기를 하다, 철학적으로 사색하다
- ￮ agonize 고민하다, 고뇌하다

[본문해석]

비록 종교적이고 도덕적으로 계몽적인 연극들(각각 기적극과 도덕극이라고 불림)의 오랜 전통이 있었지만, 영국 최초의 공공 극장은 1576년에야 지어졌다. 이것은 Gamini Salgado가 '영국이 보여준 연극적 글쓰기의 가장 위대한 전성기'라고 불렀던 촉매제임을 증명했다. 지금은 전체를 정확하게 재구성하기는 어렵지만 엘리자베스 시대의 무대 상태는 대개 원초적이었다. 이러한 부족함을 보완하기 위해 완전히 새로운 언어 매체가 창조되었다. 연극적 환상을 쌓기 위해 최소한의 속성과 효과를 지닌 맨 무대에서, 위대한 극작가인 셰익스피어는 오로지 개인화된 언어 매체, 즉 그들의 창조물이 철학적으로 사색하고, 고뇌하고, 웃고, 고통 받고, 죽을 수 있는 단어의 세계를 통해서만 특별한 다양한 경험과 캐릭터를 창조했다.

27 글의 주장 이해하기 ⑤

[정답해설]

제시문은 자신의 삶을 스스로 통제할 수 있는 심리적 강점을 신체 능력을 개발하는 것처럼 훈련을 통해 단련시킬 것을 주문하고 있다. 그러므로 ⑤의 '자신을 연약하다고 생각하지 말고 정신적으로 강해져라.'가 필자가 주장하는 내용으로 가장 적절하다.

[오답해설]

① 항상 현실적인 계획이 있어야 한다고 생각하지 마라.
② 성공하는 데 도움이 되는 조건들을 파악하라.
③ 보다 큰 꿈 중 하나를 선택하고 실현해 보라.
④ 달성 가능한 목표를 설정하고 각각의 작은 발전 단계를 즐겨라.

[핵심어휘]

- stuck 움직일 수 없는, 꼼짝 못하는
- anhedonic 쾌락을 추구하지 않는, 불쾌감의
- myth 근거 없는 믿음
- absolutely 전적으로, 틀림없이
- fall apart 허물어지다, 무너지다
- paralyzed 마비된, 쓸모없게 된
- rid oneself of ~에서 벗어나다, 버리다
- put up with 참다, 견디다
- assert 주장하다, 확고히 하다
- attainable 이룰 수 있는, 달성할 수 있는
- fragile 부서지기 쉬운, 연약한

[본문해석]

당신을 꼼짝 못하게 하는 모든 불쾌한 선택의 이면에는 규칙을 거스르면 자신(또는 삶)이 무너질 것이라는 믿음이 있다. 이것은 터무니없는 믿음이다! 그것은 당신을 완전히 마비시킬 수 있다! 그것에서 벗어날 수 있는 유일한 방법은 심리적 강점을 시험해 보는 것이다. 자신의 삶에서 문제들을 참아 내는 것을 멈추고 변화를 향한 몇 걸음을 내딛기 전까지는 자신이 얼마나 강한지 깨닫는 사람은 거의 없다. 그것은 쉽지 않을 것이다. 몇 번은 쓰러질 수도 있지만 무너지지는 않는다. 오히려 삶을 통제할 수 있는 자신의 능력을 확고히 할수록 더욱 강해질 것이다. 심리적 강점을 개발하는 것은 신체 능력을 개발하는 것과 같다. 운동을 많이 할수록 더욱 강해진다.

| 28 | 글의 주제 이해하기 | ① |

[정답해설]

제시문에 따르면 재즈에서는 연주자가 창작, 연주, 듣기의 세 가지 예술 활동을 동시에 모두 결합시킬 필요가 있으며, 재즈에서 음악 창작의 모든 행위는 연주가 창작하는 것처럼 개인적이라고 설명하고 있다. 그러므로 ①의 '연주자의 개성을 반영한 재즈의 특성'이 제시문의 주제로 가장 적절하다.

[오답해설]

② 훌륭한 공연을 위해 재즈를 작곡하는 방법
③ 재즈와 서양 음악의 유사점
④ 현대 재즈계의 유명 인사들
⑤ 전통 음악이 재즈에 미친 영향

[핵심어휘]

- clear-cut 명백한, 또렷한
- encompass 포함하다, 에워싸다
- idiom 관용구, 언어, 표현 양식
- comprise 구성되다, 이루어지다

- instantaneously 순간적으로, 즉석으로
- contribution 기여, 공헌, 이바지
- be consistent with ~와 일관되다, 일치하다
- trait 특성, 특징
- individuality 개성, 특성
- celebrated figures 유명 인사들
- scene 계, 분야

[본문해석]

모든 재즈를 포괄할 수 있는 명확한 범주는 없다. 각 연주자의 표현 양식은 그 자체로 하나의 스타일이며, 그렇지 않았다면 그 음악은 재즈가 아니었을 것이다. 재즈는 거의 모든 다른 음악과 마찬가지로 창작, 연주, 듣기의 세 가지 예술 활동으로 구성된다. 전통적인 서유럽 음악에서, 이 세 가지 활동은 항상 동일인이 수행하는 것은 아니지만 흔히 자주 수행한다. 그러나 재즈에서는 연주자가 이 세 가지를 동시에 모두 결합시킬 필요가 있다. 음악 창작은 재즈 공연의 활동적인 부분이며 창작에 대한 연주자의 이해, 즉 잘 듣는 능력에 의해서만 얻을 수 있는 이해에 달려 있다. 동료 연주자로부터 듣는 것에 즉각적으로 반응해야 하며, 자신의 참여는 전개되는 주제와 분위기에 일치해야 한다. 따라서 재즈에서 음악 창작의 모든 행위는 연주자가 창작하는 것처럼 개인적이다.

| 29 | 전체 흐름과 관계없는 문장 고르기 | ④ |

[정답해설]

제시문은 대학 교육을 받기를 원하지만 낮에는 일을 해야 하고 밤에는 근처에 야간 대학이 없는 학생들에게 원격 학습이 좋은 대안이 될 수 있다고 설명하고 있다. 그러므로 원격 학습이 일을 계속 미루거나 마감 시간을 지키지 못하는 학생들에게 좋은 선택이 될 수 없다는 ④의 설명은 글의 전체 흐름과 어울리지 않는다.

[핵심어휘]

- computer-aided 컴퓨터 지원에 의한, 컴퓨터 보조의
- instruction 교수, 교육, 지도
- distance learning 원격 학습
- enroll 등록하다, 입학하다
- entire 전체의, 전부의
- stick to deadline 마감 시간을 준수하다

[본문해석]

컴퓨터 보조 교육은 대학 수준의 교육 과정 자체를 변화시키고 있다. 점점 더 많은 학생들이 대학 교육을 원하지만, 낮에는 일을 하고 야간 교육을 제공하는 대학이 근처에 없을 수도 있다. 이 문제에 대한 해결책이 원격 학습인데, 이는 학생들이 실제로 대학에 출석하지 않고도 대학 과정에 등록할 수 있음을 뜻한다. ① 대학에서 제공되는 수강

과정은 학생들이 언제든지 이용 가능한 시간에 개인 컴퓨터로 시청할 수 있도록 녹화되어 제공된다. ② 따라서 컴퓨터 기술이 학생들에게 수강 과정을 제공하기 때문에 시간이나 공간에 구애받지 않고 수강 과정을 제공받을 수 있다. ③ 몇몇 대학에서는 현재 이 기술을 통해 학생들에게 전체 학위 프로그램을 제공하고 있다. ④ 따라서 원격 학습은 일을 계속 미루거나 마감 시간을 지키지 못하는 학생들에게는 좋은 선택이 될 수 없다. ⑤ 학생들은 실제로 대학에 다니지 않고도 대학에서 학위를 취득할 수 있다.

30 전체 흐름과 관계없는 문장 고르기 ④

[정답해설]
제시문은 데카르트의 이원론적 개념인 정신적 대상과 물질적 대상의 구성 요소들과 그 둘의 상호관계에 대해 서술하고 있다. 그런데 ④는 비판적인 검토 없이 당연하게 여겨지는 독서의 중요성에 대해 서술하고 있으므로, 글의 전체 흐름과 어울리지 않는다.

[핵심어휘]
▢ common knowledge 주지의 사실, 상식
▢ Cartesian Dualist 데카르트적 이원론
▢ consciousness 의식, 자각
▢ clockwork 시계 장치
▢ faculty 능력, 기능
▢ introspection 내성, 자기 성찰
▢ perceive 감지하다, 인지하다
▢ take for granted 당연한 일로 여기다, 대수롭지 않게 여기다
▢ independent 독립적인, 독자적인
▢ causally 원인이 되어, 인과적으로
▢ causal interaction 인과적 상호작용
▢ as it were 말하자면, 이를테면
▢ glue 아교, 접착제

[본문해석]
데카르트가 데카르트적 이원론자였다는 것은 상식이다. (아마도 상식에 지나지 않을 것이다!) ① 모두가 알다시피, 그는 정신적 대상과 동물과 인간의 몸을 포함한 물질적 대상이라는 두 가지 세계가 존재한다고 주장했다. ② 정신적 대상은 '의식의 상태' (예: 고통, 시각적 경험, 신념과 욕망, 두려움과 기쁨)이며, 물질적 대상은 다소 복잡한 '시계 장치'의 일부이다. ③ '내면 세계' 항목은 '자기 성찰'이라는 특별한 기능의 훈련을 통해 이해되며, '외부 세계'의 대상은 오감에 의해 인식된다. ④ 대부분의 '상식' 항목과 마찬가지로, 독서의 중요성은 비판적인 검토 없이 당연하게 여겨지는 경우가 많다. ⑤ 정신 상태와 신체 상태는 논리적으로 독립적이지만 인과적으로 상호 연관되어 있다. 말하자면, 인과적 상호작용은 각 개인의 몸에 정신을 결합하는 접착제와 같다.

31 주어진 문장의 위치 찾기 ⑤

[정답해설]
주어진 문장이 역접의 접속사 'But'으로 시작하므로 앞 문장은 주어진 문장과 상반되는 내용이 와야 한다. 제시문의 ①~④까지는 인류의 역사를 통틀어 나타난 기술적 변화가 우리 사회의 구조를 근본적으로 변화시킨 경우는 없었다고 설명하고 있다. 그러나 ⑤번의 마지막 문장에서는 AI가 가져올 변화의 핵심과 방식에 대해 설명하고 있다. 그러므로 주어진 문장은 ⑤에 들어가는 것이 가장 적절하다.

[핵심어휘]
▢ humanity 인류, 인간성
▢ preexisting 기존의, 이전부터의
▢ framework 뼈대, 틀, 체제
▢ recognizable 인식할 수 있는, 분간할 수 있는
▢ rifle 소총
▢ musket 머스킷총, 장총
▢ conventional 전통적인, 종래의
▢ unaltered 바뀌지 않은, 변경되지 않은
▢ encounter 마주치다, 접하다
▢ prevailing 우세한, 지배적인
▢ transformation 변화, 변신, 탈바꿈
▢ philosophical 철학의, 철학과 관련된

[본문해석]

> 하지만 AI는 인간 경험의 모든 영역을 변화시킬 것이라고 장담한다.

인류는 역사를 통틀어 기술적 변화를 경험해 왔다. 그러나 기술이 우리 사회의 사회적, 정치적 구조를 근본적으로 변화시킨 경우는 극히 드물다. (①) 우리가 사회 세계를 명령하는 기존의 틀이 적응하고 새로운 기술을 흡수하여 인식 가능한 범주 내에서 진화하고 혁신하는 경우가 더욱 많았다. (②) 자동차는 사회 구조에 전면적인 변화를 강요하지 않고 말을 대체했다. (③) 소총이 머스킷총을 대체했지만, 기존 군사 활동의 일반적인 패러다임은 크게 변하지 않았다. (④) 우리가 세상을 설명하고 명령하는 기존 방식에 도전하는 기술을 접한 경우는 극히 드물다. (⑤) 그리고 그 변화의 핵심은 궁극적으로 철학적 수준에서 발생하여 인간이 현실을 이해하는 방식과 그 안에서 우리의 역할을 변화시킬 것이다.

32 주어진 문장의 위치 찾기 ③

[정답해설]
사랑과 욕망의 신인 아프로디테와 에로스가 끔직한 괴물 타이폰과 마

주했을 때 피난처를 찾아 물고기로 변신하여 유프라테스 강으로 뛰어들었고, 이것이 물고기자리가 지금의 별자리 형태로 포착된 순간이다. 그러므로 주어진 문장은 ③에 들어가는 것이 글의 흐름상 가장 적절하다.

[핵심어휘]

- refuge 피난처, 도피처
- leap into ~에 뛰어들다
- constellation 별자리, 성좌
- Pisces 물고기자리, 쌍어궁
- lust 성욕, 욕망
- world-crushing 세상을 뒤흔드는
- alternative 대체 가능한, 대안이 되는

[본문해석]

> 피난처를 찾아 물고기로 변신한 두 사람은 안전을 위해 함께 묶여 유프라테스 강으로 뛰어들었다.

물고기자리는 주로 밧줄로 함께 묶인 물고기 한 쌍으로 상상된다. 이 이미지는 기원전 2천 년의 고대 이집트와 이후 바빌로니아 문헌에 기록되어 있다. 이 두 물고기가 왜 함께 묶여 있었는지 초기 자료에는 기록이 없지만, 이후의 그리스 로마 신화에는 일부 설명이 있다. (①) 신들이 끔찍한 괴물 타이폰을 마주했을 때, 아프로디테와 에로스는 전투에서 멀리 떨어져 있었다고 한다. (②) 사랑과 욕망의 신이었기 때문에 이 둘은 세상을 뒤흔드는 위협에 직면했을 때 할 수 있는 일이 거의 없었다. (③) 이것이 별자리의 형태로 포착된 순간이다. (④) 또 다른 버전에서는 물고기자리의 두 마리 물고기가 그들의 등에 업혀 도망친 신들을 구출하고 있다. (⑤) 그들을 도와준 보답으로 물고기들이 밤하늘에 자리 잡게 되었다.

---

33   주어진 문장의 위치 찾기   ⑤

[정답해설]

주어진 문장의 'this enterprise(이 계획)'은 전쟁에서 패한 후 정신적 회복을 위해 제도종교의 전통적 가치를 계몽된 세계관으로 대체하는 것을 목표로 한 제3공화국의 교육 개혁을 의미하므로, 주어진 문장은 글의 흐름상 ⑤에 들어가는 것이 가장 적절하다.

[핵심어휘]

- principal 주된, 주요한
- vehicle 수단, 매개체
- enterprise (대규모의) 기획, 계획
- dedicate 바치다, 전념하다
- humanism 인문주의, 인본주의

- acute 예리한, 날카로운
- abundant 많은, 풍부한
- intense 강렬한, 열정적인
- flowering 개화기, 전성기
- in the wake of ~에 뒤이어, ~을 뒤따라
- demoralize 사기를 꺾다, 의기소침하게 만들다
- humiliate 굴욕감을 주다, 창피를 주다
- siege 포위, 포위 작전
- terrify 겁을 주다, 무섭게 하다
- bourgeoisie 중산층, 자본가 계급, 부르주아
- anarchy 무정부 상태
- radical 급진적인
- the Commune 코뮌(프랑스의 최소 행정 구역)
- restoration 복원, 부활, 회복
- rejection 거절, 거부
- institutional religion 제도종교

[본문해석]

> 이 계획의 주요 수단은 교육 개혁이었으며 특히 과학, 이성, 인문주의의 이상에 전념하는 대학 시스템을 구축하는 것이었다.

제1차 세계대전이 끝난 직후에 쓴 글에서, 프랑스 철학계의 한 예리한 관찰자는 "지난 30년 동안 우리 사이에서 철학 연구가 그 어느 때보다 풍부하고 진지하며 열정적이었다"고 판단했다. (①) 이러한 전성기는 Franco-Prussian 전쟁에서 사기가 꺾인 패배에 뒤이어 제3공화국에 의해 설립된 새로운 교육 시스템에 철학이 역할을 했기 때문이다. (②) 프랑스는 Sedan에서 나폴레옹 3세가 포로로 붙잡히는 굴욕을 당했고 장기간의 포위로 파리는 폐허가 되었다. (③) 그들은 또한 대부분의 부르주아가 코뮌의 급진적 사회주의 하에서 73일간의 무정부 상태를 겪은 것에 두려움을 느꼈다. (④) 정신적 회복을 위한 새로운 공화국의 노력의 대부분은 제도종교의 전통적 가치를 거부한 데서 비롯되었으며, 이는 계몽된 세계관으로 대체하는 것을 목표로 했다. (⑤) Albert Thibaudet는 제3공화국을 "교수 공화국"이라 칭하면서 이 개혁의 중요성을 강조했다.

---

34   글의 배열순서 정하기   ④

[정답해설]

글 (C)에서 'The remark(이 발언)'는 주어진 문장의 "농부들이 더 많은 가뭄을 ~ 더 많은 도로가 필요합니다."를 가리키므로, 주어진 글 다음에 글 (C)가 와야 한다. 또한 글 (B)가 모든 주장이 설득을 시도하는 것은 아니라며 역접의 접속사 'But(그러나)'을 사용하여 글 (A)와 상반된 내용을 진술하고 있다. 그러므로 글 (A) 다음에 글 (B)가 와야 한다. 따라서 주어진 글 다음에 이어질 글의 순서로는 ④의 (C)-(A)-(B)가 가

장 적절하다.

[핵심어휘]

- national forest 국유림
- drought 가뭄
- persuade 설득시키다, 납득시키다
- distinct 서로 다른, 별개의
- enterprise (대규모의) 계획, 활동
- bother 신경 쓰다, 애를 쓰다
- notoriously 악명 높게
- undisturbed 방해받지 않는, 흔들리지 않는
- statement 성명, 진술, 서술
- portray 그리다, 묘사하다
- in a bad light 나쁘게, 부정적으로

[본문해석]

"농부들이 더 많은 가뭄을 필요로 하는 것처럼 국유림에는 더 많은 도로가 필요합니다." 누군가가 더 많은 도로가 국유림에 해로울 것이라고 청중을 설득하기 위해 이렇게 말하는 것을 들었다.

(C) 그러나 이 발언은 주장이 아니라, 숲 속 도로 건설을 부정적으로 묘사한 진술일 뿐이다. 일부 작가들은 주장을 누군가에게 어떤 것을 설득하려는 시도로 정의한다. 이것은 옳지 않다.

(A) 주장은 결론을 입증하거나 뒷받침하려고 시도한다. 누군가를 설득하려고 할 때는 그들을 자신의 관점으로 끌어들이려고 노력한다. 설득하는 것과 주장하는 것은 논리적으로 서로 다른 활동이다. 사실, 누군가에게 어떤 것을 설득하고 싶을 때는 주장을 이용할 수도 있다.

(B) 하지만 모든 주장이 설득을 시도하는 것은 아니며, 설득하려는 많은 시도에는 주장이 포함되지 않는다. 사실 주장을 하는 것이 사람들을 설득하는 가장 효과적이지 못한 방법 중 하나이며, 응당 그것이 주장에 신경 쓰는 광고주가 거의 없는 이유이기도 하다. 사람들은 가장 약한 주장에 설득되기도 하고, 때로는 꽤 그럴듯한 주장에도 흔들리지 않는 걸로 유명하다.

35 글의 배열순서 정하기 ⑤

[정답해설]

주어진 글에서 일반적으로 기술을 개발하려면 이론 학습, 신중한 연습, 올바른 태도 채택이라는 세 가지 조건이 필요하다고 설명하고 있고, 이 설명에 따라 글 (C)에서는 이론 학습, 글 (B)에서는 신중한 연습, 글 (A)에서는 올바른 태도에 대해 차례대로 서술하고 있다. 그러므로 주어진 글 다음에 이어질 글의 순서로는 ⑤의 (C)–(B)–(A)가 가장 적절하다.

[핵심어휘]

- cognitive 인식의, 인지의
- deliberate 신중한, 계획적인
- adopt 채택하다, 차용하다
- attitude 자세, 태도
- sustainable 지속 가능한, 지탱할 수 있는
- translate 번역하다, 바꾸다, 옮기다
- possess 소유하다, 보유하다

[본문해석]

좋은 비판적 사고는 인지 기술이다. 일반적으로 기술을 개발하려면 이론 학습, 신중한 연습, 올바른 태도 채택이라는 세 가지 조건이 필요하다.

(C) 이론상 우리가 기술을 보유하기 위해 알아야만 하는 것은 다시 말해 규칙과 사실이다. 예를 들어, 농구공을 차는 것은 허용되지 않는다는 사례처럼, 경기 규칙을 알지 못하면 훌륭한 농구 선수가 될 수 없다. 마찬가지로 비판적으로 생각하려면 어느 정도의 논리를 알아야 한다.

(B) 그러나 이론을 아는 것과 적용할 수 있는 것과는 다르다. 이론적으로는 자전거를 탈 때 자전거의 균형을 맞춰야 한다는 사실을 알고 있을 수 있지만, 그것이 실제로 자전거를 탈 수 있다는 의미는 아니다. 이론적 지식을 실제 능력으로 변환해야 하기 때문에 바로 이 지점에서 연습이 필요하다.

(A) 그러나 여러분의 태도가 연습이 효과적이고 지속 가능한지에 대한 큰 차이를 만든다. 피아노 치는 것을 싫어한다면 연습을 강요하는 것은 장기적으로 생산적이지 않다.

36 글의 배열순서 정하기 ③

[정답해설]

주어진 글에 따르면 이미지를 사용하면 언어 추리를 사용하여 쉽게 해결할 수 없는 문제를 해결하는 데 도움을 준다고 하였고 글 (B)에서 'For example'로 시작하며 하나의 예를 들어 설명하고 있다. 다음으로 글 (C)에서 미국 지도를 이미지화 하여 가상의 여행을 시험해 본 후, 글 (A)에서 이에 대한 해결책을 찾는다. 그러므로 주어진 글 다음에 이어질 글의 순서로는 ③의 (B)–(C)–(A)가 가장 적절하다.

[핵심어휘]

- in regard to ~에 관해서
- imagery 형상화, 이미지
- verbal reasoning 언어 추리
- salesperson 판매원
- route 경로, 노선

□ virtual 가상의

□ retrace 되짚어 가다, 되돌아가다

□ path 길, 방향

[본문해석]

> 문제 해결과 관련하여, 이미지는 언어 추리를 사용하여 쉽게 해결할 수 없는 문제를 해결하는 데 도움을 줄 수 있다.

(B) 예를 들어, 뉴욕시에 거주하는 한 영업사원은 워싱턴 DC, 버팔로, 시카고의 세 도시를 운전해야만 한다. 그 순서대로 도시를 이동한 후 뉴욕으로 돌아갈 계획이라면, 그녀는 최단 경로로 이동한 것이 아닐 수도 있다.

(C) 따라서 그녀는 미국 지도를 이미지화하고 마음속으로 여러 번 가상 여행을 할 수 있다. 워싱턴을 방문한 후 버팔로로 이동한 다음 버팔로를 방문한 후 시카고로 갔다가 뉴욕으로 돌아온다면 자신의 길을 일부 되돌아가게 될 거라는 사실을 깨닫게 된다.

(A) 그 때 그녀는 워싱턴으로 운전한 후 시카고로 갔다가 뉴욕으로 돌아오기 전에 버팔로로 가면 운행 시간을 많이 절약할 수 있다는 사실을 알게 된다.

| 37 | 한 문장으로 요약하기 | ① |

[정답해설]

(A) fewer(더 적은) / (B) intuition(직관)

제시문에 따르면 브레인스토밍 시험에서 얼굴을 마주 대하고 작업한 사람들이 생산성이 더 높을 것으로 기대했지만, 독립적으로 작업한 팀이 얼굴을 마주 대하고 작업한 팀보다 거의 두 배나 많은 아이디어를 냈다고 서술하고 있다. 즉, 브레인스토밍에서 직접 접촉하는 집단의 구성원들이 서로 물리적으로 따로 일하는 집단의 구성원들보다 (A) 적은 아이디어를 만들어냈고, 이는 우리의 (B) 직관에 반하는 것이라고 한 문장으로 요약할 수 있다.

[오답해설]

② 더 적은 … 이익

③ 더 많은 … 결론

④ 더 많은 … 직관

⑤ 더 똑똑한 … 이익

[핵심어휘]

□ obey 따르다, 순종하다

□ counterintuitive 직관에 반하는

□ independently 독립적으로, 자주적으로

□ come to light 알려지다, 밝혀지다

□ brainstorming 브레인스토밍(창조적 집단 사고)

□ thought-provoking 진지하게 생각을 하게 하는, 시사하는 바가 많은

□ emerge 생겨나다, 나타나다

□ pool 모으다, 공유[공용]하다, 생각을 서로 내놓다

□ intuition 직관, 직감

[본문해석]

정말 현명해지려면 온라인 그룹은 하나의 최종 규칙과 다소 직관에 반하는 규칙을 따라야 한다. 구성원들은 서로 너무 많이 접촉할 수 없다. 최선은 구성원들이 독립적으로 생각하고 일할 수 있어야 한다. 이 규칙은 1958년 사회 과학자들이 다양한 브레인스토밍 기술을 시험하면서 밝혀졌다. 그들은 시사하는 바가 큰 질문을 던졌다. 사람이 양손에 엄지손가락이 하나씩 더 생기면 어떤 이점과 문제점이 나타날까? 그런 다음 두 유형의 브레인스토밍 그룹이 답변을 제시했다. 한 그룹에서는 구성원들이 얼굴을 마주 대하고 작업했고, 다른 그룹에서는 구성원들이 각자 독립적으로 작업한 다음 마지막에 답변을 모았다. 얼굴을 마주 대하고 작업한 사람들이 생산성이 더 높을 것으로 기대했지만, 그렇지 않았다. 독립적으로 작업한 구성원들이 있는 팀이 거의 두 배나 많은 아이디어를 냈다. 전통적인 브레인스토밍은 혼자 생각하고 나서 결과를 모으는 것만큼 그리 효과적이지 않았다.

> 브레인스토밍에서 직접 접촉하는 집단의 구성원들이 서로 물리적으로 따로 일하는 집단의 구성원들보다 (A) 적은 아이디어를 만들어내며, 이는 우리의 (B) 직관에 반하는 것이다.

| 38 | 한 문장으로 요약하기 | ② |

[정답해설]

(A) excel(뛰어나다) / (B) limitations(한계)

제시문에 따르면 컴퓨터가 처음 등장했을 때에는 오류투성이였지만, 지금의 컴퓨터는 체스나 의학 진단과 같은 분야에서 그 성능이 (A) 뛰어난다. 그럼에도 불구하고 지금의 컴퓨터가 인간 활동의 상당 부분을 수행하는 데 어려움을 겪는 것은 컴퓨터 자체의 기술적 (B) 한계라기보다는 그것을 프로그래밍하는 프로그래머의 방식이 시대에 뒤떨어졌기 때문이라고 필자는 주장하고 있다.

[오답해설]

① 실패하다 … 문제

③ 작동하지 않다 … 문제

④ 성공하다 … 발전

⑤ 응시하다 … 한계

[핵심어휘]

- blunder 큰 실수
- tiny 아주 작은
- outlandish 이상한, 기이한
- maddening 미치게 만드는, 터무니없는
- babysit 아이를 봐 주다
- instruction-sets 명령어 세트
- attribute 속성, 특성
- deficiency 결핍, 부족
- limitation 제약, 한계
- significant 중요한, 상당한
- diagnosis 진단, 분석
- outdated 구식의, 낡은
- inherent 본래의, 내재적인
- malfunction 제대로 작동하지 않다
- stare 빤히 쳐다보다, 응시하다

[본문해석]

컴퓨터가 처음 등장한 직후, 컴퓨터의 실수는 농담의 대상이 되었다. 프로그래밍의 사소한 오류로 인해 고객의 은행 계좌가 사라지거나, 이상한 금액의 청구서가 발송되거나, 똑같은 실수를 반복하는 순환 루프에 컴퓨터가 갇혀 있었다. 이러한 터무니없는 상식의 부재로 인해 대부분의 사용자는 기계가 결코 지능화될 수 없다는 결론을 내렸다. 물론 지금의 컴퓨터는 더 나은 성능을 발휘한다. 일부 프로그램은 체스에서 사람들을 이길 수 있다. 다른 프로그램은 심장마비를 진단할 수 있다. 하지만 아직 침대를 만들거나 책을 읽거나 아이를 봐 줄 수 있는 기계는 없다. 대부분의 사람들이 할 수 있는 일들을 컴퓨터가 할 수 없는 이유는 무엇일까? 컴퓨터는 더 많은 메모리, 속도 또는 복잡함이 필요할까? 컴퓨터는 잘못된 명령어 세트를 사용하는가? 아니면 기계에는 인간의 뇌만이 가질 수 있는 마법 같은 속성이 없는 것일까? 나는 이러한 모든 한계는 오늘날 기계의 결함에는 책임이 없으며, 대신 프로그래머가 그것들을 프로그래밍하기 위해 선택한 시대에 뒤떨어진 방식에서 비롯되었다고 주장한다.

↓

초기 컴퓨터들은 상당한 오류가 있었지만, 현대의 기계는 체스나 의학 진단과 같은 작업에는 (A) 뛰어나나, 내재적인 기술적 (B) 한계보다는 시대에 뒤떨어진 프로그래밍으로 인해 기본적인 인간 활동에 어려움을 겪고 있다.

[39~40]

[핵심어휘]

- catastrophic 대변동의, 큰 재앙의
- eruption 폭발, 분화
- entomb 파묻다, 뒤덮다
- resident 거주자, 주민
- volcanic ash 화산재
- doom 죽음, 파멸, 비운
- frontier 최선단, 미개척지
- simultaneously 동시에, 일제히
- wreck 망가뜨리다, 파괴하다
- timeline 연대표, 시각표
- collapse 붕괴되다, 무너지다
- reveal 드러내다, 밝히다
- archaeological 고고학적인, 고고학상의
- seismic 지진의
- accompany 동반하다, 수반하다
- violent 격렬한, 극심한
- historical account 역사적 기록
- investigate 수사하다, 조사하다
- excavation 발굴
- archaeoseismology 고고지진학
- seismicity 지진 활동도
- speculate 추측하다, 짐작하다
- insula (고대 로마의) 집단 주택
- chaste 순결한, 순수한
- encompass 포함하다, 에워싸다
- evidently 분명히, 눈에 띄게
- interrupt 중단시키다, 가로막다
- trigger 촉발시키다, 작동시키다

[본문해석]

폼페이는 서기 79년에 베수비오산의 재앙적인 분화로 파괴되었고, 주민들은 화산재에 겹겹이 파묻혔다. 하지만 고대 로마 도시의 파멸에 대한 이야기는 더 많은 것이 있다. 「지구과학의 최전선」이란 잡지에 발표된 연구에 따르면 폼페이가 대규모 지진에 의해 동시에 파괴되었다는 증거가 있다. 이 발견은 도시 붕괴의 새로운 타임라인을 확립하고 연구에 대한 새로운 접근 방식이 잘 연구된 고고학 유적지로부터 추가적인 비밀을 (a) 밝혀낼 수 있음을 보여준다. 연구자들은 항상 지진 활동이 도시 파괴의 원인이었다는 생각을 가지고 있었다. 고대 작가 Pliny the Younger는 베수비오 화산 폭발이 격렬한 흔들림을 동반했다고 보고했다. 그러나 지금까지 이 역사적 기록을 (b) 뒷받침할 증거는 발견되지 않았다. 이탈리아의 Domenico Sparice가 이끄는 연구팀은 이 기록의 (c) 공백을 조사하기로 결정했다. Sparice 박사는 지금까지 폼페이 발굴에는 지진이 고대 건축물에 미치는 영향을 다루는 고고지진학 분야의 전문가가 포함되지 않았다고 말했다. 그는 이 분야 (d) 전문가들의 공헌이 이번 발견의 핵심이라고 말했다. Sparice 박사는 "지진의 영향은 과거 학자들에 의해 추측되었지만, 우리 연구 이전에는 실질적인 증거가 보고되지 않았다"며 이번 발견이 "매우 흥미로웠다"고 덧붙였다. 연구팀은 '순결한 연인의 집'에 초점을 맞췄다. 이 지역은 화가들이 화산 폭발로 인해 중단된 것이 분명한 (e) 색칠되지 않은 빨가게와 집을 포함한 여러 건물들로 에워싸여 있다. 발굴과 신중한 분석 끝에, 연구진은 지진으로 인해 그 집의 벽이 무너졌다는 결론을 내렸다.

39 글의 제목 유추하기 ⑤

[정답해설]
제시문에 따르면 고대 로마 도시인 폼페이가 베수비오산의 화산 폭발로 파괴되었다는 기존의 사실 외에 동시에 대규모 지진에 의해 파괴되었다는 여러 증거들이 새로운 발굴과 분석으로 밝혀졌다고 설명하고 있다. 그러므로 ⑤의 'The Eruption of Mt. Vesuvius Wasn't Pompeii's Only Killer(베수비오산의 분화가 폼페이의 유일한 살인자가 아니었다)'가 제시문의 제목으로 가장 적절하다.

[오답해설]
① 누가 화산재로 뒤덮인 폼페이를 발견하였는가
② 폼페이의 풍경에 영향을 미친 베수비오산
③ 지진으로 촉발된 베수비오산의 분화
④ 폼페이의 고고학적 발견에 의한 지진 연대표

40 문맥상 부적절한 낱말 고르기 ⑤

[정답해설]
colored → uncolored
연구팀이 초점을 맞춘 '순결한 연인의 집'이 있는 지역의 빨가게와 집은 화가들이 화산 폭발로 인해 색칠 작업을 중단한 것이 분명하다고 하였으므로, (e)의 'colored(색칠된)'는 'uncolored(색칠되지 않은)'로 고쳐 써야 옳다.

[41~42]

[핵심어휘]
- personality 성격, 개성, 인성
- obvious 분명한, 명확한
- uniqueness 독특함, 고유성
- remainder 나머지
- built in 내장된, 내재된
- theorised 이론을 제시하다[세우다]
- in a vacuum 진공 상태에서, 외부와 단절된 상태에서
- id 이드(인간의 원시적·본능적 요소가 존재하는 무의식 부분)
- ego 에고, 자아
- superego 초자아
- actualise 현실로 만들다, 실현하다
- in isolation 홀로, 따로

[본문해석]
성격은 일상생활에서 분명한 인간 상태의 한 부분이다. 우리 각자는 독특하며 이러한 독특함을 강조하는 것이 성격에 대한 연구인 반면, 심리학의 나머지 상당 부분은 사람들 간의 유사성을 강조한다. 성격의 일부는 내재되어 있는 것처럼 보이고 다른 부분은 학습된 것처럼 보인다. 물론 성격은 환경적 필요성이나 또는 신념, 가치관, 견해 및 판단을 통해서 문화에 의해 영향을 받는다.

성격을 어떤 식으로 바라보거나 이론화하든 간에, 그것이 외부와 단절된 상태로 존재하지 않는다는 것은 분명하다. 사람은 이드, 자아와 초자아, 혹은 현실의 자아, 또는 일련의 학습된 사회적 행동, 혹은 일련의 특징으로 구성될 수 있다. 이 중 어느 것이든 맥락 혹은 일련의 상황이나 경험 내에서 발생할 수 있으며, 이 두 가지 모두 동일하지는 않다. 따라서 일반적으로 또는 특히 누군가의 성격을 바라보는 가장 좋은 방법은 상호작용의 시각을 통해서이다. 사람들은 각기 타인에게 영향을 미치는 환경 없이는 존재할 수 없다. 따라서 특정 환경에 존재하는 성격을 이해하는 것이 가장 좋다. 성격은 홀로 존재할 수 없다.

41 글의 제목 유추하기 ③

[정답해설]
제시문은 성격을 이해함에 있어 성격을 인간의 독특함, 문화에 의한 영향, 상호작용의 맥락에서 설명하고 있다. 그러므로 ③의 'Understanding Personality: Uniqueness, Culture, and Context(성격 이해: 독특함, 문화, 맥락)'가 제시문의 제목으로 가장 적절하다.

[오답해설]
① 나이가 들면서 성격은 어떻게 발달하는가?
② 성격과 사회적 행동의 성별 차이
④ 성격, 사회적 행동을 결정하는 한 가지 요인
⑤ 성격과 특징의 유사점은 무엇인가?

| 42 | 빈칸 추론하기 | ④ |

[정답해설]

제시문의 마지막 부분에 사람들은 각기 타인에게 영향을 미치는 환경 없이는 존재할 수 없으므로 특정 환경에 존재하는 성격을 이해하는 것이 가장 좋다고 하였다. 따라서 성격을 바라보는 가장 좋은 방법은 상호작용의 시각을 통해서이다. 그러므로 빈칸에 들어갈 말은 ④의 'interaction(상호작용)'이 가장 적절하다.

[오답해설]

① 감정

② 창의성

③ 유용성

⑤ 생산성

[43~45]

[핵심어휘]

□ lean 기대다, 의지하다

□ graffiti (공공장소에 하는) 낙서

□ senior class president 수석 반장

□ What's up? 요즘 어때?, 잘 지냈어?

□ confident 자신감 있는, 확신하는

□ scared 겁먹은, 무서워하는

□ nervous 불안한, 걱정스러운

□ grab a coffee 커피 한 잔 마시다

□ acoustic (악기나 공연이) 전자 장치를 쓰지 않는

[본문해석]

(A)

Sophia는 North High의 벽돌 벽에 기대어 손가락으로 낙서를 따라갔다. 마지막 종이 울렸고, 학생들은 빠르게 자리를 떠나고 있었다. 그녀는 주위를 둘러보았지만 언니 Sara를 찾을 수 없었다. 한숨을 쉬며, (a) 그녀는 집으로 걸어가기 시작했다. 다음 주에는 학교 장기자랑이 있었고, 그녀는 노래 부르기를 신청했다. 그녀는 노래 부르는 걸 좋아했지만 많은 청중 앞에서 노래를 불러본 적이 없었다.

(C)

Sophia는 걸으면서 생각에 잠겼고 수석 반장인 Janet이 바로 앞에 있을 때까지 눈치 채지 못했다. Janet과 Sara는 서로 아는 사이였지만, Sophia는 그녀와 대화를 나눈 적이 없었다. "안녕, Sophia." Janet이 활짝 웃으며 말했다. "안녕, Janet. 잘 지냈어?" (c) 그녀는 깜짝 놀라며 대답했다. "장기자랑에 신청했다고 들었어." Janet이 말했다. "무슨 노래를 부를 거야?" Sophia는 걱정스러웠다. "아직 잘 모르겠어." (d) 그녀가 말했다. "아직 고심 중이야." Janet은 다시 미소를 지었다. "커피 한 잔 마시며 얘기해 볼래?"

(D)

그들은 동네 카페로 걸어가 학교와 음악에 대해 이야기했다. Janet은 대화하기에 편했고, Sophia는 (e) 그녀에게 더 편안함을 느꼈다. "어떤 종류의 음악을 좋아해?" Janet이 물었다. "나는 클래식 록을 좋아해." Sophia가 말했다. "그래서 어쿠스틱 버전의 클래식 록을 해볼까 생각 중이야." Janet의 눈이 번뜩였다. "딱 좋은데. 나는 기타를 조금 연주하는데, 같이 연주할래?"

(B)

Sophia의 눈이 휘둥그레졌다. "정말? 대단한데!" 그들은 다음 한 시간 동안 계획하고 연습했다. 마침내 작별 인사를 했을 때, Sophia는 Janet이 많은 도움을 주었기 때문에 자신감이 더욱 생겼다. 그녀가 집으로 걸어갈 때, 석양이 마을을 황금빛으로 물들였다. 그녀는 예상 밖의 순간에 새로운 친구들이 모든 것을 더 좋게 만들 수 있다는 것을 깨달았다. 장기자랑은 더 이상 두려워할 대상이 아니라 (b) 그녀가 빛날 수 있는 기회였다.

| 43 | 글의 배열순서 정하기 | ③ |

[정답해설]

글 (C)의 마지막 부분에서 Janet이 커피 한 잔 마시며 얘기해 보자고 Sophia에게 제안했고, 글 (D)의 첫 부분에서 둘이 동네 카페에서 학교와 음악에 대해 이야기하는 장면이 묘사되어 있다. 그러므로 글 (C) 다음에 글 (D)가 와야 한다. 또한 글 (D)의 마지막 부분에서 Janet이 기타 연주를 같이 하자고 Sophia에게 제안했고, 글 (B)에서 둘이 한 시간 동안 계획하고 연습하는 장면이 묘사되어 있다. 그러므로 글 (D) 다음에 글 (B)가 와야 한다. 따라서 전체적인 글의 흐름상 주어진 글 (A) 다음에 (C)-(D)-(B) 순으로 글이 이어져야 한다.

44	지칭 대상과 다른 것 고르기	⑤

[정답해설]

(a), (b), (c), (d)는 모두 Sophia를 가리키지만, (e)는 Sophia가 대화하기에 편안함을 느낀 Janet을 가리킨다.

45	내용과 불일치 문장 고르기	⑤

[정답해설]

글 (D)에서 Sophia가 어쿠스틱 버전의 클래식 록을 해보려고 한다는 말에, Janet이 자기가 기타를 조금 연주할 줄 안다면 함께 연주할 것을 제안했다. 그러므로 Sophia가 Janet에게 기타 치는 법을 가르쳤다는 ⑤의 설명은 윗글의 내용과 일치하지 않는다.

[오답해설]

① Sophia는 학교 장기자랑에 노래 부르기를 신청했다. → 글 (A)에 Sophia가 학교 장기자랑에 노래 부르기를 신청했으나, 많은 사람 앞에서 노래를 불러본 적이 없다고 서술됨

② Sophia는 Janet과 함께 연습한 후 더 자신감을 느꼈다. → 글 (B)에 Sophia가 Janet이 많은 도움을 주었기 때문에 자신감이 더욱 생겼다고 서술됨

③ Sophia의 언니와 Janet은 서로 아는 사이였다. → 글 (C)에 Janet과 Sara(Sophia의 언니)는 서로 아는 사이였지만, Sophia는 그녀와 대화를 나눈 적이 없다고 서술됨

④ Sophia는 클래식 록 노래를 부르려고 생각하고 있었다. → 글 (D)에 Sophia가 클래식 록을 좋아하므로 어쿠스틱 버전의 클래식 록을 불러볼까 생각 중이라고 서술됨

2024학년도 기출문제 **정답 및 해설**

2024학년도

[영어]

정답 및 해설

▌[영어] 2024학년도 | 정답

01	②	02	①	03	②	04	①	05	⑤
06	③	07	⑤	08	①	09	②	10	④
11	③	12	③	13	③	14	④	15	④
16	⑤	17	④	18	②	19	⑤	20	⑤
21	①	22	③	23	①	24	⑤	25	⑤
26	②	27	③	28	④	29	④	30	③
31	④	32	⑤	33	④	34	③	35	③
36	③	37	⑤	38	④	39	①	40	①
41	⑤	42	①	43	④	44	②	45	⑤

[영어] 2024학년도 | 해설

01	유사 어휘 고르기	②

[정답해설]

'advocate'는 '옹호하다, 지지하다'의 뜻으로, 'champion(싸우다, 옹호하다)'와 그 의미가 가장 유사하다.

[오답해설]

① 반대하다

③ 무시하다

④ 악화시키다

⑤ 압도하다

[핵심어휘]

▫ advocate 옹호하다, 지지하다

▫ authority 권위, 권한

▫ disregard 무시하다, 묵살하다

▫ undermine 약화시키다, 침식시키다

▫ overwhelm 압도하다, 제압하다

[본문해석]

어떤 예술도 사람들을 홀로 정복할 수 없다. 사람들은 권위에 의해 옹호되는 삶의 이상에 의해 정복된다.

02	유사 어휘 고르기	①

[정답해설]

'impartial'는 '편파적이지 않은, 공평한'의 뜻으로, 'fair(공정한, 공평한)'와 그 의미가 가장 유사하다.

[오답해설]

② 해가 없는

③ 의미 있는

④ 시기적절한

⑤ 창의적인

[핵심어휘]

▫ impartial 편파적이지 않은, 공평한

▫ harmless 해가 없는, 악의 없는

▫ meaningful 의미 있는, 중요한

▫ timely 시기적절한, 때맞춘

[본문해석]

우리는 완전히 열린 마음으로 시작하는 일이 거의 없으며, 이는 우리가 어떤 주제를 완전히 <u>공평한</u> 방식으로 논의할 수 있도록 해줄 것이다.

03 　　　유사 어휘 고르기　　　②

[정답해설]
'minutes'는 '회의록, 의사록'의 뜻으로, 'records(기록물)'와 그 의미가 가장 유사하다.

[오답해설]
① 시각
③ 순간
④ 기간
⑤ 곡조

[핵심어휘]
□ read through 다 읽다, 통독하다
□ minute 회의록, 의사록
□ duration 지속, 기간

[본문해석]
우리는 지난 회의록을 끝까지 읽었다.

04 　　　유사 어휘 고르기　　　①

[정답해설]
'confine'은 '국한하다, 한정하다'의 뜻으로, 'limit(제한하다, 한정하다)'와 그 의미가 가장 유사하다.

[오답해설]
② 확대하다
③ 분류하다
④ 촉진하다
⑤ 순응하다

[핵심어휘]
□ confine 국한시키다, 한정[제한]하다
□ statement 진술, 서술
□ conform 따르다, 순응하다

[본문해석]
막내 경찰관의 임무는 군중으로부터 진술을 받아내는 것에 국한되었다

05 　　　유사 어휘 고르기　　　⑤

[정답해설]
'it goes without saying that'은 '~은 말할 것도 없다. 두말하면 잔소리

다'의 뜻으로, 'obviously(분명히, 확실히)'와 그 의미가 가장 유사하다.

[오답해설]
① 틀림없이
② 아마도
③ 다행히도
④ 흔쾌히

[핵심어휘]
□ it goes without saying that ~은 말할 것도 없다, 두말하면 잔소리다
□ photography 사진술, 사진 촬영
□ multiply 증가하다, 배가하다
□ composition (그림·사진의) 구도
□ arguably 주장하건대, 거의 틀림없이
□ agreeably 기분 좋게, 흔쾌히
□ obviously 확실히, 분명히

[본문해석]
구도에 움직임이 더해질 때, 그리고 영상이 비칠 때 컬러 촬영의 어려움이 배가되는 것은 말할 것도 없다.

06 　　　빈칸 추론하기　　　③

[정답해설]
빈칸에 들어갈 말은 축구 경기에 가야할지 아니면 집에서 숙제를 해야 할지를 묻는 B의 질문에 대한 A의 답변이다. A의 대답에 B가 알고 있다고 말하며, 어떻게 해야 할지 결정을 내리지 못하고 있는 것으로 보아, 빈칸에 들어갈 말로는 "글쎄, 그건 네게 달려 있어."가 가장 적절하다.

[오답해설]
① 더 열심히 연습했어야 해.
② 내일은 집에 있어야 해.
④ 중요한 질문이 있어.
⑤ 우리는 어제 축구 경기를 보았다.

[핵심어휘]
□ assignment 과제, 임무
□ be up to ~에 달려 있다
□ profound 깊은, 심오한

[본문해석]
A: 숙제는 다 끝냈니?
B: 아니요, 아직이요. 오늘 밤에 하려고요.
A: 오늘 밤? 축구 경기에 가지 않니?

정답 및 해설

B: 아, 그 경기! 완전히 잊고 있었네요. 그 경기를 기대하고 있었는데요.

A: 그러게. 중요한 결정을 내려야 할 것 같아.

B: 맞아요. 경기에 가야 하나요 아니면 그냥 집에서 숙제를 해야 하나요?

A: 글쎄, 그건 네게 달려 있어.

B: 알아요. 아직 어떻게 해야 할지 모르겠어요.

A: 걱정하지 마. 네가 옳은 결정을 할 거야.

07 빈칸 추론하기 ⑤

[정답해설]

자동차 보험사에서 배터리 충전 서비스를 해 준다는 A의 말에 B가 몰랐다며 바로 전화해 본다고 하였으므로, B에 들어갈 말로는 "알려줘서 고마워."가 가장 적절하다.

[오답해설]

① 이거 정말 잘 돼 네!

② 천천히 해.

③ 등록번호가 어떻게 돼?

④ 난 잘못한 게 없어.

[핵심어휘]

- insurance company 보험 회사
- recharge 충전하다
- take your time 천천히 하다, 여유를 가지다
- registration 등록

[본문해석]

A: 뭐 하고 있어?

B: 차가 시동이 안 걸려. 뭐가 잘못됐는지 알아보고 있어.

A: 오, 이런. 너 차에 대해 아니? 뭔가 찾았어?

B: 배터리가 다 된 거 같아. 몇 주 동안 외지에 있었는데, 그 동안 아무도 내 차를 이용하지 않았어.

A: 보험사에 전화했니?

B: 무엇 때문에?

A: 보통 자동차 보험사에서 배터리 충전 서비스를 해줘. 바로 와서 충전해 줄 거야. 아주 편해.

B: 아, 난 몰랐네. 알려줘서 고마워. 지금 바로 전화해 볼 게.

A: 천만에.

08 어법상 틀린 것 고르기 ①

[정답해설]

become → becoming

'devote to'는 '~에 헌신[전념]하다'는 뜻으로, 'to'가 전치사이므로 뒤에 동사가 올 경우 동명사의 형태로 써야 한다. 그러므로 become은 becoming으로 고쳐 써야 옳다.

[핵심어휘]

- script 문자, 활자
- remedy 바로잡다, 해결하다
- preliminary 예비의, 서문의
- inadequate 부족한, 불충분한
- decade 10년
- devote to ~ing ~하는데 전념[헌신]하다
- become acquainted with ~에 정통하다, ~을 익히다[숙지하다]
- informed 잘 아는, 유식한, 정통한
- full-scale 완벽한, 전면적인
- agent 대리인, 대행사
- abridge 단축하다, 요약하다
- version 버전, 판
- illustration 삽화, 도해
- footnote 각주(각 페이지 하단에 붙이는 주석)
- abridgement 요약, 축약, 간추림
- unabridged version 무삭제판, 완본
- identification 확인, 검증, 증명
- citation 인용, 인용구

[본문해석]

아직 아무도 15세기 통신 수단이 활자에서 인쇄로 이동한 결과를 조사하려고 시도하지 않았다. 이 상황을 해결하기 위해서는 책 한 권 이상이 필요하다는 것을 깨달으면서, 나는 예비적인 노력이 아무리 불충분하더라도 없는 것보다 낫다고 느꼈고, 주로 초기 인쇄에 관한 특별한 문헌과 책의 역사를 숙지하는 데 전념하는 10년간의 연구를 시작했다. 1968년과 1971년 사이에 몇몇 예비 논문들이 학자들의 반응을 이끌어내고 정통한 비판을 이용하기 위해 출판되었다. 나의 완벽한 작품인 『변화의 대행자로서의 인쇄술』은 1979년에 등장했다. 그것은 현재 판본에서 일반 독자들을 위해 요약되었다. 삽화가 추가되었지만 이 요약본에서 각주는 삭제되었다. 요약되지 않은 완본은 모든 인용구와 참고문헌을 완전히 확인하려고 하는 독자라면 누구나 참고해야만 한다.

09 어법상 틀린 것 고르기 ②

[정답해설]

swiftly → swift

등위 접속사 and에 의한 A and B의 형태에서, 형용사 + 명사의 구조인 'autonomous mobility(자율적인 이동)'에 대응하여 'swiftly transport'는 'swift transport(신속한 운송)'가 되어야 한다. 즉, 부사 형태인 'swiftly(신속하게)'를 형용사 형태인 'swift(신속한)'로 고쳐 써야 하며, 여기서 'transport'의 품사는 동사가 아니라 명사이다.

[핵심어휘]

- neutral 중립의, 중립적인
- burden 짐, 부담
- mass-produced 대량 생산의
- autonomous mobility 자율이동
- swift 빠른, 신속한
- congestion 혼잡, 밀집
- earth-devastating 지구를 파괴하는
- inception 시작, 개시
- skeptics 회의론자
- destabilize 불안정하게 만들다
- invading 침입하는
- yellow journalism 황색 저널리즘, 선동적 언론
- invasive 급속히 퍼지는, 침략[침입]하는
- misleading 오해의 소지가 있는, 현혹시키는
- ubiquitous 어디에나 있는, 아주 흔한
- deep-fake 가짜의, 조작의
- viral 바이러스성의, 바이러스에 의한

[본문해석]

신기술의 혜택과 부담을 평가하는 데 중립적인 입장은 없다. 20세기 초 대량 생산된 포드 모델 T나 21세기의 자율주행 자동차를 생각해보라. 자동차를 통해, 인간의 혼잡과 지구를 파괴하는 오염과 대조하여 자율적인 이동과 신속한 운송의 이점을 평가한다. 그것은 사진술에서도 마찬가지이다. 시작부터 회의론자들은 광범위하고 통제되지 않은 사진술이 거짓을 퍼뜨리고 사생활을 침해함으로써 공동체와 정부를 불안정하게 할 것이라고 걱정했다. 이러한 불안은 코닥 카메라 초기에, 그것의 인기가 선동적 언론의 확산과 결합하여 침해와 오해의 소지가 있는 사진들을 만들어내면서 발생했다. 이러한 걱정은 아주 흔한 디지털 카메라 폰, 조작 영상, 그리고 바이러스성 인터넷과 더불어 오늘날에도 계속된다. 그때나 지금이나, 카메라의 작동 방법과 사진 표현력에 관한 논쟁은 사생활, 국제 정치 그리고 공공 정의에 관한 것이다.

10 문맥에 맞는 낱말 고르기 ④

[정답해설]

(A) share / (B) receptive / (C) positive

(A) 스포츠는 전 세계 사람들이 기후 위기에 대한 인식을 높이는 강력한 도구가 될 수 있으므로, 스포츠와 관련된 수십억 명의 사람들이 환경에 대한 메시지를 함께 할 수 있다. 그러므로 빈칸에 들어갈 말로는 'share(공유하다)'가 적절하다.

(B) 스포츠 팬들은 그들의 생활 습관을 바꿀 정도로 스포츠 행사에서 준비한 생태학적 계획을 적극적으로 받아들인다. 그러므로 빈칸에 들어갈 말로는 'receptive(수용적인)'가 적절하다.

(C) 스포츠 조직이 행하는 환경에 대한 노력은 가정에서 행하는 환경 목표에 또한 바람직한 영향을 미친다. 그러므로 빈칸에 들어갈 말로는 'positive(긍정적인)'가 적절하다.

[핵심어휘]

- awareness 앎, 인식, 관심
- geographical 지리적인, 지리학상의
- restrain 제한하다, 억제하다
- spectator 관중, 관람객
- practitioner 전문직 종사자
- facilitator 조력자, 협력자
- receptive 수용적인, 받아들이는
- ecological 생태학적인
- initiative 시작, 계획, 발의
- regarding ~에 관하여[대하여]
- sustainability 지속[유지] 가능성
- norm 표준, 규범, 기준
- significant 중요한, 상당한, 의미심장한
- perception 지각, 인식, 통찰력
- behavioural intention 행동 목적

[본문해석]

광범위한 인기 덕분에, 스포츠는 지리적인 위치와 사회적 배경에 관계없이 전 세계 사람들에게 기후 위기에 대한 인식을 높이는 강력한 도구가 될 수 있다. 간단히 말해서, 그 산업은 관중, 종사자 또는 협력자로서 스포츠와 관련된 수십억 명의 개인들에게 환경에 대한 중요한 메시지를 (A) 공유할 수 있다. 인식을 높이고 교육을 하는 그러한 전략은 과거에 좋은 결과를 보여주었다. 팬들이 심지어 지속해왔던 그들의 생활 습관을 기꺼이 바꿀 정도로, 스포츠 행사에서 준비된 생태학적 계획에 (B) 수용적이라는 사실이 연구에서 밝혀졌다. 이 연구는 "스포츠 행사와 관련된 규범은 가정에서 이루어지는 환경 행동 목표에도 또한 영향을 미치면서, 스포츠 조직이 행하는 노력에 대한 (C) 긍정적 인식과 상당한 관련이 있다"고 정확히 결론을 내렸다.

11 문맥에 맞는 낱말 고르기 ③

[정답해설]

(A) frequent / (B) borrowed / (C) picked up

(A) 영어 어원이 아닌 라틴어나 그리스 어원으로 개념에 대한 이름을 짓는 일은 과학적 지식이 급속히 확장함에 따라 점점 더 증가하였다. 그러므로 빈칸에 들어갈 말로는 'frequent(빈번한)'가 적절하다.

(B) 영어로 이름을 붙일 수 없는 개념을 언급하기 위해 라틴어 어원을 가져와 이름을 붙인 것이므로, 빈칸에 들어갈 말로는 'borrowed(차용했다)'가 적절하다.

(C) 일부 단어들은 즉시 사용되지 않았지만, 일부 단어들은 동시대 사람들에 의해 오늘날에도 여전히 사용되므로, 빈칸에 들어갈 말로는 'picked up(받아들였다)'가 적절하다.

[핵심어휘]

▫ rare 드문, 희귀한

▫ make up a name for ~에 대한 이름을 짓다

▫ affix 접사

▫ pick up 들이게[익히게] 되다

▫ take out 없애다, 제거하다

▫ contemporary 동년배, 동시대 사람

[본문해석]

학자들이 영어로 이름을 붙일 수 없는 개념을 언급하기 위해 전문적인 용어가 필요할 때마다, 그들은 그리스어나 라틴어에서 하나를 가져왔다. 만일 그리스어나 라틴어에도 그 개념에 대한 이름이 없다면 – 과학적 지식이 고대인들의 꿈을 넘어 급속히 확장되면서 점점 더 (A) <u>빈번해진</u> 상황 – 그들은 영어 어원이 아닌 라틴어 및/또는 그리스어 어원에서 그 개념에 대한 이름을 지을 것이다. 이 관행은 오늘날까지 계속되고 있다. 결과적으로 많은 사람들이 라틴어 용어를 (B) <u>차용</u>했고, 키케로의 시대에 전혀 사용되지 않았던 접사뿐만 아니라 라틴어 어원에서 새로 형성된 단어들이 이 시기에 영어로 들어왔다. 그 단어들의 상당수가 거의 즉시 사용되지 않았지만, 다른 많은 단어들은 동시대 사람들에 의해 (C) <u>받아들여졌고</u> 오늘날에도 여전히 함께 한다.

12 문맥에 맞는 낱말 고르기 ③

[정답해설]

(A) expansion / (B) destroyed / (C) stationary

(A) 국제 무역을 포함한 상업 활동이 엄청난 상승의 시기였다고 서술되어 있으므로, 빈칸에 들어갈 말로는 'expansion(팽창)'이 적절하다.

(B) 금전적 이익의 추구로 무서운 결과를 가져온 마이다스의 우화처럼, 그리스 사회 또한 부의 추구로 위험에 빠졌다고 설명하고 있으므로, 빈칸에 들어갈 말로는 'destroyed(파괴하다)'가 적절하다.

(C) 플라톤과 아리스토텔레스 모두 경제 성장이 바람직하지 못한 영향을 미쳤다고 생각하고 있으므로, 그들은 경제활동이 멈추길 바란다. 그러므로 빈칸에 들어갈 말로는 'stationary(정적인)'가 적절하다.

[핵심어휘]

▫ liberalization 자유화

▫ enormous 엄청난, 막대한

▫ tremendous 거대한, 굉장한

▫ disturbance 방해, 소란, 장애

▫ instability 불안정

▫ expansion 확장, 팽창

▫ reduction 축소, 감소

▫ liberate 해방시키다, 자유롭게 해주다

▫ ideal state 이상 국가

▫ constitute 구성하다, 이루다

▫ undesirable 달갑지 않은, 바람직하지 않은

▫ relatively 비교적, 상대적으로

▫ stationary 정지된, 비유동적인

[본문해석]

플라톤과 아리스토텔레스 시대 이전의 2세기는 경제적 자유화의 시기였고, 이것과 더불어 국제 무역을 포함한 상업 활동에 엄청난 상승이 왔다. 더욱이 굉장한 경제적인 혼란과 사회적인 불안정은 급속한 상업적 (A) <u>팽창</u>을 동반했고, 이것은 플라톤과 아리스토텔레스의 경제적 사고에 큰 영향을 미쳤다. 그들은 그 불안정은 마이다스의 우화가 알려준 것처럼, 무서운 결과를 가져온 금전적 이익의 추구에서 비롯되었다고 믿었다. 마이다스가 금을 쫓기 위해 자신을 (B) <u>파괴했던</u> 것처럼, 부의 추구 또한 그리스 사회를 위험에 빠뜨렸다. 플라톤과 아리스토텔레스가 이상 국가에서의 삶은 어떠한 모습인지 조사에 착수한 것은 부분적으로 이러한 위협에 대한 대응이었고, 그 상태에서 그들의 분석은 "좋은 삶"을 어떻게 이룰 것인가란 문제를 중심으로 수립되었다. 경제 성장이 바람직하지 못한 영향을 미쳤다는 것은 그들에게 분명했고, 그들은 비교적 (C) <u>정적인</u> 경제 활동 수준을 생성하는 경제 시스템의 필요성을 강조했다.

13 문맥상 부적절한 낱말 고르기 ③

[정답해설]

precision → similarity 또는 approximation

제시문에 따르면 모든 역사적 기록들은 시간이 지남에 따라 바뀔 수도 있는 일종의 재구성으로, 절대적인 확실성을 제공할 수 없다고 하였다. 즉, 진정한 역사적 기록들은 존재하지 않으며, 과거 사실의 유사성 또는 근사치만을 제공할 뿐이다. 그러므로 ③의 'precision(정확성)'은 'similarity(유사성)' 또는 'approximation(근사치)' 등으로 고쳐 써야

옳다.

[핵심어휘]

- inevitably 필연적으로, 불가피하게
- account 기록, 설명, 해석
- reconstruction 복원, 재건, 재현
- certainty 확실성, 필연성
- precision 정확, 정밀
- leeway 여지, 자유, 재량
- accommodate 담다, 수용하다
- concise 간결한, 축약된
- no way around 방도가 없는, 피할 수 없는

[본문해석]

과거의 모든 증거는 현재에서만 발견될 수 있기 때문에, 과거에 관한 이야기를 만드는 것은 필연적으로 이 증거를 그 자체의 어떤 역사를 가진 과정의 측면에서 해석하는 것을 의미한다. 그렇게 하는 것은 주변 환경과 우리 자신들 모두 그러한 과정이 되는 것을 경험하기 때문이다. 결과적으로 모든 역사적 기록들은 일종의 재구성이며, 따라서 시간이 지남에 따라 바뀔 수도 있다. 이것은 또한 역사에 관한 연구가 절대적인 확실성을 제공할 수 없고, 단지 한때 그랬던 현실의 정확성 (→ 유사성)만을 제공한다는 것을 의미하기도 한다. 다시 말해서, 진정한 역사적 기록들은 존재하지 않는다. 이것은 마치 과거를 바라보는 방식에 끝없는 자유가 있는 것처럼 들릴 수도 있다. 내 생각에는 그렇지 않다. 다른 과학 분야에서와 마찬가지로, 역사적 재구성에 대한 주요한 시험은 그것들이 기존 자료를 간결하고 정확한 방식으로 수용하는가, 그리고 어느 정도로 수용하는가이다. 그럼에도 불구하고 모든 역사적 재구성이 역사가가 생각해 낸 문맥 속에 배치된 선별된 수의 기존 자료들로 구성된다는 사실을 피할 방도는 없다.

---

14 문맥상 부적절한 낱말 고르기 ④

[정답해설]

solving → causing

일회용 비닐봉지의 대안으로 여겨졌던 재사용 가능 봉지가 탄소 발자국(carbon footprint) 즉, 이산화탄소 배출량이 오히려 더 높게 나타나는 등 새로운 환경 문제를 낳고 있다. 그러므로 ④의 'solving(해결하는)'는 'causing(일으키는)'으로 고쳐 써야 옳다.

[핵심어휘]

- single-use 일회용의
- definitely 분명히, 확실히
- restriction 제한, 제약
- in place 시행 중인, 가동 중인
- eliminate 없애다, 줄이다

- leech 달라붙어 떨어지지 않다
- microplastic 미세 플라스틱
- reusable 재사용[재활용]할 수 있는
- retailer 소매업자, 소매상
- apparently 분명하게, 명백하게
- campaigner 운동가, 활동가
- hoard 축적, 비축
- carbon footprint 탄소 발자국(온실 효과를 유발하는 이산화탄소의 배출량)
- eye-popping 눈이 튀어나올 정도의, 깜짝 놀랄 정도인
- environmentally friendly alternative 환경 친화적 대안
- conventional 전통적인, 재래식의
- replacement 교체, 대체
- straightforward 간단한, 솔직한
- boil down to ~으로 요약하다, ~으로 귀결되다

[본문해석]

일회용 비닐봉지와의 싸움은 패배할지 모르지만, 그것은 확실히 진행 중이다. 그것들의 사용에 대한 제한은 거의 12개의 미국 주들과 세계의 많은 다른 국가들에서 시행 중이다. 그리고 많은 경우, 이러한 노력들은 나무 위에 떠다니고, 수로를 막고, 미세 플라스틱을 땅과 물속에 달라붙게 하고, 해양 생물들에게 해를 끼치는 얇은 비닐봉지의 신규 판매를 줄이는데 성공적이었다. 그러나 이런 종류의 환경에 대한 성공 이야기는 또 다른 문제를 감추고 있다. 우리 중 대다수는 분명 일회용 비닐보다 더 친환경적인 대안으로 소매상들이 값싸게 팔거나 손님들에게 나눠주는 재사용 가능한 봉지에 치이고 있다. 환경운동가들은 재사용 가능한 봉지가 얇은 비닐봉지보다 훨씬 더 이산화탄소 배출량이 높으며, 이러한 봉지 꾸러미가 새로운 환경 문제를 해결하고(→ 일으키고) 있다고 말한다. 한 놀라운 추정에 따르면, 면봉지가 전통적인 비닐봉지의 진정한 환경 친화적 대안이 되려면 최소한 7,100번이 사용되어야 한다. 일회용 비닐봉지의 가장 친환경적인 대체물이 무엇인지에 대한 답은 간단하진 않지만, 그 조언은 이와 같이 요약된다. 집에 있는 어떤 봉지든 가능한 한 많이 재사용하라.

---

15 내용과 일치하는 문장 고르기 ④

[정답해설]

제시문에서 랑케가 국가의 권력을 질서와 안정의 수호자로 여긴 반면, 부르크하르트는 권력을 악과 연결된 것으로 간주했다. 즉, 권력과 악이 손을 잡고 있다고 생각했다.

[오답해설]

① 야콥 부르크하르트는 결코 목사가 되고 싶지 않았다. → 원래는 아버지를 따라 개신교 목사가 되려고 함

② 야콥 부르크하르트는 바젤에서 미술사를 공부했다. → 바젤에서 신학

을 공부했고, 미술사는 베를린에서 공부함

③ 야콥 부르크하르트와 랑케의 관계는 논란의 여지가 없다. → 부르크
하르트와 랑케의 관계는 역사학자들 사이에서 상반된 관점의 주제임. 즉 논
란의 여지가 많음

⑤ 야콥 부르크하르트는 랑케의 지적 접근법을 받아들였다. → 랑케의
개인적 야망과 직적 접근법 둘 다 거부함

[핵심어휘]

▫ Protestant minister 개신교 목사

▫ theology 신학

▫ contrary 정반대의, 상반된

▫ retain 유지[보유]하다, 지탱하다

▫ regard 존경, 높은 평가

▫ guardian 수호자, 후견인

▫ confidently 자신 있게, 당당히

▫ skeptical 회의적인, 회의론자 같은

▫ withdrawn 내성적인, 내향적인

▫ hostile forces 적군, 적대 세력

▫ reference 말, 언급

▫ reject 거절하다, 거부하다

▫ uncontroversial 논란의 여지가 없는

▫ embrace 받아들이다, 수용하다

[본문해석]

스위스 바젤에서 목사의 아들인 야콥 부르크하르트는 원래 그의 아버
지의 발자취를 따라서 개신교 목사가 되려고 하였다. 그러나 바젤에서
신학을 공부하는 동안, 그는 기독교가 신화라는 결론에 도달했다. 역
사와 미술사 연구로 눈을 돌려, 그는 베를린에서 레오폴드 랑케와 함
께 공부하며 4년을 보냈다. 부르크하르트와 랑케의 관계는 역사학자
들 사이에서 상반된 관점의 주제이다. 어떤 이들은 근본적인 그들의
차이에도 불구하고, 부르크하르트가 일생 동안 랑케를 높게 평가했다
고 주장한다. 랑케가 국가의 권력을 질서와 안정의 수호자로 여긴 반
면, 부르크하르트는 권력을 악과 연결된 것으로 간주했다. 개신교 학
자인 랑케는 과거의 사건들에서 자신 있게 관대한 신의 손을 구했지
만, 회의적이고 내향적인 부르크하르트는 역사에서 적대 세력들 사이
의 끊임없는 투쟁을 보았다. 이러한 차이로 인해 다른 역사가들은 랑
케를 '나의 위대한 주인'이라고 언급한 부르크하르트의 말에 현혹되어
서는 안 된다고 주장하였다. 오히려 부르크하르트는 랑케의 개인적 야
망과 그의 지적 접근법 둘 다 거부하게 되었다.

16   내용과 불일치 문장 고르기   ⑤

[정답해설]

제시문의 마지막 문장에서 자각몽을 꿀 수 있는 사람들은 자신의 꿈
에 영향을 미칠 수 있고, 그들이 꿈을 꾸고 있다는 것을 인식할 수 있

으며, 원한다면 스스로 깨어날 수도 있다고 서술되어 있다. 그러므로
사람들은 자신의 꿈에 영향을 미칠 수 없다는 ⑤의 설명은 제시문의
내용과 일치하지 않는다.

[오답해설]

① 사람들이 꿈을 꾸는 동안, 그들의 눈은 움직일 수 있다. → 꿈을 꾸는
것은 빠른 눈의 움직임과 특이한 뇌파 패턴에 의해 확인됨

② 모든 사람들이 무슨 꿈을 꾸었는지 기억하는 것은 아니다. → 방금
꿈을 꾼 것을 기억하려고 집중하지 않는 한 무슨 꿈을 꾸었는지 알 수 없음

③ 꿈은 우리의 마음과 생각과 연관이 있다. → 꿈은 우리 자신의 내적인
연상, 기억, 그리고 감정적 투입에 기초함

④ 꿈은 상징적이고 해석될 수 있다. → 꿈속에서 일어나는 상징과 은유로
연상을 추적할 수 있고, 꿈속 장면과 이미지가 표현했던 것이 무엇인지 해독
할 수 있음

[핵심어휘]

▫ characteristic 특유의, 특이한, 독특한

▫ bizarre 기이한, 특이한

▫ internal 내부의, 내적인

▫ association 연계, 연상, 연계

▫ metaphor 은유, 비유

▫ decode 해독하다, 이해하다

▫ sequence 연속적인 사건들

▫ lucid dream 자각몽(꿈꾸고 있음을 자각하면서 꾸는 꿈)

▫ figurative 비유적인, 표상[상징]적인

▫ interpret 설명하다, 해석하다

[본문해석]

빠른 눈의 움직임과 특이한 뇌파 패턴에 의해 확인될 수 있는 수면의
특정 단계 동안, 우리는 꿈을 꾼다. 모두가 꿈을 꾸지만, 방금 꿈을 꾼
것을 기억하려고 집중하지 않는 한, 그 이미지는 우리가 깨어나면 거
의 바로 사라진다. 꿈은 종종 외부의 자극 없이 형성되고 대신 우리 자
신의 내적인 연상, 기억, 그리고 감정적 투입에 기초하기 때문에 특이
하다. 종종 우리는 꿈속에서 일어나는 상징과 은유로 우리의 연상을
추적할 수 있다. 때때로 우리는 꿈속 장면과 이미지가 표현했던 것이
무엇인지 해독할 수 있다. "자각몽"의 존재는 조사 연구에서 확립되었
다. 자각몽을 꿀 수 있는 사람들은 자신의 꿈에 영향을 미칠 수 있고,
그들이 꿈을 꾸고 있다는 것을 인식할 수 있으며, 원한다면 스스로 깨
어날 수도 있다.

17   내용과 불일치 문장 고르기   ④

[정답해설]

제시문에서 소음 성가심의 정의가 신체적 증상뿐만 아니라 감정적 반
응을 포함하기 때문에, 연구들은 상충되는 결과를 보여주고 있다고 서

술하고 있다. 그러므로 소음 성가심이 감정적인 반응 내에서만 국한된다는 ④의 설명은 제시문의 내용과 일치하지 않는다.

[오답해설]
① 내륙 풍력 발전소에서 발생하는 소음은 과학적으로 논란의 여지가 많은 화제이다. → 내륙 풍력 발전소의 소음은 과학적 논란의 대상임
② 내륙 풍력 발전소 근처의 주민들은 아마도 정신적인 병과 신체적인 병을 모두 경험할 것이다. → 소음 성가심은 신체적 증상뿐만 아니라 감정적 반응도 포함되므로, 주민들은 정신 질환과 신체 질환을 모두 겪음
③ 과학자들은 내륙 풍력 발전소 근처의 주민들이 겪고 있는 증상의 주요 원인을 성공적으로 밝혀내지 못했다. → 과학자들은 내륙 풍력 발전소 소음이 인근 주민들에게 미치는 증상에 대한 연구 계획이나 결과들에 확신을 갖지 못함
⑤ 내륙 풍력 발전소에서 발생하는 소음에 대한 연구결과는 아직 결론이 나지 않았다. → 내륙 풍력 발전소에서 발생하는 소음에 대한 연구결과는 과학자들 사이에서도 상충되고 논란의 여지가 많음

[핵심어휘]
▫ inland 벽지의, 내륙의
▫ wind farm 풍력 발전 지역
▫ provinces 주(州), 지방, 지역
▫ controversy 논란, 논쟁
▫ resident 거주자, 주민
▫ insomnia 불면증
▫ low-frequency 저주파
▫ air pressure 기압
▫ symptom 증상, 징후
▫ sensitivity 세심함, 예민함, 민감성
▫ annoyance 시달림, 성가심
▫ extensive 아주 넓은, 광범위한
▫ interpretation 해석, 이해, 설명
▫ controversial 논란이 많은, 논란의 여지가 있는
▫ inconclusive 결정[확정]적이 아닌, 결론에 이르지 못한

[본문해석]
주로 미국 중서부 그리고 캐나다의 온타리오 주와 퀘벡 주에 위치한 성장 산업의 일부인 내륙 풍력 발전소의 소음은 과학적 논란의 대상이다. 많은 과학자들은 인근 주민들이 수면 손실, 저주파 소음, 그리고 아마도 터빈의 작동으로 인한 기압의 변화에서 비롯된 근육통, 불안, 그리고 우울증뿐만 아니라 불면증과 두통의 대상이 된다고 믿는다. 이러한 증상들이 실제 풍력 터빈의 활동 결과인지, 날씨 민감성 결과인지, 아니면 소음 성가심으로 인한 스트레스 반응의 결과인지 완전히 명확하지는 않다. 소음 성가심의 정의가 신체적 증상뿐만 아니라 감정적 반응을 포함하기 때문에, 연구들은 상충되는 결과를 보여주고 있다. 즉, 논란의 각 측은 광범위한 증거를 인용할 수 있지만, 어느 쪽도 연구 계획이나 결과들에 대한 상대방의 설명에 확신을 얻지 못한다.

18 빈칸 추론하기 ②

[정답해설]
문화 상대주의의 입장에서 다른 문화를 대할 때 판단하고 행동하기에 앞서 문화 차이의 본질, 뿌리 및 결과에 대한 정보를 먼저 이해해야 한다고 설명하고 있다. 그러므로 빈칸에 들어갈 말은 ②의 '판단과 행동에 선행하다'이다.

[오답해설]
① 우리 문화의 정체성을 구축하다
③ 전제된 목표를 형성하다
④ 객관적으로 재평가되다
⑤ 기본 원리를 설명하다

[핵심어휘]
▫ presuppose 필요조건으로 하다, 전제로 하다
▫ relativism 상대주의, 상대론
▫ normalcy 정상임, 정상 상태
▫ negotiation 협상, 교섭, 절충
▫ precede 앞서다, 선행하다
▫ cultural identity 문화 정체성
▫ reevaluate 재평가하다, 재해석하다

[본문해석]
각각의 문화 집단은 다르게 생각하고, 느끼고, 행동한다. 한 집단이 다른 집단보다 본질적으로 더 우월하거나 열등한 것으로 간주하는 과학적 기준은 없다. 집단과 사회 간의 문화 차이를 연구하는 것은 문화 상대주의의 입장을 전제로 한다. 그것은 자신을 위한 정상 상태를 의미하는 것도 아니며, 자신의 사회를 위한 정상 상태를 의미하는 것도 아니다. 그러나 자신과 다른 집단이나 사회를 대할 때는 판단을 요한다. 사회 간 문화 차이의 본질, 뿌리, 그리고 그 결과에 대한 정보가 판단과 행동에 선행되어야만 한다. 협상은 관점의 차이에 대한 이유를 관련 당사자들이 이해할 때 성공할 가능성이 더 높다.

19 빈칸 추론하기 ⑤

[정답해설]
제시문에 따르면 과학적인 진리들은 현재는 최고의 진리이지만, 그것들을 대체할 더 나은 무언가를 찾을 때까지만 임시적으로 유용한 것이지 영원한 것은 아니라는 것이다. 그러므로 ⑤의 '영원히 의존할 수 없다'가 빈칸에 들어갈 말로 가장 적절하다.

[오답해설]
① 열망의 증거가 되다
② 우리의 생활 방식을 변화시키다

③ 당신의 삶에 동기를 부여하지 않다

④ 절대적인 진리를 보여주다

[핵심어휘]

- superstructure 상부 구조, 어떤 원리 위에 선 철학
- theological 신학상의, 신학적인
- provisionally 임시로, 잠정적으로
- for the moment 잠시, 당장은, 지금은
- commitment 전념, 헌신, 책무
- wholehearted 전적인, 전폭적인
- displace 대신하다, 대체하다
- aspiration 열망, 염원, 포부
- elusive 찾기 힘든, 달성하기 힘든

[본문해석]

과학적인 상부구조들은 역사적인 진리들 또는 신의 신학적인 개념들과 닮았다. 그것들은 우리가 현재 가지고 있는 최상의 것으로서 임시적으로 유용하지만, 영원히 의존할 수 있는 것은 아니다. 그것들을 대체할 더 나은 무언가를 계속 찾는 동안, 그것들에 대한 수용은 임시적으로 남아 있고, 우리의 헌신은 전폭적이지 않다. 인간이 열망하는 어떤 영역에서든 궁극적인 목표, 즉 '진실', '신', '현실'은 우리의 손길이 미치지 않는 곳에서 영원히 찾기 어려운 채로 남아 있지만, 그것이 그곳에 있다는 우리의 믿음은 계속되는 탐구에 필요한 동기를 부여한다.

| 20 | 빈칸 추론하기 | ⑤ |

[정답해설]

곤충들과 절지동물들은 마치 다른 행성에서 온 존재들처럼 생김새나 모습이 매우 이질적으로 보이지만, 사람처럼 보고, 만지고, 듣고, 냄새 맡고, 맛을 본다. 그러므로 빈칸에는 ⑤의 '이상하게 친숙한'이 들어갈 말로 가장 적절하다.

[오답해설]

① 놀랍도록 의심스러운

② 상세히 분류된

③ 꾸준히 발전하는

④ 인간적으로 생산적인

[핵심어휘]

- estimate 평가하다, 추정하다
- virtually 거의, 사실상
- arthropod 절지동물
- alien 외계의, 이국의, 이질적인
- stare 응시하다, 빤히 쳐다보다
- unblinking 눈을 깜박이지 않는

- reproduce 재생하다, 번식하다
- finely 섬세하게, 정교하게
- tuned 조정된, 정비된
- suspicious 의심스러운, 미심쩍은
- minutely 자세하게, 상세하게

[본문해석]

오늘날 살아있는 모든 인간에게는 2억 마리나 되는 개별 곤충들이 있다고 추정된다. 세상의 모든 9천 종의 다른 개미들의 총 무게는 지구상의 모든 인간들의 무게보다 12배나 크다. 그들의 놀라운 숫자와 거의 어디에서나 발견된다는 사실에도 불구하고, 곤충들과 다른 절지동물들은 마치 다른 행성에서 온 존재들처럼 우리에게 여전히 매우 이질적이다. 그들은 여섯 개 이상의 다리로 움직이고, 깜빡이지 않는 눈으로 응시하며, 코 없이 숨을 쉬고, 고리와 판으로 이루어진 피부 없는 딱딱한 몸을 가지고 있지만, 그럼에도 그들에게 또한 이상하게 친숙한 무언가가 있다. 절지동물은 먹이를 찾고, 적으로부터 자신을 방어하고, 번식하는 것과 같이, 사람들이 생존하기 위해 하는 모든 일들을 해야 한다. 그들은 또한 자기 주변의 세상을 보고, 만지고, 듣고, 냄새 맡고, 맛을 보기 위해 정교하게 조정된 감각에 의존한다.

| 21 | 빈칸 추론하기 | ① |

[정답해설]

명상의 효과는 명상을 수행하는 사람마다 차이가 있을 수 있고, 명상을 수행하는 기술보다 명상의 결과에 더 많은 영향을 미칠 수도 있으므로 명상이 치료에 어떤 효과가 있을 지는 계속해서 연구를 해봐야 한다는 것이다. 그러므로 ①의 '명상의 물은 혼탁하다'가 빈칸에 들어갈 말로 가장 적절하다.

[오답해설]

② 명상 비판가들은 명상을 수행하려고 노력해야 한다.

③ 명상은 여러 신체적 고통을 완화시킬 수 있다.

④ 명상의 정의는 이제 명확하다.

⑤ 과학자들은 명상 방법을 조사해야 한다.

[핵심어휘]

- meditation 명상, 묵상
- physiological 생리적인, 생리학상의
- therapist 치료사, 치료 전문가
- hypertension 고혈압
- insomnia 불면증
- psychiatric disorder 정신 질환
- definitive 확정적인, 명확한
- muddy 진흙투성이의, 혼탁한
- unclouded 구름이 없는, 맑은

[본문해석]

명상이 수세기 동안 수행되었다는 것은 사실이다. 비평가들은 그 이유가 무엇이든 간에, 그것이 효과가 있는 것처럼 보인다는 것에 동의한다. 비록 생리학적인 변화가 잘 확립되어 있지 않더라도, 심리적인 이익이 존재할 수도 있다. 더욱이 연구들은 명상을 수행하기로 결정한 사람들과 그렇지 않은 사람들 사이의 가능한 차이를 통제하지 않았다. 대상마다 차이가 존재할 가능성이 있으며 그것들이 기술 자체보다 명상의 결과에 더 많은 영향을 미칠 가능성이 있다. 여기서 우리가 결론을 내릴 수 있는 것은 <u>명상의 물은 혼탁하다</u>는 것이다. 사람들은 명상을 계속할 것이며, 종종 유익한 결과도 있을 것이다. 치료사들은 고혈압, 음주 과다, 약물 남용, 불면증, 그리고 많은 다른 정신 질환들을 치료하기 위해 명상을 계속 이용할 것이다. 마찬가지로 행동 과학자들은 더 확실한 결과들이 나올 때까지 계속해서 명상과 그것의 효과를 연구할 것이다. 그러나 객관적이고 과학적인 증거를 수용과 믿음의 기준으로 받아들이기를 거부하는 사람들은 항상 존재할 것이다.

22 　　　　빈칸 추론하기 　　　　③

[정답해설]

철근 콘크리트로 된 대부분의 유럽 항구도시들의 방파제는 파도에 부서지는 반면에, 진흙과 바위 층 및 버드나무 매트로 만들어진 네덜란드의 제방은 유연하게 파도의 충격을 흡수한다. 그러므로 ③의 '자연스러운 리듬에 맞추어 유연하게 움직이다'가 빈칸에 들어갈 말로 가장 적절하다.

[오답해설]

① 객관적인 관찰자로 조용히 남아 있다
② 극적인 변화와 함께 끊임없이 변화하다
④ 생태계의 신비에 적극 대응하다
⑤ 단순히 자연계의 질서를 무시하다

[핵심어휘]

- ecological 생태계의, 생태학의
- mythological 신화의, 신화적인
- dike 제방, 둑
- willow 버드나무, 버드나무 재목
- fury 맹렬, 격렬
- flexibility 신축성, 유연성
- in tune with ~와 맞추어, ~와 조화되어
- sea wall 방파제, 방조제
- steel-reinforced concrete 철근 콘크리트
- firm 단단한, 딱딱한
- smash apart 박살나다, 산산조각 나다
- edict 칙령, 명령
- disregard 무시하다, 묵살하다

[본문해석]

생태학적 사람들은 자연에 능동적으로 작용하는 논리적 사람들과 자연에 수동적으로 작용하는 신화적 사람들과 대조적으로 자연과 상호 작용한다. 그들은 자연과 대화한다. 네덜란드의 제방은 진흙과 바위 층 및 버드나무 매트로 만들어졌다. 북대서양의 맹렬한 파도가 몰아칠 때 이 제방은 파도에 맞추어 움직임으로써 버드나무 가지의 유연성으로 그 충격을 흡수한다. 이 생태학적 해결책은 파도를 막기 위해 철근 콘크리트로 된 방파제를 건설한 대부분의 유럽 항구도시들의 논리적 해결책과 대조를 이룬다. 자연에 역행하는 이 단단한 벽들은 결국 산산조각이 나고 <u>자연의 리듬에 따라 유연하게 움직이는</u> 네덜란드의 제방들과 달리 다시 건립되어야 한다. 신화적 해결책은 단단한 벽도 유연한 제방도 건설하지 않음으로써 자연의 명령을 수동적으로 받아들이는 것이다. 신화적 해결책을 따르면, 네덜란드의 3분의 1이 물에 잠기게 된다.

23 　　　　글의 제목 유추하기 　　　　①

[정답해설]

제시문에서 주장은 사실의 반대가 아니며, 우리가 '사실'이라고 생각하는 모든 진술은 실제는 주장이라고 서술하고 있다. 즉, 사실과 주장을 잘못 구분하고 혼용하여 사용하고 있다는 의미이므로, ①의 '사실과 주장을 구분할 수 있을까?'가 제시문의 제목으로 가장 적절하다.

[오답해설]

② 진실한 주장의 표식
③ 사실, 영원한 약속!
④ 사실과 주장의 반대는 무엇인가?
⑤ 의혹에서 결단으로의 여정

[핵심어휘]

- claim 주장, 요구, 요청
- bias 편견, 편향
- suspect 의심하다, 수상하게 여기다
- unbiased 편견이 없는, 선입견이 없는
- misleading 오해의 소지가 있는, 오해를 불러일으키는
- landmark 획기적인 사건, 표식, 목표
- everlasting 영원한, 끝없는
- suspicion 혐의, 의심
- determination 결정, 확인

[본문해석]

주장은 여러분이 생각하는 것처럼 사실의 반대가 아니다. 어떤 주장이 참이라는 것을 안다고 해서 사실이 되는 것도 아니다. 어떤 주장은 항상 주장이지만, 어떤 주장의 진실은 성립한다. 그리고 어떤 주장이 개인적인 장점이나 편견을 반드시 포함하는 것은 아니다. 비록 일상

의 언어에서 우리는 진실이 의심스럽거나 편향된 진술 그리고 진실이 성립되고 편견이 없는 진술('사실'이라고 불린다)을 구별하기 위해 자주 '주장'이라는 단어를 사용하지만, 이러한 구별은 위험할 정도로 오해를 불러일으킨다. 우리가 '사실'이라고 생각하는 모든 진술은 실제는 주장이다. 즉, 그것들은 너무 광범위하고 명확하게 사실로 받아들여져서 받아들여지지 않는 주장들과 다른 것처럼 보인다. 간단히 말해서, 주장은 세상의 지금 모습이나 또는 세상 본연의 모습에 대한 신념이나 관점을 표현하는 그런 진술이다. 물론 그것들이 참인지 아닌지는 중요하지만, 그것들이 주장인지 아닌지를 결정하지는 않는다.

24 글의 제목 유추하기 ②

[정답해설]
제시문에서 시도하고 실패하는 것은 진정한 진보이며, 그것은 새로운 에너지와 다시 시도하려는 열망으로 우리를 앞으로 나가게 하는 수단이 된다고 하였다. 그러므로 ②의 '인생의 추진력, 고난을 환영하라'가 제시문의 제목으로 가장 적절하다.

[오답해설]
① 운명의 밑바닥에 머물기
③ 포기는 인생의 시련의 일부이다
④ 지식을 현실에 적용하는 방법
⑤ 새로운 경험에 마음의 문을 열어라

[핵심어휘]
▫ tolerance 관용, 관대
▫ stuck 움직일 수 없는, 꼼짝 못하는
▫ stalemate 교착 상태
▫ in every sense of the word 그 단어의 모든 의미에 있어서, 진정으로
▫ vehicle (운송) 수단, 매개체
▫ launch 시작하다, 착수하다
▫ hardship 고난, 역경

[본문해석]
시도하거나 실패하는 것을 두려워하지 마라. 그것은 여러분에게 힘과 개인적인 도전들을 극복하는 방법을 가르쳐 준다. 인생의 시련들은 여러분에게만 특별한 것은 아니다. 그것들은 정도를 달리하여 모든 사람들에게 일어나고 여러분에게 다른 사람들이 위험을 피하기 위한 도구를 제공하는 정신적 관용과 강인한 성격을 발달시키도록 돕는다. 여러분이 프로젝트나 과제에서 목표했던 결론을 달성하지 못할 때, 그것을 종종 패배로 여긴다. 이러한 사고 과정은 교착 상태에 빠트리고 포기하기 때문에 진정한 진보를 막을 수 있다. 이러한 경험을 결코 나쁜 것으로 보지 마라, 시도하고 실패하는 것은 진정한 진보이다. 그것은 새로운 에너지와 다시 시도하려는 열망으로 여러분을 정말로 앞으로 나

가게 하는 수단임을 증명할 수 있다.

25 글의 요지 파악하기 ⑤

[정답해설]
제시문에서 평범한 문제들에 대해 평범한 사람들과 평범하게 이야기하는 것이 일상생활에서 영어 사용의 압도적인 대다수를 차지하고 있기 때문에 변화에 대처하는 것은 어떤 문제도 되지 않는다고 하였다. 그러므로 ⑤의 "일상적인 영어 사용은 보통 변화에 대한 대처를 필요로 하지 않는다."가 제시문의 요지로 가장 적절하다.

[오답해설]
① 우리들 대다수는 일상적인 대화에서 부주의한 실수를 한다. → 우리들 대다수는 일상적인 대화에서 가장 편안함을 느낌
② 우리는 일상적인 일에 대해 가족과 친구들과 대립해서는 안 된다. → 일상적인 일로 가족과 친구들을 마주함
③ 언어적으로 다양한 집단의 사람들은 조화롭게 살기 위해 더 노력해야 한다. → 변화에 대한 대처가 필요 없는 일상생활에서의 무의식적인 언어 사용에 대해 서술함
④ 무의식적인 선택을 하는 것은 언어를 창조적으로 사용하는 것이 아니다. → 일상생활에서의 영어 사용에 있어 변화에 대한 대처는 무의식적일 수도 있음

[핵심어휘]
▫ confront 맞서다, 마주치다, 대립하다
▫ cope with ~에 대처하다[대항하다]
▫ variance 변화, 변동, 변천
▫ constitute of a problem 문제가 되다
▫ unconscious 무의식적인, 부지불식간의
▫ at home 편안한
▫ linguistically 언어상, 언어학적으로
▫ account for ~을 차지하다
▫ overwhelming 압도적인, 강력한
▫ vast 어마어마한, 대단한
▫ diverse 다른, 다양한

[본문해석]
우리는 언어 사용에 있어 선택을 해야 하는 필요에 정기적으로 마주친다. 대부분의 경우, 의심의 여지없이, 변화에 대처하는 것은 어떤 문제도 되지 않으며 실제로 무의식적일 수도 있다. 우리는 일상적인 일로 가족과 친구들을 상대하고 있으며, 더욱이 글을 쓰는 것이 아니라 대게 그들과 이야기를 나눈다. 언어적으로나 다른 면에서 우리가 가장 편안한 것은 바로 평범한 문제들에 대해 평범한 사람들과 평범하게 이야기하는 것이다. 그리고 다행히도 이것이 영어 사용이 필요한 압도적인 대다수를 차지하는 상황이다.

26　글의 요지 파악하기　　②

[정답해설]

플로리다 사람들에게는 다 똑같이 보이는 눈이 스웨덴 사람들이나 알류트족에게는 다른 종류의 눈으로 보이는 것은 그들만의 렌즈나 필터를 통해 눈을 바라보기 때문이다. 그러므로 ②의 "우리는 주관성의 렌즈를 통해 세상을 본다."가 제시문의 요지로 가장 적절하다.

[오답해설]

① 우리는 인식의 객관적인 필터를 유지해야 한다. → 세상을 주관적으로 바라보는 것에 대한 고찰만 있을 뿐, 객관적인 필터를 유지하라는 조언은 없음

③ 우리의 기대가 꿈을 만든다. → 기대와 꿈과의 관계가 아니라 세상을 바라보는 방법에 대한 기술임

④ 우리의 이성은 왜곡된 정보를 피해야 한다. → 의미가 통하지 않는 것을 왜곡하거나 삭제하는 것이 일반적인 경향임

⑤ 우리가 알고 있는 것을 일반화하는 데 있어 중립적인 입장을 취해야 한다. → 일반화의 방향에 대해서만 서술되어 있고, 일반화의 중립적 입장에 대한 내용은 없음

[핵심어휘]

- take note of ∼에 주목하다, 알아채다
- fall into category 범주에 들다[속하다]
- distort 비틀다, 왜곡하다
- edit out ∼을 잘라 내다[삭제하다]
- make sense 의미가 통하다, 이해가 되다
- differentiation 차별, 구별
- worldview 세계관
- inconvenience 불편, 애로
- perception 지각, 통찰력, 인식
- subjectivity 주관, 주관성

[본문해석]

"객관적인" 세계를 관찰할 때, 우리는 자신의 렌즈나 필터를 통해 그것을 본다. 우리의 일상적인 환경은 물과 물고기의 관계와 같다. 즉, 그것은 그곳에 있을 뿐이며, 우리는 그것에 주목하지 않는다. 우리의 정신 지도에 그것들을 위한 공간이 이미 있기 때문에, 대부분의 경우 우리는 정상적인 활동이라고 생각하는 것을 특별히 의식하지 않는다. 그것들은 친숙한 범주에 속한다. 언어학자들이 보여주었듯이 우리는 아는 것으로부터 모르는 것으로 일반화하고, 그러한 관점을 고려할 때 의미가 통하지 않는 것은 왜곡하거나 삭제하는(잘라 내는) 경향이 있다. 플로리다 사람들에게 모든 눈은 똑같이 보일지도 모른다. 그들의 경험은 구별을 위한 "지도"를 제공하지 않기 때문에, 눈의 종류의 차이는 무시된다. 반면에 스웨덴 사람들이나 알류트족들은 많은 다양한 종류의 눈들을 구별할 수 있는 언어를 포함한 세계관을 가지고 있다. 그 정보를 삭제하거나 왜곡하는 것은 그들을 정말 불편하게 할 것이다.

27　글의 주제 파악하기　　③

[정답해설]

글의 서두에서 켈트어학은 오랫동안 신화학과 연관된 분야라고 핵심 주제를 밝히고 있다. 그리고 켈트족 문학은 신화학자들에게 주요한 관심의 대상이었고, 켈트족의 종교와 민속 및 문학에 대한 연구는 신화적 해석의 모델이 되어 왔다고 서술되어 있다. 그러므로 ③의 '켈트학의 특징과 신화와의 연관성'이 제시문의 주제로 가장 적절하다.

[오답해설]

① 신들의 초자연적 특성을 설명하는 데 있어 되풀이되는 주제

② 고전문학에 있어서 스코틀랜드 하이랜드 문화의 중요성

④ 켈트어를 사용하는 민족들을 이해하는 방법에 대한 새로운 관점

⑤ 비교 인도유럽 문헌학에 존재하는 풍부한 전통 주제

[핵심어휘]

- Celtic 켈트족의, 켈트어의
- amongst = among
- hold up as ∼으로 보여주다[간주되다]
- recipient 수령인, 수취인
- description 기술, 묘사, 표현
- Gauls 갈리아인(지금의 북이탈리아, 프랑스, 벨기 등을 포함한 고대 켈트인)
- reappear 재현하다, 재출현하다
- oral culture 구전[구술] 문화
- supernatural 초자연적인
- discipline 규율, 훈련
- comparative 비교적, 상대적인
- philology 문헌학
- aside from ∼을 제외하고, ∼외에도
- perspective 관점, 투시, 원근법
- mythologist 신화학자, 신화 작가
- folklore 민속, 전통 문화
- interpretation 해석, 이해, 설명
- novel 새로운, 신기한

[본문해석]

켈트어학은 신화학과 오랫동안 연관된 분야이다. 서유럽 상황에서 켈트어를 사용하는 민족들은 그들 중 풍부한 '전통' 주체를 받은 사람들로 아주 흔히 간주되어 왔다. 갈리아인들의 초기 묘사부터 스코틀랜드 하이랜드 문화에 대한 현대적 설명까지 구전 문화에 대한 강조와 일상생활에서 초자연적 현상에 대한 관심이 재현되는 것을 발견한다. 현대 학문에서 켈트족 언어들은 비교 인도유럽 문헌학 및 그 부산품인 비교 신화학 이론과 강한 연관성을 발전시켰다. 이러한 외부적인 관점 외에도, 신화학자들에게 주요한 관심 대상은 켈트족 문학 자체 내에 존재하는 매우 강한 신화 감각, 즉 신, 초자연적 특성을 가진 영웅 및

정답 및 해설

먼 과거의 사건에 대한 언급이다. 이러한 이유 때문에 켈트족 종교, 민속 및 문학에 대한 연구는 종종 신화적 해석 모델의 대상이 되어 왔다.

28 전체 흐름과 관계 없는 문장 고르기 ④

[정답해설]

제시문은 동물들의 방어 기술로써 신비의 색이라고도 불리는 동물들의 위장 방법에 대해 소개하고 있다. 그런데 ④에서는 지구 거주자들의 무관심한 환경 문제에 대해 언급하고 있으므로, 글의 전체 흐름과 어울리지 않는다.

[핵심어휘]

▫ camouflage 위장, 속임수
▫ cryptic 비밀의, 신비적인
▫ coloration 천연색, 채색, 배색
▫ one-size-fits-all 누구에게나 다 맞는, 널리[두루] 적용되도록 만든
▫ boldly 선명하게, 뚜렷하게
▫ inhabitant 주민, 거주자, 서식 동물

[본문해석]

신비의 색이라고도 알려진 위장은 동물 세계에서 모두에게 적용되는 방어이다. 곤충만큼 작고 선명한 무늬가 있는 18피트(6미터) 높이의 우뚝 솟은 기린처럼 큰 동물들은 그들이 뒤섞이는 것을 돕기 위해 신비의 색에 의존한다. ① 색과 무늬는 동물이 뒤섞이는 것을 도와줄 뿐만 아니라, 그 모양을 분산시킴으로써 위장할 수도 있다. ② 그런 식으로, 포식자는 처음에 그 동물을 알아보지 못한다. ③ 동물의 색상은 몸을 납작하게 보이게 만들어서, 몸의 통통함을 숨길 수 있다. ④ 거주자들이 환경 문제에 무관심하기 때문에 우리의 행성은 계속해서 훼손된다. ⑤ 색과 무늬는 또한 동물의 그림자를 감추는 것을 도울 수 있다.

29 전체 흐름과 관계 없는 문장 고르기 ④

[정답해설]

제시문은 일정을 정하고 그것에 따라 개인의 활동을 조정하는 등 주어진 시간을 어떻게 보낼 것인지에 대한 시간의 구조화가 갖는 기능에 대해 설명하는 글이다. 그런데 ④는 순서, 단위, 주기와 같은 수학적 개념의 구성 요소에 대해 설명하고 있으므로, 글의 전체 흐름과 어울리지 않는다.

[핵심어휘]

▫ thereby 그렇게 함으로써, 그것 때문에
▫ coordinate 조직화하다, 편성[조정]하다
▫ duration 지속, 기간
▫ orientation 방향, 성향, 오리엔테이션
▫ give form to ~을 형성하다
▫ coherent 일관성 있는, 논리[조리] 정연한
▫ periodically 정기[주기]적으로
▫ building block 구성 요소
▫ impose 도입하다, 부과하다

[본문해석]

시간의 구조화는 많은 기능을 할 수 있는데, 그 중 일부는 다른 문화에서 다소 중요하다. 그러나 어디에서든 주요한 기능 중 하나는 문화의 일정을 설정하고, 그것에 따라 문화에서 개인의 활동을 조정하는 것이다. 다른 기능은 그 집단의 활동을 일부 자연 현상 또는 일부 초자연 현상과 연관시키는 것일 수도 있다. ① 구조는 과거 또는 미래에서 사건을 주문하거나, 사건의 지속 시간을 측정하거나, 서로 또는 현재로부터 얼마나 가깝거나 멀리 있는지를 측정하는 데 사용될 수도 있다. ② 무엇보다도, 구조는 방향성의 수단을 제공하며 문화에서 뿐만 아니라 개인의 삶에서 사건의 발생에 형식을 제공한다. ③ 그것은 정기적으로 반복되는 사건을 표시하고 특별한 사건을 배치하는 연속적이고 일관된 틀을 제공한다. ④ <u>순서, 단위 및 주기와 같은 근본적인 수학적 개념은 바로 그 구성 요소이다.</u> ⑤ 이와 같이 시간에 부과되는 구조는 그 이상으로, 한 문화에서 많은 것을 반영하고 영향을 미친다.

30 주어진 문장의 위치 찾기 ③

[정답해설]

주어진 문장은 오디세우스가 죽고 부상당한 부하들을 포기하고 남은 부하들을 다시 배에 태우고 떠났다는 내용이다. 즉, 부하들이 공격을 받은 것이므로, 트라키아인들이 이스마루스에서 불길이 치솟는 것을 보고 술에 취한 선원들을 복수심에 불타 공격했다고 서술된 ③에 들어가는 것이 가장 적절하다.

[핵심어휘]

▫ aboard 탄, 탑승한, 승선한
▫ in a different light 다른 시각[관점]으로
▫ priest 사제, 성직자
▫ undertake to ~할 것을 약속하다, ~할 책임[의무]를 지다
▫ spare life 목숨을 살려주다
▫ inland 내륙에, 내지에
▫ charge 공격하다, 돌격하다
▫ vengefully 복수심에 불타, 앙심을 품고
▫ fierce 거센, 사나운, 격렬한
▫ north-easterly 북동쪽에 있는, 북동쪽으로 향하는
▫ southernmost 최남단의, 가장 남쪽의
▫ oar 노, 노 젓는 사람
▫ bear (왼쪽, 북쪽 등으로) 가다[돌다]
▫ within sight of ~이 보이는 곳에

□ Lotus-eaters 로토파고스족

[본문해석]

> 오디세우스는 이들 대부분을 다시 배에 태웠으나, 그는 사망자들과 중상자들을 포기해야만 했다.

오디세우스를 다른 관점에서 보여주는 시인 「오디세이」에 따르면, 그는 트로이를 떠난 후 먼저 트라키아로 항해했다. (①) 그곳에서 그는 도시 항구인 이스마루스를 공격했고 불태웠다. (①) 그가 목숨을 살려주기로 한 아폴로의 한 사제가 감사함에 달콤한 와인 몇 병을 주었고, 그 중 절반은 그의 부하들이 해변으로 나들이 갈 때 마셨다. (②) 내지에 살았던 몇몇 트라키아인들은 이스마루스에서 불길이 치솟는 것을 보았고, 술에 취한 선원들을 복수심에 불타 공격했다. (③) 거센 북동쪽 폭풍에 그의 배들은 에게해를 횡단하여 그리스 최남단에 위치한 섬인 시테라로 향했다. (④) 갑자기 폭풍이 잠잠해지자 그는 부하들에게 노를 젓도록 시켰고, 시테라를 돌아 이타카를 향해 북서쪽으로 가려했지만, 폭풍은 전보다 더 사납게 몰아쳤고, 아흐레 동안 불었다. (⑤) 마침내 배가 도착했을 때, 오디세우스는 북아프리카 해안에서 떨어진 로토파고스족의 섬인 시링크스가 눈에 들어왔다.

| 31 | 주어진 문장의 위치 찾기 | ④ |

[정답해설]
제시문은 야외 주방에서 그릴을 사용하기 위한 여러 가지 편의 사항들이 계속해서 발전하고 있다는 내용이다. 주어진 문장은 'of course(물론)'를 사용하여 그릴이 야외 주방에서 관심이 증가하고 있는 한 요소일 뿐이라고 단정하고 있으므로, 이후의 문장에서는 '그러나(however)'라는 역접의 내용이 와야 바람직하다. 또한 ④ 다음의 문장에서 these spaces(이러한 공간들)은 주어진 문장의 'outdoor kitchens(야외 주방들)'을 가리킨다. 그러므로 주어진 문장은 ④에 들어가는 것이 적절하다.

[핵심어휘]
□ component 구성 요소, 구성 성분
□ flexibility 다루기 쉬움, 융통성, 편의성
□ outfit 갖추다, 준비하다
□ pullout drawer 이동 서랍, 접이식 서랍
□ accommodate 공간을 제공하다, 수용하다
□ charcoal 숯, 목탄
□ customize 주문 제작하다
□ on occasion 가끔, 때때로
□ opt for ~을 선택하다
□ tray 쟁반, 상자
□ invest in ~에 투자하다, ~에 돈을 쓰다

□ incorporate 포함하다, 통합하다
□ take on feature 특징을 띠다

[본문해석]

> 물론, 그릴은 야외 주방에서 관심이 증가하고 있는 한 요소일 뿐이다.

더 많은 편의성을 원하는 소비자들을 위해, 점차 더 많은 회사들이 숯과 나무를 사용할 수 있도록 팬이나 이동식 서랍을 갖춘 하이브리드 가스 그릴을 제공하고 있다. (①) 게다가 일부 바비큐는 냉장실이나 심지어 오븐을 포함한 카트로 주문 제작될 수 있어서 동시에 그릴과 구이를 할 수 있다. (②) 그리고 가끔 훈제된 고기를 좋아하는 사람들은 훈제 쟁반이나 훈제 박스와 같은 액세서리를 선택하거나 별도의 훈제기를 쉽게 추가 구매할 수 있다. (③) 또한 그릴은 주야간 활동이기 때문에, 오늘날의 바비큐들 중 상당수는 표면 조명뿐만 아니라, 날이 어두워진 후에도 온도 설정이 보이도록 제어 패널에 LED를 포함한다. (④) 그러나 이러한 공간들이 계속해서 기능적으로 확장됨에 따라 일 년 내내 즐길 수 있는 특징들을 띠게 되고, 그릴 기술의 발전 또한 그러할 것이다. (⑤) 결국, 러스 포크가 언급했듯이, "모든 것이 그릴에서 더 맛있다."

| 32 | 주어진 문장의 위치 찾기 | ② |

[정답해설]
주어진 문장은 전염병에 약한 사람들은 죽고 저항력이 더 강한 생존자들은 살아남아 공동체를 다시 형성한다고 설명하고 있다. 즉, 이것이 그러한 '도태(weeding out)'를 가리키므로, 주어진 문장은 ②에 들어가는 것이 가장 적절하다.

[핵심어휘]
□ epidemic 전염병, 유행병
□ fierce 격렬한, 극심한
□ prolonged 오래 지속되는, 장기적인
□ the Black Death 흑사병
□ repopulate 다시 사람을 살게 하다
□ population 인구, 주민, 집단
□ genetic mutation 유전적 돌연변이
□ infection 감염, 전염
□ pathogen 병원균, 병원체
□ nonmutant 비 돌연변이
□ counterpart 상대, 대응 관계에 있는 사람[것]
□ weeding out 잡초 제거, 도태
□ pre-epidemic 유행 전, 유행 이전의
□ frequency 빈도, 빈발

정답 및 해설

▫ trigger 촉발시키다, 작동시키다

▫ genetic profile 유전자 특성[개요]

[본문해석]

> 전염병이 특히 격렬하거나 장기화되면 (흑사병처럼), 약한 사람들이 대다수 사망하고 버텨낸 생존자들이 남아 그들의 공동체를 다시 사람들로 채울 것이다.

전염병이 집단에 발발할 때, 그 집단에는 감염에 더 자연스럽게 저항력을 갖게 만드는 유전적 돌연변이를 가진 개인들이 있을 것이다. (①) 병원체에 노출될 경우, 그들은 정상적인 비 돌연변이 개인들보다 생존할 가능성이 더 높을 것이다. (②) 수 세대에 걸친 그러한 "도태" 이후, 새로운 생존 집단은 본래의 유행 이전 집단보다 훨씬 더 높은 빈도의 돌연변이 개인들을 갖게 될 것이다. (③) 결과적으로, 만약 전염병이 다시 발생한다면, 그들은 유전적으로 더 잘 대비하게 될 것이다. (④) 따라서 전염병은 시간이 지남에 따라 집단의 유전자 특성에 변화를 촉발시키는 선택적인 압력으로 작용할 수 있다. (⑤) 다시 말해, 그것은 인간의 진화를 촉진할 수 있다.

33	주어진 문장의 위치 찾기	④

[정답해설]

주어진 문장에서 지중해 세계에서 온 방문객은 시칠리아 섬 출신의 티마이오스라는 그리스 역사가를 가리킨다. 그 역사가에 의해 구전되어 오던 이야기가 감명 깊은 세계사의 일부로 기록됨으로써 우리가 그 이야기에 대한 줄거리라도 개략적으로 알게 되었다는 내용이다. 그러므로 주어진 문장은 ④에 들어가는 것이 가장 적절하다.

[핵심어휘]

▫ a bare outline 기본 개요[윤곽], 개략

▫ be passed on by word of mouth 구전되다

▫ Mediterranean 지중해의

▫ windswept 바람이 많이 부는

▫ blazing 활활 타는, 맹렬한, 격렬한

▫ dwell 살다, 거주하다

▫ legendary 전설적인, 아주 유명한

[본문해석]

> 우리가 개략적이라도 알게 된 유일한 이유는 지중해 세계에서 온 방문객이 그 이야기를 기록할 때까지 그 이야기가 구전되었기 때문이다.

2천여 년 전, 춥고 바람이 많이 부는 대서양 연안에서 어떤 사람이 활활 타오르는 불 앞에 앉아 이야기를 들려주었다. (①) 오래 전에 형

제인 두 신이 있었는데, 바다의 위대한 어머니 여신에게서 함께 태어난 쌍둥이였다고 이 사람은 말했다. (②) 이 형제들이 자랐을 때, 그들은 바다를 뒤로하고 바다 근처에 사는 사람들과 함께 살게 되었다. (③) 그 이야기에는 훨씬 더 많은 부분이 있었지만, 그것이 남아 있는 이야기의 전부이다. (④) 시간이 흘러 그 기록은 알렉산더 대왕의 시대 바로 직후에 살았던 시칠리아 섬 출신의 티마이오스라는 그리스 역사가에게 흘러갔다. (⑤) 그는 전설적인 시대부터 자신의 시대까지 감명 깊은 세계사의 일부로 그 이야기를 기록했다.

34	주어진 문장의 위치 찾기	③

[정답해설]

주어진 문장에서 정복한 프랑크계 게르만인들의 많은 단어들이 프랑스 어휘에 포함되었다고 서술되어 있으므로, 다음 문장에는 어떻게 포함되었는지 그 사례를 설명한 문장이 들어가는 것이 바람직하다. ③ 다음의 문장에서 'These words(이 단어들)'가 주어진 문장의 'many words(많은 단어들)'를 받으며 그 사례에 대한 설명을 시작하고 있으므로, 주어진 문장은 ③에 들어가는 것이 적절하다.

[핵심어휘]

▫ Frankish Germans 프랑크계 독일인

▫ incorporate 포함하다, 통합하다

▫ expansion 확대, 확장

▫ subsequently 그 뒤에, 나중에

▫ tribe 부족, 민족

▫ take control of ~을 장악[지배]하다

▫ Franks 프랑크인(라인 강변의 게르만 족)

▫ prestige 명성, 신망

[본문해석]

> 프랑스에서, 정복한 프랑크계 게르만인들의 많은 단어들이 어휘에 포함되었다.

5세기에 게르만의 확장은 로마 제국의 몰락을 가져왔다. 그 후 그들을 방어할 로마 군대가 없어, 많은 땅들이 게르만족들의 지배하에 들어갔다. (①) 서양 게르만족들의 이동은 영어에 관한 이야기에서 특히 중요하다. (②) 5세기 말까지, 서게르만어를 사용하는 사람들이 프랑스와 영국의 상당 부분을 장악했다. (③) 이 단어들은 그 땅의 이름 자체를 포함했다. 즉, 로마의 지배 하에서 갈리아(골)라고 불렸던 것이 이제는 '프랑크의 땅'인 프란시아(프랑스)로 불리게 되었다. (④) 그럼에도 여전히, 라틴어는 프랑스의 언어로 남아 있었다. (⑤) 정복자들이 정복된 사람들의 언어를 사용하는 것은 아마도 놀랄 일이지만, 위대한 제국과 문명의 언어로서 라틴어의 높은 명성은 그것의 생존에 기여했을지도 모른다.

35 글의 배열순서 정하기 ③

[정답해설]

주어진 문장에서 땅 속 깊이 매장되어 있는 석유를 어떻게 찾을 수 있는지 의문을 제기하고 있다. (B)에서 석유의 성분이 대부분 탄화수소이며, (C)에서 그러한 탄화수소가 암반의 틈을 통해 지표면으로 올라온다고 하였다. 마지막으로 (A)에서 탐사자들은 석유를 먹고 사는 박테리아를 발견했을 때 그곳에 석유가 있다는 것을 알게 된다고 주어진 문장의 의문에 답하고 있다. 그러므로 주어진 글 다음에 (B)-(C)-(A) 순으로 배열되어야 글의 흐름이 가장 적절하다.

[핵심어휘]

- petroleum 석유
- distribution 분배, 분포
- detect 발견하다, 탐색하다
- quantity 양, 수량
- in reserve 비축되어 있는
- organic compound 유기 화합물
- hydrocarbon 탄화수소
- rock formation 암반
- component 요소, 성분
- leak 누설되다, 새다

[본문해석]

석유는 산업의 "피"다. 그러나 땅 속 깊이 매장되어 있기 때문에, 어떻게 그것을 찾을 수 있을까? 때때로 석유의 분포 범위를 정확히 확인하지 않아서 상당한 노동, 재료, 그리고 비용이 소모된다.

(B) 여기서 박테리아는 석유와 신비한 결합을 하고 있다고 할 수 있다. 석유는 다양한 유기 화합물로 구성되어 있는데, 그중 대다수가 탄화수소라 불리는 탄소와 수소의 화합물이다.

(C) 비록 석유가 깊이 매장되어 있지만, 일부 탄화수소가 암반의 틈을 통해 지표면으로 항상 올라온다. 석유의 가스 성분 또한 표면에 누출될 수 있다. 일부 박테리아는 석유를 먹고 산다.

(A) 그러므로, 탐사자들이 어떤 장소에서 많은 양의 그러한 박테리아를 발견했을 때, 그들은 아마도 석유가 있다는 것을 알게 된다. 샘플로 검출된 박테리아의 양에 근거하여, 그들은 또한 비축되어 있는 석유와 가스의 양을 예측할 수 있다.

36 글의 배열순서 정하기 ③

[정답해설]

주어진 문장에서 1942년에 전쟁 정보국(OWI)을 설립하였고, (B)에서 같은 달인 1942년 6월에 영화 산업을 위한 정부 정보 매뉴얼이 발표되

었다. 다음으로 (C)에서 그 매뉴얼에 대한 내용을 평가하고 있고, 마지막으로 (A)에서 1942년 후반까지 그 매뉴얼이 스튜디오 제작에 영향을 미쳤다고 서술하고 있다. 그러므로 주어진 글 다음에 (B)-(C)-(A) 순으로 배열되어야 글의 흐름이 가장 적절하다.

[핵심어휘]

- unified 통합된, 통일된
- the Office of War Information(OWI) 전쟁정보국
- agency 대행사, 대리점, 기관
- bureau 부서[국]
- publicise 알리다, 공표하다
- Allies 연합국[군], 동맹국[군]
- domestic branch 국내 지점[지부]
- administration 행정부
- appointee 지명[임명]된 사람
- New Deal 뉴딜 정책
- liberal 자유민주적인, 자유주의의
- self-defense 자기 방어, 정당방위

[본문해석]

진주만은 할리우드의 사회적 관심사의 본질을 바꾸었고, 1942년 상반기에 정부 정보 서비스에 대한 비판으로 대통령은 기존의 세 개 기관에서 하나의 통합된 기구인 전쟁 정보국(OWI)을 설립했다.

(B) 대통령의 가까운 친구이자 조언자인 Lowell Mellett는 OWI 국내 지부의 일부인 영화 산업국의 책임자가 되었다. 같은 달인 1942년 6월에, 행정부는 Mellett의 임명자인 Nelson Pointer와 그의 직원들이 쓴 문서인 영화 산업을 위한 정부 정보 매뉴얼을 발표했다.

(C) 이 매뉴얼은 '할리우드가 어떻게 전쟁에 맞서 싸워야 하는지에 대한 자유주의적 견해인 뉴딜의 가장 명확한 성명서'로 평가돼 왔다. '국민의 전쟁'은 단지 정당방위의 싸움이 아니라 민주주의를 위한 싸움이라고 강조했다.

(A) 그것은 또한 할리우드가 연합군과 노르웨이, 유고슬라비아 및 점령된 유럽의 다른 곳에 있는 저항 단체들의 노력을 알리도록 독려했다. 1942년 후반까지 이 매뉴얼은 스튜디오 제작에 영향을 미치기 시작했다.

37 글의 배열순서 정하기 ⑤

[정답해설]

주어진 문장에서 모든 과학 논문은 객관성을 확보하기 위해 출판되기 전에 저자와 별개로 확인되어야 하며, (C)에서 이러한 확인은 동료들의 성공적인 검토를 통해서라고 밝히고 있다. 다음으로 (B)에서 모든

연구자가 모든 과학 출판물에 쉽게 접근할 수 있어야 하는데, (A)에서 유료화의 벽에 막혀 그렇지 못함을 설명하고 있다. 그러므로 주어진 글 다음에 (C)-(B)-(A) 순으로 배열되어야 글의 흐름이 가장 적절하다.

[핵심어휘]

- reproducibility 복사[복제] 가능성, 재현성
- backbone 근간, 중추
- crucial 중대한, 결정적인
- independently 독립하여, 별개로
- peer-reviewed 동료 심사를 받은
- behind pay-walls 유료화의 벽에 막힌
- public fund 공금, 공적 자금
- finance 자금[재원]을 대다
- taxpayer 납세자, 과세 대상자
- heritage 유산, 상속 재산
- collectively 집합적으로, 총괄하여
- constructive 건설적인, 구조상의
- verify 확인하다, 검증[입증]하다

[본문해석]

> 발표된 결과의 복제 가능성은 과학 연구의 근간이다. 객관성은 과학에 아주 중요하며, 출판용으로 승인되기 전에 관찰, 실험 및 이론이 저자와 별개로 확인되어야 한다.

(C) 실제로 과학적으로 인정받기 위한 결과는 동료들이 검토하고 수용한 논문, 즉 연구자들이 이해하고 검증하며 필요한 경우 수정할 수 있는 글로 제시되고 설명되어야 한다. 성공적인 동료 검토를 마친 후에야 새로운 결과가 발표될 수 있고 과학적 지식에 속하게 된다.

(B) 결과적으로, 모든 과학 출판물은 연구자들이 수세기에 걸쳐 집합적으로 구축해왔고, 계속해서 발전하고 있는 공통의 유산이다. 과학의 건설적이고 보편적인 특성을 고려할 때, 어떤 연구자도 모든 과학 출판물에 가능한 한 조기에 그리고 쉽게 접근할 수 있어야 한다.

(A) 불행히도 오늘날은 그렇지 못한데, 동료 검토를 받은 대부분의 학술지들이 유료화의 벽에 막힌 과학 논문을 보관한 소수의 주요 출판사들에 속해 있기 때문이다. 전 세계적으로 대다수의 연구 프로그램들이 납세자들의 자금 지원을 받기 때문에 연구자들뿐만 아니라 모든 출신의 모든 사람들이 과학 출판물을 접할 수 있어야 한다.

38   글의 배열순서 정하기   ④

[정답해설]

주어진 문장에서 우리가 역사에 신경을 써야 하는가에 대한 답변은

(C)에서 국가의 정체성 의식을 제공하기 위해 교육적으로 필요하다는 역사 수호자들의 진부한 말처럼 빤할 수도 있다. 그러나 (A)에서 너무나 분명해 보이기 때문에 이러한 답변들을 당연한 것으로 여겨서는 안 된다며, Oliver Sacks의 박탈과 비정상의 교훈에 대해 언급한다. 마지막으로 (B)에서는 온전한 정신을 지원하기 위한 개인적 역사에 대해 설명한다. 그러므로 주어진 글 다음에 (C)-(A)-(B) 순으로 배열되어야 글의 흐름이 가장 적절하다.

[핵심어휘]

- bother 신경 쓰다, 애를 쓰다
- too obvious to labour 너무나 분명해서 수고를 필요로 하지 않는, 너무 빤한
- be deprived of ~을 빼앗기다
- realise = realize
- deprivation 박탈, 상실, 부족
- abnormality 기형, 이상, 비정상
- instructive 유익한, 교육적인, 교훈적인
- malfunctioning 오작동의, 제대로 작동하지 않는
- crucial 중대한, 결정적인
- implication 영향, 함축, 연루
- sanity 제정신, 온전한 정신, 분별
- platitude 상투어, 진부한 말

[본문해석]

> 왜 우리가 역사에 신경을 써야 하는가라는 질문에 대한 심리적 답변은 너무 빤한 것처럼 보일 수도 있다.

(C) 결국, 그 과목이 국가의 정체성 의식을 제공하기 위해 교육의 필수적인 부분으로써 필요하다는 것은 역사 수호자들의 진부한 말이 되었다. 그리고 개인적인 차원에서, 우리가 누구인지, 어디에 있는지, 심지어 가고 싶은 곳이 어디인지와 관련된 기억을 가지고 있다는 것을 우리 모두 충분히 잘 알고 있다.

(A) 그러나 단지 그것들이 너무나 분명해 보이기 때문에, 이러한 대답들은 쉽게 당연한 것으로 여겨질 수 있고, 그것들에 대한 실제적인 의존은 아니더라도, 그것들의 중요성을 깨닫는 것은 오직 우리가 과거를 빼앗겼을 때이다. 그렇기 때문에 Oliver Sacks와 다른 사람들에 의해 기록된 박탈과 비정상의 예들은 매우 교훈적이다.

(B) 그것들로부터 우리는 오작동하는 기억 혹은 완전한 기억의 상실이 개인적 정체성에 대한 우리의 의식과 그에 따라 다른 사람들과 함께 사회에서 살 수 있는 우리의 능력에 중대한 영향을 미치는 것을 볼 수 있다. 우리의 개인적 역사는 우리 자신과 우리의 온전한 정신을 위한 지원을 제공한다.

39　한 문장으로 요약하기　①

[정답해설]

(A) various(다양한) / (B) prioritize(우선시하다)

훈련을 할 때 많은 여러 요소들이 신체 적응에 영향을 미치며, 무엇을 극대화시킬 것인지 아닌지 결정하는 것이 중요하다. 또한 작은 돌에 앞서 큰 돌들을 채우고 모래에 앞서 작은 돌들을 채우는 것처럼 중요도에 따라 우선순위를 결정해야 한다고 조언하고 있다. 그러므로 훈련에서 (A) 다양한 요소를 고려하는 것이 결과를 극대화하는 데 중요하기 때문에, 중요도 피라미드는 겉보기에는 상충되는 조언보다 핵심 요소를 (B) 우선시하는 데 도움이 될 수 있다고 한 문장으로 요약할 수 있다.

[오답해설]

② 제한된 ······ 우선시하다

③ 독특한 ······ 발생시키다

④ 다양한 ······ 발생시카다

⑤ 강력한 ······ 특징짓다

[핵심어휘]

- screw up 망치다, 엉망으로 만들다
- resultant 그 결과로 생긴, 그에 따른
- adaptation 적응, 순응
- trainee 훈련생, 훈련을 받는 사람
- explosively 폭발적으로, 격정적으로
- burn (심한 운동으로) 화끈거리는 느낌
- relative to ~에 관하여, ~에 비례하여
- confusion 혼란, 혼동
- brim (잔·접시·쟁반 등의) 가장자리 cf) fill your cup to the brim 컵을 가득 채우다
- when it comes to ~에 관한 한, ~에 대해서라면
- pebble 자갈, 조약돌
- crucial 중대한, 결정적인
- prioritize 우선순위를 매기다, 우선적으로 처리하다
- diverse 다양한, 여러 가지의
- characterize 특징짓다

[본문해석]

비록 매우 단순하고 빠르게 들리지만, 사람들은 항상 이것을 망친다. 훈련을 할 때, 많은 다른 요소들이 서로 영향을 미치고 그에 따른 신체 적응이 일어난다. 지난 수십 년간의 연구와 결합하여, 지난 세기 동안 전 세계 체육관에서의 훈련생들의 경험은 당신의 훈련 노력으로부터 무엇을 극대화시킬 것인지 그렇지 않을 것인지에 대해 꽤 명확한 중요 순서를 세울 수 있도록 하였다. 어떤 훈련을 해야 할지, 얼마나 무거울지, 얼마나 많은 세트를 수행해야 할지, 실패할 때까지 훈련해야 할지, 폭발적으로 또는 천천히 '화끈거림을 느끼도록' 등 겉으로 보기

에 상충되는 조언을 볼 때, 이러한 요소들이 당신의 목표에 비례하여 얼마나 중요한지, 그리고 그것들이 훈련의 다른 측면에 어떤 영향을 미칠지 결정해야 한다. 중요도 피라미드 렌즈를 통해 이 변수들을 살펴봄으로써, 불필요한 혼란을 덜어줄 수 있을 것이다. 고전 속담에 이르길, 만일 훈련 잠재력에 대해 "컵을 가득 채우고 싶다면", 작은 돌들에 앞서 큰 돌들을 채우고 모래에 앞서 작은 돌들을 채워라.

↓

> 훈련에서 (A) 다양한 요소를 고려하는 것이 결과를 극대화하는 데 중요하기 때문에, 중요도 피라미드는 겉보기에는 상충되는 조언보다 핵심 요소를 (B) 우선시하는 데 도움이 될 수 있다.

40　한 문장으로 요약하기　①

[정답해설]

(A) fundamental(기본적인) / (B) overflow(초과)

민주주의 사회에서 관용은 필요하며 책무로써 '보통 인정되는 것보다 더 어렵고 더 긴급할 수도 있다'고 한다. 그러나 '실천적인' 사람들은 그러한 관용을 종종 허용의 과잉으로 치부하기까지 한다고 서술되어 있다. 그러므로 이론적으로 민주주의 사회에서 관용은 (A) 기본적인 것으로 간주되지만, 현실에서 일부 사람들은 허용의 (B) 초과로 보고 그것을 자주 간과한다고 한 문장으로 요약할 수 있다.

[오답해설]

② 기본적인 ······ 부족

③ 급진적인 ······ 균형

④ 관례적인 ······ 사치

⑤ 관례적인 ······ 부족

[핵심어휘]

- at odd 다투어, 불화하여, 대립하여
- presumed 당연한 것으로 여겨지는
- contemporary 동시대의, 현대의
- go one's separate ways 각자 제 갈 길을 가다, 다른 길을 가다
- theoretical 이론의, 이론상의
- coherent 통일성 있는, 일관성 있는
- comprehensive 포괄적인, 종합적인
- appropriately 적절히, 알맞게
- make the point that ~이라고 주장하다
- commitment 전념, 헌신, 책무
- urgent 긴급한, 시급한
- recognition 인정, 인식
- accommodation 적응성, 순응성, 수용성
- register 등록하다, 기입하다

- so much so that 매우 그러하므로 ~하다, 그게 어찌나 심한지 ~ 할 정도이다
- dismiss 무시하다, 묵살하다, 치부하다
- permissiveness 허용됨, 관대함, 방임주의
- zero tolerance 제로 관용 정책, 무관용
- overflow 넘침, 범람, 초과
- radical 근본적인, 급진적인
- customary 관례적인, 습관적인
- shortage 부족, 결핍

[본문해석]

이론과 실제는 자주 대립한다. 그러나 현대 사회에서 수용된 이론과 당연한 것으로 여겨지는 관용의 관행이 각각 다른 길을 가는 것처럼 보이는 데는 특히 이상한 무언가가 있다. 관용에 관한 이론적 진술들은 민주주의 사회에서 그것의 필요성과 통일성 있는 이상으로서 그것의 불가능성을 동시에 가정한다. 현대 생활에서 관용과 불관용에 관한 통합 모음집 소개에서, 수잔 멘더스는 자유주의 사회들이 관용을 해야 한다는 책무가 '보통 인정되는 것보다 더 어렵고 더 긴급할 수도 있다'는 점을 적절하게 주장한다. 이론이 주장하는 긴급성과 대조적으로, 실천은 만족스러운 것처럼 보일 수 있다. 즉, 자유 민주 사회들은 인정의 필요성과 차이의 수용성을 그것의 깊이를 명시하지 않고 받아들인 것처럼 보인다. 그게 너무 심해서 '실천적인' 사람들은 그러한 관용을 종종 허용의 과잉으로 치부하기까지 한다. '무관용'이 덜 용서받는 사회를 위한 구호로 성공한 것은 그러한 여론의 분위기가 확산되고 있음을 보여준다.

↓

이론적으로 민주주의 사회에서 관용은 (A) 기본적인 것으로 간주되지만, 현실에서 일부 사람들은 허용의 (B) 초과로 보고 그것을 자주 간과한다.

[41~42]

[핵심어휘]

- ornamentation 장식, 치장, 꾸밈
- add-on 추가[부가]물
- lay 전문 지식이 없는, 문외환의
- resort to ~에 의지[의존]하다, ~에 기대다
- debunk (정체를) 폭로하다, 틀렸음을 드러내다[밝히다]
- material 중요한, 구체적인
- externalize 외부화하다, 구체화하다
- imagery 형상화, 이미지
- integrate 통합하다, 합치다
- hidden power 잠재력

- dissociation 분리, 분열
- supplement 보충[추가](물)
- inseparable 갈라놓을 수 없는, 분리할 수 없는
- underlying 근본적인, 근원적인
- superficial 표면적인, 피상적인
- embodiment 구현, 구체화, 구체화된 것
- externalization 외부화, 구체화

[본문해석]

왜 우리는 제스처를 취할까? 많은 사람들은 제스처가 (일어나고 있는 일의 핵심이라고 가정되는) 말에 강조, 활력 그리고 장식을 준다고 말할 것이다. 간단히 말해서, 제스처는 "추가 기능"이다. 하지만 이에 반대되는 증거가 있다. 문외환의 관점에서 볼 때, 제스처는 어떤 이가 "손으로 말하는" 것이다. 단어를 찾을 수 없기 때문에 제스처에 의존한다. 마리안 걸버그는 이 구식 생각이 틀렸다는 것을 밝혀냈다. 그녀가 간단히 말했듯이, 말이 멈출 때 제스처를 시작하는 것이 아니라, 제스처 또한 멈춘다는 것이다. 우리가 제스처를 취하는 이유는 더 심오하다. 언어는 이미지와 분리할 수 없다. 제스처가 중요한 의미의 전달을 강화하는 동안, 그 핵심은 제스처와 말이 함께 한다. 그것들은 제스처가 "추가 기능" 또는 "장식"이라는 말 이상으로 더 단단히 묶여 있다. 그것들은 생각 그 자체와 통합되어 있다. 어떤 이유로 손의 사용이 제한적이고 제스처가 구체화되지 않더라도, 그것이 구현하는 이미지는 여전히 존재할 수 있고, 숨겨진 채로 말과 통합될 수 있다(예를 들어 발과 같은 신체의 다른 부분에서 나타날 수 있다).

41	글의 제목 유추하기	⑤

[정답해설]

제시문에서 많은 사람들은 제스처가 말을 강조하고 활력을 주며, 말을 꾸미는 추가적 기능을 한다고 알고 있다. 그러나 제스처가 중요한 의미의 전달을 강화하고 생각 그 자체와 통합되어 언어와 분리될 수 없는 좀 더 심오한 기능을 한다고 설명하고 있다. 그러므로 ⑤의 '제스처: 추가 이상의 기능'이 제시문의 제목으로 가장 적절하다.

[오답해설]

① 언어의 잠재력
② 제스처와 사고의 분리
③ 제스처의 필수 원칙
④ 생각의 깊이를 측정할 수 있을까?

42   빈칸 추론하기   ①

[정답해설]

제시문에서 제스처와 말은 함께 하며, 제스처가 "추가 기능" 또는 "장식"이라는 말 이상으로 더 단단히 묶여 있다고 설명하고 있다. 즉, 말과 제스처는 따로 분리된 것이 아니라 생각 그 자체와 통합되어 있는 것이다. 그러므로 ①의 'inseparable from imagery(이미지와 분리할 수 없는)'가 빈칸에 들어갈 말로 가장 적절하다.

[오답해설]

② 근본적인 의미에 의해 강조되는
③ 표면적인 형태와 다른
④ 언어 장식에 의존하는
⑤ 외부화에 의해 구축된

[43~45]

[핵심어휘]

□ duty-free shop 면세점
□ be packed with ~으로 꽉 차다[미어터지다]
□ a multitude of 다수의, 많은
□ patient 끈기 있게 일하는, 근면한
□ considerate 사려 깊은, 배려하는
□ transaction 거래, 매매
□ attendant 수행원, 승무원, 안내원
□ by the skin of one's teeth 가까스로, 간신히
□ booth 점포, 부스
□ boarding 승선, 승차, 탑승
□ make a long face 울상 짓다, 인상 쓰다, 얼굴을 찌푸리다
□ be delighted with ~을 기뻐하다

[본문해석]

(A)

"아빠, 시간 잘 보고 있어요?" 톰이 물었다. 그는 지금 탑승구로 가야 한다고 생각했지만, (a) 그의 아빠는 시간에 무심한 것처럼 보였다. "응, 톰. 걱정하지 마. 우리는 늦지 않을 거야."라고 아빠가 말했지만, 그는 적어도 20분 동안 그렇게 말하고 있었다. 아빠는 특별한 상표의 시계가 있는 면세점을 찾았다. 그들이 도착했을 때, 그 곳은 많은 사람들로 꽉 차 있었다. 공항에 있는 모든 사람들이 이 면세점에서 무언가를 원하는 것처럼 보였다.

(D)

가게 안에는 여러 물건들을 파는 작은 부스들이 많이 있었고, 아빠는 다시 시계 부스를 찾기 위해 주위를 걷고 있었다. "비행기는 4시 30분에 출발하고, 탑승은 30분 전에 시작하므로, 우리는 4시까지 탑승구에 도착해야 한다는 의미야." 톰은 마음속으로 계산을 하고 있었고, (e) 그의 시계를 보았다. 거의 4시였다. 그들은 이미 탑승구에 도착했어야만 한다. 그들이 있는 곳에서 탑승구에 도착하려면 적어도 10분은 걸릴 것이다. 톰은 아빠를 바라보며 얼굴을 찌푸렸다.

(B)

그러나 아빠는 아들을 보지도 않았다. 그는 앞에 있는 몇 개의 시계를 살펴보면서 판매원과 이야기를 나누고 있었다. 그 판매원은 매우 근면하고 사려가 깊었다. 마침내 아빠는 하나를 골랐고, 판매원은 "그럼 이걸로 포장해 드리겠습니다."라고 말했다. 아빠는 서둘러 지불했고 (b) 그로부터 포장꾸러미를 받았다. 마침내 거래는 끝이 났다. 아빠는 아들을 향해 돌아서서 "달리자"라고 말했다. 아빠가 그의 말을 마치기도 전에, 톰은 이미 뛰고 있었다.

(C)

그들은 100미터 경주자들처럼 통로를 질주했고, 포장 가방이 날아다니며 그들을 뒤쫓았다. 멀리서 (c) 그 아들이 문이 닫히는 것을 보고 "잠깐만요, 우리가 왔어요!"라고 소리쳤고, "잠깐만요, 제발!"이라고 아버지도 아들 바로 뒤에서 소리쳤다. 승무원이 그들을 보았고, 그들은 가까스로 도착했다. 자리에 앉으면서 아버지는 "봐, 내가 맞았어!"라고 말했다. 톰은 무슨 말인지 몰랐지만, (d) 그는 그저 안도의 한숨을 내쉬었다.

43   글의 배열순서 정하기   ④

[정답해설]

(A)에서는 비행기 탑승 시간이 다 되어가는 데도 느긋하게 아빠가 원하는 브랜드의 시계를 사기 위해 면세점에 들렀고, (D)에서는 비행기 탑승 시간에 늦을까봐 걱정하는 아들이 그러한 아빠를 보며 얼굴을 찌푸린다. (B)에서는 아빠가 아들의 시선은 아랑곳하지 않고 자신이 원하는 시계를 구매한 후 아들에게 탑승구로 뛰자고 말한다. 마지막으로 (C)에서 그들은 간신히 비행기에 탑승하게 되고, 아들은 안도의 한숨을 내쉰다. 그러므로 제시된 글은 (D)-(B)-(C)의 순으로 배열되어야 글의 흐름상 적절하다.

| **44** | 지칭 대상과 다른 것 고르기 | ② |

[정답해설]

(a), (c), (d), (e)는 모두 아들을 가리키지만, (b)는 아빠에게 시계를 판 판매원을 가리킨다.

| **45** | 내용과 불일치 문장 고르기 | ⑤ |

[정답해설]

톰은 비행기 탑승 시간이 다 되어 가는 데도 원하는 브랜드의 시계를 사기 위해 면세점에서 쇼핑하는 아빠를 보고 얼굴을 찌푸렸다. 그러므로 톰이 아빠가 쇼핑하는 것을 기뻐한 것은 아니다.

[오답해설]

① 톰은 시간에 대한 아빠의 태도를 걱정했다. → 톰은 비행기 탑승 시간이 다 되어 가는 데도 시간에 무심한 아빠의 태도를 걱정함

② 톰이 방문한 면세점은 매우 붐볐다. → 톰이 면세점에 도착했을 때, 그곳은 많은 사람들로 꽉 차 있었음

③ 그 판매원은 근면하고 사려 깊은 서비스를 제공했다. → 판매원은 아빠가 원하는 시계를 구입할 수 있도록 성실하게 설명함

④ 톰과 그의 아빠는 성공적으로 탑승했다. → 탑승구로 달려가 간신히 비행기에 탑승한 후 안도의 한 숨을 내쉼

2023학년도 기출문제 정답 및 해설

01 ④	02 ②	03 ①	04 ⑤	05 ⑤	06 ⑤
07 ③	08 ①	09 ③	10 ⑤	11 ④	12 ②
13 ①	14 ④	15 ③	16 ④	17 ⑤	18 ⑤
19 ③	20 ④	21 ③	22 ②	23 ②	24 ①
25 ①	26 ②	27 ③	28 ②	29 ①	30 ②
31 ③	32 ①	33 ③	34 ④	35 ④	36 ③
37 ⑤	38 ⑤	39 ②	40 ①	41 ④	42 ③
43 ④	44 ②	45 ①			

01 ④ 'persistent'는 '끊임없이 지속[반복]되는'의 의미로 'chronic(만성의, 고질적인)'과 의미가 가장 유사하다.

어휘
- trainee doctor : 수련의, 견습 의사
- persistent : 끊임없이 지속[반복]되는
- fatal : 죽음을 초래하는, 치명적인
- occasional : 가끔의, 간헐적인
- irregular : 불규칙적인, 비정규의
- infectious : 전염되는, 병을 옮길 수 있는

오답풀이
① fatal → 치명적인
② occasional → 가끔의
③ irregular → 불규칙적인
⑤ infectious → 전염되는

해석
내가 수련의였을 때, 첫 환자들 중 한 명은 만성 기침 이 있는 노인이었다.

02 ② 'contradicted'는 '상충되다, 엇갈리다'라는 의미로 'opposed (반대하다, 맞서다)'와 그 의미가 가장 유사하다.

어휘
- televised : TV로 방송되는, TV로 중계된
- court case : 법정 사건
- witness statements : 목격자[증인] 진술

- contradict : 모순되다, 상충되다, 엇갈리다
- confirm : 확인하다, 확정하다
- duplicate : 복사[복제]하다, 사본을 만들다
- appreciate : 인정하다, 고마워하다, 감상하다

오답풀이
① agreed → 동의하다
③ confirmed → 확인하다
④ duplicated → 복사하다
⑤ appreciated → 인정하다

해석
그 법정 사건이 TV로 중계되는 동안, 목격자 진술이 서로 엇갈렸다.

03 ① 'advent'는 '도래, 출현'의 의미로 'emergence(출현, 나타남)'와 그 의미가 가장 유사하다.

어휘
- advent : 도래, 출현
- agribusiness : 기업식 농업[영농]
- emergence : 출현, 나타남
- transformation : 변신, 변형, 탈바꿈
- collapse : 붕괴, 실패
- manipulation : 조작, 처리
- supplement : 보충, 보완

오답풀이
② transformation → 변형
③ collapse → 붕괴
④ manipulation → 조작
⑤ supplement → 보충

해석
농업의 출현이 없었더라면 무려 20억이나 되는 사람들이 지금 존재하지 않았을지도 모른다.

04 ⑤ 'exceptional'은 '예외적인, 이례적인'의 의미로 'unusual(특이한, 드문)'과 그 의미가 가장 유사하다.

어휘
- promotion : 승진, 승격

- exceptional : 예외적인, 이례적인
- circumstances : 사정, 상황
- adverse : 부정적인, 불리한
- suspicious : 의심스러운, 의혹을 갖는
- customary : 관례적인, 습관적인
- profitable : 이익이 되는, 유리한
- unusual : 특이한, 드문

오답풀이

① adverse → 부정적인
② suspicious → 의심스러운
③ customary → 관례적인
④ profitable → 이익이 되는

해석

첫 해 승진은 <u>이례적인</u> 일이다.

05 ⑤ 'substandard'는 '수준 이하의, 열악한'의 의미로 'insufficient (부족한, 불충분한)'와 그 의미가 가장 유사하다.

어휘

- bias : 편견, 편향
- substandard : 수준 이하의, 열악한
- sophisticated : 세련된, 정교한
- considerate : 사려 깊은, 배려하는
- temporary : 일시적인, 임시의
- conventional : 관습적인, 전통적인
- insufficient : 부족한, 불충분한

오답풀이

① sophisticated → 세련된
② considerate → 사려 깊은
③ temporary → 일시적인
④ conventional → 관습적인

해석

간호사가 환자에게 편견을 가질 때, <u>수준 이하</u>의 치료를 제공한다.

06 ⑤ A가 빨간 셔츠를 건조기에서 찾았지만 아직 마르지 않았다고 하였고, 빈칸의 다음 대화에서 통학 버스가 금방 올 것을 염려하고 있다. 그러므로 빈칸에는 대화의 흐름상 ⑤의 "it's going to take at least twenty more minutes.(적어도 20분 이상은 걸릴 거야.)"가 들어갈 말로 적절하다.

어휘

- top drawer : 맨 위 서랍
- any minute : 금방, 금세
- at least : 적어도

오답풀이

① You can buy a new shirt instead.(대신 새 셔츠를 살 수 있어.)
② Then you can wear it right away.(지금 바로 입을 수 있어.)
③ Just put it in the washing machine.(그냥 세탁기에 넣어.)
④ I hope you find your favorite shirt soon.(네가 제일 좋아하는 셔츠를 빨리 찾길 바래.)

해석

A: 엄마, 내가 제일 좋아하는 빨간 셔츠가 어디 있는지 알아요?
B: 네 방의 맨 위 서랍은 확인해봤니?
A: 네. 하지만 거기엔 없었어요.
B: 그럼 건조기 안을 한 번 보렴.
A: 아, 여기 있네요. 근데 아직 마르지 않았어요.
B: 적어도 20분 이상 걸릴 거야.
A: 이런! 통학 버스가 금방 올 거예요.
B: 음, 그러면 그냥 다른 셔츠를 입어야 해.

07 ③ B가 명예 훈장을 받은 것에 대해 A가 빈칸 다음에서 겸손하다고 하였으므로, 빈칸에는 B가 자신이 한 일에 대해 겸손함을 드러내는 표현이 들어가야 한다. 그러므로 빈칸에는 글의 흐름상 ③의 "I'm sure anyone else would have done the same.(다른 사람들도 그와 똑같이 했을 겁니다.)"가 들어갈 말로 적절하다.

어휘

- the Medal of Honor : 명예 훈장
- Sergeant : 병장, 하사, 경사
- deserve : ~을 받을 만하다, ~할 가치가 있다
- Commissioner : 위원, 경찰청장
- modest : 겸손한
- department : 부서, 학과
- be doing well : 회복 중이다, 건강하다
- cherish : 소중히 여기다, 간직하다
- right person : 적임자
- criminal : 범인, 범죄자

오답풀이

① I've never been afraid of anything.(저는 아무런 걱정도 없습니다.)
② I've always considered myself to be a hero.(전 항상 스스로를 영웅이라고 생각했습니다.)
④ I'm not sure if you're the right person for this medal.(당신이 이 훈장의 적임자인지 잘 모르겠네요.)
⑤ I think arresting criminals should come before everything.(저는 무엇보다도 범인들을 검거하는 것이 우선이라고 생각합니다.)

해석

A: 명예 훈장을 수여한 것을 축하합니다. 박 경사님.

B: 제가 그럴 자격이 있는지 모르겠네요. 청장님.

A: 물론 그럴 자격이 있습니다. 그 젊은이의 생명을 구한 것은 매우 용감했습니다.

B: 다른 사람들도 그와 똑같이 했을 겁니다.

A: 정말 겸손하네요. 당신은 우리 부서의 자랑입니다.

B: 감사합니다. 그 젊은이가 건강하다니 기쁠 뿐입니다.

A: 덕분에 우리 도시의 거리가 좀 더 안전하고 따뜻해졌습니다.

B: 이 순간을 영원히 간직하겠습니다.

08 ① 'translate'가 포함된 문장에서 관계대명사 'which'의 선행사는 'control of food production'이다. 이때 관계대명사 'which'가 이끄는 종속절의 수와 시제는 앞의 선행사에 일치시켜야 하므로, ①의 'translate'는 3인칭 단수 현재 시제인 'translates'로 고쳐 써야 옳다.

어휘

• common theory : 통설

• physical power : 육체적인 힘, 물리력, 체력

• force into submission : 복종[굴복]시키다

• subtle : 미묘한, 예민한

• version : 설명, 생각, 견해

• claim : 주장, 요청, 권리

• monopolise : 독점하다, 독차지하다

• manual labour : 육체노동

• ploughing : 쟁기질

• in turn : 차례대로, 교대로, 번갈아

• translate : 번역[통역]하다, 바뀌다, 전환되다

• with regard to : ～과 관련하여

• resistant to : ～에 대해 저항하는

• fatigue : 피로, 피곤

• problematically : 문제가 많게, 의심스럽게

• exclude : 제외하다, 거부하다, 배제하다

• priesthood : 사제직, 성직

• craft : 공예, 기술, 기교

해석

남성이 여성보다 강하며, 남성이 여성을 복종시키기 위해 더 큰 물리력을 사용해 왔다고 보는 것이 통설이다. 이 주장에 대한 더 미묘한 견해는 그들의 힘이 쟁기질이나 수확과 같은 힘든 육체노동을 필요로 하는 일들을 남성들이 독점하게 한다고 주장한다. 이것이 그들이 식량 생산을 통제하게 하고, 이는 다시 정치권력으로 전환된다. 그러나 '남성이 여성보다 강하다'는 말은 평균적이거나 특정 형태의 힘에 대해서만 타당하다.

여성은 일반적으로 남성보다 배고픔, 질병 그리고 피로에 더 저항력이 강하다. 또한 대다수 남성들보다 더 빨리 달리고 더 무거운 것을 들 수 있는 여성들도 많다. 게다가, 이 이론에서 가장 문제가 되는 것은 여성들은 역사를 통틀어 현장에서, 작업장에서 그리고 가정에서 힘든 육체 노동에 종사하는 반면, 주로 성직, 법률, 정치와 같은 육체적 노력을 거의 필요로 하지 않은 직업에서 배제되어 왔다는 것이다. 만약 사회 권력이 체력과 직접적 연관성이 있는 분야로 나뉘었다면, 여성들은 훨씬 더 많은 것을 얻었어야 했다.

09 ③ 글의 문맥상 동시동작의 부대상황을 나타나는 분사구문으로 '～while they asked about hugs received.'의 의미이다. 그러므로 ③의 'asked'는 'asking'으로 고쳐 써야 옳다.

어휘

• play a role in : ～에서 역할을 하다

• physical intimacy : 신체적 친밀감

• interplay : 상호 작용

• social support : 사회적 지원, 사회 복지

• exposure : 노출, 폭로

• buck : 달러, 루피

• inhale : 들이마시다, 흡입하다

• nasal drops : 콧물

• draw blood : 피를 뽑다, 혈액을 채취하다

• confirm : 확인해 주다, 사실임을 보여주다

• volunteer : 자원 봉사자, 지원자

• immune : 면역성이 있는

• survey : (설문) 조사하다

• consecutive : 연이은, 순차적인

• symptom : 증상, 징후

• mucus : 점액, 콧물

• quarantine : 격리, 차단

• impervious : 영향받지 않는, 통과시키지 않는

해석

포옹은 신체적 친밀감과 건강 사이에서 어떤 역할을 담당한다. 연구원들이 질병에 대한 노출, 사회 복지, 그리고 매일의 포옹 사이의 상호 작용을 조사했다. 과학이라는 미명하에 (아마 백 달러의 비용을 받고), 404명의 건강한 성인들이 일반적인 감기에 걸리도록 콧물을 들이마시는 것에 동의했다. 우선 연구원들은 지원자들이 면역력이 없다는 것을 확인시키기 위해 혈액 샘플을 채취했다. 그리고 나서 14일 동안 연이어 참가자들을 조사했고, 받은 포옹에 대해 물었다. 마지막으로, 그들은 지원자들을 감기 바이러스에 노출시키고 닷새 동안 격리시킨 상태에서 점액 생성과 같은 증상을 관찰했다. 매일 포옹하는 사람들은 아플 확률이 32퍼센트나 낮았다. 포옹이 감기에

정답 및 해설

281

걸리지 않게 만드는 것이 아니라는 사실도 밝혀졌다. 하지만 감기에 걸린 포옹자들은 덜 아팠다. 그들은 증상이 심하지 않았고 더 빨리 나았다.

10 ⑤ (A) 하이브리드 자동차가 도시 운전자들에게 유용한 경우를 설명하고 있으므로, 연비가 '훌륭한', '뛰어난'의 의미인 'superb'가 적절하다.

(B) 하이브리드 자동차가 고속도로 상에서 전기 모터에 의존할 경우 더 빠른 속도를 낼 수 없다는 의미가 되어야 하므로, 앞의 부정어 'doesn't'와 호응하여 'higher'가 적절하다.

(C) 하이브리드 자동차가 생각한 것보다 친환경적이지 못하다는 내용이 와야 하므로 'less'가 적절하다.

어휘

- hybrid : 잡종, 혼성체
- environmentally : 환경적으로
- rely on : ~에 의지하다, ~을 필요로 하다
- emission : 배출, 배기가스
- stationary : 움직이지 않는, 정지해 있는
- crucially : 결정적으로, 중요하게
- superb : 최고의, 최상의, 뛰어난
- fuel economy : 연비
- fall back on : ~에 기대다[의지하다], 후퇴하다, 물러서다
- petrol engine : 가솔린 기관
- comparable : 비슷한, 비교할 만한
- conventional : 전통적인, 재래식의, 기존의
- petrol-powered car : 가솔린 자동차
- take into account : ~을 고려하다, 계산에 넣다
- manufacturing : 제조업
- decommission : 해체하다, 감축하다

해석

하이브리드 자동차는 정말 친환경적일까? 어떻게 사용하느냐에 달려있다. 하이브리드 자동차가 소음이 적고 배기가스를 발생시키지 않는 전기 모터에 거의 전적으로 의존할 수 있을 때, 차가 정지해 있을 때 완전히 꺼져 결정적으로 (A) 뛰어난 연비를 제공할 때 도시 운전자들에게는 아주 유용하다. 하지만 고속도로 상에서 차를 몰면 전기 모터는 (B) 더 빠른 속도로 차를 운전할 수 있는 동력이나 먼 거리를 달릴 수 있는 에너지가 없기 때문에 하이브리드는 가솔린 엔진에 의존해야 할 것이다. 이러한 경우 하이브리드는 유사한 연비와 동일한 배기가스를 배출하는 기존의 가솔린 자동차와 똑같다. 하이브리드 자동차용 배터리를 제조하려면 많은 에너지가 필요하다는 점도 고려해야 한다. 불과 몇 년 후, 배터리 수명이 다해 그것들을 해체하고 재활용하려면 더 많은 에너지를 필요로 한다.

이러한 점과 개발 영향 때문에 실제로 하이브리드 자동차는 제조업체가 믿길 바라는 것보다 (C) 덜 친환경적이다.

11 ④ (A) 미국 사회의 다양성을 고려할 때 학교 조직과 교육 과정을 두고 집단 간에 의견 차이가 있다는 의미가 되어야 하므로, '불일치'나 '의견 차이'를 뜻하는 'disagreements'가 적절하다.

(B) 이익 단체들이 교사, 학교 관계자, 그리고 교과서 출판 업자들에게 그들의 관점을 강요한다고 하였으므로 교육과정을 정치에 개입시키는 'politicize'가 들어갈 말로 적절하다.

(C) 이익 집단들이 자신의 의제를 내세우며 극단주의의 선을 넘게 되면 교육과정 전체가 이익 집단들에 의해 좌지우지 되고 공교육이 위협받게 된다는 의미이므로, '취약한'의 의미를 지닌 'vulnerable'이 들어갈 말로 적절하다.

어휘

- given : ~을 고려하면, 특정한, 정해진
- diversity : 다양성
- insulate : 보호하다, 격리하다
- result from : 기인하다, 원인이다
- tension : 긴장감, 긴장 상태
- disagreement : 불일치, 의견 차이
- turn up : 나타나다, 도착하다
- racial segregation : 인종차별
- interest group : 이익 단체[집단]
- retain : 유지하다, 보유하다
- politicize : 정치에 개입시키다, 정치화하다
- impose A on B : B에게 A를 강요하다
- school officials : 학교 관계자
- local school boards : 지역 학교 이사회
- myths and fables : 신화와 우화
- imaginative : 창의적인, 상상력이 풍부한
- inject : 주사하다, 주입하다
- creationism : 천지창조설, 천지창조론
- biology : 생물학
- extremism : 극단주의, 극단론
- agenda : 의제, 강령
- without regard to : ~을 고려하지 않고, ~에 상관없이
- vulnerable : 취약한, 연약한

해석

미국 사회의 다양성을 고려할 때, 학교들을 집단 간의 차이와 긴장으로 인한 압박으로부터 격리시키는 것은 불가능했다. 사람들이 기본 가치관이 다를 때, 그러한 (A) 불일치는 학교가

어떻게 조직되는지 혹은 학교가 무엇을 가르쳐야 하는지에 대한 논쟁에서 조만간 나타난다. 때때로 이러한 논쟁은 인종차별과 같은 끔찍한 불공평을 제거한다. 그러나 때때로 이익 단체들은 교육과정을 (B) 정치화하고 교사, 학교 관계자, 그리고 교과서 출판업자들에게 그들의 관점을 강요하려고 한다. 전국적으로, 심지어 지금도, 이익 단체들은 어린 독자들로부터 신화와 우화 그리고 다른 창의적인 문학들을 없애고 생물학에 창조론의 가르침을 주입하도록 지역 학교 이사회를 압박하고 있다. 집단들이 이성이나 타인을 가리지 않고 자신의 의제를 내세우며 극단주의의 선을 넘을 때, 그들은 공교육 자체를 위협하여 어떤 문제도 정직하게 가르치기 어렵고 교육과정 전체가 정치 운동에 (C) 취약해진다.

12 ② (A) 백상아리가 먹이를 몰래 잡기 위해 색깔을 바꾸는 것이므로, '위장'이나 '변장'의 의미인 'camouflage'가 들어갈 말로 적절하다.

(B) 연구원들이 바다표범 미끼를 보트 뒤에 매단 것은 상어들을 유인하기 위한 것이므로 '유인하다', '유도하다'의 의미인 'entice'가 들어갈 말로 적절하다.

(C) 턱에 있는 자국은 해당 상어가 다른 상어들과 구별되는 신체적 특징이므로, '식별할 수 있는'의 의미를 지닌 'identifiable'이 들어갈 말로 적절하다.

〔어휘〕

- predatory fish : 포식 어류
- white shark : 백상아리
- impressive : 인상적인, 인상 깊은
- intrigue : 강한 호기심, 흥미진진함
- oceanic beast : 해양 동물
- camouflage : 위장, 변장
- cluster : 무리, 군집
- strategy : 계획, 전략
- sneak up : 살금살금 다가가다, 몰래 다가가다
- prey : 먹이, 희생자
- seal : 바다표범, 물개
- decoy : 미끼
- dispel : 떨쳐 버리다, 없애다
- entice : 유인하다, 유도하다
- identifiable : 알아볼 수 있는, 식별할 수 있는
- jaw : 턱
- verify : 확인하다, 입증하다, 검증하다
- variable : 변수

〔해석〕

지구상에서 가장 큰 포식 어류인 백상아리는 300개 이상의 날카로운 이빨로 무장하고 5,000파운드에 달하는 무게로 이

미 인상적이다. 이제, 새로운 연구는 그 해양 동물에게 더 많은 흥미를 더하며, 아마도 먹이를 몰래 잡기 위한 (A) 위장 전략으로 그 동물이 색깔을 바꿀 수 있다는 것을 보여준다. 남아프리카 앞바다의 새로운 실험에서, 연구원들은 바다표범 미끼를 보트 뒤에 매달고 흰색, 회색, 검은색 판으로 특별 제작된 색판 근처에서 물 밖으로 뛰어오르는 몇 마리 상어들을 (B) 유인했다. 연구팀은 상어가 점프할 때마다 사진을 찍으며 하루 종일 실험을 반복했다. 턱에 있는 자국 때문에 쉽게 (C) 식별할 수 있는 한 상어는 어두운 회색과 훨씬 밝은 회색으로 그때그때 다르게 나타났다. 과학자들은 컴퓨터 소프트웨어를 사용하여 날씨, 조명 수준, 카메라 설정과 같은 변수들을 수정해 가며 이것을 검증했다.

13 ① 윗글은 비위생적 접촉이 면역력을 강화시킨다는 위생 가설에 대해 설명하고 있다. 즉, 유아기 때 더러워지는 것에 대해 무관심하거나 방치함으로써 비위생적인 접촉에 의해 전염되는 유아기 감염이 튼튼한 면역 체계를 형성하는데 도움이 된다는 설명이다. 그러므로 ①의 'distaste(혐오감)'은 'indifference(무관심)'이나 'negligence(방치)'등으로 바꿔 써야 적절하다.

〔어휘〕

- left to one's own devices : 제멋대로 하게 내버려 둔
- hesitate : 주저하다, 망설이다
- doorknob : 문고리, 손잡이
- wipe snot : 콧물을 닦다
- sleeve : 소매
- distaste : 불쾌감, 혐오감
- date to : 연대를 추정하다, ~로 거슬러 올라가다
- allergy : 알레르기
- city slicker : 전형적인 도시인
- epidemiologist : 유행병학자, 전염병학자
- sibling : 형제자매
- susceptible : 민감한, 예민한, 걸리기 쉬운
- hay fever : 꽃가루 알레르기
- eczema : 습진
- infection : 감염, 전염병
- transmit : 전송하다, 전염시키다
- unhygienic : 비위생적인
- foster : 조성하다, 발전시키다
- robust : 튼튼한, 탄탄한
- immune system : 면역 체계
- hygiene hypothesis : 위생 가설
- convenient : 편리한, 적절한, 알맞은
- asthma : 천식
- autoimmune disorder : 자가 면역 질환

- multiple sclerosis : 다발성 경화증
- Crohn's disease : 크론병
- microbiologist : 미생물학자

【오답풀이】

② foster → 형성하다

③ convenient → 적절한

④ fearful → 겁내는

⑤ active → 작동하다

【해석】

제멋대로 하게 나두면, 대부분의 아이들은 주저하지 않고 손잡이를 핥거나 소매로 코를 닦는다. 하지만 더러워지는 것에 대한 혐오감(→ 무관심)이 그들의 건강에 이로울 수 있다는 생각에 어떤 근거가 있는가? 그 이론은 1800년대까지 거슬러 올라가는데, 농부들이 전형적인 도시인들보다 알레르기로 덜 고생한다는 사실을 유럽의 의사들이 깨달았던 때이다. 하지만 그 이론은 1989년이 되어서야 비로소 폭넓은 관심을 얻기 시작했는데, 영국의 전염병학자인 David Strachan은 손위의 형이나 누나가 있는 어린 아이들이 다른 아이들보다 꽃가루 알레르기와 습진에 덜 걸린다는 사실을 발견했다. Strachan은 "비위생적인 접촉에 의해 전염되는" 유아기 감염이 튼튼한 면역 체계를 형성하는데 도움이 된다고 말했다. 위생 가설이라고 불리는 그의 이론은 알레르기와 천식뿐만 아니라 다발성 경화증과 크론병과 같은 자가 면역 질환이 1950년대 이후 미국에서 300% 이상 증가한 이유에 대해 적절한 설명을 제공한다. 아마도 서구 사회는 자신의 건강을 위해 지나치게 청결했고, 부모들은 조금의 먼지 도 겁내했다. "현대 세계에서 일어나고 있는 일이 무엇이든 간에, 그것은 불필요할 때 면역 체계가 작동하는 원인이 되고 있다"고 런던 대학의 미생물학자인 Graham Rook이 말한다.

14 ④ 생물학적 나이와 실제 나이가 다른 만큼 과학자들이 노화 시계를 개발한 것은 생물학적 나이를 감추기 위해서가 아니라 밝히기 위해서이다. 그러므로 ④의 'veil(감추다)'은 'reveal(드러내다, 밝히다)' 등으로 바꿔 써야 적절하다.

【어휘】

- clock : 기록하다, 재다, 세다
- cope with : ~에 대처하다[대응하다]
- wear and tear : 마모, 소모, 손상
- factor : 요인, 요소
- biological age : 생물학적 나이[연령]
- chronological age : 실제 나이[연령]
- reflection : 반사, 반영
- mortality : 사망자 수, 사망률
- straightforward : 간단한, 솔직한

- decade : 10년
- assess : 재다, 평가하다, 측정하다
- veil : 베일을 쓰다, 가리다, 감추다
- degrade : 저하시키다, 퇴화시키다

【오답풀이】

① clocked → 세다

② reflection → 반영

③ straightforward → 간단한

⑤ degraded → 퇴화하다

【해석】

나이는 당신이 센 생일 숫자보다 훨씬 더 많다. 스트레스, 수면, 그리고 식습관 모두 우리의 장기가 일상생활의 손상에 어떻게 대응하는지에 영향을 미친다. 이와 같은 요소들은 같은 날에 태어난 사람들보다 당신을 더 빨리 혹은 더 천천히 늙게 만들 수도 있다. 그것은 생물학적 나이가 실제 나이, 즉 여러분이 살아온 나이와 상당히 다를 수 있다는 것을 의미한다. 생물학적 나이는 실제 나이보다 신체적 건강과 심지어 사망률을 더 잘 반영한다. 그러나 그것을 계산하는 것은 그리 간단하지 않다. 과학자들은 지난 10년 동안 생물학적 나이를 감추기(→ 밝히기) 위해 신체적 표식을 측정하는 노화 시계라고 불리는 도구를 개발하는데 보냈다. 노화 시계 이면의 큰 개념은 기본적으로 여러분의 장기가 얼마나 퇴화되었는지를 표시하여 건강한 시간이 얼마나 남았는지를 예측하는 것이다.

15 ③ 글의 서두에 도자기 탑(Porcelain Tower)은 15세기 초 중국 명나라 영락제가 그의 어머니를 기리기 위해 세웠다고 서술되어 있다. 그러므로 "It was built to honor the Emperor's mother.(그것은 황제의 어머니를 기리기 위해 세웠다.)"는 ③의 설명이 제시문의 내용과 일치한다.

【어휘】

- the Yongle Emperor : 영락제(명나라 제3대 황제)
- Ming dynasty : 명 왕조(명나라)
- construction : 건설, 건축
- towering : 우뚝 솟은, 높이 치솟은
- monument : 기념물, 기념비
- Porcelain Tower : 도자기 탑
- imperial capital : 제국의 수도
- Buddhist Temple complex : 불교사원
- white porcelain : 백자, 백자기
- glisten : 반짝이다, 번득거리다
- adorn with : ~으로 꾸미다[장식하다]
- vibrant : 활기찬, 강렬한, 생생한
- glazed : 유약을 바른, 유약을 입힌
- the remnants : 유적, 유물

- replicate : 모사하다, 복제하다
- slab : 평판, 조각
- fade : 바래다, 사라지다
- decade : 10년
- rural : 시골의, 지방의

오답풀이

① Its bricks were all the same size.(그것의 벽돌은 크기가 모두 같았다.) → 벽돌의 크기가 모두 같은 것은 아님

② It stood in a temple of a rural area.(그것은 지방의 사원에 세워졌다.) → 황실의 수도인 난징시의 바오엔 불교 사원에 세워짐

④ It was decorated with the shapes of the sun.(그것은 태양 모양으로 장식되었다.) → 동물, 풍경으로 장식됨

⑤ Its porcelain slabs have been successfully replicated today.(그것의 도자기 평판은 오늘날 성공적으로 복제되었다.) → 성공적으로 복제하지 못함

해석

15세기 초, 중국 명나라 영락제는 그의 어머니를 기리기 위해 우뚝 솟은 기념비를 세우라고 명령했다. 도자기 탑은 당시 황실 수도였던 난징시에 웅장한 바오엔 불교 사원의 일부로 세워진 거대한 탑이었다. 그 탑은 백자 벽돌로 건축되어 햇빛에 반짝거렸고, 동물, 하층부, 풍경 등이 녹색, 노란색, 갈색의 생생한 유리로 장식되었다. 유물을 연구하는 역사학자들은 유약을 입힌 도자기 벽돌들이 고도의 숙련공들에 의해 만들어졌다고 말하지만, 안타깝게도 그것들을 만드는 방법은 역사 속으로 사라졌다. 가장 큰 벽돌들 중 몇 개는 두께가 50센티미터 이상이고 무게가 150킬로그램이나 나갔으며, 그 색유리는 수 세기 동안 선명하게 남아 있었다. 오늘날 이 도자기 평판들을 복제하려고 하는 노동자들은 5센티미터 이상의 두께로 만들기 위해 애쓰고 있으며 그 색깔은 불과 10년 후에 사라진다.

16 ④ 글의 서두에서 남아프리카 공화국의 소설가 Nadine Gordimer는 뛰어난 문학 능력뿐만 아니라 흑인과 백인을 엄격히 분리하는 제도인 인종 차별 정책에 대해 일관되고 용기 있는 비판으로 1991년 노벨 문학상을 받았다고 서술되어 있다. 그러므로 "She was acknowledged for her strong stance against racial discrimination.(그녀는 인종 차별에 반대하는 강경한 태도로 그 공적을 인정받았다.)"는 ④의 설명이 제시문의 내용과 일치한다.

어휘

- apartheid : (남아프리카공화국의) 인종 차별 정책
- segregating : 차별, 분리
- in all spheres of : 모든 영역에서
- racism : 인종 차별 주의, 민족주의
- for one thing : 우선, 첫째로
- racist system : 인종 차별 제도
- in one's own way : 자기 나름대로
- concentrate on : ~에 집중하다, ~에 초점을 맞추다
- moral : 도덕적인, 도덕과 관련된
- dilemma : 딜레마, 진퇴양난
- unambiguous : 모호하지 않은, 분명한
- delicate : 미묘한, 민감한
- inequality : 불평등, 불균등
- injustice : 불공정, 부당함, 불의
- neglect : 방치하다, 소홀히 하다
- ethical : 윤리적인, 도덕적인
- be attributed to : ~의 탓이다, ~의 덕분이다
- be acknowledged for : 공적을 인정받다
- strong stance : 강경한 태도[입장]
- racial discrimination : 인종 차별

오답풀이

① Her novels neglected the ethical problems faced by the whites.(그녀의 소설은 백인들이 직면한 윤리적 문제를 소홀히 했다.) → 백인들의 도덕적 딜레마에도 초점을 맞춤

② Her fight against apartheid was mainly driven by political ambition.(인종 차별 정책에 대한 그녀의 투쟁은 주로 정치적 야망에 의해 추진되었다.) → 인간적인 측면에 관심을 둠

③ Her growth as a writer was attributed to her middle-class black parents.(작가로서의 그녀의 성장은 중산층 흑인 부모의 덕분이었다.) → 중산층 백인 부모의 덕분임

⑤ She was praised for her ability to avoid delicate issues on South African politics.(그녀는 남아프리카 공화국의 정치에 관한 민감한 문제를 회피하는 능력으로 칭찬을 받았다.) → 일관되고 용기 있는 비판을 함

해석

남아프리카 공화국 소설가 Nadine Gordimer는 뛰어난 문학 능력뿐만 아니라 모든 삶의 영역에서 흑인과 백인을 엄격히 분리하는 제도인 인종 차별 정책에 대해 일관되고 용기 있는 비판으로 1991년 노벨 문학상을 받았다. 인종 차별 정책에 대한 그녀의 투쟁은 주로 정치적 제스처가 아니었다. 소설가로서 그녀는 인종 차별 정책과 민족주의의 인간적 측면에 더 큰 관심을 두었다. 우선 그녀는 남아프리카에 사는 백인 중산층 지식인으로서 그 제도의 혜택을 받았다는 것을 알고 있었다. 그녀는 또한 인종 차별 제도를 유지하는 데 책임이 있는 백인들이 나름대로의 고통을 받았다는 사실도 알고 있었다. 그래서 그녀의 소설이나 단편소설은 남아프리카의 사회적 관계에 의해 개인들에게 부과된 도덕적 딜레마에 초점을 맞추고 있다. 비록 지식인으로서 그녀는 민감한 사회적 문제에 대해 분

명한 정치적 발언을 할 수 있지만, 소설가로서 그녀는 불평등과 불공정에 바탕을 둔 사회에서 살아가는 인간의 보다 불명확한 측면에 더 관심이 많다.

17 ⑤ 칸트의 관점에서는 물에 빠진 아이를 구하는 것이 중요한 것이 아니라, 그들을 구하려는 의지나 의도가 중요하다. 즉, 결과론자가 행위의 결과를 중시하는 반면, 칸트는 행위의 동기를 중시한다고 볼 수 있다. 그러므로 빈칸에는 'motivation(동기)'이 들어갈 말로 적절하다.

어휘

• moral : 도덕적인, 도덕상의
• perspective : 관점, 시각
• count : 중요하다
• intention : 의도, 의향
• consequentialist : 결과론자, 결과주의자
• obviously : 분명하게, 명확하게
• be concerned with : ~에 관계가 있다, ~에 관심이 있다
• repression : 탄압, 진압, 억압
• intuition : 직관, 직감
• motivation : 동기

오답풀이

① repression → 억압
② decision → 결정
③ intuition → 직관
④ satisfaction → 만족

해석

물에 빠진 아이를 구하기 위해 강으로 뛰어든다고 생각해보라. 이것은 아마도 대부분의 사람들에게 좋은 일처럼 보일 것이다. 그러나 칸트에게는 물에 빠진 아이를 구하기 위해 강물에 뛰어들어야 하는 것이 자신의 도덕적 의무라는 것을 알았기 때문에 그렇게 하는 것이 좋은 일일 뿐이다. 당신을 멋지게 보이게 할 수도 있고, 친구들에게 감동을 줄 수도 있고, 텔레비전에 나올 수도 있고, 심지어 당신이 아이를 돌봤기 때문에 강물에 뛰어들어 아이를 구한다면, 칸트의 관점에서 그것은 더 이상 도덕적인 행위가 아니다. 칸트에게는 물에 빠진 아이를 구하는 것이 꼭 중요한 일은 아니다. 중요한 것은 그들을 구하려는 의지나 의도이다. 분명한 것은 결과론자가 결과에 주로 초점을 맞추는 반면, 칸트는 선택과 동기에 관심을 갖는다.

18 ⑤ 윗글에 따르면 정보를 측정하고 기록하는 일은 원시 사회와 문명 사회를 구분 짓는 경계선이며, 초기 문명 사회에서 데이터화의 초기 기반이 되었다. 따라서 빈칸에는 정보를 측정하고 기록하는 것이 데이터 생성을 촉진시켰다는 의미가 되어야 하므로 'facilitated'가 들어갈 말로 적절하다.

어휘

• demarcation : 경계, 구분
• primitive : 초기의, 원시의
• conceptual : 개념의, 구상의
• millennium : 천년, 새로운 천년이 시작되는 시기
• significantly : 크게, 상당히, 중요하게,
• accuracy : 정확성, 정확도
• evolution : 진화, 발전
• script : 문자
• precise : 정확한, 정밀한
• method : 방법, 수법
• transaction : 거래, 처리
• retrieve : 되찾다, 검색하다
• datafication : 데이터화
• reverse : 뒤바꾸다, 반전[역전]시키다
• imitate : 모방하다, 흉내내다
• hinder : 방해하다, 저지하다
• facilitate : 가능하게[용이하게] 하다, 촉진시키다

오답풀이

① complicated → 복잡하게 만들다
② reversed → 뒤바꾸다
③ imitated → 모방하다
④ hindered → 방해하다

해석

정보를 기록하는 능력은 원시 사회와 선진 사회의 경계선 중 하나이다. 길이와 무게에 대한 기본적인 계산과 측정은 초기 문명의 가장 오래된 개념적 도구 중 하나였다. 기원전 3천년 경에 기록된 정보에 대한 개념은 인더스 계곡, 이집트, 메소포타미아에서 상당히 발전하였다. 일상생활에서 측정의 사용이 증가함에 따라 정확성이 향상되었다. 메소포타미아에서 문자의 진화는 생산과 사업상 거래를 추적하는 정확한 방법을 제공했다. 문자 언어는 초기 문명이 현실을 측정하고, 기록하고, 나중에 검색할 수 있도록 하였다. 측정과 기록 모두 데이터 생성을 촉진시켰다. 그것들은 데이터화의 초기 기반이다.

19 ③ 기술 기업들이 온라인 광고 시장을 지배하면서 언론 본연의 임무인 진실 보도보다는 상업적으로 돈벌이가 되는 자극적인 낚시성 기사를 우선시 하여 '가짜 뉴스'를 양산하였다. 그러므로 빈칸에는 'boring truth(지루한 진실)'이 들어갈 말로 적절하다.

어휘

• bulletin : 뉴스 단신, 공고, 회보
• a profusion of : 많은, 풍성한
• spring up : 휙 나타나다, 갑자기 생겨나다

- compete with : ~와 경쟁하다[겨루다]
- online-only : 온라인 전용
- article : 글, 기사
- curated : 전문적인 식견으로 엄선한, 관장한
- algorithm : 알고리즘
- struggle : 투쟁하다, 몸부림치다
- dominate : 지배하다, 두드러지다
- print circulation : 발행부수
- collapse : 붕괴되다, 폭락하다
- go bust : 파산하다, 망하다
- prioritise : 우선순위를 매기다, 우선적으로 처리하다
- attention-grabbing : 눈길을 끄는, 주목을 끄는
- clickbait : 낚시성 기사, 클릭 미끼
- propel : 추진하다, 나아가게 하다
- declare : 단언하다, 선언하다
- fake news : 가짜 뉴스
- neologism : 신조어, 새로운 표현
- racy : 흥분되는, 짜릿한, 야한
- exaggerated : 과장된, 부풀린

오답풀이

① subjective opinion(주관적인 의견)

② racy headlines(짜릿한 제목)

④ online etiquette(온라인 에티켓)

⑤ exaggerated ads(과장된 광고)

해석

뉴스가 예전 같지 않다. 요즘 대부분의 소비자들은 뉴스 단신의 대부분을 온라인으로 받는다. 온라인 발행이 저렴하기 때문에, 많은 새로운 소식통이 갑자기 생겨난다. 기성 신문이 운영하는 웹사이트는 페이스북과 트위터와 같은 소셜 미디어 사이트의 알고리즘에 의해 엄선된 논평, 디지털 체인 레터 및 기사의 편집은 말할 것도 없고, 보다 새로운 온라인 전용 매체 및 전문(또는 아마추어) 블로그와 경쟁한다. 기성 매체는 어려움을 겪어왔다. 기자들의 월급을 주던 광고의 많은 부분이 온라인 광고 시장을 지배하는 두 개의 큰 기술 회사 페이스북과 구글에게 돌아갔다. 발행 부수가 폭락했다. 지역 신문들이 특히 큰 타격을 입었고, 많은 신문사들이 파산했다. 소셜 미디어 알고리즘은 <u>지루한 진실</u>보다 눈길을 끄는 낚시성 기사를 우선시하며, 전 세계적으로 말도 안 되는 일을 추진하는 데 일조한다. 사전 편찬사인 콜린스는 "가짜 뉴스"를 2017년 올해의 신조어로 선언했다.

20 ② 범죄가 만연한 거리, 주차장. 쇼핑몰 등에 클래식 음악을 틀어 놓으면, 그러한 음향 환경을 좋아하지 않는 부랑자들이 그곳을 배회하지 않게 됨으로써 범죄를 막을 수 있다는

논리이다. 그러므로 앞의 부정어 'won't'와 호응하여 ②의 'want to loaf around there(그곳에서 배회하고 싶다)'가 빈 칸에 들어갈 말로 적절하다.

어휘

- team up : 한 팀이 되다, 협력[협조]하다
- pump : 주다, 공급하다
- crime-ridden : 범죄가 많은, 범죄가 만연한
- deter : 단념시키다, 그만두게 하다, 막다
- pipe : 보내다, 송신하다
- a tube station : 지하철역
- robbery : 강도
- vandalism : 공공 기물 파손 행위
- slice : 썰다, 자르다, 줄어들다
- light-rail : 경전철
- transit hubs : 교통 중심지
- Port Authority : 항만청
- vagrancy : 부랑, 부랑률
- crime-stopping : 범죄 예방
- maestro : 명연주자, 거장
- logic : 논리, 타당성
- calming : 진정, 차분함
- loiter : 어슬렁거리다, 빈둥거리다
- vandalize : 공공 기물을 파손하다
- soundscape : 음향 풍경
- annoy : 괴롭히다, 짜증나게 하다
- apparently : 분명하게, 명백하게
- scare away birds : 새를 놀라게 하여 쫓다
- blare : 요란하게[쾅쾅] 울리다
- stable : 안정된, 차분한
- loaf around : 빈둥거리다, 배회하다

오답풀이

① (won't) get emotionally stable(정서적으로 안정되지 않다)

③ (won't) be in the mood for classical music(클래식 음악을 듣고 싶어 하지 않다)

④ (won't) commit a serious crime on the spot(현장에서 중범죄를 저지르지 않다)

⑤ (won't) pay attention to the music any more(음악에 더 이상 귀를 기울이지 않다)

해석

1990년대 이래로, 기업과 경찰은 범죄가 만연한 거리, 주차장, 쇼핑몰에 클래식 음악을 공급하기 위해 협력해왔다. 왜 그럴까? 그것은 바로 한 소절이 범죄를 막을 수 있다는 증거가 있기 때문이다. 2005년, 런던 지하철은 특정 지하철역에 클래식 음악을 방송하기 시작했고, 1년 내에 강도와 공공 기물 파

손 행위가 3분의 1로 줄어들었다. 오리건주 포틀랜드의 경전철 역과 뉴욕 항만청 버스 터미널과 같은 다른 교통 중심지들도 비발디와 같은 바로크 거장들의 범죄 예방 덕택에 부랑률이 감소했다고 보도됐다. 원리는? 우선, 클래식 음악은 마음을 진정시킬 수 있다. 그러나 더욱 중요한 것은, 종종 십대들인 어슬렁거리고 공공 기물을 파손하는 이들은 대개 관현악을 즐기지 않는다는 것이다. 그리고 음향 환경에 짜증이 난다면, 그곳에서 배회하고 싶지 않을 것이다. 분명 이것은 동물에게도 또한 효과가 있다. 영국 Staverton에 있는 Gloucstershire 공항에서, 공항 책임자들은 새들을 놀라게 하여 쫓는 가장 좋은 방법은 티나 터너의 빅 히트곡을 튼 밴을 모는 것이라는 사실을 알고 있다.

21 ③ Kenneth와 Mamie Pipps Clark의 실험에서 흑인 아이들이 피부색 때문에 스스로를 열등하게 생각한다는 사실을 알아냈다. 즉, 이것은 흑인 아이들이 피부색 때문에 인종차별을 받고 있다는 자의식이 내재되어 있다는 증거였다. 그러므로 ③의 'internalized the social values of their environment(그들 환경의 사회적 가치를 내면화한)'가 빈칸에 들어갈 말로 적절하다.

어휘

- segregation : 인종 차별
- sense of self : 자아감, 자의식, 자존감
- pale : 창백한, 연한, 옅은
- take A as B : A를 B로 여기다[간주하다]
- internalize : 내면화하다, 내재화하다
- inferior : 못한, 열등한
- attorney : 변호사, 대리인
- lawsuit : 소송 사건
- testify : 증언하다, 증명하다
- self-hatred : 자기 혐오[증오]
- Supreme Court : 대법원
- ruling : 결정, 판결
- integrate : 통합시키다, 합치다
- spur : 원동력이 되다, 박차를 가하다
- burden : 짐을 나르다, 부담을 지우다
- oppressive : 억압하는, 숨이 막힐 듯한
- norm : 표준, 규범, 기준

오답풀이

① felt the need to free themselves to succeed(성공에서 스스로 벗어날 필요성을 느꼈다)
② were burdened with expectations from their elders(어른들로부터의 기대감에 부담감을 가졌다)
④ learned how to avoid oppressive norms and conventions

(억압적인 규범과 관습을 피하는 방법을 배웠다)
⑤ had the desire to develop and realize their own potential(잠재력을 개발하고 실현하려는 욕망이 있었다)

해석

아프리카계 미국인 심리학자인 Kenneth와 Mamie Pipps Clark은 1940년대 인종 차별 속에 살고 있는 흑인 아이들이 어떻게 자의식을 발달시키는지 이해하기 위해 일부는 하얀 피부이고, 일부는 갈색 피부인 아기 장난감 세트를 이용했다. 두 가지 옵션 모두를 제시받은 흑인 아이들은 피부색이 옅은 인형을 선호했고, 어떤 인형들이 그들과 닮았는지 물었을 때 심지어 울기도 했다. Clark 연구원들은 이것을 아이들이 그들 환경의 사회적 가치를 내면화한 증거로 받아들였다. 즉, 그들은 피부색 때문에 스스로를 열등하다고 생각했다. 이 실험은 유명한 브라운 대 교육위원회 소송에서 변호사들에게 깊은 인상을 남겼고, Kenneth는 인종 차별이 자기혐오로 이어졌다고 증언했다. 1954년 대법원의 판결은 마침내 학교들을 통합시켰고 민권 운동 부흥에 박차를 가했다.

22 ② 중국의 궁정 점성가들은 부정확한 예측을 하게 되면 처형되었기 때문에, 어떤 점성가들은 단순히 기록을 조작하여 나중에 해당 사건과 일치시켰다. 그러므로 빈칸에는 ②의 'they were in perfect conformity with events(그 기록들이 사건들과 완벽하게 부합하도록 했다)'가 들어갈 말로 적절하다.

어휘

- astrology : 점성술, 점성학
- contend : 주장하다, 다투다
- constellation : 별자리
- profoundly : 큰, 매우, 완전히
- fate : 운명, 숙명
- Constellation of the Goat : 염소자리
- subtle : 민감한, 예민한
- capital offense : 사형, 죽을 죄
- overthrow : 뒤집다, 전복시키다
- regime : 정권, 정부
- inaccurate : 부정확한, 오류가 있는
- execute : 처형하다, 실행하다
- doctor : 조작하다, 변조하다
- conformity : 순응, 부합
- record-keeping : 기장, 기록 관리
- fuzzy : 흐릿한, 어렴풋한, 모호한
- fraud : 사기, 가짜, 엉터리
- cautious : 조심스러운, 신중한
- descendant : 자손, 후손

오답풀이

① a more cautious position would be adopted(좀 더 신중한 입장을 취할 것이다)

③ people would pay close attention to the stars(사람들은 별에 세심한 주의를 기울일 것이다)

④ descendants could learn from their ancestors(후손들은 그들의 조상들로부터 배울 수 있었다)

⑤ observations of the planets could be encouraged(행성들의 관측은 장려될 수 있었다)

해석

점성술은 여러분이 태어났을 때 행성들이 어느 별자리에 있는지가 여러분의 미래에 큰 영향을 미친다고 주장한다. 수천 년 전에 행성의 움직임이 왕, 왕조, 제국의 운명을 결정한다는 생각이 발달했다. 점성가들은 행성의 움직임을 연구했고, 가령 지난 번 금성이 염소자리에서 떠오를 때 무슨 일이 있었는지 자문했다. 그리고 아마 이번에도 비슷한 일이 일어날 것이다. 그것은 민감하고 위험한 일이었다. 점성가들은 오직 국가에만 고용되었다. 많은 나라에서 공식 점성가가 아닌 다른 사람이 하늘의 징조를 읽는 것은 죽을 죄였고, 정권을 전복시키는 좋은 방법은 그것의 몰락을 예측하는 것이었다. 부정확한 예측을 한 중국 궁정 점성가들은 처형되었다. 다른 이들은 단순히 기록들을 조작하여 나중에 <u>그 기록들이 사건들과 완벽하게 부합하도록 했다.</u> 점성술은 관측, 수학, 그리고 모호한 생각과 거짓으로 신중하게 기록 관리된 이상한 조합으로 발전했다.

23 ② 윗글은 십대들의 침묵에 대해 신뢰, 이해, 유연성의 분위기를 조성해 십대들의 감정을 이해하고 인정하는 방법에 대해 설명하고 있다. 그러므로 빈칸에는 ②의 'Acknowledge and legitimize a teenager's feelings(십대의 감정을 인정하고 정당화하라)'가 들어갈 말로 적절하다.

어휘

• noted : 저명한, 유명한
• reprimand : 질책하다, 문책하다
• suspended animation : 가사상태, 무기력감
• establish : 설립하다, 조성하다
• atmosphere : 대기, 공기, 분위기
• flexibility : 유연성, 신축성
• legitimize : 정당화하다, 합법화하다
• outfit : 옷, 복장
• awful : 끔찍한, 형편없는
• refrain from : ～을 삼가다
• peer : 또래, 친구
• mean : 비열한, 저속한, 못된
• temptation : 유혹, 꾐

• ritual : 의식, 절차
• adolescent : 청소년

오답풀이

① Resist the temptation to control and keep silent(통제하고 싶은 유혹을 뿌리치고 침묵하라)

③ Encourage teens to accept criticism from others(십대들이 다른 사람들의 비판을 받아들이도록 격려하라)

④ Maintain family rituals as a way of staying in touch(연락하고 지내는 방법으로 가족 의례를 유지하라)

⑤ Take adolescent mood swings and silences personally(사춘기의 감정 동요와 침묵을 개인적으로 받아들여라)

해석

십대들은 부모들과 왜 말을 하지 않는가? "기본적으로, 그들은 부모님이 이해하지 못할 거라고 생각합니다."라고 한 저명한 심리학자가 말한다. "계속해서 질책과 지시를 받을 때, 그들은 부모가 자신들의 기분을 신경 쓰지 않는다고 느낄지도 모릅니다." 십대들에게 침묵은 무기다. 그것은 "더 이상 날 통제할 수 없어."라고 말하고 있는 것이다. 하지만 그렇다고 해서 앞으로 수년 간 가사 상태로 살아야 한다는 뜻은 아니다. 그것은 신뢰, 이해, 유연성의 분위기를 조성해야 한다는 것을 의미한다. <u>십대의 감정을 인정하고 정당화하는</u> 방법은 다음과 같다. 만일 딸이 가장 친한 친구가 자신의 새 옷을 형편없다고 말했다면, "너는 제니퍼의 말에 왜 신경을 쓰니?"라고 말하는 것을 삼가라. 십대들은 자기 또래들이 어떻게 생각하는지 매우 신경을 쓰며, 현명한 부모는 그것을 정상으로 받아들인다. 대신, "그게 너를 마음 아프게 했을 거야. 좋아하는 사람들이 못된 말을 하면 마음이 아파."라고 해라.

24 ① 제시문의 마지막 문장에 나와 있는 'Golden Dustmen(황금 청소부)'처럼 빅토리아 시대에 런던에서 부자가 될 수 있는 직업은 석탄 가루를 치우는 청소부였다. 쓰레기통에서 도시 외곽까지 석탄 가루를 나르는 청소부들이 없었다면 도시의 거리가 막혔을 것이다. 그러므로 윗글의 제목으로 ①의 'When Victorians Got Rich on Dust(빅토리아 시대의 사람들이 먼지로 부자가 되었을 때)'가 가장 적절하다.

어휘

• dig through : ～를 파나가다[파헤치다]
• junkyard : 고철상, 고물상
• resell : 되팔다, 전매하다
• scraps of metal : 고철 조각
• rag : 해진 천, 누더기
• furrier : 모피상
• prized : 소중한, 귀중한
• coal dust : 석탄 가루

- brickmaker : 벽돌제조업자, 벽돌공
- clay : 점토, 찰흙, 진흙
- scarce : 부족한, 결핍한
- open-hearth : 평로, 덮개가 없는 난로
- ash : 재, 잿더미
- clog : 막다, 방해하다
- dustman : (옥외 쓰레기를 치우는) 청소부
- lug : 나르다, 끌다
- dustbin : 휴지통, 쓰레기통
- outskirts : 변두리, 근교, 외곽
- thigh-deep : 허벅지 깊이의
- filthy rich : 대단히 부유한
- outstrip : 앞지르다, 능가하다
- tarnish : 흐려지다, 퇴색하다
- foolproof : 극히 간단한, 바보라도 해 낼
- coal mine : 탄광

오답풀이

② A Foolproof Recipe for Brickmaking(아주 손쉽게 벽돌을 만드는 법)

③ How Bad Is Working in a Coal Mine?(탄광에서 일하는 것이 건강에 얼마나 나쁜가?)

④ Child Labor During the Industrial Revolution(산업 혁명 시대의 소년 노동)

⑤ Air Pollution: Why London Struggled to Breathe(대기 오염: 런던이 숨쉬기 힘든 이유)

해석

빅토리아 시대에 런던에서 아이들이 고물상을 파헤치며 되팔 수 있는 모든 것을 찾는 것은 드문 일이 아니었다. 단추와 비누를 만드는 데 사용될 수 있는 금속 조각, 누더기, 뼈, 그리고 심지어 죽은 고양이까지 그들은 모피상에게 팔았다. 하지만 가장 귀중한 발견물은 석탄 가루였다. 벽돌을 만들기 위해 그것을 진흙과 섞은 벽돌공들은 석탄 가루에 꽤 많은 돈을 지불했다. 석탄 가루가 부족했던 것은 아니다. 사실 덮개 없는 난로 때문에 재가 사방에 날렸고, 쓰레기통에서 도시 외곽까지 그것을 나르는 청소부들이 없었다면 도시의 거리가 막혔을 것이다. 그 장면은 흡사 여자, 남자, 그리고 아이들이 허벅지까지 먼지를 뒤집어쓰고 일하는 디킨스 소설의 정기적인 재활용 작업처럼 보였다. 그들의 상사들은 엄청 부유했지만 런던의 먼지 공급이 수요를 앞지르면서 수익이 감소했다. 19세기 후반까지, 한때 '황금 청소부'였던 이들에 대한 전망은 이미 퇴색되었다.

25 ① 제시문에 따르면 점점 더 많은 세계적인 회사들이 메타버스 내의 공간을 사들여 상점을 차리고 있고, 그 공간을

지배하기 위해 각축을 벌이고 있다고 설명하고 있다. 그러므로 제시문의 제목으로 ①의 'Setting up Shop in the Metaverse(메타버스에서의 상점 개설)'가 가장 적절하다.

어휘

- metaverse : 가상공간, 메타버스
- eventually : 결국, 드디어
- avatar : 화신, 아바타
- fanciful : 상상의, 허황된, 비현실적인
- retailer : 소매업자, 소매상
- dominant : 우세한, 우성의, 지배적인
- fade away : 사라지다, 쇠퇴하다
- obscurity : 무명, 모호함
- ecosystem : 생태계
- eco-friendly : 친환경적인, 환경 친화적인
- climb the social ladder : 출세하기

오답풀이

② Opening Electronic Bank Branches(전자 은행 지점 개설)

③ Building Virtual Eco-friendly Environments(환경 친화적 가상공간 구축)

④ Climbing the Social Ladder in the Metaverse(메타버스에서 출세하기)

⑤ Dominating the Shopping Space with Avatars(아바타로 쇼핑 공간 장악하기)

해석

이전에 페이스북으로 알려진 이 회사는 메타버스가 인터넷의 미래라고 확신해 작년에 이름을 메타로 바꾸었다. 메타와 그 회사 사장인 마크 주커버그는 결국 우리들 대다수가 메타버스에서 일하고, 놀고, 쇼핑할 것이라고 생각한다. 아니면 적어도 우리의 아바타들이 그럴 것이다. 많은 이들에게 이 모든 것이 허황되게 들리겠지만, 점점 더 많은 회사들이 메타버스 내의 공간을 사들여 그곳에 가게를 차리고 있다. 이 회사들은 아디다스, 버버리, 구찌, 토미 힐피거, 나이키, 삼성, 루이비통 그리고 심지어 HSBC와 JP 모건 같은 은행들도 포함한다. 그러나 그러한 사업체들의 문제는 그들이 어떤 장소를 선택하느냐이다. 현재 메타버스 내에는 샌드박스, 디센트럴랜드, 복셀, 솜니움 스페이스 및 메타 소유의 호라이즌 월드를 포함한 가장 인기 있는 50여 개의 세계적 공급사들이 있다. 소매업체와 다른 투자자들은 이들 중 어떤 업체가 우리의 아바타로부터 가장 많은 방문을 받으며 메타버스의 지배적인 세력이 될지 도박을 하고 있다. 그리고 어떤 다른 세계가 무명으로 사라질지 모른다. 더욱이 승리의 생태계 속에서 기업은 가장 인기 있는 영역을 선택하기 위해 노력해야만 한다.

26 ② 제시문에서 화가 많이 난 고객에게 더 많은 보상을 해줄

거라는 일반적인 통념과 달리 문화적 특성과 개인의 수용 수준에 따라 다르다는 것을 실험을 통해 증명하고 있다. 그러므로 제시문의 제목으로는 ②의 "Does the Squeaky Wheel Get the Most Oil?(삐거덕 거리는 바퀴가 기름을 가장 많이 얻을까?)"가 가장 적절하다.

어휘

• compensation : 보상, 배상
• intense : 강한, 강렬한
• service reps : 서비스 직원들
• hierarchy : 계급, 계층
• simulate : 모의 실험하다, 시뮬레이션하다
• service interaction : 서비스 상호작용
• inevitable : 불가피한, 필연적인
• subject : 연구[실험] 대상, 피실험자
• inappropriate : 부적절한, 부적합한
• perception : 지각, 인식, 통찰력
• mitigate : 완화시키다, 경감시키다
• squeaky : 끼익 하는 소리가 나는
• broth : 수프, 죽
• stitch : 바늘땀, (뜨개질의) 코

오답풀이

① Does Time Really Fly When You're Having Fun?(즐거운 시간을 보내면 시간이 정말 빨리 갈까?)
③ Can a Rolling Stone Gather Any Moss?(구르는 돌에 이끼가 낄 수 있을까?)
④ Can Too Many Chefs Spoil the Broth?(요리사가 많으면 스프를 망칠까?)
⑤ Can a Stitch in Time Save Nine?(제때 꿰맨 한 땀이 아홉 땀의 수고를 덜까?)

해석

새로운 연구는 사람들이 서비스 실패 후 더 화가 난 것처럼 보일수록 더 많은 보상을 받을 것이라는 일반적인 통념을 시험하고 종종 그 반대가 사실이라는 것을 보여준다. 연구원은 강한 분노가 서비스 직원들에게 미치는 영향은 권력 거리 또는 PD로 알려진 문화적 특성, 즉 권력 차이와 위계에 대한 개인의 수용 수준에 따라 다르다는 것을 발견했다. 모의실험을 거친 서비스 상호 작용을 포함한 네 가지 실험에서 PD가 높은 참가자(권력 차이를 자연스러운 또는 불가피한 것으로 받아들인 참가자)는 몹시 화가 난 고객보다 조금 화가 난 고객에게 더 많은 보상을 제공했고, 반면에 PD가 낮은 참가자는 정반대였다. 왜 그럴까? PD가 높은 피실험자들은 강한 분노의 표현을 부적절하다고 보고 그들을 응징한 반면 PD가 낮은 피실험자들은 그 표현을 위협적인 것으로 보고 그들에게 보상을 했다. 그러나 위협에 대한 인식이 완화되었을 때(참가자들

은 고객들이 자신들에게 해를 가할 수 없다고 들었다), PD가 낮은 사람들도 조금 화가 난 고객들에게 더 많은 보상을 해주었다.

27 ③ 세계 각국의 보호무역주의, 전염병과 전쟁으로 인한 공급 부족 및 인플레이션의 심화 등으로 세계화가 정체되면서 각국 정부는 자국의 글로벌 기업들이 우호적인 국가에서 사업하는 것을 선호한다고 하였다. 그러므로 ③의 'the switch to a security-first model of globalisation(세계화의 안보 제일주의 모델로의 전환)'이 제시문의 주제로 가장 적절하다.

어휘

• go-go : 호경기의
• economic integration : 경제 통합
• stall : 멈추다, 지연되다, 지체되다
• aftershock : (큰 지진 후의) 여진
• populist : 포퓰리즘
• revolt : 반란, 혐오
• stagnate : 침체되다, 정체되다
• postpone : 미루다, 연기하다
• give way to : 바뀌다, 대체되다
• wait-and-see : 관망하는
• globalisation : 세계화
• blip : 깜박 신호, 일시적인 상황[문제]
• extinction : 멸종, 소멸
• pandemic : 전국적인 유행병, 전염병
• trigger : 촉발시키다, 방아쇠를 당기다
• reimagine : 재상상하다
• boardroom : 중역 회의실, 이사회실
• trillion : 1조
• inventory : 물품 목록, 재고
• stockpile : 비축하다, 사재기하다
• insurance : 보험, 보장
• prioritise : 우선순위를 매기다, 우선적으로 처리하다
• descend : 내려오다, 내려앉다
• protectionism : 보호주의
• usher : 안내하다, 알려 주다
• efficiency : 효율성, 효율화
• security-first : 안전 제일
• disruption : 방해, 붕괴, 파괴

오답풀이

① the era of globalisation ushered in by new businesses(신생 사업들이 이끄는 세계화 시대)
② the promotion of globalisation through cost efficiency(비용

의 효율성을 통한 세계화 촉진)

④ the disruption of globalisation caused by war(전쟁으로 인한 세계화의 붕괴)

⑤ the threat of globalisation to workers' rights(노동자의 권리에 대한 세계화의 위협)

해석

1990년대와 2000년대의 호경기 이후, 기업들이 금융 위기의 여진, 개방된 국경에 대한 포퓰리즘 반란, 도널드 트럼프 대통령의 무역전쟁으로 어려움을 겪으면서 2010년대에 경제 통합의 속도는 지체되었다. 상품과 자본의 흐름이 정체되었다. 많은 사장들이 해외 투자에 대한 큰 결정을 미루었고, 그에 맞추어 관망하는 쪽으로 선회하였다. 세계화가 일시적인 문제에 직면했는지 아니면 소멸에 직면했는지 아무도 몰랐다. 우크라이나에서 전염병과 전쟁이 한 세대에 한 번꼴로 세계 자본주의를 이사회와 정부에서 재상상하는 계기가 되었기 때문에 이제 기다림은 끝났다. 보이는 모든 곳에서 공급망은 9조 달러의 재고에서 공급 부족과 인플레이션에 대한 보험으로 비축되었고, 글로벌 기업들이 중국에서 베트남으로 옮겨감에 따라 노동자들의 싸움으로 바뀌어 가고 있다. 이러한 새로운 종류의 세계화는 여러분의 정부가 우호적인 국가들에서 여러분이 신뢰할 수 있는 사람들과 사업하는 것을 우선시한다. 그것은 보호무역주의, 큰 정부, 그리고 심화된 인플레이션으로 주저앉을 수 있다.

28 ② 아메리칸 드림은 원래 신분에 관계없이 누구나 열심히 일하면 '무일푼에서 벼락부자로' 성공할 수 있다는 믿음이었으나, 1920년대 이후 미국의 현실과 모순되고 동떨어져 연구원들과 사회 과학자들로부터 비판을 받아왔다고 설명하고 있다. 그러므로 ②의 'the fallacy of the great American Dream(위대한 아메리칸 드림의 오류)'가 제시문의 주제로 가장 적절하다.

어휘

• the Lost Generation : 잃어버린 세대, 가치관을 잃은 세대(제1차 세계 대전 무렵의 환멸과 회의에 찬 미국의 젊은 세대)
• deception : 속임, 기만, 사기
• prominent : 중요한, 유명한
• vast : 방대한, 막대한
• misery : 고통, 빈곤, 비참
• live the dream : 꿈을 성취[실현]하다
• self-sufficient : 자급자족할 수 있는
• stunningly : 놀랍도록, 기막히게
• prosperity : 번영, 번창
• assumption : 추정, 가정
• perseverance : 인내, 참을성

• risk-taking : 위험을 각오한[무릅쓴, 감수한]
• from rags to riches : 무일푼에서 벼락부자로
• mobile : 이동하는, 움직이는
• misplaced : 부적절한, 잘못된
• contradict : 부정하다, 모순되다
• repentance : 뉘우침, 회개
• self-reliance : 자기 의존, 자립심
• fallacy : 오류, 착오
• revision : 수정, 변경

오답풀이

① the repentance of self-reliance through hard work(열심히 일해서 자립한 것에 대한 회개)

③ the revision of the American Dream(아메리칸 드림의 수정)

④ the criticism of material success in America(미국의 물질적 성공에 대한 비판)

⑤ the realization of the Lost Generation's ideals(잃어버린 세대의 이상 실현)

해석

잃어버린 세대의 일원들은 '아메리칸 드림'에 대한 생각을 거창한 속임수로 보았다. F.S. 피츠제럴드의 위대한 개츠비에서 이 이야기의 서술자 닉 캐러웨이가 개츠비의 막대한 재산이 엄청난 고통으로 보상받았다는 것을 깨닫게 되면서 이것은 유명한 주제가 되었다. 피츠제럴드에게, 열심히 일하면 성공한다는 아메리칸 드림의 전통적인 비전은 변질되었다. 잃어버린 세대에게 '꿈을 실현하는 것'은 더 이상 단순히 자급자족하는 삶을 구축하는 것이 아니라, 필요한 어떤 수단을 써서라도 엄청난 부자가 되는 것이었다. '아메리칸 드림'이란 용어는 그들이 어디에서, 어떤 사회 계층에서 태어났는지에 관계없이 누구나 번영과 행복을 추구할 권리와 자유를 가지고 있다는 믿음을 말한다. 아메리칸 드림의 핵심 요소는 열심히 일하고, 인내하고, 위험을 감수함으로써 누구나 '무일푼에서 벼락부자로' 상승하여 재정적으로 부유하고 사회적으로 출세한 성공 비전을 실현시킨다는 가정이다. 1920년대 이후, 아메리칸 드림은 현대 미국의 현실과 모순된 잘못된 믿음으로 종종 연구원들과 사회 과학자들에 의해 의문의 제기와 비판을 받아왔다.

29 ① 반세기 전에 유행했던 오래된 기술이지만 큰 회사나 정부 기관에서 필수적인 기술이었기 때문에 Mooney는 구직 활동 당시 여러 고용주들로부터 고위직을 제안 받았다. 그러므로 ①의 "Old technology can still be of great use. (오래된 기술도 여전히 큰 도움이 될 수 있다.)"가 윗글의 요지로 가장 적절하다.

어휘

• passionate : 열정적인, 열광적인

- Sputnik : 세계 최초의 구소련 인공위성
- stuff : 잡동사니, 하찮은 것
- cool point : 좋은 점수
- insurance : 보험
- government agency : 정부 기관, 정부 당국
- institution : 기관, 시설
- potential : 가능성이 있는, 잠재적인
- expertise : 전문 지식[기술]
- senior position : 상급직, 고위직
- resilience : 회복력, 복원력, 반동
- decades-old : 수십 년 된
- specialize in : ~을 전문으로 하다

【오답풀이】

② Keep up with the changing times in the tech world.(기술 세계에서 변화하는 시대에 뒤떨어지지 않도록 해라.)

③ The best job is one that makes full use of your abilities.(가장 좋은 직업은 당신의 능력을 최대한 활용하는 것이다.)

④ Silicon Valley is always in the market for new technology. (실리콘 밸리는 항상 새로운 기술을 위한 시장이다.)

⑤ The future of digital technology lies within academic institutions.(디지털 기술의 미래는 학술 기관 안에 있다.)

【해석】

Caitlin Mooney는 24살이며 스프트닉 시대의 과거 기술에 열정적이다. 최근 뉴저지 공대 컴퓨터 공학과를 졸업한 Mooney는 컴퓨터 메인프레임과 이를 구동하는 코볼이라고 불리는 소프트웨어를 포함하여, 반세기 전에 유행했던 기술의 팬이다. 그런 것들은 실리콘 밸리에서 어떤 좋은 점수도 얻지 못하겠지만, 큰 은행, 보험 회사, 정부 기관 및 다른 큰 기관들에서는 필수적인 기술이다. Mooney의 구직 기간 동안, 잠재적인 고용주들은 그녀의 전문성을 보았고 그녀가 찾고 있던 것보다 더 높은 고위직에 관해 상담하고 싶어 했다. "그 고위직들은 정말 기대됩니다."라고 Mooney는 말했다. 그녀는 지금 여러 일자리 제안 중 하나를 결정하려고 노력하고 있다. 수십 년 된 컴퓨터 기술과 이를 전문으로 하는 사람들의 복원은 새로운 기술이 종종 많은 옛 기술 위에 구축된다는 것을 보여준다.

30 ② Enron 스캔들로 물러난 CEO Jeff Skilling과 7년간 12억 달러의 과다 수익 처리로 불명예 퇴진한 도시바의 Hisao Tanaka의 사례처럼 성공 속에 사기와 기만이 감춰져 있을 수도 있다는 내용이다. 그러므로 ②의 "All that glitters is not gold.(반짝인다고 모두 금은 아니다.)"가 윗글의 요지로 가장 적절하다.

【어휘】

- multigenerational : 다세대의, 여러 세대의

- midsize : 중형의, 중견의
- sheer : 순전한, 온전한
- longevity : 장수, 수명
- architect : 건축가, 설계자
- attest to : 증명하다, 증언하다
- navigator : 조종사, 항해사
- sustained : 한결같은, 지속적인
- conceal : 숨기다, 은폐하다
- trickery : 사기, 기만, 속임수
- hail : 환영[환호]하다, 축하하다
- well-regarded : 인정받는, 존경받는
- resign : 퇴임하다, 물러나다
- disgrace : 불명예, 치욕
- overstatement : 과장, 과대
- unearth : 파헤치다, 밝혀내다
- feather : 털, 깃털

【오답풀이】

① A watched pot never boils.(지켜보는 냄비는 결코 끓지 않는다.)

③ Time and tide wait for no man.(세월은 사람을 기다리지 않는다.)

④ Birds of a feather flock together.(깃털이 같은 새들끼리 모인다.)

⑤ Don't put all your eggs in one basket.(한 바구니에 모든 달걀을 담지 마라.)

【해석】

과거의 성공을 좋은 판단의 표식이라고 가정하는 것은 유혹적이며, 일부 경우에는 그럴 수도 있다. 다세대에 걸친 몇몇 독일 중견기업의 성공과 워런 버핏의 장기간 투자 실적 등은 자주 인용되는 사례다. 하지만 성공은 다른 부모를 가질 수 있다. 나폴레옹이 그의 장군들에게 요구했던 것으로 유명한 특성인 행운은 종종 인정받지 못한 성공의 설계자이다. 스포츠인들은 기술뿐만 아니라 행운의 중요성을 증언할 수 있다. 네 번의 아메리카 컵 요트 경기에서 승리한 항해사이자 설계자인 Grant Simmer는 경쟁자들의 실수로 인한 행운의 도움을 인정했다. 때로는 지속적인 성공으로 보이는 것이 속임수를 숨길 수도 있다. Enorn 스캔들이 터지기 전인 2001년, CEO Jeff Skilling은 매우 성공적인 리더로 환영받았다. 도시바의 존경받는 상사 Hisao Tanaka는 7년간 12억 달러의 과다 수익이 밝혀진 후 2015년에 불명예 퇴진했다.

31 ③ 머리에 이가 많으면 건강한 사람이라는 뉴헤브리디스 원주민들의 생각은 오랜 관찰 결과 사실이 아닌 걸로 밝혀졌다. 건강한 사람들은 이가 서식하기에 알맞은 체온을 유지했기

때문에 이가 많은 것이지 이가 건강의 원인은 아니다. 그러므로 "이의 증식이 인체의 건강을 증진시키는 데 중요한 결정 요인이었다"는 ③의 내용은 전체적인 글의 흐름과 어울리지 않는다.

어휘

- lice : louse(이)의 복수
- observation : 관찰, 관측
- accurate : 정확한, 정밀한
- statistics : 통계, 통계학
- correlation : 연관성, 상관관계
- proliferation : 급증, 확산, 증식
- determinant : 결정 요인
- flesh : 살, 피부
- scatter : 뿌리다, 흩어지다
- prey on : ~을 먹이로 하다, 잡아먹다

해석

수세기 동안 뉴헤브리디스 제도의 원주민들은 이로 가득 찬 머리를 건강의 표시로 여겼다. "수세기에 걸친 관찰로 건강한 사람들은 대개 이가 있고 아픈 사람들은 그렇지 않은 경우가 많다는 사실을 알게 되었습니다. 관찰 자체는 정확하고 믿을 만 했습니다."라고 Darrell Huff는 「통계로 거짓말하는 방법」이란 책에 썼다. ①그러나 그 상관관계가 이가 건강의 열쇠라는 것을 의미하는 것은 아니었다. 오히려 그 반대였다. ②건강한 사람들은 그들의 몸이 딱 알맞은 온도, 즉 벌레를 위한 완벽한 집이었기 때문에 이가 있었다. ③따라서 이의 증식은 인체의 건강을 증진시키는 데 중요한 결정 요인이었다. ④그러나 사람들이 고열이 날 때, 그들의 몸은 뜨거워졌고 이로 인해 이가 흩어졌다. ⑤이는 건강의 원인이 아니라 건강을 해쳤다.

32 ① 제시문에 따르면 암호화폐는 그동안 실제 거래에서 큰 역할을 한 적이 없으며, 실물 경제에 활용도가 높은 제품을 결코 내놓은 적이 없다고 서술되어 있다. 그러므로 "실제 거래에서 유용함을 충분히 입증한 Venmo와 같은 디지털 결제 앱을 사용한다고 가정하자"는 ①의 설명은 전체적인 글의 흐름과 어울리지 않는다.

어휘

- transaction : 거래, 처리
- much-hyped : 대대적으로 과장된, 엄청 선전된
- bitcoin : 비트코인
- national currency : 자국 통화
- disaster : 재앙, 재난
- payment app : 결제 앱
- amply : 광범위하게, 충분하게
- rein in : 억제하다, 고삐를 죄다

- stablecoin : 가격 변동성을 최소화하도록 설계된 암호화폐
- supposedly : 추정상, 아마
- peg : 정하다, 고정시키다
- unregulated : 비규제의, 규제받지 않는
- cascading : 폭포같은, 계속되는, 연속적인
- collapse : 붕괴, 실패
- reminiscent : 연상시키는, 추억에 잠긴
- the Great Depression : 대공황
- crypto industry : 암호화폐 산업
- come up with : ~을 생산하다, 제시하다
- spectacularly : 눈부시게, 극적으로
- cutting edge : 최첨단
- cultivate : 경작하다, 양성하다
- prominent : 저명한, 유명한

해석

암호화폐는 2009년 무렵부터 있었으며, 그동안 실제 거래에서 큰 역할을 한 적이 없는데도 비트코인을 자국 통화로 만들려는 엘살바도르의 대대적인 시도는 재앙이 되었다. ①예를 들어, 실제 거래에서 유용함을 충분히 입증한 Venmo와 같은 디지털 결제 앱을 사용한다고 가정하자. ②그렇다면 어떻게 암호화폐가 절정에 달했을 때 거의 3조 달러의 가치가 되었을까? ③추정컨대 미국 달러에 고정돼 있었지만 분명 비규제 은행의 모든 위험 대상이었고, 대공황에 일조했던 은행 부도의 물결을 연상시키는 연쇄 붕괴를 경험한 지금 '스테이블코인'을 억제하기 위해 왜 아무런 조치도 취해지지 않았는가? ④내 대답은 암호화폐 산업이 실물경제에 활용도가 높은 제품을 결코 내놓은 적이 없지만, 마케팅 자체는 눈부시게 성공해 최첨단이자 존경할 만한 이미지를 만들어냈다는 것이다. ⑤특히 저명한 인물과 기관을 양성함으로써 그렇게 했다.

33 ③ 고생물학자들은 빙하기 황새 렙탑틸로스 로부스투스가 날지 못하는 종(種)이라고 생각했지만, 왕립학회 오픈 사이언스지에 발표된 렙탑틸로스 로부스투스의 날개 뼈 화석을 통해 이 사실이 잘못되었다는 것을 알았다. 그러므로 주어진 문장은 날지 못하는 종(種)이라고 생각했지만, 12피트 길이의 날개폭은 황새가 머리 위로 날아오르도록 했을 것이라고 서술되어 있는 ③에 들어가는 것이 가장 적절하다.

어휘

- analyze : 분석하다, 조사하다
- fossil : 화석
- hobbit : 호빗(가상의 난장이)
- immense : 엄청난, 거대한
- stork : 황새
- tower over : ~보다 훨씬 높다

- paleontologist : 고생물학자
- previously : 이전에, 미리
- flightless : 날지 못하는
- wingspan : 날개 길이, 날개폭
- soar : 솟구치다, 날아오르다
- prompt : 즉각[지체 없이] ~하다, 촉발하다
- revise : 변경하다, 개정하다
- anatomy : 해부학
- scavenger : 청소부, 죽은 동물을 먹는 동물
- prehistoric : 선사의, 선사 시대의

해석

> 그러나 오늘 왕립학회 오픈 사이언시스지에 발표된 날개 뼈를 포함한 새롭게 분석된 화석들이 이 이야기를 바꾸어 놓았다.

인도네시아 동부의 섬인 고대 플로레스에서, '호빗' 크기의 인간은 거대한 새와 그 풍경을 공유했다. (①) 크기가 5피트 이상인 빙하기 황새 렙탑틸로스 로부스투스는 6만 년 이전에 살았던 3피트 크기의 호모 플로레시엔시스보다 더 컸다. (②) 이전에 고생물학자들은 그 큰 새가 고립된 섬 생태계에 적응해 살아가는 날지 못하는 종(種)이라고 생각했다. (③) 황새의 크기에도 불구하고, 12피트 길이의 날개폭은 황새가 머리 위로 날아오르도록 했을 것이다. (④) 이 새로운 사실에 고생물학자들은 L. 로부스투스의 해부학과 행동에 대해 이전에 생각했던 것을 즉각 수정했다. (⑤) 이 새로운 연구는 그 새가 작은 먹이를 사냥하기보다 아마도 죽은 동물들에게서 먹이를 구했던 것으로 알려진 다른 선사시대의 나는 황새들처럼 청소부였을 거라는 사실을 시사한다.

34 ④ 고대 이집트인들이 사용한 아이라이너의 일반적인 제조법에는 납이 포함되어 있었고, 납 이온은 다른 면에서 여전히 독성이 있지만 박테리아가 눈을 감염시키기 전에 죽이는 활성산소인 일산화질소를 생성하는 데 도움을 주었다. 이러한 사실을 파리의 화학 팀이 밝혀낸 것이므로 주어진 문장은 ④에 들어가는 것이 가장 적절하다.

어휘

- lead ions : 납 이온
- toxic : 독성의, 독이 있는
- nitric oxide : 일산화질소
- free radical : 활성 산소
- infect : 감염시키다, 오염시키다
- rim : 가장자리[테를 이루다[두르다]
- makeover : 미용, 화장
- ritual : 의식상의, 의례적인

- slaughter : 도살, 학살
- manuscript : 원고, 사본
- wearer : 착용하는 사람, 사용하는 사람
- skeptical : 의심 많은, 회의적인
- formula : 공식, 화학식, 제조법
- scraped : 긁어낸
- onto something : 말이 맞는, 뭔가 이루어낸, 좋은 결과의
- compound : 화합물
- deliberately : 의도적으로, 일부러
- dub : 별명을 붙이다, 재녹음하다

해석

> 납 이온은 다른 면에서 여전히 독성이 있지만 또한 박테리아가 눈을 감염시키기 전에 죽이는 활성산소인 일산화질소를 생성하는 데 도움을 주었다.

이집트인들은 눈가에 검은 화장을 하는 것으로 유명하다. 이 화장은 단지 사람만을 위한 것이 아니라, 기원전 2500년의 예술에서 보듯이 도살 의식에 끌려가는 소들 또한 머리에 칠을 했다. (①) 그 시대의 기록들은 아이라이너가 눈의 감염으로부터 사용자들을 보호한다고 주장했지만, 현대 과학자들은 회의적이었다. (②) 결국 가장 일반적인 제조법에는 납이 포함되어 있었다. (③) 하지만 2009년, 파리의 Pierre와 Marie Curie 대학의 연구원이 이끄는 화학 팀은 무덤에서 긁어낸 샘플을 분석했고 고대인들의 말이 맞다는 것을 발견했다. (④) 게다가, 아이라이너의 일부 화합물은 이집트가 원산지가 아니어서, 연구원들은 이 화장품이 단지 수중에 있었기 때문에 사용된 것이 아니라 의도적으로 제조된 것이라고 믿게 되었다. (⑤) 이 연구의 저자들은 그 아이라이너를 우리에게 알려진 최초의 대규모 화학 제조 공정이라고 이름 붙였다.

35 ④ 고대 그리스는 국민 주권에 대한 개념을 제시한 반면 로마는 공화주의 개념을 제시했다. 즉, 그리스와 로마의 정부 형태는 달랐지만 수세기에 걸쳐 공화주의와 민주주의가 얽히면서 오늘날 우리가 알고 있는 현대 자유민주주의 체제를 만들어냈다. 그러므로 비록 고대 그리스와 로마의 정부 형태는 (A)달랐지만(dissimilar), 그들은 함께 현대 민주주의의 (B)토대(foundation)를 마련했다고 한 문장으로 요약할 수 있다.

어휘

- governing decision : 통치 결정
- lay out : 제시하다, 설계하다
- republicanism : 공화주의
- representation : 대표, 대리
- popular sovereignty : 국민 주권

정답 및 해설

• derive : 끌어내다, 유도하다, 도출하다
• legislative body : 입법부, 입법 기관
• senate : 원로원
• liberal democracy : 자유민주주의
• intertwine : 뒤얽히다, 엮이다
• regime : 정권, 제도, 체계
• deficiency : 결핍, 결점
• interchangeable : 교환[교체]할 수 있는, 호환할 수 있는
• dissimilar : 다른, 같지 않은
• groundbreaking : 획기적인, 신기원을 이룬

오답풀이

① (A) primitive → 원시적인
   (B) deficiencies → 결점
② (A) interchangeable → 교환할 수 있는
   (B) inspiration → 영감
③ (A) ideal → 이상적인
   (B) riddles → 수수께끼
⑤ (A) groundbreaking → 획기적인
   (B) groundwork → 기반

해석

고대 그리스 민주주의는 대중이 정부의 일에 직접 참여하여 정책을 선택하고 통치 결정을 내리도록 하였다. 이런 의미에서 국민은 국가였다. 이와 대조적으로, 로마 제국은 국가 내의 권력 분립과 선출된 관리들을 통한 대중의 대표성을 강조하는 공화주의의 개념을 제시했다. 따라서 그리스가 국민 주권에 대한 개념을 제시한 반면, 원로원과 같은 입법 기관의 개념을 도출한 것은 로마이다. 그들의 초기 형태에서, 그리스의 민주주의도 로마의 공화주의도 오늘날의 기준으로 자유 민주주의로 정의되지는 않을 것이다. 둘 다 특정의 민주적 요소를 강조했지만 근본적인 방법으로 제한했다. 수세기에 걸쳐 정치적 권리와 제도가 확대되면서 공화주의와 민주주의가 얽혀 오늘날 우리가 알고 있는 현대 자유민주주의 체제를 만들어냈다.

⬇

비록 고대 그리스와 로마의 정부 형태는 (A)달랐지만, 그들은 함께 현대 민주주의의 (B)토대를 마련했다.

36 ③ (A) 꽃은 수분을 위해 그리고 양봉가는 꿀을 위해 각각의 입장에서 꿀벌의 목적을 예로 들어 설명하고 있다. 그러므로 (A)에 들어갈 연결어구는 예시의 의미를 나타내는 'For instance(예를 들어)'가 가장 적절하다.
(B) 특정한 목적을 위해 무언가를 이용하고 있지만, 자연에서는 누가 누구를 이용하고 있는지 명확하지 않다고 했으므

로, (B)에는 역접의 의미를 나타내는 'Yet(하지만)'이 들어갈 연결어구로 가장 적절하다.

어휘

• perceived : 인지된, 감지된
• pollinate : 수분하다, 꽃가루를 주다
• beekeeper : 양봉가
• hive : 벌집
• be relative to : 관계가 있다
• exploit : 이용하다, 착취하다
• tick : 진드기
• hide : (짐승의) 가죽
• rhinoceros : 코뿔소
• rid : 없애다, 제거하다

해석

우리가 목적을 바라보는 방법은 종종 인지된 중요성과 관련이 있다. (A)예를 들어, 꽃을 주된 관심의 대상으로 본다면 꿀벌의 목적은 꽃을 수분시키는 것이라고 말한다. 하지만 우리가 양봉가라면, 꿀벌의 목적은 벌집에 공급할 꿀을 생산하는 것이라고 말할 가능성이 더 높다. 여기서 목적은 꽃을 위해 씨앗을 운반하거나 벌집을 위해 꿀을 생산하는 더 큰 맥락과 관련이 있다고 볼 수 있으며, 특정한 목적을 위해 무언가를 착취하거나 이용하는 것과 관련이 있다. (B)하지만, 자연에서는 누가 누구를 이용하고 있는지 종종 명확하지 않다. 코뿔소 가죽의 진드기를 먹는 작은 새는 코뿔소를 모두가 먹을 수 있는 큰 뷔페로 이용하는가, 아니면 코뿔소가 성가신 진드기를 없애는 수단으로 그 새를 이용하는가? 그 둘은 서로가 필요하다. 그래서 목적은 상대적인 것이며, 어떤 사물이나 사람의 상대적인 중요성과 관련이 있다.

37 ⑤ 주어진 문장에서 화자는 최근에 여성 운동이 활발하지 못한 것에 의문을 던졌고, 글 (C)에서 실제 여성 운동이 유럽과 미국 전역에서 폭발했던 당시 상황을 설명하였다. 다음으로 글 (B)의 마지막 문장에서 일본 여성에 대한 사례를 언급했고, 글 (A)에서 그에 대한 구체적인 설명을 제시하였다. 그러므로 주어진 글 다음에 (C) – (B) – (A)의 순으로 글이 이어져야 한다.

어휘

• burst : 터뜨리다, 폭발하다
• enormous : 거대한, 엄청난
• dissipate : 소멸되다, 사라지다
• extremely : 매우, 극도로
• explosion : 폭발, 폭파
• end up with : 결국 ~하게 되다
• narrow section : 좁은 부분

• population : 인구, 주민

해석

60년대 이후 여성 운동은 전통적인 남성의 사고방식을 그대로 반영하는 방향으로 발전했다. 그것은 마치 뇌 속으로 타들어가는 모양과 같아서 밖으로 빠져나갈 수 없다. 나는 최근에 왜 여성 운동이 전체적으로 잠재력을 발휘하지 못하는지 생각해 보았다.

(C) 여성 운동은 유럽과 미국 전역에서 엄청난 에너지를 내며 현장에서 폭발했다. 하지만 에너지는 사라졌고, 실제로 성취된 것은 모든 유럽 국가들과 아마도 60년대에 젊고 현재 중년이 된 미국과 캐나다의 중산층 여성들이 오히려 더 잘 해냈다는 것이다.

(B) 그들은 대개 텔레비전과 라디오, 신문 등과 같은 문화적인 일에 좋은 직업을 갖고 있다. 이것은 일본처럼 여성들이 매우 힘든 시간을 보내는 나라들도 또한 사실이다.

(A) 오늘날 일본에는 공적인 생활을 하는 여성이 극히 드물고, 서구의 어느 곳보다 훨씬 적으며, 그들이 있을 때는 거의 항상 문화적인 일에 있다. 그래서 모든 엄청난 에너지의 폭발은 결국 여성 인구의 극히 일부만이 이전보다 더 잘하게 되었다.

38 ⑤ 주어진 글에서 문화를 숙주의 몸 속에 기생하는 기생충에 비유하여 화제를 던지고 있고, 글 (C)에서 한 숙주에서 다른 숙주로 증식하며 퍼지는 기생충의 특성에 대해 설명하고 있다. 글 (B)에서 이런 식으로 문화적인 사상 또한 인간의 마음속에 기생하여 전파된다고 설명하고 있으며, 마지막으로 글 (A)에서 기생충에 잡아먹힌 숙주처럼 인간은 죽지만 그 사상은 퍼지며, 문화는 정신적 기생충이라고 결론을 내린다. 그러므로 주어진 글 다음에 (C) – (B) – (A)의 순으로 글이 이어져야 한다.

어휘

• infection : 감염, 전염병
• parasite : 기생충
• unwitting : 자신도 모르는, 부지불식간의, 무의식적인
• host : 주인, 성체, 숙주
• organic parasite : 유기[생물에서 나온] 기생충
• multiply : 증가하다, 증식하다
• feed off : ～을 먹다
• pass along : 전달하다, 부담시키다, 떠넘기다
• in this fashion : 이런 식으로
• dedicate : 바치다, 헌신하다
• conspiracy : 음모, 모의

• emerge : 나오다, 드러나다

해석

점점 더 많은 학자들이 문화를 정신적인 감염이나 기생충의 일종으로 보고 있으며, 인간을 무의식적인 숙주로 여긴다. 바이러스와 같은 유기 기생충은 숙주의 몸 속에 기생한다.

(C) 이 기생충들은 한 숙주에서 다른 숙주로 증식하여 퍼지면서 숙주를 먹고, 약화시키고, 때로는 죽이기도 한다. 숙주가 기생충에게 물려줄 만큼 충분히 오래 사는 한 숙주의 상태는 거의 신경 쓰지 않는다.

(B) 바로 이런 식으로, 문화적인 사상은 인간의 마음속에 살아 있다. 이들은 증식하여 한 숙주에서 다른 숙주로 전파되며, 때로는 숙주를 약화시키고 때로는 죽이기도 한다. 문화적인 사상은 심지어 죽음의 대가를 치르더라도 그 사상을 퍼뜨리기 위해 사람의 생명을 바치도록 강요할 수 있다.

(A) 인간은 죽지만, 그 사상은 퍼진다. 이 접근법에 따르면, 문화는 다른 사람들을 이용하기 위해 어떤 사람들에 의해 꾸며진 음모가 아니다. 오히려 문화는 우연히 나타난 정신적 기생충이며, 그 이후에 감염된 모든 사람들을 이용한다.

[39~40]

어휘

• liberally : 듬뿍, 아낌없이
• troop : 병력, 부대
• overthrow : 타도하다, 전복하다
• be preoccupied with : ～에 골몰하다[몰두하다]
• hyperorganized : 과조직화된
• monarchy : 군주국, 왕정
• side with : ～의 편을 들다, 두둔하다
• the Confederacy : 남부연합(미국의 남북전쟁 당시 북부에 대항하는 남부 연방)
• defeat : 패배시키다, 물리치다
• Latino : (미국에 사는) 라틴 아메리카인
• spontaneous : 자발적인, 즉흥적인
• take place in : ～에서 열리다, 일어나다
• slavery : 노예, 노예제도
• significance : 중요성, 중대성, 의의
• fall by the wayside : 도중에 실패하다, 사라지다
• spirits industry : 양주 산업, 양주 업계
• seize : 붙잡다, 장악하다
• ubiquitous : 어디에나 있는, 도처에 있는

- rage : 노하다, 맹위를 떨치다, 성행하다
- geographically : 지리적으로
- conspiracy : 음모, 모의
- ridden : 시달리는, 사로잡힌
- distorted : 왜곡된, 비뚤어진
- cuisine : 요리, 요리법
- immigration : 이민, 이주
- restoration : 부활, 회복

해석

많은 미국인들에게, 싱코 데 마요는 멕시코 음식을 먹고 아낌없이 마시는 날이다. 그러나 실제 역사는 훨씬 더 정치적 사안이다.

그것은 1860년대에 시작되었다. 프랑스는 멕시코로 제국을 확장하고 싶어 했고, 나폴레옹 3세는 아브라함 링컨이 내전에 몰두하는 동안 멕시코에서 민주적으로 선출된 대통령 베니토 후아레스를 타도하기 위해 그의 군대를 멕시코시티로 진격하도록 명령했다. 과조직화된 프랑스군은 승리할 것으로 크게 기대되었고, 이는 남부연합의 편에 설 새로운 멕시코 군주국을 탄생시켰다.

그러나 1862년 5월 5일, 멕시코군은 푸에블라 전투에서 프랑스를 물리쳤다. 그 뜻밖의 승리는 골드러시 기간 동안 북쪽으로 온 라틴 아메리카인들을 하나로 모았고, 자발적인 축하행사로 이어졌다고 「미국의 전통인 엘 싱코 데 마요」(첫 번째는 캘리포니아의 투올룸네 카운티에서 열렸다.)의 저자 데이비드 E. 헤이스-바티스타는 말한다. 곧 그들은 멕시코와 미국의 두 노예제도에 대항하는 투쟁을 지원하기 위해 단체들을 조직하기 시작했다.

그러나 1930년대에 남북 전쟁에 대한 기억이 더 멀어지면서 민권 공휴일로서의 싱코 데 마요의 중요성은 점차 사라지기 시작했다. 1980년대와 1990년대까지 히스패닉 소비자의 수가 급격히 증가했고, 특히 양주 업계 판매자들이 그 순간을 장악했다. 그들은 그 공휴일을 멕시코-미국 문화의 일반적인 축제로 전환시켜 어디에서나 열었고, 파티는 오늘날에도 성행하고 있다.

39 ② 싱코 데 마요는 푸에블라 전투, 남북 전쟁, 노예제도에 대한 투쟁 등의 역사에 비추어 볼 때, 멕시코-미국 문화의 일반적인 축제 이상의 정치적으로 훨씬 무게가 실린 사안이다. 그러므로 ②의 'politically charged(정치적 사안의)'가 빈칸에 들어갈 말로 가장 적절하다.

오답풀이

① geographically driven(지리적으로 추진된)
③ conspiracy ridden(음모에 사로잡힌)
④ culturally distorted(문화적으로 왜곡된)

⑤ economically balanced(경제적으로 균형 잡힌)

40 ① 제시문에 싱코 데 마요는 멕시코군이 푸에블라 전투에서 프랑스군을 물리친 후 라틴 아메리카인들의 자발적인 축하행사에서 비롯되었고, 이후 1980년대와 1990년대에 히스패닉 소비자의 수가 급격히 증가하면서 양주 업계 판매자들이 그 날을 멕시코-미국 문화의 일반적인 축제로 전환시켰다고 서술되어 있다. 그러므로 ①의 'The Surprising Evolution of Cinco de Mayo(싱코 데 마요의 놀라운 진화)'가 윗글의 제목으로 가장 적절하다.

오답풀이

② The Political Significance of Mexican Cuisine(멕시코 요리의 정치적 중요성)
③ Revisiting the History of Mexican Immigration(멕시코 이민의 역사 다시보기)
④ All Against Slavery: Struggles of the Confederacy(노예 제도에 반대하는 모든 것: 남부 연합의 투쟁)
⑤ The Restoration of Civil Rights Through Cinco de Mayo(싱코 데 마요를 통한 시민권 회복)

[41~42]

어휘

- gasp at : ~에 놀라 숨이 막히다
- glance up : 흘낏[휙] 보다, 언뜻 보다
- shrink : 줄어들다, 움츠리다
- dub : 별명을 붙이다, 더빙하다
- moon illusion : 달 착시
- phenomenon : 현상, 사건
- trickery : 사기, 속임수
- disagree : 의견이 다르다, 일치하지 않다
- deceive : 속이다, 기만하다
- supermoon : 슈퍼문, 초대형 달
- coincide with : ~와 일치하다, 동시에 일어나다
- lunar orbit : 달의 (공전) 궤도
- roughly : 대략, 거의
- naked eye : 육안
- barely : 겨우, 거의
- juxtapose : 병치하다, 옆에 놓다, 나란히 놓다
- foreground : 전경, 앞 경치
- hypothesis : 가설, 추정
- intrigue : 강한 흥미[호기심]
- take the time to : ~하는데 시간을 내다[할애하다]
- savor : 맛, 풍미, 음미

- lunar eclipse : 월식
- breathtaking : 숨이 막히는, 숨이 멎는 듯한
- optical illusion : 착시, 착시 현상

해석

여러분은 밤의 지평선을 보고 엄청나게 큰 달이 뜨는 광경에 가슴이 벅찬 적이 있는가? 몇 시간 후에 하늘을 올려다보면, 대게는 달이 작아진 것처럼 보일 것이다. 달 착시라고 불리는 이 현상은 수천 년 동안 목격되어 왔으며, 모두가 마음속에서 일어나는 시각적 속임수이다. 그리고 그렇게 오랜 시간이 지난 후에도, 과학자들은 여전히 우리의 뇌에서 정확히 무슨 일이 일어나고 있는지에 대해 의견이 분분하다. 그것을 시험해 보려면, 지평선에서 떠오르는 달 사진을 찍어 그날 밤 늦게 찍은 이미지와 비교하면 된다. 눈은 순간적으로 속을지언정, 그 크기는 일정하게 유지될 것이다. (A)마찬가지로 슈퍼문 기간 동안 보름달의 날짜가 달의 궤도에서 지구와 가장 가까운 곳에 일치하고 달이 약 7% 더 크게 보일 때, 비록 다르다고 확신하더라도 육안으로는 그 차이를 거의 볼 수 없다.

그 착각에 대한 일반적인 설명은 달이 지평선 가까이 있을 때, 하늘과 마주하여 나란히 있는 나무나 건물들이 뇌를 속여 달이 지구에 더 가깝고 따라서 더 크다고 인식하는 것이다. (B) 그러나, 궤도상의 우주 비행사들 또한 앞에 물체가 없는데도 달 착시를 목격하기 때문에, 이 설명이 문제를 완전히 해결하지는 못한다. 다른 가설들이 많지만, 달 착시는 여전히 과학자들과 이 달의 신비를 편안히 앉아 음미하는데 시간을 할애하는 사람들에게 약간의 흥미를 유발한다.

41 ④ 주어진 제시문은 수천 년 동안 목격된 달의 착시 현상에 대해 설명하고 있으며, 달이 작아지는 것처럼 보이는 이유에 대한 다양한 가설을 제공하고 있다. 그러므로 ④의 'The Optical Illusion of the Size of the Moon(달의 크기에 대한 착시 현상)'이 윗글의 제목으로 가장 적절하다.

오답풀이

① Traveling to the Moon Made Easy(손쉬운 달 여행)
② Lunar Eclipse During Supermoons(슈퍼문 기간 동안의 월식)
③ The Breathtaking View from Outer Space(우주에서 바라본 숨막히는 광경)
⑤ The Shrinking Universe: A Cause for Worry?(작아지는 우주: 걱정거리인가?)

42 ③ (A) 달 착시를 시험하기 위해 그 결과가 유사한 두 가지 방법을 제시하고 있다. 그러므로 'Similarly(마찬가지로)'가 빈칸 (A)에 들어갈 연결어구로 가장 적절하다.
(B) 나무나 건물들 때문에 달 착시가 나타난다는 앞의 설명

과 달리 우주 비행사들은 앞에 물체가 없는데도 달 착시를 목격한다고 서술하고 있다. 그러므로 역접의 접속사 'However(그러나)'가 빈칸 (B)에 들어갈 연결어구로 가장 적절하다.

[43~45]

어휘

- be stuck in : ~에 처박혀 있다, ~에 갇히다
- polio : 소아마비
- antidote : 해독제, 해결책
- supposedly : 추측컨대, 아마도
- grab : 붙잡다, 움켜쥐다
- butcher paper : 고기 포장용지
- grasp : 완전히 이해하다, 파악하다
- instruction : 지시, 설명
- delicious-sounding : 맛있는 소리를 내는
- ward : 실, 병동
- keep under wraps : 숨기다, 비밀로 하다
- decade : 10년
- epidemic : 유행병, 전염병
- bowling alley : 볼링장
- moviegoer : 영화 관람객
- wary : 경계하는, 조심하는
- coupled with : ~와 결부된, 동반된
- eradicate : 근절하다, 뿌리 뽑다
- be inducted into : ~에 가입되다, 헌액[추대]되다
- the National Toy Hall of Fame : 국립 장난감 명예의 전당
- humble : 겸손한, 겸허한
- keep a low profile : 겸손함을 유지하다
- devote : 바치다, 헌신하다
- exploration : 탐사, 탐구
- royalty check : 저작권료
- bittersweet : 달콤한, 달콤쌉싸름한
- boost : 높이다, 신장시키다
- arithmetic : 산수, 산술
- be struck with : ~에 휩싸이다
- hospitalize : 입원시키다

해석

(A) 1948년이었고, 엘리너 애벗은 지루했다. 퇴임한 선생님은 그녀처럼 소아마비를 앓고 있는 어린 아이들에게 둘러싸여 샌디에이고 병원에 갇혀 있었다. 아이들은 외롭고 슬퍼했으며, 달리 할 일이 없었던 애벗은 유쾌한 보드 게임이 완벽한 해결책이 될 수 있으리라 생각했다. 그래서 그녀는

아마도 고기 포장용지 한 장을 쥐고 도안을 그리기 시작했다.

(D) 최종 결과 어린 아이들은 대만족이었다. 세거나 읽을 필요 없이, 참가자는 단순히 색을 파악하여 카드 상의 지시에 따라 보드를 여행하고, 도중에 맛있는 소리를 내는 여러 위치에 멈추면 되었다. 그녀는 소아마비 병동의 아이들과 그 게임을 함께 했고, 아이들은 좋아했다. 1년 후 밀턴 브래들리가 그 게임을 사들였는데, 그것은 공전의 히트작인 캔디랜드였다.

(B) 밀턴 브래들리는 수십 년 동안 그 이야기를 비밀에 부쳤지만, 그 게임과 병과의 연관성은 거기서 멈추지 않았다. 소아마비가 캔디랜드를 유명하게 만드는 데 일조했을 가능성이 있다. 1950년대 초, 소아마비 전염병이 전국을 휩쓸었다. 건강을 지키는 가장 좋은 방법은 사람들을 만나지 않는 것이었다. 공공 수영장, 놀이터, 그리고 볼링장은 폐쇄되었다. 영화 관람객들은 극장에서 서로 멀리 떨어져 앉도록 안내 받았다. 조심스러운 부모들은 아이들을 밖에서 놀도록 내버려두지 않았다. 건강하든 아프든, 모두가 시간을 보내는데 도움이 될 오락거리가 필요했다. 전후 미국인들이 그 어느 때보다 많은 돈과 여가 시간을 가졌다는 사실과 더불어, 그것은 어린이 보드 게임이 인기를 끌기 위한 이상적인 조건을 제공했다. 게다가, 그것은 사탕에 관한 것이지 않은가!

(C) 오늘날, 소아마비는 사실상 지구상에서 근절되었다. 그러나 캔디랜드는 계속해서 기부를 하고 있다. 그 게임은 4천만 장 이상이 팔렸고 2005년에 국립 장난감 명예의 전당에 헌액되었다. 하지만 애벗은 남은 여생 동안 겸손함을 유지했다. 뉴욕 로체스터에 있는 박물관인 더 스트롱의 니콜라스 리케츠에 따르면, 애벗은 첫 저작권료를 받았을 때, 그 돈의 상당 부분을 병동에서 만난 아이들에게 바로 돌려주었다. 얼마나 자상한가!

43 ④ 우선 글 (A)에서 엘리너 애벗이 소아마비 병동에서 보드 게임을 만든 상황을 설명하고 있다. 다음으로 보드 게임을 하는 방법에 대해 설명한 글 (D)가 이어져야 한다. 글 (D)의 말미에 밀턴 브래들리가 그 게임을 사들여 히트시킨 것이 캔디랜드였고, 그것이 유명하게 된 이유를 글 (B)에서 설명하고 있다. 마지막으로 글 (C)에서 캔디랜드를 처음 도안한 엘리너 애벗의 훈훈한 미담에 대해 설명하고 있다. 그러므로 글 (A) 다음에 (D)-(B)-(C)의 순서로 글이 이어져야 한다.

44 ② 캔디랜드는 엘리너 애벗이 샌디에이고 병원에 입원중일 때 소아마비에 걸린 아이들을 위해 고안했고, 소아마비가 사라진 이후에도 계속해서 기부를 이어가고 있으며, 애벗이

첫 저작권료를 받았을 때도 그 돈의 상당 부분을 병동에서 만난 아이들에게 돌려주었다고 서술하고 있다. 그러므로 ②의 'The Bittersweet History of Candy Land(캔디랜드의 달콤한 역사)'가 윗글의 제목으로 가장 적절하다.

[오답풀이]

① How to Play Candy Land with Kids(아이들과 캔디랜드 놀이하는 방법)

③ Using Candy Land as an Educational Tool(캔디랜드를 교육 도구로 사용하기)

④ Candy Land: Boosting Children's Confidence(아이들의 자신감을 높여주는 캔디랜드)

⑤ The Decline of the Popularity of Candy Land(캔디랜드의 인기 하락)

45 ① 글 (D)에서 세거나 읽을 필요 없이, 참가자는 단순히 색을 파악하여 카드 상의 지시에 따라 보드를 여행하고, 도중에 맛있는 소리를 내는 여러 위치에 멈추면 된다고 그 게임에 대해 설명하고 있다. 그러므로 "Candy Land requires basic arithmetic skills.(캔디랜드는 기본적인 산술 능력을 필요로 한다.)"는 ①의 설명은 윗글의 내용과 일치하지 않는다.

[오답풀이]

② America was struck with an epidemic in the 1950s.(미국은 1950년대에 전염병이 유행하였다.)

③ Eleanor Abbott made Candy Land while hospitalized.(엘리너 애벗은 입원 중에 캔디랜드를 만들었다.)

④ Eleanor Abbott shared her first royalty check with others.(엘리너 애벗은 처음 받은 저작권료를 다른 사람들과 나누었다.)

⑤ At first, Milton Bradley did not reveal the origin story of Candy Land.(처음에 밀턴 블래들리는 캔디랜드의 유래를 밝히지 않았다.)

경찰대학 10개년 영어 ▼

2022학년도 기출문제 정답 및 해설

제2교시 **영어영역**

01 ③	02 ⑤	03 ⑤	04 ①	05 ③	06 ④
07 ④	08 ①	09 ①	10 ③	11 ①	12 ②
13 ④	14 ④	15 ②	16 ⑤	17 ④	18 ④
19 ⑤	20 ⑤	21 ③	22 ⑤	23 ③	24 ①
25 ④	26 ①	27 ③	28 ②	29 ⑤	30 ③
31 ①	32 ②	33 ③	34 ②	35 ①	36 ⑤
37 ②	38 ②	39 ③	40 ⑤	41 ①	42 ②
43 ③	44 ②	45 ②			

01 ③ 'ubiquitous'는 '어디에나 있는, 아주 흔한'이라는 의미로 'omnipresent(어디에나 있는)'와 의미가 가장 유사하다.

오답풀이
① 소리 높여 표현하는
② 모호한
④ 거침없는
⑤ 무료의

어휘
• Track : 추적하다
• stray : (자기도 모르게) 제 위치[길]를 벗어나다
• thanks to : ~의 덕분에, 때문에
• soon : 곧
• microchip : 마이크로칩
• vociferous : 소리 높여 표현하는
• equivocal : 모호한
• inexorable : 거침없는
• complimentary : 무료의

해석
어디에서나 볼 수 있는 마이크로칩 덕분에 길 잃은 개를 추적하는 것이 곧 쉬워질 것이다.

02 ⑤ 'unscrupulous'는 '부도덕한'이라는 의미로 'dishonest(정직하지 못한)'과 가장 의미가 유사하다.

오답풀이
① 신중한
② 비정상적인
③ 근면한
④ 무관심한

어휘
• Through : …을 통해[관통하여]
• public : 일반인[대중]의
• education : 교육
• advocacy : (생각·행동 노선·신념 등에 대한 공개적인) 지지[옹호]
• protests : 항의[반대/이의] (운동), 시위
• prudent : 신중한

해석
공교육, 정치적 옹호, 시위를 통해 개방된 공간과 숲을 부도덕한 개발자들로부터 보호하고자 했다.

03 ⑤ 'ostracized'는 '외면하다'의 의미로 'excluded(제외되는)'과 가장 의미가 유사하다.

오답풀이
① 당혹한
② 정류한
③ 범람한
④ 스며들다

어휘
• Individual : 각각[개개]의
• risk : 위험
• fellow : 동료
• worker : 노동자
• bewildered : 당혹한
• rectified : 정류한
• inundated : 범람한

해석
그런 행동을 한 개인들은 동료들로부터 외면을 당할 위험이 있었다.

04 ① 'nemesis'는 '강적'의 의미로 'adversary(적수)'와 가장 의미가 유사하다.

오답풀이
② 촉매
③ 관습
④ 영재
⑤ 천정

어휘
- Stuttering : 말을 더듬는
- embarrassing : 난처한
- struggled : 투쟁[고투]하다
- throughout : 도처에
- childhood : 어린 시절
- catalyst : 촉매
- convention : 관습

해석
말을 더듬는 것은 티모시가 어린 시절 내내 고군분투했던 당혹스러운 강적이었다.

05 ③ 'banal'은 '지극히 평범한'이라는 의미로 'ordinary(일상적인)'와 가장 유사하다.

오답풀이
① 다정한
② 혐오의
④ 걱정되는
⑤ 과장된

어휘
- exchanged : 교환
- climbers : 등반가
- inwardly : 마음속으로
- frantic : 정신없이[미친 듯이]
- affectionate : 다정한
- aversive : 혐오의

해석
등반가들과 지극히 평범한 축하 인사를 주고받다 보니 속으로 걱정이 앞섰다.

06 ④ A는 지난밤 국제 우주 정거장을 봤다고 말한다. B의 말에 A는 '나는 쉽게 그것과 별들 사이의 차이점을 쉽게 구별할 수 있어.' 라고 답한다. 따라서 B가 무엇을 물어봤는지 예상할 수 있다. ④의 "How did you know that it was the ISS (어떻게 구별을 했어?)"가 빈칸에 들어갈 말로 가장 적절하다.

오답풀이
① ISS와 NASA의 차이점을 설명해줄래?
② 구름의 중심에 있는 별이 보여?
③ ISS를 본 이유가 뭐야?
⑤ 지구에서 얼마나 떨어져 있니?

어휘
- International Space Station : 국제 우주 정거장(ISS)
- amazing : (감탄스럽도록) 놀라운
- possible : 가능한
- Earth : 지구, 세상
- across : 건너서
- location : (…이 일어나는 · 존재하는) 장소[곳/위치]
- neat : 정돈된

해석
A : 이봐, 그거 알아? 어젯밤에 국제 우주 정거장을 봤어!
B : 정말? 대단해! 정말 ISS를 볼 수 있어? 지구에서?
A : 응. 하늘을 가로지르는 밝은 별처럼 보였어.
B : 어떻게 구별을 했어?
A : 그것은 굉장히 빨리 움직여서 그 주변의 별들 사이에서 쉽게 구별할 수 있었어. ISS 위치를 보려면 NASA 웹사이트에서 확인할 수 있어.
B : 정말 깔끔하게 들리네. 한번 해볼게.

07 ④ B는 블로그를 통해 접한 Nessie라고 불리는 스코틀랜드 호수의 괴물에 대해 이야기 하고 있다. 빈칸 이후 A는 사진이 수정 되었을 수도 있으니 보이는 모든 것을 믿지 말라고 이야기 한다. 따라서 ④의 "There are lots of photos of Nessie, though(하지만 Nessie의 사진이 많아.)"가 적절하다.

오답풀이
① 실제로 과학자들은 그것의 존재를 믿었어.
② 하지만 그것은 나의 실수인 것 같아.
③ 괴물은 자연의 질서를 어지럽혀.
⑤ 응, 그것들은 실존함이 입증되었어.

어휘
- interesting : 흥미로운
- quite : 꽤
- proven : 입증[증명]된
- modified : 수정된
- approach : 접근법
- reasonable : 타당한
- suspicion : 의심
- authentic : 진본[진품]인

A : 뭐 하고 있어?

B : 블로그를 통해 몇 가지 흥미로운 것들에 대해 살펴보고 있어.

A : 뭐가 그렇게 흥미로운데?

B : 이 블로그에 따르면, 스코틀랜드의 한 호수에 Nessie라는 괴물이 살고 있대.

A : 오, 꽤 흥미롭긴 한데, 믿지 않는 게 좋을 거야. 이런 종류의 것들은 증명되지 않았어.

B : 하지만 Nessie의 사진이 많아.

A : 사진이 수정되었을 수 있어. 보이는 모든 것을 믿는 것보다 합리적인 의심을 가지고 접근하는 것이 중요하다고 생각해.

B : 알겠어. 명심할게.

08 ① 능동인지 수동인지 고르는 것이 관건이다. factors가 고려하는 요소인지 고려되는 요소인지 확인해본다. factors는 고려되는 요소이다. 따라서 ①의 'considering'을 'considered'로 고쳐 써야 한다.

어휘

- illness : 병, 아픔
- chemical : 화학의
- imbalance : 불균형
- factors : 요인, 인자
- environment : (주변의) 환경
- injury : 부상
- opinions : (개인의) 의견[견해/생각]
- society : (공동체를 이루는 일반적인) 사회
- supervision : 감독
- psychiatrist : 정신과 의사
- treatment : 치료, 처치
- pioneered : (특정 지식문화 부문의) 개척자[선구자]
- whereby : (그것에 의하여) …하는
- receives : 받다, 받아들이다
- above : (위치나 지위 면에서) …보다 위에[위로]

해석

정신질환은 여러모로 우리에게 수수께끼로 남아 있다. 어떤 과학자들은 그것이 유전적이라고 생각한다. 다른 사람들은 이것이 신체의 화학적 불균형에 의한 것이라고 생각한다. 고려되는 다른 요인으로는 사람의 환경이나 뇌손상 등이 있다. 전문가들은 무엇이 정신질환을 유발하는지에 대해 각기 다른 의견을 가지고 있고, 그것을 어떻게 치료할지에 대해서는 다른 생각을 가지고 있다. 정신질환자를 병원이나 교도소에 배치해 사회로부터 격리시키는 것도 한 방법이다. 또 다른 방법은 정신과 의사의 감독 아래 약을 투여해 행동을 수정하는 것이다. 약물 치료를 받고 있는 정신환자들은 감독된 주택에서 생활하는 경우가 많다. Sigmund Freud가 개척한 또 다른 치료 방법은 정신분석으로, 환자는 정신과에서 많은 시간 동안 상담과 상담치료를 받는 것이다. 위의 치료법들은 종종 결합된다.

09 ① (A) 위험을 향해 달려가는 사람들의 이야기가 전개 되어야 하므로 안전하게 사는 것을 불안해 한다는 문장이 나와야 한다. 'nervous(불안)'이 적절하다.

② (B) 과학자들은 왜 고의적으로 상해, 죽음을 얻으려고 하는지 궁금해 하므로 'court(…을 얻으려고 하다)'가 적절하다.

③ (C) 육체적 또는 정신적으로 스트레스를 받는 상황이 유발 되는 것을 의미하므로 'arises(발생하다)'가 적절하다.

어휘

- nervous : 불안해[초조해/두려워] 하는
- relaxed : 느긋한, 여유 있는
- placidly : 잔잔하게
- surely : 확실히
- minuscule : 극소의
- deliberately : 고의로, 의도[계획]적으로
- evade : (어떤 일이나 사람을) 피하다[모면하다]
- interplay : 상호 작용
- ingredient : (특히 요리 등의) 재료[성분]
- adrenaline : 아드레날린
- chemical : 화학의, 화학적인 (변화를 수반한)
- adrenal : 신장 부근의
- arises : 생기다, 발생하다
- disappears : (눈앞에서) 사라지다
- swiftly : 신속히
- forcefully : 힘차게

해석

어떤 사람들은 차분하고 안전하게 살면 (A) 불안해한다. 그들은 대부분의 사람들이 위험으로부터 도망치는 것처럼 확실하게 위험을 향해 달려간다. 번지점프를 하거나 산악자전거를 타고 자갈길을 미끄러져 내려가거나 벼랑 앞 틈에 끼어 손끝으로 매달리거나 심지어 위험한 모험을 하기 위해 안전한 직장을 그만두기도 한다. 그들은 위험을 감수하는 사람들이고, 과학자들은 오랫동안 궁금해해왔다. 왜 고의적으로 상실, 상해, 심지어 죽음에 대한 (B) 구애를 하는지. 그 질문에 대한 대답은 심리적인 요인과 생리적인 요인의 복잡한 상호작용을 포함한다. 위험에 대한 신체의 생리학적 반응의 핵심 요소는 아드레날린이다. 신체는 이 화학물질을 신장의 부신 중앙에서 생산한다. 육체적으로나 정신적으로 스트레스를 받는 상황이

(C) 발생했을 때, 혈류로 흘러 들어가는 아드레날린은 신체가 스스로를 보호하기 위해 신속하고 강력하게 행동할 수 있도록 준비시킨다.

10　③ (A) 사냥감의 속도와 지구력, 민첩성이라는 지문이 나오므로 'Fleeing(도망치는)'이 적절하다.

　　(B) 사자, 표범, 치타가 단거리의 폭발적인 스피드만 낼 수 있다는 것을 알고 있다고 했으므로 'panic(허둥지둥함)'할 일이 거의 없다는 것이 적절하다.

　　(C) 개들은 고양이만큼 빠르지는 않지만, 몸이 약하거나 늙거나 병든 먹이를 소진시킬 정도로 오랫동안 달릴 수 있다는 의미가 되어야 하므로 'exhaust(소진시키다)'가 적절하다.

어휘

• Fleeing : 도망치는
• Hunting : 사냥
• inspiring : (…하도록) 고무[격려/자극]하는
• endurance : 인내(력), 참을성
• antelopes : 영양
• against : …에 반대하여[맞서]
• hoofed : …한 발굽이 있는
• rarely : 좀처럼 …하지 않는
• idle : 게으른, 나태한
• panic : 허둥지둥함
• predator : 포식자
• deadly : 치명적인
• prey : (사냥 동물의) 먹이[사냥감]
• depend : 의존하다
• endurance : 인내(력)
• exhaust : 다 써 버리다, 고갈시키다
• invigorate : 활성화하다

해석

(A) 도망치는 것은 사냥감의 속도와 지구력, 민첩성의 신화적 수준에 영감을 주며 정교한 예술로 완성되었다. 영양, 가젤, 얼룩말과 같은 평범한 동물들 또한 공격자들의 재능과 자신의 능력을 비교하는 법을 배웠다. 사자, 표범, 치타가 단거리의 폭발적인 스피드만 낼 수 있다는 것을 알고 있는 발굽이 달린 것들은 달리기와 유리한 출발이 가능한 한 고양이를 보고 (B) 허둥지둥 하는 일이 거의 없다. 중요한 것은 맹수가 "기지를 공격"하지 않고 치명적인 전력 질주를 할 수 있을 만큼 가까이 가지 않도록 감시하는 것이다. 그러나 사냥개와 늑대에 맞서는 먹잇감 동물은 지구력만으로는 의존할 수 없다는 것을 알고 있다. 개들은 고양이만큼 빠르지는 않지만, 몸이 약하거나 늙거나 병든 먹이를 (C) 소진시킬 정도로 오랫동안 달릴 수 있다.

11　① (A) 멜로디가 올라가면 최저음을 떨어뜨리며, 대조적인 모션을 취하고 있으므로 'contrary(대조적으로)'가 적절하다.

　　(B) 방향이 반대로 가는 것을 의미하므로 'separating(분리시키다)'가 적절하다.

　　(C) 단 하나의 선이 곡조를 전달하는 것으로 식별될 수 있게 하기 위해 다른 부분은 조화를 이루어야 함을 의미하므로 'harmony(조화)'가 적절하다.

어휘

• struggling : 발버둥이 치는
• contrary : ~와는 다른[반대되는]
• parallel : (두 개 이상의 선이) 평행한
• In other words : 다시 말해서
• fall : 떨어지다, 빠지다, 내리다
• equally : 똑같이, 동일[동등]하게
• separating : 분리
• discord : 불화, 다툼
• harmony : 조화, 화합
• identified : 확인된, 인정된, 식별된
• Somehow : 어떻게든

해석

만약 여러분이 선율적이고 조화로운 결합체에 대해 생각하고 있다면 두 가지 요소들을 결합시키는 방법은 (A) 대조적인 모션을 해야 효과가 있다. 너의 선율이 올라감에 따라 화음진행에 가장 낮은음을 떨어뜨리도록 노력해라. 마찬가지로 너의 멜로디가 떨어질 때 최저음을 위쪽으로 올려라. 대조적인 움직임은 두가지의 파트와 그들사이의 미러가 있다고 상상하고 (B) 분리시켜라. 한 방향으로의 움직임이 유발한다. 다른 부분이 다른 방향으로 움직이도록. 단 하나의 선이 곡조를 전달하는 것으로 확인 될 수 있게 하기 위해 (C) 조화를 이루어야 곡조가 전달이 된다.

12　② 제시문은 콘벨트에 대한 내용이다. 강우량이 풍부하며, 길고 따뜻한 생장기가 있고 이 모든 것이 땅을 매우 가치 있게 만든다고 했으므로 ②의 'futile(쓸데없는)'이 아니라 'useful(유용한)'등으로 바꿔 써야 적절하다.

오답풀이

① (특히 가축을 도살하기 전에) 살찌우다
③ 소작인
④ 공급하다
⑤ 설치되다

어휘

• running : 운영, 경영

- farm : 농장, 농원
- operation : (대규모) 기업, 사업체
- particularly : 특히, 특별히
- grown : 재배하다
- rainfall : 강우(량)
- valuable : 가치가 큰
- machinery : (특히 큰 기계를 집합적으로 가리켜) 기계(류)
- fertilizer : 비료
- owned : [복합어를 이루어] …이 소유하는
- insurance : 보험
- rent : 임대
- equipped with : …을 갖춘
- electric lighting : 전기 조명
- round-the-clock : 24시간[밤낮 없이] 계속되는

해석

오늘날 중서부에서 농장을 운영하는 것은 매우 돈이 많이 드는 운영이 될 것 같다. 이는 특히 가축의 대부분을 살찌우는 옥수수가 재배되는 콘벨트에서 더욱 그렇다. 콘벨트의 중심은 아이오와, 일리노이, 인디애나에 있다. 토양은 극히 쓸데없고 (→유용하고), 강우량이 풍부하며, 길고 따뜻한 생장기가 있다. 이 모든 것이 땅을 매우 가치 있게 만든다. 토지에 가축, 종자, 기계, 연료, 비료 등의 비용을 더하면 농사는 매우 돈이 많이 드는 운영이 된다. 그러므로 많은 농부들이 소작인들이고 땅의 많은 부분은 은행, 보험 회사 또는 부유한 사업가들이 소유하고 있다. 이 주인들은 일반적으로 기계와 노동력을 제공하는 농부들에게 땅을 임대해준다. 일부 농장은 제분업체와 계약하여 운영된다. 기업들은 농장을 매입하고 경영자를 투입해 농사를 짓게 하고 농사를 지을 수 있는 기계를 공급하며 농산물을 자체 용도로 가져간다. 기계에는 24시간 작동이 가능하도록 전기 조명이 설치되는 경우가 많다.

13 ④ 제시문은 디지털 정보와 지식의 불확실성에 대해 설명하고 있다. 지식의 위상이 도전받는 이유는 접근할 수 있는 것의 품질이 종종 알려져 있지 않기 때문이라고 한다. 그러므로 ④의 'unveiled(공개되다)'가 아닌 'cover(감추다)'로 바꿔 써야 적절하다.

오답풀이

① 방해하다
② (통계 조사의) 표본
③ 알려지지 않은
⑤ 상대적인

어휘

- uncertainty : 불확실성, 반신반의
- infinitude : 무한

- response : 대답, 응답
- esoteric : 소수만 이해하는
- disciplines : 규율, 훈육
- stature : 지명도, 위상
- accessed : (장소로의) 입장[접근]
- publisher : 출판인
- affiliation : (개인의 정치 · 종교적) 소속[가입]
- clearly : 또렷하게
- deliberately : 고의로, 의도[계획]적으로
- simplistic : 지나치게 단순화한
- correct : 맞는, 정확한
- overcome : 극복하다
- nevertheless : 그렇기는 하지만, 그럼에도 불구하고
- caveat : 통고[경고]

해석

디지털 정보는 지식의 불확실성을 증가시키는 데 한몫을 한다. 첫째, 인터넷을 통해 접근할 수 있는 정보의 무한성은 어떤 주제에 숙달하려는 어떠한 시도도 어렵게 만든다. 어떤 분야에서든 무엇이 알려져야 하는지를 더 이상 알 수 없다. 그 응답은 점점 더 좁혀지거나 난해해지는 것에 초점을 맞추는 것이다. 훈련이나 관심사를 인정하거나, 할 수 있는 모든 것은 그 분야를 시도하는 것이다. 둘째, 지식의 위상이 도전받는 이유는 접근할 수 있는 것의 품질이 종종 알려져 있지 않기 때문이다. 인쇄된 책에는 대개 품질 출판사, 저자 소속 등의 표시가 선명하게 표시되어 있다. 그러나 인터넷 정보의 질이 항상 그렇게 명백하고, 때로는 의도적으로 공개되고(→감추어지고), 때로는 단순하지만 시끄럽지는 않다. 백과 사전도 보장되지 않는다. 위키백과는 다음과 같이 주장한다. 누구나 편집할 수 있는 무료 백과사전. 올바른 소재가 대개 잘못된 것을 극복한다는 이론에도 불구하고, 지식은 항상 상대적이라는 주의사항이 있다.

14 ④ 카페의 절반 이상의 손님들이 정기적으로 방문 한다고 하였으므로, 'More than half of the customers visit this cafe regularly. (이 카페는 고객의 절반 이상이 정기적으로 방문합니다.)'는 ④의 설명이 제시문의 내용과 일치한다.

오답풀이

① Songbird House는 1904년에 유명한 유적지였다.
② Songbird House에서는 조식이 제공되지 않는다.
③ 신입사원들은 자주 채용된다.
⑤ Songbird House는 거실을 개조하는 회사이다.

어휘

- located : …에 위치한
- historic : 역사적으로 중요한, 역사에 남을 만한, 역사적인

- pastries : 패스트리
- proud : 자랑스러워하는, 자랑스러운
- personally : (다른 사람을 통하거나 하지 않고) 직접, 개인적으로
- assured : 확실한, 확실시 되는
- variety : 여러 가지, 갖가지, 각양각색
- creatives : 창의적인 사람, (창작 활동을 하는) 작가
- nursing mothers : 양모, 수양어머니
- comfortable : 편(안)한, 쾌적한
- extension : (세력 · 영향력 · 혜택 등의) 확대
- frequently : 자주, 흔히
- renovates : 개조하다

해석

Songbird House는 2012년 7월 23일 오픈하였으며 이 건물은 1904년 지어진 역사적인 집입니다. 저희는 커피와 차에 중점을 두고 있지만, 여러분은 수제 페이스트리와 아침 샌드위치를 좋아하실 것입니다. 우리는 낮은 직원 이직률을 자랑스럽게 여겨서 우리 모두가 고객을 개인적으로 알게 되고 고객은 한결같은 것에 대해 확신하게 됩니다. 우리가 환영하는 얼굴의 60%는 단골이지만, 우리는 매일 각계각층의 아름다운 다양한 사람들을 만나는 것이 즐겁습니다. 당신이 누구이든, 누구를 사랑하든, 당신이 어디에 있든 간에 방문하세요. 사업가, 학생, 작가, 양모 편안히 계세요. Songbird House는 당신의 거실의 연장선입니다.

- insects : 곤충
- distinct : 뚜렷한, 분명한
- boggy : 늪지, 습지, 수렁
- devoid : ~이 전혀 없는
- nutrition : 영양
- attracts : 마음을 끌다
- fuel : 연료
- trapping : 덫, 올가미
- digesting : (음식을) 소화하다[소화시키다], 소화되다
- prey : (사냥 동물의) 먹이[사냥감]
- enzymes : 효소
- rainwater : 빗물

해석

코브라 백합은 코브라 뱀의 머리를 닮은 독특한 잎 덕분에 눈길을 끄는 식물이다. 그것의 웅크러진 잎은 식물의 밑부분에서 솟아올라 후드 잎으로 둥글게 된다. 이 육식성 식물은 놀라운 외모와 함께 작은 척추동물뿐만 아니라 곤충도 잡아먹는다. 북아메리카가 원산지인 코브라 백합은 종종 영양이 부족한 습지대에서 뚜렷한 집단으로 자란다. 후드를 쓴 잎은 곤충을 유인하는 향기를 분비하고, 식물이 먹이를 가두고 소화시켜 연료를 모을 수 있게 한다. 일단 안으로 들어가면 곤충들이 탈출하기 어렵고, 식물은 또한 동물성 물질을 분해하는 것을 돕기 위해 소화효소를 분비할 것이다. 그러나 다른 많은 낭상엽 식물들과 달리 코브라 백합 식물들은 먹이를 가두기 위해 빗물을 모을 수 없다.

15 ② 제시문은 코브라 백합에 대한 내용을 이야기 하고 있다. 코브라 백합은 놀라운 외모와 함께 작은 척추동물뿐만 아니라 곤충도 잡아먹는다고 서술되어 있으므로 'It is eaten by small animals with a backbone. (그것은 척추 동물들에게 먹힌다.)'라는 ②의 설명은 제시문의 내용과 일치하지 않는다.

오답풀이

① 잎은 코브라의 머리를 닮는다.
③ 습지대에서 종종 발견된다.
④ 그것은 기분 좋은 냄새를 분비하여 곤충을 유인한다.
⑤ 빗물을 모아 먹잇감을 가두지 않는다.

어휘

- eye-catching : (단번에) 눈길을 끄는
- dramatic : 극적인
- curling : (둥그렇게) 감기다[감다], (몸이[을]) 웅크러지다[웅크리다]
- foliage : 나뭇잎
- appearance : (겉)모습, 외모
- carnivorous : 〈식물이〉 식충성의
- feed on : ~을 먹고 살다

16 ⑤ 한국음식의 인기와 그에 따른 위기를 설명하고 있는 내용이므로 ⑤의 'Popularity and Crisis of Korea's National Dish (대한민국 국민요리의 인기와 위기)'가장 적절하다.

오답풀이

① 김치 : 치솟는 인기
② 김치는 건강에 어떤 영향을 미치나요?
③ 한국, 중국과의 무역전쟁에서 승리하다
④ 김장 : 유네스코 선정

어휘

- unmistakable : 오해의 여지가 없는, 틀림없는
- permeates : 스며들다, 침투하다
- admirer : (유명한 사람 · 물건을) 찬미하는 사람, 팬
- valued : 존중되는, 귀중한, 소중한
- refrigerators : 냉장고
- peninsulA : 반도
- cabbage : 양배추
- traditionally : 전통적으로
- communal : (한 공동체 내의) 집단들이 관련된

- heritage : (국가 · 사회의) 유산
- copious : 엄청난 (양의), 방대한
- damage : 손상, 피해
- Health : (몸 · 마음의) 건강
- Award : (부상이 딸린) 상

<해석>

이 냄새는 출퇴근 시간대에 서울 지하철 객차에 스며들며, 찬미자들은 이 냄새가 지구상에서 가장 건강에 좋은 음식이라고 주장한다. 냉장고가 들어오기 전에 비타민C 의 원천으로 평가받던 김치는 이제 한반도에서 멀리 떨어진 메뉴에서 떠오르고 있다. 맵고 마늘 냄새가 나는 양배추 요리는 영국, 호주, 미국에서 피자 토핑과 소를 채운 타코 음식으로 발견된다. 김치를 담그는 전통적인 공동 행위인 김장은 최근 유네스코부터 세계문화유산으로 인정받았다. 그러나 로스앤젤레스부터 런던까지 한국 국적의 레스토랑에서 인기가 높아졌음에도 불구하고 요리는 원산지에서 위기에 처해있다. 배추, 마늘, 양념. 고춧가루 등 김치의 기본 재료에 중국과의 무역전쟁이 한국 문화의 정체성에 지속적인 손상을 우려하는 목소리가 더해진다.

17 ④ 제시문은 전체적으로 기술 준비 상태에 도달한 솔루션은 거의 없었고 효율성 및 환경 영향에 대해 검증된 솔루션은 없었다고 한다. 그러므로 제시문의 제목으로는 ④의 'Want to Heal the Ocean? More Work Needed (바다를 치유하고 싶나요? 더 많은 작업이 필요함)'이 적절하다.

<오답풀이>
① 해양 동물 구하기 : Microlitter 대상 지정
② 해양 발견을 위한 소극적 여정
③ 인류에 대한 해양 위협
⑤ 해양폐기물 재활용의 효용성에 대한 의문

<어휘>
- Innovative : 획기적인
- solutions : (문제 · 곤경의) 해법, 해결책
- restore : (이전의 상황 · 감정으로) 회복시키다
- developed : (산업 · 경제 · 기술 등이) 발달한, 선진의
- implemented : 시행하다
- scattered : 산발적인
- accessible : 접근[입장/이용] 가능한
- prevention : 예방, 방지
- wastewater : 폐수, 하수
- inconsistent : 일관성 없는
- harmonization : 조화
- assess : (특성 · 자질 등을) 재다[가늠하다]
- targeted : 목표가 된
- Overall : 종합[전반]적인, 전체의

- readiness : 준비가 되어 있음
- validated : 적합하며
- environmental : (자연) 환경의

<해석>

해양 쓰레기를 예방, 감시, 청소하기 위한 혁신적인 솔루션은 건강한 해양을 복원하고 시간이 지남에 따라 그것의 안녕을 유지하기 위해 필요하다. 또한, 이러한 솔루션 중 몇 개가 개발 및 구현되었는지, 플랫폼 전체에 정보가 분산되어 쉽게 액세스할 수 없는 상황에서 어느 정도까지 효과적인지 거의 알려지지 않았다. 글로벌 분석 또한 Nature Sustainability에서도 177개의 PMC 솔루션을 식별한 연구진은 그 중 106개가 모니터링, 33개는 (대부분 폐수 처리를 통해) 33개는 예방, 30개만 청소하는 것으로 나타났다. 그들은 또한 다양한 개발자에 걸쳐 쓰레기 크기 용어의 일관되지 않은 사용을 발견한다. 이는 처리 대상 쓰레기의 유형을 평가하기 위한 조화와 노력이 필요했으며, 이는 해결책 중 137개가 Microlitter를 대상으로 한다는 것을 보여준다. 전체적으로 기술 준비 상태에 도달한 솔루션은 거의 없었고 효율성 및 환경 영향에 대해 검증된 솔루션은 없었다.

18 ④ 제시문은 미국에서 노인들을 대상으로 한 '케어'를 관찰한 결과, 그 문화에서의 개인화는 특정한 상징과 지위의 획득뿐만 아니라 일련의 성공의 성취도 포함한다고 결론지을 수 있을 뿐이라고 이야기 한다. 따라서 제시문의 제목으로는 ④의 'one aspect of personalization in the United States (미국의 개인화의 한 측면)'이 적절하다.

<오답풀이>
① 개인화의 여러 가지 전략
② 노인에 대한 전형적인 오해
③ 미국의 노인요양문제
⑤ 미국 경제에 대한 소비의 기여

<어휘>
- observing : 관찰하는
- aged : 고령의, 연로한
- personalization : 개인화, 인격화
- acquisition : 습득
- achievement : 업적, 성취한 것
- a series of : 일련의
- individual : 각각[개개]의
- withdrawn : (뒤로) 물러나다, 철수하다
- displaced : 추방된
- scarcely : 거의 …않다
- symbolize : 상징하다
- retention : 보유

• machinery : 기계 부품들

• adequate : 충분한

• indispensable : 없어서는 안 될

해석

미국에서 노인들을 대상으로 한 '케어'를 관찰한 결과, 그 문화에서의 개인화는 특정한 상징과 지위의 획득뿐만 아니라 일련의 성공의 성취도 포함한다고 결론지을 수 있을 뿐이다. 그 징표에 따르면 성공할 능력이 상실되거나 실패한 개인은 성공 메커니즘에서 물러났기 때문에 덜한 사람으로 간주된다. 미국의 노인들은, 그들이 직업 체계에서 물러났거나 쫓겨났기 때문에, 성공하거나 실패할 수 있는 능력을 박탈당한다; 그들은 여전히 지속적인 소비 능력으로 그들의 과거의 성공을 상징할 수 없는 한, 거의 없는 사람으로 보여진다. 이런 식으로 개인의 소비능력 보유는 성공 시스템에서 물러난 후에도 다음과 같이 받아들여진다. 이러한 소비를 통해, 경제에 없어서는 안 될 서비스가 제공되기 때문에, 성공을 대체할 적절한 수단이 된다.

19 ⑤ 제시문은 어떤 사람들은 주어진 기술을 사용하기로 선택하지만, 다른 사람들은 그렇지 않으며 어떤 기술이든, 개인이 사용하지 않기로 선택하는 경우가 될 수 있다고 하였다. 따라서 ⑤의 'the destiny of a technology determined by individual choices (개인의 선택에 의해 결정되는 기술의 운명)'이 제시문의 주제로 가장 적절하다.

오답풀이

① 자율성에 대한 기술적 비판

② 윤리가 혁신 기술에 미치는 영향

③ 윤리 기술을 이해하고 활용하는 방법

④ 사람들이 좋아하는 기술을 홍보해야 하는 이유

어휘

• unclear : 불확실한, 분명하지 않은

• inevitable : 불가피한, 필연적인

• perspective : 관점, 시각

• autonomous : 자주적인, 자치의

• individuals : 각각[개개]의

• elect : (선거로) 선출하다

• competitor : (특히 사업에서) 경쟁자[경쟁 상대]

• arise : 생기다, 발생하다

• argument : 논쟁; 언쟁, 말다툼

• implemented : 시행하다

• decisions : 결정, 판단

• Insofar : …하는 한에 있어서는

• reflect : 반영하다

해석

적어도 윤리적인 관점에서 기술이 어떻게 불가피할 수 있는지, 어떻게 자율적일 수 있는지 알 수 없다. 어떤 사람들은 주어진 기술을 사용하기로 선택하지만, 다른 사람들은 그렇지 않다. 어떤 기술이든, 모든 개인이 사용하지 않기로 선택하는 경우가 될 수 있다. 경쟁자가 생기거나 도덕적 논쟁이 나타나 다수의 사람들이 더 이상 기술을 사용하지 않도록 설득할 수 있다. 그 기술은 개인의 결정으로 인해 구현되지 않는다. 따라서 기술 또는 적어도 구현이 불가피한 것은 아니다. 그것을 유지하기로 한 개인의 선택에 의존하는 한, 그것은 자율적이지 않다. 기술의 필연성과 자율성을 바탕으로 기술 윤리를 구현하려는 노력은 사람들이 선택을 하는 방식을 반영하지도 않고, 윤리적 의사결정을 내리지도 않으며, 개인과 기술의 전체 관계를 반영하지도 않는다.

20 ⑤ 제시문에 따르면 이민자들이 미국의 어떤 주류 문화를 형성했는지에 대해 설명하고 있다. 그러므로 ⑤의 'The immigrants released their own cultures into the American mainstream. (이민자들은 그들만의 문화를 미국 주류로 내보냈다.)'가 제시문의 요지로 적절하다.

오답풀이

① 미국의 국경들은 예상치 못한 문제들을 극복했다.

② 그 위험한 피해는 새로운 사람들에 의해 일어났다.

③ 다양한 이민자들이 르네상스를 일으켰다.

④ 소문화는 미국의 공공생활에 적합하도록 변화된다.

어휘

• foreign–born : 외국 태생의

• native–born : 토박이

• minority : 소수자의

• professionals : 전문가

• priests : 사제들

• ministers : 장관들

• religions : 종교

• politics : 정치학

• institutions : 기관

• feast : 연회, 잔치

• emptied : 비어 있는, 빈

• Day of Atonement : 속죄일(금식하고 참회의 기도를 드리는 날)

• fraternal : 공제(共濟)의(사상·이해관계가 같은 개인·집단이 서로 돕기 위한 것)

• ghetto : (흔히 소수 민족들이 모여 사는) 빈민가[게토]

• ragtime : 래그타임

해석

물밀 듯이 밀려오는 외국태생과 토착태생, 백인, 흑인 등 다양한 인종. 소수만이 전문직 종사자였다: 사업가, 교사, 의사와 변호사, 성직자, 목사, 랍비. 대부분의 사람들은 공장을 가득 채우고, 집을 짓고, 바닥을 닦고, 유복한 자들의 아기들을 돌보는 일꾼들이었다. 그러나 이 새로운 거주자들은 더 많은 것을 도시로 가져왔다. 그들은 그들의 종교, 정치, 제도, 예술을 가져왔다. 그들은 마을 잔치에는 거리를 가득 메웠고 속죄일에는 거리를 비웠다. 그들은 작은 가게 앞 교회와 공제조직을 만들었다. 그들은 유대 연예인들이 그들의 기술을 연마하는 보드빌 극장들과 래그타임 밴드들이 미국 음악의 경계를 허무는 게토 댄스홀로 서둘렀다. 그리고 그들은 도시의 공공의 생활에 나타났다.

21 ③ 제시문은 대등하지 못한 지위를 누리고 있었지만 사과를 함으로써 독일의 도움을 받을 수 있게 된 체코에 대한 내용이다. 그러므로 ③의 'Apologies restore equilibrium in domestic and international relations. (사과는 국내외 관계의 평형을 회복하게 해준다.)'가 제시문의 요지로 가장 적절하다.

오답풀이

① 독일은 체코가 전후 행동에 대해 사과할 때까지 체코 피해자들에게 돈을 주지 않았다.
② 사과는 부유한 나라와 가난한 나라 사이의 분열을 바로잡는 데 도움을 준다.
④ 사과는 사람으로 하여금 지나간 일을 잊게 만든다.
⑤ 미국은 매독 치료를 거부당한 흑인들에게 사과했다.

어휘

- apologies : 사과
- veritable : (강조의 뜻으로 쓰여) 진정한
- Government : 정부, 정권
- demonstrate : 증거[실례]를 들어가며 보여주다, 입증[실증]하다
- wronged : 부당한 취급을 받은, 학대받은
- experiment : (과학적인) 실험
- effective : 효과적인
- restitution : 배상, 보상
- persecution : 박해, 학대
- formally : 정식으로, 공식적으로
- expulsion : (어떤 장소에서의) 축출[추방]
- receiving : 받는
- reparations : 배상금, 배상물
- responded : 대답[응답]하다, 답장을 보내다

해석

배려의 표시로서의 사죄의 힘은 우리가 지금 공식적으로 보고 있는 진정한 사태의 핵심에 있다. 예를 들어, 정부는 1997년 미국이 의학 실험의 일환으로 매독 치료를 거부당한 흑인들에게 사과했을 때처럼 부당했던 집단에 대해 관심이 있다고 발표할 수 있다. 다른 나라에 사과를 하는 것은 향후 협력의 토대를 마련하는 효과적인 방법이다. 1990년대 후반, 체코는 유럽 국가 중 유일한 국가로 남아 있었다. 2차 세계 대전 동안 있던 나치에 박해에 있어 독일이 배상금을 제공하지 않은 유일한 국가는 체코다. 독일은 체코가 전후 Sudetenland에서 독일계 동포를 추방한 것에 대해 공식적으로 사과할 때까지 체코 피해자들에게 배상금을 지불하기를 거부했다. 체코 정부는 1997년 나토 가입에 대한 독일의 지원과 배상금을 모두 받기 위해 사과의 뜻을 밝혔다. 독일은 체코의 이익을 위해 기금을 마련하는 것으로 대응했고, NATO와 유럽연합은 체코를 그들의 멤버에 합류하도록 초청했다.

22 ⑤ 이 제시문은 최악의 실수 중 하나는 당신이 무엇을 하든 모든 전화를 받는 습관을 들이는 것이라고 하며 전화를 다루는 방법에 대해 설명하고 있다. 그러므로 ⑤의 'Insulate yourself as much as possible from interruption. (방해를 받지 않도록 최대한 차단하라)'가 제시문의 요지로 가장 적절하다.

오답풀이

① 편안함과 즐거움을 함께 계획하라
② 성공에 대한 두려움이 사라지지 않도록 주의하라.
③ 자연스러운 최적의 작업 주기를 알아두어라
④ 성공을 최종 목적지가 아닌 과정으로 생각하라

어휘

- jarring : 삐걱거림, 진동; 부조화
- nervous : 신경이 과민한
- repeated : 반복[되풀이]되는
- interruptions : 중단(시키는 것), 중단(된 기간)
- midst : 중앙, 한가운데
- concentrating : (정신을) 집중하다[집중시키다], 전념하다
- worst : 가장 나쁜[못한], 최악의
- segment : 부분
- rude : 무례한, 예의 없는, 버릇없는
- wise : 지혜로운, 현명한, 슬기로운
- victim : (속임수를 당한) 피해자
- consciously : 의식[자각]하여
- enjoyment : 즐거움, 기쁨
- Beware : 조심[주의]하다
- fears : 공포, 두려움

(해석)

중요한 문제에 집중하고 있을 때 반복되는 방해만큼 신경계에 거슬리는 것은 없다. 최악의 실수 중 하나는 당신이 무엇을 하든 모든 전화를 받는 습관을 들이는 것이다. 전화를 다루는 좋은 방법은 오전 9시에서 10시 사이, 오후 4시에서 5시 사이 등 한 번에 통화를 집중시키는 것이다. 그 시간 동안 당신은 모든 전화를 받고, 당신에게 전화한 사람들에게 다시 전화해라. 바쁘다고 전화를 거절하는 건 무례한 행동이 아니다. 당신은 현명한 것이다. 만약 당신이 전화의 희생자라면, 전화 심사는 당신의 직장생활을 바꿀 수 있다.

23 ③ 제시문에서는 텔레비전이라는 단어를 사용하여 그 묶음의 다양한 부분, 즉 산업, 콘텐츠, 그리고 다른 모든 부분에 대해 이야기하기 때문에 텔레비전을 어렵게 생각할 필요가 없다고 한다. 또한 만약 우리가 삶의 모든 시스템의 모든 세부사항을 항상 생각해야 한다면, 우리는 과다 노출로 기절할 것이라고 했으므로 빈칸에는 'ambiguity(모호함)'이 들어갈 말로 가장 적절하다.

(오답풀이)

① 일관성
② 글을 읽고 쓸 줄 아는 능력
④ (자유) 재량(권)
⑤ 인기

(어휘)

- expressed : (감정의견 등을) 나타내다, 표(현)하다
- seems : (…인·하는 것처럼) 보이다
- confusing : (무엇이) 혼란스러운
- various : 다양한
- industry : 산업, 공업, 제조업
- content : (어떤 것의) 속에 든 것들, 내용물
- overexposure : 노출 과다
- bundling : 일괄 판매, 시스템 판매
- collect : 모으다, 수집하다
- preserve : (원래 상태좋은 상태를 유지하도록) 보존[관리]하다
- rare : (존재하는 수가 많지 않아서) 진귀한[희귀한]
- first editions : (책의) 초판
- mass-market : 일반 대중을 대상으로 한, 대량 판매 시장용의
- novel : (장편) 소설
- legitimately : 합법적으로, 정당하게

(해석)

가게에서 텔레비전을 살 수 있기 때문에 집에서 텔레비전을 볼 수 있지만, 당신이 사는 텔레비전은 당신이 보는 텔레비전

이 아니며 당신이 보는 텔레비전은 당신이 사는 텔레비전이 아니다. 그렇게 표현하면 혼란스러워 보이지만 일상 생활에서는 전혀 혼란스럽지 않다. 텔레비전이 무엇인지에 대해 너무 어렵게 생각할 필요가 없고, 텔레비전이라는 단어를 사용하여 묶음의 다양한 부분, 즉 산업, 콘텐츠, 가전제품에 대해 이야기하기 때문이다. 언어는 우리가 적절한 수준의 모호함을 가지고 일할 수 있게 해준다. 만약 우리가 삶의 모든 시스템의 모든 세부사항을 항상 생각해야 한다면, 우리는 과다 노출로 기절할 것이다. 이와 같은 객체 및 산업, 제품 및 서비스, 비즈니스 모델의 묶음들은 텔레비전에서만 볼 수 있는 것이 아니다. 희귀한 초판본을 수집보존하는 사람들, 그리고 대량 판매 시장용의 로맨스 소설을 사서 다음 주에 나눠주는 사람들은 모두 합법적으로 label book 애호가에게 권리를 주장할 수 있다.

24 ① 제시문에서 역사적 증언은 진위에 달려 있기 때문에, 전자 역시 실질적인 기간이 더 이상 중요하지 않게 되면 재생산에 의해 위태로워진다고 말하고 있다. 그러므로 빈칸에는 'authority(권한)'이 들어갈 말로 가장 적절하다.

(오답풀이)

② 소극성
③ 승진
④ 실적
⑤ 국한

(어휘)

- situations : 상황, 처지, 환경
- product : (어떤 과정에 의한) 산물
- mechanical : 기계적인
- reproduction : 복사, 복제
- bring : 가져오다, 데려오다
- presence : (특정한 곳에) 있음, 존재(함)
- depreciated : 가치가 떨어지다[절하되다]
- landscape : 풍경
- spectator : 관중
- nucleus : 중심
- interfered : 간섭[개입/참견]하다
- vulnerable : (~에) 취약한, 연약한
- transmissible : 보낼[전할, 전도할] 수 있는; 전염하는
- substantive : 실질적인
- duration : 지속, (지속되는) 기간
- testimony : 증거

(해석)

기계적 재생산의 산물을 가져올 수 있는 상황은 실제 미술 작품에 영향을 미치지 않을 수 있지만, 그 존재의 질은 항상 절하된다. 이는 영화가 관객보다 먼저 심사하는 풍경은 물론 미

술 작품까지 적용된다. 가장 민감한 중심인 미술 대상의 경우 진위성이 방해받는 반면, 점수에 취약한 자연 대상은 그렇지 않다. 사물의 진위는 그 실체적 지속 시간부터 그 실체적 증언, 그 실체가 경험한 역사까지 모든 것의 본질이다. 역사적 증언은 진위에 달려 있기 때문에, 과거 역시 실질적인 기간이 더 이상 중요하지 않게 되면 재생산에 의해 위태로워진다. 그리고 역사적으로, 정말로 위태로운 것은 증언은 대상의 권한에 영향을 받는다.

저 있다. 짝이 없는 전자를 가진 과산화물과 같은 원자와 분자를 자유라디칼이라고 한다. 자유 라디칼의 짝이 없는 전자는 원자나 분자를 불안정하게 만든다. 원자의 전자는 쌍으로 존재하지 않는다. 짝을 이루지 않은 전자를 가진 원자는 다시 안정되기를 원하기 때문에 다른 원자나 분자로부터 "훔쳐올" 또 다른 전자를 재빨리 찾는다. 활성산소의 불안정성은 DNA, RNA, 단백질, 그리고 지방산과 같은 거대 분자에 위협을 가하는 것이다.

25 ④ 제시문은 짝이 없는 자유라디칼에 대해 설명하고 있다. 자유라디칼의 짝이 없는 전자는 원자나 분자를 불안정하게 만든다. 원자들은 다시 안정되기를 원하기 때문에 훔쳐올 무언가를 찾는다고 한다. 그러므로 빈칸에는 ④의 'another electron(다른 전자)'이 들어갈 말로 가장 적절하다.

(오답풀이)

① 다른 세포
② 강력한 에너지
③ 안정된 핵
⑤ 영양분이 많은 단백질

(어휘)

• remember : 기억하다
• electrons : 음전하를 가지는 소립자
• orbiting : 궤도를 선회하는
• nucleus : (원자)핵
• atom : 원자
• stable : 안정된
• stability : 안정, 안정성[감]
• depend on : ~에 의존하다
• orbit : (특정 개인조직 등의) 영향권[세력권]
• pairs : (둘씩) 짝을 짓다
• unpaired : 짝이 없는
• superoxide : 슈퍼옥사이드
• molecules : 분자
• free radical : 짝짓지 않은 전자를 가지는 원자단
• steal : 훔치다, 도둑질하다
• instability : 불안정
• fatty acids : 지방산

(해석)

원자의 핵을 돌고 있는 전자를 기억해라. 이 전자들은 에너지를 포함하고 있지만, 이 에너지가 항상 안정적이지는 않다. 안정성은 원자 안에 있는 전자의 수에 따라 달라진다. 원자는 전자가 짝을 지어 공전할 때 더 안정적이다. 홀수 전자를 가진 원자는 짝이 없는 전자를 가져야 한다. 산소가 짝을 이루지 않은 전자 하나를 가지고 있을 때 그것은 슈퍼옥사이드로 알려

26 ① 귀인 이론이란 자신이나 다른 사람들의 행동의 원인을 찾아내기 위해 추론하는 과정을 설명하는 이론을 뜻한다. 사람들이 자신의 성공과 실패의 원인을 어떻게 설명하느냐에 초점을 맞춘다고 한다. 언어 수업에서 좋은 점수를 받지 못하였을 때 여러 가지 원인에 초점을 맞출 것이다. 그러므로 빈칸에는 ①의 'just plain old bad luck (그저 오래된 불운을 드러내기 위함)'이 들어갈 말로 가장 적절하다.

(오답풀이)

② 이전의 학습 경험
③ 언어 학습에 대한 지나친 자부심
④ 부적절한 교수법 사용
⑤ 자기 효능감의 부족

(어휘)

• underlying : (겉으로 잘 드러나지는 않지만) 근본적인[근원적인]
• self-esteem : 자부심
• learning : 학습
• fundamental : 근본적인
• attribution : 귀착시킴, 귀속, 귀인(歸因)
• self-efficacy : 자기 효능감
• failures : 실패
• describes : (~이 어떠한지를) 말하다[서술하다], 묘사하다
• explanations : 해명, 이유; 설명
• ability : (~을) 할 수 있음, 능력
• perceived : 인지된
• luck : 좋은 운, 행운
• internal : 내부의
• dimensions : 면적
• judged : (…로 미루어) 판단하다[여기다]

(해석)

언어 학습에서 자존감의 역할에 대한 이슈의 근본은 귀속과 자기 효율성의 개념이다. 귀인 이론은 사람들이 자신의 성공과 실패의 원인을 어떻게 설명하느냐에 초점을 맞춘다. Bernard Weiner는 성공 및/또는 실패에 대한 네 가지 설명(능력, 노력, 업무의 어려움 인식, 행운)으로 귀인 이론을 설명한

다. 이 네 가지 요소 중 두 가지는 학습자의 내부 요인, 즉 능력과 노력이다. 그리고 두 가지는 학습자의 내부 요인이다. 학습자 이외의 외부 상황(과제 난이도 및 행운)에 기인한다. Weiner에 따르면, 학습자들은 이 4차원의 과제를 성공적으로 수행했다고 설명하는 경향이 있다고 한다. 개인에 따라 여러 가지 인과적 결정 요인이 인용될 수 있다. 그러므로, 언어 수업 기말고사에서 높은 점수를 받지 못하는 것은 그들의 부족한 능력이나 노력의 결과라고 판단될 수 있고, 다른 사람들은 시험의 난이도가 높다고 여기고, 다른 사람들은 그저 오래된 불운을 드러내기 위해서라고 판단될 수도 있다.

27 ③ 제시문은 히스패닉계의 뉴요커들은 이 도시 인구의 51%를 차지하지만, Covid-19 사망자의 62%를 차지한다고 하며 그것은 그들의 여러 결과의 요인일 수 있음을 강조한다. 적절한 의료 서비스가 부족하며 여러 이유로 진단을 받기를 거부하는 요소들이 나열된다. 그러므로 ③ 'the virus exploits weaknesses (그 바이러스는 나약함을 이용한다)' 가 들어갈 말로 적절하다.

오답풀이
① 의사들은 그들의 역할을 하는 것을 꺼린다.
② 소수민족이 적합한 정책을 개발하다.
④ 우리는 긴급한 일을 이해했다.
⑤ Covid-19의 변종에 대한 치료는 교육을 필요로 한다.

어휘
• population : 인구, (모든) 주민
• account for : 설명하다
• compared with : ~과 비교하여
• adjusted : 조절[조정]된
• disparity : (특히 한쪽에 불공평한) 차이
• strongly : 튼튼하게
• associated : 관련된
• poorly : 좋지 못하게, 저조하게, 형편없이
• Lack of : ~이 부족하다
• appropriate : 적절한
• health care : 의료 서비스
• trust : 신뢰, 신임
• undiagnosed : 진단 미확정[회피]의
• potentially : 가능성 있게, 잠재적으로; 어쩌면
• diagnosis : 진단
• explanation : 해명, 이유; 설명

해석
흑인 및 히스패닉계 뉴요커들은 이 도시 인구의 51%를 차지하지만, Covid-19 사망자의 62%를 차지한다. 나이를 조절하여 봤을 때 백인에 비해 사망률이 두 배나 된다. 이러한 차이

는 여러 요인의 결과일 가능성이 높다. 고혈압과 당뇨병과 같은 병적 질환은 Covid-19로 인한 사망과 밀접한 관련이 있으며 흑인과 히스패닉의 사회에서 더 흔하다. 하지만 무엇이 고혈압과 당뇨병의 높은 비율을 야기할까? 적절한 의료 서비스가 부족하다. 돈, 시간, 위치 또는 믿음에 대한 이유로 집에 머물며 바이러스를 퍼뜨릴 가능성이 높을 수 있으며 치료와 진단의 지연을 경험할 수 있다. 이 설명은 이탈리아, 뉴올리언스, 그리고 아마도 이란과 같은 뉴욕시에 대해서도 마찬가지다: 이 바이러스는 나약함을 이용한다. 건강과 건강관리의.

28 ② 제시문은 창의성을 어떻게 정의해야 하는지 그 어려움에 관해 설명하고 있다. 심리학자와 사회학자들의 예시를 들며 어떤 논쟁을 벌이는지 서술하고 있다. 또한 역사적, 문화적 시대에 따라 그 정의가 달라짐을 설명하고 있다. 그러므로 창의성의 정의에 대해 설명하기 위해서는 그것이 무엇인지 동의해야 함을 이야기 한다. ②의 'first need to agree on what it is (그것이 무엇인지에 대해 동의)'가 들어갈 말로 적절하다.

오답풀이
① 일련의 규칙을 정해야 한다.
③ 이 단어에 대한 광범위한 연구를 해야한다.
④ 그 용어의 심리학적인 결과를 조사한다.
⑤ 주로 그 의미의 본질에 집중한다.

어휘
• sociocultural : 사회 문화적인
• attacking : 공격하다
• creativity : 창조적임, 창조성
• surprisingly : 놀랍게도
• argue : (논거를 들어) 주장하다, 논증하다
• definitions : (어떤 개념의) 의미[정의]
• intelligence : 지능
• institution : (특정 집단 사이에서 오랫동안 존재해 온) 제도 [관습]
• defining : 본질적인 의미를 규정하는
• creative : 창조적인, 창의적인
• complimentary : 칭찬하는
• praise : 칭찬, 찬사, 찬양
• whether : …인지 (아닌지)·(아니면 ~인지)
• useful : 유용한, 도움이 되는, 쓸모 있는
• scientific : 과학의

해석
사회문화적 접근은 문제의 핵심을 공격하는 것으로 시작된다. 창의성이란 무엇인가? 창의성을 설명하기 위해서는 먼저 그것이 무엇인지에 대해 동의해야 하는데, 이것은 놀랄 만큼 어

려운 것으로 나타났다. 모든 사회과학은 일상적이고 친숙해 보이는 개념을 정의해야 하는 과제에 직면해 있다. 심리학자들은 지능, 감정, 기억의 정의에 대해 논쟁을 벌인다; 사회학자들은 집단, 사회 운동, 그리고 제도의 정의에 대해 논쟁을 벌인다. 하지만 창의성을 정의하는 것은 사회과학이 직면한 가장 어려운 일 중 하나일 수 있다. 왜냐하면 모두가 창의적이라고 믿고 싶어하기 때문이다. 사람들은 일반적으로 "창의력"을 칭찬의 표현으로 사용한다. 역사적, 문화적 시대에 따라 창의적이라고 불리는 것이 달라졌다는 것이 밝혀졌다. 심리학자들은 때때로 우리가 창의성에 대한 합의를 이끌어낼 수 있을지, 심지어 그것이 과학 연구에 유용한 주제일지에 대해서도 궁금해 했다.

되었다. 신문은 세계를 움츠러들게 만들었다. 그리고 전신은 그것을 훨씬 더 극적으로 축소시켰다. 모든 혁신과 함께, 예언자들은 우리가 기술적 종말론에 직면하고 있는지 아니면 유토피아에 직면하고 있는지에 대해 언쟁을 했다. 빅토리아 시대 전문가에게 물어본 바에 따르면, 전신은 세계 평화의 시대를 안내하거나 바보 같은 잡동사니로 우리를 빠져들게 할 것이다. 물론 어느 예측도 옳지 않았지만, 어느 것도 틀리지 않았다. 종말론자와 유토피아가 모두 이해하고 동의하는 한 가지는 모든 새로운 기술이 우리를 새롭고 친숙한 행동으로부터 멀어지게 하면서 새로운 형태의 행동으로 내몰고 있다는 것이다. 기술이 우리의 일상생활에 어떻게 편향시키는지 이해하는 것을 의미한다.

29 ⑤ 제시문은 새로운 기술로 사는 것은 사고방식과 행동에 영향을 미친다는 이야기이다. 따라서 사고와 행동에 영향을 미친다는 문장이 나와야 한다. 그러므로 빈칸에는 ⑤ 'how they bias everyday life (기술이 우리의 일상생활에 어떻게 편향시키는가)'가 들어갈 말로 적절하다.

(오답풀이)

① 왜 기술이 과거에 무시당했는지
② 전신이 제 기능을 하는 방법
③ 미래에는 어떤 혁신이 이루어져야 하는가
④ 기술 혁신을 일으키는 요소

(어휘)

• shapes : (중요한 영향을 미쳐서) 형성하다
• cognition : 인식, 인지
• enlarging : 확대[확장]하다, 확대[확장]되다
• knowledge : 지식
• dramatically : 희곡[연극]적으로, 극적으로
• bickered : 다투다
• technological : 과학[공업] 기술의[에 관한], (과학) 기술(상)의
• apocalypse : (성서에 묘사된) 세상의 종말
• pundit : 전문가
• wrong : 틀린, 잘못된
• pushes : (힘으로) 밀어붙이다[젖히다], 밀치다
• nudging : (…을 특정 방향으로) 살살[조금씩] 밀다[몰고 가다]
• familiar : 익숙한, 친숙한
• understanding : (특정 주제·상황에 대한) 이해
• functions : (사람·사물의) 기능
• bias : 편견, 편향

(해석)

모든 새로운 기술은 우리의 사고방식을 형성한다. 인쇄된 단어는 우리의 지식을 저장하는 것을 크게 확장시키는 것과 함께 우리의 인식을 선형적이고 추상적으로 만드는 데 도움이

30 ③ 제시문은 도덕적인 주장에 관한 설명이다. 도덕적인 논쟁의 혼란은 우리가 다른 사람들에게 강요할 권리가 없다는 생각에서 생겨난다. 즉, 우리의 견해를 다른 사람들에게 강요해서는 안 된다는 하나의 주장이 있다고 설명한다. 도덕적인 논쟁은 입장을 고려하기를 거부할 때 중단된다고 했으므로 빈칸에는 ③의 'that is just your opinion(그것은 단지 당신의 의견)'이 들어갈 말로 가장 적절하다.

(오답풀이)

① 말보다는 행동이 중요하다.
② 당신의 의견에 전적으로 동의한다.
④ 나도 같은 처지야
⑤ 겉만 보고 판단하지 마라

(어휘)

• argument : 논쟁; 언쟁, 말다툼
• stopped : 멈춘, 정지된; 저지된
• refuses : (요청·부탁 등을) 거절[거부]하다
• opinion : (개인의) 의견[견해/생각]
• implication : (행동·결정이 초래할 수 있는) 영향[결과]
• judgement : 판단력
• bearing : 관련, 영향
• similarly : 비슷하게, 유사하게
• implied : 함축된, 은연중의, 암시적인, 언외의
• disapprove : 탐탁찮아[못마땅해] 하다
• relevance : (표현 등의) 적절, 타당성
• confusion : (정신 상태의) 혼란
• deny : (무엇이) 사실이 아니라고 말하다, 부인[부정]하다
• asserting : (사실임을 강하게) 주장하다
• respect : 존중, 정중

(해석)

도덕적인 논쟁은 누군가가 '그것은 단지 당신의 의견'이라고 말하면서 입장을 고려하기를 거부할 때 종종 중단된다. 그 의

미는 누군가의 판단력이 다른 사람만큼 뛰어나고, 아무도 다른 사람에게 말할 권리가 없다는 것이다. 내가 바나나를 좋아하지 않는다는 사실은 나에 대한 사실일 수 있지만, 당신이 무엇을 좋아하는지와는 상관이 없다. 이와 비슷하게, 내가 어떤 것에 동의하지 않는다면, 그것은 나에 대해 말해 줄 수 있지만, 그것은 당신이 해야 할 일과 관련이 없다. 이 모든 것의 혼란은 우리가 다른 사람들에게 말 할 '권리'가 없다는 생각에서 나타난다. 우리는 도덕적 주장이 모두를 구속할 수 있다는 것을 부인하는 동시에, 우리 모두가 존중해야 할, 즉 우리의 견해를 다른 사람들에게 강요해서는 안 된다는 최소한 하나의 도덕적 주장이 있다고 하는 것 같다.

31 ① (A) 애착의 성격이 매우 중요하며 나중에 만들 수 있는 믿음에 강한 영향을 미친다고 한다. 처음에 경험한 애착에 관하여 설명하고 있으므로 빈칸에 들어갈 연결어구는 예시의 의미를 나타내는 'for example(예를 들어)'가 가장 적절하다.

(B) 처음 경험한 애착이 애증이 엇갈리는 감정을 느꼈다면 결국 그만두는 경향으로 이어진다고 한다. 이어지는 내용은 안정된 애착을 경험한 사람에 대한 설명이 나오므로 비교의 의미를 나타내는 'In comparison(~와 비교하여)'이 가장 적절하다.

어휘

- initial : 처음의, 초기의
- attachments : 애착
- crucial : 중대한, 결정적인
- development : 발달, 성장
- social : 사회의, 사회적인
- influence : 영향
- ambivalent : 반대 감정이 병존하는, 애증이 엇갈리는
- insecure : (자기 자신에 대해서나 다른 사람과의 관계에 대해) 자신이 없는
- commitment : 헌신
- reluctantly : 마지못해서, 꺼려하여
- enthusiastic : 열렬한, 열광적인
- alert : (문제·위험 등을) 경계하는
- perceived : 인지된
- straightforward : 간단한, 쉬운, 복잡하지 않은
- reasonably : 합리적으로
- steadfast : (태도·목표가) 변함없는
- membership : 회원 (자격·신분)

해석

우리가 삶에서 처음 경험한 애착의 성격은 나중에, 우리의 발달과 사회적, 정서적 경험에 매우 중요하다. 이러한 애착은 우

리가 나중에 만들 수 있는 믿음에 강한 영향을 미친다. (A) 예를 들어, 만약 처음에 경험한 애착이 애증이 엇갈리는 감정이었다면, 안전하다고 느끼는 것과 불안하다고 느끼는 것 사이를 왔다갔다 한다면, 그것은 또한 집단에 대한 개인의 헌신이 될 수 있다. 어떤 사람은 마지못해 이익집단에 가입하거나, 잠시 동안 열성적이 되기는 하지만, 그 집단의 다른 구성원들이 초래한 사회적 경시나 지위 상실에 대해 끊임없이 경계하게 된다. 이것은 그만두는 경향으로 이어질 것이다. (B) 이와 비교하여 처음에 경험한 애착이 안정적이었던 사람은 그룹에 가입하고 회원 자격을 합리적으로 확고하게 유지하는 데 직접적인 방법으로 끌릴 수 있다.

32 ② 제시문은 보편적인 창조예술의 의문에 관해 서술하고 있다. 재즈와 록의 혁신은 인간의 경험에서 더 직접적으로 생겨난다고 하며 해답을 알려줄 수 있을 것이라고 한다. 그러나 ②의 할리우드 작곡가들이 재즈의 어휘와 록의 구조화 모델을 실험하였다는 문장은 전체적인 글의 흐름과 어울리지 않는다.

어휘

- deeper : (위에서 아래까지) 깊은
- probe : 캐묻다, 캐다, 조사하다
- different : 다른, 차이가 나는
- depth : (위 표면에서 아래쪽 바닥까지의) 깊이
- exploring : 탐구[분석]하다
- causation : (다른 사건의) 야기
- dominated : (...의) 가장 중요한[두드러지는] 특징이 되다
- arising : 생기다, 발생하다
- directly : 곧장, 똑바로
- excavate : 발굴하다, 출토하다
- Nevertheless : 그럼에도 불구하고
- composers : (특히 클래식 음악) 작곡가
- experimenting : 실험하기
- entail : 수반하다
- universal : 보편적인
- evolutionary biology : 진화 생물학
- literate : 글을 읽고 쓸 줄 아는

해석

다른 시각에서 다른 시각으로 더 깊이 들어가 인과관계를 탐구할 때. 창조 예술이 역사를 통틀어 모든 곳에서 인간의 마음을 빼앗은 이유는 무엇일까? 우리는 최고의 미술관과 심포니 홀에서도 답을 찾지 못할 것이다. ① 재즈와 록의 혁신은 인간의 경험에서 더 직접적으로 생겨나는데, 아마도 우리에게 그 답을 더 잘 알려 줄 수 있을 것이다. ② 그럼에도 불구하고 할리우드 작곡가들은 재즈의 용어와 록의 구조화 모델을 실험

하기 시작했다. ③ 창조 예술은 보편적이고 유전적인 특성을 수반하기 때문에 답은 진화 생물학에 있다. ④ 호모 사피엔스는 약 10만년 동안 존재해 왔지만 문맹 문화는 그 중 10분의 1도 되지 않았다. ⑤ 그래서 왜 보편적인 창조 예술이 있는지에 대한 미스터리는 인간이 존재의 처음 10분의 9동안 무엇을 하고 있었는지에 대한 질문으로 귀결된다.

33 ③ 제시문은 유리가 깨지지 않도록 작업하는 방법에 대해 서술하고 있다. pull-type 스크레이퍼를 사용하며, 유리고정핀을 제거하려면 pull-type 스크레이퍼의 날카로운 모서리를 부드러운 metal points에 걸고 퍼티와 함께 당겨 빼내라고 한다. 그러나 ③의 유리 제조사들이 생산 원가를 줄이기 위해 공장을 동아시아 일부 국가로 이전하기 시작했다는 것은 전체적인 글의 흐름과 어울리지 않는다.

어휘

- keep : (특정한 상태·위치에)계속 있다[있게 하다]
- break : 깨어지다, 부서지다; 깨다, 부수다
- movement : (몸·신체 부위의) 움직임
- parallel : (두 개 이상의 선이) 평행한
- pressure : 압박, 압력
- scraping : (무엇을 긁거나 깎아서 생긴) 부스러기
- scraper : (흙·성에 등을) 긁어내는 도구
- away from : ~에서 떠나서
- glazing points : 유리고정핀(퍼티가 완전히 굳기 전까지 유리를 고정시키기 위해 설치하는 끝이 뾰족한 작은 못)
- manufacture : (기계를 이용하여 대량으로 상품을) 제조[생산]하다
- factories : 공장
- production cost : 생산비
- beside : 옆에
- edge : (가운데에서 가장 먼) 끝, 가장자리, 모서리
- loose : (떨어질 것처럼) 헐거워진[풀린]

해석

유리가 깨지지 않도록 하려면 유리 근처와 유리의 모든 움직임이 평행이어야 하며(긁을 때 유리에 압력을 가하지 않아야 함), 항상 pull-type 스크레이퍼를 사용해야 한다. ① 그렇게 하면 모든 힘이 유리에서 떨어져서 깨지지 않는다. ② 유리고정핀을 제거하려면 pull-type 스크레이퍼의 날카로운 모서리를 부드러운 metal points에 걸고 퍼티와 함께 당겨 빼낸다. ③ 유리 제조사들은 생산 원가를 줄이기 위해 공장을 동아시아 일부 국가로 이전하기 시작했다. ④ 유리 부분이 모두 제거되었는지, 유리 가장자리 옆과 아래에 있는 오래된 퍼티가 느슨한지 다시 확인한다. ⑤ 그렇지 않다면, 당신은 다시 한 번의 열기가 필요하다.

34 ③ 주어진 문장에서 심리학자들과 행동 생태학자들은 유전적 전달보다 학습능력을 우선시 해야 한다고 하였다. 그러므로 글 (B)에서 그러한 전달 수단은 학습 비용을 피하고 자손이 접하는 환경은 부모의 환경과 비슷하기 때문이라고 설명한다. 뒤에 이어질 내용으로 (C) 과거의 경험은 예측 가치가 없고 학습된 반응보다 고정된 반응의 유전적 전달이 선호된다고 한다. 마지막으로 (A) 데이비드 스티븐스는 위와 같은 의견에 동의하면서도 다양한 유형의 안정성은 분리되어야 한다며 환경 안정성에 대한 가정에 이의를 제기해 왔다고 설명하고 있다. 그러므로 주어진 글 다음에 (B) - (C) - (A)의 순으로 이어져야 한다.

어휘

- Psychologists : 심리학자
- ecologist : 생태학자
- favoured : (조건 등이) 좋은
- environment : (주변의) 환경
- often : 자주, 흔히, 보통
- In such a case : 그런 경우
- stable : 안정된, 안정적인
- enough : 필요한 만큼의[충분한]
- stability : 안정, 안정성[감]
- separated : 갈라선
- genetic : 유전의, 유전학의
- rarely : 드물게, 좀처럼 …하지 않는
- learning : 학습
- Past experience : 과거 경험
- predictive : 예측[예견]의
- fixed : 고정된
- Somewhere : 어딘가에[에서/에로]
- worth : …의 가치가 있는[되는]

해석

심리학자들과 행동 생태학자들은 동물이 사는 환경이 자주 변하지만 적당히 변할 때 고정된 특성의 유전적 전달보다는 학습 능력이 우선시 되어야 한다고 생각한다.

(B) 정보는 환경이 거의 변하지 않을 때 유전적 전달에 의해 전달되는 것이 가장 좋다. 왜냐하면 그러한 전달 수단은 학습 비용을 피하고 자손이 접하는 환경은 부모의 환경과 비슷하기 때문이다. 하지만 환경이 끊임없이 변화한다면 배운 것이 다음 상황에서 완전히 무관한 것이므로 배울 가치가 없다.

(C) 따라서 과거의 경험은 예측 가치가 없다. 학습된 반응보다는 고정된 반응의 유전적 전달이 좋다. 변하지 않는 환경과 항상 변하지 않는 환경 사이 어디쯤에서 배움은 학습 비용을 지불할 가치가 있기 때문에 고정된 반응의 유전적

전달보다 좋다.

(A) 이 경우 환경은 학습에 유리할 정도로 안정적이지만 유전적 전달에 유리할 정도로 안정적이지 않다. 데이비드 스티븐스는 위와 같은 의견에 동의하면서도 다양한 유형의 안정성은 분리되어야 한다며 환경 안정성에 대한 가정에 이의를 제기해 왔다.

35 ① 주어진 문장에서 최근 창의성 이론 중 하나는 심리경제학이라고 하였다. 그것은 창의성을 뒷받침하는 교육을 설계하는데 문제의 이유를 명확히 하는데 도움이 된다고 한다. 그에 대한 예시가 나와야 하므로 (A) 예를 들어 교육 목표에 대한 개념을 고려한다고 한다. 이어지는 문장은 커리큘럼이 명확한 보상을 받아야 함을 의미하지만 창의성을 그렇지 않다는 (C)가 와야 한다. 마지막으로 (B) 창의적 사고는 독창적이기 때문에 문제의 효익이 불확실하고 비용을 정당화하기 어렵다는 설명이 있어야 한다. 그러므로 주어진 글 다음에 (A) - (C) - (B)의 순으로 이어져야 한다.

어휘

- psychoeconomic : 심리학과 경제학의 특성을 가지고 있는
- applies : 쓰다, 적용하다
- clarify : 명확하게 하다, 분명히 말하다
- designing : 설계의, 도안의
- creativity : 창조적임, 창조성; 독창력, 창조력
- Consider : 사례[고려/숙고]하다
- educational : 교육의, 교육적인
- objectives : 목적, 목표
- accountability : 책임 (있음), 의무
- original : 독창적인
- definition : (어떤 개념의) 의미[정의]
- educator : 교육자
- open-ended : 제약[제한]을 두지 않은
- uncertain : 불확실한, 불안정한
- justify : 정당화시키다[하다], 해명[옹호]하다

해석

가장 최근의 창의성 이론 중 하나는 심리경제학이다. 이것은 교육에 직접적으로 적용되는 것처럼 들리지는 않겠지만, 실제로 교실에서 해야 할 일이 무엇인지, 그리고 창의성을 뒷받침하는 교육을 설계하는 데 문제가 있는 이유를 명확히 하는 데 도움이 된다.

(A) 예를 들어, 교육 목표에 대한 개념을 고려한다. 교육자들은 학교생활에 많은 시간과 자원을 가지고 있을 뿐이며, 적어도 미국에서는 오늘날의 학교에서는 많은 책임감이 있다.

(C) 이는 커리큘럼이 명확한 보상을 받아야 함을 의미한다. 창

의성은 그렇지 않다. 그것은 종종 학생의 본질적인 동기부여와 개별 학생의 자기표현에 달려있다.

(B) 또한 창의적 사고는 독창적이기 때문에, 교육자가 실제로 창의적 사고를 할 수 있는 열린 과제를 제시한다면 그 결과가 어떻게 될지 알 수 없다. 따라서 문제는 효익이 불확실하고 비용(즉, 시간의 투자)을 정당화하기 어렵다는 것이다.

36 ⑤ 주어진 문장은 일부 사업은 회계기간이 경과함에 따라 각 매각을 특정 판매원가와 일치시키는 것이 실용적이지 않다고 한다. 그러므로 판매 수익을 판매 당시 판매된 상품의 원가와 일치시킨다는 문장의 뒤인 ⑤에 위치하는 것이 가장 적절하다.

어휘

- practical : 현실[실질/실제]적인
- figure : (특히 공식적인 자료로 제시되는) 수치
- period : 기간, 시기
- identified : 확인된, 인정된, 식별된
- inclusion : 포함
- income : 소득, 수입
- statement : 성명, 진술, 서술
- retailers : 소매업자, 소매상; 소매업
- devices : 장치
- simultaneously : 동시에
- particular : 특정한
- relatively : 비교적
- revenue : (정부·기관의) 수익[수입/세입]
- accounting : 회계 (업무)
- period : 기간, 시기

해석

그러나 일부 사업(예: 소규모 소매업체)은 회계기간이 경과함에 따라 각 매각을 특정 판매원가와 일치시키는 것이 실용적이지 않다고 생각한다.

기간 동안의 판매원가(또는 판매된 재화의 원가) 수치는 다른 방법으로 식별할 수 있다. (①) 일부 사업장에서는 판매시점에 판매원가를 파악한다. (②) 매출액은 매출원가와 밀접하게 일치하므로 손익계산서에 포함하기 위한 매출원가를 식별하는 것은 문제가 되지 않는다. (③) 많은 대형마트(예: 슈퍼마켓)는 각각의 판매를 기록하는 동시에 특정 판매의 대상이 되는 상품의 원가를 픽업하는 POS(Point-of-Sale) 장치를 보유하고 있다. (④) 상대적으로 적은 수의 고부가가치 품목을 판매하는 다른 사업체들도 판매 수익을 판매 당시 판매된 상품의 원가와 일치시키는 경향이 있다. (⑤) 이들은 회계기간 말에 판매원가를 보다 쉽게 파악할 수 있다.

[37~38]

어휘

- mustered : (특히 병사들이) 소집[동원]되다, 소집[동원]하다
- completing : 완료하다, 끝마치다
- duty : 직무, 임무
- hostility : 적의, 적개감, 적개심
- fellow : 같은 처지에 있는, 동료의
- parades : 열병식
- unpopular : 인기 없는
- incident : (국가 간의, 흔히 무력이 개입되는) 사건[분쟁]
- chain-smoking : 줄담배를 피우다
- isolation : 외로운[고립된] 상태
- appeared : 나타나다, 보이기 시작하다
- timidly : 겁많게, 소극적으로
- gesture : (특정한 감정의도의) 표시[표현]
- undoubtedly : 의심할 여지없이, 확실히
- continuing : 연속적인, 계속적인
- survived : 살아남다, 생존[존속]하다
- stranger : 낯선[모르는] 사람

해석

1970년 6월 23일, 나는 베트남에서 1년간의 군복무를 마치고 막 전역했다. 나는 23세의 육군 참전용사로 캘리포니아 오클랜드에서 텍사스 달라스로 귀국하는 비행기에 타고 있었다. 나는 당시 많은 동포들이 적개심을 느꼈다는 경고를 받았다. 우리가 그 평판이 좋지 않은 전쟁에서 집으로 돌아왔을 때 우리를 위한 고향의 열병식은 없었다. 수만 명의 다른 사람들처럼, 나도 아무런 일도 없이 집에 가려고 했다.

나는 제복을 입고 창가 좌석에 앉아 줄담배를 피우며 동료 승객들과 눈을 마주치지 않았다. 옆자리에 아무도 앉지 않아 고립감을 더했다. 10살이 채 안 된 어린 소녀가 갑자기 통로에 나타났다. 그녀는 미소를 지으며 말없이 소심하게 나에게 잡지 한 권을 건넸다. 나는 그녀의 잡지를 받아들였다. "집에 온 것을 환영한다." 라는 말에 "고맙다"는 말밖에 할 수 없었다. 그녀가 어디에 앉았는지, 누구와 함께 있었는지 모른다. 왜냐하면 그녀에게서 잡지를 받은 직후, 나는 창문 쪽으로 몸을 돌려 눈물을 흘렸기 때문이다. 그녀의 작은 연민의 몸짓이 내가 오랜만에 경험하는 것이었다.

저 어린 소녀는 의심의 여지없이 수년 전 일에 대한 기억이 없다. 나는 그녀가 커서 다른 사람들을 보듬어 주고 그녀의 아이들에게도 똑같이 하도록 가르친다고 생각한다. 어머니로부터 나에게 "선물"을 주라는 말을 들었을 수도 있다는 걸 안다. 그녀의 아버지는 그 시점에 아직 베트남에 있었을 수도 있고 전쟁에서 살아남지 못했을 수도 있다. 그녀가 왜 나에게 그 잡지를 주었는지는 중요하지 않다. 중요한 건 그녀가 그랬다는 사실이다.

그 이후로, 나는 그녀를 본받았고, 다른 방식으로 그들을 위해 똑같이 하려고 노력했다. 오래 전에 비행기를 탔던 나처럼, 그들은 왜 낯선 사람이 시간을 내어 손을 뻗었는지 결코 알 수 없을 것이다. 하지만 그 이후로 내 시도는 모두 그 어린 소녀 때문이라는 것을 알고 있다. 그녀가 지치고 겁에 질려 외로운 군인에게 잡지를 주었다는 것은 내 인생에서 상기된다.

37 ② 제시문은 환영받지 못한 군인에게 베푼 낯선 소녀의 위로에 대한 내용이다. 낯선 소녀의 작은 친절에 군인은 크게 감동을 느끼며 그녀를 본받기 위해 노력한다고 했다. 그러므로 제시문의 제목으로는 ②의 'A Small Act of Kindness Matters (작은 친절의 중요성)'이 가장 적절하다.

오답풀이

① 전투에서 승리할 수 있을까?
③ 용기있는 병사의 승리
④ 참전용사들의 마음의 고통
⑤ 어린 소녀 찾기

38 ② 서술자는 군인 중 한 사람으로 1970년 6월 23일, 베트남에서 1년간의 군복무를 마치고 막 전역했다. 그러므로 ②의 'The narrator had been one of the military personnel. (서술자는 군인 중 한 사람이다.)'은 제시문의 내용과 일치한다.

오답풀이

① 서술자는 한 달 후에 베트남으로 돌아가야 한다.
③ 서술자는 어린 소녀로 하여금 감정적으로 상처를 받았다.
④ 그 어린소녀는 서술자의 좋은 친구였다.
⑤ 어린 소녀는 서술자의 발자취를 따라갔다.

[39~40]

어휘

- twentysomething : 20대 풋내기
- period : 기간, 시기
- adulthood : 성인(임), 성년
- equivalent : (가치·의미·중요도 등이) 동등한[맞먹는]
- quarterlife crisis : 청년위기
- overwhelming : 압도적인, 너무도 강력한[엄청난], 저항[대응]하기 힘든
- instability : 불안정
- apprehension : 우려, 불안
- encounter : (특히 반갑지 않은 일에) 맞닥뜨리다[부딪히다]
- disorientation : 방향 감각 상실, 혼미
- confusion : (정신 상태의) 혼란

정답 및 해설

- independence : (개인의) 자립
- premature : 너무 이른, 시기상조의
- emerging : 최근 생겨난, 최근에 만들어진
- infinite : (수량이) 무한한[무한정의]
- mind : 마음, 정신
- steel : (~에 대비해서) 마음을 단단히 먹다

해석

20대 연령대를 성인이 된 시기라고 부르는 경우가 많다. 어떤 사람들은 30살이 되는 것이 이제 한 세대 전에 21살이 되는 것과 같다고 말한다. 청년 위기라는 용어는 20대들이 직면하고 있는 문제와 문제들을 묘사하기 위해 만들어졌다. 최근 대학 졸업자들에 따르면, 분기별 위기는 "압도적인 불안정성, 끊임없는 변화, 너무 많은 선택, 그리고 극심한 공포의 무력감"이라고 한다. 가족과 대학의 보호 영역을 떠날 때 20대는 정체성, 직업 선택, 생활 준비, 독립성 확립, 삶의 열정을 발견하고 활용하고 새로운 소셜 네트워크를 만드는 것에 대한 방향 감각과 혼란을 겪는다. 주요한 삶의 결정을 내리고 책임을 받아들이는 경험이 거의 없는 20대들은 무엇을 해야 하고, 어디로 가야 하고, 누가 되어야 하는지에 대한 지침을 찾으려는 전환의 영역에 놓여 있다. 시행착오의 시기로 조급한 결심을 하고 때로는 우유부단으로 마비되기도 한다.

39 ③ 제시문은 청년위기라는 용어를 사용하며 20대들이 겪는 불안감에 대해 서술하고 있다. 삶의 결정을 내리고 책임을 받아들이는 경험이 없는 20대들은 전환의 영역에서 큰 혼란스러움을 겪는다고 한다. 그러므로 ③ 'Challenges : What the Emerging Adult Faces (도전 : 성인에 직면하다)'가 제시문의 제목으로 가장 적절하다.

오답풀이
① 20대의 전성기
② 20대의 청춘
④ 20대의 무한한 가능성
⑤ 20대의 강한 정신

40 ⑤ 주요한 삶의 결정을 내리고 책임을 받아들이는 경험이 거의 없는 20대들은 무엇을 해야 하고, 어디로 가야하고, 누가 되어야 하는지에 대한 지침을 찾으려는 전환의 영역에 놓여 있다고 한다. 그러므로 빈칸에는 ⑤의 'trial and error(시행착오)'가 들어갈 말로 가장 적절하다.

오답풀이
① 몸과 마음
② 원인과 결과
③ 자랑거리
④ 장단점

[41~42]

어휘

- filial imprinting : 부모 각인
- range : (변화차이의) 범위[폭]
- elicit : (정보·반응을 어렵게) 끌어내다
- imprinting : 각인
- visual : 시각의, (눈으로) 보는
- auditory : 청각의
- olfactory : 후각의
- Movement : (몸·신체 부위의) 움직임
- stationary : 움직이지 않는, 정지된
- important : 중요한
- properly : 제대로, 적절히
- individual : 각각[개개]의
- odor : 냄새
- chain : 일련, 띠(처럼 이어진 것)
- demonstrates : 증거[실례]를 들어가며 보여주다, 입증[실증]하다
- shrews : 땃쥐류

해석

모체에 대한 반응을 부모 각인이라고 한다.

어린 새들의 접근과 애착을 이끌어낼 수 있는 물체의 범위는 매우 크다. 각인 자극은 시각, 청각 또는 후각일 수 있다. 시각 자극의 범위에는 제한이 없는 것 같다. 움직임은 번쩍이는 불빛처럼 주의를 끌도록 돕는다. 정지된 물체는 배경과 대비되는 경우라면 어린 새들을 유인할 수 있다.

청각 자극은 많은 어린 새들에게 매력적인 것으로 밝혀졌다. 예를 들어, 청둥오리 새끼들에게 있어 소리는 어미를 따라가도록 유도하는 데 매우 중요하다. 미국원앙새는 나무 구멍에 둥지를 튼다. 둥지 구멍 밖의 물에서 어머니의 부름은 어린 아이들이 어머니를 제대로 보지 못했음에도 불구하고 어미에게 다가가게 된다.

냄새 자극의 예는 생후 5일에서 14일 된 아기 땃쥐에 의해 제공된다. 아기 땃쥐들은 그들을 돌보는 어미의 냄새에 각인된다. 어린 땃쥐들은 일찍부터 어미의 냄새를 알게 되어 캐러밴을 형성하게 되며, 그 냄새를 따라가게 된다. 생후 5~6일 된 땃쥐를 다른 종의 어미가 돌보게 되면 이 돌봐준 어미의 냄새가 땃쥐에게 각인된다.

나중에, 그 땃쥐들이 15일이 되면, 그들은 그들의 진짜 어미에게로 돌아간다. 이 형제들은 그녀를 따라가지도 않고, 어떤 형제들에게도 사슬처럼 캐러밴을 형성하지도 않는 것으로 보였다. 하지만, 그들은 그들을 돌봐준 어머니의 냄새가 스며든 천 조각을 따라갔다. 어린 땃쥐들이 어렸을 때 그들을 돌보는 어미의 냄새로 각인된다는 것을 보여주는 반응이다.

41 ① 주절의 주어 'The range'가 단수 이므로 동사도 단수가 되어야 한다. 따라서 'are'는 'is'로 고쳐야한다.

42 ② 아기 땃쥐들은 그들을 돌보는 어미의 냄새에 각인된다. 어린 땃쥐들은 일찍부터 어미의 냄새를 알게 되어 캐러밴을 형성하게 되며, 그 냄새를 따라가게 된다. 생후 5~6일 된 땃쥐에게 다른 종의 어미를 대신하면 이 어미의 냄새가 땃쥐에게 각인된다고 하였으므로 빈칸에는 ②의 'odor of whoever nurses them when they are young (어렸을 때 그들을 돌보는 어미의 냄새)'가 들어가는 것이 가장 적절하다.

⟨오답풀이⟩
① 그들이 돌봐준 어머니를 따라다니며 보낸 시간
③ 둥지를 떠나기 전에 돌봐주는 어미를 부른다
④ 그들의 친모에 대한 시각적 관심의 양
⑤ 그들이 자라서 친모를 돌본다

[43~45]

⟨어휘⟩
• handgun : 근접 전투용 · 호신용 총기
• expressionless : 표정[감정]이 없는
• sideways : 옆으로, 옆에서
• awning : (창이나 문 위의) 차양, 비[해] 가리개
• seasick : 뱃멀미
• mottle : 얼룩덜룩하게 하다
• obscured : 잘 알려져 있지 않은, 무명의
• admission : 입장료
• Canadian : 캐나다 사람
• intensity : 강렬함, 강함, 격렬함
• deck : (배의) 갑판
• deprived : 궁핍한, 불우한
• whenever : …할 때는 언제든지
• locker : 로커, (자물쇠가 달린) 개인 물품 보관함
• wristband : 손목 밴드
• warm : (더) 따뜻해지다, 데워지다
• psyched : (특히 곧 있을 일에 대해) 들뜬[흥분한]

⟨해석⟩
(A) "과일이나 권총을 소지하고 계십니까?"
"물론, 트렁크에는 3킬로그램의 키위가 있고 그녀의 지갑에는 44구경 매그넘이 들어 있습니다."
아니, 국경수비대엔 그렇게 말하지 않았다. 이 사람들하고는 농담하지 않는 게 좋다. 그들은 유머 감각이 별로 없고 차를 뒤지는 것을 좋아한다. 국경수비대는 나를 긴장시킨다. 그 무표정한 눈과 얼어붙은 얼굴을 벗어나자마자 기분

이 좋아졌다.

(B) 비가 옆으로 내리면서 덮개로 쓰려고 했던 비 가리개 안으로 다시 들어가게 된다. 페리가 흔들리기 시작했다. 마가렛은 디젤 연기와 파도로 인해 뱃멀미를 할 때 시칠리아에서 몰타까지 페리를 타고 갔던 이야기를 들려준다. 몇몇 아이들은 플라스틱 시트를 위 아래로 움직이며 장난감 자동차를 운행하고 있다. 빗방울 창을 통해 보는 산꼭대기는 안개 속에 가려져 있다. 곧 우리는 저편 부두로 차를 몰고 들어간다. 배에서 차들이 줄이어 떨어지고, 온천까지 9마일이라는 소리가 들렸다. 캐나다인의 입장료는 $4.00이다.

(C) Kootenai 호수를 따라 50마일을 도는데, 자동차가 전체 길을 통과할 수 있는 지점은 약 3개뿐이다. 우리는 마지막 탑승차였다. 남색 옷을 입은 항해사가 아래쪽 갑판에 있는 주차 공간으로 안내한다. 우리는 승객 층까지 가파른 계단을 오른다. 여객선이 부두에서 벗어나 호수를 가로질러 향할 때 바람과 비가 강렬해진다. 단 1분 동안만, 갑판 위로 걸어갈 뿐이지만.

(D) 하지만 Ainsworth의 여행은 백 명의 국경 수비대를 맞닥뜨릴 가치가 있는 곳이다. Ainsworth Hot Springs. 몇 년 전부터 가고 싶었다. 내가 아는 사람들은 전부 그곳을 방문했다. 누가 Ainsworth 얘기를 할 때마다 박탈감이 들 정도였다. 그래서 내 친구 마가렛과 나는 춥고 비가 오는 11월 화요일에 온천에 가기엔 나쁘지 않은 하루를 보낸다. 캐나다 몇 마일 들어가면 길이 바뀐다.

(E) 사물함은 없다. 각자 옷을 넣을 비닐봉지를 준비한다. 접수번호가 적힌 벨크로 손목밴드를 나눠주는 점원에게 확인한다. 내 것은 380이다. 수영장으로 향할 때 비가 내 몸에 얼룩덜룩 묻게 내린다. 따뜻한 커다란 수영장, 기분전환하기에 좋은 장소, 위쪽의 수영장과 동굴들. 동굴들! 그게 바로 Ainsworth가 특별한 이유다. 우리는 뜨거운 물을 따라 다시 산중턱으로 노를 저어 들어간다. 희미한 불빛이 놀라운 광경을 보여준다.

43 ③ 국경수비대에게는 농담을 하지 않는 것이 좋다며 여행의 서막을 알리는 지문이 나온다. 하지만 Ainsworth의 여행은 백 명의 국경 수비대를 맞닥뜨릴 가치가 있는 곳이라며 Ainsworth Hot Springs에 대하여 그 가치를 서술하는 (D)가 나오는 것이 적절하다. 캐나다로 몇 마일을 돌면 길이 바뀐다고 하였고 이어지는 (C)로 자동차가 전체 길을 통과할 수 있는 지점은 약 3개뿐이며, 필자는 마지막 탑승차라는 것이 이어짐이 적절하다. 페리가 부두에서 벗어나 호수를 가로질러 향할 때 바람과 비가 강렬해진다고 하였으므로 비가 옆으로 내리면서 필자가 덮개로 쓰려고 하는 비 가리개 안으로 다시 들어가게 된다는 설명의 (B)가 이어지는 것이 적절하다. 마지막으로 (E)의 동굴들! 그게 바로 Ainsworth가

정답 및 해설

특별한 이유라고 하였다. 마침내 Ainsworth를 마주한 필자의 감동적인 심정이 이어지는 것이 적절하다.

44 ② 필자는 누군가 Ainsworth얘기를 할 때마다 박탈감이 들 정도로 그곳에 가고 싶었다. 따라서 Ainsworth에 가고싶은 마음이 확고하였다(determined). 마침내 Ainsworth에 도착한 순간 신이 나고 흥분한(excited) 모습을 보인다.

오답풀이

① 안도하는 → 정신적으로 긴장한

③ 겁먹은 → 놀란

④ 유감스러워 하는 → 열성적인

⑤ 낙담한 → 무관심한

45 ② Ainsworth가 캐나다 국경에서 얼마나 떨어져 있었는지는 언급되지 않았다. 그러므로 ②의 'Ainsworth was nine miles away from the anadian border. (Ainsworth는 캐나다 국경에서 9마일 떨어져 있었다.)'는 제시문의 내용과 일치하지 않는다.

오답풀이

① 해설자는 국경수비대와 가벼운 대화를 나누지 않았다.

③ 여행객들은 페리에서 폭우와 바람을 만났다.

④ Margaret은 필자와 함께 여행을 갔다.

⑤ 동굴은 Ainsworth를 다른 온천과 구별하게 만든 핵심이다.

2021학년도 기출문제 정답 및 해설

제2교시 영어영역

01 ②	02 ③	03 ②	04 ③	05 ④	06 ③
07 ⑤	08 ①	09 ①	10 ③	11 ⑤	12 ④
13 ⑤	14 ①	15 ③	16 ⑤	17 ②	18 ⑤
19 ③	20 ④	21 ①	22 ④	23 ②	24 ①
25 ①	26 ②	27 ①	28 ⑤	29 ③	30 ①
31 ②	32 ②	33 ③	34 ④	35 ③	36 ⑤
37 ⑤	38 ④	39 ④	40 ①	41 ③	42 ④
43 ③	44 ④	45 ③			

01 ② 'tawdry'는 '저속한'의 의미로 'immoral(음란한)'과 그 의미가 가장 유사하다.

오답풀이
① 합법적인
③ 열정적인
④ 뜻밖의
⑤ 기이한

어휘
• rock star : 록 스타
• tawdry : (싸구려 티가 나게) 번쩍거리는[야한], 저속한, (도덕적으로) 지저분한
• affair : 일[사건], 불륜(관계), 정사
• shockwave : 충격파, (나쁜 일로 인한) 충격적인 여파
• passionate : 열정적인
• weird : 기이한, 섬뜩한

해석
그 록 스타의 저속한 불륜 소식은 전 세계 팬들을 충격에 빠뜨렸다.

02 ③ 'irk'는 '짜증스럽게 하다'의 의미로 'annoy(짜증나게 하다, 귀찮게 하다)'와 그 의미가 가장 유사하다.

오답풀이
① 몰아내다
② 속임수를 쓰다

④ 실망한
⑤ 설득하다

어휘
• suburb : 교외
• irk : 짜증스럽게[귀찮게] 하다
• apartment : 아파트, 콘도
• neighbor : 이웃, 옆자리 사람
• ousted : 몰아내다

해석
Joanne은 아파트 이웃들에게 쉽게 짜증이 나기 때문에 교외의 한 집으로 이사했다.

03 ② 'parsimonious'는 '(돈에 지극히) 인색한'의 의미로, 'stingy((특히 돈에 대해) 인색한[쩨쩨한])'와 그 의미가 가장 유사하다.

오답풀이
① 무관심한
③ 먼
④ 목적
⑤ 사려 깊은

어휘
• philanthropist : 독지가, 자선가
• pass away : 사망하다
• relative : 친척
• reveal : 드러내다[밝히다/폭로하다]
• parsimonious : (돈에 지독히) 인색한
• lifestyle : 생활 방식
• apathetic : 무관심한, 심드렁한

해석
자선가가 세상을 떠난 후, 가까운 친척들은 그가 자신의 생활 방식에 관해서라면 인색했었다는 것을 밝혔다.

04 ③ 'languid'는 '나른한'의 의미로 'peaceful(평화로운)'과 그 의미가 가장 유사하다.

오답풀이
① 더딘

② 습한
④ 변덕스러운
⑤ 매력적인

어휘

• favorite : 매우 좋아하는
• pastime : 취미
• porch : 현관
• languid : (움직임이) 힘없는, 나른한
• tardy : 더딘, 늦은[지체된]
• capricious : 변덕스러운, 잘 변하는

해석

Brown 씨가 가장 좋아하는 취미 생활은 나른한 여름 오후의 현관에 앉아 있는 것이었다.

05　④ 'arcane'은 '신비로운'의 의미로 'secretive(비밀스러운)'와 그 의미가 가장 유사하다.

오답풀이

① 동일한
② 향상된
③ 상속한
⑤ 변화가 많은

어휘

• cheesecake : 치즈 케이크
• popular : 인기 있는
• among : ~중에서
• New Yorker : 뉴욕시민
• recipe : 조리[요리]법
• arcane : 신비로운, 불가사의한
• generation : 세대[대]
• identical : 동일한, 똑같은
• inherited : 상속한, 유전의
• diversified : 변화가 많은

해석

Marley의 치즈 케이크는 뉴욕시민들 사이에서 매우 인기가 있으며, 그들의 레시피는 대대로 신비로웠다.

06　③ Dan's 백화점에 가는 길을 묻는 A에게 B는 처음에는 30분 정도 걸어가야 한다고 말했다. 그러나 A가 너무 멀다며 다른 방법을 묻자 여기서 두 블록 떨어진 곳에서 M11 버스를 타고 가면 된다고 말한다. 그 뒤에 이어지는 A의 질문에 Houston Street 정류장이라고 답하였으므로, ③의 "Where do I get off?(어디서 내려야 하죠?)"가 빈칸에 들어갈 말로 가장 적절하다.

오답풀이

① 버스로 얼마나 걸릴까요?
② 걷기로 하면 어때요?
④ Dan's까지 길을 안내해줄 수 있나요?
⑤ 몇 시에 문을 여는지 아나요?

어휘

• department store : 백화점
• half-hour : 30분
• besides : ~외에, 게다가, 뿐만 아니라
• get off : 떠나다, (타고 있던 것에서) 내리다
• direction : 방향[위치]
• lead : 안내하다[이끌다/데리고 가다]

해석

A : 실례합니다만, Dan's 백화점으로 가는 길을 아십니까?
B : 물론이죠. 하지만 여기서 30분 정도 걸으면 좋아요.
A : 그건 꽤 머네요. 걷는 것 말고 다른 방법은 없을까요?
B : 여기서 두 블록 떨어진 곳에서 M11 버스를 타도 돼요.
A : 어디서 내려야 하죠?
B : Houston Street 정류장. Dan's는 거기서 멀지 않아요.
A : 내릴 때 누군가에게 길을 물어볼게요. 정말 고마워요.
B : 괜찮아요. 행운을 빌어요.

07　⑤ 이제 졸업을 하며 정식으로 경찰이 되어 Tonawanda 경찰서에서 일을 하게 될 Lee 생도에게 Louis 경사가 축하 인사를 전하고 있다. 빈칸에는 마지막으로 자신에게 해줄 지혜로운 말이 있느냐는 Lee 생도의 물음에 대한 답변이 들어가야 한다. 그에 대해서 Lee 생도가 "I won't"라고 하며 항상 시민들을 위해 일을 하겠다고 다짐을 하였으므로 경찰로서의 좌우명을 잊지 말라는 ⑤의 "Never forget our motto, "to serve and to protect.""("봉사와 보호"라는 우리의 좌우명을 절대 잊지 마라.)"가 빈칸에 들어갈 말로 가장 적절하다.

오답풀이

① 경찰로서의 특전을 활용하라
② 열심히 하면 훌륭한 경찰이 될 수 있다
③ 누구든 범인이 될 수 있으니 항상 의심하라
④ 이 일이 네게 맞지 않는다면 내게 알려주렴

어휘

• cadet : (경찰·군대의) 간부[사관] 후보생, 생도
• sergeant : 병장, 경사
• deserve : …을 받을 만하다
• parting words : 결별의 인사
• citizen : 시민, 주민

- perk : 특전
- officer of the law : 경(찰)관
- suspicious : 의혹을 갖는, 수상쩍은
- criminal : 범죄의, 범죄자, 범인
- motto : 모토, 좌우명

해석

A : 축하해, Lee 생도.

B : 감사합니다, Louis 경사님.

A : 오늘 졸업식이 끝나면 Tonawanda 경찰서에서 정식으로 경찰관이 될 거야.

B : 네. 스스로 믿겨지지가 않네요.

A : 넌 그럴 자격이 있어. 너 정말 열심히 했잖아.

B : 감사합니다. 해주실 지혜로운 결별 인사가 있으십니까?

A : "봉사와 보호"라는 우리의 좌우명을 절대 잊지 마.

B : 그럴게요. 저는 항상 우리 도시의 시민들을 위해 일할 것입니다.

A : 나는 네가 우리를 자랑스럽게 만들 거라고 확신해.

08 ① 'which' 뒤의 문장이 불완전한 문장이기 때문에 이때의 which는 관계부사로 쓰인 것이 아니다. 그러므로 전치사 + 명사절을 만들기 위해서 선행사를 포함하는 관계대명사 what을 써서 ①의 'which'를 'what'으로 고쳐 써야 한다.

어휘

- complicated : 복잡하게 만들다
- intelligent : 총명한, 똑똑한, 지능이 있는
- out of touch with : ～과 동떨어져 있다
- hiccups : 딸꾹질
- singultus : 딸꾹질
- physician : 의사, 내과 의사
- ridiculous : 웃기는, 터무니없는
- diaphragm : 횡격막
- irritate : 짜증나게 하다, 거슬리다, 자극하다
- rapidly : 빨리, 급속히, 신속히, 순식간에
- irregular : 고르지[가지런하지] 못한, 불규칙적인
- distension : 팽창, 확대
- gastric : 위(胃)의
- tobacco : 담배
- excess : 지나침, 과도, 과잉
- excitement : 흥분, 신남

해석

의사들은 복잡한 단어들을 사용하는 것으로 알려져 있는데, 복잡한 단어들은 매우 지능적이거나 대부분의 사람들이 이해할 수 있는 것과 완전히 동떨어지게 들리게 한다. 딸꾹질을 뜻하는 의학 용어인 singultus는 의사들이 우스꽝스럽게 들렸을

때를 보여 주는 완벽한 예다. 딸꾹질은 횡격막이 자극되어 불규칙한 소리를 내는 방식으로 공기를 빠르게 밀어올릴 때 발생한다. 횡격막을 자극하고 딸꾹질을 유발하는 것은 음식, 알코올 또는 공기, 위가 팽창하는 현상, 위 온도의 급격한 변화 또는 알코올 및/또는 담배를 과도하게 사용하는 것이다. 딸꾹질은 또한 흥분이나 스트레스에 의해 유발될 수 있다. 대부분의 딸꾹질은 몇 분밖에 지속되지 않지만, 딸꾹질의 몇몇 경우는 며칠 또는 몇 주 동안 지속될 수 있다. 하지만 이것은 매우 이례적인 일이긴 하지만, 이것은 보통 또 다른 의학적 문제의 징후다.

09 ① 'since' 뒤에 완전한 문장이 왔으므로 이 문장에서 'since'는 '～이후로'의 의미를 지닌 시간의 접속사이다. 이때 주절의 동사는 현재완료 또는 현재완료진행을 쓰고 부사절인 since절에는 과거시제를 써야하므로 'was'로 고쳐 써야 한다.

어휘

- wrench : 확 비틀다, 삐다
- tinker with : ～을 서투르게 만지작거리다[손을 대다]
- mechanic : 정비공
- population : 인구, (모든) 주민
- rural area : 시골 지역
- ethos : (특정 집단·사회의) 기풍[정신]
- carry over : (다른 상황에서 계속) 이어지다
- encourage : 격려[고무]하다, 권장[장려]하다

해석

Tim Richardson의 엄마인 Doris Bohannon은 그가 세 살 때부터 자전거를 탔고 그 후 얼마 되지 않아 비틀거렸다고 말한다. 그리고 그녀는 알아야 한다. 그녀는 쓰레기 더미에서 망가진 자전거를 집으로 가져와 아이들이 만질 수 있도록 그에게 자전거를 고치는 법을 가르쳐준 사람이다. 인구 832명의 웨스트 버지니아 주 Odd에서 자란 Richardson은 "엄마는 집안에서 정비공이다"라고 말한다. "농촌에 살면서 당신은 직접 자전거 수리하는 법을 배웠거나, 타지 않았거나 중 하나이다." 그 정신은 버지니아주 해리슨버그에 있는 그의 자전거 가게인 Shenandoah 자전거 회사로 이어졌고, 그곳에서는 고객들이 그들 자신의 자전거 문제를 알아내도록 격려한다.

10 ③ (A) 8월은 여름이라 덥고 햇빛이 강하기 때문에 아스팔트가 뜨거워진다는 내용이 전개되어야 하므로 'heat(열)'이 적절하다.

(B) 도로의 색을 밝게 하는 것이 지구 온난화를 낮추는 데 도움이 된다는 이야기를 하면서 '알베도'에 대한 설명을 해야 하므로 표면에서 태양 에너지를 'reflective(반사하

정답 및 해설

는)'가 적절하다.

(C) 뒷부분에 'cool roof'가 냉방비를 20% 이상 줄일 수 있다고 하였으므로 열 흡수율이 낮은 지붕 재질을 선택하면 에너지를 절약할 수 있다는 내용이 되므로 'absorbs(흡수하는)'가 적절하다.

어휘

- parking lot : 주차장, 주차 지역
- blacktop : 아스팔트, 아스팔트 도로
- soak up : 빨아들이다, 흡수하다
- rethink : 다시 생각하다[재고하다]
- pavement : 인도, 보도
- calculate : 계산하다, 산출하다, 추정하다
- keep out of : ~에 들이지 않다
- global warming : 지구 온난화
- billion : 10억
- roughly : 대략, 거의, 거칠게
- equivalent : 동등한[맞먹는]
- elegantly : 우아하게, 고상하게
- albedo : 알베도(달·행성이 반사하는 태양 광선의 비율)
- abrasive : 거친, 거슬리는
- reflective : 빛[열]을 반사하는
- consciousness : 의식, 자각
- climate : 기후, 분위기, 풍조
- absorb : 흡수하다, 빨아들이다
- repel : 격퇴하다, 쫓아 버리다
- substantial : 상당한

해석

8월에 주차장을 건넌 사람은 아스팔트가 (A) 열을 많이 흡수한다는 것을 알고 있다. 우리 주변의 표면의 색을 재고하는 것이 지구를 식히는 데 도움이 될 수 있을 것이 드러났다. 지붕과 보도는 도시 지역의 60%를 차지한다. 과학자들은 전세계적으로 그들의 색깔을 밝게 하는 것이 485억 톤의 이산화탄소를 대기 중에 배출하지 못하게 하는 것과 같은 효과를 지구 온난화에 가져올 수 있다고 계산한다. 그것은 대략 18년 동안 세계의 모든 자동차를 도로에서 떼어내는 것과 맞먹는다. 이 우아하고 간단한 해결책은 알베도-표면에서 태양 에너지를 (B) 반사하는 정도의 증가 때문에 효과가 있다. 집으로 갈수록, 색채 의식이 기후변화와 싸우는 것보다 더 많은 것을 한다. 열을 덜 (C) 흡수하는 지붕 재질을 선택하는 것은 상당한 에너지 절감을 의미할 수 있다. "쿨루프"가 냉방비를 20% 이상 줄일 수 있다는 연구결과가 나왔다.

11 ⑤ (A) 70억 명의 사람들이 각자 가지고 있는 70억 개의 의제들 중 큰 그림(지구 온난화나 자유 민주주의와 같은)을 생각하는 것은, 당장 하루하루 생존의 위기에 놓인 사람들에게는 부족할 것 없는 자들의 배부른 소리라고 느껴질 수 있으므로 'luxury(사치)'가 적절하다.

(B) 큰 그림을 사치라 말하면서 지금 당장 생존의 위기에 놓인 사람들의 예를 들고 있는 문장이므로 바다 한가운데서 발 디딜 땅을 찾는 'refugees(난민들)'가 적절하다.

(C) 끼니를 걱정하고, 정착할 땅을 찾고, 조금이라도 삶을 더 살아보려는 노력이 지구 온난화나 자유 민주주의와 같은 문제보다 훨씬 생존과 직결되는 문제이므로 'urgent(시급한)'가 적절하다.

어휘

- agenda : 의제[안건]
- relatively : 비교적
- frugality : 절약, 검소
- struggling : 발버둥 치는, 기를 쓰는, 분투하는
- refugees : 난민
- vacationers : 휴가객, 피서객
- Mediterranean : 지중해
- overcrowded : 너무 붐비는, 초만원인
- trivial : 하찮은, 사소한
- urgent : 긴급한, 시급한
- crisis : 위기, 최악의 고비
- liberal democracy : 자유 민주주의

해석

70억의 사람들이 70억의 의제를 가지고 있는데, 큰 그림을 생각하는 것은 비교적 보기 드문 사치다. 뭄바이 빈민가에서 두 아이를 키우느라 고군분투하는 미혼모 한 명이 다음 식사에 집중하고, 지중해 한복판에 있는 배를 탄 난민들이 지평선을 살피며 육지의 흔적을 살피고, 초만원인 런던 병원에서 죽어가는 한 남자가 한 번 더 숨을 들이쉬기 위해 남은 모든 힘을 모은다. 그들 모두는 지구 온난화나 자유 민주주의의 위기보다 훨씬 더 시급한 문제를 안고 있다.

12 ④ 제시문은 해양 플라스틱이 해양에 미치는 환경적 문제에 대한 내용이다. 수많은 해양 동물들이 이로 인해 피해를 보고 있는데, 글쓴이는 이를 하와이의 빅아일랜드에서 해변을 걷다가 플라스틱을 밟으며 심각한 문제로 인식하게 되었다고 하였다. 문맥상 오염되어 있지 않은 해변에서조차 미세플라스틱이 발견되었다는 내용이 와야 하므로 ④의 'tainted(오염된)'을 'untainted(더럽혀지지 않은)' 등으로 바꿔 써야 적절하다.

오답풀이

① 멸종위기에 처한
② 눈에 띄게

③ 크기

⑤ 재앙

어휘

- estimate : 추산[추정]하다
- million : 백만
- marine animal : 해양 동물
- endangered : 멸종위기에 처한
- affected : 영향을 미치다
- visibly : 눈에 띄게, 분명히
- strangle : 교살하다, 옭죄다
- abandon : 버려진, 유기된
- discard : 버리다, 폐기하다
- zooplankton : 동물성 플랑크톤
- microplastic : 미세 플라스틱 조각
- taint : 더럽히다, 오염시키다
- paved road : 포장도로
- ankle-deep : 발목까지 올라오는
- crunch : 으드득[뽀드득], 아작아작 씹다
- looming : 어렴풋이 보이기 시작하는, 무시무시한
- catastrophe : 참사, 재앙
- mention : 말하다, 언급[거론]하다

해석

해양 플라스틱은 매년 수백만 마리의 해양 동물을 죽일 것으로 추정된다. 멸종위기종을 포함한 700여 종이 피해를 본 것으로 알려졌다. 일부는 버려진 어망이나 버려진 6팩 고리에 의해 눈에 띄게 목이 죄인 채 해를 입는다. 아마도 눈에 보이지 않게 해를 입은 경우도 많을 것이다. 동물성 플랑크톤에서 고래에 이르기까지 모든 크기의 해양 종들은 현재 가로 세로 5분의 1인치보다 작은 미세 플라스틱을 먹는다. 하와이 빅아일랜드의, 오염되어온(→ 더럽혀지지 않은) 것 같은 해변에서, 포장도로가 없이 이어진 길을, 나는 발목까지 올라오는 미세 플라스틱 사이로 걸어왔다. 그들은 내 발밑에서 라이스 크리스피들처럼 으드득거렸다. 그 후, 나는 왜 몇몇 사람들이 해양 플라스틱을 기후 변화와 같이 언급할만한 다가오는 재앙으로 보는지 이해할 수 있었다.

13 ⑤ 제시문은 위기에 대처하는 자아의 힘에 대해 설명하면서 어떠한 위기 상황에서 자아의 힘이 줄 수 있는 여러 가지 긍정적인 영향을 나열하고 있다. 위기에서 발생하는 두려움을 약화시키는 것도 자아의 힘의 긍정적 영향 중 하나일 것이다. 그러므로 ⑤의 'reinforcing(강화하는)'을 'weakening(약화하는)' 등으로 바꿔 써야 적절하다.

오답풀이

① 광범위한

② 쾌히 받아들이는

③ 인정

④ 용인하다, 참다, 견디다

어휘

- factor : 요인, 인자
- cope : 대처[대응]하다
- crisis : 위기, 최악의 고비
- psychologist : 심리학자
- strength : 힘
- independent : 독립된
- dependent on : …에게 의존하고 있는
- approval : 인정, 찬성, 승인
- tolerate : 용인하다, 참다, 견디다
- perceive : 감지[인지]하다
- accurately : 정확히
- sound : 건전한, 건강한, 소리
- essential : 필수적인
- reinforce : 강화하다
- paralyze : 마비시키다, 무력[무능]하게 만들다
- arise : 생기다, 발생하다

해석

위기에 대처하는 데 중요하고 사람마다 다른 요인은 심리학자들이 '자아의 힘'이라고 부르는 것이다. 그것은 자신감을 포함하지만 훨씬 더 광범위하다. 자아의 힘이란 자기 자신에 대한 감각을 가지고 있고, 목적 의식을 가지고 있으며, 자신을 있는 그대로 받아들이는 것을 의미하며, 인정이나 생존을 위해 다른 사람에게 의존하지 않는 자랑스러운 독립된 인격체로 자신을 받아들이는 것을 의미한다. 자아의 힘은 강한 감정을 참을 수 있고, 스트레스 안에서 집중을 유지할 수 있으며, 자신을 자유롭게 표현하고, 현실을 정확하게 인지하며, 건전한 결정을 내릴 수 있는 것을 포함한다. 그러한 연계된 자질들은 새로운 해결책을 모색하고 위기에서 종종 발생하는 마비되는 두려움을 강화하는 데(→ 약화하는 데) 필수적이다.

14 ① 식당에는 가금류가 들어오는 것이 허용되지 않는 것이 보통이지만, San Marcos 카페는 다양한 가금류가 식당 주변에 돌아다니는 것으로 유명하다. 특히 Buddy라는 레그혼 수탉은 오랫동안 카페에서 비공식 웨이터 주임으로 있었을 정도였으므로, 'Various poultry can be spotted around the cafe. (카페 주변에서 다양한 가금류를 발견할 수 있다)'는 ①의 설명이 제시문의 내용과 일치한다.

⑤ 그의 사진작품은 Science지에 실렸다.

어휘

⑤ 그의 사진작품은 Science지에 실렸다.

오답풀이

② 수탉이 식탁 공간에 들어갈 수 있도록 한다.

③ 수탉 한 마리가 10년 전부터 웨이터 역할을 했다.

④ Buddy의 의상은 빨간 넥타이로 구성되었다.

⑤ 그들은 더 이상 계피롤을 제공하지 않는다.

어휘

• quite : 꽤, 상당히

• mismatched : 짝을 잘못 짓다

• flock : 떼, 무리

• peacock : (수컷) 공작

• peahen : (암컷) 공작

• cavort : 신이 나서 뛰어다니다

• poultry : 가금(닭·오리·거위 따위)

• tenure : 임기, 재임 기간

• maitre d' : 웨이터 주임, 호텔 지배인

• notwithstanding : …에도 불구하고, 그래도

• cozy : 아늑한, 친밀한

• ranchhouse : 목장주 주택, 랜치 하우스

• spot : 점, 얼룩, 발견하다

해석

San Marcos 카페를 방문했을 때 상당한 인사를 기대하라. 어울리지 않는 수컷 공작과 암컷 공작, 야생 칠면조, 그리고 수탉의 무리들은 모두 식당 앞과 뒤쪽을 돌아다닌다. 식당에는 가금류가 허용되지 않지만, 약 15년 전에 Buddy라는 이름의 아주 유명한 레그혼 수탉 한 마리가 있었는데, 그는 이 식당의 비공식적인 웨이터 주임으로 오랫동안 복역했다. 검은 넥타이를 맨 Buddy는 문앞에서 기분 좋게 손님을 맞았고 아침식사 시간 내내 울었다. 방황하는 닭들에도 불구하고, San Marcos 카페는 진정한 발견이다. 시골 부엌 스타일로 꾸며진 아늑하고 매력적인 목장으로, 최고의 계피롤 중 하나를 제공한다.

15 ③ 제시문은 생태학자이자 생물학자인 Thomas Eisner의 연구들과 업적에 대한 이야기를 하고 있다. 그는 곤충과 절지동물에 대한 연구를 하고 Jerrold Meinwald를 도와 화학 생태학 분야를 연구하는 등의 업적이 많은데, 그의 아내와는 여러 자연 속의 사진을 찍어 Science지에 실리기도 하였다고 서술되어 있다. 그러므로 'His wife founded the field of chemical ecology. (그의 아내와 화학 생태계를 세웠다)'라는 ③의 설명은 제시문의 내용과 일치하지 않는다.

오답풀이

① 파킨슨병 합병증으로 81세에 사망했다.

② 그는 곤충이 먹이를 어떻게 잡는가에 관심이 있었다.

④ 그의 의제는 열대우림의 생물 다양성을 보호하는 것을 포함했다.

어휘

• ecologist : 생태학자

• evolutionary biologist : 진화 생물학자

• complications : 합병증

• bombardier beetles : 폭탄먼지벌레

• arthropod : 절지동물(곤충, 거미, 게 등)

• capture : 포로로 잡다, 포획하다

• prey : 먹이[사냥감]

• collaborator : 공동 연구자, 합작자

• outspoken : 노골적으로[거침없이] 말하는

• conservationist : 환경 보호 활동가

• biodiversity : 생물 다양성

• larval hook : 유충 갈고리

• grace : 우아함, 품위, 꾸미다[장식하다]

해석

코넬 대학의 생태학자 겸 진화 생물학자인 Thomas Eisner는 지난주 81세의 나이로 파킨슨병으로 인한 합병증으로 사망했다. 거미줄에서부터 폭탄먼지벌레에 이르기까지 다양한 주제에 대한 수백 편의 저널 기사에서, Eisner는 곤충과 절지동물이 어떻게 스스로를 방어하고 먹이를 잡으며 때때로 복잡한 방법으로 짝을 유혹하는지를 탐구했다. 코넬의 협력자 Jerrold Meinwald와 함께, 그는 화학 생태학 분야, 즉 동물과 식물이 어떻게 화학물질을 사용하여 의사소통을 하는지에 대한 연구를 하는 것을 도왔다. 노골적인 환경 보호 활동가인 Eisner는 생물 다양성을 보호하기 위한 기금을 마련하기 위해 기업들이 유용한 화학물질을 얻기 위해 열대우림에서 "생물자원 탐사"를 할 수 있도록 하는 아이디어를 홍보했다. Eisner는 또한 유명한 과학 작가이자 피아니스트였고, 그의 아내 Maria와 함께, 유충 갈고리, 딱정벌레 털, 그리고 다른 미세한 경이로운 사진들로 Science지의 많은 페이지와 표지를 장식했던 자연 사진작가였다.

16 ⑤ 제시문에 따르면 인플레이션 이후 미국의 평범한 중위 가계소득은 정체되어 있고, 기업들은 생산성과 임금 문제를 더욱 해치고 있다. 그러므로 제시문의 제목으로는 ⑤의 'Economic Outlook for the Average Joe: Cloudy with Rain(평범한 사람의 경제전망: 흐리고 비)'이 가장 적절하다.

오답풀이

① 인플레이션: 경제의 큰 장애물

② 기업투명성에 대한 국민의 요구

③ 테크노크라트가 재채기를 하면 은행들은 감기에 걸릴까?

④ 유럽경제 약세의 나비효과

어휘

- median : 중앙에 있는, 중앙값
- household : (한 집에 사는 사람들을 일컫는) 가정
- income : 수입, 소득
- adjust : 조정하다, 적응하다
- stagnate : 침체되다, 부진해지다
- soar : 급증[급등]하다[치솟다]
- stark : 삭막한[황량한], 냉혹한, 극명한
- direction : (위치·이동의) 방향, (발전·전개해 나가는) 방향
- corporate : 기업[회사]의, 법인(체)의
- productivity : 생산성
- wage : 임금
- accompany : 동반하다
- hollowing : 산업공동화
- democracy : 민주주의
- replacement : 교체, 대체
- hurdle : 허들[장애물]
- demand : 요구, 요구하다, 따지다
- transparency : 투명도[투명성]
- faltering : 비틀거리는
- outlook : 관점, 전망

해석

1967년 이후 인플레이션에 맞춰 조정된 미국의 중위 가계소득은 미국 최고 부자들의 부와 소득이 급증했음에도 불구하고 인구의 하위 60%에 대해 정체되었다. 유럽의 변화는 덜 극명하지만 같은 방향을 가리키고 있다. 기업 이익은 1960년대 이후 최고 수준이지만 기업들은 투자보다는 저축을 선택함으로써 생산성과 임금을 더욱 해치고 있다. 그리고 최근, 이러한 변화들은 민주주의의 공동화와 세계화된 엘리트들에 의한 기술정치적 통치로 대체되는 것을 동반하고 있다.

17 ② 개인 병실에 누워서 Fred에 대해 회고하고 있는 내용이므로, ②의 'Reminiscing About a Bedfellow on a Dark Morning(어두운 아침의 잠동무에 대한 회고)'이 가장 적절하다.

오답풀이
① 책 대 애완동물: 누가 더 좋은 동반자를 만들까?
③ 사랑하는 닥스훈트로부터의 희망의 메세지
④ 예상치 못한 강아지의 도착: 새로운 시작
⑤ 의료정치 이면의 진실

어휘
- starlings : 찌르레기
- vantage : 우세, 유리, 유리한 점[위치]
- democrat : 민주주의자, 민주당원
- lack : 부족, 결핍
- dachshund : 닥스훈트(몸통과 귀가 길고 다리가 짧은 작은 개)
- occasion : 때[기회/경우], 행사
- everlasting : 영원한, 변치 않는, 끊임없는
- attend : 주의를 기울이다, 참석하다
- lecherous : 호색의
- physician : 의사, 내과 의사
- reluctantly : 마지못해서, 꺼려하여
- rumple : 헝클다
- oppressive : 억압적인, 후텁지근한, 답답한
- fraudulent : 사기를 치는
- improvement : 향상, 개선, 호전
- rudeness : 버릇없음, 무례함, 오만함
- pretension : 허세, 가식, 주장, 자처
- versus : …대(對)
- companion : 동반자, 동행
- medical care : 의료, 건강 관리

해석

난 지금 2번가와 3번가 사이에 있는 마을 동쪽에 있는 내 개인 병실에 누워 침대의 유리한 지점에서 찌르레기를 보고 있다. 민주당원 3명: Harry Truman(타임즈의 케케묵은 사본), Adlai Stevenson(하퍼스), Dean Acheson('그의 당을 바라보는 한 민주당원'이라고 불리는 책의)이 나와 함께 침대에 누워 있다. 민주당원들은 닥스훈트가 부족하기 때문에 나와 함께 잠자리에 드는데, 사실 이런 경우에 나는, 몇 년 동안 죽어가고 있는 나의 닥스훈트인 Fred의 유령이 방문할 것을 거의 확신한다. 인생에서 Fred는 항상 병자를 간호했고, 어떤 음란한 늙은 의사처럼 환자와 함께 침대로 바로 올라갔으며, 나쁜 상황을 더 악화시켰다. 이 어두운 아침 내내, 나는 구겨진 담요 위에서 마지못해 그를 즐겁게 해주었고, 그의 강압적인 몸무게를 느꼈으며, 그의 사기 보고를 들었다. 그는 살아있을 때 불편한 침대 동료였다: 죽음은 별로 나아지지 않았다–나는 여전히 붐비고, 그의 타고난 무례함과 그의 가식을 왜 참아냈는지 여전히 궁금하다.

18 ⑤ 제시문에 따르면 정책입안자들은 경제체제의 본질적 취약성을 해결하고 금융시스템의 탄력성을 높이기 위한 개혁을 설계해야 한다고 설명하고 있다. 그러므로 ⑤의 'reforming an economic system to withstand distress(고난에 견딜 수 있는 경제체제 개혁)'가 제시문의 주제로 가장 적절하다.

오답풀이
① 통계에 근거한 경제정책 입안
② 특색있는 사건들을 바탕으로 한 경제 건설
③ 기업보다 사람들의 요구를 앞세우는 것

④ 경제체제의 잠재적 문제점 예측

어휘

- inherent : 내재하는
- fragility : 부서지기 쉬움, 여림, 허약, 허무함
- reform : 개혁[개선]하다, 개혁[개선]
- objective : 목적, 목표, 객관적인
- eliminate : 없애다, 제거[삭제]하다
- failure : 실패
- institution : 기관[단체/협회]
- spur : 박차, 원동력[자극제]이 되다
- efficiency : 능률, 효율(성)
- strive : 분투하다
- enhance : 높이다[향상시키다]
- resilience : 회복력, 탄성, 탄력
- transfer : 옮기다, 이동[이송/이전]하다
- idiosyncratic : 특유한, 기이한, 색다른
- insulated : 절연[단열/방음] 처리가 된

해석

경제체제의 본질적인 취약성은 그것이 더 안전하게 만들어질 수 없다는 것을 의미하지 않는다. 많은 것들이 행해질 수 있고, 행해져 왔으며, 여전히 행해질 수 있다. 그러나 개혁을 설계할 때는 신중하게 목표를 선택하는 것이 중요하다. 개별 은행이나 대형 기관의 부실 위험을 없애는 게 목표가 돼서는 안 된다. 실패에는 장점이 있다. 올바른 인센티브를 창출하고 혁신을 촉진하며 효율성을 촉진하는 것이 중요하다. 오히려 정책입안자들은 보다 광범위한 금융시스템의 탄력성을 높이기 위해 노력해야 한다. 시스템이 극심한 스트레스를 받을 때도 결제, 재산권 처분 서비스 제공, 신용 제공, 리스크 이전 등의 기본적인 기능을 수행할 수 있어야 한다. 즉, 정책입안자들은 독특한 사건이 시스템적인 위기로 바뀌지 않는 시스템을 구축하도록 노력해야 한다. 이는 재정적인 고통의 확률을 낮출 뿐만 아니라 실물경제가 그것으로부터 절연되어 있을 확률을 높이려는 것을 의미한다.

19 ③ 제시문에 따르면 언어가 의사소통 체계로 발전한 후 인간은 꾸준히 음악을 통해 누구와 의사소통을 해야 하는지에 대해 의문을 가져왔다고 하였다. 인간들 사이에서의 의사소통은 음악보다는 언어를 이용하는 것이 훨씬 나았고, 결국 현대인들은 초자연적인 존재들과 소통하기 위해서 음악을 이용하게 되었다고 설명하고 있다. 그러므로 ③의 'music as a means to communicate with the supernatural(초자연적인 사람들과 소통하기 위한 수단으로서의 음악)'이 제시문의 주제로 가장 적절하다.

오답풀이

① 음악이 우리의 초자연적 관점에 미치는 영향
② 언어에 비해 음악의 기능적 다양성
④ 의사소통 수단으로서의 언어의 장점
⑤ 음악이 언어발전에 미치는 영향

어휘

- principal : 주요한, 주된
- communicative : 말을 잘 하는, 의사 전달의
- compulsion : 강요, 충동
- among : …간에, …중에서
- fulfill : 실현[성취]하다
- achieve : 달성하다, 성취하다
- prelinguistic : 전언어적
- infant : 유아, 젖먹이, 아기
- entity : 독립체
- propensity : 경향[성향]
- shaman : 샤먼, 주술사, 무당
- composition : 구성, 작품, 작곡

해석

언어가 현대 인류의 주요 의사소통 체계로 발전한 후, 사람들은 음악을 통해 누구와 의사소통을 해야 하는지에 대한 질문을 남겨두었다. 음악은 결국 '흥'의 파생물로서, 그 자체가 의사소통의 수단으로 진화했기 때문에 의사소통 기능은 쉽게 떨어질 수 없었다; 오늘날에도 여전히 존재하는 것처럼 현대 인간들 사이에는 음악과 의사소통해야 하는 강박 관념이 남아 있었다. 어떻게 이것이 실현될 수 있었을까? 다른 인간들과의 의사소통은 이제 언어 이전기의 유아들을 제외하고, 음악보다는 언어에 의해 훨씬 더 잘 성취되었다. 그러나 현대 인간들의 마음 속에는 이제 그들이 소통할 수 있고 소통해야 할 또 다른 유형의 실체인, 초자연적인 존재들이 있었다. 그래서 음악을 통해 의사소통을 하는 인간의 성향은 무당의 북을 치거나 바흐의 작품을 통해 초자연적인 것에 초점을 맞추게 되었다.

20 ④ 제시문에 따르면 무탄소 문명을 이뤄나가기 위해서는 유럽연합, 미국, 중국 세 나라가 서로 협력하여 규정, 기준 등을 정하고 다른 나라를 이끌어야 한다고 설명하고 있다. 그러므로 ④의 'Cooperation among the key members is essential for a zero-carbon world. (무탄소 세계를 위해서는 주요 구성원 간의 협력이 필수적이다)'가 제시문의 요지로 가장 적절하다.

오답풀이

① 인구 문제는 탄소 시대 이후로 질주하기 전에 해결해야 한다.
② 코끼리 3마리가 모두 동시에 행진하는 상황에서 어느 경쟁자도 우승할 수 없다.

③ 중국의 참여는 배출제로 경제를 위한 낙관적 신호이다.
⑤ 무탄소 문명은 20년 안에 역효과를 낼 운명이다.

어휘

- lead the charge : 먼저 책임을 지고 이끌다, 임무를 선도하다
- emission : 배출, 배출물, 배기가스
- roar : 으르렁거리다, 함성[아우성]을 지르다
- transition : 이행[과도]
- era : 시대
- poised : 태세를 갖추고 있는, 준비가 다 된
- herd : 떼, 사람들[대중]
- marching : 행진하는
- in sync : (동작·작업 등이 속도를 맞추어) 동시에 이뤄지는, 화합하는
- common : 공동의, 공통의
- regulations : 규칙, 법령
- standard : 기준
- humanity : 인류, 인간, 인간성
- fold : 접다, (가축, 특히 양의) 우리
- participation : 참가, 참여
- optimistic : 낙관적인, 낙관하는
- backfire : 역효과를 낳다

해석

5억 1천 2백만 명의 시민이 살고 있는 유럽연합은 최근까지 배출제로의 녹색 경제를 선도했다. 14억에 가까운 인구를 가진 중화인민공화국은 최근 몇 년 동안 탄소 시대 이후로의 전환 계획으로 아우성쳐왔다. 그리고 이제 3억 3천 2백만 명의 시민이 있는 미국은 이 무리에 동참할 준비가 되어 있다. 세 마리 코끼리가 모두 동조하여 행진하고, 우수사례를 공유하고, 공통의 코드, 규정, 기준, 인센티브를 제정하고, 나머지 인류를 우리로 끌어들이기 위해 손을 내밀지 않으면, 20년도 채 안 되어서 무탄소 문명화를 향한 경주에서 우리는 지고 말 것이다.

21 ① 제시문은 내 주변의 사람(배우자와 같은)에 의해서 목표 추구에 영향을 받는다는 내용이다. 특히 행복한 관계에서 오는 안정감은 목표 추구를 더 쉽게 해준다고 하였다. 그러므로 ①의 'The chances of achieving your goals hinge on your spouse. (목표 달성의 가능성은 배우자에게 달려 있다)'가 제시문의 요지로 가장 적절하다.

오답풀이

② 심리적 안정감이 웰빙의 주요 지표다.
③ 현실적인 목표를 설정하는 것은 파트너의 영향을 많이 받는다.
④ 개인적인 감정은 목표를 추구하는 것과 직결된다.

⑤ 배우자의 성실성은 성공적인 결혼으로 이어진다.

어휘

- treat : 대하다, 여기다, 치부하다
- pursuit : 추구, 좇음, 추격
- solitary : 혼자 하는
- endeavor : 노력, 시도, 애씀
- foster : 조성하다, 발전시키다
- impede : 지연시키다[방해하다]
- tofu : 두부
- influence : 영향, 영향력
- conscientious : 양심적인, 성실한
- organized : 조직화된, 조직적인
- reliable : 믿을 수 있는
- predict : 예측[예견]하다
- posit : 사실로 상정하다[받아들이다]
- predictable : 예측[예견]할 수 있는
- feel in control : 무엇이든 할 수 있다고 느끼다, 자신에 차 있다
- hinge on : …에 달려있다
- spouse : 배우자
- psychological stability : 심리적 안정성
- indicator : 지표, 계기[장치]
- conscientiousness : 성실성

해석

전통적으로, 연구는 목표 추구를 독단적인 노력으로 취급해왔다. 그러나 일상적인 경험은 우리의 관계가 우리의 발전을 촉진하거나 방해할 수 있다는 것을 보여 준다. 매일 아침 일찍 일어나려면 밤 10시에 침대 옆 램프를 끄는 배우자와 함께 사는 것이 좋다. 채식주의자가 되고 싶다면 두부 vs 스테이크에 대한 배우자의 감정이 아마도 영향을 미칠 것이다.

현재 연구원들은 그 영향을 조사하고 있다. 워싱턴 대학의 한 연구는 성실한 배우자, 즉 조직적이고 신뢰할 수 있는 자와 결혼하는 것은 미래의 직업 만족도와 더 높은 수입을 예견한다는 것을 발견했다. 독일 쾰른 대학의 Wilhelm Hofmann의 연구는 높은 관계 만족도가 목표 추구에 대한 통제 감정에 긍정적인 영향을 미친다는 것을 보여 준다. Hofmann은 행복한 관계의 안정성이 집중을 더 쉽게 한다고 단언한다. Hofmann에 따르면, "사람들의 일상이 안정되고 예측 가능하다고 느낄 때, 그들은 목표를 추구하는 능력에 대해 더 자신감을 느낀다"라고 한다.

22 ④ 제시문에 따르면 풍차가 매년 최소 4만 5천 마리의 새와 박쥐를 죽이지만 사실 이것은 많은 수가 아니라고 설명하며 그에 대한 방증으로 고양이 한 마리가 죽이는 새의 수

를 보여 주었다. 그러므로 ④의 'Windmills do not threaten avian wildlife as much as outdoor cats. (풍차는 야외 고양이만큼 조류 야생동물을 위협하지 않는다)'가 제시문의 요지로 가장 적절하다.

오답풀이

① 새와 박쥐에 대한 정책은 통계에 근거해야 한다.

② 고양이 주인에게 고양이가 야외에서 자유롭게 돌아다니지 못하게 하기를 권고한다.

③ 풍차는 환경기준에 적합하도록 규제할 필요가 있다.

⑤ 생태적 균형을 위해 야외 고양이 개체 수를 억제해야 한다.

어휘

• windmill : 풍차, 풍차 터빈
• estimate : 추산[추정]하다
• in perspective : 원근법에 의하여, 전체적 시야로, 긴 안목에서
• measure : 측정하다[재다]
• toll : 사용세, 요금, 사상자[희생자] 수
• equivalent to : ~와 같음, 상응함
• statistic : 통계, 통계학
• roam : 돌아다니다, 배회[방랑]하다
• regulate : 규제하다, 조절하다
• avian : 새[조류]의
• curb : 억제[제한]하다

해석

미국에서 풍차는 매년 최소 4만 5천 마리의 새와 박쥐를 죽일 것으로 추정된다. 그것은 많은 수의 새와 박쥐처럼 들린다. 그 숫자를 원근법에 넣기 위해, 주인의 집을 드나드는 것을 허용하는 애완 고양이들이 고양이 한 마리당 평균 300마리 이상의 새를 죽이는 것으로 측정되었다고 생각해 보라. 만약 미국의 야외 고양이 개체 수가 약 1억 마리로 추산된다면, 미국에서는 풍차에 의해 연간 4만 5천 마리의 새와 박쥐가 죽는 것에 비해, 고양이는 최소한 300억 마리의 새를 죽이는 것으로 계산될 수 있다. 그 풍차의 희생자 수는 단지 150마리의 고양이의 일과 맞먹는다.

23 ② 제시문에서 우리가 통계적 샘플을 기하학의 원리나 중력처럼 생각한다고 하였는데, 이들은 결코 변하지 않는 과학적 진리이다. 또한 우리가 그렇게 생각하는 것과는 달리 요즘과 같은 빅데이터의 시대에 통계적 샘플에 의존하는 것은 자동차 시대에 말의 채찍을 잡고 있는 것과 같이 뒤떨어진 행동이라고 말하고 있다. 그러므로 빈칸에는 'immutable(불변의)'이 들어갈 말로 가장 적절하다.

오답풀이

① 무례한

③ 미숙한

④ 임박한

⑤ 공정한

어휘

• statistical : 통계적인, 통계학상의
• bedrock : 기반
• geometry : 기하학
• concept : 개념
• constraint : 제약
• clutch : (꽉) 움켜잡다
• whip : 채찍
• predominant : 두드러진, 뚜렷한, 우세한
• aim : (무엇을 성취하는 것을) 목표하다
• impertinent : 무례한
• immutable : 불변의
• immature : 미숙한
• imminent : 임박한
• impartial : 공정한

해석

우리는 통계적 샘플링을 기하학의 원리나 중력의 법칙과 같이 일종의 불변의 기반이라고 생각하는 경향이 있다. 그러나 그 개념은 1세기도 안 된 것이며, 특정한 기술적 제약 속에서 특정한 순간에 특정한 문제를 해결하기 위해 개발되었다. 그러한 제약조건은 더 이상 같은 정도로 존재하지 않는다. 빅데이터 시대에 무작위 표본에 도달하는 것은 자동차 시대에 말의 채찍을 움켜쥐는 것과 같다. 우리는 여전히 특정 상황에서 샘플링을 사용할 수 있지만, 대규모 데이터 세트를 분석하는 방법이 될 필요는 없으며 앞으로도 없을 것이다. 점점 더 우리는 모든 것을 추구하는 것을 목표로 할 것이다.

24 ① 제시문에 따르면 기술 혁신이 이루어짐에 따라 여성들이 가질 수 있는 임신에 대한 선택권이 확대되었고, 개개인은 기술적 수단을 통해 생물학적 번식을 조절할 수 있게 되었다. 또한 입양과 이혼을 통해 가족의 재구성이 이루어진다고 하였으므로 그동안 널리 통용되던 가족의 의미가 약화되었다고 볼 수 있다. 그러므로 빈칸에는 'undermine(약화시키다)'이 들어갈 말로 가장 적절하다.

오답풀이

② 복사하다

③ 요약하다

④ 통합하다

⑤ 단순화하다

어휘

- fetus : 태아
- invisible : 보이지 않는, 무형의
- innovation : 혁신, 쇄신
- decade : 10년
- physical : 육체[신체]의, 물질[물리]적인
- prevent : 막다[예방/방지하다]
- redefine : 재정립하다
- terminate : 끝내다, 종료하다
- pregnancy : 임신
- conflict : 갈등[충돌]
- contraception : 피임
- abortion : 낙태
- dispute : 분쟁, 논란, 논쟁
- uncouple : 분리시키다
- reproduction : 생식, 번식, 복제, 재생
- parenting : 육아
- artificial insemination : 인공 수정
- in vitro fertilization : 체외 수정
- embryo implantation : 배아 삽입
- reconfiguration : 구조 변경
- adoption : 입양
- divorce : 이혼
- unconventional : 색다른, 독특한
- undermine : 약화시키다
- duplicate : 복사하다
- consolidate : 통합하다

해석

인간 태아는 최근까지 대부분 보이지 않고 말없이 사는 사회 구성원이었다. 지난 몇 십 년 동안의 기술 혁신은 태아에게 더 큰 물리적 현실과 법적 권리에 대한 새로운 주장을 제공하는 동시에 여성들에게 임신을 예방하고, 재정의하며, 심지어 종료할 수 있는 더 많은 근거를 제공했다. 피임과 낙태를 위한 기술적 선택권 확대와 관련된 갈등은 이 문제들에 대한 하나의 유리한 점을 제공한다. 또 다른 일련의 분쟁은 인공수정, 체외수정, 배아삽입과 같은 기술적 수단을 통해 사회적 양육으로부터 생물학적 번식을 점진적으로 분리하는 것에 관한 것이다. 입양과 이혼을 통해 가족의 재구성과 교차하면서, 이러한 색다른 생식 경로는 "어머니", "아버지", "자식", "가족"이라고 통용되는 의미를 약화시키기 시작했다.

25　① 우리의 눈, 코, 귀, 입 등은 정보를 수집하고, 팔과 다리는 행동을 할 수 있게 해준다. 살아가면서 여러 가지 선택을 하거나 협상을 하게 될 때 우리는 이러한 능력에 의존하게 되는데 진정으로 선택할 수 있으려면 고무망치에 맞은 무

류이 경련을 일으키는 것처럼 단순한 감각정보에 대한 반응 이상을 행해야 한다. 그러므로 빈칸에는 ①의 'reacting to sensory information(감각정보에 대한 반응하기)'이 들어갈 말로 가장 적절하다.

오답풀이

② 극도의 욕망에 굴복하기
③ 가장 유익한 것 선택하기
④ 즉각적인 만족감 찾기
⑤ 타고난 본능 억누르기

어휘

- instrument : 기구, (차량·기계에서 측정용)계기
- capability : 능력, 역량
- negotiate : 협상[교섭]하다
- satiation : 포만감
- vulnerability : 취약성
- twitch : 씰룩거리다, 경련하다, 홱 당겨지다
- mallet : 망치
- evaluate : (양·가치·품질 등을) 평가하다
- vital : 필수적인
- sensory : 감각의
- utmost : 최고의, 극도의
- gratification : 만족감
- instinct : 본능
- suppress : 금하다, 참다[억누르다]

해석

우리가 거울을 볼 때, 우리는 선택에 필요한 몇 가지 "기구"를 본다. 우리의 눈, 코, 귀, 입이 우리의 환경으로부터 정보를 수집하는 반면, 우리의 팔과 다리는 우리가 그것에 대해 행동할 수 있게 해준다. 우리는 배고픔과 포만감, 안전과 취약성, 심지어 삶과 죽음 사이에서조차 효과적으로 협상하기 위해 이러한 능력에 의존한다. 그러나 우리의 선택하기 위한 능력은 단순히 감각정보에 반응하는 것 이상을 포함한다. 의사의 고무망치로 적당한 곳을 맞히면 무릎이 경련을 일으킬 수도 있지만, 아무도 이 반사작용을 선택으로 여기지 않을 것이다. 진정으로 선택할 수 있으려면 가능한 모든 선택권을 평가하고 가장 좋은 선택을 해야 하며, 정신을 육체처럼 선택에 필수적인 것으로 만들어야 한다.

26　② 젊었을 때 창업을 하는 것이 더 쉬운 것은 사실이지만, 일부 산업에서는 나이로부터 오는 경험 덕분에 젊지 않은 나이에도 창업에 성공하였음을 알 수 있다. 이는 곧 재정적인 자원, 올바른 네트워크, 훌륭한 아이디어를 가지고 있다면 창업을 하는 데에 나이는 상관 없음을 의미한다. 그러므로 빈칸에는 ②의 'age is nothing but a number (나이는 숫자

에 불과하다)'가 들어갈 말로 가장 적절하다.

[오답풀이]

① 내면의 성공은 보상이다

③ 모든 것이 당신이 아는 사람에게 전해진다

④ 퍼즐의 마지막 조각은 자본이다

⑤ 젊은은 언제나 승리할 수 있는 길을 찾을 것이다

[어휘]

• responsibility : cordia(맡은 일), 책무

• capitalist : 자본가, 자본주의자

• gush : 솟구치다, 쏟아 내다

• entrepreneur : 사업가[기업가]

• obstacle : 장애물

• founder : 창립자, 설립자

• capital : 수도, 자본금, 자금

• prevail : 승리하다[이기다], 만연[팽배]하다

[해석]

젊었을 때 창업이 더 쉽다는 것은 의심의 여지가 없다. 비업무에 대한 책임감이 적을수록 새로운 벤처기업에 피와 땀과 눈물을 쏟을 가능성이 높다. 하지만 그렇다고 해서 당신이 어리다고 해서 학교를 떠나거나 회사를 차려야 한다는 뜻은 아니다. 벤처 투자자들은 종종 신선한 고기를 선호한다. 실리콘밸리의 가장 큰 VC 회사 중 하나인 세쿼이아캐피탈의 Michael Moritz는 20대 중후반 기업가들에 대해서 "그들이 넘을 수 없는 경계도, 한계도, 장애물은 없다고 본다"라고 입을 모았다. 그러나 생명공학이나 비즈니스 소프트웨어와 같은 일부 산업의 창업자들은 창업자의 나이와 함께 오는 경험으로부터 우위를 점하고 있다. 한 기술 사업가의 연구에 따르면, 이들 및 기타 고성장 산업에서 성공적인 창업자의 평균 연령은 40세였다. 그것은 만약 여러분이 재정적인 자원, 올바른 네트워크, 그리고 가장 중요한, 훌륭한 아이디어를 가지고 있다면, <u>나이는 숫자에 불과하다는 것</u>을 보여 준다.

27 ① 굴절되지도 않고 피부를 통과하여 뼈 사진을 찍을 수 있게 하는 엑스레이라는 새로운 광선이 발견되자 과학계는 혼란스러우면서도 열띤 연구에 돌입하였다. 뿐만 아니라 이러한 신비한 광선은 광고, 노래, 만화 등에서도 선풍적인 인기를 끌었다. 그러므로 빈칸에는 ①의 'Popular culture was equally mesmerized(대중문화도 똑같이 매혹되었다)'가 들어갈 말로 가장 적절하다.

[오답풀이]

② 광고주와 정치인이 뒤를 이었다

③ 이 발견은 많은 사람들의 도전을 받았다

④ 금융권에서 충격을 받았다

⑤ 대중적 열풍을 반영하는 경우는 드물다

[어휘]

• notion : 개념, 관념, 생각

• unrefractable : 굴절되지 않는

• indifferent : 무관심한

• befuddle : 어리둥절하게 하다

• precipitate : 촉발시키다, 치닫게 하다

• feverish : 몹시 흥분한, 과열된

• implication : 영향[결과], 함축, 암시

• mesmerize : 완전 넋을 빼놓다

• penetrate : 관통하다, 침투하다

• flesh : 피부, 살, 고기

• intoxicating : 도취시키는

• prose : 산문

• follow suit : 방금 남이 한 대로 따라 하다

• be taken aback : ~에 깜짝 놀라다[충격을 받다]

• craze : 대유행[열풍]

[해석]

우르츠부르크 바이에른 대학의 Wilhelm Roentgen 교수는 1895년 12월에 처음으로 엑스레이를 발견했다. 굴절되지 않고 전자기장에 무관한 새로운 종류의 광선의 개념은 과학계를 혼란스럽게 했고 그들의 본성과 빛과 물질의 오랜 이론에 대한 함의에 대한 열띤 연구를 촉발시켰다. <u>대중문화도 똑같이 매혹되었다.</u> 유리처럼 쉽게 피부를 관통하고 골격의 사진 이미지를 연출할 수 있는 '어두운 빛'이라는 개념은 도취적이었다. 하룻밤 사이에 이 신비로운 광선은 광고, 산문, 노래, 만화에서 끊임없이 마주치는 인기 있는 아이콘이 되었다. 1896년 한 해에만 이 주제에 관한 1,000여 편의 기사와 50여 권의 책이 출판되었다.

28 ⑤ 제시문은 효과적으로 위협하는 발언을 하는 방법에 대한 글이다. 노골적으로 위협하지 않더라도 청자가 스스로 그 위협의 내용을 예측하고 이해한다는 내용이 들어와야 한다. 그러므로 빈칸에는 ⑤의 'negative consequences to the addressee(수신인에게 부정적인 결과)'가 들어갈 말로 가장 적절하다.

[오답풀이]

① 수족관으로의 다정한 초대

② 향후 조치의 명시적 철회

③ 현황 유지

④ 협력의 무언의 동의

[어휘]

• threat : 협박, 위협

• utterer : 발언자, 공표자

• utterance : 표현함, 발언

- carry out : 수행하다
- addressee : 수신인
- prompting : 설득[유도]
- forecast : 예측, 예보, 예측[예보]하다
- consequence : 결과, 중요함
- explicitly : 명쾌하게, 명백하게
- remark : 발언[말/논평/언급]
- overtly : 명백히, 공공연하게
- chilling : 으스스한
- imminent : 목전의, 임박한
- doom : 죽음, 파멸, 비운
- cordial : 화기애애한, 다정한
- explicit : 분명한, 명쾌한, 명백한
- withdrawal : 철회, 취소, 기권
- maintenance : 유지[지속]
- cooperation : 협력, 합동, 협조

해석

위협이 효과적이 되려면, 발언자는 위협을 수행할 수 있는 수단을 가지고 있어야 하며 수신인이 발언의 설득이 없는 경우와는 다르게 행동을 하기를 바란다. 그렇다면 일단 화자가 대상에게 그러한 힘의 위치에 있는 것으로 보이면, 비록 명백하게 발언자 자신의 행동을 수반하는 것으로 프레임을 씌우지 않더라도, 수신인에게 부정적인 결과를 예측하는 어떤 발언도 위협으로 합리적으로 이해될 수 있다. 노골적으로 위협적인 내용이 담기지 않은 발언의 이치다. 예를 들어 영화 속 마피아 보스가 "오늘 밤 물고기들과 함께 자자"고 했을 때, 수족관이 있는 방에 있는 화자의 집에서 자고 가자는 초대장이 아니라, 임박한 파멸의 소름끼치는 메시지로 받아들여진다.

29 ③ 네안데르탈인과 호모 사피엔스와 현대 사람들의 뇌 크기에 대해 설명하면서 뇌 크기와 영리함은 연관이 없다고 하였다. 추운 기후에 사는 사람들은 더 큰 뇌를 가지고 있고, 뼈 역시 그보다 컸으며, 큰 근육이 있으면 지능과는 무관하게 더 큰 뇌를 필요로 한다. 그러므로 빈칸에는 ③의 'is also related to muscularity and climatic conditions (근육 및 기후 조건과도 관련이 있다)'가 들어갈 말로 가장 적절하다.

오답풀이

① 불가피하게 지능과 체중을 결정한다
② 근육 손실 및 영양실조에 대한 보상
④ 서식지와 주변 환경을 나타낸다
⑤ 인류를 위한 지성의 그릇으로 오랫동안 알려져 왔다

어휘

- specimen : 견본, 샘플, 표본, 시료
- clever : 영리한, 똑똑한, 재주가 있는

- massive : (육중하면서) 거대한, 엄청나게 큰
- stocky : (체격이) 다부진
- correlate : (밀접한) 연관성[상관관계]이 있다
- neuroanatomist : 신경 해부학자
- measurement : 측정, 측량, 치수[크기/길이/양]
- independent of : …와는 관계없이, …와는 별도로
- inevitably : 필연적이다시피, 예상한대로, 불가피하게
- determine : 결정하다, 알아내다, 밝히다
- compensation : 보상(금), 보상[이득]
- malnutrition : 영양실조
- muscularity : 근골의 건장함, 강건, 근육질
- indicate : 나타내다[보여 주다], 내비치다[시사하다]
- vessel : (대형) 선박[배], 그릇[용기/통]

해석

네안데르탈인의 뇌 용적은 1,200~1,750 cc로 현대 호모 사피엔스의 초기 및 현재 표본(1,200~1700 cc)과 거의 같은 범위였다. 이것은 그들이 현대인만큼 영리했다는 것을 의미하지는 않는데, 뇌의 크기는 근육과 기후 조건과도 관련이 있기 때문이다. 더 추운 기후에 사는 사람들은 더 큰 뇌를 갖는 경향이 있고 네안데르탈인은 추운 기간 동안 유라시아에서 살았다. 네안데르탈인의 뼈 또한 그들이 거대했다는 것을 보여 준다. 그들은 짧고 다부진 몸매를 가지고 있었는데, 수컷은 아마도 몸무게가 약 145파운드였고 키는 5피트 7인치도 되지 않았다. 또한 뇌 용적은 밀접하게 연관된 종에서 더 무거운 근육과 몸무게와 상관관계가 있다. 독일의 신경 해부학자 Heinz Stephan은 지난 40년 동안 많은 종에서 뇌의 크기와 다양한 부분을 연구해왔다. 그의 세밀한 측정은 큰 근육은 지능과 무관하게 더 큰 뇌를 필요로 한다는 것을 보여준다.

30 ① 제시문에 따르면 기술이 발전하면서 디지털 기계를 이용한 재택근무, 은행 계좌 업무 등이 늘어나고 있다. 그러면서 사람 대 사람으로 처리했던 일들을 기계가 대신하게 되었다. 그러므로 빈칸에는 ①의 'technology is isolating us(기술이 우리를 고립시키고 있다)'가 들어갈 말로 가장 적절하다.

오답풀이

② 직원들이 과로하고 있다
③ 인공 지능은 인간에게 유익하다
④ 재정 관리가 최우선이다
⑤ 인력이 균등하게 배분된다

어휘

- secretary : 비서, 총무[서기]
- accountant : 회계사
- terminals : 단자
- actually : 실제로, 정말로, 사실은

- impersonal : 인간미 없는, 비인격적인
- credit : 신용거래, 입금하다
- eliminate : 없애다, 제거[삭제]하다, 탈락시키다
- paycheck : 급료(지불 수표), 봉급(으로 받는 수표)
- coworker : 함께 일하는 사람, 협력자, 동료
- detache : 떼다[분리하다]
- interact : 소통하다[교류하다]
- deposit : 보증금
- withdraw : 빼내다, 철수하다
- loan : 대출[융자](금), 빌려주다, 대출[융자]하다
- reject : 거부[거절]하다
- isolate : 격리하다, 고립시키다, 분리[구분]하다
- overwork : 과로하다, 혹사하다
- artificial intelligence : 인공 지능
- priority : 우선 사항
- evenly : 고르게, 반반하게, 균등하게
- allocate : 할당하다

해석

비즈니스 세계는 기술이 우리를 고립시키고 있는 한 영역이다. 많은 사람들이 이제 집에서 혼자 일한다. 대형 중앙컴퓨터를 이용할 수 있게 되면서 비서, 보험대리점, 회계사 등 직원들이 자택 내 디스플레이 단말기에서 업무를 수행한다. 그들은 더이상 그들이 상대하는 사람들을 실제로 볼 필요가 없다. 게다가 직원들은 비인격적인 방법으로 급여를 받는 경우가 많다. 근로자의 급여는 자동으로 은행 계좌에 입금돼, 급료 지급 수표가 필요 없게 된다. 급여를 받거나 수표를 현금으로 바꾸기 위해 동료들과 줄을 서는 사람들이 더 적다. 마지막으로 개인 뱅킹은 분리된 과정이 되고 있다. 고객들은 계좌에서 돈을 입출금하기 위해 사람들이 아닌 기계와 교류한다. 심지어 일부 은행 대출도 대출 담당자와의 인터뷰가 아닌 컴퓨터 프로그램에 의해 승인되거나 거부된다.

31 ② (A) 생물학자들은 뇌가 수십억 개의 뉴런에서의 생화학 반응을 통해 마음을 생산한다고 추측한다. 하지만 아직까지 이 추측에 대한 정확한 근거를 찾아내지는 못하였다고 설명하고 있다. 그러므로 빈칸에 들어갈 연결어구는 역접의 의미를 나타내는 'However(그러나)'가 가장 적절하다.

(B) 마음이 뇌에서 나온다고 추측하고는 있지만 아직까지 그에 대한 근거를 찾지 못하였기 때문에 실제로 이것이 사실이라 할지라도 적어도 지금으로서는 뇌와 마음을 개별적으로 연구해야 한다고 설명하고 있다. 그러므로 빈칸에 들어갈 연결어구는 인과의 의미를 나타내는 'Hence(이런 이유로)'가 가장 적절하다.

어휘

- neurons : 뉴런
- synapses : 시냅스
- biochemical : 생화학의, 생화학 물질
- subjective : 주관적인
- assume : 추정[상정]하다
- somehow : 어떻게든, 왠지
- reaction : 반응, 반작용
- so far : 지금까지
- absolutely : 전적으로, 틀림없이, 전혀, 극도로
- explanation : 해명, 이유, 설명
- emerge : 나오다, 드러나다, 알려지다, 생겨나다
- particular : 특정한, 특별한
- how come : 어째서, 왜
- clue : 단서, 실마리, 힌트
- undertaking : 일[프로젝트], 약속

해석

많은 과학자들을 포함한 많은 사람들은 뇌와 마음을 혼동하는 경향이 있지만, 그것들은 정말 매우 다른 것이다. 뇌는 뉴런, 시냅스, 생화학 물질의 물질적 네트워크다. 마음은 고통, 쾌락, 분노, 사랑 등 주관적인 경험의 흐름이다. 생물학자들은 뇌가 어떻게든 마음을 생산하고, 수십억 개의 뉴런에서 생화학 반응이 어떻게든 고통과 사랑 같은 경험을 만들어 낸다고 추측한다. (A) 그러나, 지금까지 우리는 뇌에서 어떻게 정신이 나오는지에 대한 아무런 설명도 가지고 있지 않다. 어째서 수십억 개의 뉴런이 특정 패턴으로 전기 신호를 발사하고 있을 때 나는 고통을 느끼고, 뉴런이 다른 패턴으로 발화했을 때 나는 사랑을 느낄 수 있을까? 전혀 감이 안 잡혔다. (B) 이런 이유로, 비록 마음이 실제로 뇌에서 나온다고 해도, 적어도 지금으로서는 마음을 연구하는 것이 뇌를 연구하는 것과는 다른 일이다.

32 ② 제시문은 IoT를 여러 산업 분야에 어떻게 적용할 수 있는지, 그로 인해 얻을 수 있는 혜택은 무엇인지에 대해 설명하고 있다. 그러나 ②는 IoT를 동원할 수 있는 기반시설이 없는 산업도 많다고 하고 있으므로 전체적인 글의 흐름과 어울리지 않는다.

어휘

- revolutionize : 대변혁[혁신]을 일으키다
- landscape : 풍경, 조경을 하다
- bridge : 다리, 가교, 다리를 놓다[형성하다]
- previously : 이전에, 미리
- reliant : 의존[의지]하는
- infrastructure : 사회[공공] 기반 시설
- mobilize : 동원되다, 동원하다

- specific : 구체적인, 명확한
- optimize : …을 최대한 좋게[적합하게] 만들다[활용하다]
- occupancy : 사용
- spoilage : (음식 · 식품의) 부패[손상]
- generate : 발생시키다, 만들어 내다
- revenue : 수익

해석

사물인터넷(IoT)은 디지털과 물질세계를 연결함으로써 기업과 소비자 지형을 혁신할 수 있다. ① 기존에 인터넷에 연결되지 않았던, 물체를 제작하고, 이동하고, 판매하던 것에 의존하던 산업은 누구나 혜택을 받을 수 있다. ② 그러나 IoT를 동원할 수 있는 5세대(5G) 광대역통신 기반시설이 없는 산업도 많다. ③ IoT가 기업에 가져올 수 있는 구체적인 혜택은 기술 활용 방법에 따라 달라진다. ④ 일례로 센서 활용으로 사용 수준에 따라 조명이나 난방을 최적화하여 폐기물을 줄이거나, 온도 모니터링으로 운반 중인 제품의 변질을 줄일 수 있다. ⑤ IoT는 파이프라인을 통해 활동을 분석하여 출력을 극대화하고 새로운 자원 풀의 식별을 돕는 음향 해상 유전 센서 등 수익 창출과 생산성 향상도 가능하다.

33 ③ 우리가 지금 마약이라고 생각하는 물질들도 처음에는 일반 약물들과 다르게 취급되지 않았고 심지어는 식품첨가물로도 쉽게 구할 수 있었다. 그러다 1914년 해리슨 법이 통과되고 나서부터 본격적으로 마약이 범죄라는 것을 인식하게 되었다고 설명하고 있다. 그러나 지난 40년을 언급하며 특정 약물의 억제를 위해 마약전쟁을 선포했다는 ③은 전체적인 글의 흐름과 어울리지 않는다.

어휘

- criminology : 범죄학, 형사학
- unaware : …을 알지[눈치 채지] 못하는
- criminalization : 유죄로 하기
- construe : ~을 ~으로 이해[해석]하다
- array : 집합체[모음/무리], 배열
- arguably : 주장할 수 있는
- enhance : 높이다, 향상시키다
- hard drug : 중독성 마약
- readily : 손쉽게, 순조롭게
- stimulating : 자극이 되는, 고무적인
- enforcement : 시행, 집행, 강조
- aggressively : 공격적으로
- contemporary : 동시대의, 현대의, 당대의
- opiate : 아편제
- legislation : 제정법

해석

일반 시민뿐 아니라 범죄학 학생들도 마약의 범죄화가 20세기 미국 창작물이라는 사실을 모르는 경우가 많다. 이전에, 우리가 지금 "마약"이라고 해석하는 것은 건강을 해칠(혹은 향상시킬) 가능성이 있는 방대한 양의 다른 물질들과 다르게 다루어지지 않았다. ① 지금 우리가 생각하는 '중독성 마약'은 한때 의약품으로, 식품첨가물로도 쉽게 구할 수 있었다. ② 코카콜라는 코카인을 자극성 재료로 포함시켜 '진짜'라고 광고에 부응한 적이 있으며, 이후 카페인으로 대체되었다. ③ 지난 40년간 법 집행부가 특정 약물을 적극적으로 제거해야 한다는 생각을 근거로 한 '마약 전쟁'이 목격되어왔다. ④ 의회가 1914년 해리슨 법을 통과시키면서 약물에 대한 우리의 현대적 관점은 아편제의 판매와 소유를 효과적으로 범죄화하면서 시작되었다. ⑤ 마리화나를 불법화하는 법률은 1930년까지 16개 주에서, 1937년까지 모든 주에서 시행되었다.

34 ④ 주어진 문장은 애벌레들이 시력이 있든 없든 막대기의 색에 맞추어 자신들의 몸 색깔을 변화시켰다는 실험에 대한 결과이다. 그러므로 실험의 준비단계에 해당하는 문장의 뒤인 ④에 위치하는 것이 가장 적절하다.

어휘

- caterpillar : 애벌레
- vision : 시력, 눈, 시야
- Peppered moth : 얼룩나방
- camouflage : 위장, 위장하다
- blend : 섞다, 혼합하다, 섞이다
- obscure : 보기[듣기/이해하기] 어렵게 하다
- adapt : 맞추다, 적응하다
- finding : (조사 · 연구 등의) 결과
- evidence : 증거, 흔적
- dermal : 피부의, 진피의
- photoreception : 광선 감수성

해석

> 연구원들이 상자를 열었을 때, 그들은 시력이 있든 없든 거의 모든 애벌레들이 상자 안의 막대기에 맞추어 몸의 색깔을 바꾸었다는 것을 발견했다.

얼룩나방은 위장술의 달인이다. (①) 애벌레 단계에서, 그들은 주변 환경을 보지 않고도 피부색을 그들의 환경에 섞이게 바꿀 수 있다는 새로운 연구결과가 나왔다. (②) 300마리 이상의 얼룩나방 유충을 기른 후 영국 연구진은 검은 페인트로 일부 유충의 시야를 가렸다. (③) 유충은 흰색, 녹색, 갈색 또는 검은 막대기가 들어있는 상자에 넣어 적응할 시간을 부여했다. (④) 연구자들은 그 애벌레들을 두 가지 다른 색깔의

막대기가 들어있는 새 상자로 옮겼고, 약 80%의 곤충들이 자신의 몸 색깔에 맞는 막대기에 의지하여 휴식을 취하기로 선택했다. (⑤) 연구진은 이 연구결과가 얼룩나방 유충이 피부로 볼 수 있는 피부 광선 감각 능력이 있다는 강력한 증거를 제공한다고 밝혔다.

35 ① 주어진 문장에서 미국에 전기가 공급되기 시작하면서 공장이 전기화되고, 자동차를 중심으로 양산품 시대가 문을 열었다고 하였다. 그러므로 전기로 인한 자동차의 대량 생산이 사회의 방향을 바꾸었다고 한 글 (A)가 그 다음에 와야 한다. 글 (C)에서 점점 자동차의 수요가 증가하게 되고, 글 (B)에서 증가한 자동차들을 위한 콘크리트 고속도로가 만들어졌다고 설명하고 있다. 그러므로 주어진 글 다음에 (A) – (C) – (B)의 순으로 이어져야 한다.

어휘

- urban : 도시의, 도회지의
- electrify : 전기를 통하게 하다
- onset : 시작
- rural : 시골의
- kingpin : 중심인물
- affordable : 줄 수 있는, (가격이) 알맞은
- alter : 변하다, 달라지다, 바꾸다
- temporal : 시간의, 시간의 제약을 받는
- spatial : 공간의, 공간적인
- orientation : 방향, 지향, 성향
- stretch : 늘이다, 뻗은 지역
- culminating : 절정에 달하는, 궁극의
- seamless : 아주 매끄러운
- interstate highway : 주간 고속도로
- impetus : 자극, 추진력
- emerge : 나오다, 드러나다
- suburb : 교외
- nascent : 발생기의, 초기의
- rev up : 활성화되다, 활기띠다
- assembly line : 조립 라인

해석

1900년부터 대공황이 시작되기 전인 1929년까지 미국의 도시 지역은 전기가 공급되었고, 1936년부터 1949년 사이에 미국의 시골 지역 뒤를 이었다. 공장의 전기화는 자동차를 중심으로 양산품 시대를 열었다.

(A) 전기가 없었다면 Henry Ford는 노동자들에게 일을 제공하고 수백만 명의 미국인들이 사용할 수 있는 적당한 가격의 자동차를 제조할 수 있는 전력 도구가 없었을 것이다. 가

솔린 모델 T 자동차의 대량 생산은 사회의 시간적, 공간적 방향을 바꾸었다.

(C) 수백만 명의 사람들이 말과 벌레를 자동차와 교환하기 시작했다. 증가하는 연료 수요를 충족시키기 위해 초창기 석유 산업은 탐사 및 시추에 박차를 가하고 전국에 송유관을 건설했으며 조립 라인에서 나오는 수백만 대의 자동차에 동력을 공급하기 위해 수천 개의 주유소를 설치했다.

(B) 미국 전역에 콘크리트 고속도로가 설치되었고, 세계 역사상 가장 큰 공공 사업인 미국 주간 고속도로 시스템이 절정에 달해 완벽한 해안 간 도로 시스템을 만들었다. 주간 고속도로는 도시 지역에서 고속도로 출구에서 튀어 나오는 새로 생겨난 교외 지역으로 수백만 가구의 대규모 이주를 촉발했다.

36 ⑤ 주어진 글에서 자신의 감정이 타인에게 미치는 영향에 대해 언급했고, 그 감정이 적절하다 할지라도 문제로 이어질 수 있다고 하였다. 그에 대한 설명이 글 (C)에 나와 있고 감정은 일치하거나 일치하지 않을 수도 있다고 하였으므로 일치하는 경우에 대해 설명한 글 (B)가 다음에 와야 한다. 실제의 감정과 드러난 말과 말투가 다를 때 오는 문제를 글 (A)에서 정리하고 있으므로 주어진 글 다음에 (C) – (B) – (A)의 순으로 이어져야 한다.

어휘

- be aware of : ~을 알다
- appropriate : 적절한
- intensity : 강렬함, 격렬함, 강도
- inappropriate : 부적절한, 부적합한
- recipient : 받는 사람, 수령[수취]인
- facilitate : 가능하게[용이하게] 하다
- derail : 탈선하다[시키다]
- psychotherapy : 심리 요법, 정신 치료
- congruent : 알맞은, 적절한, 합동의
- indicate : 나타내다[보여 주다]
- refer to : 언급하다, …에 적용되다
- verbal : 언어[말]의, 구두의
- incongruent : 맞지 않는, 조화하지 않는

해석

모든 사람이 자신의 감정이 인생에서 다른 사람에게 어떤 영향을 미치는지 알고 있는 것은 아니다. 감정이 적절할 때에도, 그들의 강도는 문제로 이어질 수 있다. 물론 어떤 감정은 부적절하다.

(C) 감정이 적절한 것으로 간주되는지 여부는 감정이 표시되는 맥락과 관련된 사람들과 관련이 있다. 감정은 또한 일

치하거나, 일치하지 않을 수도 있다.

(B) 그들이 일치할 때, 그 감정은 전달되고 있는 메시지와 들어맞는다. 어떤 사람들은 그들의 말과 말투로 다른 감정을 나타낼 수도 있다. 때때로 이것은 언어적 행동과 비언어적 행동의 차이점이라고 일컬어진다.

(A) 그러한 메시지는 그 감정의 수신자를 혼란스럽게 하는 경향이 있고 문제를 일으킬 수 있다. 사람들이 감정을 표현할 때, 그들은 관계를 촉진하거나 그들을 탈선시킬 수 있다. 감정표현의 영향을 이해하는 것이 심리치료의 핵심이다.

[37~38]

어휘

- barely : 간신히, 가까스로, 겨우
- fiercely : 사납게, 맹렬하게
- chores : 잡일, 허드렛일
- regardless : 개의치[상관하지] 않고
- hold back : 기다리다, 저지[억제]하다
- velvety : 벨벳같은, 아주 부드러운
- soapy water : 비눗물
- beat : 이기다, 통제[억제]하다
- pitching : 투구
- ranch : 목장
- annual : 연간의, 매년의
- driveway : 진입로[차도]
- platter : 접시
- grin from ear to ear : 활짝 웃다[싱글벙글하다]
- folks : 사람들
- cuisine : 요리법, 요리
- custom : 관습, 풍습

해석

어느 날 아침, 잠에서 깨어 보니 기온이 겨우 5도였고 바람도 매섭게 불고 있었다. 아빠와 다른 카우보이들은 상관없이 집 안일을 했지만 엄마는 나를 제지했다. "너와 내가 오늘 초콜릿 케이크를 만드는 게 어때?"라고 그녀가 말했다.

엄마는 내가 찾아야 할 재료들을 말해주셨고 밀가루와 설탕을 그릇에 숟가락으로 떠서 넣기 시작했다. "사용량을 어떻게 알아요?" 하고 나는 물었다. 나는 그녀가 요리 레시피를 보는 것을 본 적이 없다.

"적당한 균형을 찾는 거야. 처음에는 실수를 하겠지만 그렇게 배우는 거란다."라고 말했다.

곧 그 집은 풍성하고 벨벳 같은 초콜릿의 달콤한 향기로 가득 찼다. 오븐에서 나오는 열기는 따뜻하고 반가웠다.

"다음엔 무슨 일이 생길지 알지?" 엄마가 내게 물었다.

"먹어요!" 하고 나는 말했다.

엄마는 웃었다. "먼저 청소를 하러 와야지." 그녀가 싱크대를 뜨거운 비눗물로 가득 채우며 말했다. 음, 심지어 재미있는 일도 힘든 일을 필요로 했다. "요리의 즐거움은 먹는 것에 관한 것이 아니다. 사람들 얼굴에 비친 미소를 보는 거야."

나는 몇 살 더 먹었을 때까지 미소가 초콜릿 케이크 한 조각을 어떻게 이길 수 있는지 잘 보지 못했다. 나는 15살이었고, 아빠, 오빠, 그리고 나는 친구의 목장에서 이웃집이라고 불리는 연례 행사인 일을 하고 있었다. 한낮쯤, 구슬땀을 얼굴에 흘리는 아빠가, "오늘은 봉급을 잘 받는 게 좋겠다."라 하는 것을 들었다. 와우, 현금 받는구나, 하고 나는 생각했다. 그리고 차도를 따라 내려오는 차를 보기 위해 고개를 들었고, 사람들이 프라이드 치킨 접시와 빵가루 입힌 돼지고기, 각종 샐러드, 케이크와 파이를 들고 왔다. 카우보이들은 활짝 웃고 있었다. 오늘에 이르기까지, 나는 아침에 열심히 일한 후에 먹은 그 음식이 얼마나 맛있었는지 기억한다. 그날 오후, 카우보이들은 웃고 떠들며 두 배나 열심히 일했다. 나는 엄마가 왜 요리하는 것을 좋아했는지에 대해 뭐라고 말했는지 생각해 보았다. 사람들에게 그렇게 많은 즐거움을 줄 수 있다는 건 꽤 특별해 보였다.

37 ⑤ 엄마가 말한 요리의 즐거움은 음식을 먹는 것이 아니고 그 음식을 먹는 사람들의 행복한 얼굴을 보는 것이다. '나'는 이것을 처음에는 이해하지 못하였지만, 나중에 직접 경험해 보고 그 말을 이해하게 된다. 그러므로 제시문의 제목으로는 ⑤의 'A Lesson on the Joy of Cooking(요리의 즐거움에 대한 교훈)'이 가장 적절하다.

오답풀이

① 오래된 습관은 쉽게 사라지지 않음
② 당신이 먹는 것이 당신을 만든다
③ 당신은 좋은 이웃인가?
④ 다양한 카우보이 요리

38 ④ 나는 아버지가 말한 '지불'이 돈인줄 알았으나, 실제로 그들이 받은 것은 맛있는 음식들이었다. 그러므로 ④의 'What the old man meant by payment was the food. (아빠가 말한 지불을 의미하는 것은 음식이었다)'는 제시문의 내용과 일치한다.

오답풀이

① 엄마가 요리를 할 때는 레시피를 충실히 따랐다.
② 엄마는 요리에 있어 가장 중요한 것은 맛이라고 했다.
③ 이웃을 부르는 풍습은 매달 행해졌다.
⑤ 카우보이들은 오후에 일하는 것을 좋아하지 않았다.

정답 및 해설

[39~40]

어휘

- interface : 인터페이스, 접속기
- exploit : 이용하다, 착취하다
- fort : 보루, 요새, 진지
- arithmetic : 산수, 연산, 계산
- transmission : 전염, 전파, 전송
- outperform : 능가하다
- demonstrate : 증거를 들어가며 보여 주다, 입증하다
- complications : 합병증
- hemorrhage : 출혈
- stimulating : 자극이 되는, 고무적인
- subthalamic nucleus : 시상밑핵
- immobilize : 움직이지 못하게 하다, 고정시키다
- lurk : 숨어 있다
- cognitive : 인식[인지]의
- complaint : 불평[항의], 통증
- alleviate : 완화하다
- functionality : 기능성, 목적, 기능
- breakthrough : 돌파구
- augment : 늘리다, 증가시키다
- dwindle : 줄어들다
- neuroscience : 신경 과학
- deprivation : 박탈[부족]
- authoritative : 권위적인, 권위 있는
- establishments : 시설, 기관, 지배층

해석

때때로 뇌와 컴퓨터 간 직접 연결 체계, 특히 임플란트는 인간이 디지털 컴퓨팅, 즉 완벽한 리콜, 빠르고 정확한 산술 계산, 고대역폭 데이터 전송의 요새를 이용할 수 있게 해줌으로써 결과적으로 하이브리드 시스템이 증강되지 않은 뇌를 획기적으로 능가할 수 있게 해 줄 수 있다고 제안된다. 그러나 인간의 두뇌와 컴퓨터 사이의 직접적인 연결 가능성은 입증되었지만, 그러한 인터페이스가 가까운 시일 내에 향상으로 널리 사용될 것 같지는 않다.

우선, 뇌에 전극을 이식할 때 감염, 진극 번위, 출혈, 인지 저하 등 의학적으로 심각한 합병증의 위험이 있다. 아마도 뇌 자극을 통해 얻을 수 있는 이점에 대한 현재까지 가장 생생한 예시는 파킨슨병 환자들의 치료일 것이다. 파킨슨 임플란트는 뇌와 실제로 소통하는 것이 아니라 단지 시상밑핵에 자극적인 전류를 공급한다는 점에서 비교적 간단하다. 실험 비디오는 실험 대상자가 의자에 털썩 주저앉아 질병에 의해 움직이지 못하다가 전류가 켜졌을 때 갑자기 살아나는 모습을 보여준다: 실험 대상자는 이제 팔을 움직이고, 일어서서 방을 가로

질러 걷고, 돌아서서 피루엣을 공연한다. 그러나 이 특히 간단하고 거의 기적적으로 성공한 절차 뒤에는 부정적인 면이 숨어 있다. 심뇌 임플란트를 받은 파킨슨 환자들에 대한 한 연구는 언어 유창성, 선택적 주의력, 색상 이름 지정, 언어 기억력 등이 대조군에 비해 감소하는 것으로 나타났다. 치료 대상자들은 또한 더 많은 인지적 불만을 보고했다. 그러한 위험과 부작용은 심각한 장애를 완화하기 위해서라면, 이 수술을 사용하는 것을 견딜 수 있을 것이다. 하지만 건강한 피실험자들이 신경외과에 자원하기 위해서는, 정상적인 기능성을 <u>상당히 향상시켜야</u> 할 것이다.

39 ④ 제시문은 뇌 자극을 통해 파킨슨병 환자가 움직임을 보이는 긍정적인 결과가 있는 반면에 언어 유창성, 선택적 주의력, 색상 이름 지정, 언어 기억력 등은 대조군에 비해 감소한다는 것을 언급한다. 그러므로 ④의 'Direct Brain-Computer Interfaces: Pros and Cons(뇌와 컴퓨터 간 직접 연결 체계: 장단점)'이 제시문의 제목으로 가장 적절하다.

오답풀이
① 뇌와 컴퓨터 간 연결 체계를 통한 전체 기능 확보
② 파킨슨병 치료의 돌파구
③ 임플란트를 통한 뇌의 힘 증가시키는 최고의 방법
⑤ 신경 과학에서의 성공에 대한 희망의 감소

40 ① 파킨슨병에 걸린 환자들은 뇌 자극 실험에 여러 가지 부작용이 있음에도 병을 완화시킬 수 있다면 견딜 수 있다고 한다. 하지만 건강한 사람이 이 실험을 하려면 여러 부작용에 대비하여 미리 정상적인 기능들을 향상시켜 놓아야 할 것이다. 그러므로 빈칸에는 ①의 'substantial enhancement(대폭 향상)'가 들어갈 말로 가장 적절하다.

오답풀이
② 보편적 허용
③ 복잡한 업적
④ 완전 박탈
⑤ 권위 있는 시설들

[41~42]

어휘

- disabled : 장애를 가진, 장애인들
- inflict : (괴로움 등을) 가하다
- definition : 정의, 의미
- proof : 증거(물), 증명(서)
- fascinated : 매료된
- obedient : 순종적인, 복종하는

- divine : 신[하느님]의, 신성한
- liberate : (사회적 제약 · 편견에서) 해방된[자유로운]
- deduce : 추론[추정]하다, 연역하다
- centre : 중심, 중앙, 가운데
- orbit : 궤도, 영향권, 궤도를 돌다
- cast : (빛을) 발하다, (그림자를) 드리우다
- chink : 틈, 가늘게 새어 들어오는 빛
- contemporary : 동시대의, 현대의, 당대의
- stunning : 굉장히 아름다운[멋진], 깜짝 놀랄
- realisation : 깨달음, 자각, 인식, 실현
- decipher : 판독하다, 해독하다
- reveal : 드러내다, 밝히다
- transcend : 초월하다

해석

수세기 동안 나 같은 장애인들은 신이 가한 시련을 받으며 살고 있다고 믿어졌다. 글쎄, 내가 저 위에서 누군가를 (A) 속상하게 했을 가능성이 있다고 생각하지만, 나는 모든 것이 자연의 법칙에 의해 다른 방식으로 설명될 수 있다고 생각하는 것을 선호한다. 만약 당신이 나처럼 과학을 믿는다면, 당신은 항상 지켜지는 어떤 법칙이 있다고 믿는다. 원한다면 율법은 신의 일이라고 할 수 있지만 그것은 신의 존재에 대한 증거라기보다는 신의 정의라고 할 수 있다. 기원전 300년경, Aristarchus라는 철학자는 특히 월식에 매료되었다. 그는 그들이 정말 신들에 의해 야기된 것인지 의문을 제기할 만큼 (B) 용감했다. Aristarchus는 진정한 과학의 선구자였다. 그는 천하를 주의 깊게 연구하여 대담한 결론에 도달했다. 그는 월식이 실제로 달 위를 지나가는 지구의 그림자라는 것과 (C) 신성한 사건이 아니라는 것을 깨달았다. 이 발견으로 자유로워진 그는 머리 위에서 실제로 무슨 일이 일어나고 있는지 알아낼 수 있었고, 태양과 지구와 달의 진정한 관계를 보여주는 도표를 그릴 수 있었다. 거기서 그는 더욱 주목할 만한 결론에 도달했다. 그는 모두가 생각했던 것처럼 지구가 우주의 중심이 아니라 태양을 공전하는 것이라고 추론했다. 사실, 이 배열의 이해는 모든 일식과 월식을 설명한다. 달이 지구에 그림자를 드리울 때, 그것은 일식이다. 그리고 지구가 달을 음영으로 가리면, 그것은 월식이다. 그러나 Aristarchus는 그것을 더 이어나갔다. 그는 그의 동시대인들이 믿었던 것처럼 별들이 천국의 바닥에서 쨍그랑거리는 것이 아니라, 별들은 우리와 같은, 아주 먼 곳에 있는 다른 태양들일 뿐이라고 제안했다. 얼마나 놀라운 현실이었을까. 우주는 <u>인간의 정신으로 이해될 수 있는 원리나 법칙에 의해 지배되는</u> 기계다.

41 ③ (A) 장애는 신으로부터 받은 시련이라고 믿고 있는 사람들이 있다고 하였으므로, 'upset(속상하게 하다)'이 적절하다.

(B) 월식과 같은 자연 현상이 정말로 신들에 의해 야기된 것일지에 대해 의문을 가진 것이므로, 신의 권능에 도전하는 것이라고 볼 수 있다. 그러므로 'brave(용감한)'가 적절하다.

(C) 월식은 신의 능력이 아니라 단지 지구의 그림자가 달을 지나가는 자연적인 현상일 뿐이라는 것을 발견해낸 것이므로, 'divine(신성한)'이 적절하다.

42 ④ 장애나 일식, 월식 등의 자연 현상은 과학이 발전하기 이전에는 인간이 이해할 수 없는 신의 권능이라고 생각되었지만, 여러 연구를 통해 그것들 역시 어떠한 원리나 법칙에 의해 움직인다는 것을 알게 되었다. 그러므로 빈칸에는 ④의 'can be understood by the human mind (인간의 정신으로 이해될 수 있다)'가 들어가는 것이 가장 적절하다.

오답풀이

① 신의 암호를 해독하다
② 신의 존재를 밝혀내다
③ 인간의 과학적 역량을 초월하다
⑤ 신과 자연의 유대를 강화하다

[43~45]

어휘

- frizzy-hair : 곱슬곱슬한 머리
- bachelorette : 미혼[독신] 여성
- variation : 변화, 변형, 변주곡
- composer : 작곡가
- foyer : 로비, 현관[입구]
- opus : 작품
- weasel : 족제비
- experiment : 실험을 하다
- atonal : 무조의
- desperately : 절망적으로, 필사적으로
- exceedingly : 극도로, 대단히
- jackass : 멍청이
- occasional : 가끔의
- allusion : 암시
- dissonance : 불협화음
- brutality : 잔인성, 야만성, 무자비
- commotion : 소란, 소동
- choreographer : 발레 편성가, 안무가
- discordant note : 불협 화음
- jubilant : 승리감에 넘치는, 의기양양한
- impartial : 공정한

- amusing : 재미있는, 즐거운
- candid : 솔직한
- reserved : 내성적인
- dexterity : 재주
- suffer from : ~로 고통받다
- knack : 재주, 요령
- overshadow : 빛을 잃게[무색하게] 만들다
- comprehensive : 포괄적인, 종합적인
- riot : 폭동, 모임[집합]

해석

나는 사실 Stravinsky에 대해 아주 일찍부터 알고 있었다. 나는 12살쯤이었다. 나는 멋지고 곱슬머리에 30대 미혼인 Denise에게서 피아노 레슨을 받고 있었는데, 그는 바흐의 변주곡인 Für Elise와 내 흥미를 유지하기 위한 스타워즈의 테마를 가르쳐 주기 위해 우리 아파트로 오곤 했다. 음악적 재능을 전혀 보이지 않는다는 사소한 문제에도 불구하고, 나는 어떻게든 그것을 다음 단계로 가야겠다고 결심했다. 나는 작곡가가 되어야 했다.

그래서 어느 주에는 매일 오후 몇 시간씩 우리 현관의 피아노 주위를 어슬렁거리고, 메모를 쓰고, 지우고, 또 몇 개 더 썼다. 마침내 금요일에 Denise가 왔고, 나는 그녀를 위해 내 작품을 연주했다. Madison 거리의 교통체증, 팩스기, 그리고 발정난 족제비들이 합쳐진 소리 같았다.

"잘했어, A.J."라고 그녀가 말했다. "너는 무조 구성에서 실험을 하고 있구나."

"네, 저는 무조 구성에 관심이 많아요." 물론, 나는 무조 작곡이 무엇인지 전혀 알지 못했다. 사실, 나는 필사적으로 조성 작곡을 하려고 노력하고 있었다. 단지 (A) 내 귀가 100% 깡통이었던 것이다.

"Stravinsky가 생각나는구나."라고 그녀가 말했다.

"아, 네, Stravinsky." 나는 고개를 끄덕이며 대답했다. Denise는 아주 친절하게 대해주고 있었다. 그녀는 나를 좌절시키고 싶지 않아 했지만, Stravinsky를 떠올릴 수 있는 유일한 방법은 Stravinsky가 우연히 건반에 앉는 것이었다.

그렇게 해서 러시아 거장을 처음 알게 되었다. 그 후, 대학에서는 Stravinsky에 대한 지식을 The Rites of Spring(봄의 제전)이라는 네 단어만큼 넓혔다. 봄의 제전을 쓴 무조 작곡가. 그것이 나의 견해였다.

Britannica로부터 나는 두 가지 중요한 것을 배웠다. 먼저, 봄의 제전이다. 단 하나의 의식이었다. 그래서 내가 Stravinsky를 가끔 넌지시 말할 때 나는 내내 얼간이처럼 들렸다. 둘째, '봄의 제전'은 1913년 5월 29일 테레 드 샹젤리제스에서 데뷔했을 때 '개야 폭동'을 일으키기에 충분했다. Stravinsky의 점수는 "스캔들한 불협화음과 율동적인 야만성"으로 시크한 파리 관객들 사이에서 소란을 일으켰다. 소동이

너무 커서 발레 무용수들은 근처 구덩이에서 오케스트라의 소리를 들을 수 없었다. 그러나 무용수들은 어쨌든 무대 옆의 의자에 서서 소리를 지르고 리듬을 흉내내는 안무가의 재촉을 받으며 계속 춤을 추었다.

난 이게 너무 좋다. 1세기 전만 해도 불협화음을 낸 발레가 실제 폭동을 일으킬 수 있다는 사실이 믿기지 않는다. 요즘 발레단의 관객은 거의 폭동을 일으키지 않는다. 그들은 종종 잠이 들기에 너무 바쁘다. 혹은 그들이 정말로 화가 났다면, 그들은 어디선가 멋진 파스타 저녁을 먹기 위해 첫 번째 연극이 마치고 떠난다.

43 ③ 자신이 연주하는 음악에 대해 표현하는 태도나 불협화음을 내는 무조음악을 듣고 솔직하게 반응했던 1세기 전의 분위기를 사랑했다고 하는 것으로 보아 필자의 태도는 'amusing and candid(재미있고 솔직한)'하다고 할 수 있다.

오답풀이

① 낙천적이고 의기양양한
② 객관적이고 공정한
④ 짜증이 나고 비판적인
⑤ 차분하고 내성적인

44 ④ 제시문에 따르면, '나'는 무조 음악에 대해 알지도 못하였고, 음조 음악을 쓰려고 하였으나 선생님의 귀에는 무조 음악처럼 들렸다. 그러므로 (A)가 의미하는 바로는 ④의 'I could not hear the differences between musical notes. (나는 음악적 음의 차이점을 들을 수 없었다)'가 가장 적절하다.

오답풀이

① 나는 작곡가의 기대에 못 미치는 건반 실력을 가졌었다.
② 나는 내 귀를 향한 Denise의 강타로 고통받았다.
③ 나는 무조 음악과 음조 음악을 작곡하는 데 재주가 있었다.
⑤ 내 연주로 인해 내 작곡 실력은 무색해졌다.

45 ③ 나는 Stravinsky에 대해 원래 알고 있었고, 그에 대해 대학에서는 그의 작품 '봄의 제전'에 대한 지식이 넓어졌다는 서술만 되어 있으므로 ③의 'I gained a comprehensive understanding of Stravinsky in college. (나는 대학에서 Stravinsky에 대한 포괄적인 이해를 얻었다)'가 제시문의 내용과 일치하지 않는다.

오답풀이

① 나의 피아노 선생님은 미혼이고 30대였다.
② 나는 피아노로 스타워즈 테마를 배운 적이 있다.
④ Britannica는 Stravinsky에 대한 나의 오해를 깨닫게 해주었다.
⑤ 나는 불협 화음이 폭동을 일으킨 것에 놀랐다.

2020학년도 기출문제 정답 및 해설

01 ②	02 ⑤	03 ①	04 ①	05 ⑤	06 ④
07 ④	08 ⑤	09 ③	10 ④	11 ③	12 ③
13 ①	14 ③	15 ④	16 ②	17 ④	18 ①
19 ⑤	20 ①	21 ②	22 ③	23 ②	24 ⑤
25 ①	26 ③	27 ②	28 ②	29 ③	30 ⑤
31 ②	32 ①	33 ④	34 ①	35 ④	36 ④
37 ③	38 ⑤	39 ⑤	40 ④	41 ⑤	42 ②
43 ②	44 ①	45 ③			

01 ② 'procrastination'은 '미루는 버릇, 지연, 연기'의 의미로 'postponement(지연, 연기, 미루기)'와 그 의미가 가장 유사하다.

오답풀이

① 조급함
③ 자발적임
④ 걱정
⑤ 과장

어휘

• procrastination : 미루는 버릇, 지연, 연기
• slipshod : 대충하는, 아무렇게나 하는
• inadequate : 불충분한, 부적당한
• properly : 제대로, 적절히, 올바르게
• hastiness : 조급함, 성급함, 경솔
• postponement : 지연, 연기, 미루기
• spontaneity : 자발적임, 즉흥적임
• exaggeration : 과장, 허풍

해석

중요한 업무나 책무가 끝나지 않거나 대충 완료되었을 때 그 업무를 제대로 완수하는 데 시간이 부족하기 때문에 <u>미루는 버릇</u>은 직장 생활에서 큰 문제가 된다.

02 ⑤ 'plummeted'는 '곤두박질치다, 급락하다'의 의미로 'drop sharply(폭락하다, 급락[급감]하다)'와 그 의미가 가장 유사하다.

오답풀이

① 갑작스럽게 호황을 맞다
② 다시 회복되다
③ 꼼짝 못하게 되다
④ 차이를 만들다

어휘

• financial crisis : 금융 위기
• the last half : 후반기, 하반기
• currency : 통화, 통용, 유통
• plummet : 곤두박질치다, 급락하다
• boom : 호황을 맞다, 번창[성공]하다
• bounce back : 다시 회복되다
• get stuck : 꼼짝 못하게 되다
• drop sharply : 폭락하다, 급락[급감]하다

해석

세계 금융 위기는 1997년 하반기에 시작되었는데, 그 때 몇몇 아시아 경제의 통화가치가 폭락했다.

03 ① 'abjure'는 '포기하다, 영구히 버리다'의 의미로 'abandon (포기하다, 버리다)'과 그 의미가 가장 유사하다.

오답풀이

② 구성하다
③ 수정하다
④ 영감을 떠올리다
⑤ 정성 들여 만들다

어휘

• quotation : 인용, 인용구[문]
• deftly : 솜씨 좋게, 능숙하게
• fabric : 직물, 구조, 뼈대
• prose : 산문
• abjure : 포기하다, 영구히 버리다
• paraphrase : 다른 말로 바꾸어 표현하다, 바꾸어 쓰다[말하다]
• abandon : 포기하다, 버리다
• brainstorm : 브레인스토밍을 하다, 영감[멋진 생각]을 떠올리다

정답 및 해설

• elaborate : 정성 들여 만들다, 공들여 해내다

해석

산문의 구조에 능숙하게 인용구를 엮을 수 없다면, 그것들을 모두 버리고 대신 다른 말로 바꾸어 표현하라.

04 ① 'rudimentary'는 '기초적인, 기본적인'의 의미로 'basic(기본적인, 근본적인)'과 그 의미가 가장 유사하다.

오답풀이

② 깊은
③ 최적의
④ 의식하는
⑤ 추상적인

어휘

• application : 응용프로그램
• responsive : 즉각 반응[대응]하는, 호응하는
• spelling checker : 철자법 검사기
• rudimentary : 기초적인, 기본적인
• optimal : 최적의, 최상의
• conscious : 의식하는, 지각하는

해석

개인용 컴퓨터의 성능 향상은 사용자에게 더 똑똑하고 더 즉각 반응하는 응용프로그램의 개발을 가능하게 하고 있다. 철자법이나 문법 검사기를 사용해 본 사람이라면 매우 기초적인 수준에서 이런 유형의 응용프로그램을 경험해 본 적이 있다.

05 ⑤ 'tenacious'는 '질긴, 끈질긴'의 의미로 'persistent(끈질긴, 집요한)'과 그 의미가 가장 유사하다.

오답풀이

① 독단적인
② 믿을 수 있는
③ 유용한
④ 도식의

어휘

• written language : 문어(文語), 문자 언어
• more or less : 거의, 액[대략]
• extremely : 극히, 매우
• tenacious : 질긴, 끈질긴, 집요한
• arbitrary : 제멋대로인, 독단적인
• reliable : 믿을 수 있는, 신뢰할 만한
• persistent : 끈질긴, 집요한

해석

문자 언어가 지금과 거의 비슷해 보일 것이라고 생각하는 한

가지 이유는 지금까지 그것들이 매우 끈질긴 것으로 판명되었기 때문이다. 중국어 체계는 3천 년 이상 거의 변하지 않았고, 현대 그리스어는 거의 오랫동안 사용되어 온 알파벳으로 쓰여 왔다.

06 ④ 'haphazardly'는 '무턱대고, 되는 대로'의 의미로 'randomly(무작위로, 닥치는 대로)'와 그 의미가 가장 유사하다.

오답풀이

① 은밀히
② 변함없이
③ 명쾌하게
⑤ 정확하게

어휘

• formula : 식, 공식, 방식
• reactive : 반응을 보이는
• fall back on : ~에 기대다[의지하다]
• haphazardly : 무턱대고, 되는 대로
• covertly : 은밀히, 몰래, 살며시
• invariably : 변함없이, 언제나
• explicitly : 명쾌하게, 명확하게
• randomly : 무작위로, 닥치는 대로
• precisely : 바로, 꼭, 정확히

해석

결정을 내리는 데 명확한 방식이 부족하면, 우리는 반응을 보이게 되고 무엇을 해야 할지 결정하는 데 익숙하고 편안한 방법에 의지하게 된다. 결과적으로, 우리는 우리의 목표를 지지하지 않는 방법을 무턱대고 선택한다.

07 ④ 'that' 이하의 종속절의 주어는 앞의 'the Description del'Egyptek'이므로, 이를 대신하는 지시대명사는 복수 형태인 'they'가 아니라 단수 형태인 'it'을 사용해야 한다.

오답풀이

① 선행사 'the date'를 수식하기 위한 형용사절로 '전치사 + 관계대명사'의 형태인 'at which'를 사용한 것은 적절하며, 때를 나타내는 관계부사 'when'으로 바꿔쓸 수 있다.
② 'become' 다음에 과거분사가 와서 형용사의 역할을 대신하므로, 과거분사 'transformed'를 사용한 것은 적절하다.
③ 글의 문맥상 '~에서 기인하다[비롯되다]'의 의미인 'result from'을 사용한 것은 적절하다.
⑤ 분사구문의 형태로 현재분사인 'providing'을 사용한 것은 적절하다.

어휘

- antiquarianism : 골동품 연구[취미]
- supersede : 대체하다, 대신하다
- archaeology : 고고학
- antiquity : 고대, (고대의) 유물
- discipline : 학과, 학문, 지식 분야
- Egyptology : 이집트학
- expedition : 탐험[대], 원정[대]
- remains : 유적, 유물
- pharaonic : 파라오의[같은]
- multi-volume : 권수가 많은, 여러 권으로 된
- accuracy : 정확[도], 정밀[도]
- constitute : 구성하다, 이루다
- internally : 내부로, 내적으로
- consistent : 한결같은, 일관된, 변함없는
- appraisal : 평가[회], 평가제
- assessment : 평가, 부과
- entirety : 전체, 전부 cf) in one's entirety 통째로, 전부

해석

유럽의 골동품 연구가 고고학으로 대체된 날짜의 문제와 마찬가지로, '조기 여행자'의 저술과 이집트 유물의 수집이 현대 이집트 학문 분야에 근접한 것으로 변형된 구체적인 날짜를 제시하기는 쉽지 않다. 그러나 이집트 고고학의 대부분의 역사는 19세기 초 나폴레옹의 탐험을 이집트의 파라오 입석 유적을 기록하고 묘사하려고 한 최초의 조직적 시도로 여긴다. 탐험으로 비롯된 여러 권의 출판물인 '델 이집택의 묘사'의 중요성은 높은 수준의 정확성뿐만 아니라 학자들 집단에 의한 지속적이고 내적으로 일관된 평가회를 구성하였다는 사실에 있으며, 이로 인해 고대 이집트에 대한 최초의 실제 평가를 제공했다.

08 ⑤ 선행사 'a worry'를 수식하기 위한 형용사절이 와야 하므로 관계대명사를 사용해야 하고, 종속절이 완전한 문장이므로 '전치사 + 관계대명사'의 형태인 'about which'로 바꿔 써야 한다.

오답풀이

① 'million'은 수의 단위를 나타내며 앞에 수사가 있어도 복수형으로 하지 않는다. 따라서 단수 형태의 'million'을 사용한 것은 적절하다.
② 'half'는 한정사보다 앞에 쓰여서 명사를 수식하는 전치한정사로써 적절하게 사용되었다.
③ 글의 문맥상 'bad'의 최상급 형태인 'worst'를 사용한 것은 적절하다.
④ 글의 문맥상 '~함에 따라(비례 용법)'의 의미를 지닌 접속사 'as'를 사용한 것은 적절하다.

어휘

- ha : 헥타르(hectare)
- illegal : 불법적인, 비합법적인
- logging : 벌목
- land clearing : 개간, 개척지
- hazard : 위험, 모험
- sub-Saharan : 사하라 사막 이남의
- account for : (부분·비율을) 차지하다
- corrupt : 부패하게 만들다, 타락시키다
- ineffective : 비효과적인, 무능한, 무력한
- poverty : 빈곤, 가난
- civil unrest : 사회 불안
- internal : 내부의, 국내의
- refugee : 난민, 망명자
- drought : 가뭄
- infestation : 침입, 습격, 만연
- catastrophically : 파멸로, 비극으로

해석

화재는 매년 약 3억 5천만 헥타르(1,350 평방미터)의 숲을 파괴한다. 어떤 화재는 사람들이 불법적인 벌목이나 토지 개간을 은폐하기 위해 계획된다. 다른 화재는 자연적인 원인에 의해 시작된다. 세계에서 가장 큰 화재 위험은 전 세계의 약 절반 비율을 차지하는 사하라 사막 이남 아프리카에 있다. 방치된 화재는 부패하거나 무능한 정부 그리고 높은 수준의 빈곤, 시민 불안 및 내부 난민을 가진 나라에서 최악이 되기 쉽다. 세계 기후 변화로 세계 각 지역에 가뭄과 곤충이 들끓음에 따라, 산불이 비극적으로 증가할 우려가 있다.

09 ③ 'Had Clinton not been as agile as ~'는 'If Clinton had not been as agile as ~'에서 접속사 'If'가 생략되고 주어와 동사가 도치된 가정법 과거완료 구문이다. 따라서 주절의 동사인 'would be'도 가정법 과거완료 구문에 해당하는 동사인 'would have been'으로 바꿔 써야 한다.

오답풀이

① 종속절의 주어가 3인칭인 'experience'이므로, 현재완료 시제로 'has + p.p'의 형태인 'has taught'를 사용한 것은 적절하다.
② 동사 'succeed'는 '성공하다'와 '뒤를 잇다'의 두 의미로 사용되는데, 전자의 명사형은 'success(성공)'이며 후자의 명사형은 'succession(연속)'이다. 본문에서 'a succession of'는 '일련의, 연이은'의 의미로 문맥상 올바르게 사용되었다.
④ 'just the opposite'은 '정반대'의 의미로 올바르게 사용되었다.

⑤ 'even if(비록 ~일지라도, ~라 하더라도)'는 양보를 나타내는 접속사로 문맥상 올바르게 사용되었다.

어휘

• contemporary : 동시대의, 현대의, 당대의
• hit the ground running : (성공적으로) 잘 나가다, 의욕적으로 시작하다
• stumble : 비틀거림, 실수, 잘못, 실착
• succession : 연속, 잇따름, 계승
• legislative : 입법의, 입법부의
• debacle : 대실패, 와해, 붕괴
• Congress : 의회, 국회
• agile : 날렵한, 민첩한, 재빠른
• one-term : 한 임기의, 단임의
• transformational : 변형의, 변화의, 변혁적인
• the head of a union : 노조위원장
• stature : 지명도, 위상, 지위
• presidency : 대통령 직[임기], 회장 직[임기]
• evaporate : 증발하다, 사라지다
• Hundred Days : 백일 의회(루즈벨트 대통령의 뉴딩 정책 등 중요 법안 가결)

해석

만약 동시대의 경험이 우리에게 무언가를 가르쳐준다면, 확실히 대통령이 의욕적으로 시작할 필요가 있다. 레이건의 빠른 출발과 클린턴의 비틀거림의 차이로 하나는 입법부의 승리가 계속되는 길에 접어들었고 다른 하나는 의료의 붕괴와 의회의 패배로 가는 길에 들어섰다. 만약 클린턴이 1993년 말에 회복 중에 있는 것만큼 민첩하지 못했더라면, 1995년에 다시 그는 한 임기의 대통령이 되었을 것이다. 그 상황이었다면, 그는 결코 자신이 바라던 변혁적인 인물이 되지 못했다. 대부분의 기관에서 지도자의 권력은 시간이 지남에 따라 커진다. CEO, 대학 총장, 노조위원장은 장기간의 실적을 통해 지위를 얻는다. 대통령직은 정반대이다. 즉, 권력이 빠르게 사라지기 쉽다. 대통령이 그의 첫 100일 동안 프랭클린 루즈벨트에 필적해야 하는 것은 아니지만, 취임 첫 달은 그가 두 번의 임기를 모두 채우더라도, 보통 그에게 열린 가장 넓은 기회의 창이다. 그래서 그는 서둘러 움직여야만 한다.

10 ④ 제시문에 따르면 미래에 대한 예측을 분석하는 방법도 의학과 마찬가지로 엄격하게 적용하기를 바라지만, 20세기 초의 의학이 여전히 증거보다는 주로 명성에 토대를 두고 있었으므로 그것은 쉽지 않은 싸움이 될 것이다. 그러므로 ④의 'easy(쉬운)'는 문맥상 'difficult(어려운)' 등으로 바꿔 써야 적절하다.

오답풀이

① 완전히 발달한
② 무관한
③ 분석하다
⑤ 명성

어휘

• superforecasting : 초예측
• prediction : 예측, 예견
• medicine : 의학, 의술, 의료
• black art : 마법, 마술
• fledged : 깃털이 다 난, 날 수 있게 된 cf) fully fledged 완전히 발달한, 필요한 자격을 다 갖춘
• controversial : 논란이 많은, 논란의 여지가 있는
• qualification : 자격, 자격증
• eminence : 명성, 저명
• confidence : 신뢰, 믿음
• irrelevant : 무관한, 상관없는
• treatment's effectiveness : 치료 효과
• statistically : 통계상으로, 통계적으로
• rigorously : 엄격히, 엄밀히
• bring about : 야기하다, 초래하다
• rigor : 엄격, 준엄, 엄격한 적용
• evidence : 증거, 증언

해석

'초예측 : 예측 기법과 과학'이란 저서는 1909년에 태어난 스코틀랜드 의사인 Archie Cochrane에 대한 토론으로 시작되는데, 그는 아마 누구 이상으로 의학을 마법에서 완전히 발달한 과학으로 탈바꿈시켰다. 반세기 전에 심도 깊은 논란이 되었던 그의 통찰력은 의사의 자격, 명성 및 신뢰는 무관한 것이며 치료 효과에 대한 유일한 시험은 통계적으로나 엄밀하게 효과를 보여줄 수 있는 지의 여부였다. 이 책의 저자인 'Tetlock'씨는 사람들이 미래에 대한 예측을 분석하는 방법도 마찬가지로 엄격하게 적용하기를 희망했다. 그것은 쉬운(→ 어려운) 싸움이 될 것이다. 예측은 20세기 초의 의학과 마찬가지로 여전히 증거보다는 주로 명성에 토대를 두고 있다.

11 ③ 제시문의 마지막 문장에서 응답자의 1/4에서 1/30이 실제로 투표하지 않았을 때 투표했다고 말한 것으로 일관되게 나타났다고 서술되어 있으므로, 응답자들은 자신들이 투표하지 않는다는 것을 인정하지 않을 수도 있다. 그러므로 ③의 'deny(부인하다)'는 'admit(인정하다)' 등으로 바꿔 써야 적절하다.

오답풀이

① 진실성

② 가리다

④ 진실성

⑤ 분류하다

어휘

• polling : 투표, 여론조사

• wiggle : 흔들림 cf) wiggle room 자유 재량권

• veracity : 진실성, 정직함

• shade : 그늘지게 하다, 가리다, 감추다

• embarrassing : 당혹스러운, 난처한

• overstate : 과장하다, 부풀리다

• integrity : 완전, 무결, 흠 없음

• crucially : 결정적으로, 중요하게

• sort : 분류하다, 구분하다

• pollster : 여론 조사원[조사자]

• self-reported : 자가 보고된, 스스로 보고하는 형식의

• consistently : 지속적으로, 끊임없이, 항상

해석

여론조사는 인터넷 데이트와 같다. 제공된 정보의 진실성에는 약간의 흔들림의 여지가 있다. 특히 질문이 난처하거나 민감할 때, 우리는 사람들이 진실을 가린다는 것을 알고 있다. 응답자들은 그들의 수입을 부풀릴 수 있다. 그들은 자신들이 투표하지 않는다는 것을 부인하지(→ 인정하지) 않을 수도 있다. 그들은 평판이 나쁘거나 사회적으로 용납될 수 없는 견해를 밝히는 데 주저할 수도 있다. 이 모든 이유로, 가장 세심하게 계획된 여론조사조차도 응답자들의 답변의 진실성에 의존한다. 선거 여론조사는 선거일에 투표할 사람과 그렇지 않은 사람을 분류하는 데 결정적으로 달려 있다. 사람들은 여론 조사원들이 듣고 싶은 말이라고 생각하기 때문에 종종 그들이 투표할 거라고 말한다. 자체 보고된 투표 행동과 선거 기록을 비교한 연구에 따르면 응답자의 1/4에서 1/30이 실제로 투표하지 않았을 때 투표했다고 말한 것으로 일관되게 나타난다.

12 ③ (A) 불독과 스패니얼처럼 서로 짝짓기를 해서 계속 자손을 번식할 수 있다면 같은 종에 속한다고 할 수 있으므로 'fertile(생식력 있는)'이 적절하다.

　　(B) 말과 당나귀는 서로 다른 두 종(種)이기 때문에 짝짓기를 한다 해도 그 새끼는 번식력이 없으므로 'sterile(불임의)'이 적절하다.

　　(C) 말과 당나귀는 결과적으로 서로 다른 두 종이기 때문에 그 진화 경로가 다르다. 즉 분리된 진화 경로에 따라 움직이므로 'separate(분리된)'가 들어갈 말로 적절하다.

어휘

• biologist : 생물학자

• organism : 유기체, 생물

• species : 종(種)

• mate with : ~와 짝짓기하다

• give birth to : 낳다, 출산하다

• fertile : 새끼를 많이 낳는, 번식력이 있는

• sterile : 불임의, 새끼를 낳지 못하는

• offspring : 자식, 새끼

• trait : 특성, 특징

• induce : 유도하다, 유발하다

• mutation : 돌연변이, 변화[변형]

• vice versa : 거꾸로, 반대로

• consequently : 결과적으로, 그 결과

• distinct : 별개의, 서로 다른, 구별되는

• evolutionary : 진화의

• bulldog : 불독

• spaniel : 스패니얼(기다란 귀가 뒤로 처져 있는 작은 개)

• pair off with : ~와 짝이 되다

해석

생물학자들은 생물을 종으로 분류한다. 동물들이 서로 짝짓기를 해서 (A) 생식력 있는 새끼를 낳는다면 같은 종(種)에 속한다고 한다. 말과 당나귀는 현세의 공통 조상을 가지고 있고 많은 신체적 특징들을 함께한다. 그러나 그 동물들은 서로에게 성적인 관심을 거의 보이지 않는다. 그 동물들은 그렇게 하도록 유도되면 짝짓기를 하겠지만 그 새끼는 (B) 불임이다. 따라서 당나귀 DNA의 돌연변이는 결코 말에게 건너갈 수 없으며, 그 반대도 마찬가지이다. 이 두 종류의 동물은 결과적으로 서로 다른 두 종으로 여겨지며, (C) 분리된 진화 경로를 따라 움직인다. 이와 대조적으로 불독과 스패니얼은 매우 다르게 보일 수도 있지만, 그 동물들은 같은 종의 일원으로 동일한 DNA 풀을 공유하고 있다. 그들은 행복하게 짝짓기를 할 것이고 그들의 강아지들은 자라서 다른 개들과 짝짓기를 하여 더 많은 강아지를 낳을 것이다.

13 ① (A) 정보 범람의 속도가 데이터를 신속하고 효율적으로 처리하는 속도를 넘어서는 것이므로, 'overwhelm(능가하다)'이 적절하다.

　　(B) 빅데이터를 효과적으로 이용하기 위한 방법과 도구들을 찾지 못한다면 정보의 홍수에 계속해서 빠지는 것이므로, 'drown(물에 빠지다)'이 적절하다.

　　(C) 빅데이터의 힘을 성공적으로 이용하기 위해 이미 취해진 조치들과 더불어 지금 취할 수 있는 조치가 많다는 의미이므로, 'harness(이용하다)'가 적절하다.

어휘

- drawback : 단점, 결점, 문제점
- overwhelm : 압도하다, 능가하다
- maximize : 극대화하다
- take action : 조치를 취하다, 행동에 옮기다
- appropriate : 적절한, 타당한
- methodology : 방법론
- evolve : 진화하다, 발달하다
- drown : 물에 빠져 죽다, 익사하다
- security : 보안, 경비, 안전
- adequate : 충분한, 적절한
- deadly : 치명적인, 극도의
- ensure : 보장하다, 보호하다
- harness : 마구를 채우다, 이용하다
- renounce : 포기하다, 단념하다

해석

빅데이터에는 단점이 있다. 정보의 범람은 일부는 유용하고 일부는 그렇지 않은데, 신속하고 효율적으로 데이터를 처리하고 적절한 조치를 취하는 능력을 (A) 능가할 수 있다. 만약 우리가 빅데이터를 효과적으로 이용하기 위해 방법론과 도구를 만들어 활용하지 못한다면, 우리는 계속해서 그 속에 (B) 빠질 지도 모른다. 국가 안보의 맥락에서, 적절한 빅데이터 도구가 없다면 엄청나고 심지어 치명적인 결과를 초래할 수 있다. 하지만, 우리가 빅데이터의 힘을 성공적으로 (C) 이용하기 위해 많은 경우에 이미 취해진 조치들, 즉 지금 취할 수 있는 조치들이 있다.

14 ③ 제시문에 따르면 미국 사회는 인종적, 종교적, 언어적 다양성의 존재를 인정하고 피부색, 성별, 나이에 상관없이 모든 사람들이 동등한 권리를 보장받는다고 서술하고 있다. 그러나 ③은 갈등적 요소에 대해 언급하고 있으므로 전체적인 글의 흐름과 어울리지 않는다.

어휘

- melting pot : 용광로, 도가니
- diversity : 다양성, 포괄성
- attitude : 자세, 태도, 사고방식
- constitutional : 입헌의, 헌법적인
- separation : 분리, 분열
- principle : 원리, 원칙
- guarantee : 보장하다, 약속하다
- worship : 예배, 숭배
- diverse : 다양한, 가지각색의
- conflict : 충돌, 갈등
- regardless of : ~에 상관없이

- gender : 성, 성별
- geographical : 지리학의, 지리적인

해석

미국은 서로 다른 배경의 사람들이 어떤 식으로든 모두 똑같아진다는 점에서 사실 '용광로'가 아니다. 미국은 항상 생각, 태도, 행동의 다양성을 내재하고 있다. ① 예를 들어, 미국의 초기부터 존재한 기본 원칙인 교회와 주(州)의 헌법적 분리는 모든 종교인들이 숭배와 종교 행위에 대해 똑같은 자유와 권리를 갖는다는 것을 보장한다. ② 다양한 종교적 배경을 가진 사람들이 함께 하나의 종교로 '융합'될 것으로 기대되지 않는다. ③ 갈등은 배경이 같든 다르든 간에, 단순히 사람들 사이에서 일어난다. ④ 다른 법들은 피부색, 성별, 나이에 상관없이 모든 사람들의 동등한 권리를 보장한다. ⑤ 미국은 심지어 공식적인 국가 언어조차 가지고 있지 않으며, 다양한 지역에서 많은 정부 간행물과 다른 출판물 또한 다양한 언어로 제공된다. 요컨대, 한 국가로서 미국은 다양성의 현실과 이점을 항상 인식해 왔다.

15 ④ 제시문에 따르면 기계 기술의 발전은 일시적으로 개별 근로자를 대체하여 고용 위기를 불러오지만, 장기적으로 비용과 가격을 낮추고 수요를 증가시킴으로써 새로운 고용 기회를 창출한다고 하였다. 따라서 기계가 인간 기술의 필요성을 감소시킨다는 ④의 내용은 전체적인 글의 흐름과 대치되므로 적절하지 못하다.

어휘

- displace : 대신하다, 대체하다
- obsolete : 더 이상 쓸모가 없는, 한물간, 구식의
- fireman : (증기기관차의) 화부(火夫), 기관 조수
- employee : 종업원, 직원
- shovel : 삽질하다, 삽으로 푸다
- locomotive boiler : 기관차 보일러
- union support : 노조 지원
- cease : 그만두다, 멈추다
- temporary : 일시적인, 임시의
- reduce : 줄이다, 감소하다
- hold down : 억제하다, 견뎌내다
- employment : 고용, 취업
- establish : 설립하다, 구축하다

해석

기계가 특정 직업에서 개별 근로자를 대체하고 단기적으로는 이것이 종종 어려운 문제를 일으킨다는 것에 대해 아무도 의문을 제기하지 않는다. ① 예를 들어, 철도에 디젤 엔진과 전력의 사용으로 화부(火夫), 즉 기차의 증기기관용 증기를 생산하는 기관차 보일러에 삽으로 석탄을 퍼넣는 직원의 자리는

쓸모없게 되었지만, 노조의 지원 때문에 철도회사는 기차에 사용된 증기 동력이 중단된 후 수년 동안 이 자리를 채워야만 했다. ② 그러나 그러한 문제들은 일시적이다. ③ 궁극적으로, 기계 기술의 발전은 비용과 가격을 낮추거나 그것을 억제하는 경향이 있고, 사람들이 더 많은 상품을 구입할 수 있도록 함으로써 새로운 고용 기회를 창출한다. ④ 기계는 인간 기술의 필요성을 감소시킨다. ⑤ 만약 어떤 산업에서 더 적은 노동자를 고용한다면, 다른 산업에서 더 많은 노동자를 고용한다. 동시에 신상품이 도입되고 신산업이 구축된다.

16 ② 제시문은 법적 성인은 어떤 치료도 거부할 권리가 있으나 정신병은 예외적으로 강제적인 치료를 규정하고 있다는 내용이다. 그러므로 빈칸에는 'compulsory(강제적인, 의무적인)'가 들어갈 말로 가장 적절하다.

[오답풀이]

① 대체 가능한
③ 부가적인
④ 증가의
⑤ 예방을 위한

[어휘]

- competent : 유능한, 법적 능력[자격]이 있는
- treatment : 치료, 처치
- apply to : ~에 적용되다
- Mental Health Act : 정신보건법
- mental disorder : 정신 장애[이상]
- alternative : 대체 가능한, 대안이 되는
- compulsory : 강제적인, 의무적인, 필수의
- adjunctive : 부속의, 첨부의, 부가적인
- incremental : 증가의, 증대하는
- preventive : 예방[방지]을 위한

[해석]

법적 성인은 심지어 생명을 구하는 어떤 치료도 거부할 권리가 있다는 것이 많은 법체제의 원칙이다. 이 원칙은 신체 질병의 치료에 적용된다. 그러나 많은 나라에서 정신병을 앓고 있는 사람들에게는 적용되지 않는다. 영국의 경우를 보면, 정신병 환자의 강제적인 치료를 규정한 정신보건법이 있다.

17 ④ 제시문에 따르면 테니스, 수영, 골프, 스키를 포함한 일부 스포츠는 비용이 많이 들어서 주로 부유층이 참여하지만, 축구, 야구, 농구는 모든 소득수준의 사람들이 접할 수 있다고 하였다. 즉, 부의 정도나 사회적 지위에 따라 스포츠의 종류를 선택할 수 있는 것이므로, 빈칸에는 'standing(지위, 평판)'이 들어갈 말로 가장 적절하다.

[오답풀이]

① 속박
② 요구
③ 유행
⑤ 선호

[어휘]

- social-conflict : 사회적 갈등
- analysis : 분석
- inequality : 불평등, 불균형
- participation : 참여, 참가
- well-to-do : 부유한, 잘사는
- accessible : 접근 가능한, 이용 가능한
- reflect : 반사하다, 반영하다
- bonds : 구속, 굴레
- standing : 지위, 평판
- preference : 선호, 애호

[해석]

사회 갈등 분석은 스포츠가 사회적 불평등과 밀접하게 관련이 있다고 지적하는 것에서 시작된다. 테니스, 수영, 골프, 스키를 포함한 일부 스포츠는 비용이 많이 들어서 참여는 주로 부유층에 국한된다. 그러나 축구, 야구, 농구는 모든 소득수준의 사람들이 접할 수 있다. 요컨대, 사람들이 하는 게임은 단순히 선택의 문제가 아니라 사회적 지위를 반영한다.

18 ① 제시문에서 동기부여적 자극은 중간 난이도로 추정되는 작업에서 가장 좋다고 나타나므로, 만약 성공률이 매우 높거나 또는 매우 낮다고 여겨지면 동기부여적 자극은 약해지게 된다. 그러므로 빈칸에는 'weakened(약화시키다)'가 들어갈 말로 가장 적절하다.

[오답풀이]

② 동원하다
③ 등락을 거듭하다
④ 안정시키다
⑤ 교체하다

[어휘]

- expectancy : 기대치, 기대하는 것
- motivational : 동기부여적인
- arousal : 자극, 흥분
- assumption : 가정, 추정
- indicate : 나타내다, 보여주다
- moderate : 보통의, 중간의
- difficulty : 어려운 정도, 난이도
- mobilize : 동원하다, 집결시키다

정답 및 해설

• fluctuate : 변동[등락]을 거듭하다

• stabilize : 안정시키다, 고정시키다

• alternate : 번갈아 나오다, 교대[교체]하다

해석

성공이 동기부여에 미치는 영향은 무엇인가? 동기는 반드시 높여야 하는가? 앞선 주장은 일부 활동에서 성공적인 성과가 목표로 이어진다는 것을 학습자가 깨닫게 되면 기대치가 상승할 가능성이 높다는 것을 시사한다. 이것은 성공이 동기부여를 증가시키는 경향이 있다고 말하는 것처럼 보이지만, 문제는 그렇게 간단하지 않다. 이 주장은 잠재적인 동기는 고려하고 동기부여적 자극은 무시한다. 동기부여적 자극은 활동을 올바르게 수행하기 위해 얼마나 많은 노력이 필요한지에 대한 한 사람의 추정에 근거한다. 연구에 따르면 동기부여적 자극은 중간 난이도로 추정되는 작업에 가장 좋다고 나타난다. 만약 성공률이 매우 높거나 매우 낮다고 여겨지면, 동기부여적 자극은 약해진다. 다시 말해서, 우리가 도전적이라고 생각하지만 거의 불가능하지 않은 것들을 위해 우리는 가장 열심히 노력한다.

19 ⑤ 지네딘 지단은 마르세유에서 태어나고 자란 프랑스인이자 그의 부모가 알제리에서 이민 온 북아프리카 사람이기도 하다. 또한 이슬람교도이자 유명한 축구선수이다. 이러한 지네딘 지단의 정체성은 그가 어디에서 어떻게 생각하느냐에 따라 달라지므로, 그의 정체성은 유동적이라는 것이다. 그러므로 빈칸에 들어갈 말로는 'fluid(유동적인)'가 가장 적절하다.

오답풀이

① 독특한

② 민족의

③ 정치적인

④ 토종의

어휘

• identity : 신원, 신분, 정체성

• tricky : 힘든, 까다로운

• compilation : 편집, 편찬, 편성

• claim : 주장하다, 요청[요구]하다

• impose : 강요하다, 부과하다

• outsider : 외부인, 국외자

• aftermath : 여파, 후유증 cf) in the aftermath of ~의 여파로

• emigrate : 이민을 가다, 이주하다

• reportedly : 전하는 바에 따르면, 들리는 바로는

• fiercely : 사납게, 맹렬하게, 지독하게

• ancestral : 조상의, 전래의

• multifaceted : 다면적인

• unique : 고유의, 독특한

• ethnic : 민족의, 종족의

• indigenous : 토종의, 토착의

• fluid : 유동적인, 가변적인

해석

아프리카의 역사가들에게 정체성은 까다로운 이지적 문제가 될 수 있다. 어느 곳의 사람들과 마찬가지로 아프리카인들은 수많은 정체성을 구성하고 있는데, 그 중 일부는 개인적으로나 집단적으로 주장되고, 다른 일부는 외부인에 의해 강요된다. 만약 사람들에게 누가 현존하는 가장 유명한 아프리카인이냐고 묻는다면, 통상적 대답은 '넬슨 만델라'이다. 그러나 2006년 월드컵의 여파로 이것에 답할 때, 현존하는 가장 유명한 아프리카인이 지네딘 지단이라고 말하는데 충분한 사유가 있다. 이 한 사람을 지세히 살펴보자. 지단이 누구며 어떤 사람인가? 그는 마르세유에서 태어나고 자란 프랑스인이다. 그러나 또한 북아프리카 사람이고, 부모는 알제리에서 이민을 왔다. 그리고 가족의 뿌리인 베르베르족(族)은 카빌 산에 있으며, 들리는 바로는 자기 조상 마을에 대해 매우 자랑스러워한다고 한다. 그는 또한 자신을 이슬람교도라고 설명한다. 그리고 물론 그는 축구선수다. 지단 스스로 선택해 사용할 이 꼬리표 중 어느 것이든 그가 어디에 있는지 그리고 그때 어떻게 생각하고 있는가에 달려 있다. 즉, 정체성은 다면적인 것 만큼 유동적이다.

20 ① 피카소, 마야 안젤로, 아인슈타인 등은 각 분야에서 많은 작품과 논문을 발표했지만 정작 호평을 받은 것은 소수에 불과했다. 즉, 위인의 명성은 하루 아침에 이루어진 것이 아니라 부단한 작품 활동과 끊임없는 연구의 결과이므로, ①의 'do a lot of work (많은 일을 해라)'가 빈칸에 들어갈 말로 가장 적절하다.

오답풀이

② 채무불이행을 거부하다

③ 급진적인 위험을 무릅쓰다

④ 새로운 통찰력을 얻다

⑤ 더 나은 방법을 탐구하다

어휘

• oeuvre : 일생의 작품, 모든 작품, 전작(全作)

• sculpture : 조각, 조소, 조각품

• ceramic : 도자기

• drawing : 그림, 소묘, 데생

• not to mention : ~은 말할 것도 없이, 물론이고

• rug : 깔개, 양탄자, 무릎덮개

• tapestry : 태피스트리(색실로 짠 추단)

• fraction : 부분, 일부

- garner : 얻다, 모으다
- acclaim : 찬사, 칭찬, 호평
- poetry : 시, 시가
- recite : 암송하다, 낭송하다
- memoir : 회고록, 전기
- pay attention to : ~에 주의를 기울이다
- autobiography : 자서전, 수기
- relativity : 상대성, 상대성 이론
- reject : 거부하다, 거절하다
- default : 불이행, 태만
- radical : 과격한, 급진적인

해석

피카소 일생의 작품에는 인쇄물, 러그, 태피스트리는 물론이고, 1,800여 점의 그림, 1,200여 점의 조각품, 2,800여 점의 도자기, 그리고 12,000여 점의 소묘가 포함되어 있는데, 이 중 극히 일부만이 호평을 얻었다. 시 분야에서, 우리가 마야 안젤로의 고전 시인 "Still I Rise"를 낭송할 때, 우리는 그녀가 165편의 다른 시를 썼다는 것을 잊어버리기 쉽다. 우리는 그녀의 감동적인 회고록 "I Know Why the Caged Bird Sings"를 기억하나 그녀의 다른 6편의 자서전에는 관심을 덜 기울인다. 과학 분야에서, 아인슈타인은 물리학에 변혁을 가져온 일반 상대성 이론과 특수 상대성 이론에 관한 논문을 썼지만, 그의 248권의 출판물 중 상당수가 최소한의 영향을 미쳤다. 'This American Life'와 팟캐스트 'Serial'의 제작자인 아이라 글래스는 만약 당신이 독창적인 사람이 되고 싶다면 "당신이 할 수 있는 가장 중요한 일은 많은 일을 하는 것이다."라고 말한다.

21 ② 제시문에서 Witmer가 박사학위를 받을 당시, 심리학은 본질적으로 학문적 연구 분야였지 그 분야를 특징짓는 응용 기능은 거의 없었다고 하였다. 그러므로 빈칸에는 1800년대 후반의 심리학의 특징을 설명한 ②의 "psychologists didn't practice psychology, but studied it (심리학자들은 심리학을 실습하지 않고 연구했다)"이 들어갈 말로 가장 적절하다.

오답풀이

① 실험심리학 분야는 인기가 없었다
③ Lightner Witmer는 독일의 대표적인 심리학자였다
④ 심리학 박사학위를 받는데 많은 노력을 했다
⑤ Wilhelm Wundt는 임상심리학 탄생의 장을 마련했다

어휘

- doctorate : 박사학위
- experimental psychology : 실험심리학
- pioneer : 개척자, 선구자
- essentially : 근본적으로, 본질적으로

- academic discipline : 학과, 교과
- apply : 신청하다, 지원하다, 적용하다
- characterize : 특징짓다, 특징 지우다
- doctoral degree : 박사학위
- set the stage for : ~을 위한 장을 마련하다, ~의 기초를 닦다
- clinical psychology : 임상심리학

해석

Lightner Witmer는 1892년 독일에서 심리학 박사학위를 받았는데, 많은 사람들이 실험심리학의 창시자로 여긴 Willhelm Wundt 수하에 있었다. 그는 또한 실험심리학의 또다른 개척자인 James KcKeen Cattell 수하에서 연구했다. Witmer가 박사학위를 받을 당시, 심리학은 본질적으로 학문 연구 분야였다. 오늘날 그 분야를 특징짓는 응용 기능은 거의 없었다. 요컨대 1800년대 후반에 심리학자들은 심리학을 실습하지 않고 연구했다.

22 ③ 제시문에 따르면 물의 효용성은 생사의 문제가 될 만큼 엄청난 가치를 지니고 있지만 공짜이거나 매우 낮은 가격에 팔리는 반면, 다이아몬드는 필수품이라고 생각하는 사람이 거의 없는데도 매우 높은 가격에 팔린다. 그러므로 ③의 'a good's utility may have little influence on its price(재화의 효용이 가격에 거의 영향을 미치지 않을 수도 있다)'가 빈칸에 들어갈 말로 가장 적절하다.

오답풀이

① 재화의 가격은 효용성에 달려 있을 수도 있다
② 재화의 가격은 가치와 밀접한 관계가 있을 수도 있다
④ 재화의 효용은 공급과 수요에 달려 있을 수도 있다
⑤ 필요한 재화의 양은 가격에 달려 있지 않을 수도 있다

어휘

- lecture : 강의하다, 강연하다
- demand : 수요, 요구
- pose a puzzle : 수수께끼를 내다
- commodity : 상품, 물품
- utility : 효용, 유용성
- enormous : 거대한, 막대한
- availability : 효용, 유효성, 활용성
- necessity : 필수품, 생필품
- intertwine : 엮다, 뒤얽히다, 밀접하게 관련되다
- quantity : 양, 수량

해석

애덤 스미스는 1760년대에 Glasgow 대학에서 강의할 때, 수수께끼를 내서 수요에 관한 연구를 소개했다. 상식적으로 상품의 가격은 그 재화가 소비자들에게 어느 정도의 가치가 있

느냐 즉, 상품이 제공하는 효용의 양에 달려 있다고 그는 말했다. 그러나 스미스는 일부 사례에서 재화의 효용이 가격에 거의 영향을 미치지 않을 수도 있다고 지적했다. 스미스는 다이아몬드와 물을 예로 들었다. 그는 물은 대부분의 소비자들에게 엄청난 가치를 지니고 있다고 언급했는데 사실, 물의 효용성은 생사의 문제가 될 수 있다. 그럼에도 불구하고 물은 일반적으로 공짜이거나 매우 낮은 가격에 팔리는 반면, 다이아몬드는 필수품이라고 생각하는 사람이 거의 없는데도 매우 높은 가격에 팔린다.

23 ② 제시문에 따르면 받은 편지함의 최신 메일이 항상 맨 앞에 위치한다고 해서 모두 다 중요한 메일은 아니듯, 가장 큰 소리를 낸다고 해서 우선순위가 가장 높은 것은 아니라는 것이다. 그러므로 빈칸에는 ②의 'don't always scream the loudest(항상 가장 큰 소리를 내는 것은 아니다)'가 들어갈 말로 가장 적절하다.

오답풀이

① 쉽게 나쁜 길로 빠지게 할 수 있다
③ 때때로 우리의 성공을 깎아내린다
④ 우리가 가장 먼저 생각했던 것들이다
⑤ 가장 중요치 않은 일에 휘둘리다

어휘

- to-do list : 해야 할 일을 적은 목록
- intention : 의도, 의향 cf) good intention 선의
- tyrannize : 압제[압박]하다, 폭군같이 굴다
- trivial : 사소한, 하찮은
- stuff : 것, 물건, 잡동사니
- obligate to : 어쩔 수 없이[억지로] ~하다
- love-hate relationship : 애증 관계
- priority : 우선순위, 우선권, 상위, 중요함
- inbox : 받은 편지함
- dictate : 받아쓰게 하다, 구술하다, 지시[명령]하다
- masquerade : 가장하다, 꾸미다 cf) masquerade as ~으로 가장하다, ~인 체하다
- tackle : 씨름하다, 태클을 걸다
- squeaky : 끼익 소리가 나는, 삐걱거리는
- deserve : ~을 받을만한 가치가 있다
- grease : 기름, 윤활유
- prime minister : 수상, 총리
- duly : 적당히, 알맞게
- astray : 길을 잃은, 못된 길에 빠진
- undermine : 약화시키다, 깎아내리다, 해치다
- at the mercy of : ~에 좌우되어, ~에 휘둘리는

해석

해야 할 일을 적은 목록은 좋은 의도로 유용한 것을 모아놓는 역할을 하는 반면, 그것들은 또한 목록에 있기 때문에 어쩔 수 없이 해야 하는 사소하고 중요치 않은 일들로 우리를 옥죈다. 그런 연유로 우리들 대부분은 해야 할 일을 적은 목록과 애증 관계에 있다. 허락된다면 그 목록은 받은 편지함이 우리의 하루 일과를 불러줄 수 있는 것처럼 우리의 우선순위를 정한다. 대부분의 받은 편지함은 우선권을 가장한 체 중요하지 않은 이메일로 넘쳐난다. 우리가 받은 순서대로 이 과제들과 씨름하는 것은 마치 삐걱거리는 바퀴에 즉시 기름칠을 하는 것처럼 행동하는 것이다. 그러나 호주 총리 Bob Hawke가 적절하게 언급했듯이, "가장 중요한 것은 항상 가장 큰 소리를 내는 것은 아니다."

24 ⑤ 블록체인이 이중 지출 문제를 방지하기 위해 공유 원장을 제공한 것처럼 부패 또는 사기 행위를 방지하기 위한 효과적인 도구를 제공하기 위해서는 또 하나의 불변성이 필요하다. 그것은 어떤 당사자가 문서 또는 디지털 기록으로 처리할 수 있기 때문에 과거의 입력 내용을 변경하는 것을 방지하는 것이다. 그러므로 빈칸에는 공통으로 ⑤의 'immutability(불변성, 불역성)'이 들어갈 말로 가장 적절하다.

오답풀이

① 활용성
② 혁신
③ 다양성
④ 유연성

어휘

- blockchain : 블록체인(공공 거래 장부)
- bitcoin : 비트코인(디지털 화폐)
- double-spend : 이중 지출의
- digital currency : 디지털 통화[화폐]
- ledger : (거래 내역을 적은) 원장
- ensure : 보증하다, 보장하다
- transact : 거래하다, 사무를 보다
- detect : 알아내다, 감지하다
- fraudulent : 사기를 치는, 정직하지 못한
- premised on : ~을 전제한
- innovation : 혁신, 쇄신
- alter : 바꾸다, 변경하다
- multiplicity : 다수, 다양성
- flexibility : 구부리기 쉬움, 유연성
- immutability : 불변성, 불역성

(해석)

블록체인은 이중 지출 문제를 방지하기 위해 비트코인에 사용된다. 비트코인 이전의 디지털 화폐의 문제는 누군가가 똑같은 단위의 디지털 화폐를 여러 곳에서 동시에 사용할 수 있다는 것이었다. 블록체인은 공유 원장을 제공함으로써 이러한 문제를 해결하는데, 이것은 모든 사람이 어느 시점에서 사용자들 사이에 얼마나 많은 디지털 화폐가 거래되었는지를 알고 동의하도록 한다. 블록체인은 부패 또는 사기 행위를 알아내고 방지하는 효과적인 도구를 제공할 수 있다고 생각된다. 이러한 생각은 블록체인의 불변성을 전제로 한다. 그 불변성은 어떤 당사자가 문서 또는 디지털 기록으로 처리할 수 있기 때문에 과거의 입력 내용을 변경하는 것을 방지한다.

25 ① (A) 일하는 여성이 늘어난 것은 가정을 지키고 다른 식구들을 부양해야 하기 때문이므로, 실제 자신의 필요에 의해서가 아니라 사회적인 필요 때문이라고 설명하고 있다. 그러므로 빈칸에 들어갈 연결어구는 인과관계를 나타내는 'Therefore(그러므로)'가 가장 적절하다.

(B) 최근에 일하는 여성이 많이 늘어났지만, 사실 흑인과 다른 소수 여성들에게 일은 백인 여성들보다 훨씬 오래 동안 필수적이었다고 설명하고 있다. 그러므로 빈칸에 들어갈 연결어구는 역접의 의미를 나타내는 'However(그러나)'가 가장 적절하다.

(어휘)

• former : 이전의, 전자의
• Congresswoman : 여성 하원의원
• pinpoint : 정확히 찾아내다[보여주다]
• workforce : 노동자[직원], 노동인구[노동력]
• unprecedented : 전례[선례, 유례]가 없는, 공전의 cf) unprecedented numbers 엄청난 수
• meet : 충족시키다
• minority : 소수, 소수집단
• female : 암컷, 여성
• working age : 취업 연령
• analyst : 분석가
• high-income : 고소득

(해석)

Patricia Schroeder 전 하원의원은 유례없이 많은 여성이 이처럼 일을 하는 주된 이유는 가정을 지켜야 하기 때문이라고 주장하면서 여성들이 직장에 들어가는 가장 중요한 이유 중 하나를 정확히 찾아냈다. 많은 가정주부들이 어쩔 수 없이 일을 한다. 비록 가족은 더 작아졌지만, 다른 식구들을 위해 필요한 것은 더 많아졌다. (A) 그러므로 이러한 가정주부들에게 일은 실제 필요한 것이 아니라 사회적 필요이다. 그것은 가족이

자신의 욕구를 충족시킬 수 있는 유일한 방법이다. (B) 하지만 흑인과 다른 소수 여성들에게 일은 백인 여성보다 훨씬 오래 동안 필수적이었다. 전체 취업 연령 여성 중 일하는 여성의 비율이 1972년 32%에서 2000년대 초반 70% 이상으로 높아졌다. 이러한 추세를 연구하는 분석가들은 일부 고소득 여성들이 일을 그만두고 아이들과 함께 집에 있는 것을 선택할 수도 있지만 자녀를 둔 일하는 여성의 비율은 계속해서 증가할 것으로 예상된다고 말한다.

[26~27]

(어휘)

• convinced that : ~라고 확신하는
• derive from : ~에서 유래하다, 파생하다
• address : 다루다, 처리하다
• activate : 작동시키다, 활성화시키다
• judiciously : 사려 깊게, 신중하게
• evolve : 진화하다, 발전하다
• cluster : 무리, 송이
• evocative : 생각나게 하는, 환기하는, 연상되는
• spinning wheel : 물레
• ply : 연장을 부지런히 쓰다, 능숙하게 다루다
• rebel : 반란을 일으키다, 저항[반항]하다
• denounce : 맹렬히 비난하다, 고발하다
• dignity : 존엄, 위엄, 가치, 중요성
• rural : 시골의, 지방의
• elite : 엘리트, 정예
• mass : 대중, 무리
• emblem : 상징, 표상
• manual labor : 육체노동
• despise : 경멸하다, 멸시하다
• compassion : 동정, 연민
• proceeds : 수입, 매상
• urge : 재촉하다, 촉구하다
• give away : 주다, 기부하다, 인도하다
• needy : 어려운, 궁핍한
• infinitely : 대단히, 엄청, 무한히
• moral : 도덕상의, 도덕적인
• patronize : 후원하다, 지원하다
• donation : 기부, 기증

(해석)

인간의 행동이 그들의 감정 에너지를 '심장'으로부터 끌어냈고, 이는 신중하게 선택된 상징들에 의해서만 처리되고 활성화될 수 있다고 확신하면서, 간디는 물레, 소, 그리고 '간디 모

자(그에 의해 대중화된 하얀 면 모자)'를 포함한 문화적으로 연상되는 한 무리의 강력한 상징을 발전시켰다. 예를 들어 간디가 모두에게 부지런히 쓰도록 요구했던 물레는 몇 가지 상징적인 목적을 수행했다. 그것은 현대 기술 문명에 대해 조용하게 저항하고 인도의 농촌 생활 방식의 가치를 비난하는(→ 찬양하는) 방법이었다. 그것은 도시와 마을, 서구화된 엘리트들과 대중들을 하나로 묶었고, '유대감의 상징'이 되었다. 물레는 또한 육체노동과 그것에 종사하는 사람들의 가치를 확립하고 이 둘 모두를 경멸하는 전통적인 인도 문화에 맞섰다. 그것은 사회적 연민을 상징했는데, 그 생산품의 수입을 필요로 하지 않는 사람들이 궁핍한 사람들에게 그 생산품을 나누어주도록 재촉받았기 때문에, 이는 기부금을 후원하는 사람들에게 대단히 우월한 도덕적 행위였다. 그리고 그것은 또한 그 사람을 혼자 있게 둬서 적어도 얼마 동안은 침묵을 지키도록 했다. 간디는 이런 종류의 수많은 상징들을 발전시켰을 뿐만 아니라 스스로도 하나의 상징이 되었다.

26 ③ 간디가 모두에게 부지런히 쓰도록 요구했던 물레는 현대 기술 문명에 대한 조용한 저항과 인도의 농촌 생활 방식의 가치를 찬양하는 상징적인 목적을 수행했다. 그러므로 ③의 'denouncing(비난하는)'은 'admiring(찬양하는)' 등으로 바꿔 써야 적절하다.

오답풀이
① 연상되는
② 저항하는
④ 도전하는
⑤ 후원하는

27 ② ①, ③, ④, ⑤의 'it'은 모두 여러 가지 상징적 의미를 지녔던 'the spinning wheel(물레)'을 가리키나, ②의 'it'은 앞의 'manual labor(육체노동)'을 가리킨다.

28 ② Annemarie는 독일군 병사가 기차 안에까지 있어 긴장했고 어디로 가냐고 검문을 받았을 때 몹시 겁이 났다(terrified). 그러나 분위기를 누그러뜨리는 Kirsti의 유쾌한 대화에 독일군 병사들이 지나가자 안도하였다(relieved).

오답풀이
① 희망적인 → 실망한
③ 흥분된 → 불쾌한
④ 놀란 → 속상한
⑤ 비참한 → 부끄러운

어휘
• tense : 긴장한, 긴박한
• stroll : 거닐다, 산책하다
• glance at : ∼을 힐끗 보다
• stick : 찌르다, 박다
• probe : 캐묻다, 조사하다
• distort : 비틀다, 일그러뜨리다
• frightened : 겁먹은, 무서워하는
• fascination : 매혹, 매료, 심취
• calmly : 고요히, 침착하게, 태연하게
• stare at : ∼을 응시하다, 뚫어지게 쳐다보다
• puzzled : 당황하는, 어리둥절한
• exclaim : 소리치다, 외치다
• sink : 빠지다, 가라앉다
• chatter : 수다를 떨다, 재잘거리다
• chirp : 짹짹거리다, 재잘거리다
• brand-new : 신품의, 신상품의
• chuckle : 빙그레[싱긋] 웃다, 껄껄 웃다
• gaze : 응시하다, 바라보다
• blur : 희미한[흐릿한] 것
• relieved : 안도하는, 안심하는
• offended : 불쾌한, 화가 난
• upset : 속상한, 마음이 상한
• miserable : 비참한, 불행한

해석

기차가 다시 출발했다. 그들의 차량 끝에 있는 문이 열리면서 두 명의 독일군 병사가 나타났다. Annemarie는 긴장했다. 여기 말고 기차에도? 그들은 어디에나 있었다. 병사들은 승객들을 힐끗 보며 함께 차량 안을 거닐었고, 여기저기 멈춰 서서 질문을 던졌다. 그들 중 한 사람은 이빨에 무언가 끼어 있었고, 혀로 더듬느라 자신의 얼굴을 찡그렸다. Annemarie는 두 사람이 다가오자 겁에 질린 표정으로 지켜보았다. 병사들 중 한 명이 따분한 표정을 지으며 내려다보았다. "어디로 갑니까?" 그가 물었다. "Gilleleje"라고 Mama가 침착하게 대답했다. "오빠가 거기 살아요, 그를 방문할 예정이에요." 병사가 돌아서자 Annemarie는 안도했다. 그때 아무런 예고 없이, 그가 뒤로 돌아섰다. "새해를 맞아 오빠를 찾아가는 겁니까?"라고 그가 갑자기 물었다. Mama는 당황한 표정으로 그를 응시했다. "새해?"라고 그녀가 물었다. "이제 겨우 10월이에요." "맞춰 보세요!"라고 Kirsti는 갑자기 큰 목소리로 병사를 바라보며 소리쳤다. Annemarie는 가슴이 철렁 내려앉으며 어머니를 바라보았다. Mama의 눈은 겁에 질려 있었다. "쉬, Kirsti", Mama가 말했다. "그렇게 수다 떨지 마." 그러나 Kirsti는 여느 때처럼 Mama에게 전혀 주의를 기울이지 않았다. 그녀는 쾌활하게 병사를 바라보았고, Annemarie는 그녀가 무슨 말을 하려는지 알았다. 이 애는 우리 친구 Ellen이고 그녀가 새해를 맞아요! 그러나 그녀는 아니었다. 대신에 Kirsti는 그녀의 발을 가리켰다.

"Henrik 삼촌을 만나러 갈 거예요."라고 그녀는 재잘거렸고, "그리고 나는 신상품의 윤이 나는 검은 신발을 신었어요!"라고 말했다. 병사는 껄껄 웃으며 움직였다. Annemarie는 다시 창문을 바라보았다. 해안을 따라 북쪽으로 계속 갈 때, 나무와 발트해 그리고 흐린 10월의 하늘이 희미하게 지나갔다.

29 ⑤ 제시문에 따르면 고양이들은 고기의 다른 맛들을 구별하기 위해 '달콤한' 미뢰를 개조했는데, 이것이 애완 고양이들이 가끔 주인에게 괜찮아 보이는 음식을 멀리하는 이유라고 설명하고 있다. 그러므로 "고양이는 고기의 다른 맛을 구별하지 못한다."는 ⑤의 설명은 제시문의 내용과 일치하지 않는다.

(오답풀이)

① 고양이의 조상은 수백만 년 전에 유전적 변이를 겪었다.
② 고양이는 많은 양의 동물성 단백질을 필요로 한다.
③ 고양이는 번식에 필수적인 호르몬을 만들 수 없다.
④ 고양이는 설탕 맛을 느끼지 못한다.

(어휘)

• genetic : 유전의, 유전학의
• felid : 고양이과 동물
• lock : 고정되다
• animal protein : 동물성 단백질
• amino acid : 아미노산
• taurine : 타우린(아미노산의 일종)
• prostaglandin : 프로스타글란딘(호르몬 물질)
• essential : 필수적인, 근본적인
• reproduction : 생식, 번식, 복제
• niacin : 니아신(비타민 B3)
• thiamine : 티아민(비타민 B1)
• retinol : 레티놀(비타민 A)
• extract from : ～에서 뽑아내다, 추출하다
• adapt : 개조하다, 개작하다
• taste bud : 미뢰, 맛봉오리
• flavor : 맛, 풍미
• come to light : 알려지다, 밝혀지다
• captive breeding : 포획 사육
• clouded leopard : 구름무늬 표범, 타이완 표범

(해석)

수백만 년 전, 대략 열두 번의 유전적 변이가 오늘날의 모든 고양이과 동물 조상에서 일어났는데, 그 이후로 그들은 고기를 먹도록 정해졌다. 모든 고양이들은 먹이에 다량의 동물성 단백질을 필요로 한다. 식물성 단백질에는 고양이가 필요로 하는 타우린과 같은 특정 아미노산이 부족하지만 다른 포유류들(인간 포함)은 그렇지 않다. 고양이들은 번식하는 데 필수적

인 호르몬인 프로스타글란딘을 직접 만들 수 없기 때문에 고기로부터 이것을 얻을 필요가 있다. 다른 포유류들에 비해, 모든 고양이들은 니아신, 티아민, 레티놀과 같은 많은 양의 비타민을 필요로 하는데, 이것은 식물보다 고기에서 추출하는 것이 더 쉽다. 그리고 익은 과일과 익지 않은 과일의 차이를 구별할 필요가 없기 때문에, 고양이들은 설탕 맛을 볼 수 있는 능력을 잃어버렸다. 고양이들은 고기의 다른 맛들을 구별하기 위해 '달콤한' 미뢰를 개조했는데, 이것이 애완 고양이들이 가끔 주인에게 괜찮아 보이는 음식을 멀리하는 이유이다. 이러한 지식은 지난 40년 동안 밝혀졌고, 애완용 고양이뿐만 아니라 구름무늬 표범과 같은 멸종위기에 처한 고양이과 동물의 포획 사육에도 도움을 주었다.

30 ③ 제시문에 따르면 Philip은 이후 20년 동안 홀로 떠나기로 선택한 Sparta를 제외하고 그리스 본토 전체를 조직적으로 정복했다고 서술되어 있다. 그러므로 "Sparta를 정복했다."는 ③의 설명은 제시문의 내용과 일치하지 않는다.

(오답풀이)

① 창의 길이를 약 18피트로 늘렸다.
② 기병을 전선에 추가하였다.
④ Athens와 Thebes의 연합군을 격퇴했다.
⑤ 그리스 본토를 통합했다.

(어휘)

• throne : 왕좌, 왕위
• spear : 창, 투창
• sarissa : 사리사(고대 그리스의 마케도니아군이 사용한 창)
• hoplite : (고대 그리스의) 장갑(裝甲) 보병
• retain : 유지하다, 보유하다
• wedge formation : 설대 대형
• cavalry : 기갑부대
• incorporate : 합병하다, 편입하다
• element : (소)부대, 분대
• phalanx : (고대 그리스의) 방진(方陣)
• mainland : 본토
• defeat : 패배시키다, 물리치다, 격퇴하다
• combined forces : 연합군
• era : 시대, 대(代)
• territory : 영토, 영역

(해석)

왕위에 오르자마자, Philip은 마케도니아 군대를 Thebes에서 보았던 것보다 더욱 성공적인 모습으로 변모시키기 시작했다. Philip은 Thebans가 사용했던 이미 긴 창을 더 길게 늘여, 길이가 약 18피트의 창인 마케도니아의 사리사를 만들었는데, 이는 전통적인 그리스 호블라이트 창의 두 배였다. 그는

정답 및 해설

Thebans의 설대 대형을 유지하면서도 또한 중무장 기병을 전선에 추가하여, 마케도니아의 가장 강한 부대를 방진(方陣)에 편입시켰다. 그 결과는 자명했는데, Philip은 이후 20년 동안 홀로 떠나기로 선택한 Sparta를 제외하고 그리스 본토 전체를 조직적으로 정복했다. Philip의 마지막 대승은 Chaeronea 전투(B.C. 338년)에서였는데, 이 전투에서 마케도니아 군대는 Athens와 Thebes의 연합군을 격퇴하였다. Philip이 본토 전체를 정복한 것은 한 시대의 끝이었고, 처음으로 영토 전체가 한 왕의 지배 아래 통합되었다.

31 ② 제시문에 따르면 함무라비 법전은 주로 결혼과 상속, 가족 관계, 재산권, 그리고 상업적 관습과 같은 민사 업무를 다루었다고 서술되어 있다. 그러므로 "법전은 형법을 주로 다루었다."는 ②의 설명은 함무라비 법전에 대한 제시문의 내용과 일치히지 않는다.

오답풀이

① 법전이 새겨진 비석이 19세기에 발견되었다.
③ 신분에 따라 동일 범죄에 대한 처벌이 달랐다.
④ 사형제도가 포함되었다.
⑤ 재판관들은 상해의 고의성 여부를 구별하였다.

어휘

- the code of laws : 법전
- bear name : 이름을 붙이다
- authority : 권한, 권위
- to that effect : 그런 취지로
- subject : 백성, 국민, 신하
- decree : 법령, 법칙, 판결
- collectively : 집합적으로, 총괄하여, 통틀어
- term : 부르다, 칭하다, 일컫다
- inscribe : 쓰다, 새기다
- stone stelae : 석비(石碑)
- erect : 건립하다, 세우다
- civil affairs : 민정, 민사
- inheritance : 유산, 상속
- property rights : 재산권
- business practice : 상업적 관습, 실무
- criminal offense : 형사 범죄
- severity : 혹독, 엄격
- offender and victim : 가해자와 피해자
- commoner : 평민, 서민
- restitution : 반환, 배상, 보상
- noble : 상류층, 귀족
- trial : 재판, 공판
- ordeal : 시련, 고난

- retribution : 응징, 징벌
- retaliatory action : 보복 행위
- capital punishment : 사형, 극형
- intentional : 의도적인, 고의로 한
- injury : 피해, 상해
- monetary : 화폐의, 통화의, 금전의
- fine : 벌금, 과태료
- malicious : 악의적인, 적의 있는
- intent : 의사, 의도, 목적
- manifest : 나타내다, 드러내 보이다
- morality : 도덕(성), 윤리
- restrict : 제한하다, 한정하다
- application : 적용, 응용
- apply to : ~에 적용하다

해석

기원전 약 1792년부터 약 1750년까지 메소포타미아를 통치했던 바빌로니아 황제 함무라비는 자신의 이름을 붙인 법전으로 가장 유명한데, 그것은 지금까지 발견된 가장 초기의 법전 중 하나이다. 그의 주된 관심사는 그의 권한을 통해 제국의 질서를 유지하는 것이었는데, 이는 그의 백성들의 요구에 부응하는 것이었다. 그런 취지로, 그는 신하들에게 복잡한 법전을 하사했다. 통틀어 함무라비 법전이라 불리는 282개의 법령은 비석이나 기둥에 새겨졌고 여러 곳에 세워졌다. 하나는 19세기에 페르시아의 Susa에서 발견되었고 현재 파리의 루브르 박물관에 있다.

이 법전은 주로 결혼과 상속, 가족 관계, 재산권, 그리고 상업적 관습과 같은 민사 업무를 다루었다. 형사 범죄는 가해자와 피해자의 사회적 지위에 따라 엄격함의 정도가 다르게 처벌되었다. 상류층의 권리와 평민의 권리는 분명한 차이가 있었다. 일반적으로 귀족들이 평민들에게 입힌 손해에 대한 배상금은 지급이 허용된다. 그러나 귀족에게 손해를 입힌 평민은 죽음으로 지불해야 할지도 모른다. 시련에 의한 재판, 보복 행위에 의한 응징, 그리고 사형은 일반적인 관행이었다. 그러나 재판관들은 고의적인 상해와 의도하지 않은 상해를 구별하였고, 금전적인 벌금은 일반적으로 악의적인 의도가 드러나지 않는 처벌에 사용되었다. 종종 함무라비 법전과 관련된 '눈에는 눈'의 도덕성은 그 적용이 상대적으로 제한되었고, 사회적 평등에 반하여 저질러진 범죄에만 적용되었다.

32 ① 제시문에 따르면 동시에 두 가지 일을 하려고 하다가 어느 한 쪽도 제대로 할 수 없다. 즉, 멀티태스킹이 더 많은 일을 할 수 있는 효과적인 방법이라고 생각하지만 그것은 잘못된 생각이라는 것이다. 그러므로 제시문의 제목으로는 ①의 'Fallacy of Multitasking(멀티태스킹에 대한 잘못된 생각)'이 가장 적절하다.

오답풀이

② 멀티태스킹의 기초

③ 멀티태스킹: 이유와 방법

④ 멀티태스킹 수요의 대응 전략

⑤ 위대한 결과 뒤의 단순한 진리: 멀티태스킹

어휘

• chew : 씹다, 깨물다

• repercussion : 영향, 반향

• airliner : 여객기

• clear : 승인하다, 허가하다

• medicine : 약, 약물

• toddler : 유아, 걸음마를 배우는 아이

• unattended : 방치된, 돌보지 않는

• tragedy : 비극

• multitasking : 다중 작업, 멀티태스킹

• get it backward : 거꾸로 하다

• get less done : 덜 끝내다

• fallacy : 틀린 생각, 오류, 착오

• ABC : 기본, 기초, 입문

• coping : 대응[대항]하다, 맞서다

• strategy : 계획, 전략

해석

사람들은 실제로 걷기와 말하기, 껌을 씹고 지도를 읽는 것과 같은 두 가지 이상의 일을 동시에 할 수 있다. 하지만 컴퓨터처럼 우리가 할 수 없는 것은 동시에 두 가지 일에 집중하는 것이다. 우리의 관심은 앞뒤로 왔다 갔다 한다. 이것은 컴퓨터에게는 괜찮지만, 인간에게는 심각한 영향을 미친다. 두 대의 여객기가 같은 활주로에 착륙하도록 허가된다. 어떤 환자에게 약을 잘못 투여한다. 유아가 욕조에 방치된다. 이 모든 잠재적 비극들이 공통적인 것은 사람들이 동시에 너무 많은 일을 하려고 노력하다가 그들이 해야 할 일을 잊어버린다는 것이다. 동시에 두 가지 일을 하려고 할 때, 둘 중 어느 쪽도 할 수 없거나 잘 하지 못할 것이다. 만약 멀티태스킹이 더 많은 일을 할 수 있는 효과적인 방법이라고 생각한다면, 그것을 거꾸로 행한 것이다. 덜 하는 것이 효과적인 방법이다.

33 ④ 제시문에 따르면 통계상 오늘날의 이혼율이 과거보다 높아진 것은 가정 불행의 결과만은 아니며, 이혼한 사람들의 가능성이 높아지고 이혼을 하는 것이 더 쉬워졌기 때문이라고 설명하고 있다. 그러므로 ④의 'cautious interpretation of divorce statistics(이혼 통계에 대한 신중한 해석)'가 제시문의 주제로 가장 적절하다.

오답풀이

① 이혼 통계의 용도

② 이혼 통계의 수집

③ 사람들이 이혼을 하는 이유

⑤ 이혼과 가정 파탄에 대한 대처

어휘

• divorce : 이혼, 분리

• statistics : 통계, 통계 자료

• disorganization : 해체, 분열

• cite : 인용하다, 소환하다

• entirely : 전적으로, 완전히, 전부

• ostracism : 외면, 배척

• poverty : 빈곤, 가난

• route : 길, 노선

• cautious : 신중한, 조심스러운

• interpretation : 해석, 이해, 설명

• cope with : ~에 대처[대응]하다

• breakdown : 고장, 와해, 붕괴, 파탄

해석

이혼 통계는 가족 해체의 척도로 흔히 사용되며, 현재의 높은 이혼율은 미국 가정이 심각한 문제에 처해 있다는 증거로 인용되고 있다. 그러나 오늘날의 이혼율이 과거보다 높아진 것은 전적으로 가정 불행의 결과만은 아니다. 이전 세대에는 결혼 생활이 불행했음에도 불구하고 많은 부부들이 이혼을 피했다. 여성의 경우에 그것은 사회적 외면 혹은 잘 살 수 있는 기회가 거의 없기 때문에 가난을 의미했다. 이혼한 사람들의 가능성이 높아지고 이혼을 하는 것이 더 쉬워지면서, 더 많은 불행한 부부들이 이 길을 택했다.

34 ① 제시문에 따르면 후진국은 유아 사망률이 높은데, 영양 섭취, 건강 관리, 전염병 예방 접종 등으로 유아 사망률이 감소되었을 때 대부분의 지역에서 출산율 하락을 동반했다고 설명하고 있다. 그러므로 ①의 "Infant mortality rates affect birth rates. (유아 사망률은 출생률에 영향을 미친다)"가 제시문의 요지로 가장 적절하다.

오답풀이

② 전 세계의 유아 사망률이 매우 빠르게 감소하고 있다.

③ 부의 불균형은 유아 사망률에 반영된다.

④ 유아 사망률의 주된 원인은 수질이 나쁘기 때문이다.

⑤ 산전 관리를 잘 하면 유아 사망률을 낮출 수 있다.

어휘

• infant : 유아, 젖먹이

• mortality rate : 사망률

- ensure : 보장[보증]하다, 확신하다
- sustained : 지속된, 한결같은, 일관된
- birth rate : 출생률
- precede : 선행하다, ~에 앞서다
- demographically : 인구 통계학상의
- nutrition : 영양, 영양 섭취
- rehydration : 재수화, 복원 cf) oral rehydration therapy 경구 수분 보충 요법(설사로 인한 탈수증 완화 요법)
- immunization : 면역, 예방주사
- infectious disease : 전염병
- reduction : 감소, 축소
- preventable : 막을 수 있는, 예방할 수 있는
- communicable : 전달되는, 전염성의 cf) communicable disease 전염병
- disparity : 차이, 격차
- prenatal : 태어나기 전의, 태아기의 cf) prenatal care 산전 관리

해석

개발도상국의 대부분이 그렇듯이 유아 사망률이 높을 때, 부모들은 몇 명의 아이들이 성년기까지 살아남는 것을 보장하기 위해 아이를 많이 갖는 경향이 있다. 유아 사망률이 지속적으로 감소하기 전에 먼저 선행되지 않았던 출생률이 지속적으로 감소한 적은 없었다. 인구 통계학적으로 분류된 세계에서 가장 중요한 차이점 중 하나는 후진국의 유아 사망률이 높다는 것이다. 더 나은 영향 섭취, 개선된 건강 관리, 간단한 경구 수분 보충 요법, 그리고 전염병 예방 접종은 유아 사망률을 획기적으로 감소시켰으며, 이는 대부분의 지역에서 출산율 하락을 동반했다. 쉽게 예방할 수 있는 전염병으로부터 매년 5백만 명의 아이들의 목숨을 구하면 2,000만 명 혹은 3,000만 명의 추가 출산을 피할 수 있을 것으로 추정된다.

35 ④ 주어진 문장에서 'ubiquity(편재성)'란 골고루 있지 않고 하나에 치우쳐 있다는 의미로, 우주 질량의 80% 이상이 암흑 물질로 구성된 것은 암흑 물질의 편재성을 의미한다. 또한 그런 편재성에도 불구하고 천문학자들이 암흑 물질을 구성하는 입자에 대해 실감하지 못하고 있으므로, 주어진 문장은 이를 추정하고 있는 ④에 위치하는 것이 가장 적절하다.

어휘

- ubiquity : 도처에 있음, 편재(성)
- astronomer : 천문학자
- constitute : 구성하다, 본질을 이루다
- dark matter : 암흑 물질
- infer : 추론하다, 뜻하다, 암시하다
- gravitational : 중력의

- distribution : 분배, 분포, 유통
- galaxy cluster : 은하단
- mass : 덩어리, (물체의) 질량
- subatomic particle : 아원자 입자(원자보다 작은 입자)
- neutrino : 중성자, 중성미립자
- hypothetical : 가설의, 가상의
- axion : 악시온(원자보다 작은 입자)
- elude : 피하다, 빠져 나가다
- detection : 발견, 간파, 탐지
- elementary particle : 소립자
- weakly interacting massive particles(WIMPs) : 약한 상호작용을 하는 거대 입자
- apparently : 분명하게, 명백하게
- electromagnetic radiation : 전자기 방사선, 전자기 복사
- conventional : 전통적인, 관례적인

해석

> 그러나, 그것의 편재성에도 불구하고, 천문학자들은 무엇이 암흑 물질을 구성하는지에 대해 실감하지 못하고 있다.

암흑 물질을 측정할 수 있지만, 단지 보이지 않을 뿐이다. (①) '어두워서' 보이지 않는다. (②) 천문학자들은 은하가 어떻게 스스로를 지탱하는지, 중력 렌즈가 어떻게 작용하는지 그리고 은하단에서 보이는 고온 가스의 관측된 온도 분포를 설명하기 때문에 암흑 물질의 존재를 추론한다. (③) 결론은 우주 질량의 80% 이상이 우리가 단지 볼 수 없는 형태라는 것이다. (④) 무거운 중성미자와 같은 아원자 입자나 악시온 같은 여타 가상 입자를 포함할 수 있다. (⑤) 그 중 일부는 단지 탐지를 막는 물체에 갇혀 있을 수도 있다. 현재 천문학자들은 대부분의 암흑 물질이 약한 상호작용을 하는 거대한 입자(WIMP)로 불리는 새로운 소립자로 구성되어 있다고 믿는데, 그것은 분명 전자기 방사선이나 원자와 상호작용하지 않는다. 그러므로 그것들은 전통적인 탐지 방법으로 보이지 않는다.

36 ④ 주어진 문장에서 심신이 소모된 근로자들은 그들이 도와야 할 사람들을 비인격화시키고 물건이나 사물로 생각한다고 시술되어 있다. 그러므로 심신이 소모된 사회복지사가 위탁 아동을 대하는 태도를 예로 들어 설명한 ④에 위치하는 것이 가장 적절하다.

어휘

- burned-out : 소진된, 녹초가 된
- depersonalize : 비인격화하다, 인격을 박탈하다
- burnout : 극도의 피로, 심신 소모
- afflict : 괴롭히다, 피해를 입히다
- employee : 종업원, 고용인, 직원

- day in and day out : 매일, 연일, 언제나
- social worker : 사회복지사
- due to : ~ 때문에, ~에 기인하는
- exhaustion : 탈진, 소진, 고갈
- be worn out : 지치다, 고단하다, 기진맥진하다
- desperate : 필사적인, 절실한
- foster child : 수양 자녀, 위탁 아동
- scared : 겁먹은, 무서워하는
- behavioral : 행동의, 행동에 관한

해석

심신이 소모된 근로자들은 때때로 그들이 도와야 할 사람들을 비인격화시키고, 그들을 인간으로 대하기보다 물건이나 사물로 생각한다.

심신 소모는 특별한 종류의 심리적 스트레스 결과로, 연일 연장 근무로 높은 수준의 업무 스트레스를 겪는 일부 직원들을 괴롭힌다. 그것은 특히 직원들이 다른 사람들을 돕거나 보호하거나 돌보는 책임을 질 때 발생할 가능성이 높다. 간호사, 의사, 사회복지사, 교사, 변호사, 경찰관은 직업 특성상 심신 소모로 발전할 위험이 크다. (①) 심신 소모의 세 가지 주요 증상은 낮은 개인적 성취감, 정서적 피로감, 그리고 비인격화이다. (②) 심신이 소모된 근로자들은 종종 자신이 남을 돕거나 해야 할 만큼 성취하지 못하고 있다고 느낀다. (③) 감정상 그들은 때때로 도움이 절실한 사람들을 대해야 하는 끊임없는 스트레스로 지쳐버린다. (④) 예를 들어, 심신이 소모된 사회복지사는 신규 도움이 필요한 위탁 아동을 매우 겁먹은 12살짜리 아이가 아니라 사례 번호로 생각할 수도 있다. (⑤) 이러한 심리적 결과는 심신이 소모된 사회복지사가 아이를 냉담하고 동떨어진 태도로 대할 때 행동 결과로 이어질 수도 있다.

37 ③ 주어진 문장에서 합리적 분석 방식은 의사결정 과정의 속도가 느리므로 속도와 효과의 절충에 대해 언급한 글 (B)가 다음에 와야 한다. 글 (B)에서 직관력이 합리적 모델보다 더 나은 결과를 산출할 수 있다고 하였으므로, 업무 유형에 따라 합리적 의사결정보다 직관이 더 효과적이라고 설명한 글 (C)가 다음에 와야 한다. 마지막으로 글 (C)의 업무 유형은 글 (A)에 설명되어 있다. 그러므로 주어진 글 다음에 (B) – (C) – (A)의 순으로 이어져야 한다.

어휘

- analytic : 분석적인, 분해적인
- superior : 우세한, 우월한
- intuition : 직관(력), 직감
- human resource management : 인적자원 관리

- strategic : 전략상 중요한, 전략적인
- aesthetic : 미학적인, 심미적인
- judgmental : 판결상의, 판단상의, 주관적 판단의
- holistic : 전체론의, 전체론적인
- versus : ~에 비해, ~와 대조적으로, ~대(對)
- trade-off : 균형, 절충
- at hand : 가까운, 머지않은, 당면한
- put simply : 간단히 말해
- prim : 대비시키다, 준비시키다
- subdivide : 더 작게 나누다, 세분하다, 하위 구분하다
- chunk : 덩어리, 상당히 많은 양

해석

역사적으로 합리적 분석 방식은 종종 직관에 비해 우세한 결과를 제공하는 것으로 보여지지만, 이러한 의사결정 과정은 훨씬 더 느리다.

(B) 따라서 어떤 사람들은 의사결정에 있어서 속도 대 효과의 절충에 대해 이야기한다. 그러나 의사 결정자의 경험 수준과 당면한 업무의 성격에 따라 직관력이 합리적 모델보다 더 나은 결과를 산출할 수 있다.

(C) 간단히 말해, 특정 분야에서 많은 경험을 가진 개인(즉, 전문가)은 그들이 직면하는 업무의 유형에 따라 합리적인 의사결정을 하는 것보다 직관으로 더 효과적인 대비를 한다. 일반적으로 전문가들은 당면한 업무가 하나 이상의 정답이 있거나 업무를 더 작은 덩어리로 쉽게 세분화할 수 없을 때 직관적인 의사결정의 사용에 가장 효과적이다.

(A) 이러한 유형의 업무는 인적자원 관리, 전략적, 미학적, 투자 결정 등에서 흔히 볼 수 있다. 요컨대, 직관은 전문가들이 판단력이 필요한 전체론적 업무를 수행할 때 가장 효과적이다.

38 ⑤ 주어진 문장에서 효과적인 의사소통의 필요성에 대해 언급했고, 이에 대한 사례를 글 (C)에서 보여주고 있다. 글 (C)에서 에어 플로리다 737기가 Potomac 강 위의 다리와 충돌했을 때의 원인을 글 (B)에서 설명하고 있다. 마지막으로 이에 대한 대책으로 글 (A)에서 효과적인 의사소통 능력을 갖추기 위한 적극성과 감수성 훈련에 대해 설명하고 있다. 그러므로 주어진 글 다음에 (C) – (B) – (A)의 순으로 이어져야 한다.

어휘

- cabin crew : 객실 승무원
- flight attendant : 스튜어디스, 승무원
- vital : 필수적인, 매우 중대한
- Federal Aviation Administration : 미 연방항공국

357

- assertiveness training : 적극성 훈련
- sensitivity training : 감수성 훈련
- mandatory : 법에 정해진, 의무적인
- investigator : 수사관, 조사관
- crash : 추락, 충돌
- in part : 부분적으로는, 어느 정도는
- copilot : 부[보조] 조종사, 부기장
- engine power readings : 엔진 출력 측정치
- tragic : 비극의, 비극적인
- take off : 이륙하다, 출발하다

해석

오늘날 항공사 객실 승무원, 조종사, 승무원 등이 서로 간에 그리고 승객들과 효과적으로 의사소통할 수 있는 능력이 위기를 예방하는 데 필수적이라는 사실을 우리 모두 알고 있다.

(C) 효과적인 의사소통이 아주 중요하다는 것을 보여준 비극적인 사례가 에어 플로리다 737기가 워싱턴 D.C.의 국립공항에서 이륙한 후 Potomac 강 위의 다리와 충돌했을 때 일어났다.

(B) 미 연방항공국 조사관들은 부기장이 엔진 센서의 얼음으로 인해 발생한 엔진 출력 측정치에 대한 문제를 조종사에게 알리지 않았기 때문에 부분적으로 추락의 결과가 나왔다고 판단했다.

(A) 이 사건과 부족한 의사소통이 원인이 된 다른 위험한 사건들 때문에, 미 연방항공국은 모든 항공사 승무원들이 효과적으로 의사소통할 수 있는 능력을 갖추도록 하기 위해 의무적으로 적극성과 감수성 훈련을 실시했다.

[39~40]

어휘

- facilitate : 용이하게 하다, 촉진하다, 조장하다
- festivity : 축제, 행사
- stimulus : 자극, 고무, 격려
- celebrity : 유명 인사, 명사
- pair : 짝을 짓다, 부부가 되다
- evident : 분명한, 눈에 띄는
- relative : 비교상의, 상대적인
- enormous : 거대한, 엄청난
- expose : 드러내다, 노출시키다, 폭로하다
- parental : 부모의, 아버지[어머니]의
- predictor : 예측 변수, 예언자, 예보자
- peer : 또래, 동배

- facilitation : 용이[간편]함, 촉진, 조장
- liking : 애호, 기호, 취향
- internalized : 내면화된, 내재화된
- sensory : 감각의, 감각상의
- property : 특성, 속성
- craving : 욕구, 갈망, 열망
- innate : 타고난, 선천적인
- judicious : 신중한, 판단력 있는
- child rearing : 육아

해석

어린 시절부터 가족 내에서든 다른 집단과이든 사회적 상호작용은 대부분의 음식 경험이 발생하는 맥락을 제공하고, 이에 따라 좋아하는 음식에 대한 학습이 촉진된다. 예를 들어, 친구와 함께 하는 음식 축제와 같은 그러한 싱호작용과 관련된 슬거움은 단 것만큼이나 새로운 음식 맛을 위한 조건부 자극에 긍정적일 수도 있다. 따라서 음식점에서 음식에 대한 평가는 요리사의 솜씨와 같은 사회적 환경과 많은 관련이 있을 수도 있다. 아이들의 경우 음식을 친구들의 존재, 좋아하는 유명인 또는 어른들의 관심과 짝을 짓는 것은 모두 이러한 음식에 대한 호감을 증가시키며, 의심의 여지 없이 이 집단들의 긍정적인 가치를 아이에게 반영한다. 이러한 과정은 다양한 사회적 상호작용이 아이들의 음식 선호도에 미치는 상대적인 영향에서 강하게 나타난다. 놀랍게도, 부모들이 먹는 음식을 자녀들이 접할 수 있는 가정에서 엄청난 기회에도 불구하고, 부모의 선호도는 자녀의 음식 선호도의 강한(→ 약한) 예측 변수이다. 사실, 그들은 다른 어른들의 선호도보다 더 나은 예측 변수는 아니다. 이것은 이러한 선호도의 범위가 가족 내의 특정한 음식 습관보다 더 넓은 문화와 관련이 있음을 시사한다. 한 아이의 음식에 대한 호불호는 부모의 음식보다 또래, 특히 특정 친구와 훨씬 더 연관이 있을 가능성이 높다. 음식 선택의 사회적 촉진에 대한 궁극적인 영향은 그 취향이 결국 내면화 된다는 것이다. 즉, 다른 사람들이 그렇게 하기 때문에 선택된 음식들은 그들 자신의 감각적 특성으로 좋아지게 된다.

39 ⑤ 제시문에 따르면 아이들의 음식에 대한 선호도는 다양한 사회적 상호작용에 강하게 영향을 받아 그 취향이 내면화 되는 것이라고 설명하고 있다. 그러므로 ⑤의 "How is Food Preference Socially Constructed? (음식 선호도는 사회적으로 어떻게 만들어지는가?)"가 제시문의 제목으로 가장 적절하다.

오답풀이

① 단 것에 대한 갈망
② 냠냠!: 음식에 대한 타고난 반응
③ 새로운 맛을 위한 조건부 자극

④ 육아를 위한 신중한 음식 선택

40 ④ 아이들의 음식 선호도는 다양한 사회적 상호작용의 영향을 강하게 받으므로, 부모의 음식 선호도가 자녀의 음식 선호도에 미치는 영향은 적다는 것이다. 그러므로 (d)의 'strong(강한)'은 'weak(약한)'로 바꿔 써야 한다.

오답풀이

① 촉진되다
② 사회적인
③ 상대적인
⑤ 내면화된

[41~42]

어휘

• meerkat : 미어캣(몽구스의 일종인 남아프리카산의 작은 육식 동물)
• boast : 뽐내다, 자랑하다
• formidable : 가공할, 어마어마한
• rhino's horn : 코뿔소의 뿔
• cheetah : 치타
• subterranean : 지하의
• play host to : ~를 초대하다, ~의 수용처가 되다
• colony : 집단, 군집, 군단
• communally : 공동으로
• mongoose : 몽구스(사향고양잇과의 포유동물)
• claw : 발톱
• acute : 예리한, 예민한, 잘 발달된
• handy : 유용한, 편리한, 가까운
• spot : 발견하다, 찾다, 알아채다
• burrow : 굴을 파다, 파고들다
• sentry : 보초, 감시
• birds of prey : 맹금류
• lookout : 망보는 곳, 망보는 사람, 보초
• shrill : 날카로운, 째는 듯한
• bark : 짖는[우는] 소리, 큰 소리
• make a dash for : ~을 향해 돌진하다
• bolthole : 빠져나갈 구멍, 도피처
• cover : 숨을 곳, 잠복 장소
• signify : 의미하다, 뜻하다, 나타내다
• territorial : 영토의, 세력의
• alpha : 첫째가는 것, 우두머리
• pitch in : 착수하다, 협력하다
• babysit : 아이를 봐 주다

• room : 묵다, 유숙[하숙]하다, 재우다
• pup : 새끼, 아동
• play-fighting : 싸움 놀이
• scorpion : 전갈
• biology : 생물학, 생명 작용[활동]
• harsh : 가혹한, 혹독한, 냉혹한
• vast : 방대한, 막대한, 광대한
• predator : 포식자, 포식 동물
• make a meal of : ~을 먹다
• burrow : 굴, 피난처, 은신처

해석

(A) 미어캣은 아프리카 평원에서 가장 큰 동물이 아닐 수도 있고, 코뿔소의 뿔처럼 특별히 가공할 무기나, 치타의 속도처럼 인상적인 기술을 자랑하는 것처럼 보이지도 않을 것이다.

(D) 그럼에도 불구하고, 강인한 생명력과 영리한 속임수 그리고 독특한 공동체 정신의 결합을 통해, 이 포유류들은 가혹한 환경에 완벽하게 적응했다. 그들은 땅속 굴에서 살며 그들을 잡아먹으려는 많은 포식자들뿐만 아니라 남아프리카의 극한 기온에서 벗어난다.

(B) 이 땅속 굴 중 일부는 보통 한 군집이 동굴 크기의 약 절반이지만, 두세 가족이 공동으로 함께 생활하며, 최대 50마리 이상을 수용할 수 있다. 몽구스의 일종인 그들은 땅을 파거나 자기방어에 사용되는 뾰족하고 구부러진 발톱과 위험을 알아채는 데 매우 유용한 잘 발달된 시력을 갖추고 있다. 사실 그들이 먹이를 찾아 위험을 무릅쓰고 굴 밖으로 나올 때, 주로 그들의 가장 중요한 적인 맹금류들을 찾아 하늘을 쳐다보며 적어도 한 마리의 미어캣이 바위 위나 덤불 속에서 항상 보초를 설 것이다.

(C) 어떤 위험이라도 감지되는 즉시, 보초가 날카로운 경고음으로 울부짖으면 다른 미어캣들은 즉시 근처 구멍이나 다른 숨을 곳을 향해 돌진할 것이다. 미어캣은 다양한 위험을 알리기 위해 수십 가지의 다른 소리를 내는 것으로 여겨진다. 미어캣은 영역 내에서 함께 사냥을 하는 것뿐만 아니라, 육아 의무도 함께한다. 일반적으로 이 군집의 우두머리 쌍만이 짝짓기를 하지만, 다른 모든 미어캣들도 새끼를 돌보고 재우고 먹이는 것뿐만 아니라, 어디에서 먹이를 구할 것인지, 싸움 놀이를 할 것인지 그리고 전갈의 어느 부분을 먹을 것인지와 같은 소중한 삶의 기술을 보여주기 위해 협력한다.

41 ⑤ 글 (A)에서 평범한 미어캣의 신체적 특성에 대해 설명하고 있고, 글 (D)에서는 그럼에도 불구하고 가혹한 환경에 완벽하게 적응했다고 서술되어 있다. 글 (D)에 이어 글 (B)에서 미어캣의 땅굴 생활을 자세히 설명하고 있으며, 글 (B)에

이어 글 (C)에서 위험에 대처하는 미어캣의 생활 모습을 설명하고 있다. 그러므로 글 (A) 다음에 (D) – (B) – (C)의 순서로 이어져야 한다.

42 ② 제시문에 따르면 미어캣은 최대 50마리 이상을 수용할 수 있는 땅속 굴에서 두세 가족이 공동으로 함께 생활한다고 하였다. 그러므로 "미어캣은 일반적으로 독립적인 생활을 한다."는 ②의 설명은 제시문의 내용과 일치하지 않는다.

오답풀이

① 미어캣은 몽구스의 한 종류이다.
③ 미어캣은 땅을 파거나 자기방어를 위한 뾰족한 발톱이 있다.
④ 미어캣은 우두머리만 짝짓기를 한다.
⑤ 미어캣은 위협이 있을 경우 보초가 즉시 동료에게 알린다.

[43~45]

어휘

- spacial reasoning test : 공간추리 시험
- observation : 관찰[관측], 논평[의견]
- doting : 맹목적으로 사랑하는, 애지중지하는
- around the clock : 24시간 내내, 밤낮으로
- obviously : 확실히, 분명히, 명확히
- suspicious : 의심스러운, 수상쩍은
- evidence : 증거, 증언
- spatial intelligence : 공간 지각 능력
- infant : 유아, 젖먹이
- disconfirm : 확신하지 않다, 부정하다
- narrated story : 구연동화
- alert : 기민한, 민첩한, 주의 깊은
- prodigy : 영재, 천재, 신동
- fidelity : 충실, 충성
- pedagogical : 교육학의
- implication : 암시, 함축, 연루, 관계
- duplicate : 복사[복제]하다, 다시[중복해서] 하다

해석

[가] 두 명의 연구원들은 대학생들이 모차르트 피아노 소나타를 듣고 난 후 공간추리 시험에서 더 높은 점수를 받았다고 보고했다. 이 논평이 뉴스에 나간 직후, 맹목적인 부모들은 밤낮으로 그들의 아기에게 모차르트를 들려줬다. 분명 그들은 대학생들처럼 그들의 아기가 더 똑똑해지기를 바랐다. 그러나 부모들은 그러한 마법의 혜택을 제공한다고 주장하는 어떠한 행위도 의심해 봐야 한다.

[다] '모차르트 효과'의 가장 큰 (B) 문제점은 원래의 실험이 성인에게 이루어졌다는 것이다. 즉, 그것은 우리에게 유아

에 관한 말은 아무것도 없었다. 또한, 이 연구는 다른 유형의 음악을 시험하지 않았다. 왜 그 문제에 바흐나 슈베르트의 음악을 사용하지 않나? 더욱 중요한 물음은 모차르트 효과가 실제로 존재하는가이다.

[나] 그 증거가 시사하는 바는 무엇인가? 몇몇 연구들은 모차르트의 음악을 들은 후 공간 지각 능력이 조금 향상된다는 것을 알았다. 그러나 대부분의 연구원들은 그 효과를 (B) 반복할 수 없었다.

[라] 왜 일부 연구들은 그 효과를 지지하고 다른 연구들은 부정하는가? 대부분의 연구는 음악을 들은 학생들과 조용히 쉬는 학생들을 비교했다. 하지만, 두 심리학자는 이야기를 듣는 것도 시험 점수를 향상시킨다는 사실을 발견했다. 이것은 이야기를 듣기 좋아하는 학생들에게 특히 사실이었다. 따라서 모차르트를 듣고 더 높은 점수를 받은 학생들은 그저 더 주의 깊거나 기분이 더 좋을 뿐이었다.

43 ② 글 [가]에서는 대학생들에게 행한 모차르트 효과가 아기들에게도 과연 효과가 있는지 의문을 제기하고 있다. 다음으로 글 [다]에서 이러한 모차르트 효과의 여러 문제점들을 지적하고 있으며, 글 [나]에서는 모차르트 효과가 반복해서 나타나지 않아 우연한 것임을 설명하고 있다. 마지막으로 글 [라]에서 모차르트 효과가 실제로 효과가 없음을 결론 내리고 있다. 그러므로 글 [가] 다음에 전체적인 글의 흐름 상 [다] – [나] – [라]의 순서로 배열되어야 한다.

44 ① 제시문은 모차르트 효과의 실효성에 대해 의문을 제기하고 여러 증거들을 통해 모차르트 효과가 실제 효력이 없음을 설명하고 있다. 그러므로 ①의 "Mozart Effect: Nothing Magical (모차르트 효과: 마법은 없다.)"가 제시문의 제목으로 가장 적절하다.

오답풀이

② 모차르트: 신동 만들기
③ 클래식 음악이 왜 아기에게 좋은가?
④ 모차르트의 소나타: 최고의 음악적 충실도
⑤ 모차르트 음악과 교육적인 영향

45 ③ (A) 글 [나]에서는 일부 나타난 모차르트 효과도 반복되어 나타나지 않아 우연한 것임을 설명하고 있다. 그러므로 빈칸에는 'duplicate(반복해서 하다)'가 들어갈 말로 가장 적절하다.
(B) 글 [다]에서는 원래의 실험과 그 대상이 다른 것, 모차르트 음악에 한정된 것, 그리고 모차르트 효과의 실효성 여부에 관한 것 등 '모차르트 효과'가 갖는 문제점을 열거하고 있다. 그러므로 빈칸에는 'problem(문제점)'이 들어갈 말로 가장 적절하다.

2019학년도 기출문제 정답 및 해설

01 ④	02 ⑤	03 ④	04 ①	05 ②	06 ④
07 ⑤	08 ③	09 ④	10 ⑤	11 ③	12 ⑤
13 ⑤	14 ③	15 ⑤	16 ⑤	17 ①	18 ②
19 ⑤	20 ②	21 ④	22 ①	23 ③	24 ②
25 ①	26 ④	27 ②	28 ①	29 ②	30 ⑤
31 ③	32 ④	33 ①	34 ①	35 ③	36 ④
37 ③	38 ④	39 ②	40 ②	41 ⑤	42 ①
43 ③	44 ③	45 ③			

01 ④ 'pensive'는 '깊은 생각에 잠긴, 수심 어린'의 의미로 'thoughtful(생각에 잠긴, 심사숙고하는)'과 그 의미가 가장 유사하다.

[오답풀이]
① 명시적인, 공공연한
② 지나친, 과도한
③ 만연하는, 스며드는
⑤ 낙관적인, 낙천적인

[어휘]
• pensive : 깊은 생각에 잠긴, 수심 어린
• gentleness : 상냥함, 온화함, 관대함
• overt : 명시적인, 공공연한
• excessive : 지나친, 과도한
• pervasive : 만연하는, 스며드는

[해석]
수심에 잠긴 온화함에도 불구하고, 이 편지의 어조보다 더 단호한 것은 없다.

02 ⑤ 'exhaustive'는 '철저한, 완전한'의 의미로 'thorough(빈틈없는, 철두철미한)'와 그 의미가 가장 유사하다.

[오답풀이]
① 보람 있는, 수익이 많이 나는
② 혁명적인, 획기적인
③ 관대한, 온화한
④ 독립적인, 독자적인

[어휘]
• assert : 주장하다, 단언하다
• genome : 게놈, 유전체
• by no means : 결코 …이 아닌
• exhaustive : 철저한, 완전한
• rewarding : 보람 있는, 수익이 많이 나는
• revolutionary : 혁명적인, 획기적인
• lenient : 관대한, 온화한
• independent : 독립적인, 독자적인
• thorough : 빈틈없는, 철두철미한

[해석]
그 의사는 인간 게놈에 관한 자신의 평생 연구가 결코 완전하지 못했다고 단언했다.

03 ④ 'conundrum'은 '난제, 수수께끼'의 의미로 'puzzle(퍼즐, 수수께끼)'와 그 의미가 가장 유사하다.

[오답풀이]
① 기구, 도구
② 강도, 강탈
③ 범인, 범죄자
⑤ 시위, 설명

[어휘]
• conundrum : 난제, 수수께끼
• instrument : 기구, 도구
• robbery : 강도, 강탈
• criminal : 범인, 범죄자
• puzzle : 퍼즐, 수수께끼
• demonstration : 시위, 설명

[해석]
이 수수께끼는 그 경찰관들이 이전에 직면했던 것과는 전혀 달랐다.

04 ① Jack과의 다툼 후 A의 말에 B가 그것은 용기가 필요하다고 했으므로, ①의 "It's never too late to apologize(사과하

기에는 결코 늦지 않았어)"가 빈칸에 들어갈 말로 가장 적절하다.

오답풀이

② 항상 모든 사람들을 기쁘게 할 수는 없어

③ 때로는 다툼이 팀에 도움이 되기도 해

④ 다른 것들과 마찬가지로, 시간이 모든 상처를 치유해 주지

⑤ 말하기에 앞서 생각해야 하는 이유야

어휘

• ounce : 온스, 아주 적은 양

• apologize : 사과하다, 사죄하다

• quarrel : 다툼, 언쟁, 싸움

• heal : 고치다, 치료하다

• wound : 상처, 부상

해석

A : 어제 데이트는 어땠어?

B : 최악이었어.

A : 무슨 일이 있었어?

B : 내가 해서는 안 된 말을 해서 Jack은 이제 나랑 말도 안 해.

A : 사과하기에 결코 늦지 않았어.

B : 그렇게 하려면 모든 용기를 끌어 모아야 해.

05 ② Mills 형사가 범죄현장에서 나온 지문과 용의자의 지문을 대조해 보지 않은 상태에서 목격자의 진술로만 체포 영장을 발부받기에는 충분하지 않다고 했으므로, ②의 "We move on evidence, not feelings(느낌이 아니라 증거로 움직입니다.)"가 빈칸에 들어갈 말로 가장 적절하다.

오답풀이

① 바로 체포 영장을 청구할게요

③ 이미 필요한 모든 증거를 확보했다고 생각해요

④ 목격자의 진술에 집중합시다

⑤ 우리의 주 임무는 시민의 안전을 보장하는 것입니다

어휘

• detective : 형사, 수사관, 탐정

• print : 흔적, 자국, 지문

• the scene of the crime : 범죄현장

• witness : 목격자, 증인

• description : 묘사, 서술, 인상착의

• arrest warrant : 체포 영장, 구속 영장

• perpetrator : 가해자, 범인

• concentrate on : ~에 집중하다

• ensure : 보장하다, 확실하게 하다

해석

A : Mills 형사님, 이 사람이 우리가 찾고 있는 사람인거 같아요.

B : 그의 지문을 범죄현장에서 나온 것과 대조해 봤나요. Flaherty 경관님?

A : 결과가 아직 나오지 않았지만, 두 명의 목격자가 그와 같은 인상착의를 지닌 사람을 봤다고 말했어요.

B : 그것만으로 체포 영장을 발부받기에는 충분하지 않아요.

A : 하지만, 난 이 사람이 범인이라고 확신해요.

B : 우리는 느낌이 아니라 증거로 움직입니다.

A : 알겠어요. 그렇다면 감식반에서 나올 결과를 기다려야겠군요.

06 ④ 'those'는 앞의 'standpoint(견지, 관점)'를 받는 지시대명사로 단수이기 때문에 'that'으로 고쳐 써야 옳다.

어휘

• recurrent : 되풀이되는, 반복되는, 재발되는

• court : 법정, 법원

• adopt : 택하다, 채택하다

• disclose : 밝히다, 폭로하다, 공개하다

• medical practitioner : 의사, 개업의

• specialty : 전공

• be grounded in : ~에 근거하다

• therapeutic : 치료상의, 치료법의

• privilege : 특권, 특전

• preeminent : 탁월한, 현저한

• withhold : 보류하다, 주지 않다

• deferential : 경의를 표하는, 공손한

• standpoint : 견지, 관점

• adequacy : 적절, 타당성

해석

법정에서 반복되는 이슈는 환자들의 의학적 치료에 관해 얼마만큼 환자들에게 공개해야 하는지를 결정하는 데 있어 누구의 관점을 선택하느냐 하는 것이다. 대다수의 주(州)들은 전문가들을 선호하며, 같은 공동체와 같은 전공 내의 '합리적인 의사'에 의해 합리적이라고 여길 만큼만 의사들이 공개에 책임이 있다는 입장을 취한다. 이러한 접근법은 소위 치료적 특권에 근거하며, 환자에게 해가 될 수 있는 어떤 정보도 알려주지 않을 의사의 현저한 특권을 인정한다. 이를 덜 옹호하는 소수자의 규칙은 공개의 적절성이 '합리적인 의사'의 관점에서가 아니라 '합리적인 환자'의 관점에서 결정되어야 한다는 입장을 취한다. 비록 이러한 일반적인 규칙들이 잘 정착된다 하더라도, 공개의 타당성에 관한 의문들은 여전히 제기된다.

07 ⑤ 'make + 목적어 + 목적보어'의 구문에서 목적보어인 'satisfy'의 형태는 'the practice of raku'가 사물이므로 'satisfying(만족시키는)'이 적절하다. 목적어가 사람이라면 만족하는 것이므로 수동의 의미인 과거분사 'satisfied'가 와야 한다.

어휘

- low-temperature : 낮은 온도, 저온
- fast-firing : 급속으로 굽는
- chance : 우연한
- ceramic ware : 도자기류, 세라믹 제품
- crackle : 잔금, 잔금을 넣어 구은 도자기
- glaze : 유약
- humble : 변변치 않은, 작은
- sculptural : 조각의, 조각술의
- abstract : 추상적인, 관념적인
- figurative : 구상의, 조형의
- vibrant : 활기찬, 생기가 넘치는
- infinite : 무한한, 한계가 없는
- ceramist : 도예가, 요업가
- relatively : 비교적, 어느 정도

해석

라쿠는 도자기 제품에 흥미롭고 우연한 표면 효과를 내며 저온에서 급속히 굽는 대중적인 공정이다. 소박한 하얀 잔금 무늬 유약에서 놀랄 말한 스펙트럼 색상까지, 그리고 작은 찻잔에서 추상적이고 구상의 조각 형태에 이르기까지, 라쿠 작업에 존재하는 가능성과 혁신의 범위는 그것을 항상 참신하고 생기 넘치게 해준다. 그것의 목적과 마찬가지로, 이 고대 공정의 현대적인 서구식 작업은 동양의 뿌리와는 다르지만, 다양성, 에너지 그리고 미(美)에 있어서 라쿠의 결과는 여전히 무한하다. 일본과 서양 라쿠는 도예가에게 굽기의 최종 결과물을 비교적 단기간에 경험할 기회를 제공해주며, 바로 이러한 특징이 라쿠 작업을 매우 만족스럽게 만든다.

08 ③ (A) 해마의 꼬리가 지속적인 손상 없이 평상시 크기의 절반까지 줄어드는 것이므로 '확장되는(expanded)'이 아니라 '압축되는(compressed)'이 들어갈 말로 적절하다.

(B) 해마는 4개의 골 판으로 된 약 36개의 정사각형 마디 구조로 인해 그것의 꼬리가 평상시 크기의 절반까지 압축되었다가 다시 회복하는 것이므로 'resilience(복원력)'가 들어갈 말로 적절하다.

(C) 척추의 등뼈를 콜라겐으로 연결하여 해마의 척추를 안전한 상태로 유지하는 것이므로 'safe(안전한)'가 들어갈 말로 적절하다.

어휘

- manta ray : 쥐가오리

- crush : 으스러뜨리다, 쭈그러뜨리다
- armor : 갑옷, 철갑
- compress : 압축하다, 꾹 누르다
- expand : 확장하다, 넓히다
- resilience : 회복력, 복원력, 탄성, 탄력
- rigidity : 단단함, 강직, 경직
- approximately : 대략, 대충, 약
- segment : 부분, 조각, 마디
- bony plate : 골 판
- spinal column : 척추
- vertebrae : 척추뼈, 등골, 등뼈
- collagen : 콜라겐
- glide : 미끄러지다
- spine : 척추, 등뼈
- vulnerable : 취약한, 연약한
- mimic : 흉내 내다, 모방하다
- flexible : 신축성 있는, 유연한
- excursion : 유람, 여행
- detonate : 폭발시키다, 터뜨리다

해석

게, 새, 쥐가오리가 저녁거리로 해마를 계속해서 으스러뜨리려 하지만, 해마는 독특한 보호 갑옷을 입고 있다. 해마의 꼬리는 지속적인 손상 없이 평상시 크기의 절반까지 (A) 압축될 수 있는 것으로 샌디에이고에 있는 캘리포니아 대학 연구원들이 최근 밝혀냈다. 그 꼬리의 (B) 복원력은 각각 4개의 골 판으로 만들어진 약 36개의 정사각형 마디인 그것의 구조에서 비롯된다. 그 판은 척추의 등뼈를 콜라겐과 연결하고, 척추를 (C) 안전한 상태로 유지하면서 서로 미끄러질 수 있다. 궁극적으로 연구원들은 3D 프린터로 해마의 유연하고 튼튼한 꼬리를 모방한 로봇 팔을 만들고 싶어 하며, 수중여행을 위해 또는 폭탄을 폭발시키기 위해 그것을 사용하고 싶어 한다.

09 ④ (A) 윗글은 점화 효과의 예시로 투표소의 위치나 노출이 투표 행위에 영향을 미친다는 내용이다. 그러므로 점화 효과로 인해 개인의 자아를 '확인하는(confirm)' 것이 아니라 '위협하게(threaten)' 된다.

(B) 투표는 정책에 대한 가치와 평가를 반영하며 이와 관련이 없는 것으로부터 영향을 받아서는 안 되는 행위이다. 그러므로 '무관한 것(irrelevancies)'이 들어갈 말로 적절하다.

(C) 점화 효과에 따라 교실과 학교 사물함의 모습을 공개하는 것은 참석자들이 학교 법안 발의를 지지하는 경향을 '감소시킨(minimized)' 것이 아니라 '증가시켰음(increased)'을 보여준다.

어휘

- priming effect : 점화 효과
- confirm : 사실임을 보여주다, 확인해 주다
- autonomous : 자주적인, 자율적인
- vote : 투표
- deliberate : 사려 깊은, 신중한
- assessment : 평가, 사정
- consensus : 의견 일치, 합의
- irrelevancy : 논외, 무관함
- affect : 영향을 미치다, 발생하다
- polling station : 투표소
- precinct : 구역[지구], 선거구
- proposition : 제안, 제의, 과제
- expose : 드러내다, 폭로하다, 노출시키다
- tendency : 성향, 기질, 경향
- initiative : 주민 법안 발의

해석

점화 효과에 대한 연구는 우리의 판단과 선택에 대한 의식적이고도 자율적인 작가로서 우리의 자아상을 (A) 위협하는 발견을 낳았다. 예를 들어, 우리들 대부분은 투표를 정책에 대한 가치와 평가를 반영하며 (B) 무관한 것에 의해 영향을 받아서는 안 되는 신중한 행위라고 생각한다. 예를 들어, 투표는 투표소의 위치에 의해 영향을 받아서는 안 되지만, 그것은 영향을 받는다. 2000년에 애리조나 선거구에서의 투표 패턴에 관한 연구는 투표소가 가까운 곳에 위치해 있을 때보다 학교 내에 위치해 있을 때, 학교 기금을 늘리자는 제안에 대한 지지가 훨씬 더 크다는 것을 보여주었다. 또 다른 실험에서 교실과 학교 사물함의 모습을 공개하는 것이 참석자들이 학교 법안 발의를 지지하는 경향을 (C) 증가시켰음을 또한 보여주었다. 그 이미지의 효과는 부모들과 다른 투표자들 간의 차이보다 더 컸다.

10 ⑤ 어떤 해답이 폭넓은 이론화를 위한 구축물의 역할을 한다는 의미로만 즉시 사용되는 곳에서 추가 작업이 그 자체로 중요하고 긴급한 경우, 조금이라도 더 빨리 해답을 구하는 것이 대단히 가치 있는 경우이므로 문맥상 'later(l 나중에)'가 아니라 'earlier(더 일찍)'가 적절하다.

어휘

- point in time : 때, 어떤 시점
- elude : 피하다, 빠져나가다
- benefit : 유익하다, 유용하다
- slightly : 약간, 조금
- immensely : 엄청나게, 대단히
- plausible : 그럴듯한, 이치에 맞는

- deploy : 배치하다, 효율적으로 사용하다
- serve as : …의 역할을 하다
- theoretical : 이론적인, 이론상의
- urgent : 긴급한, 시급한, 다급한

해석

'발견'을 더 나중의 시점에서 더 이른 시기로 정보의 도달을 옮기는 행위라고 생각해보라. 발견의 가치는 발견된 정보의 가치와 ① 동등하지 않으며, 오히려 그렇지 않았을 때보다 더 일찍 이용 가능한 정보를 소유하는 가치와 동등하다. 과학자나 수학자는 많은 사람들이 ② 회피한 해답을 찾는 데 첫 번째 존재가 됨으로써 위대한 기술을 보여줄 지도 모르나, 그 문제가 어떤 식으로든 빨리 풀리게 된다면, 그 일은 아마도 세상에 많은 ③ 도움이 되지 못했을 것이다. 조금이라도 더 빨리 해답을 구하는 것이 대단히 가치 있는 경우가 있지만, 그러나 이것은 그 해답이 즉각 활용될 때 가장 그럴듯하며, 몇몇 실용적인 목적을 위해 ④ 효율적으로 사용되거나 혹은 더 나아가 이론적인 작업의 토대 역할을 한다. 그리고 후자의 경우 어떤 해답이 폭넓은 이론화를 위한 구축물의 역할을 한다는 의미로만 즉시 사용되는 곳에서, 추가 작업이 그 자체로 중요하고 긴급한 경우에만 해답을 조금 더 ⑤ 나중에 얻는 것이 엄청난 가치가 있다.

11 ③ 과학은 항상 확률적이고 수정의 대상이며, 언제라도 우리의 이해에 대한 망설임과 불확실성을 인식하고 있는 가치 시스템이라고 했으므로, 세상에 대한 '확고부동한 (steadfast)' 일반화가 아니라 '변경 가능한(changeable)' 일반화이다.

어휘

- be committed to : ~에 헌신[전념]하다
- persuade A of B : A에게 B를 확신시키다
- and therefore : 그 때문에
- tacitly : 암암리에, 암묵적으로
- validity : 유효함, 타당성
- theorem : (수학) 정리(定理), 일반 원리, 법칙
- be entitled to : ~할 권리가 있다
- observation : 관찰, 감시
- steadfast : 변함없는, 확고부동한
- dazzling : 눈부신, 휘황찬란한
- manipulate : 조작하다, 처리하다
- albeit : 비록 …일지라도
- probabilistic : 개연론의, 확률적인, 가망성의
- revision : 수정[정정], 검토
- institution : 기관, 단체, 협회
- evaluate : 평가하다, 감정하다

• candidate : 후보자, 지원자

• cognizant of : …를 인식하고 있는

• tentativeness : 시험[실험]적임, 망설임

• uncertainty : 불확실성, 반신반의

해석

우리는 이성에 전념한다. 만일 우리가 질문을 하고, 가능한 대답들을 평가하고, 다른 사람들에게 그러한 대답들의 가치를 확신시키려 노력한다면, 그 때 우리는 추론하게 되고 그 때문에 이성의 ① 타당성에 대해 암묵적으로 동의하게 된다. 우리는 수학과 논리의 정리(定理)처럼 이성의 세심한 적용에서 나오는 결론은 무엇이든 또한 전념하게 된다. 비록 우리가 물리적인 세계에 관한 어떤 것도 논리적으로 ② 입증할 수 없더라도, 그것에 관한 어떤 믿음에 확신을 가질 권리가 있다. 세상에 대한 ③ 확고부동한 일반화를 발견하는 이성과 관찰의 적용은 우리가 과학이라 부르는 것이다. 세상을 설명하고 조작하는 데 눈부신 성공을 거둔 과학의 진보는, 비록 항상 확률적이고 수정의 대상이지만 우주에 관한 지식이 ④ 가능함을 보여준다. 과학은 사실 우리가 지식을 얻는 방법에 대한 패러다임이며, 이는 과학의 특정한 방법이나 제도가 아닌, 말하자면 세상에 대한 설명을 추구하고, 후보 설명들을 ⑤ 객관적으로 평가하며, 언제라도 우리의 이해에 대한 망설임과 불확실성을 인식하고 있는 가치 시스템이다.

12 ⑤ 야생동물에게 미치는 플라스틱의 피해 사례로, 수년 간 질긴 플라스틱에 옥죄어 거북의 껍데기가 상처가 없는(unscathed) 것이 아니라 상처가 생긴 것이므로 'scathed' 또는 'wounded'를 사용해야 한다.

어휘

• biologist : 생물학자

• plier : 집게, 펜치

• extract : 추출하다, 뽑다

• nostril : 콧구멍

• writhe in agony : 고통으로 몸부림치다

• profusely : 풍부하게, 잔뜩

• tick : 째깍[똑딱]거리다, 작동하다

• log : 기록하다, 항해[비행]하다

• desperate : 필사적인, 발악하는

• dislodge : 제거하다, 내몰다, 쫓아내다

• raw : 날것의, 가공되지 않은

• lay bare : 발가벗기다

• toll on : (~에 끼치는) 피해, 손해

• albatross : 알바트로스 새, 신천옹

• burst with : …으로 터질 듯하다

• refuse : 쓰레기, 찌꺼기

• stuck : 움직일 수 없는, 꼼짝 못하는, 갇힌

• unscathed : 다치지 않은, 상처 없는

• strain : 잡아당기다, 죄다

• snare : 덫, 올가미

• discard : 버리다, 폐기하다

해석

코스타리카에서 떨어진 보트 위에서, 어떤 생물학자가 바다거북의 콧구멍에서 플라스틱 빨대를 뽑아내기 위해 스위스 군용 칼의 집게를 사용하고 있다. 그 거북이는 잔뜩 피를 흘리며 고통으로 ① 몸부림을 치고 있다. 고통스러운 8분 동안 유튜브 비디오가 작동하고, 시청하기가 아주 힘들지만 2천만 명 이상의 시청 ② 기록을 달성했다. 결국, 점점 더 필사적인 생물학자들이 그 동물의 코에서 4인치 길이의 빨대 한 개를 간신히 ③ 제거한다. 야생동물에게 끼치는 플라스틱의 피해를 ④ 발가벗기는 이와 같은 가공되지 않은 장면들에 익숙해지고 있다. 배가 쓰레기로 터질 듯이 죽은 신천옹, 수년 간 질긴 플라스틱에 옥죄어 ⑤ 상처 없는 껍데기가 여섯 개의 팩 고리에 갇힌 거북이, 버려진 어망에 잡힌 바다표범. 누구에게 책임이 있는가? 거울을 잘 들여다보라.

13 ⑤ 지구가 다양한 생물들을 수용하는 유일한 존재인지 아니면 우리가 지구에 존재하는 것들만큼이나 복잡한 생명체로 가득한 우주에 살고 있는 지에 대한 물음에 후자가 점점 가능성이 높아지고 있다고 답하고 있다. 또한 우주에는 잠재적으로 사람이 거주할 수 있는 무수히 많은 외계행성과 외계위성들이 존재한다고 설명하고 있으므로, ⑤의 'Is Anybody Out There? (밖에 누구 있어요?)'가 윗글의 제목으로 가장 적절하다.

오답풀이

① 지구, 그 놀라운 서식지

② 은하계 사이의 초고속도로

③ 미생물이 정말 우리의 조상인가?

④ 우주 동물원: 엄청난 속임수

어휘

• rare : 드문, 진귀한, 희귀한

• exceptional : 예외적인, 이례적인, 특출한

• pretty much : 거의

• diversity : 다양성, 포괄성

• microbe : 미생물

• teem with : 바글[와글]거리다, 풍부하다, 가득하다

• vast : 방대한, 막대한

• rage : 몹시 화를 내다, 격노하다

• exoplanet : 태양계 외 행성, 외계행성

• trillions of : 무수히 많은

• habitable : 거주할 수 있는, 살 수 있는

• exomoon : 외계위성

• emerge trom : ~에서 벗어나다, 나오다

• property : 속성, 특성

• intergalactic : 은하계 사이의

• hoax : 농간, 거짓말, 속임수

해석

우리는 진귀한 지구에 살고 있는가? 다른 행성들이 기껏해야 단순한 미생물의 서식지가 될 때, 아주 이례적으로 생명체의 풍부한 다양성을 수용하는 거의 유일한 존재인가? 또는 우리가 거대한 우주 동물원의 일부로 존재하는 것을 의미하면서, 여기에 존재하는 것들만큼이나 복잡한 생명체로 가득한 우주에 살고 있는가? 이에 관한 논쟁이 한창이지만, 우리는 후자가 매우 가능성이 높다는 것을 받아들일 때가 되었다고 말한다. 지금까지 우리는 적어도 3,700개의 외계행성에 대해 알고 있으며, 잠재적으로 거주할 수 있는 무수히 많은 외계행성들과 외계위성들이 우리 은하계 내에 그리고 그 너머에 존재하는 것 같다. 우리는 생명체가 보통 그 행성 위에서 어떻게 생겨나는지 모르지만, 많은 과학자들은 그것이 어떤 적합한 행성의 화학적이고 물리적인 특성에서 아마 생겨났을 거라고 생각한다.

14 ③ Frank O'Connor는 1931년부터 미국에서 잡지를 정기적으로 발행하였고 몇 년 동안 하버드와 노스웨스턴 대학에서 가르쳤다. 이 때부터 그의 작가 경력이 자리 잡기 시작했으므로 "His writing career in the US took off in the early 1930s. (그의 작가 경력은 1930년대 초반 미국에서 시작했다.)"는 ③의 설명이 윗글의 내용과 일치한다.

오답풀이

① 그는 하버드 대학에서 학위를 딴 아일랜드 극작가이다.

② 그는 Abbey 극장에서 무대 요원의 일원이었다.

④ 그는 이야기꾼의 목소리에서 리듬을 모호하게 하였다.

⑤ 그의 이야기는 초기 미국의 관습과 관련이 있다.

어휘

• struggle for independence : 독립 투쟁

• briefly . 대략, 잠시, 잠깐

• librarian : 사서

• declared : 공표한, 선언한, 공언한

• prolific : 다작의, 다산의

• playwright : 극작가, 각본가

• stage crew : 무대 요원, 무대계원

• take off : 도약하다, 출발하다

• blur : 흐릿해지다, 희미해지다

해석

Frank O'Connor는 너무 가난해서 대학교육을 시켜줄 수 없었던 아일랜드 Cork의 한 가정에서 태어났다. 아일랜드의 독립 투쟁 동안에 그는 잠시 아일랜드 공화국 군대의 일원이었다. 그 후 그는 Cork와 Dublin에서 도서관 사서로 일했으며, 단편 소설의 작가로 자리 잡기 전까지 Abbey 극장의 감독이었다. 1931년부터 그는 미국에서 잡지를 정기적으로 발행하였으며, 몇 년 동안 하버드와 노스웨스턴 대학에서 가르쳤다. 그가 공언한 목표는 소재를 만드는 데 있어 이야기꾼의 목소리에서 자연스러운 리듬과 강세를 찾는 것이었다. 그는 사실 아일랜드의 관습과 아일랜드의 인물에 관한 다작의 역사가였다.

15 ⑤ 윗글의 마지막 문장에서 세계 야생동물 기금(WWF)은 그 종들이 발견되거나 소생될 경우를 대비하여 양쯔강돌고래가 서식 가능한 어떤 지역이든 보존을 요청하였다고 서술하고 있으므로, "The World Wildlife Fund has given up all hope in reviving the species. (세계 야생동물 기금은 그 종을 소생시키려는 모든 노력을 포기했다.)"는 ⑤의 설명은 윗글의 내용과 일치하지 않는다.

오답풀이

① 그것의 유일한 서식지는 양쯔강이었다.

② 그것은 중국의 흰색 돌고래와 혼동되지 않는다.

③ 산업화는 그것의 개체수를 감소시키는 역할을 하였다.

④ 그것은 2006년 탐사 기간 동안 나타나지 않았다.

어휘

• baiji : 민물돌고래, 양쯔강돌고래

• extinct : 멸종된, 사라진

• freshwater : 담수, 민물

• be confused with : ~과 혼동되다

• drastically : 과감하게, 철저하게

• decade : 10년

• hydroelectricity : 수력 전기

• extinction : 소멸, 멸종

• conserve : 아껴 쓰다, 보호[보존]하다

• expedition : 탐험, 탐사, 원정

• reportedly : 전하는 바에 따르면, 소문에 의하면

• preservation : 보존, 보호, 유지

• habitat : 서식지

• revive : 회복하다, 소생하다

• decline : 감소하다, 줄어들다

• population : 인구, 개체수

해석

양쯔강돌고래는 이전에 중국의 양쯔강에서만 발견된 담수 돌

고래로 기능상 멸종된 종이다. 그것은 또한 중국의 민물돌고래로 불린다. 그것은 중국의 흰색 돌고래와 혼동되지 않는다. 중국이 산업화가 되고 어획, 운송, 수력전기를 위해 강을 과도하게 사용하게 됨에 따라 양쯔강돌고래의 개체수는 수십 년간 급격히 감소했다. 양쯔강돌고래는 역사상 인간이 멸종으로 내몬 첫 번째 돌고래 종이 될 수도 있었다. 그 종들을 보존하기 위한 노력이 있었지만, 2006년 후반 탐사대는 그 강에서 한 마리의 양쯔강돌고래도 발견하지 못했다. 2007년 8월, 소문에 의하면 한 중국인 남성이 양쯔강에서 헤엄치고 있는 양쯔강돌고래로 추정되는 커다란 하얀 동물을 촬영했다고 한다. 세계 야생동물 기금(WWF)에서는 그 종들이 발견되거나 소생될 경우를 대비하여, 양쯔강돌고래가 서식 가능한 어떤 지역이든 보존을 요청하고 있다.

16 ⑤ 윗글은 새로 이사 온 이웃의 십대 아이들이 음악을 크게 틀어 놓아서 이웃 주민 중 한 사람이 그 부모에게 볼륨을 줄여달라고 정중히 부탁하는 내용이다. 그러므로 ⑤의 'to complain about a neighbor's loud music (이웃의 큰 음악 소리에 대해 항의하기 위해)'가 윗글의 목적으로 가장 적절하다.

(오답풀이)
① 어려운 이웃을 위한 기부를 요청하기 위해
② 주민 파티에 이웃을 초대하기 위해
③ 떠나는 가족에게 행복을 빌기 위해
④ 더 좋은 스테레오 스피커로 교환을 요구하기 위해

(어휘)
• opportunity : 기회
• address as : …라고 부르다[호칭하다]
• unofficial : 비공식적인, 공인되지 않은
• appreciate : 고마워하다, 감사하다
• turn down : (볼륨을) 줄이다, 낮추다
• solicit : 간청[요청]하다, 얻으려고 하다
• donation : 기부, 기증
• a block party : 주민 파티

(해석)
이번 기회에 제 소개를 하며 이웃으로 오신 것을 환영합니다. 새로 이사 온 집의 도로 바로 위에 있는 19번지에서 제 아내 Monica와 제가 살고 있습니다. 우리는 Meadow Street에서 지난 20년간 살아왔습니다. 아마도 제가 이 주변에 있는 모든 사람들보다 나이가 더 많기 때문에, 마을의 비공식적인 '시장'으로 종종 불립니다.
저는 당신이 이사 온 이래 발생한 문제들에 관하여 우리의 몇몇 이웃들로부터 그들의 요청을 전해달라는 부탁을 받았습니다. 우리 모두 음악을 사랑하고 우리 중 대부분은 10대 자녀가

있거나 생길 겁니다. 그래서 당신의 십 대 자녀에게 볼륨을 줄여달라고 부탁하면 감사하겠습니다.
제대로 정착이 된 후 우리 모두 만나서 인사할 것을 고대합니다.

17 ① 윗글은 진지함만을 토대로 하는 관계 보다는 웃음을 기반으로 하는 관계가 유익하다고 설명하고 있다. 그러므로 ①의 "A key to a healthy relationship is laughing together. (유익한 관계의 핵심은 함께 웃는 것이다.)"가 윗글의 요지로 가장 적절하다.

(오답풀이)
② 말뿐인 실천은 관계 실패의 근원이다.
③ 진지한 말은 끊임없이 서로를 비판하게 된다.
④ 놀라움이 당신의 관계에 웃음을 준다.
⑤ 많이 웃어라, 그러면 결국 새로운 관계를 형성할 것이다.

(어휘)
• laughter : 웃음
• compatibility : 양립[공존] 가능성, 호환성
• child : 만들어낸 것, 소산
• beware of : …에 주의하다
• intimate : 친한, 친밀한, 사적인
• dour : 시무룩한, 재미없는
• seed : 씨, 씨앗, 종자
• end up with : 결국 ~하게 되다

(해석)
웃음은 양립 가능한 하나의 실마리이다. 웃음은 장기간에 걸쳐 얼마나 서로 어울릴지를 말해준다. 만일 당신과 함께한 웃음이 다른 이들을 상하게 하지 않으면서 유익하고 건강하다면, 당신은 세상과 좋은 관계를 맺고 있는 것이다. 웃음은 놀라움의 소산이다. 만일 서로를 웃게 만들 수 있다면, 당신은 항상 서로를 놀라게 할 수 있다. 만일 당신이 서로를 항상 놀라게 할 수 있다면, 당신 주변의 세계를 새롭게 할 수 있다. 웃음이 없는 관계를 조심하라. 단지 진지함을 토대로 한 가장 친밀한 관계조차도 시무룩하게 되는 경향이 있다. 시간이 지남에 따라, 세상에 관한 공통의 진지한 관점을 공유하는 것은 당신으로 하여금 같은 관점을 공유하지 않는 사람들에게서 등을 돌리게 하는 경향이 있으며, 당신의 관계는 함께 비판적인 것에 근거할 수 있다.

18 ② 아프리카의 해안선이 아메리카의 해안선과 일치하는 이유에 대해 지리학자뿐만 아니라 지질학자도 물리학자도 동원되므로, 이를 설명하기 위해 모든 과학자가 필요하다는 의미이다. 그러므로 빈칸에는 'dispensable(불필요한)'이 들어갈 말로 가장 적절하다.

정답 및 해설

④ 유동성, 환금성

어휘

- annual : 매년의, 연례의
- sustain : 계속시키다, 지속시키다
- per capita : 1인당
- twenty-five-fold : 20배
- spectacularly : 구경거리로, 극적으로
- velocity : 속도, 속력
- originality : 독창성, 창의력
- transparency : 투명성, 투명도
- liquidity : 유동성, 환금성
- consistency : 일관성, 지속성

해석

연간 경제성장률의 작은 차이조차도, 수십 년 또는 수 세기 동안 지속된다면 결국 경제적 행복의 수준도 엄청난 차이가 난다. 예를 들어 미국의 1인당 국민 총생산(GNP)은 1820년에서 1998년의 기간 동안 해마다 연 1.7%씩 성장했다. 이것은 생활 수준에서 25배의 증가를 가져왔는데, 이는 1820년도에 1인당 약 1,200 달러에서 오늘날 1990년의 달러로 약 30,000 달러의 1인당 소득이 증가한 것이다. 미국이 세계에서 가장 부유한 경제대국이 된 핵심은 연간 8퍼센트의 성장을 보이는 중국의 최근 실적처럼 극적인 빠른 성장에 있지 않다. 그 핵심은 <u>지속성</u>이며, 이는 미국이 거의 두 세기 동안 소득성장률을 유지했다는 사실이다.

오답풀이

① 무죄의, 결백한

③ 꼼꼼한, 세심한

④ 자격이 있는, 제한적인

⑤ 연결된, 접촉된

어휘

- reductionism : 환원주의, 환원론
- unify : 통합하다, 통일하다
- put …under the microscope : …을 철저히 조사하다
- geographer : 지리학자
- coastline : 해안 지대, 해안선
- landmass : 광대한 토지, 대륙
- adjacent : 인접한, 가까운
- drift : 떠돌다, 표류하다
- geologist : 지질학자
- upwelling : 용승
- push apart : 떠밀다
- innocent : 무죄의, 결백한
- dispensable : 없어도 되는, 불필요한
- meticulous : 꼼꼼한, 세심한
- qualified : 자격이 있는, 제한적인

해석

훌륭한 환원주의란 한 분야의 지식을 또 다른 지식으로 대체하는 것이 아니라 그것들을 연결하거나 통합하는 형태로 이루어진다. 한 분야에 사용된 빌딩블록은 다른 분야에 의해 철저히 조사된다. 어떤 지리학자는 아프리카의 해안선이 아메리카의 해안선과 꼭 맞는 이유를 대륙이 한 때 인접해있었으나 서로 떨어져 각기 다른 판에 안착했다고 설명할 수도 있다. 그 판들이 이동하게 된 이유를 묻는 질문은 그 판들을 떠미는 마그마의 용승에 호소하는 지질학자들을 거쳐 가게 된다. 마그마가 어떻게 그렇게 뜨거워졌는지에 대해 말하면, 그들은 지구의 핵과 맨틀에서의 반응을 설명하기 위해 물리학자들을 소환한다. 과학자들 중 어느 누구도 <u>불필요한</u> 사람은 없다.

---

19 ⑤ 미국이 세계에서 가장 부유한 경제대국이 될 수 있었던 핵심은 최근의 중국처럼 고속 성장에 있는 것이 아니라 누 세기 동안 소득성장률을 꾸준히 유지한 것에 기인한다. 그러므로 빈칸에는 'consistency(지속성)'가 들어갈 말로 가장 적절하다.

오답풀이

① 속도, 속력

② 독창성, 창의력

③ 투명성, 투명도

---

20 ② 어떤 이유에 관한 믿음을 추론할 때 그 자체가 반드시 분명하지는 않더라도 자기 자신의 믿음에 관한 이성적인 설명을 표현하는 능력을 필연적으로 수반한다고 하였으므로, 빈칸에는 ②의 "need not be the result of any conscious process at all (어떤 의식적인 과정의 결과일 필요가 전혀 없다)"가 들어갈 말로 가장 적절하다.

오답풀이

① 종종 상호 반박의 상황에 기인한다

③ 어떤 결론을 검토하는 그 주제의 능력 속에 있을 수도 있다

④ 전제와 결론의 존재를 거의 부정한다

⑤ 관련 원칙에 따라 지속적으로 중재되어야만 한다

어휘

- explicit : 분명한, 명쾌한
- introspection : 자기 성찰, 반성
- self-observation : 자기 성찰
- relevant : 관련 있는, 연관된
- manifest : 나타나다, 분명해지다
- expressive : 표현적인, 표현이 풍부한

- self-explanation : 자기 설명
- mutual : 서로의, 상호간의
- contradiction : 모순, 반박
- premise : 전제, 근거
- constantly : 지속적으로, 거듭, 한결같이
- mediate : 중재하다, 조정하다

해석

이유에 관한 믿음은 어떤 의식적인 과정의 결과일 필요가 전혀 없다. 나는 내 이웃이 아무도 그를 방문한 적이 없다는 이유로 친구가 거의 없다고 믿을지도 모른다. 나는 결코 이러한 추론을 나 자신이나 그 밖의 다른 누구에게도 명백히 해본 적이 없을 수도 있다. "왜 당신은 그가 친구가 거의 없을 거라고 생각하나요?"라고 묻는다면, 여전히 나는 어떠한 반성이나 자기 성찰 없이 대답할 수 있다. "왜냐하면 아무도 그를 방문한 적이 없으니까요."라고 말이다. 어떤 주제가 연관된 상황 속에 있다는 것은 그 추론을 의식적으로 검토할 때, 반드시 그 자체가 분명하지는 않지만, 입증의 형태 그리고 표현이 풍부한 자기 설명의 형태로, 즉 사람이 그저 할 수 있는 자기 자신의 믿음에 관한 이성적인 설명을 표현하는 능력을 필연적으로 수반한다.

21 ④ 인간 공학이 몇몇 분야에서는 이미 진화보다 훨씬 뛰어나며 남은 영역에서도 머지않아 뛰어나게 될 것이므로, 진화가 지능을 만들었듯이 마찬가지로 인간 공학도 그렇게 할 수 있다는 것이다. 그러므로 빈칸에는 ④의 'soon be able to do the same (곧 같은 일을 할 수 있다)'가 들어갈 말로 가장 적절하다.

오답풀이
① 슈퍼지능과 경쟁하다
② 진화 과정보다 훨씬 뒤처지다
③ 스스로 사람 수준의 인공지능으로 위장하다
⑤ 비슷한 실수를 반복하다

어휘
- blind : 눈이 먼, 맹목적인
- evolutionary : 진화의, 진화적인
- foresight : 예지력, 선견지명
- genetic : 유전적인
- efficiency : 효율, 능률
- theoretically : 이론적으로, 이론상
- feasible : 실현가능한, 그럴듯한
- vastly : 대단히, 엄청나게
- compete against : ~과 경쟁하다
- lag behind : …보다 떨어지다, 뒤쳐지다
- disguise : 변장[위장]하다, 숨기다

해석

우리는 맹목적인 진화의 과정이 인간 수준의 보통 지능을 만들어낼 수 있다는 사실을 안다. 왜냐하면 한 때 적어도 이미 그렇게 해봤기 때문이다. 예지력이 있는 진화 과정, 즉 지적인 인간 프로그래머에 의해 설계되고 유도된 유전적 프로그램은 훨씬 더 효율적으로 비슷한 결과를 도출할 수 있어야만 한다. 인간 수준의 인공지능이 이론상 가능할 뿐만 아니라 금세기 내에 실현가능하다고 주장하는 몇몇 철학자들과 과학자들에 의해 이러한 관찰이 행해졌다. 그 개념은 우리가 진화와 지능을 만들어내는 인간 공학의 상대적인 역량을 추정할 수 있다는 것이며, 그리고 인간 공학이 몇몇 분야에서는 이미 진화보다 훨씬 뛰어나며 남은 영역에서도 머지않아 뛰어나리라는 것을 알게 된다는 것이다. 진화가 지능을 만들어 냈다는 사실인 즉 인간 공학이 곧 같은 일을 할 수 있을 것임을 시사한다.

22 ① 전기 자동차의 폭발적인 증가로 인한 배터리 재활용 문제를 언급하고 이로 인한 환경오염 문제를 나열하고 있으므로, 빈칸에는 ①의 "This has an environmental cost (이것은 환경상의 대가가 따른다)"가 들어갈 말로 가장 적절하다.

오답풀이
② 더 많은 조치가 금지되었다
③ 그 원인을 파악했다
④ 이것은 파리 기후 협약을 비준한다
⑤ 이것은 현 에너지 정책을 지지한다

어휘
- International Energy Agency(IEA) : 국제 에너지 기구
- Paris climate agreement : 파리 기후 협약
- give off : 발산하다, 방출하다
- toxic : 유독성의
- ingredient : 재료, 성분, 구성 요소
- finite : 한정된, 유한한
- extraction : 뽑아냄, 추출
- depletion : (자원의) 고갈, 소모
- prohibit : 금지하다, 못하게 하다
- take steps : 조치를 취하다
- identify : 확인하다, 알아보다
- ratify : 비준하다, 인준하다

해석

전 세계의 전기 자동차 수는 작년에 2백만 대를 넘어섰으며 만일 국가들이 파리 기후 협약의 목표치를 충족시킨다면, 국제 에너지 기구는 2030년까지 전 세계적으로 1억 4천만 대의 차량이 될 것으로 추산한다. 이러한 전기 자동차 호황은 지금부터 2030년 사이에 재활용이 필요한 소모된 리튬이온 전지

1100만 톤이 남게 될 수 있다. 그러나 EU에서는 겨우 5%의 리튬이온 전지들만이 재활용된다. 이것은 환경상의 대가가 따른다. 전지들이 만약 손상될 경우 유독 가스를 방출하는 위험을 수반할 뿐만 아니라, 리튬과 코발트와 같은 핵심 성분들은 유한하고 추출은 수질 오염과 다른 환경적 결과들 사이에서 자원의 고갈을 야기할 수 있다.

23 ③ 전자는 거대한 대양의 한 방울의 물처럼 그리고 밤중에 몰아치는 바람 속의 돌풍처럼 그 위치를 알아낼 수 없는 자기장의 일부라고 했으므로, 빈칸에는 ③의 "they have no identity of their own (그것들은 자신만의 독자성을 갖지 못한다)"가 들어갈 말로 가장 적절하다.

오답풀이

① 그것들은 우주의 중심에 매개체를 제공한다
② 그것들은 양자기장에서 파급 효과를 생성한다
④ 그것들은 완벽한 전위(電位)를 하지 못한다
⑤ 그것들은 기폭제로서 여러 반응을 제공한다

어휘

- electromagnetic field : 전자기장
- electron : 전자
- identical : 동일한, 똑같은
- quantum field : 양자기장
- macroscopic : 육안으로 보이는, 거시적인
- gust : 세찬 바람, 돌풍
- localize : …의 위치를 알아내다
- mingle : 섞다, 어울리다
- entity : 실재, 존재, 독립체
- vector : 벡터, 매개체, 진로
- ripple effect : 파급 효과
- identity : 정체, 독자성
- potential : (물리) 전위(電位), 자위(磁位)
- catalyst : 촉매, 기폭제

해석

전자기장은 어디에나 있으며 우주에 존재하는 모든 단일 전자는 그곳에 속할 뿐만 아니라 언제 어디서든 다른 전자와 정확히 동일하다. 그것들 중 두 개를 교환해보라. 그러면 우주는 알아차리지 못할 것이다. 그런 이유로, 그것들이 표출하는 양자기장 때문에, 전자는 육안으로 보이는 물체를 묘사하는 것처럼 묘사될 수 없다. 그것들은 그 자기장에 속해 있다. 그것들은 거대한 대양의 한 방울의 물처럼, 혹은 밤중에 몰아치는 돌풍처럼, 그 위치를 알아낼 수 없는 한 방울 혹은 하나의 돌풍 같은 자기장의 일부이다. 하나가 보이지 않는 한, 방울들과 돌풍들은 바람이나 대양 그 자체와도 같다. 그것들 자신보다 훨씬 더 거대한 실체에 섞인 채, 그것들은 자신만의 독자성을 갖지 못한다.

24 ② 생산비 개념은 전체 경제에 대한 이해에서 그다지 유용하지 않은 요소인데, 비경제학자들은 생산비에 대한 지나친 의존으로 생산비를 한정된 분석이 아니라 하나의 목표로 여기게 된다. 그러므로 빈칸에는 ②의 'an end rather than a tool with limited analytic capability (한정된 분석적 능력을 가진 도구라기보다는 하나의 목표)'가 들어갈 말로 가장 적절하다.

오답풀이

① 농업 투자 결정에 쓸모 있는 자원
③ 장기간의 시장 성장에 가장 미약한 지수 중 하나
④ 연관 산업의 합동 평가에 관한 시험
⑤ 시장 지산에 관한 모호한 측정

어휘

- appropriate : 적절한, 적합한
- comparison : 비교, 비유
- reliance : 의존, 의지
- inherent : 내재하는, 타고난, 본질적인
- devote to : …에 전념하다[쏟다]
- relate well to : ~을 잘 이해하다
- length-of-run : 실행 기간
- obvious : 분명한, 명확한
- instrumental : 쓸모 있는, 도움이 되는
- analytic : 분석적인
- indices : 지수(index의 복수)
- inter-industry : 연관 산업
- collaboration : 공동 작업[연구], 협력
- assessment : 평가, 사정
- obscure : 모호한, 막연한
- asset : 자산, 재산

해석

생산비 개념은 마치 피자를 만드는 비용이 피자 산업을 이해하는데 그다지 유용하지 않은 것처럼, 농업경제학을 이해하는데 그다지 유용하지 않다. 농업에 있어서 공동 생산의 본질을 고려해 볼 때, 더 적절한 비유는 피자의 생산 비용과 외식산업의 구조적 이해와의 관계이다. 뒤 이은 분석의 내재적 취약성 때문에 생산비에 대한 지나친 의존은 위험한데, 다른 곳에서 더 잘 사용될 수 있는 생산비에 몰입하는 자원들, 그리고 생산비의 강조가 원인이 될 수 있는 문제들의 제한된 집중이 그것이다. 표면적으로 볼 때, 생산비는 경제학적 분석에서 유용하고 기본적인 요소처럼 보인다. 더욱이 공급함수, 투입 수요함수, 실행 기간과 다른 중요한 사안들은 덜 명확한 개념인 반면에, 비경제학자들은 생산비의 개념을 잘 이해한다. 그 결과 생

산비는 종종 한정된 분석적 능력을 가진 도구라기보다는 하나의 목표로 간주된다.

25 ① 윗글에서 먹을 수 있는 유아식이 모유 밖에 없는 수렵채집인들의 양육 기간은 그렇지 않은 사람들보다 더 길었다고 설명하고 있다. 그러므로 ①의 'relationship between the age of weaning and available food (젖을 떼는 나이와 먹을 수 있는 음식 사이의 관계)'가 윗글의 주제로 가장 적절하다.

【 오답풀이 】
② 수렵채집 사회에서 일찍 젖을 떼야 할 필요성
③ 아이들의 건강에 있어 젖떼기의 역할 논쟁
④ 아이들이 일찍 젖을 떼기 위한 농사 독려
⑤ 농부와 수렵채집인 사이의 인구학적 비교

【 어휘 】
• proportion : 부분, 비율, 몫
• infant : 유아, 아기, 젖먹이
• nurse : 양육하다, 기르다
• wean : 젖을 떼다, 이유를 시작하다
• hunter–gather : 수렵채집인
• baby formula : 유아용 유동식, 분유
• replacement : 교체품, 대체물
• nourish : 영양분을 공급하다, 키우다
• chew : 씹다, 깨물다, 물어뜯다
• controversy : 논란, 논쟁
• demographic : 인구학의
• contrast : 대조, 비교

【 해석 】
미국에서 어머니에 의해 조금이라도 양육된 유아의 비율과, 그렇게 양육된 유아가 젖을 때는 연령은 20세기 대부분 감소했다. 예를 들어, 1970년대까지 미국 아이들 중 5%만이 6개월의 나이에 양육을 받았다. 그와 달리, 농부들과 접촉하지 않고 경작된 식품을 이용하지 못한 수렵채집인들 사이에서, 유아는 6개월 이상 양육을 받는다. 왜냐하면 그들이 먹을 수 있는 적합한 유아식은 모유뿐이기 때문이다. 그 유아들은 젖소의 우유, 아기용 분유, 부드러운 음식 대체품에 접근할 수 없다. 7개월 이상의 수렵채집인 집단에서 젖을 떼는 평균 연령은 약 3살이며, 이는 아이들이 충분히 딱딱한 음식을 씹어 마침내 영양공급을 스스로 할 수 있는 연령이다.

26 ④ 채무 불이행으로 인한 피해액이 채권시장의 0.1%에 불과하고, 중국 정부가 어려움에 빠진 큰 회사를 지원할거라고 설명하고 있으므로, ④의 'the unwarranted concern about China's bond market (중국의 채권시장에 대한 불필요한 걱정)'이 윗글의 주제로 가장 적절하다.

【 오답풀이 】
① 중국 경제의 복병
② 중국의 사회기반시설에 대한 위험한 투자
③ 중국 정부 개입의 비판 필요성
⑤ 중국 누적 부채의 암울한 미래

【 어휘 】
• bond market : 채권 시장
• default : 채무 불이행
• second quarter : 2분기
• cost of credit : 대손비용
• shoot up : 급증하다, 급등하다
• state–owned company : 국영 기업
• infrastructure : 사회기반시설
• sacrosanct : 신성불가침의, 아주 신성한
• backlog : 잔무, 재고
• casualty amount : 피해액
• rescue : 구조하다, 구출하다
• recent past : 가까운 과거
• a hidden pitfall : 숨어있는 함정, 복병
• intervention : 개입, 간섭
• unwarranted : 불필요한, 부적절한
• doomed : 불운한, 어두운, 암울한

【 해석 】
중국의 채권시장이 이렇게 폭풍우가 몰아치는 봄을 맞이한 적은 없었다. 이미 2분기에 채무 불이행 기록을 달성했다. 기업에 대한 대손비용은 급증했다. 심지어 사회기반시설에 투자하는 신성불가침의 국영 기업들조차 위험해 보인다. 무엇이 잘못되었을까? 질문에 대한 답은 전혀 없다. 채무 불이행은 중국을 위한 발전이며, 이는 누적 부채의 잔고를 정리할 필요가 있다. 올해 피해액은 채권시장의 0.1%에 불과하다. 하지만 투자자들이 정부가 어려움에 빠진 큰 회사를 지원할거라고 예상할 때, 그것은 여전히 가까운 과거에 대한 향상이다.

27 ② (A) 타고난 재능 중 부족한 점은 노력을 통해 보완할 수 있는데, 명작을 읽고 사고하는 것이 그 작품을 창작한 많은 기술을 이해할 수 있는 것처럼 노력을 통해 재능을 습득할 수 있다. 그러므로 'create(창조하다, 만들다)'가 빈칸에 들어갈 말로 적절하다.

(B) 우리가 위대하고 특별한 재능이라고 부르는 것은 보통 질적인 것이라기보다는 속도의 우월성을 의미하지만, 과학자의 경우 생산 속도가 아니라 품질로 그 결과물을 판단한다. 그러므로 'speed(속도)'가 빈칸에 들어갈 말로 적절하다.

(B) 반감

⑤ (A) 불일치

(B) 열정

어휘

- expertise : 전문 지식[기술]
- prestige : 위신, 명성, 선망
- autonomy : 자치권, 자주성, 자율성
- dignity : 존엄, 위엄, 품위
- incompatible : 양립할 수 없는, 공존할 수 없는
- purge A of B : A에게서 B를 제거하다
- party hack : 정당의 일꾼, 정치인
- librarian : 도서관 사서
- censor : 검열관, 감시관
- ideologue : 이론가, 공상[몽상]가
- bureaucracy : 관료제, 관료주의, 관료정치
- impediment : 장애, 방해, 걸림돌
- federal : 연합의, 동맹의
- bluntly : 직설적으로, 노골적으로
- resistance : 저항, 반대
- antipathy : 반감, 증오
- congruence : 일치, 조합, 합동
- affinity : 친밀감, 친화력
- incompatibility : 양립할 수 없음, 불일치, 상반성
- aspiration : 열망, 포부

해석

직업은 전문 지식, 명성, 자율성, 품위 및 정규 학습, 정치와 종종 양립할 수 없는 가치를 구현한다. 스스로 정치와 단절하기 위한 공공 직업의 역사적 투쟁, 예를 들어 도시 관리자 대 정치인들, 도서관 사서 대 무지한 검열관, 환경 과학자 대 정치적 몽상가, 모두는 이러한 (A) 저항을 반영한다. 전문가들 또한 관료주의를 좋아하지 않는데, 그들은 관료주의를 종종 자신의 전문 분야를 자유롭게 행사하는 데 장애로 여긴다. 연방 정부에서 근무하는 과학자 및 기술자와 같은 특수한 전문가들은 연방 행정관보다 업무에 대한 만족도가 훨씬 낮다. 직설적으로 말해서, 공직을 선택하는 전문가는 종종 공직의 두 가지 주요 특징인 정치와 관료주의에 대한 (B) 반감을 극복해야 한다.

29 ② 호기심은 다루기 힘든 것이라고 제시문에서 설명한 후 글 (B)에서 그것의 특성을 열거하여 서술하고 있다. 이어 글 (A)에서 역사적인 인물들을 들어 이를 요약한 후 글 (C)에서 진보, 혁신, 창의력을 믿는 사회에서의 호기심에 대한 대처 방식을 보여주고 있다. 그러므로 (B) - (A) - (C)의 순으로 글이 배열되는 것이 적절하다.

어휘

- deficiency : 부족, 결핍
- innate : 타고난, 선천적인
- compensate for : 보상하다, 보충하다, 보완하다
- persistent : 끈질긴, 집요한, 지속[반복]되는
- concentration : 집중, 전념
- substitute : 대리자, 대용품, 대체품
- provided that : 만약 ~하다면, ~을 전제로
- plasticity : 가소성, 신축성
- assimilate : 완전히 이해하다, 동화하다
- expeditious : 신속한, 급속한, 빠른 속도의
- qualitative : 질적인
- undertaking : 일, 사업, 업적
- suppress : 진압하다, 억제하다

해석

타고난 능력 중 부족한 점은 지속적인 노력과 집중을 통해 보완될 수 있다. 노력은 재능을 대신하는 것이거나, 더 나아가 노력이 재능을 (A) 만든다고 누군가 말할 수도 있다. 자신의 능력을 향상시키기로 확고히 결심한 사람은 그렇게 할 것이며, 이는 신경 세포의 신축성이 크게 감소하는 시기에, 교육이 너무 늦게 시작되지 않는다는 것을 전제로 한다. 명작을 읽고 사고하는 것이 그 작품을 창작한 많은 기술을 이해시킨다는 것을 잊지 마라. 물론 저자의 통찰력, 지도 원칙, 심지어 스타일까지 결론을 넘어 확장시키는 것을 전제로 한다. 우리가 위대하고 특별한 재능이라고 부르는 것은 보통 질적인 것이라기보다는 속도의 우월성을 의미한다. 그러나 과학적 업적에서 예술가처럼 과학자들은 생산 (B) 속도가 아니라 그들이 생산한 것의 품질에 의해 판단되기 때문에 느린 것이 빠른 것만큼이나 유용한 것으로 판명된다.

28 ① (A) 직업은 정치와 종종 양립할 수 없는 가치를 구현하는데, 스스로 정치와 단절하기 위한 공공 직업들 모두 이러한 투쟁을 해왔다. 그러므로 빈칸에는 'resistance(저항)'가 들어갈 말로 적절하다.

(B) 전문가들 또한 관료주의를 좋아하지 않는데, 공직을 선택하는 전문가는 정치와 관료주의에 대한 좋지 않은 감정을 극복해야 한다. 그러므로 빈칸에는 'antipathy(반감)'가 들어갈 말로 적절하다.

오답풀이

② (A) 일치

(B) 친밀

③ (A) 저항

(B) 친밀

④ (A) 일치

어휘

- distraction : 주의산만, 혼란
- corrosive : 좀먹는, 갉아 먹는
- unruly : 다루기 힘든, 제멋대로의
- deviant : 벗어난, 일탈적인
- be liable to : ∼할 것 같다
- attest : 증명하다, 증언하다, 입증하다
- provisional : 임시의, 일시적인, 잠정적인
- laceration : 괴롭힘, 상처
- disdain : 무시하다, 멸시하다, 경시하다
- diversion : 전환, 바꾸기
- excursion : 여행, 유람
- impulsive : 충동적인, 충격적인
- constitute : 구성하다, 여겨지다
- probe : 조사하다, 살피다, 탐색[탐구]하다
- stamp on : ∼을 짓밟다, 각인시키다

해석

대부분의 서양 역사에서, 호기심은 기껏해야 주의 산만이며, 최악의 경우 영혼과 사회를 좀먹는 독약이다. 이것에는 이유가 있다. 호기심은 다루기가 힘들기 때문이다.

(B) 그것은 규칙을 싫어하며, 적어도 모든 규칙은 임시적이라고 생각하여 아직 아무도 물어볼 생각을 하지 못한 현명한 질문에 상처를 낸다. 그것은 승인된 경로를 무시하고, 전환, 계획되지 않은 여행, 충동적인 좌회전을 선호한다.

(A) 요컨대, 호기심은 일탈적이다. 그것을 추구하는 것은 갈릴레오에서 찰스다윈과 스티브 잡스에 이르기까지 모든 이들이 입증했던 것처럼, 어느 시점에서 권위와 충돌하게 한다. 무엇보다 질서를 중시하는 사회에서는 호기심을 억누르려고 애쓸 것이다.

(C) 그러나 진보, 혁신, 창의력을 믿는 사회는 사람들의 탐구심이 사회의 가장 중요한 자산을 구성함을 인정하면서, 그것을 육성할 것이다. 계몽주의 시대까지 유럽 사회는 그들의 미래가 호기심에 있다는 것을 알고 그것을 짓밟기 보다는 탐구하는 질문을 독려했다.

30 ⑤ 제시문에서 드론을 비행하는 것은 법적으로 숙련된 기사가 하도록 되어 있다고 설명한 후 글 (C)에서 법적 안정성 고지에 대해 서술하고 있다. 또한 글 (B)에서는 글 (C)에서 언급한 '무인상자'에 대한 용어를 설명하고 있으며, 마지막으로 글 (A)에서 드론의 역할에 대해 설명하고 있다. 그러므로 (C) – (B) – (A)의 순으로 글이 배열되는 것이 적절하다.

어휘

- maintenance : 지속, 유지 보수
- autonomously : 자체적으로, 독자적으로
- remotely : 원격으로
- operative : 직공, 정보원, 첩보원
- aspire : 열망하다, 염원하다
- associated : 관련된, 연합의[지지의]
- a base station : 기지국
- implication : 함축, 암시, 내포된 뜻
- be up to : ∼에 달려 있다, ∼가 할[결정할] 일이다
- hence : 이런 이유로, 이로부터

해석

대부분의 기존 드론은 숙련된 기사가 비행을 조정해야 한다. 사실, 법도 이것을 종종 요구한다. 또한 드론은 기술적인 지원과 유지 보수가 필요하다.

(C) 그리고 드론을 조종하는 사람들은 하는 일에 대한 법적 안전성 고지를 이해하도록 권고 받는다. 이런 까닭에 '무인상자'에 매력이 있다.

(B) 이것은 관련 걱정 없이 드론의 장점을 판매하기를 열망하는 몇몇 회사의 제공품에 적용되는 용어이다. 문제의 상자는 드론을 보관하고, 그것을 재충전하며, 드론이 수집한 데이터를 고객에게 전송하는 기지국이다.

(A) 드론은 미리 프로그램 된 일정에 따라 독자적으로 비행할 수 있으며, 방문하도록 명령을 받은 지점까지 자동으로 그것의 경로를 찾거나, 지구 어느 곳에서나 통제 센터에서 시스템을 공급하는 회사 직원에 의해 원격으로 조종될 수 있다.

31 ③ 윗글은 생존을 위해 피를 서로 빌려주는 흡혈박쥐의 습성에 대해 설명하고 있다. 그러므로 진화와 관련된 설명을 한 ③의 내용은 글 전체의 흐름과 연관성이 떨어진다.

어휘

- loan : 대출, 대부, 대여
- lender : 빌려주는 사람, 대출자
- vampire bat : 흡혈박쥐
- congregate : 모으다
- prey : 먹이, 사냥감, 희생자[피해자]
- incision : 절개, 벤 자리, 벤 상처
- suck : 빨다, 흡입하다
- victim : 피해자, 희생자, 제물
- cope with : …에 대처[대응]하다, …에 대항하다
- uncertainty : 불확실성, 반신반의

- alleviate : 완화하다, 가볍게 하다
- regurgitate : 토하다, 게우다
- debtor : 채무자, 빚쟁이
- reciprocate : 화답하다, 응답하다
- favour : 호의, 친절

해석

많은 동물들은 효과적으로 협력하고, 몇몇 동물들은 심지어 빌려주기도 한다. 자연에서 가장 유명한 대출자는 흡혈박쥐이다. 이 박쥐들은 동굴 내부에 수천 마리가 모여 매일 밤 먹이를 찾아 날아다닌다. 잠자는 새나 부주의한 포유류를 발견하면, 그것의 피부에 작은 상처를 내고 피를 빨아먹는다. ① 하지만 모든 흡혈박쥐가 매일 밤 먹이를 구하는 것은 아니다. ② 불확실한 삶에 대처하기 위해, 흡혈귀들은 피를 서로에게 빌려준다. ③ (그러나 흡혈귀들은 진화적 압박을 완화하고자 대출을 하지 않는다.) ④ 먹이를 구하는 데 실패한 흡혈귀는 둥지로 돌아와 좀 더 운이 좋은 친구가 훔친 피를 게워내도록 부탁할 것이다. ⑤ 흡혈귀들은 피를 빌려준 녀석을 아주 잘 기억하여, 그래서 나중에 그 친구가 배가 고파 둥지로 돌아오면, 그 호의를 빚진 녀석에게 다가갈 것이다.

32 ④ 윗글은 철의 녹과 물의 관계를 예로 들어 풀의 색깔과 녹색의 관계에 대한 인식의 전환에 대해 설명하고 있다. 즉, 녹슨 것이 실제로 물 자체의 속성이 아니라 물이 철과 반응한 속성임을 볼 때, 녹색은 풀에서 방출한 빛이 뇌의 신경세포와 반응할 때 생기는 경험이라고 서술하고 있다. 이것은 인간의 인식이므로 주어진 문장은 ④에 들어가는 것이 가장 적절하다.

어휘

- A is no more B than C is D : A가 B가 아닌 것은 C가 D가 아닌 것과 같다
- property : 속성, 특성
- rustish : 녹이 슨
- perception : 지각, 자각, 인식
- a bar of : (금, 철, 비누 등) 한 덩이의, 한 개의
- inconvenient : 불편한, 곤란한
- perspective : 관점, 시각
- bounce off : 튀어나오다, 방출하다
- neuron : 뉴런, 신경 세포
- rust : 녹

해석

당신이 풀을 녹색으로 볼 때, 녹슨 것이 물의 속성이 아니듯 녹색은 풀의 속성이 아니다.

당신이 한 조각의 철이라고 상상해보라. 그래서 물 한 방울이 다가올 때, 당신은 평소처럼 아무것도 하지 않고 앉아 있다. 당신은 그 물에 대해 어떻게 인식할 것인가? 물론 한 덩이의 철은 뇌가 없고, 전혀 인식하지 못할 것이다. 하지만 그 불편한 사실을 무시하고, 한 조각의 철이 물을 감지할 수 있다면 어떤 기분이 들지 상상해보자. 한 조각의 철의 관점에서 볼 때, 물은 우선 녹이 슬게 하는 것이다. (①) 이제 인간의 관점으로 돌아가라. (②) 녹슨 것이 실제로 물 자체의 속성이 아니라 물이 철과 반응하는 속성임을 안다. (③) 인간의 인식도 마찬가지이다. (④) 녹색은 풀에서 방출한 빛이 뇌의 신경세포와 반응할 때 생기는 경험이다. (⑤) 녹이 철 조각에 들어 있는 것처럼 녹색은 우리 내부에 있다.

33 ① 필자가 브뤼셀을 향해 기차를 타고 가던 중에 주머니에 숨긴 반지를 독일 세관원들에게 들킬까봐 불안감이 극에 달했으나, 무사히 지나치자 조용한 안도의 한숨이 입에서 흘러나왔다. 그러므로 필자의 심경은 불안하고 초조한(nervous) 마음에서 안도의(relieved) 마음으로 바뀌었다.

오답풀이

② 기쁜 → 낙담한
③ 무관심한 → 격분한
④ 짜증 난 → 무서운
⑤ 놀란 → 실망한

어휘

- distressing : 괴로움을 주는, 고통스러운
- customs officials : 세관원
- forewarn : 미리 경고하다, 미리 주의를 주다
- initial : 이름의 첫 글자
- anxiety : 근심, 걱정, 염려
- unbearable : 참을 수 없는, 견딜 수 없는
- undisturbed : 방해받지 않은, 평온한
- faint : 희미한, 약한
- sigh : 한숨, 탄식
- discouraged : 낙담한, 실망한
- outraged : 화가 난, 격분한
- irritated : 짜증 난, 귀찮은

해석

나는 1939년 4월 기차 편으로 브뤼셀을 향해 떠났다. 내가 겨우 아홉 살 때, 부모님을 두고 떠난 것은 몹시 괴로웠다. 독일과 벨기에 사이의 국경에 다다랐을 때, 기차는 잠시 멈추었고 독일 세관원들이 탑승했다. 그들은 내가 가진 보석과 다른 귀중품들을 보여 달라고 요구했다. 나는 함께 여행 중인 젊은 여성으로부터 이러한 요청에 대해 미리 경고를 받았다. 그래서 나는 내 이니셜이 적힌 작은 금반지를 주머니에 숨겨두었는

데, 그것은 일곱 번째 생일 선물로 받은 것이었다. 그들이 기차에 탑승했을 때, 나치 장교들이 모습을 드러내자 불안감은 거의 극에 달했고, 그들이 반지를 발견할까봐 나는 두려웠다. 다행히도 그들은 내게 거의 관심을 기울이지 않았고, 내가 방해받지 않은 채로 가게 해주었다. 그들의 발소리가 점차 희미해짐에 따라, 조용한 한숨이 입에서 흘러나왔다.

[34~35]

어휘

• extract : 추출하다, 뽑다
• mental model : 심성 모형
• mastery : 숙달, 통달, 지배
• representation : 묘사, 표현
• instant : 순간, 찰나
• decipher : 판독하다, 해독하다
• subtle : 민감한, 예민한, 미묘한
• seam : 솔기, 이음매, 접합선
• winnow : 골라내다, 추려내다
• extraneous : 관련 없는
• perceptual : 지각의, 인지의
• distraction : 주의산만, 혼란
• variation : 변화, 변형
• stay on top of : ~을 잘[완히] 알다, 최신 정보를 알다
• cull out : 골라내다, 발췌하다, 제외하다
• identifying : 감별, 확인, 식별
• split-second : 순식간의, 눈 깜짝할 사이의
• go wild : 미쳐 날뛰다, 미친 듯이 열중하다
• baseball 101 : 야구의 기초[기본]
• anatomy : 해부, 분석
• endowment : 기부, 기금
• de facto : 사실상의, 실질적인

해석

새로운 자료로부터 핵심 아이디어를 추출하여 심성 모형을 조직하고 기존 지식에 이 모형을 연결하는 법을 배우는 사람은 복잡한 숙달 과정을 배우는 데 있어 유리함을 보여준다. 심성 모형은 어떤 외부 현실의 정신적 표현이다. 투구를 기다리는 야구 타자를 생각해 보라. 그는 그것이 커브볼인지, 체인지업인지, 아니면 다른 볼인지를 해독하는데 찰나도 걸리지 않는다. 어떻게 그럴 수 있는가? 투수가 예비동작을 하는 방식, 던지는 방식, 공의 솔기 회전 등 몇 가지 미묘한 신호가 도움이 된다. 훌륭한 타자는 아무 관련 없는 지각의 산만함을 골라내고, 투구에서의 이러한 변화만을 보며, 연습을 통해 각 종류의 투구에 대한 다른 단서들을 기반으로 뚜렷한 심성 모형을

형성한다. 그는 볼의 구질을 잘 알기 위해서, 타격 자세, 스트라이크 존 및 스윙에 관해 그가 알고 있는 것과 이 모형을 연결한다. 이것들은 선수 위치에 따라 심성 모형과 연결한다. 즉, 1위와 2위를 차지한 사람을 주자로 두었다면, 아마도 그는 주자를 전진시키기 위해 희생 플레이를 할 것이다. 그는 각 종류의 투구를 식별하고 응답하는 가장 중요한 요소를 제외한 모든 요소를 골라내고, 그 학습으로부터 심성 모형을 구축하고, 이 복잡한 게임의 다른 필수 요소에 대한 숙달 과정에 그러한 모형을 연결했기 때문에, 전문 선수는 매번 플레이트에 올라갈 때마다 직면한 거대하고 가변적인 정보를 이해할 수 없는 경험이 부족한 선수보다 득점을 올릴 확률이 더 높다.

34 ① 야구의 타자는 투수가 던지는 볼의 구질이 커브볼인지, 체인지업인지, 아니면 다른 볼인지를 순간적으로 파악하여 기존의 지식과 연결한다. 이렇게 함으로써 훌륭한 타자는 불필요한 요소를 골라내고 투구에서의 변화에만 집중하여 심성 모형을 구축한다. 그러므로 윗글의 제목으로는 ①의 'Split-Second Decisions Made Easy (순간의 결정이 일을 쉽게 만든다)'가 가장 적절하다.

오답풀이

② 야구 선수가 미친 듯이 열중할 때
③ 야구의 기본: 오른손 타자를 선택하라
④ 야구 투수에 대한 분석
⑤ 타자가 볼을 얼마나 멀리 칠 수 있는가?

35 ③ 야구의 타자가 투수가 던지는 볼의 구질을 파악하기 위해 타격 자세, 스트라이크 존, 스윙 등 기존에 알고 있던 지식을 동원하는 것처럼, 새로운 자료로부터 핵심 아이디어를 추출하여 심성 모형을 조직하고 기존 지식에 이 모형을 연결하는 법을 배우는 사람들은 복잡한 숙달 과정을 배우는 데 있어 유리함을 보여준다. 그러므로 ③의 'prior knowledge (기존 지식)'이 빈칸에 들어갈 말로 가장 적절하다.

오답풀이

① 향후의 사건 경로
② 운동선수의 기부
④ 실질적인 원칙
⑤ 통제된 동기부여

[36~37]

어휘

• vernacular : 사투리, 방언, 자국어
• take exception to : ~에 반대하다, ~에 이의를 제기하다

• relentlessly : 가차 없이, 용서 없이, 끊임없이

• wage : 벌이다, 계속하다

• in full swing : 한창 진행 중인, 무르익은

• reiterate : 반복하다, 되풀이하다

• contentment : 만족, 자족

• encapsulate : 요약하다, 압축하다

• spectacularly : 구경거리로, 극적으로

• dialect : 방언, 사투리

• extinction : 멸종, 소멸

• diversity : 다양성, 포괄성

• for one's sake : ∼을 위해

• prestige : 위신, 명성, 품위

해석

사실 세계의 영어권 지역의 대부분이 그렇듯이, 내가 자란 서부 뉴욕 주에서는 'doesn't'의 형태가 모국어에는 (a) 거의 존재하지 않는다. 내가 어디 출신인지에 대해 거의 모든 사람이 'It don't matter' 그리고 'He don't need that'이라고 말한다.

물론, 고등학교 영어 선생님인 Breck 부인은 이러한 어법을 강하게 반대했으며, 이에 대한 자신만의 작은 전쟁을 끊임없이 (b) 벌였다. 나는 그녀의 캠페인이 한창 진행 중인 어느 날 수업 시간에 앉아 있던 것이 잘 기억난다. 그날 나의 반 친구 노먼이 700번째로 "그는 그걸 몰라요(don't)"처럼 말하는 것을 듣고 그녀는 지적하기로 결심했다. "그는 그걸 몰라(doesn't)란다, 노먼" 노먼은 "네, 그게 맞네요."라고 대답했다. Breck 부인은 얼굴에 흥분한 표정을 지으며 "he don't."의 "dont'가 아니야, 노먼." "그는 그걸 몰라(DOESN'T)라고 말해"라고 반복해서 말했다. "하지만… 하지만…" 노먼의 얼굴에 (c) 만족스러운 모습이 나타났다. "하지만 그것은 올바르게 들리지 않아요(don't)!"

이 작은 에피소드는 우리가 표준 영어라고 부르는 특정 형태의 영어와 우리가 통틀어 비표준 영어라고 칭하는 모든 다양한 다른 영어 사이의 (d) 대조를 아주 깔끔하게 요약한다. 대다수의 영어 사용자는 표준 영어와는 거의 항상 상당히 다르고, 때때로 극적으로 다른 (e) 현지 자국어 형태의 영어를 배우고 말하면서 자란다.

36 ④ 윗글은 부정문에서 3인칭 단수 현재일 때 대동사 'doesn't'를 사용해야 하는데, 'don't'를 사용하는 문제를 두고 표준영어와 비표준영어의 사용에 대한 에피소드를 전하고 있다. 그러므로 ④의 "Standard vs. Non-standard English: Don't It Matter? (표준영어 대 비표준영어: 'Don't'가 문제인가요?)"가 윗글의 제목으로 가장 적절하다.

오답풀이

① 좋았던 옛 시절: 나의 영어 선생님의 모습

② 다양성을 위해 방언의 소멸을 막아라

③ 올바른 소리: 정책 입안자를 위한 딜레마

⑤ 자국어 대 정통 영어 : 그 전쟁의 결말

37 ③ 반 친구 Norman이 선생님의 지적에 틀린 말 같다고 수긍하지 못하는 표정을 짓고 있으므로, (c)의 'contentment(만족)'은 'discontent(불만족)'으로 고쳐 써야 옳다.

[38∼39]

어휘

• induce : 설득하다, 유도[유발]하다

• soothing : 달래는, 위로하는, 진정하는

• despondency : 낙담, 의기소침, 허탈감

• duration : 지속, 지속 기간

• questionnaire : 설문지, 질문지

• dismiss : 물러가게 하다, 해산시키다

• experimenter : 실험자

• volunteer : 자원봉사자, 지원자

• adverse : 부정적인, 불리한

• instill : 스며들게 하다, 서서히 주입시키다

• assistance : 도움, 원조

• contradict : 부정[부인]하다, 반박하다

해석

음악이 좋은 기분을 유발함으로써 협력과 도움을 증대시킬 수 있다는 사실이 실험으로 입증되었다. Rona Fried와 Leonard Berkowitz는 Wisconsin 대학에서 학생들과 함께 연구에 착수했다. 그들은 4개 그룹으로 나누고 그들 중 3그룹에 다양한 음악 작품을 연주하여 각기 다른 분위기를 유도했다. 멘델스존의 'Songs Without Words'에서 두 곡이 한 그룹에 차분한 분위기를 심어주기 위해 선택되었다. 듀크 엘링턴의 'One O'clock Jump'는 다른 그룹에 신나는 기분이 들도록 연주되었다. 존 콜트레인의 'Meditations'은 세 번째 그룹에서 슬픔과 낙담의 부정적인 감정을 주입하는 데 사용되었다. 네 번째 통제 그룹은 음반이 연주되는 7분 내내 침묵 속에 앉아 있었다. 학생들은 음악을 듣기 전과 후의 기분에 관한 설문지를 작성해야 했으며, 이것은 음악으로 인해 그들의 감정에 상당한 차이를 보였음을 확인했다.

그들이 해산되기 직전에 실험자들은 지원자들에게 15분에서 2시간 정도의 시간을 필요로 하는 전혀 무관한 다른 실험을 도와달라고 부탁했다. 그들은 도울 준비가 되었는지를 명시하기 위해 양식을 작성하도록 요구받았고, 만약 그렇다면 총 시간의 양도 함께 작성하도록 요구받았다. 물론 이것은 실험자가 그들이 들었던 음악 유형에 따라 도움을 주려는 의지가 네 그

룹에서 변경되었는지를 알아내려는 도움에 관한 실험이었다. 이것은 사실로 판명되었다. 두 번째 실험을 도울 의지와 도와줄 준비가 되어 있는 시간의 길이를 측정했을 때, 멘델스존의 음악 작품을 들은 사람들이 가장 도움이 되는 것으로 나타났다. 두 가지 측정 모두에서 부정적인 감정을 주는 콜트레인의 음악을 들은 학생들이 도움이 될 의지가 가장 적었다.

38 ④ 윗글은 실험을 통해 차분한 음악인 멘델스존의 음악을 들은 사람들이 부정적인 감정을 주는 음악인 콜트레인의 음악 유형보다 남을 도우려는 의지가 강했음을 밝히고 있다. 그러므로 ④의 "Types of music influenced people's willingness to help. (음악의 유형은 돕고자 하는 사람들의 의지에 영향을 미쳤다.)"가 윗글의 요지로 가장 적절하다.

오답풀이

① 협력 그룹은 멘델스존의 음악을 선호하는 경향이 있다.
② 고전 음악은 사람들에게 차분한 분위기를 심어준다.
③ 협력과 도움은 음악적인 재능에 의해 영향을 받는다.
⑤ 신나는 기분은 사람들에게 더 많은 도움을 준다.

39 ② 음악 유형에 따라 도움을 주려는 의지가 변경되었는지를 파악하기 위한 두 번째 실험 결과 그것이 사실로 나타났으므로, 빈칸에는 ②의 'proved to be the case (사실로 판명되었다)'가 들어갈 말로 가장 적절하다.

오답풀이

① 사전에 검증되었다
③ 많은 이들에게 도전 받았다
④ 앞선 결과들을 반박했다
⑤ 더 많은 지지를 필요로 했다

[40~42]

어휘

• insignificant : 대수롭지 않은, 사소한, 하찮은
• dominate : 지배하다, 군림하다
• elusive : 찾기 힘든, 파악하기 어려운
• ingredient : 재료, 성분, 구성 요소
• correlation : 연관성, 상관관계
• aptitude : 소질, 적성
• flunk : 낙제하다, 떨어지다
• push up the daisy : 죽다, 사라지다
• in no time : 곧, 즉시
• acute : 뾰족한, 날카로운, 예리한
• stone-tipped : 돌로 깎은, 돌로 다듬은

• spear : 창
• mammoth : 맘모스, 매머드
• dexterous : 솜씨 좋은, 능수능란한
• crucial : 중대한, 결정적인
• nimble-fingered : 손이 빠른
• chimp : 침팬지
• crafty : 술수가 뛰어난, 교활한
• deft : 날랜, 재빠른, 능숙한
• eternally : 영원히, 영구히
• prey : 먹이, 사냥감, 희생자[피해자]
• split : 쪼개다, 찢다
• flint stone : 부싯돌
• uranium : 우라늄
• dexterity : 재주, 솜씨

해석

지능에 관한 대부분의 정의에 따르면, 100만 년 전 인류는 세계의 1등 도구 제작자였을 뿐만 아니라 이미 지능이 가장 높은 동물이었지만, 주변 생태계에 거의 영향을 미치지 못하는 하찮은 생명체였다. 그들은 지능과 도구 제작 이외의 몇 가지 핵심 특징이 분명히 부족했다.

어쩌면 인류는 결국 지구를 지배하게 되었는데, 그것은 어떤 찾기 힘든 세 번째 핵심 요소 때문이 아니라, 단지 훨씬 높은 지능과 훨씬 우수한 도구 제작 능력의 진화 때문일까? 그렇게 보이지는 않는다. 왜냐하면 역사적 기록을 조사할 때, 우리는 인간 개인의 지능 및 도구 제작 능력과 전체로서의 우리 종의 능력 사이의 직접적인 연관성을 보지 않기 때문이다. 2만 년 전, 평균적인 사피엔스는 오늘날의 평균적인 사피엔스보다 더 높은 지능과 더 나은 도구 제작 능력을 지녔다. 현대의 학교와 고용주들은 때때로 우리의 소질을 시험할 수 있지만, 아무리 불량하더라도 복지국가는 항상 기본적인 필수품은 보장한다. 석기시대에 자연의 선택은 매일 매 순간마다 당신을 시험했고, 만일 무수히 많은 시험들 중 하나에서 떨어지면, 즉시 데이지 꽃을 들어 올렸을 것이다. 그러나 석기시대 조상들의 뛰어난 도구 제작 능력과 날카로운 정신 및 훨씬 더 예리한 감각에도 불구하고, 2만 년 전 인류는 오늘날보다 훨씬 약했다.

이렇게 2만 년 이상 인류가 돌로 다듬은 창으로 매머드를 사냥하는 것에서 우주선으로 태양계를 탐험한 것은 더 솜씨 좋은 손이나 더 큰 두뇌의 진화 덕분이 아니다. 대신 우리가 세상을 정복하는 데 중요한 요소는 많은 인간들을 서로 연결하는 능력이었다. 오늘날 인간은 지구를 완전히 지배하고 있는데, 이는 인간 개개인이 침팬지나 늑대보다 훨씬 영리하고 손이 더 빠르기 때문이 아니라, 지구상에서 호모 사피엔스가 유연하게 수없이 협력을 할 수 있는 유일한 종이기 때문이다. 지능과 도구 제작 역시 분명히 매우 중요했다. 그러나 만약 인간

이 수없이 유연하게 협력하는 법을 배우지 못했다면, 우리의 뛰어난 두뇌와 솜씨 좋은 손은 여전히 우라늄 원자가 아닌 부싯돌을 쪼개고 있을 것이다.

40 ② 밑줄 친 (A) 'were pushing up the daisies in no time(즉시 데이지 꽃을 들어 올렸을 것이다.)'의 의미는 죽음을 의미한다. 즉, 석기시대에 인간은 자연의 선택에 따라 매 순간 시험을 치렀고, 그 시험에 떨어지면 도태되어 살아남지 못했을 거라는 의미이므로 ②의 'would die soon(곧 죽었을 것이다)'을 뜻한다.

오답풀이

① 영원히 번영을 이루었다

③ 도구를 천천히 갈았다

④ 꽃들을 빨리 꺾었다

⑤ 결국 농부가 되었다

41 ⑤ 본문에서 인간이 침팬지나 늑대보다 훨씬 영리하고 손이 빠르기 때문이 아니라, 유연하게 무수히 협력을 할 수 있는 유일한 종이기 때문에 지구를 지배하는 것이 가능했다고 설명하고 있다. 그러므로 빈칸에는 인간이 협력하는 법을 배우지 못했다면 있을 수 있는 일을 추론해야 하므로, ⑤의 'splitting flint stones rather than uranium atoms (우라늄 원자가 아닌 부싯돌을 쪼개다)'가 빈칸에 들어갈 말로 가장 적절하다.

오답풀이

① 훨씬 더 예리한 감각을 키우다

② 생태계에 중요한 영향을 미치다

③ 야생에서 수많은 난관을 극복하다

④ 무리지어 쉽게 먹이를 구하다

42 ① 호모 사피엔스의 세계 (D) 지배에서 핵심적인 역할을 한 것은 더 높은 지능이나 더 나은 (C) 솜씨가 아니라, 대대적인 유연한 협동 능력이다.

오답풀이

② (C) 솜씨

  (D) 탐험

③ (C) 진화

  (D) 경작

④ (C) 복지

  (D) 지배

⑤ (C) 복지

  (D) 탐험

[43~45]

어휘

• in perspective : 전체적 시야로, 긴 안목에서

• innocent : 순수한, 결백한

• be weighed down : 억제받다, 짓눌리다

• a day-care center : 아동, 노인 탁아시설

• relate : …에 대하여 이야기하다[들려주다]

• annual : 매년의, 연례의

• multicultural : 다문화의

• diversity : 다양성, 포괄성

• enthusiasm : 열광, 열정

• in the midst of : ~중에[가운데에]

• commotion : 소란, 소동, 야단법석

• get out of : 회피하다, 비리다

• charge down : 몸으로 막다

• in advance : 미리, 사전에

해석

(A) 어린아이 같은 세계관이 자주 어른의 삶을 긴 안목에서 볼 수 있게 한다는 사실을 알고 있는가? 아이들의 순수한 관점은 어른들이 그들의 문제에 짓눌리지 않는데 도움이 될 수 있다. 탁아소의 관리자인 Nancy Craver는 아이의 관점이 어떻게 큰 문제를 작은 문제로 바꾸는 데 (a) 그녀에게 도움이 되었는지 다음 이야기를 통해 들려준다. 그 일은 탁아소의 연례행사인 다문화 저녁 식사에서 있었던 일인데, 부모와 자녀 및 직원이 그들의 다양성과 모두가 일을 잘 할 수 있는 능력을 축하하기 위해 마련되었다.

(C) 작년의 축하 행사는 Nancy가 마치 새로운 관리자로 고용된 것처럼, 그녀에게는 크나 큰 도전이었다. 올해 (d) 그녀는 안심하고 저녁 식사에 참여할 수 있도록 일찌감치 계획을 세웠다. 처음에는 단지 사소한 일들이 잘못되었다. 그후 누군가가 저녁 식사 후 프레젠테이션에 사용될 예정이었던 슬라이드 프로젝트를 떨어뜨렸다. 바로 그 저녁 식사가 끝났을 때, 아이들을 다른 곳으로 데려가 놀게 하려고 고용된 여자가 나타나지 않았다. 아이들은 쉬지 않고 뛰어다니기 시작했다.

(D) 이렇게 소동이 벌어지는 가운데, 어떤 노인이 주차장에서 자기 차를 막고 있는 차를 이동시켜 달라고 누군가에게 말했다. 긴장과 체온이 상승한 Nancy는 그가 주차장에서 빠져나가도록 도우러 갔다. (e) 그녀가 막 건물로 돌아오는 순간, 어린아이 하나가 계단을 몸으로 막고 그녀에게 몸을 던졌다. 아이가 공중에 떠올랐을 때, Nancy의 마음속에 문득 떠오른 상상은 다친 아이, 충격을 받은 부모, 그리고 사람들이 "거봐. 그녀는 우리 아이들을 통제하거나 보호조차 할 수 없어!"라고 말하는 내용이 포함되어 있었다.

(B) (b) 그녀가 본능적으로 팔을 뻗었을 때, 그 어린아이를 잡았을 뿐만 아니라 웃음과 흥분 또한 붙잡았다. 즉시 그러한 첫 번째 끔찍한 상상들이 사라졌다. (c) 그녀를 흔들면서, Nancy는 아이의 열정으로 이것이 축하 행사라는 생각이 떠올랐다. 그녀의 웃음과 놀이는 상황을 바꾸지는 못했지만, 그러나 그 일은 Nancy의 관점을 바꾸었다. 그리고 저녁은 그녀와 주변 사람들을 위해 계속해서 더욱 잘 진행되었다.

43 ③ 글 (D)의 'commotion(소동)'이란 글 (C)의 슬라이드 프로젝트가 떨어지고, 아이들을 돌봐줄 사람이 나타나지 않고, 아이들이 쉬지 않고 뛰어다니기 시작하는 것을 말하므로 글 (C) 다음에 글 (D)가 와야 한다. 그리고 계단을 몸으로 막고 Nancy에게 몸을 던져 공중에 떠오른 아이를 글 (B)에서 Nancy가 본능적으로 팔을 뻗어 그 아이를 잡았으므로 글 (D) 다음에 글 (B)가 와야 한다. 그러므로 글의 배열순서는 (C) – (D) – (B) 순이다.

44 ③ (c)의 'her'는 Nancy가 붙잡은 어린 여자 아이를 가리키며, (a), (b), (d), (e)는 모두 Nancy를 지칭한다.

45 ③ 윗글은 탁아소의 관리자인 Nancy가 겪은 경험담을 서술한 글로, 그녀가 언제 관리자가 되었는지는 글에 나타나 있지 않다. 그러므로 ③의 "She became the director three years ago. (그녀는 3년 전에 관리자가 되었다.)"라는 설명은 윗글의 내용과 일치하지 않는다.

오답풀이
① 그녀는 탁아소의 책임을 맡고 있었다.
② 그녀는 공중에 떠 있는 아이를 붙잡았다.
④ 그녀는 올해의 저녁 식사를 미리 준비했다.
⑤ 그녀는 주차 문제를 도와주었다.

2018학년도 기출문제 정답 및 해설

제2교시 영어영역

01 ②	02 ①	03 ④	04 ①	05 ④	06 ②
07 ⑤	08 ⑤	09 ②	10 ④	11 ④	12 ②
13 ①	14 ④	15 ⑤	16 ⑤	17 ③	18 ③
19 ①	20 ⑤	21 ①	22 ⑤	23 ①	24 ④
25 ①	26 ③	27 ③	28 ②	29 ⑤	30 ②
31 ③	32 ②	33 ①	34 ④	35 ②	36 ⑤
37 ④	38 ③	39 ①	40 ⑤	41 ⑤	42 ①
43 ③	44 ③	45 ③			

01 ② 'vanguard'는 '선봉, 선두'의 의미로 'forefront(맨 앞, 선두)'와 그 의미가 가장 유사하다.

오답풀이
① 혼란, 소란
③ 보호, 보장
④ 반대, 항의
⑤ 준비, 대비

어휘
• deceive into : 속여서 ~하게 하다
• vanguard : 선봉, 선두
• turmoil : 혼란, 소란
• forefront : 맨 앞, 선두
• preparation : 준비, 대비

해석
그 시위에 참여한 학생들은 속아서 그들이 혁명의 선봉에 있다고 생각했다.

02 ① 'collude'는 '공모하다', '결탁하다'는 뜻으로 'collaborate(협력하다, 협업하다)'와 그 의미가 가장 유사하다.

오답풀이
② 제안하다, 제의하다
③ 가장하다, ~인 체하다
④ 의도하다, 작정하다
⑤ 개입하다, 끼어들다

어휘
• collude : 공모하다, 결탁하다
• minor : 미성년자
• collaborate : 협력하다, 협업하다
• intervene : 개입하다, 끼어들다

해석
정부는 제조사들이 미성년자들에게 제품을 판매하기 위해 결탁했다고 결론지었다.

03 ④ 'penchant'는 '기호, 애호'의 뜻으로 'inclination(성향, 경향)'과 그 의미가 가장 유사하다.

오답풀이
① 고정 관념, 집착
② 소질, 적성
③ 비난, 책망
⑤ 낭비, 사치

어휘
• penchant : 기호, 애호
• demise : 종말, 죽음, 사망
• obsession : 고정[강박] 관념, 집착
• aptitude : 소질, 적성
• reproach : 비난, 책망
• inclination : 의향, 성향, 경향
• extravagance : 낭비, 사치

해석
살면서 더 좋은 것만을 추구하는 그의 성향 때문에 가족의 재산을 탕진했다.

04 ① 'cabin'은 '오두막 집[좁은 곳]에 가두다'라는 뜻의 동사로, 'confine(가두다, 국한시키다)'와 그 의미가 가장 유사하다.

오답풀이
② 비난하다, 꾸짖다
③ 소개하다, 도입하다
④ 보호하다, 보장하다

⑤ 예시하다, 예증하다

어휘

- stern : 엄중한, 심각한
- cabin : 오두막 집[좁은 곳]에 가두다
- relevant : 관련 있는, 적절한
- confine : 넣다[가두다], 국한시키다
- rebuke : 비난하다, 꾸짖다
- safeguard : 보호하다, 보장하다
- exemplify : 예시하다, 예증하다

해석

롤스에게 가장 엄격한 비평가들은 종종 그를 "단지 미국인이나 기껏해야 영국계 미국인 독자에게만 관계된 것"으로 <u>국한시키려고</u> 노력했다.

05 ④ 'circumlocutory'는 '빙 둘러 말하는', '완곡한'의 뜻으로 'roundabout(우회적인, 둘러대는)'와 그 의미가 가장 유사하다.

오답풀이

① 명백한, 분명한
② 간결한, 간략한
③ 근거 없는, 사실 무근의
⑤ 달래는, 회유적인

어휘

- pending lawsuit : 계류[심리] 중인 소송
- circumlocutory : 빙 둘러 말하는, 완곡한
- pharmaceutical : 약학의, 제약의
- representative : 대표, 대리인
- unequivocal : 명백한, 분명한
- succinct : 간결한, 간략한
- unfounded : 근거 없는, 사실 무근의
- roundabout : 우회적인, 둘러대는
- conciliatory : 달래는, 회유적인

해석

심리 중인 소송에 관한 심문은 제약 회사 대표의 <u>우회적인</u> 답변에 부딪혔다.

06 ② ②의 'announce'는 해당 문장에서 '이름을 말하다[부르다], 호명하다'는 뜻의 타동사로 사용되었는데, 뒤에 목적어가 없으므로 'was announced'의 수동태 형태로 쓰여야 한다.

오답풀이

① 'where'는 앞의 'the Gold Room'을 선행사로 하는 관계부사의 계속적 용법으로 사용되었으며, 'in which'로 바꿔 쓸

수 있다.

③ 'that'은 앞의 'walk'를 선행사로 하는 주격 관계대명사로 사용되었다.
④ 'making'은 현재분사의 형태로 능동형 분사구문을 이끈다.
⑤ 'the other'는 둘 중의 다른 하나로, 해당 문장의 'the other end'는 '반대편'을 의미한다.

어휘

- legislative staff : 국회 보좌진, 의회 보좌진
- incoming : 새로 당선[선출]된
- House and Senate members : 상원과 하원 의원들
- sixteen hundred hours : 16:00, 오후 4시
- on the dot : 제 시간에, 정각에
- announce : 이름을 말하다[부르다], 호명하다
- podium : 연단, 강단
- vigorous : 활발한, 격렬한, 활기찬
- jaunty : 의기양양한, 쾌활한
- determined : 단호한, 완강한, 단단히 결심한
- on a schedule : 일정대로, 예정대로
- detour : 둘러 가는 길, 우회로
- refreshment : 다과, 가벼운 식사, 음료

해석

나는 백악관의 의회 보좌진에게 직접 인사를 받고 Gold Room으로 안내되었다. 그곳에는 새로 당선된 대부분의 상하원 의원들이 이미 모여 있었다. 오후 4시 정각에, Bush 대통령이 호명되어 연단으로 걸어 나왔다. 활기차고 건강한 모습이었으며, 의기양양하면서도 단호한 걸음걸이로 그는 예정대로 진행할 것이며 우회 수단은 최소한도로 유지하고 싶다고 말했다. 십여 분에 걸쳐 그는 몇 마디 농담과 함께 국가의 단합을 요구하며 그 방에서 연설을 했고, 이에 앞서 다과와 함께 대통령 내외와 사진을 찍도록 백악관 반대편으로 우리를 초대했다.

07 ⑤ ⑤의 문장은 'without(~이 없었더라면)'과 함께 과거사실의 반대를 나타내는 가정법 과거완료 구문이므로, 'would have + p.p' 형식에 따라 'be'를 'have been'으로 고쳐 써야 옳다.

오답풀이

① 'offers'는 관계대명사 'which'의 선행사인 'deck'이 단수이므로, 3인칭 단수 현재 시제에 맞게 수와 시제가 일치되었다.
② 'where'는 관계부사로 뒤에 완전한 문장이 왔으므로 옳게 사용되었다.
③ 'as'는 'name A as B(A를 B로 임명[지명]하다)' 구문으로 옳게 사용되었다.
④ 'has been'은 현재완료 시제로 해당 문장의 내용상 과거부터 지금까지 '동화 같은 한 시즌을 보냈다'는 의미이므로

정답 및 해설

옳게 사용되었다.

어휘

- the Fourth of July : (7월 4일의) 독립기념일
- firework : 폭죽, 불꽃놀이
- rooftop deck : 옥상
- a breathtaking view : 너무나 아름다운 전망
- landmark : 역사적인 건물[장소], 랜드마크
- toast : 건배하다, 축배를 들다
- improbable : 사실[진실] 같지 않은, 있을 것 같지 않은
- itinerant : 떠돌아다니는, 순회하는
- chronicle : 연대기
- candidate : 출마자, 후보자
- ERA earned run average : (투수의) 방어율
- accomplishment : 업적, 공적, 성적
- overshadow : 그늘지게 하다, 가리다, 무색하게 하다
- toil : 수고, 노력, 고역
- odyssey : 오디세이, 대서사시, 긴 모험

해석

샌프란시스코 자이언츠의 투수인 Ryan Vogelsong과 그의 부인인 Nicloe은 아파트 옥상에서 독립기념일에 하는 불꽃놀이를 구경했는데, 그곳은 Baby Bridge, Alcatraz Island와 Coit Tower와 같은 랜드마크 건물들의 너무나 아름다운 전망을 제공했다. 또한 그곳에서 그들은 적어도 지금까지는 없을 법한 떠돌이 경력의 정점인, National League의 올스타 팀에 선정된 것을 샴페인으로 축하하고 있었다. 샌프란시스코 자이언츠의 크로니클은 최근에 그를 사이영 상 후보로 지명했다. 34살의 Vogelsong에게는 일종의 동화 같은 한 시즌이었는데, 그는 월드시리즈 결승전에서 8대 1의 스코어와 방어율 2.23을 기록했다. 비록 올해의 성적이 Vogelsong이 야구에서 이전에 이루었던 모든 성적을 무색하게 했지만, 그 성적은 샌프란시스코, 피츠버그, 일본, 베네수엘라에 더해 10개의 마이너리그 도시들에서 체류한 극적인 노력이 없었다면 불가능했을 것이다.

08 ⑤ ⑤ 'have me'는 앞의 'the impressions'와 'other people' 사이에 목적격 관계대명사 'that' 또는 'which'가 생략되어 있으므로, 'have' 다음에 목적어가 생략되어 있어야 한다. 즉, 'have the impressions of me'의 구조가 되어야 하므로 'have me'는 'have of me'로 고쳐 써야 옳다.

오답풀이

① 'have evolved'는 앞의 'yet'과 함께 현재완료 시제로 사용되었으며, 뒤의 'the mind'를 목적어로 취한다.

② 'wins'는 앞의 'a quality'가 주어이므로 3인칭 단수 현재의 형태가 알맞다.

③ 'that'은 명사절을 이끄는 접속사로 뒤에 완전한 문장이 왔

으므로 맞게 사용되었다.

④ 'what'은 뒤의 'think'의 목적어에 해당하는 의문사로 맞게 사용되었다.

어휘

- comparison : 비교, 비유
- crucial : 중대한, 결정적인
- sustained : 지속된, 한결같은
- evolve : 발달하다, 진화하다
- inequality : 불평등, 불균등
- get to the point : 핵심에 이르다, 요점을 언급하다
- be derived from : ~로부터 파생되다[나오다]

해석

루소에게 중요한 것은 자연 상태와 비교되지 않는 것이다. 지속적인 유내 관계 없이 사는 피조물은 아직까지 지성이 사람과 대등할 정도로 진화될 수 없을 거라고 주장하며 루소는 두 가지 결론을 이끌어 냈다. 첫째, 더 센 체력, 더 좋은 목소리, 더 나은 지능과 같은 타고난 불평등은 우리가 우연히 소유한 특질이 타인의 시각에서 존경, 칭찬, 가격, 가치를 얻을 때만 중요하다. 두 번째 결론은 혼자 있는 자연인만이 순수하다는 것이다. 항상 남이 우리를 어떻게 생각할지 신경 써야 되는 사회 속에서, 우리는 다른 사람으로부터 명예와 존경을 얻으려고 무언가를 행한다. 나의 자의식은 타인이 나에 대해 가지고 있는 인상에서 비롯된다는 점이 바로 핵심이다.

09 ② (A) 정서적인 삶과 육체적인 삶이 다르지 않다는 의미가 되어야 하는데, 앞에 부정어 'no'가 사용되었으므로 'distinct(별개의)'가 들어갈 말로 가장 적절하다.

(B) 다음에 오는 문장이 역접의 의미인 'On the contrary(반대로)'로 시작되고 그 내용이 긍정적이므로, (B)에는 부정적인 어휘인 'despair(절망)'가 들어갈 말로 가장 적절하다.

(C) 만족시킬 수 없는 욕망과 죽음에 대한 두려움은 이성의 실행을 통해 극복될 수 있다고 했으므로, (C)에는 극복되기 위한 객체인 'obstacles(장애물)'이 들어갈 말로 가장 적절하다.

어휘

- realization : 깨달음, 자각, 인식
- void : 빈 공간, 진공
- providential : 신의, 섭리의, 신의 뜻에 의한
- distinct : 뚜렷한, 분명한, 별개의
- indistinct : 분명하지 않은, 희미한
- mortal : 죽을 운명의, 영원히 살 수 없는
- grasp : 완전히 이해하다, 파악하다
- unappeasable : 만족시킬 수 없는, 채울 수 없는

- path : 길, 방향
- obstacle : 장애(물), 방해(물)
- surmount : 극복하다, 이겨내다
- reason : 이성, 사고, 판단

해석

우주가 원자와 빈 공간으로 구성되어 있으며 다른 무엇도 없다는 깨달음. 세상이 우리를 위해 창조주의 섭리로 만들어진 것이 아니라는 깨달음. 우리가 우주의 중심이 아니라는 깨달음. 정서적인 삶이 육체적인 삶과 (A) 별개의 것이 아니며 다른 모든 피조물의 육체적인 삶과 다를 바 없다는 깨달음. 우리의 정신은 우리의 몸과 마찬가지로 물질적인 것이며 영원히 살 수 없다는 깨달음 – 이 모든 것들이 (B) 절망의 원인은 아니다. 반대로 상황을 있는 그대로 이해하는 것은 행복의 가능성으로 가는 중요한 단계이다. 인간이 행복한 삶을 사는 것은 가능하지만, 그것은 그들이 우주의 중심이라고 생각하기 때문이 아니다. 만족시킬 수 없는 욕망과 죽음에 대한 두려움은 인간의 행복에 대한 주요한 (C) 장애물이지만, 그것들은 이성의 실행을 통해 극복될 수 있다.

10 ④ (A) 윗글은 음악이 환자의 치료에 어떤 효과를 보이는지 의학적 특성을 설명한 글이므로, (A)에는 'medicinal(의학적)'이 들어갈 말로 가장 적절하다.

(B) 제2차 세계대전 동안 일부 군대 병원과 공장에서 이용했던 음악 치료는 이제 환자들에게 보편적으로 이용되고 있으므로, (B)에는 'widely(널리)'가 들어갈 말로 가장 적절하다.

(C) 지금은 음악 치료가 보편화 되어 음악이 긴장완화에 효과가 있다는 내용이 되어야 하므로, (C)에는 'conducive(도움이 되는)'가 들어갈 말로 가장 적절하다.

어휘

- therapy : 치료, 요법
- explicit : 분명한, 명쾌한
- physiological : 생리학의, 생리적인
- cognitive : 인지의, 인식의
- the wounded : 부상자들
- aesthetic : 심미적, 미학적
- medicinal : 약효가 있는, 치유력이 있는
- property : 속성, 특성
- disability : 상해, 장애
- surgery : 수술, 진료
- notably : 특히, 현저히, 뚜렷이
- dental : 치아의, 치과의
- burns : 화상
- coronary : 관상동맥의

- attest : 증명[입증]하다
- legato passage : 부드러운 음조
- predictable : 예측[예견]할 수 있는
- detrimental : 해로운, 불리한
- conducive to : ~에 도움이 되는, ~에 좋은
- relaxation : 휴식, 긴장완화

해석

명백한 의료 행위인 음악 치료는 20세기, 특히 제1차 세계대전 동안 서양에서 처음 발전했는데, 그때의 의사와 간호사들은 음악이 부상자들의 심리적, 생리적, 인지적, 감정적 상태에 미치는 효과를 목격했다. 음악의 (A) 의학적 특성에 관한 최초의 주요 연구는 1948년에 발표되었는데, 제2차 세계대전 동안 일부 군대 병원과 공장에서 계속 이용한 음악 치료 반응이었다. 음악 치료는 이제 정신적 혹은 신체적 장애나 병이 있는 사람들에게 (B) 널리 이용된다. 음악 치료의 가장 중요한 기능들 가운데 하나는, 특히 치과나 화상 그리고 관상동맥 치료에서 수술을 준비하거나, 수술을 하거나, 수술에서 회복중인 환자들의 긴장을 풀어주는 것이다. 지금은 느리고 안정된 템포, 부드러운 음조, 온화한 리듬, 예측 가능한 변화와 단순하게 지속되는 멜로디의 음악이 긴장완화에 (C) 도움이 된다는 사실이 충분히 입증되었다.

11 ④ 현실에서 영적인 것은 복잡하고 다차원적인 현상이므로, 영적인 것에 대한 이해를 넓히기 위해서는 폭넓을 해석을 포함해야 한다. 그러므로 ④의 'excludes'는 '포함하다'는 의미를 지닌 'includes'로 수정해야 옳다.

어휘

- spiritual dimension : 영적 차원
- controversial : 논쟁상의, 논란이 많은
- a holistic approach : 전체론적 접근법
- be identified as : ~로써 판명되다[밝혀지다]
- vital : 필수적인, 중요한, 중대한
- spirituality : 영적인 것, 영혼, 정령
- resilience : 회복력, 탄력, 탄성
- single entity : 단일 실체
- multi-dimensional : 다차원의
- exclude : 배제하다, 제외하다
- appropriate : 적절한, 적당한, 타당한
- anti-discriminatory : 반차별적인

해석

비록 영적 차원은 노동의 육체적, 정신적 그리고 감정적 측면에 큰 영향을 미치는 ① 중요한 요소로 점차 밝혀지고 있지만, 그것은 복잡하고 논란의 소지가 많은 영역이며, 종종 전체론적 접근법 내에서는 간과된다. 유감스럽게도 영적인 것과

회복력을 탐구하는 대다수 연구들이 영적인 것을 ② 쉽게 측
정되고 통제되는 단일 실체로 취급하고 있다. 현실에서 영적
인 것은 복잡하며, ③ 다차원적인 현상이다. 따라서 영적인 것
의 폭넓은 해석을 ④ 배제하는 연구는 우리의 이해를 넓히는
데 중요하다. 영적인 것을 단지 종교적 정의만을 사용하여 해
석하는 사람들이 있다. 영적인 것에 대한 이러한 ⑤ 협의의 종
교적 해석은, 종종 미국이나 영국에서 보는 기도교적인 해석
으로, 반차별적 관행을 과시하는 정부 기관들에게는 적합하지
않다.

12 ② 모든 사람이 모든 주제에 대해 똑같은 사고방식과 신념을
가지게 된다면 의사소통의 필요성이 없게 되므로, 그 대화
는 생동감이 있는 것이 아니라 지루해질 것이다. 그러므로
②의 'lively(생동감 있는)'는 'bored(지루한)' 또는 'dull(따분
한)'로 수정해야 옳다.

어휘

- pervasive : 넘치는, 충만한, 만연한
- attitude : 태도[자세], 사고방식
- in almost every respect : 거의 모든 면에서
- dissimilar : 같지 않은, 다른
- common ground : 공통점, 공통적인 입장
- at hand : 직접적인, 당면한
- prevail : 만연[팽배]하다, 퍼지다

해석

한 이론에 따르면, 특정 범위 내에서 의사소통자들이 더 동일
할수록, 그들의 의사소통은 더욱 효율적이 된다. 한 가지 제한
적인 조건은 사람들 사이의 동일성이 너무 ① 만연해서 그들
이 모든 주제에 똑같은 사고방식과 신념을 가지게 된다면, 의
사소통의 필요성이 없어진다. 예를 들면, 누구나 다 영화부터
정치까지 모든 주제가 일치하는 파티에서, 대화는 아마 ② 생
동감이 있을 것이다. 반면에, 거의 모든 면에서 ③ 일치하지
않는 사람들은 공통점, 즉 경험을 공유하고 생각을 교환하는
근거가 부족할 것이다. 이 이론에 따르면, 이상적인 상황은 사
람들이 많은 동일성을 가지고 있지만 당면한 주제에 대해서는
그들의 사고방식으로 소통하고 어쩌면 서로의 사고방식에 영
향을 미칠 수 있을 만큼 일치하지 않는 상황이다. 그러나 동일
성은 분명 ④ 만연하게 된다. 결국, 사고방식이 영향을 미치는
목표는 당신의 사고방식과 점점 ⑤ 닮아가도록 다른 사람의
사고방식을 변화시키는 것이다.

13 ① 윗글에서 현대전의 양상이 점차 예측할 수 없는 방법으로
전술들이 결합되면서 그 성격이 변질되고 있다고 하였으
므로, 전쟁과 평화의 구별 그리고 누가 호전적이고 비호전
적인지 구별하는 것은 명확한 것이 아니라 불명확하다. 그

러므로 ①의 'clarified(명확한)'는 'vague(불명확한)' 또는
'ambiguous(애매모호한)'로 수정해야 옳다.

어휘

- distinction : 구별, 차별, 차이
- combatant : 전투적인, 호전적인
- noncombatant : 비전투적인, 비호전적인
- principally : 주로
- recruit : 뽑다, 모집하다
- hybrid : 잡종, 변종, 혼합
- be associated with : ~와 관련[연관]되다
- non-state actor : 비국가 활동 세력
- fuse : 융합되다, 결합되다
- unpredictable : 예측[예상]할 수 없는
- magnitude : 규모, 중요도
- appreciate : 진가를 알아보다, 인정하다

해석

4차 산업혁명은 갈등의 성격뿐만 아니라 갈등의 크기에도 영
향을 미칠 것이다. 전쟁과 평화의 구별 그리고 누가 호전적이
고 비호전적인지 구별하는 것은 불편하게도 ① 명확해지고 있
다. 마찬가지로 전쟁터는 점차 국지적인 동시에 세계화 되고
있다. ISIS와 같은 조직들은 중동의 한정된 지역에서 ② 주로
활동했지만 그들은 또한 대게 소셜 미디어를 통해 100개 이
상의 나라에서 투쟁자들을 모집하고 있고, 반면에 테러리스트
관련 공격은 지구상 어디에서든지 발생할 수 있다. 현대의 갈
등은 재래식 전술과 이전에 주로 비국가 무장 세력과 관련 있
던 요인들과 결합하면서, 점차 그 성격이 ③ 변질되고 있다.
그러나 점차 예측할 수 없는 방법으로 전술들이 ④ 결합되고
국가와 비국가 무장 세력이 서로 알게 되면서, 변화의 가능성
의 크기는 아직까지 널리 ⑤ 알려지지 않고 있다.

14 ④ 윗글에서 게르는 크기에 따라 다르지만, 하나의 게르가 한
시간에서 세 시간 내에 조립될 수 있다고 서술하고 있다.
그러므로 "It can be built in three hours or less. (게르는 세
시간 이내에 지을 수 있다.)"는 ④의 설명이 윗글의 내용과
일치한다.

오답풀이

① 대부분의 몽고인들은 게르를 'yurt'라고 부르기를 원한다.
② Ulaan Baatar라는 도시 지역에서만 게르를 볼 수 있다.
③ 게르는 목재와 벽돌로 지어진다.
⑤ 게르를 지금의 여행객에게는 권하지 않는다.

어휘

- ger : 게르(몽고인의 둥근 주거 천막)
- identifiable : 인식 가능한, 알아볼 수 있는

• offend : 불쾌감을 주다, 비위를 거스르다

• nationalistic : 국수주의적인, 민족적인

• sensibility : 감정, 감성, 감수성

• steppe : 스텝(나무가 없는 대초원) 지대

• hide : 가죽

• nomadic : 유목의, 방랑의

• flexible : 융통성 있는, 유연한

• assemble : 모으다, 조립하다

해석

몽골 전역에서 볼 수 있는 게르라고 부르는 크고 흰 천막은 아마 그 나라의 가장 대표적인 상징물이다. ('yurt'라는 단어는 러시아 사람에 의해 서양에 소개된 터키의 단어이다. 몽고인들의 민족적인 감성을 자극하고 싶지 않다면, 'ger'라는 단어를 사용해라.) Ulaan Baatar라는 교외지역에서 조차, 대부분의 몽골 사람들은 여전히 게르에 살고 있다. 그리고 그 이유를 이해하기란 어렵지 않다. 특히 대초원의 외부 지역에서 목재와 벽돌은 귀하고 비싸지만, 동물의 가죽은 싸고 쉽게 구할 수 있다. 유목민들은 분명 유연성 및 기동성이 있어야 했고 게르는 쉽게 옮길 수 있다. – 크기에 따라 다르지만, 하나의 게르가 한 시간에서 세 시간 내에 조립될 수 있다. 만약 기회가 생긴다면, 게르를 방문하거나 체류해 볼 초대를 놓치지 말아야 한다.

15 ⑤ 윗글에서 1967년에 사람들이 혐오하여 공원 관리국이 엘크의 사살을 멈추었다고 했으므로, "여론 때문에 늑대 사살이 중단되었다. (Public opinion halted the shooting of wolves.)"는 ⑤의 설명은 옳지 못하다.

오답풀이

① 야생동물은 1900년대에 과학적으로 관리되기 시작했다.

② 1872년에 정확한 동물 개체수는 알려지지 않았다.

③ 천적이 없어진 후에 엘크가 번성했다.

④ 총 4,619마리의 엘크가 1962년에 사살되었다.

어휘

• geyser basin : 간헐천 지대

• feeding behavior : 섭식 행동

• ranger : 공원 관리원[경비원]

• elk : 엘크(북 유럽이나 아시아에 사는 큰 사슴)

• bison : 들소

• federal : 연합의, 동맹의, 연방 정부의

• directive : 지시, 명령

• eliminate : 제거하다, 없애다

• overpopulate : 인구가 넘치다, 과밀화하다

• distaste : 불쾌감, 혐오감

• flourish : 번창하다, 번성하다

• predator : 포식자, 포식[육식] 동물

cf. natural predator : 천적

• halt : 멈추다, 중단하다

• public opinion : 여론

해석

옐로우스톤 국립공원은 간헐천 지대를 보호하기 위해 1872년에 설립되었다. 그러나 200만 에이커에 달하는 공원 때문에 정부는 야생 동물 관리를 시작했고, 불행히도 과학적인 야생 동물 관리는 반세기가 지나고 난 후에야 시작되었다. 그 공원이 설립될 당시에 그 지역 동물들의 개체수와 섭식 행동에 대한 세부 기록이 없었다. 초창기 관리원들은 소에게 먹이를 주는 것처럼 엘크나 들소에게 먹이를 주었고 늑대들을 사살하기 시작했다. 1926년까지, 연방 정부의 지시에 따라 마지막 늑대들이 사살되었다. 그 이후 엘크는 풀과 덤불 그리고 닿는 곳이라면 나무의 어느 부분이든 다 먹어 치우면서 공원에 넘쳐났다. 그래서 1934년에 관리원들은 엘크들도 사살하기 시작했고, 기록에 의하면 1962년에만 4,619마리의 엘크가 사살 당했다. 1967년에 사람들의 혐오로 공원 관리국은 사살을 멈추었다. 그러나 그 공원은 회복되지 않았다.

16 ⑤ 수십억 달러의 초현대적 장비인 로켓을 발사하기 위한 최적지가 바로 세계에서 가장 빈곤한 지역이라는 것은 직관에 반하는 모순이므로, 빈칸에 들어갈 말로는 ⑤의 'counterintuitive(반 직관적인, 직관에 어긋나는)'가 가장 적절하다.

오답풀이

① 장엄한, 위풍당당한

② 순식간의, 잠깐 동안의

③ 대재앙의, 파멸의

④ 보편적인, 일반적인

어휘

• launch : 출시, 진수, 발사

• unpopulated : 사람이 살지 않는, 무인의

• patch : 작은 땅, 지역

• preferable : 더 좋은, 나은, 선호하는

• get showered with : ~의 공세를 받다, 쏟아져 내리다, 퍼붓다

• wayward : 변덕스러운, 불규칙한, 불안정한

• flaming : 격렬한, 불타는

• equator : 적도

• axis : 축

• rocket booster : 로켓 추진체

• oomph : 정력, 활력, 박력

• futuristic : 초현대적인, 미래의

• rainforest : 열대우림

• shantytown : 판자촌, 빈민가

• majestic : 장엄한, 위풍당당한

• fleeting : 순식간의, 잠깐 동안의

• catastrophic : 대재앙의, 파멸의

• counterintuitive : 직관에 반대되는[어긋나는], 납득이 잘 안 되는, 감이 잘 오지 않는

해석

좋은 로켓 발사 장소는 몇 가지 중요한 특징들을 가지고 있다. 해안가 근처 사람이 거주하지 않는 지역이 좋은데, 아무도 어느 방향에서 날아올지 모르는 불타는 금속 파편을 뒤집어쓰지 않아도 되기 때문이다. 만일 그곳이 적도상이라면 또한 좋다. – 축으로 도는 모든 회전체처럼, 지구도 중간 부분이 가장 빨리 도는데, 그것이 로켓 추진체에 추가 화력을 제공한다. 다시 말하면, 가장 좋은 장소는 멀리 떨어진 열대지역이다. 그러한 장소가 또한 세계에서 가장 빈곤한 지역이라는 사실은 많은 로켓 발사 즉, 열대우림과 빈민가 위로 쏘아 올린 초현대적 장비에 들어간 수십억 달러의 돈에 반(反) 직관적인 느낌이 든다.

17 ③ 윗글은 분석가들조차 사실과 추론을 구별하지 못하거나 논리적인 증명을 거치지 않고 결론을 도출하는 등 잘못된 추론을 하고 있음을 설명하고 있다. 그러므로 빈칸에 들어갈 말로는 ③의 'Examples of the inability to reason well abound (추론을 잘못하는 사례들이 많다)'가 가장 적절하다.

오답풀이

① 용어의 혼동은 논리적인 결함을 더욱 가중시킨다.

② 논리적인 사고는 과학적인 연구를 선도한다.

④ 일반화는 엄격한 시험을 거친다.

⑤ 귀납적 논리가 학계에 만연하다

어휘

• inference : 추론, 추리, 추정

• assumption : 가정, 추정

• inductively : 귀납적으로

　cf. reason inductively : 귀납적으로 추론하다

• be subject to : ~의 대상이다, ~을 거치다[당하다]

• alien concept : 이상한[생소한] 개념

• infer : 추론하다, 뜻하나, 암시하다

• terminology : 술어, 전문 용어

• unfamiliarity : 잘 모름, 생소, 낯설음

• underlying : 근본적인, 근원적인

• confusion : 혼란, 혼동

• aggravate : 악화시키다, 가중시키다

• flawed : 결함[결점/흠]이 있는

• precursor : 선도자, 선구자

• inability : 무능, 불능

• rigorous : 철저한, 엄격한

• prevail : 퍼지다, 만연[팽배]하다

• academia : 학계

해석

추론을 잘못하는 사례들은 많다. 사실과 추론을 구별하지 못하는 분석가들을 발견하거나 추론이 사실이라는 가정 하에 일을 처리하는 분석가들을 발견하는 것은 특별한 일이 아니다. 분석가들이 비록 귀납적으로 도달한 일반화가 논리적인 증명을 거친 것이 아니라고 할지라도, 그의 결론이 증거로부터 '논리적으로' 도출된 것이라고 말하는 것을 듣는 것은 특별한 일이 아니다. 각기 다른 종류의 탐구는 각기 다른 종류의 '증명'을 거쳐야 한다는 사실은 많은 연구가들에게 생소한 개념이다. 그리고 '추론하다'와 '함축하다'라는 단어의 빈번한 오용은 용어에 관한 지식 부족뿐만 아니라 논리의 기본 개념에 익숙하지 않음을 보여준다.

18 ③ 윗글은 사실을 호도하기 위한 정부의 이중화법에 대한 사례들을 예시한 글로, 한 공무원이 월급 인상을 요구했을 때 '증액을 지지하는 것은 금전상 부적절하다'는 말은 '월급 인상이 없다'는 것을 의미하는 이중화법에 해당된다. 그러므로 빈칸에 들어갈 말로는 ③의 'no pay raise(임금 인상은 없음)'가 가장 적절하다.

오답풀이

① 해고 통지서

② 전체 청원 중단

④ 신규 일자리가 없음

⑤ 조기 퇴직

어휘

• doublespeak : 이중화법, 사실을 호도하기 위한 말, 모호한 말, 돌려 말하기

• the Bureau of Land Management : (내무부의) 토지 관리국 (BLM)

• a press release : 보도 자료, 언론 발표

• administrative procedure : 행정절차

• compliance : 준수, 승낙, 이행

• statutory : 법에 명시된, 법률상의

• rulemaking : 규칙제정, 입법

• federal : 연방제의, 연방 정부의

• lease : 임대차 계약

• qualification : 자격, 자질

• crack down : 엄중 단속, 강력 탄압

• the Department of Commerce : 상무부, 상무국

• fluctuational : 끊임없이 변동하는[오르내리는]

• predisposition : 성향, 경향

- juxtaposed with : 병치된, 나란히 놓인
- monetarily : 화폐로, 금전상으로
- injudicious : 지혜롭지 못한, 부적절한, 무분별한
- advocate : 지지하다, 옹호하다
- increment : 임금 인상, 증가, 증액
- pink slip : 해고 통지서
- petition : 진정, 탄원, 청원
- suspend : 유예[중단]
- early retirement : 조기 퇴직

[해석]

정부에 있는 사람들이 대중에게 이야기 하든 서로에게 이야기 하든, 이중화법이 정부에 넘쳐나고 있다. 토지 관리국은 1986년에 "법률 요건을 이행하려는 행정절차를 포함하기 위해, 내무부의 토지 관리국이 오늘 연방 정부의 석탄 임대차 계약 자격에 관한 규칙 제정을 발간했다."는 말로 시작하는 언론 발표를 했다. 이러한 이중화법은 간단히 토지 관리국이 석탄의 임대를 엄중 단속하겠다는 것을 의미한다. 월급 인상을 요구했던 상무부의 한 공무원은 "정부 기준과 병치되는 것으로 귀하의 직위상 생산 능력의 변동성 때문에, 증액을 지지하는 것은 금전상 부적절하다."라는 말을 들었다. 바꾸어 말하면, <u>임금 인상은 없다</u>는 것이다.

19 ① 윗글은 나이든 쥐에게 오스테오칼신이라는 호르몬을 투여했을 때 젊은 쥐들처럼 다시 근력이 회복되는 연구 결과를 설명한 글이다. 그러므로 빈칸에 들어갈 말로는 ①의 'Wind back the clock(시간을 되돌려라)'이 가장 적절하다.

[오답풀이]

② 제때의 바늘 한번이 아홉 바느질을 던다. → 호미로 막을 데를 가래로 막는다.
③ 세월은 사람을 기다리지 않는다.
④ 노인들을 공경하라.
⑤ 시간을 단축하라.

[어휘]

- rejuvenate : 다시 젊어보이게 하다, 활기를 되찾게 하다
- Osteocalcin : 오스테오칼신
- secrete : 분비하다
- boost : 북돋우다, 부양하다, 촉신시키다
- inject : 주사하다, 주입하다
- counterpart : 상대, 한 짝[쌍]
- stitch : 바늘, 바늘땀, 바늘코

[해석]

<u>시간을 되돌려라</u>. 우리는 나이든 쥐들의 근육을 회복시켜 주는 호르몬을 발견했다. 뼈에서 분비되는 호르몬인 오스테오칼

신이 연료를 태우고 에너지를 발생시키기 위한 근력을 촉진시킨다고 콜럼비아 대학의 연구진들이 발견했다. 연구팀이 나이든 쥐들에게 그 호르몬을 투여했을 때, 그 동물들은 쥐들의 나이에서 오랜 시간인 한 살이나 나이를 먹었음에도 불구하고, 젊은 쥐들이 달리는 만큼 멀리 달릴 수 있었다. 그 호르몬을 투여 받지 못한 늙은 쥐들은 반 밖에 달리지 못했다. 오스테오칼신 수치는 사람과 쥐들 둘 다 나이를 먹어감에 따라 감소하는데, 그 연구팀은 이제 그 호르몬이 사람의 경우에도 또한 근육의 기능을 향상시킬 수 있는지 실험을 계획하고 있다.

20 ⑤ 창의력과 혁신 또한 제도화된 과학과 학문의 영역에서 특정 성취 기준에 맞추어야 한다고 했으므로, 현대 세계의 과학도 또한 앞의 '자본주의 철창'처럼 감옥이 되어 가고 있다는 것이다. 그러므로 빈칸에는 ⑤의 'the prison house of the mind(지성의 감옥)'가 들어갈 말로 가장 적절하다.

[오답풀이]

① 지성의 길에서 빛나는 횃불
② 관료주의적 요구로부터 해방된
③ 어떤 공격에도 끄떡없는 난공불락의 요새
④ 당면한 도덕 문제에 취약한

[어휘]

- exigency : 긴급 사태, 급박
- domain : 영역, 분야, 범위
- institutionalized : 제도화된
- accommodate : 수용하다, 부응하다, 적합하다
- criteria : 표준, 기준
- discipline : 규율, 훈련
- torchlight : 불빛, 횃불
- emancipate : 해방시키다, 자유를 주다
- bureaucratic : 관료적인, 요식적인
- a fortress impregnable : 난공불락의 요새
- vulnerable : 취약한, 연약한

[해석]

인간의 욕구가 급박한 생산으로 희생되는 자본주의 철창처럼, 어떤 의미에 있어서 현대 세계의 과학은 또한 <u>지성의 감옥</u>이 되어 가고 있다. 즉, 제도화된 과학과 학구적인 학문의 영역에서, 창의력과 혁신은 다양한 전문적 훈련을 지배하는 특정 성취 기준에 적합해야만 한다.

21 ① '방귀쟁이' Joseph Pujol은 대포 같은 방귀 소리를 내거나 직장(直腸)으로 15피트의 거리까지 물줄기를 뿜어내는 등 마음대로 방귀를 뀌는 능력을 소유하고 있었다. 그러므로 빈칸에 들어갈 말로는 ①의 'at will(마음대로)'이 가장 적절하다.

정답 및 해설

② 말없이, 조용히

③ 간헐적으로, 간간히

④ 보람 없이, 헛되이

⑤ 무심코, 우연히

어휘

• fart : 방귀를 꾸다

• anus : 항문, 똥구멍

• fartiste : 방귀쟁이

• rumble : 우르르[우르릉]거리는 소리를 내다

• cannon–fire : 대포

• spectacularly : 구경거리로, 볼만하게

• rectally : 직장(直腸)으로

• punctuate : 긴간이 끼어들다

• intermittently : 간헐적으로, 쉬엄쉬엄, 간간이

• to no avail : 보람 없이, 헛되이

• inadvertently : 무심코, 우연히

해석

19세기 후반에서 20세기 초반 동안에, 프랑스 사람인 Joseph Pujol은 공기를 그의 항문으로 빨아들여 마음대로 방귀를 꾸는 능력으로 유명했다. 그는 자신을 프랑스어로 '방귀쟁이'를 의미하는 Le Pétomane라 칭하며, 무대 위에서 쇼를 펼쳤다. 격식을 갖춰 옷을 입고서, 그는 우르르 울리는 대포 같은 방귀 소리로 쇼를 시작하곤 했다. 다양한 프로그램들이 뒤를 이었고, 가장 볼만한 것은 1906년의 샌프란시스코 지진을 흉내낸 것이었다. 그는 직장(直腸)으로 거의 15피트의 거리까지 물줄기를 뿜어낼 수 있었고, 쇼를 마칠 때에는 다양한 동물 소리처럼 들리는 방귀소리를 간간히 내며 농장 노래를 불렀다.

22 ⑤ (A) 똑같은 과거의 일이라도 (A) 앞의 내용은 시간을 거슬러 기억력을 재구성해야 되지만, (A) 뒤의 내용은 '섬광 기억'이라고 해서 원래 사건에 대한 기억이 촬영된 것처럼 완벽히 남아 있다고 설명하고 있다. 그러므로 빈칸 (A)에는 역접의 접속 부사 'However(그러나)'가 들어가는 것이 알맞다.

(B) 섬광 기억에 대한 첫 연구 사례로 John F. 케네디 대통령의 암살 사건을 예로 들어 설명하고 있으므로, 빈칸 (B)에는 'For example(예를 들어)'이 들어갈 말로 알맞다.

어휘

• reconstruct : 재건하다, 재구성하다

• flashbulb memory : 섬광 기억

• charged : 열정적인, 격렬한, 흥분된

• vivid : 생생한, 선명한

• incident : 일, 사건

• assassination : 암살, 시해

해석

과거의 인생 경험 대부분이라면, 아마도 기억력을 재구성해야 한다는 것에 동의할 것이다. 예를 들어, 누군가가 3년 전에 생일을 어떻게 축하했었는지 물어본다면, 뒤로 시간을 거슬러 올라가 그 상황을 재구성하려 할 것이다. (A) 그러나 사람들의 기억력이 원래 사건에 완벽히 충실하게 남아 있다고 믿는 몇 가지 상황이 있다. 이러한 형태의 기억들을 섬광 기억이라고 부르는데, 사람들이 감정적으로 흥분된 사건을 경험했을 때 발생한다. 즉, 사람들의 기억들이 너무나 생생해서 그 기억들은 원래의 사건이 거의 촬영이 된 것처럼 보인다. 섬광 기억에 관한 첫 연구는 공적인 사건들에 대한 사람들의 회상에 초점을 맞추었다. (B) 예를 들어, 연구원들은 참가자들에게 John F. 케네디 대통령의 암살 사건에 대해 처음에 어떻게 알게 되었는지 물어보았다. 80명의 참가자들 가운데 한 사람을 제외하고 모든 사람들이 생생한 회상을 전했다.

23 ① (A) 학생들에게 매트와 쿠션뿐만 아니라 음식과 음료를 가져오게 함으로써 교실 분위기가 바뀐 것이므로, 빈칸 (A)에는 'altered(변경되었다)'가 들어갈 말로 가장 적절하다.

(B) 사회 문화적 대화에 활기를 주는 음식과 음료는 공동체의 유대 관계를 결속시키는 중요한 역할을 하므로 빈칸 (B)에는 'cement(결속시키다)'가 들어갈 말로 가장 적절하다.

오답풀이

	(A)	(B)
②	유지되다	용해되다
③	변경하다	약화되다
④	유지되다	굳어지다
⑤	수정하다	늦춰지다

어휘

• engagement : 관계, 참여, 유대

• pillow : 베개

• stuffed toy : 봉제 완구

• slumber party : 파자마 파티

• strategically : 전략상, 전략적으로

• draft : 원고, 초안

• vital : 활기 있는, 생생한

• sociocultural : 사회문화적인

• enhance : 높이다, 향상시키다, 강화하다

• atmosphere : 대기, 공기, 분위기

• communal bond : 공동체[유대] 관계

- alter : 바꾸다, 변경하다
- cement : 시멘트를 바르다, 접합하다, 결속시키다
- dissolve : 녹다, 용해되다
- solidify : 굳어지다, 응고하다

해석

학생들의 사회적 유대를 촉진시키기 위해, 나는 그들에게 매트와 쿠션뿐만 아니라 음식과 음료를 교실로 가져오라고 독려했다. 이러한 물품들 덕에, 교실 공간은 '사회적' 측면을 획득했기 때문에 형태와 기능이라는 면에서 (A) 변경되었다. 반사 운동을 하는 동안에, 나는 비록 학생들이 파자마 파티에 참석하고 있는 중이었지만, 어떻게 학생들이 매트와 쿠션뿐만 아니라 베개와 봉제 인형을 가지고 왔는지 관찰했다. 매트와 쿠션이 사용되지 않을 때, 학생들은 서로의 원고에 대해 토론하거나 평가하면서, 테이블 주변에 전략적으로 배치된 의자에 앉아 먹고 마셨다. 음식과 음료가 어떠한 사회 문화적 대화에서도 활기를 주므로, 음식과 음료는 사교적인 분위기를 강화시키는 데 도움을 주었고, 공동체 유대 관계를 (B) 결속시키고, 학생들의 동질감을 높였다.

24 ④ 윗글은 유럽의 주요 철광석 매장 지역 중의 하나인 독일의 Augsburg에서 광업과 갑옷 사업이 번창했던 이유를 설명하고 있다. 그러므로 ④의 'Germany, the Hub of Armor Technology(갑옷 기술의 중심지, 독일)'가 윗글의 제목으로 가장 적절하다.

오답풀이

① 무기와 갑옷과의 고별
② 갑옷 사업의 과거와 미래
③ 석기 대 철기 : 분명한 선택
⑤ 고품질 저가의 양날 검

어휘

- mining : 채굴, 광산
- armor : 갑옷, 철갑
- coincidence : 우연의 일치, 동시 발생
- deposit : 매장층, 광상
- iron ore : 철광석
- feudal state : 봉건 국가
- annoyance : 짜증, 성가심
- alternative : 대안, 선택 가능한 것
  cf. have no alternative : 선택의 여지가 없다, 대안이 없다
- sally : 돌격하다, 출격하다
- underwirte : 서명하다, 동의하다
- lavish : 풍성한, 엄청난, 막대한
- extensive : 아주 넓은[많은], 대규모의
- visor : 복면, 가면, (투구의) 면갑

- double-edged : 양날의, 서로 상반된

해석

광산과 갑옷 기술의 중심은 독일의 Augsburg였는데, 그것은 우연의 일치가 아니었다. Augsburg는 유럽의 주요 철광석 매장 지역 중의 하나로, 갑옷을 입은 기사들로 군사력을 강화시킨 봉건 국가들의 금속 수요 때문에 광업이 호황을 이루고 갑옷 사업도 또한 빠르게 번창하였다. 봉건 유럽 전체가 짜증을 낼 정도로, 독일인들은 손님들이 다른 대안이 없다는 것을 알고 있었으므로, 매우 높은 가격을 책정했다. 독일의 갑옷은 세계에서 최고였고, 만약 손님들이 그 가격이 맘에 들지 않는다면, 그 손님은 다음 전쟁에서 막대기와 돌을 들고 앞으로 돌격할 수밖에 없었다. 이렇듯 막대한 이익을 낸 독일의 갑옷 제조업자들은 광범위한 연구와 개발 노력을 할 수 있었다. 그것은 결과적으로 더 강력한 갑옷, 예를 들어 머리 전체를 덮으면서 움직이는 면갑이 있는 강철 투구를 만들어 냈다.

25 ① 윗글은 흥정을 시도한 사람들이 흥정을 하지 않은 사람들에 비해 상당한 비용을 절약했다고 설명하고 있다. 또한 윗글의 마지막 문장에서 값을 흥정하지 않는 사람들은 테이블 위에 돈을 버리고 있는 것과 마찬가지라고 하였으므로, ①의 'Can't Hurt to Ask(물어본다고 손해날 건 없어)'가 윗글의 제목으로 가장 적절하다.

오답풀이

② 흥정의 기초 입문
③ 가구 흥정 수월하게 하기
④ 쇼핑하기 : 보상받기
⑤ 흥정이 실제로 물가를 올리는가?

어휘

- haggle : 값을 깎다, 흥정을 하다
- bargain : 상당하다, 흥정하다
- chicken : 겁쟁이
- health-related charge : 의료비
- inflate : 부풀리다, 올리다

해석

흥정하기가 싫으세요? 당신 혼자만 그런 것은 아니다. 국가 통계 조사에 따르면 과거 3년 동안 모든 재화와 용역에 대해 단지 48%의 쇼핑객들만이 더 나은 거래를 하기 위해 흥정을 시도했고, 그 수치는 2007년의 61%에서 감소된 것이다. 그러나 겁쟁이라면, 당신이 흥정에서 진 것이다. 흥정을 한 사람들 가운데 89%는 적어도 한번은 보상을 받았다. 성공적인 가구 흥정가들은 평균 300$를 아꼈으며, 의료비에 의문을 제기한 사람들도 마찬가지였다. 휴대폰 요금에 흥정을 시도했던 사람들도 80$를 아꼈다. 분명히 말하자면, 값을 흥정하지 않는 사람

정답 및 해설

들은 테이블 위에 돈을 버리고 있는 것이다.

26 ③ 윗글에서는 어떤 세속적인 직업을 갖고 상거래를 하는 것이 헌신의 증거이기 때문에 개신교의 믿음이 자본주의 경제 사회를 이끌었다고 보고 있다. 그러므로 ③의 'influence of Protestantism on economic ideals(개신교가 경제 사상에 미친 영향)'이 윗글의 주제로 가장 적절하다.

오답풀이

① 사회적 평등을 위한 종교의 역할
② 개신교 믿음이 흥성한 이유
④ 경제 활동에서 도덕의 중요성
⑤ 개신교와 가톨릭의 차이점

어휘

• Catholicism : 가톨릭교, 천주교
• God-given : 하느님이 주신, 천부적인
• vocation : 직업, 천직
• priesthood : 사제직
• Protestant : 개신교
• be called to : 신의 뜻에 따라 ~을 맡다[하다]
• secular : 세속적인, 종교와 관련 없는
• craft : 재주, 기술, 직업
• fervor : 열렬, 열정
• inevitably : 필연적으로, 불가피하게
• devotion : 헌신, 전념
• morally : 도덕상, 도덕적으로
• greed : 탐욕, 욕심
• predestination : 운명, 숙명, 운명예정설
• morality : 도덕, 도덕성

해석

가톨릭은 하나님이 주신 유일한 천직은 사제직이라고 생각하나, 개신교는 사람들이 신의 뜻에 따라 어떤 세속적인 직업이나 상거래를 할 수도 있다고 생각한다. 그들이 하나님을 섬긴다는 믿음은 더 많은 재화를 생산하고 더 많은 돈을 벌면서, 종교적인 열정을 가지고 일하도록 격려한다. Weber는 개신교의 믿음이 결국 자본주의 경제 사회를 이끌었다고 믿었는데, 왜냐하면 그 믿음이 도덕적으로 남용이나 야망과 같은 동기들을 의심하는 증거라기보다는 헌신의 증거로 이익을 추구할 기회를 제공했기 때문이다. 운명예정설에 관한 생각은 또한 신자들이 사회적 불평등과 가난에 대해서 걱정할 필요가 없다는 것을 의미하는데, 물질적인 부유함이 영적인 부유함을 상징하기 때문이다.

27 ③ 윗글은 최초의 상업용 유리 거울이 베니스에서 만들어졌고, 오늘날 사용하는 은도금 방식의 유리 거울은 독일 화학

자에 의해서 개발되었다고 설명하고 있다. 그러므로 ③의 'development of commercial glass mirror technology(상업용 유리 거울 기술의 발전)'가 윗글의 주제로 가장 적절하다.

오답풀이

① 거울을 발명하게 된 숨은 경제적 동기
② 독일 화학자의 뛰어난 업적
④ 상업용 유리 거울 속에 감춰진 인간의 욕망
⑤ 유럽 고대 거울 기술의 공통성

어휘

• vanity : 자만심, 허영심
• polish : 닦다, 광[윤]을 내다
• blow : 불다, 날리다
• flatten : 납작하게 하다, 반반하게 만들다
• coat with : ~을 바르다, ~을 씌우다
• amalgam : 아말감, 혼합물, 결합물
• mercury : 수은
• tin : 주석
• come up with : ~를 생각해내다
• silvering : 은박, 은도금
• compound : 복합체, 화합물
• agent : 물질, 제
• invert sugar : 전화당
• Rochelle salt : 로셸염
• formaldehyde : 포름알데히드
• metallic : 금속성의, 금속이 함유된
• a pane of glass : 창 유리 한 장
• commonality : 공통성, 공용성

해석

호기심, 허영심 아니면 아직까지 탐구되지 않은 이유에서든, 사람들은 여러 시대에 걸쳐 자신의 반사된 모습을 보고 싶어 했다. 기원전 2,500년 초기 이집트인들은 대개 청동이지만, 가끔 은이나 금으로 만들어진 아주 광이 나는 금속 거울을 지니고 있었다. 최초의 상업용 유리 거울은 1564년에 베니스에서 만들어졌다. 이 유리 거울은 입으로 불어 납작해진 유리로 만들었고 수은과 주석의 혼합물로 코팅되었다. 베니스인들은 유럽에 수세기동안 거울을 공급하면서 발전했다. 1840년이 되고 나서야 Justus Liebig라는 독일 화학자가 우리가 오늘날 사용하는 은도금 방식을 생각해 냈다. 이 기술에 의해, 은과 암모니아의 화합물이 전화당, 로셸염, 포르말알데히드와 같은 불순물을 감소시키는 화학 반응을 거치게 되었고, 그 결과 금속성의 은이 매끄러운 판유리 뒷면에 고르게 발라졌다.

28 ② 윗글은 나이가 들거나 또는 근육이나 관절에 문제가 있는 애완동물에게 치료용 침대가 도움이 된다는 내용이다. 그

러므로 ②의 'to promote specialized pet furniture(애완용 전문 가구를 판촉하기 위해)'가 윗글의 목적으로 가장 적절하다.

오답풀이

① 가축의 학대를 막기 위해

③ 숙면이 주는 이점을 설명하기 위해

④ 애완동물 소유자에게 가구의 위험성을 알리기 위해

⑤ 애완동물 소유자에게 애완동물의 나쁜 잠버릇을 경고하기 위해

어휘

• curl up : 몸을 웅크리다, 몸을 동그랗게 말다
• blissful : 더없이 행복한, 즐거운
• restful : 편안한, 평화로운
• muscular : 근육의, 근육질의
• joint : 관절, 연결 부위
• pace : 서성거리다, 왔다 갔다 하다
• relocate : 이전[이동]하다, 새 자리로 옮기다
• companion : 동지, 동반자, 반려 동물
• therapeutic : 치료상의, 치료법의
• impromptu : 즉흥적으로, 즉석에서
• muscular-skeletal : 근육과 뼈의 근골격계의
• rejuvenate : 다시 젊어 보이게 하다, 활기를 되찾게 하다
• healing : 치유, 치료
• abuse : 남용, 오용, 학대
• hazard : 위험, 모험

해석

개나 고양이가 웅크리며 꿀잠을 자는 것보다 더 편안한 것은 무엇일까? 개와 고양이 둘 다 하루의 거의 절반을 잠을 자면서 보낸다. 그러나 모든 잠이 휴식을 주는 것은 아니다. 나이 든 동물들, 근육이나 관절에 문제가 있는 동물들 또는 매우 활동적인 개들은 자주 왔다 갔다 하거나 자리를 새로 옮긴다. 만일 당신의 반려동물이 이 부류 중 하나에 해당된다면, 치료용 침대가 도움이 될 수 있다. 이러한 전문 제품은 일반 침대나 즉석 잠자리와 달리 도움과 편안함을 준다. 나이와 건강과는 상관없이, 훌륭한 침대는 근골격계의 건강을 향상시키며 더불어 활력과 치유의 이점을 제공한다.

29 ⑤ 윗글은 크리스마스 계절을 맞이하여 주변의 불우한 이웃들을 보살펴줌으로써 그들이 행복을 찾도록 도와주라는 내용이다. 그러므로 ⑤의 'Find happiness by helping the needy around you(주변의 곤궁한 사람들을 도와 행복을 찾아라)'가 윗글의 요지로 가장 적절하다.

오답풀이

① 선의의 행동으로 진정한 행복 수치를 측정하라

② 지역 사회에서 행복 바이러스를 붙잡아라

③ 이웃에게 자기의 행복을 강요하지 마라

④ 정신 건강을 위해 자기만족을 연습하라

어휘

• secure : 획득하다, 확보하다
• contentment : 만족, 만족감
• ill-fate : 나쁜 운명, 불행
• in need : 어려움에 처한, 궁핍한
• the needy : 빈곤한 사람들, 영세민

해석

행복을 살 수는 없다. 가장 가까운 식료품 가게에 가서 1파운드의 버터를 주문하듯이 1파운드의 행복을 주문할 수는 없다. 그러나 행복은 내부로부터 오는 것이기 때문에, 자신의 행동을 통해 행복의 척도를 확보할 수 있다. 불우한 동료들을 도와줌으로써 만족감을 느낄 수 있다. 그들과 함께 나누지 않는다면 불행으로 인해 행복한 크리스마스를 보낼 수 없는 사람들을 도울 수 있다. 이 평화와 선의의 계절에, 어려움에 처한 사람들에게 우리의 눈을 통해 행복을 보도록 강요하지 맙시다. 오히려 그들이 자신의 눈을 통해 행복을 보고 찾도록 도와줍시다. 지역 사회의 불행을 반드시 살핍시다.

30 ② 윗글은 불굴의 의지로 스스로를 독려하며 영국 해협을 헤엄쳐 횡단하는 필자의 심경을 표현한 글이다. 그러므로 윗글에 나타난 'I'의 심경은 ②의 'determined and persistent(결연하고 끈기 있는)'이다.

오답풀이

① 좌절했지만 회복이 빠른

③ 기죽고 실망한

④ 놀랐지만 유쾌한

⑤ 위축되고 낙담한

어휘

• sprinting : 스프린팅, 전력질주
• stroke : 스트로크, 수영법
• summit : 정상, 산꼭대기
• frustrated : 실망한, 좌절한
• resilient : 회복력 있는, 회복이 빠른
• persistent : 불굴의, 끈기 있는
• daunted : 겁먹은, 기죽은
• exhilarated : 기분이 들뜬, 유쾌한
• overwhelmed : 압도된, 위축된

해석

깊은 숨을 들이마시고, 나는 다시 전속력으로 역주를 시작했다. 스트로크 횟수를 세면서 나는 스스로에게 천 번의 스트로크로 수영을 할 때까지 다시는 위를 쳐다보지 않겠다고 말했다. 나는 천천히 한걸음씩 시작해서 몇 백 야드를 나아갔다. 이제 나는 영국 해협이 왜 수영을 하는데 에베레스트 산과 같은 존재인지 깨달았다. 비록 모든 사람의 목표가 정상에 도달하는 것이지만, 산꼭대기는 공기가 희박하고 모든 것이 도전적이 된다. 500번의 스트로크를 할 때까지는 위를 쳐다보지 마라. 가능한 한 빨리 가라. 힘껏 밀어라. 전력을 다해 팔을 저어라. 킥을 해라. 그래. 다리를 킥해라. 더 깊게 더 빨리 저어라. 자. 힘내자. 저어라.

31 ③ 윗글에 따르면 의사가 되는 것은 선택 사항이지만, 일단 의사가 되어 환자들과 직업적인 관계를 시작하게 되면 그들의 치료에 최선을 다해야 하는 것이 의사들의 의무이다. 그러므로 의사가 환자를 치료하는 데 갈등이 생긴다는 것은 의사의 의무에 반하는 것이므로, ③의 내용은 전체적인 글의 흐름과 어울리지 않는다.

어휘

• as a rule : 대체적으로, 통례로, 통상
• physician : 의사, 내과 의사
• altruistic : 이타적인
• altruism : 이타주의
• discharge : 면하게 하다, 해제하다
• obligation : 의무, 책무
• compromise : 타협[절충]하다, 위태롭게 하다
• integrity : 고결, 성실, 청렴
• therapeutic : 치료상의, 치료법의
  cf. therapeutic treatment : 치료적 처우
• transfer : 옮기다, 이동하다
• obligatory : 의무적인, 이행해야 할

해석

통상 의사들은 환자들의 최선의 이익을 위해 행동할 때 보통 이타주의와 관련된 행동에 선택의 여지가 없기 때문에 이타적으로 여겨져서는 안 된다. 의사들은 환자들에게 선택의 문제로 면할 수 없는 직업적인 의무가 있다. 물론 의사가 되어 환자들과의 직업적인 관계를 시작하는 것은 선택적인 행위이다. ① 그러나 일단 의사가 이러한 관계를 시작하면, 의무를 선택할 수는 없다. ② 의사는 만일 치료를 하는 것이 개인적이고 직업적인 고결함을 위태롭게 한다면 특별한 상황에서 특정 환자를 치료하지 않을 선택을 할 수 있다. ③ 따라서 환자를 치료적 처우가 필요한 개인으로 보는 의사에게는 잠재적인 갈등이 발생한다. ④ 그러나 의사는 환자의 치료가 다른 의사에게

전달되도록 보장해야만 한다. ⑤ 일단 의사가 되면, 그 사람은 자기 환자에 대해 의학적인 최선의 이익을 다하겠다고 약속을 한다. 이것은 선택이 아니라, 의무이다.

32 ② 윗글은 열로 인한 물의 부피 팽창과 빙하가 녹는 것이 해수면 상승의 원인이라고 설명하고 있다. 그러므로 해수면 상승을 막기 위해 물의 분자 구조를 이해하는 것이 가장 중요하다는 ②의 내용은 전체적인 글의 흐름과 어울리지 않는다.

어휘

• molecular : 분자의, 분자로 된
• sink into : ~에 빠져들다, 가라앉다
• mercury : 수은
• thermal : 열의, 보온성이 좋은
• account for : ~을 차지하다
• mountain glacier : 산악 빙하
• ice sheet : 빙상, 대륙 빙하
• Antarctica : 남극 대륙

해석

다른 기후 문제와 달리, 해수면 상승에 관한 과학은 매우 간단하다. ① 해수면은 여러 상황으로 인해 주로 열이 물에 가하는 작용 때문에 상승한다. ② 해수면 상승을 막기 위해서는 물의 분자 구조를 이해하는 것이 가장 중요하다. ③ 지구의 온도가 상승함에 따라, 약 90%인 대기권에서 초권된 열의 대부분은 바다에 흡수된다. ④ 물이 따뜻해짐에 따라, 물은 온도계의 수은처럼 팽창한다. ⑤ 이러한 열의 팽창은 해수면 상승의 3분의 1을 차지한다. 나머지 3분의 2는 산악 빙하 그리고 그린랜드와 남극의 빙상이 녹은 것이다.

33 ① 윗글에 따르면 동물을 대상으로 한 실험적 연구는 윤리적인 문제가 발생하기는 하지만, 각종 질병을 예방하고 치료하는 의학 분야의 발전에 중요한 도구가 되었다. 그러므로 빈칸 (A)에는 'experimental(실험적인)', 빈칸 (B)에는 'instrumental(도구적인)'이 들어갈 말로 가장 적절하다.

오답풀이

	(A)	(B)
②	통계적인	성공적인
③	분야	중요한
④	발전적인	그럴 듯한
⑤	실험실	사소한

어휘

• diet : 식사, 음식, 식습관
• electrode : 전극

- implantation : 이식, 전이
- injection : 주사, 주입
- experimentation : 실험, 실험법
- prevention : 예방, 방지
- polio : 소아마비
- diabetes : 당뇨병
- measles : 홍역
- smallpox : 천연두
- massive burns : 중증 화상
- stroke : 뇌졸중
- disorder : 장애, 질병
- ethical : 윤리적인, 도덕적인
- statistical : 통계적인, 통계의
- plausible : 정말 같은, 그럴 듯한
- negligible : 무시해도 될 정도의, 보잘 것 없는, 사소한

해석

어떠한 경우에, 연구원들은 하루 중 다른 시간, 년 중 다른 계절, 식습관의 변화 등등의 목적으로 자연에 있는 동물을 단순히 관찰한다. 이러한 과정은 어떠한 윤리적인 문제도 발생하지 않는다. 그러나 다른 연구들에서, 동물들은 뇌 손상, 전극 이식, 약이나 호르몬 투여 그리고 분명 동물들에게는 이익이 되지 않는 다른 과정을 당했다. (과학자를 포함하여) 양심이 있는 사람은 누구든지 이러한 사실에 괴로워한다. 그럼에도 불구하고 동물 실험은 소아마비, 당뇨병, 홍역, 천연두, 중증 화상, 심장병 그리고 다른 심각한 병세의 예방과 치료 방법을 이끄는 의학 연구에 매우 중요했다. 대부분의 노벨 물리학상이나 의학상들은 인간이 아닌 동물들을 대상으로 한 연구에 수여되었다. AIDS, 알츠하이머 병, 뇌졸중 그리고 많은 다른 질병들을 치료하거나 예방하는 방법을 찾을 수 있는 희망은 주로 동물 연구에 달려있다. 의학과 생물심리학의 여러 분야에서, 동물들이 없었다면 연구는 느리게 진척되거나 전혀 진척될 수 없었을 것이다.

> 단순히 관찰만 하는 연구와 달리, 비록 몇몇 동물들을 대상으로 한 (A) 실험적인 연구는 윤리적인 문제가 발생하기는 하지만, 그 연구들은 다양한 의학 분야의 발전을 이루는데 (B) 도구적인 것들이었다.

34 ④ 윗글에 따르면 지도는 그 목적에 적절하지 않다고 여기는 엄청난 양의 정보를 단순화시키는데, 주어진 문장에서 지도는 적절한 정보는 유지하고 가끔은 더 심하게 단순화시킨다고 하였으므로 그에 대한 예시들을 설명한 ④에 들어가는 것이 가장 적절하다.

어휘

- representation : 묘사, 표현
- relevant : 관련 있는, 적절한
- assumption : 가정, 추측
- constraint : 제약, 제한, 통제
- tractability : 순종, 유순, 다루기 쉬움, 용이성
- abstract : 추출하다, 요약하다
- tremendous : 거대한, 엄청난
- deem : 여기다, 생각하다, 간주하다
- irrelevant : 무관한, 상관없는
- topology : 위상 기하학, 지세학
- architectural : 건축학의, 건축술의
- blueprint : 계획, 청사진
- prototype : 원형, 모형

해석

> 그것은 적절한 정보는 유지하고, 가끔은 더 심하게 단순화시킨다.

일반적으로 말하면, 모델은 어떤 목적에 부합하도록 만든 실물의 단순화된 표현이다. (①) 그것은 특정 목적에 무엇이 중요하고 중요하지 않은지에 관한 몇 가지 가정에 근거하여, 혹은 가끔 정보의 제약이나 용이성에 근거하여 단순화되었다. (②) 예를 들면, 지도는 현실 세계에 대한 모델이다. (③) 그것은 지도 제작자가 그 목적에 적절하지 않다고 여기는 엄청난 양의 정보를 요약시켜 버린다. (④) 예를 들면, 도로 지도는 도로, 기본 지세, 사람이 가고 싶은 장소와 도로와의 관계, 그리고 다른 관련 정보를 기록하고 강조한다. (⑤) 여러 전문직들은 잘 알려진 모델 유형 즉, 건축물의 청사진, 공학적인 모형 등을 가지고 있다. 이들 각각은 주된 목적에 적절하지 않은 세부사항은 요약하고 적절한 것은 유지한다.

35 ② 윗글은 판례법에 대한 서술인데, 글 (B)에서 판례법이 판사들에게 중요한 이유를 설명하고 있고, 글 (A)에서 낙태법을 예로 들어 판사들의 역할인 법 해석에 대해 서술하고 있다. 마지막으로 글 (C)에서 그로 인한 판결의 결과를 설명하고 있으므로, 글의 흐름상 (B) – (A) – (C)의 순으로 이어져야 한다.

어휘

- common law : 관습법, 불문법
- case law : 판례법
- ruling : 결정, 판결
- precedent : 선례, 판례, 전례
- be bound by : 묶이다, 얽매이다, 구속되다

• Parliament : 의회, 국회

• Abortion Act : 낙태법

• secretary : 서기, 비서, 사무관

• decline to : ~을 거부[거절]하다

• referral : 소개, 추천, 위탁

• termination : 임신 중절 수술, 인공 유산, 낙태

• take into account : ~을 고려하다, 참작하다

• plug the gap : 틈새를 메우다

• enact : 법을 제정하다, 입법하다

• procedure : 절차, 방법, 수술

해석

관습법은 판례법이라고도 알려져 있는데, 그 법은 특정 사건을 판결(혹은 선고)하는 판사들에 의해 발달된 법이다. 판사들은 이전의 학설이나 원칙을 따르는데, 이것은 이전에 선고된 '선례'에 구속된다는 것을 의미한다.

(B) 이 법은 본질적으로 과거에 판결되었던 유사한 판례들, 특히 최상급 법원에서 판결된 판례들을 고려해야 한다는 것을 뜻한다. 이렇게 판사가 제정한 법은 국회가 법을 제정하지 않아 판사들이 그 틈을 메울 책임을 떠안은 상황이 되기 때문에 중요하다.

(A) 마찬가지로 판사들은 가끔 국회가 통과시킨 법들을 해석해야만 한다. 한 가지 사례가 1967년에 제정된 낙태법이다. 한 비서가 양심적으로 낙태에 참여하는 것을 반대할 권리가 그녀의 낙태 거부를 보호한다고 주장하면서, 낙태 추천 서류의 타이핑을 거부했다.

(C) 판사들은 '참여'라는 단어를 보았고 그 비서는 그 수술과 연관성이 부족하기 때문에, 죄가 없다고 판결했다.

36 ⑤ 윗글에 따르면 로봇시대의 성공 여부는 로봇을 대하는 문화의 차이에 달려 있다고 설명하고 있다. 글 (C)에서 서양과 동양의 문화가 로봇을 대하는 방식이 다르다고 정의하고, 이어 글 (B)에서 일본 문화의 예를 든 다음, 글 (A)에서 그 결과에 대해 설명하고 있다. 그러므로 글의 흐름상 (C) – (B) – (A)의 순으로 이어져야 한다.

어휘

• robotics : 로봇 공학

• companion : 동반자, 동료, 친구

• soulless : 영혼[정신]이 없는, 비열한

• differentiate : 구별하다, 구분 짓다

• predisposition : 성향, 경향, 기질

해석

로봇 공학이 확산됨에 따라, 어느 나라가 로봇시대에 성공할지의 여부는 문화적으로 사람들이 로봇을 그들의 삶에 얼마나 잘 받아들이는가에 달려 있다.

(C) 서양과 동양의 문화는 로봇을 대하는 방식이 매우 다르다. 일본은 로봇에 대해 경제적인 필요성과 기술적인 노하우를 가지고 있을 뿐만 아니라, 문화적인 성향도 또한 가지고 있다.

(B) 80%의 일본인들이 믿었던 고대 Shinto 종교는 사물과 인간 모두에 영혼이 있다는 애니미즘을 신봉하고 있다.

(A) 결과적으로 일본 문화는 로봇을 영혼이 없는 기계로 보는 서양 문화보다 로봇 친구를 실제 친구만큼이나 더 잘 받아들이는 경향이 있다.

[37~38]

어휘

• yearn for : ~을 그리워하다, 동경하다

• sous chef : 부주방장

• chop : 썰다, 다지다

• eggplant : 가지

• zucchini : 애호박

• chore : 집안일, 허드렛일

• peel : 껍질을 벗기다[깎다]

• faucet : 수도꼭지

• nope : 아니, 아니오

• executive chef : 주방장

• be confronted with : ~에 직면하다, 맞서다

• versus : ~대, ~에 비해, ~와 대조적으로

• gender : 성, 성별

• end in a draw : 동점으로 끝나다, 무승부로 끝나다

• aftermath : 여파, 후유증

• attest : 증명하다, 입증하다

해석

우리는 미국으로 돌아왔지만, Julie의 마음은 여전히 이탈리아에 있었다. 그녀는 이탈리아의 피자를 조금 더 그리워하고 있었다. 그녀는 나를 부주방장으로 여기고 피자를 직접 만들기로 결심했다. 나는 가지와 애호박을 썰었다. 우리 둘 다 조용히 일에 집중했다. 다음으로 양파를 썰 차례이다. 나는 양파 껍질을 벗기고 싱크대로 가져가 수도꼭지를 틀고 흐르는 물속에서 양파를 썰기 시작했다.

"뭐하고 있어?"

"물속에서 양파를 썰고 있어."

"왜?"

"눈물을 흘리지 않으려면 그렇게 하라고 브리태니커 백과사전에 나와 있어."

이것은 브리태니커 백과사전에 수록된 유용한 팁 중의 하나인 Heloise식 팁이었고, 나는 그것을 실행해 보는 것에 꽤나 신이 나 있었다.

"안 돼, 너무 불안해."

"그러나 브리태니커 백과사전에 그렇게 나와 있어."

"안 돼, 내가 주방장이고 당신이 부주방장이야."

여기서 나는 불행한 상황에 닥치게 된다. 바로 브리태니커 백과사전 대 내 아내. 거대한 두 권력이다. 난 어느 것을 선택해야 할까? 자, 브리태니커 백과사전은 꽤 신뢰할만하다. 그러나 내가 아는 한, 브리태니커 백과사전이 내 아이를 업어주거나 며칠 동안 나를 모른척하거나 싫어하는 티셔츠를 버릴 수는 없다.

그래서 나는 Julie가 브리태니커 백과사전을 이겼다고 결정했다. 물 없이 양파를 썰어야 했고 나는 울어야 했다.

37 ④ 윗글은 가정에서 아내의 말을 들을 수밖에 없는 한 남편의 처지를 다룬 재미있는 에피소드로, ④의 'Real Boss in My Home(우리 집 진짜 보스)'가 윗글의 제목으로 가장 적절하다.

오답풀이

① 눈물 없이 물속에서 양파 까기

② 무승부로 끝난 성(性) 대결

③ 이탈리아 요리 팁의 후유증

⑤ 브리태니커의 부주방장

38 ③ 바로 앞 문장에서 아내 Julie가 브리태니커 백과사전을 이겼다고 결정했으므로, 빈칸에는 아내의 주장을 수용하는 내용이 와야 한다. 그러므로 ③의 "The onion will be cut without water and I will cry(물 없이 양파를 썰어야 했고 나는 울어야 했다)."가 빈칸에 들어갈 내용으로 가장 적절하다.

오답풀이

① 여성들이 얼마나 강도 높게 일하는지를 증명하는 것은 어느 것인가.

② 나는 수정사항 때문에 브리태니커 백과사전에 전화를 해야만 했다.

④ 나는 다음 며칠 동안 아내를 모른 척 할 것이다.

⑤ 그러나 나는 내일 주방장이 될 것이다.

[39~40]

어휘

- raven : 큰까마귀
- birdbrain : 새대가리, 멍청이, 바보
- spot : 발견하다, 찾다, 알아채다
- cache : 은닉하다, 숨겨두다, 저장하다
- deceive : 속이다, 기만하다
- twist : (예상 밖의, 뜻밖의) 전환[전개], 반전
- cognitive : 인식의, 인지의
- replicate : 모사하다, 복제하다
- pellet : 알갱이, 작은 알[공], 둥글게 뭉친 것
- distracter : 정답 이외의[틀린] 선택지
- bulky : 부피가 큰, 덩치가 큰
- barter with : ~와 교환[교역]하다
- pass up : 거절하다, 퇴짜놓다, 포기하다
- treat : 대접, 한턱, 선물
- emergency : 비상사태, 돌발 사건

해석

우리는 오랫동안 큰까마귀가 바보가 아니라는 것을 알고 있었다. 큰까마귀는 매달려 있는 먹이를 잡아당기기 위해 끈을 모으고 심지어 서로를 속이기 위해 노력하면서, 나중을 위해 먹이를 숨겨두는 일이 목격되었다. 사이언스 지(紙)에 오늘 발표된 한 연구는 특히 인상적인 예상 밖 반전을 보여준다. 즉, 큰까마귀는 자연에서 결코 접하지 못했던 장래에 필요한 것들을 계획할 수 있다.

그 새로운 연구는 스웨덴의 인지 동물학자들이 주도하였는데, 그들은 이전에 유인원들의 계획능력을 테스트하기 위해 사용했던 일련의 실험들을 이번에는 큰까마귀를 이용하여 똑같이 따라했다. 큰까마귀들은 처음에 퍼즐 박스로부터 둥글게 뭉친 먹이를 부수기 위해 돌을 사용하는 것을 배웠다. 다음날 박스가 없었을 때, 그 새들에게 돌로 된 도구와 너무 가볍고 부피가 커서 도구로 사용할 수 없는 장난감인 '틀린 선택지' 중에서 고르도록 했다. 박스는 선택 후 15분 뒤에 다시 가져왔다. 비록 늦긴 했지만, 큰까마귀들은 당시에 거의 80%가 올바른 도구를 선택했고, 당시에 선택한 도구의 86%를 성공적으로 사용했다. 그 새들은 실험자에게 먹이 한 덩이를 교환하는 대가로 병뚜껑을 주어야 했을 때도 거의 잘 수행했다. 그 새들은 비록 그것을 교환하기 위해 15분을 기다려야 했지만, 거의 항상 잘못된 선택지보다 병뚜껑을 선택했다. 곧 필요해질 물건에 대한 선호는 큰까마귀들이 도구나 교환할 징표 중의 하나를 위해 더 작은 것을 포기해야 했을 때, 그리고 각 물건을 17시간이 지나고 나서야 사용할 수 있게 되었을 때조차도 계속되었다.

정답 및 해설

39 ① 'be used to 동사원형'은 '~하기 위해 사용되다'는 의미이고, 'be used to ~ing'는 '~하는데 익숙하다'는 의미다. 해당 문장은 문맥상 전자에 해당하므로 ①의 'testing'은 'test'로 고쳐 써야 옳다.

40 ⑤ 윗글에 따르면 큰까마귀는 즉각적인 보상이나 필요성이 없어도 장차 무엇이 필요한지 이해하고 준비할 수 있는 '계획 능력(planning abilities)'을 소유하고 있음을 실험을 통해 알 수 있었다. 그러므로 빈칸에 들어갈 말은 ⑤의 'plan for future needs(장래에 필요한 것들을 계획하다)'이다.

오답풀이

① 돌발 상황을 위해 도구를 지키다
② 상황을 대비해 무리지어 일하다
③ 앞으로 일어날 사건을 예측하다
④ 잠재적인 경쟁자들을 속이다

[41~42]

어휘

• reed : 갈대
• swamp : 늪, 습지
• mud : 진흙
• solid : 확실한, 중단 없는, 한결같은
• interrupt : 방해하다, 가로막다, 중단시키다
• right off : 즉각, 곧
• chickabiddy : 삐악삐악, 병아리
• ornery : 성질 더러운, 성미 고약한
• stubborn : 완고한, 고집스러운

해석

난 가기로 결정했고 갈 것이며, 어머니 생일 때까지 그곳에 가야만 했다. 이것은 굉장히 중요했다. 나는 어머니를 집으로 데리고 올 기회가 있다면 어머니 생일날이어야 한다고 믿었다. 만일 이 내용을 우리 아버지나 조부모님에게 큰 소리로 말하면, 내가 공중에서 고기를 잡는 편이 더 낫다고 말씀하셨을 것이다. 그래서 나는 그 말을 크게 하지는 않았다. 그러나 나는 그것을 믿었다. (①) 우리 아버지는 내가 부러진 갈대에 기대고 있고 언젠가 늪의 진흙이 얼굴을 다 덮을 거라고 말씀하신다.
마침내 Gram과 Gramps Hiddle 그리고 내가 여행의 첫째 날을 시작했을 때, 나는 처음 30분 동안 중단 없이 기도했다. 나는 사고가 나지 않게 해달라고 기도했고 (나는 차와 버스를 무서워했다), 7일이 남은 어머니 생일 날 거기에 도착할 수 있게 해달라고 기도했고, 어머니를 집에 데리고 올 수 있

게 해달라고 기도했다. 반복해서 나는 똑같은 기도를 했다. 나는 나무들에게도 기도했다. 이것이 하느님에게 직접 기도하는 것보다는 쉬웠다. 거의 항상 근처에 나무들이 있었다. 하나님의 모든 창조물들 가운데 가장 평평하고, 가장 똑바른 길인 Ohio Turnpike에 다다랐을 때, Gram이 내 기도를 막았다. "Salamanca". (②)
나는 즉시 내 진짜 이름이 Salamanca Tree Hiddle임을 설명해야만 했다. 내 부모님은 Salamanca가 우리 증조할머니가 속한 인디언 부족의 이름이라고 생각했다. (③) 우리 부모님은 실수를 했었다. 그 부족의 이름은 Seneca였지만 부모님들은 내가 태어나고 나서야 실수를 발견했기 때문에, 그때까지 내 이름으로 사용되었고, 여전히 Salamanca로 남아있었다. (④) 내 가운데 이름은 Tree인데, 그것은 우리 어머니가 너무 아름다워 하셔서 내 이름의 일부로 만든 나무의 이름에서 따온 것이다. 그녀는 더욱 구체적이길 원해서 가장 좋아하는 Sugar Maple Tree를 사용했지만, Salamanca Sugar Maple Tree Hiddle은 그녀에게는 훨씬 더 평범했다. (⑤) 우리 어머니는 나를 Salamanca라고 부르곤 했지만 그녀가 떠난 후, 단지 Hiddle 조부모님들만 나를 Salamanca(그들이 나를 병아리라고 부르지 않고 있었을 때)라고 불렀다. 대부분의 다른 사람들에게 나는 Sal이었고, 특별히 재미있다고 생각하는 몇몇 소년들에게 나는 Salamander였다.

41 ⑤ 윗글의 마지막 줄에서 대부분의 다른 사람들에게 나는 Sal이었고, 특별히 재미있다고 생각하는 몇몇 소년들에게 나는 Salamander였다고 했으므로, 대부분의 사람들이 그녀를 Salamanca 또는 Salamandar라고 불렀다는 ⑤의 내용은 옳지 못하다.

오답풀이

① 그녀의 여행 목적은 어머니를 집으로 데리고 오는 것이었다.
② 그녀의 조부모님들은 그녀의 여행에 동행했다.
③ 그녀는 신보다 나무에게 기도하는 것이 더 쉽다고 생각했다.
④ 그녀의 부모들은 그녀의 이름을 지었을 때 오해가 있었다.

42 ①

> 때때로 나는 늙은 당나귀처럼 성미가 고약하고 고집이 세다.

다른 사람들은 어머니를 생일날 집으로 데리고 오는 것을 불가능하다고 생각하지만, 그녀는 그렇지 않다고 굳게 믿고 있는 것에서 필자의 고집과 완고함을 엿볼 수 있다. 그러므로 그녀가 부러진 갈대에 기대고 있고 언젠가 늪의 진흙이 얼굴을 다 덮을 거라고, 아버지가 그녀의 고집 센 성격을 언급한 ①에 들어가는 것이 가장 적절하다.

[43~45]

어휘

- disembark : 내리다, 상륙시키다
- fascia : 간판
- illuminated : 조명장식을 한, 환한[빛나는]
- suspend : 매달다, 걸다
- strut : 지주, 버팀목
- duct : 배관, 도관
- mundanity : 세속적임, 평범함
- delight : 기쁨, 즐거움
- apt : 적절한, 적합한
- neighborliness : 친밀, 긴밀, 밀접, 근접
- subtitle : 자막, 부제
- provoke : 유발하다, 불러일으키다
- genuine : 진짜의, 정말의
- distinctive : 독특한, 특별한
- casual eye : 평상시의 눈
- typeface : 활자면, 서체
- nostalgic : 향수의, 향수를 불러일으키는
- mind-set : 심적 경향[태도], 사고방식
- elicit : 끌어내다, 꾀어내다
- vaguely : 모호하게, 희미하게
- intensely : 몹시, 강렬하게
- lie beyond : ~너머에 있다, 미치지 않다
- congenial : 마음이 맞는[통하는], 적합한, 알맞은
- temperament : 기질, 성품
- esoteric : 비밀의, 난해한
- bewilderment : 어리둥절함, 당황, 난처
- platter : 접시
- intimacy : 친밀, 친교

해석

암스테르담의 Schipol 공항에 내리자마자, 나는 터미널 안으로 몇 발자국 걸어가서 입국장과 출구 그리고 환전 데스크를 보여주는 천장으로부터 매달린 표지판의 모습과 마주했다. 그것은 밝은 노란색 표지판이었으며, 높이는 1미터 폭은 2미터였고, 디자인은 단순했으며, 케이블과 에어컨 배관들로 얽힌 천장으로부터 강철 버팀목에 매달려 조명이 비추는 알루미늄 박스 안의 플라스틱 간판이었다. 단순하고 심지어 평범해 보임에도 불구하고, 그 표지판은 나를 기쁘게 했고, 특별하긴 하지만, '이국적인'이라는 형용사가 그 기쁨을 표현하기에 적절해 보였다. 이국적 정취는 특별한 곳에 존재한다. 즉, Aankomst의 a 두 개, Uitgang의 u와 l의 근접, 영어 자막용으로 "desk"를 의미하는 단어인 balies, 그리고 Frutiger나 Univers라는 실용적이고 현대적인 서체의 선택이 그렇다.

만일 그 표지판이 내게 진정한 기쁨을 불러 일으켰다면, 그것은 부분적으로 내가 다른 어딘가에 도착했다는 첫 번째 결정적인 증거를 제공했기 때문이다. 그것은 해외에 있다는 상징이다. 평상시의 눈에 특별하게 보이는 것 같지는 않지만, 그러한 표지판은 우리나라에서는 결단코 이러한 형태로 존재하지 않는다. 우리나라에서는 노란색이 덜 했고, 서체는 더 부드럽고 향수를 불러일으켰으며, 외국인들의 혼동에 너무 무관심한 나머지 자막도 없었고, 그 언어는 내가 다른 역사나 사고방식의 존재를 혼란스럽게 느끼는 반복인, as를 두 번 쓰는 일도 없다.

표지판이 다른 장소에서 다를 수도 있다는 것은 단순하지만, 즐거운 생각이란 증거이다. 즉, 나라는 다양하고, 국경을 건너 관습은 변화한다. 그러나 다르다는 것 하나만으로 기쁨을 이끌어 내기에는 충분하지 않고, 오래가지도 못한다. 그 상이함은 내 나라가 개선할 수 있는 것처럼 보인다. 만일 내가 Schipol 표지판을 이국적이라고 부른다면, 그것은 모호하지만 강렬하게, 표지판을 만들고 uitgang 너머에 위치한 그 나라가 결정적인 방법으로 우리나라보다 나의 성품이나 관심사에 더 적합하다는 것을 입증하는데 성공했기 때문이다. 그 표지판은 행복의 징표이다.

43 ③ 윗글은 암스테르담의 Schipol 공항에 도착한 필자가 단순하고 평범해 보이지만 기분 좋고 특별해 보이는 표지판을 보고, 자신의 나라에서는 결코 볼 수 없는 이국적인 느낌을 서술한 글이다. 그러므로 ③의 'Sweet Bewilderment: Am I Elsewhere? (기분 좋은 어리둥절함 : 내가 있는 곳은 어디인가?)'가 윗글의 제목으로 가장 적절하다.

오답풀이

① 이국적인 동시에 향수적인
② 지나치게 난해한 표지판은 호기심을 없앤다.
④ 같은 접시 위에 다양한 언어
⑤ 국경을 넘어 : 선구적 여행가

44 ③ 암스테르담의 Schipol 공항의 표지판에 대한 자국 표지판의 다른 점 중의 하나는 다른 언어로 된 자막이 없다는 것이므로, 이는 외국인들의 혼동에 무관심하다는 의미이다. 그러므로 빈칸에는 ③의 'confusion(혼동)'이 들어갈 말로 가장 적절하다.

오답풀이

① 재능
② 흥분
④ 친밀
⑤ 숫자

45   ③ 필자는 Schipol 공항의 표지판에 대해 단순하고 평범해 보임에도 불구하고 나를 기쁘게 했고 이국적이라고 표현했다. 그러므로 그 표지판의 단순함이 이국적인 정취를 느끼는 주요 이유라는 ③의 설명은 윗글의 내용과 일치하지 않는다.

오답풀이

① 그 표지판의 폭은 높이의 두 배이다.

② 그 표지판은 두 가지 언어로 적혀 있다.

④ 그 표지판은 다른 나라에 도착했다는 증거를 제시한다.

⑤ 필자는 집으로 돌아와서 그와 같은 표지판을 볼 수 없었다.

2017학년도 기출문제 정답 및 해설

제2교시 **영어영역**

01 ①	02 ③	03 ①	04 ①	05 ⑤	06 ④
07 ②	08 ②	09 ①	10 ③	11 ④	12 ②
13 ④	14 ②	15 ⑤	16 ⑤	17 ⑤	18 ④
19 ②	20 ③	21 ①	22 ①	23 ③	24 ④
25 ③	26 ③	27 ①	28 ②	29 ⑤	30 ②
31 ⑤	32 ④	33 ④	34 ③	35 ⑤	36 ③
37 ①	38 ④	39 ②	40 ②	41 ④	42 ②
43 ②	44 ③	45 ④			

01 ① 'categorically'는 '절대적으로', '명확히'의 뜻으로 내용상 가장 비슷한 단어는 'unequivocally(모호하지 않게, 명백히)'이다.

〔오답풀이〕
② 전형적으로, 보통
③ 버릇없이, 무례하게
④ 마지못해서, 꺼려하여
⑤ 악의를 갖고, 심술궂게

〔어휘〕
• devise : 창안[고안]하다, 궁리하다
• attorney : 변호사, 법률 대리인

〔해석〕
변호사들이 우리의 제안을 <u>명확히</u> 거절했으므로 새로운 행동 계획을 궁리할 시간이다.

02 ③ 'opulent'는 '부유한', '호사스러운'의 의미로 글의 내용상 'luxurious(사치스러운, 호화로운)'와 가장 유사한 뜻이다.

〔오답풀이〕
① 비도덕적인, 부도덕한
② 자랑스러운, 자부심이 강한
④ 건강에 해로운, 유해한
⑤ 무능한, 쓸모없는

〔어휘〕
• emerge : 나타나다, 출현하다
• victorious : 승리한, 승리를 거둔
• long-fought : 장기 투쟁
• bout : 한바탕, 병치레
• cancer : 암
• tycoon : 거물, 대군
• turn over a new leaf : 새사람이 되다
• denounce : 맹렬히 비난하다, 고발하다

〔해석〕
암과의 긴 투병에서 승리를 거둔 후, 언론계의 거물인 그는 <u>호사스러운</u> 생활 방식을 자책하고 새사람이 되려고 노력했다.

03 ① 'contentious'는 '논쟁을 초래할', '논쟁하기 좋아하는'의 의미로 'controversial(논란이 많은, 논쟁을 좋아하는)'과 그 의미가 동일하다.

〔오답풀이〕
② 복잡한, 복합의
③ 찾기 힘든, (교묘히) 피하는
④ 비밀스러운, 숨기는
⑤ 성과 없는, 헛된

〔어휘〕
• sanction : (국제법을 위반한 국가에 대하여 국제 연합이 취하는) 제재, 처벌
• issue : 문제, 쟁점, 사안

〔해석〕
그 나라에 대한 제재는 가장 <u>논쟁을 초래할</u> 쟁점이 될 것으로 예상된다.

04 ① 'be numbered'는 숫자가 다 세어졌다는 의미로 해당 문장에서 '얼마 남지 않은', '한정된'의 뜻으로 사용되었다. 그러므로 'limited(제한된, 한정된)'가 가장 비슷한 단어이다.

〔오답풀이〕
② 오래 계속되는, 장기적인
③ 보존된, 저장된
④ 속도가 붙은, 가속된

⑤ 겹쳐진, 포개진

어휘

- capitalism : 자본주의
- capitalist : 자본주의자, 자본가
- era : 시대, 시기
- give way to : 양보하다, ～로 바뀌다[대체되다]
- socialism : 사회주의
- assumption : 가정, 추정
- intellectual : 지식인, 지성인

해석

자본주의 시대가 얼마 남지 않았고, 자본주의자 시대가 이제 사회주의로 바뀌어야만 한다. 이러한 추정이 대서양 양쪽 지식인들에게 폭넓게 퍼졌다.

05 ⑤ 'presumptuous(주제넘은, 건방진)'의 뜻으로 풀어서 설명하면 'arrogant and disrespectful(오만하고 무례한)'과 같은 의미이다.

오답풀이

① 주의를 기울이고 경계하는
② 정확하고 정밀한
③ 근면 성실하고 부지런한
④ 성취할 수 있고 실용적인

어휘

- politician : 정치인, 정치가
- hegemony : 패권, 헤게모니
  cf. economic hegemony : 경제패권

해석

많은 정치인들은 그 나라의 경제패권을 주제넘다고 보았다.

06 ④ recovering → recovered

지구로부터 '재생된' 화석 연료이므로 수동의 의미를 지닌다. 그러므로 수동의 의미를 나타내는 과거분사 'recovered'를 사용해야 한다.

such fossil fuels (which are) recovered from the earth.

어휘

- interruption : 중단, 방해, 두절
- apparently : 분명하게, 명백하게
- marine organism : 해양 생물
- exceed : 넘다, 초과[초월]하다
- decomposer : 분해자(박테리아 · 균류 등)
- accumulate : 쌓다, 축적하다

- coal : 석탄
- overlie : (지층이 다른 지층의) 위에 겹치다, ～의 위에 눕다
- molecular : 분자의, 분자로 된
- release : 풀어 주다, 석방[해방]하다, 방출하다
- immense : 엄청난, 어마어마한
- fossil fuel : 화석 연료
- environment : (주변의) 환경
- atmosphere : 대기, 공기, 분위기
- carbon dioxide : 이산화탄소
- be removed from : ～로부터 제거되다

해석

육지 식물과 해양 생물의 성장이 재생하기 위한 분해 능력을 초과했을 때, 수백만 년 전에 평상시의 에너지 흐름에 중대한 중단이 분명 발생했다. 에너지가 풍부한 유기체의 축적된 층들이 점차 겹겹이 쌓인 땅의 압력을 받아 석탄과 석유로 변했다. 우리가 이제 연소시켜 방출할 수 있는 에너지가 석탄과 석유의 분자 구조 속에 저장되어 있다. 그리고 우리의 현대 문명은 지구로부터 재생된 그러한 화석 연료에서 나오는 엄청난 양의 에너지에 의존하고 있다. 화석 연료를 연소시킴으로서 우리는 대부분의 저장된 에너지를 최종적으로 주변 환경에 열로 내보낸다. 우리는 또한 수백만 년에 걸쳐 천천히 제거되어 왔던 엄청난 양의 이산화탄소를 상당히 짧은 시간에 대기 중에 돌려보내고 있다.

07 ② which → of which

'be composed of(～으로 구성되어 있다)'의 목적어에 해당되는 'the elements'가 관계대명사 'which'의 선행사이므로, 전치사＋관계대명사의 형태인 'of which'를 사용해야 문법적으로 옳다.

어휘

- readily : 손쉽게, 쉽사리
- renewable : 재생 가능한, 갱신할 수 있는
- comprise : ～으로 구성되다[이뤄지다]
- property : 재산, 소유물, 속성, 특성
- element : 요소, 성분
- compose : 구성하다, 조립하다
- abundance : 풍부, 부유
- range from A to B : 범위가 A에서 B에 이르다, A에서 B까지 다양하다
- unlimited : 무제한의, 무한정의
- extract : 뽑다, 얻다, 추출하다
- industrial material : 공업 원료
- copper : 구리, 동
- deplete : 덜다, 줄이다, 고갈시키다

해석

지구는 인간 생활에 매우 중요한 자원을 많이 가지고 있다. 일부는 손쉽게 재생이 가능하고, 일부는 재생하는 데 상당한 비용이 들며, 일부는 전혀 재생할 수 없다. 지구는 매우 다양한 광물들로 구성되어 있는데, 그 광물들의 특성은 광물들을 구성하고 있는 성분뿐만 아니라 그 광물들이 어떻게 형성되었는지 그 역사에 따라서도 달라진다. 광물들의 양은 희소한 것부터 거의 무제한까지 다양하다. 그러나 자연 환경으로부터 그 광물들을 추출해 내는 어려움은 그 광물들의 양만큼이나 중요한 문제이다. 매우 다양한 광물들은 가령 철, 알루미늄, 마그네슘, 구리와 같은 필수적인 공업 원료를 위한 자원들이다. 상당수의 최고의 자원들이 고갈되어 가고 있고, 그 광물들을 구하기가 점점 더 어려워지고 비용이 많이 들고 있다.

08 ② being noted → noting

주어인 J.S. Mill이 언급된 것이 아니라 Wilhelm von Humboldt를 언급한 것이므로, 수동태 분사구문인 'being noted'는 능동 형태의 'noting'으로 바꿔 써야 옳다.

어휘

- continent : 대륙, 본토
- reject : 거부하다, 거절하다
- utilitarian : 공리주의의, 실용적인
- liberalism : 자유주의, 진보[개혁]주의
- put forward : 제안하다, 내세우다, 지명하다
- compatible : 호환이 되는, 양립될 수 있는
- autonomy : 자치권, 자주성, 자율성
- inspiration : 영감, 고취, 격려
- liberal : 자유주의의, 개혁주의의
- frontispiece : (책의) 권두 삽화, 머리 그림
- contemporary : 동시대인, 동년배
- convergence : 집중, 수렴, 통합
- deficiency : 결핍, 부족, 결점, 결함
- ethic : 윤리, 도덕
- individualism : 개성, 개인주의
- transmission : 전달, 전송, 전파
- rival : 경쟁[대항]하다, ~에 필적하다[비할 만하다]

해석

유럽 대륙에서 Kant는 자유주의의 공리주의 옹호를 거부했지만 바른 생활에 관한 자신만의 생각을 자유롭게 선택할 수 있는 사람에게만 오는 자율성과 양립 가능한 경우를 내세웠다. J.S. Mill은 다른 독일 자유주의자들에게 영감을 스스로 얻었고, 「자유론」이란 저서의 권두 삽화에서 동시대 사람인 Wilhelm von Humboldt를 언급했다. 그러나 독일과 영미 자유주의에 집중하던 시기는 곧 지나갔다. Hegel, Marx 그리고 독일 지식인들은 자유주의 사회의 특징을 보여준 개인주의의 도덕 결함을 집중적으로 탐구했다. Kant에서 Hegel과 Marx에 이르는 사상의 전파는 Plato에서 Aristotle과 Augustine에 이르는 초기 사상의 흐름과 견줄만큼 매우 극적이다.

09 ① (A) 광대역 인터넷을 사용하는데 통신 회사와 소비자 사이에 갭이 발생하는 이유는 통신회사들은 멀리 떨어진 가정에 비용 때문에 설치를 꺼리고, 반면에 저소득 가정은 감당하기에 요금이 비싸기 때문이다. 그러므로 'prohibitive(엄두를 못 낼 정도로 비싼)'이 적합하다.

(B) 현대 생활의 중요한 도구인 고속 인터넷을 통해 아이들이 배우고 어른들이 일하는 것을 가능하게 한다는 의미이므로, 'enabling'이 적합하다.

> - enable + 목적어 + to 부정사 : ~가 ~하는 것을 가능하게 하다
> - constrain + 목적어 + to 부정사 : ~가 ~하는 것을 못하게 하다

(C) 진정한 해결책은 가격을 낮추고 서비스를 높이기 위해 통신 회사 간 경쟁을 유도하는 것이므로, 'increased(증가된)'가 적합하다.

어휘

- broadband : 광대역, 고속 데이터 통신망
- take for granted : ~을 당연하게 여기다
- the Federal Communications Commission (FCC) : 연방 통신 위원회
- rural : 시골의, 지방의
- telecom company : 통신 회사
- balk : 멈칫하다, 꺼리다
- wire : 전선을 연결[가설]하다, 배선 공사를 하다
- far-flung : 먼, 멀리 떨어진
- low-income : 소득이 낮은, 저소득의
- fee : 요금, 수수료
- prohibitive : (가격 · 비용이) 엄두도 못 낼 정도로 높은[비싼]
- affordable : (가격이) 구입할 수 있는, 알맞은
- stream : 데이터 전송을 연속적으로 이어서 하다
- critical : 비판적인, 대단히 중요한[중대한]
- constrain : 제한[제약]하다, 못하게 하다
- digitally : 숫자로, 디지털 방식으로
- cloud : 클라우드 서비스(인터넷으로 연결된 데이터센터에 소프트웨어와 콘텐츠를 저장해 두고 필요할 때마다 꺼내 쓸 수 있는 서비스)
- subsidy : 보조금, 장려금
- competition : 경쟁, 대회, 시합

- notoriously : (나쁜 뜻으로) 유명하게, 악명 높게
- consolidated : 합병된, 통합된

<해석>

우리들 대부분은 광대역 인터넷을 당연한 것으로 여기지만, 그러나 거의 미국인 5명 중 1명은 그것에 접속하기가 어렵다고 연방 통신 위원회는 말한다. 교외 지역에서 통신 회사들은 멀리 떨어진 가정에 비용 때문에 설치를 꺼리는 반면에, 저소득 가족은 요금이 (A) 너무 비싸다고 한다. 광대역의 격차를 좁히는 것은 최신의 TV 드라마를 전송하는 것 이상으로 중요하다. 고속 인터넷은 현대 생활의 중요한 도구이며, 아이들이 디지털 방식으로 배우고 어른들이 클라우드 서비스를 통해 일하는 것을 (B) 가능하게 한다. 연방 통신 위원회는 최근에 소형 광대역 보조금을 승인했지만, 진짜 해결책은 악명 높은 합병 회사의 경쟁을 (C) 고조시키는 데 있다.

10 ③ (A) 후천적으로 획득된 것이 아니라, 개인들이 세상에 태어날 때부터 가지고 나오는 아이디어와 성향이므로, 'innate (선천적인, 타고난)'가 적합하다.

(B) 인간의 뇌는 선천적인 성향(호기심) 때문에 다른 모든 것을 무시하고 단지 가장 중요하고 흥미로운 것에만 관심을 보이므로, 'ignore(무시하다)'가 적합하다.

(C) 다른 모든 것을 무시하고 중요하고 흥미로운 것에 집중하는 능력이므로, 구별해 내는 유전자의 본성을 말한다. 그러므로 'discriminating(구별해 내는)'이 적합하다.

<어휘>

- evolutionary : 진화의, 진화론에 의한
- organism : 유기체, 생물
- conserve : 아껴 쓰다, 보호[보존]하다
- selectively : 선택적으로, 선별적으로
- criteria : 표준, 기준, 규준
- collective : 수집된, 모여진, 집합적인
- gene pool : 유전자 풀, 유전자 공급원
- species : 종(種)
- dole out : ~을 조금씩 나눠 주다
- innate : 선천적인, 타고난
- acquired : 후천적인, 획득한
- predisposition : 성향, 경향
- savannah : 사바나, 대초원
- adopt : 채택하다, 취하다
- home in on : ~을 향해 곧장 나아가다
- spear : 창, 작살
- annoyingly : 성가시게, 귀찮게
- infinite : 무한한, 한계가 없는
- trail : 흔적, 자취, 길

- in vain : 헛되이, 보람 없이
- worthwhile : 가치[보람] 있는, ~할 가치가 있는
- discriminating : 구별해 내는, 식별력[분별력]이 있는, 안목 있는
- integrating : 통합의
- grab : 붙잡다, 움켜잡다

<해석>

진화론 학자인 Henry Plotkin이 말하기를, 유기체가 수많은 세대를 거쳐 세상의 지식을 획득하면서, 진화는 필요의 기준에 따라 선택적으로 관련 지식을 보존하고, 그 수집된 지식은 종의 유전자 풀 내에 보관된다. 그렇게 수집된 지식은 개인에게 조금씩 나눠지고, 그 개인들은 특정한 방법으로 어떤 것들을 배우기 위해 (A) 타고난 아이디어와 성향을 가지고 세상에 태어난다. 바꾸어 말하면, 당신이 사바나에서 사냥을 하든 혹은 유튜브에서 수백만의 비디오들 중에서 고르든 간에, 당신의 뇌는 거의 모든 것을 (B) 무시하고 오로지 가장 중요하고 흥미로운 것을 향해 곧장 나아가도록 프로그래밍 되어 있다. 그와 달리, 당신은 마치 귀찮다는 듯이 아무 나무나 바위에 창을 찌르는 것처럼 무한한 비디오 링크들 속에서 길을 잃고 그 중 가치 있는 것을 찾아내기를 헛되이 바란다. 유전자의 (C) 구별해 내는 본성을 이해함으로써, 우리는 기억 속에 남아 관심을 사로잡을 만한 이야기의 토대를 구축하기 시작한다.

11 ④ drop → rise

그린란드와 남극 대륙의 대규모 빙상이 녹으면 가장 가까운 곳의 해수면이 가장 크게 상승할 것이라고 생각하기 쉽다. 그런데 글의 마지막 부분에서 '그것은 정말로 놀랍고 다소 직관에 반하는 결과'라고 했으므로, 인근의 해수면은 오히려 낮아지고 빙하가 녹는 곳으로부터 가장 멀리 떨어진 곳의 해수면이 가장 크게 상승한다는 것을 알 수 있다. 그러므로 ④의 'drop'은 'rise'로 바꿔 써야 옳다.

<어휘>

- sea level : 해수면
- globe : 지구, 지구본
- stretch of coast : 길게 펼쳐진 해안가
- ice bucket : 얼음 통
- Antarctica : 남극 대륙
- massive : 거대한, 엄청나게 큰
- exert : 가하다[행사하다], 노력하다, 애쓰다
- gravitational pull : 중력
- attraction : 끌어당기는 힘, 인력
- burden : 짐, 부담
- uplift : 들어 올리다, 융기하다
- diminish : 줄어들다, 약해지다

- meltwater : 해빙수, 빙하수
- counterintuitive : 반직관적인, 직관에 어긋나는
- geophysicist : 지구 물리학자

(해석)

어느 길게 펼쳐진 해안가를 따른 해수면의 상승은 지구의 커다란 두 얼음 통인 그린란드와 남극 대륙으로부터 해안이 얼마나 멀리 떨어져 있는가에 달려 있다. 가장 가까운 나라들이 빙상이 녹을 때 가장 크게 상승하리라는 것은 쉽게 생각할 수 있지만, 그것은 그리 간단하지만은 않다. 그린란드와 남극 대륙의 대규모 얼음덩이는 그 주위 바다에 강력한 중력을 가하지만, 빙하가 녹을 때 끌어당기는 힘이 약화되어 인근의 해수면이 낮아진다. 게다가 빙상의 무게에 대한 하중이 없어지면서 육지가 상승하고, 수면 위로 약간 올라오게 된다. 그 효과는 거리가 멀어지면 약해지는 데, 실제로 빙하가 녹는 곳으로부터 가장 멀리 떨어진 곳의 해수면이 가장 크게 상승하는 것을 볼 수 있다. "그것은 정말로 놀랍고 다소 직관에 반하는 결과이지만, 그것은 사실이다."라고 Harvard 대학의 지구 물리학자인 Jerry Mitrovica가 말한다.

12 ② endangers → defines

Adelie 펭귄들은 남극 대륙의 추운 바다 속에서 크릴새우를 먹이로 완벽하게 적응하여 살고 있으므로, 빙하가 그들의 존재를 위험에 빠뜨리는 것이 아니라 분명하게 드러내는 것이다. 그러므로 ②의 'endangers'는 'defines'로 바꿔 써야 옳다.

(어휘)

- pop up : 튀어나오다, 불쑥 나타나다
- simultaneously : 동시에, 일제히
- surround : 둘러싸다, 에워싸다, 포위하다
- as far as the eye can see : 끝이 안 보이게, 끝도 없이
- hesitate : 주저하다, 망설이다
- reluctant : 꺼리는, 주저하는
- watery : 물의, 물기가 많은
- effortlessly : 노력 없이, 쉽게
- endanger : 위험에 빠뜨리다, 위태롭게 만들다
- leap : 뛰어오르다, 껑충 뛰다
- excitedly : 흥분[격분]하여, 기를 쓰고
- frigid : 몹시 추운, 냉랭한
- literally : 문자[말] 그대로
- frozen : 냉동된, 얼어붙은
- microscopic : 현미경으로만 볼 수 있는, 미세한
- algae : 말, 조류(물속에 사는 하등 식물의 한 무리)
- in profusion : 풍부하게
- graze : 풀을 뜯다, 방목하다

- dense : 빽빽한, 밀집한
- swarm : 떼, 무리
- krill : 크릴새우
- shrimplike : 작은 새우 같은
- crustacean : 갑각류 동물(게 · 가재 · 새우 등)

(해석)

네 개의 작은 머리들이 끝도 없이 빙하로 둘러싸인 짙은 남빛 바다 속에서 동시에 튀어 오른다. 그들은 물고기만큼이나 쉽게 헤엄을 칠 수 있으므로 수중 세계를 떠나는 것을 망설이고 주저한다. 그들은 Adelie 펭귄이며, 빙하는 그들의 존재를 분명하게 드러낸다. 펭귄들은 촘촘한 원을 이루어 기를 쓰듯 뛰어오르고, 남극 대륙의 해안가를 둘러싼 이 추운 바다 속에서 완벽하고 쉽게 물속을 들락거린다. 펭귄의 먹이는 말 그대로 꽁꽁 얼어붙은 바다에 묶여 있다. 해빙의 층 속으로, 햇살이 넘칠 흐를 때 미세한 조류들이 풍부하게 꽃을 피운다. 여름이 시작될 무렵 해빙이 녹을 때, 얼음 속 조류는 물속에서 나와 작은 새우 모양의 갑각류 형태인 빽빽한 크릴새우 떼에게 뜯어 먹힌다. 크릴새우는 차례로, Adelie 펭귄의 주요 먹이 거리가 된다.

13 ④ unpredictable → predictable

사람의 성격이나 특징은 후천적인 환경에 의해서가 아니라 선천적인 유전적 요인에 의해 결정되며, 따라서 생애 초기에 나타나는 사람의 기질과 성격은 평생 동안 꽤 예측 가능한 상태로 남아 있다는 것이다. 그러므로 ④의 'unpredictable'은 'predictable'로 바꿔 써야 옳다.

(어휘)

- genome : 게놈(세포나 생명체의 유전자 총체)
- enormous : 거대한, 엄청난
- construction : 건설, 건축, 구조
- organism : 유기체, 생물
- gene : 유전자
- cognition : 인식, 인지
- psychological trait : 심리적 특성
- variation : 변화, 변형, 차이
- identical twins : 일란성 쌍생아
- fraternal twins : 이란성 쌍생아
- biological siblings : 생물학적 형제자매
- adoptive siblings : 입양으로 맺어진 형제자매
- raise : 기르다, 키우다
- temperament : 성질, 기질
- emerge : 나타나다, 출현하다
- unpredictable : 예측할 수 없는, 예측이 불가능한
- lifespan : 수명

- rear : 기르다, 양육하다
- neuroscience : 신경 과학
- architecture : 건축학, 건축 양식
- genetic : 유전의, 유전학의

해석

인간 게놈은 복잡한 생명체의 구조를 알려줄 엄청난 양의 정보를 포함하고 있다. 상당수의 경우, 특정 유전자들은 인지적 측면, 언어적 측면, 그리고 성격적 측면과 연관 지을 수 있다. 심리적 특성이 다를 때, 그 차이의 상당수는 유전자의 다름에서 온다. 즉, 함께 자랐던 따로 자랐던 간에, 일란성 쌍둥이가 이란성 쌍둥이보다 더 비슷하고, 생물학적 형제자매가 입양으로 맺어진 형제자매보다 더 비슷하다. 사람의 기질과 성격은 생애 초기에 나타나며 평생 동안 꽤 예측 가능한 상태로 남는다. 성격과 지능 둘 다 문화 내의 아이들의 특정 가정환경에 거의 영향이 없음을 보여준다. 동일한 가족 내에서 자란 아이들이 비슷한 것은 대게 공유된 유전자 때문이다. 더욱이 신경 과학은 뇌의 기본 구조가 유전적 통제 하에 발달된다는 것을 보여준다.

14 ② 의사 Walter Reed는 1869년에 Virginia 대학에서 의학 박사 학위를 수료했고, 1870년에 New York 대학의 Bellevue 의학 단과 대학에서 두 번째 의학 박사 학위를 취득했다.

오답풀이

① yellow fever가 모기에 의해 전염된다는 사실을 밝혀냈을 뿐, 백신을 개발했다는 내용은 없다.
③ 중국 아이가 아니라, 아메리카 원주민 소녀를 입양했다.
④ 그가 curator를 역임한 곳은 후에 국립 의료 박물관이 된 군 의학 박물관이다.
⑤ 그가 쿠바에 간 이유는 황열병을 연구하기 위해서이다.

어휘

- army physician : 군의관
- yellow fever : 황열병
- transmit : 전염시키다, 전송하다
- mosquito : 모기
- species : 종(種)
- M.D. degree : 의학 박사 학위
- adopt : 입양하다
- curator : 큐레이터(박물관·미술관 등의 전시 책임자)
- station : 배치하다, 주둔시키다, 가 있다, 보내다
- confirm : 확인하다, 확정하다
- commemorate : 기념하다
- achievement : 업적, 성취, 달성
- name after : ~의 이름을 따서 짓다[명명하다]

해석

의사 Walter Reed는 미국의 군의관으로 1901년에 황열병이 특정 모기 종에 의해 전염된다는 사실을 발견했다. 그는 Virginia에서 태어나 1869년에 Virginia 대학에서 의학 박사 학위를 수료했다. Reed는 1870년에 New York 대학의 Bellevue 의학 단과 대학에서 두 번째 의학 박사 학위를 취득했다. Reed는 의사로서 미군에 입대했다. 그리고 1876년에 결혼했다. 그 부부는 아들과 딸을 하나씩 두었고, 후에 아메리카 원주민 소녀를 입양했다. 그는 또한 나중에 국립 의료 박물관이 된 군 의학 박물관에서 큐레이터를 역임했다. 그는 황열병을 연구하기 위해 Cuba로 갔는데, 그 병으로 수천 명의 병사들이 숨졌다. 다른 의사들의 도움으로, Reed는 그 질병이 모기에 의해 전염된다는 사실을 확인했다. 이 발견으로 무수히 많은 생명을 구했다. 그의 업적을 기념하기 위해, 많은 미국의 병원들이 Reed의 이름을 따서 지어졌다.

15 ⑤ 탐사 중에 Sacajawea라는 16살 난 아메리카 원주민 여성을 알게 되었고, 그녀의 도움으로 인디언으로부터 말들을 얻어 아무런 문제없이 인디언 지역을 통과했다.

오답풀이

① 미국은 영국이 아니라 프랑스로부터 Louisiana 지역 전체를 매입했다.
② 미시시피 강이 어디서 시작되고 로키 산맥이 정확히 어디에 위치하는지 아무도 확신하지 못했다.
③ 탐사 대원들은 추천이 아닌 자발적인 미군 지원자들로 구성되었다.
④ 탐사는 1804년 5월부터 1806년 9월까지 계속되었으므로, 모든 탐사를 마치기까지 2년 4개월의 기간이 걸렸다.

어휘

- purchase : 구입하다, 매입하다
- territory : 지역, 영토, 영역
- commission : 의뢰하다, 주문하다
- expedition : 탐험, 탐사, 원정
- comprise : ~으로 구성되다[이뤄지다]
- captain : (미국 육군·공군·해병대의) 대위
- a first(second) lieutenant : 중(소)위
- volunteer : 지원자, 자원 봉사자
- command : 관할부대, 지휘부, 사령부
- perilous : 아주 위험한
- objective : 목적, 목표
- depart : 출발하다, 떠나다
- become acquainted with : ~을 알게 되다, ~와 아는 사이이다

해석

1803년에 미국 정부는 프랑스로부터 Louisiana 지역 전체를 매입했다. 그 지역은 미시시피 강에서 로키 산맥의 중앙에 이르지만, 미시시피 강이 어디서 시작되고 로키 산맥이 정확히 어디에 위치하는지 정말 아무도 확신하지 못했다. Thomas Jefferson 대통령은 이 지역에 탐사를 의뢰했다. 탐사대는 대위 Meriwether Lewis와 소위 William Clark의 통솔 하에 미군 지원자들의 선발팀으로 구성되었다. 그들의 위험한 탐사는 1804년 5월부터 1806년 9월까지 계속되었다. 그들의 주요 목적은 새로 얻은 영토를 탐험하고 지도를 만들어, 그 대륙의 서쪽 절반을 가로지르는 실제 길을 찾아내는 것이다. Lewis와 Clark은 43명의 사람들과 출발해 2년 동안 지원했다. 그들은 Bird Woman이란 의미인 Sacajawea라는 16살 난 아메리카 원주민 여성을 알게 되었다. 그녀의 도움으로 Lewis와 Clark은 인디언으로부터 말들을 얻어 아무런 문제없이 인디언 지역을 통과했다.

16 ⑤ Halibut은 현재 태평양(The Pacific) 지역이 아니라, 대서양(The Atlantic) 지역 사람들에 의해 남획으로 고갈되어 멸종위기 종으로 공표되었다.

어휘

• principally : 주로
• apply to : ~에 적용되다
• flatfish : 넙치류 생선
• flounder : 가자미과의 바닷물고기
• underbelly : 아랫배 부분
• scale : 비늘
• naked eye : 육안, 나안
• embedded : 내장된, 삽입된
• migrate : 이동하다, 이주하다
• boiled : 끓은, 삶은
• deep-fried : 튀긴
• grilled : 석쇠에 구운
• salmon : 연어
• ultra-low fat : 초저지방
• depleted : 열화된, 감손된
• overfishing : 남획
• declare : 선언하다, 공표하다

해석

Halibut은 북대서양과 북태평양에 서식하는 오른 눈 가자미 과의 양눈 넙치와 생선에 주로 붙여지는 이름이다. Halibut은 위쪽은 어두운 갈색이고 아랫배 부분은 하야며 껍질에 박혀서 육안으로는 잘 보이지 않는 아주 작은 비늘이 있다. 부화할 때, 그것은 머리 양쪽에 눈이 달려 있다. 6개월 후 한 쪽 눈이

다른 쪽 눈으로 이동한다. Halibut은 신선할 때 삶거나 튀기거나 구워 먹는다. Halibut은 지방 함유량이 매우 낮기 때문에 연어보다 훈제하기는 더 어렵다. 현재 대서양 사람들의 남획으로 고갈되어 멸종위기 종으로 공표되었다.

17 ⑤ 마지막 문장에서 Rosenzweig 교수가 비록 왜래종이 멸종을 초래하더라도, 결국 그 멸종 단계는 끝나며, 새로운 종이 진화를 시작할 것이라고 설명하고 있으므로 ⑤의 설명은 윗글의 내용과 일치하지 않는다.

어휘

• alien species : 외래 종
• ecologist : 생태학자, 생태[환경] 운동가
• define : 정의하다, 규정하다, 분명히 밝히다
• inadvertently : 무심코, 우연히, 부주의로
• deliberately : 고의로, 의도적으로
• habitat : 서식지
• ecology : 생태(계), 생태학
• evolutionary biology : 진화 생물학
• appearances : 외모, 외관, 모습
• deceive : 속이다, 기만하다
• caution : 조심, 경고, 주의
• exotics : 외래종
• non-native : 토종이 아닌, 외래종의
• innocuous : 악의 없는, 무해한
• decades : 10년
• invasive : 급속히 퍼지는, 침투[침략]하는
• uncertainty : 불확실성, 반신반의
• approach : 접근법, 처리 방법
• natural ecosystem : 자연 생태계
• roll back : 되돌리다, 복원하다
• impractical : 터무니없는, 비현실적인
• a prevailing view : 우세한 견해
• biodiversity : 생물의 다양성
• extinction : 멸종, 소멸
• phase : 국면, 단계
• evolve : 진화하다, 발달하다

해석

생태학자들은 일반적으로 외래종을 사람들이 무심코 혹은 일부러 새로운 장소로 옮겨놓은 것이라고 규정하고 있다. "아주 소수의 왜래종도 새로운 서식지에서 문제를 일으킨다."라고 어는 생태학 교수이자 진화 생물학자가 말한다. 그럼에도 불구하고 겉모습에 속기 쉽고, 생태학자들이 이러한 외래종의 상당수가 단지 아무런 해를 끼치지 않은 것으로 보고되었다는 이유만으로 받아들여도 된다고 경고했다. 더욱이 이 외래

종은 수십 년 동안 무해한 모습으로 있다가 돌연 급속히 퍼질 수 있다. 그러한 불확실성 때문에, 많은 생태학자들은 강한 조치가 취해져야 한다고 주장한다. 그들의 처리 방법은 자연 생태계에서 왜래종을 제거하는 것이다. 그러나 많은 전문가들은 더 자연적이었던 때로 생태계 복원을 시도하는 과학적 지식에 의문을 제기한다. 심지어 생태계에서 모든 외래종을 제거하고자 하는 많은 생태학자들도 이런 목표가 비현실적이라는 것을 인정한다. 나아가 Arizona 대학의 Rosenzweig 교수는 침투 왜래종이 생물의 다양성을 감소시킨다는 다수의 견해를 반박한다. 왜래종은 자연 환경에서 종(種)의 수를 증가시킨다. 비록 왜래종이 멸종을 초래하더라도, 결국 그 멸종 단계는 끝나며, 새로운 종이 진화를 시작할 것이라고 그는 설명한다.

18 ④ 지역사회가 200년 전에 기술된 헌법에 의해 통제받는 것이 늘 빈가운 것은 아니지만, 헌법을 개성하는 절차가 워낙 까다롭기 때문에 기존의 헌법을 유연하게 해석하여 사용토록 압박을 받는다는 의미이므로, 빈칸에 들어갈 말로는 'flexible(유연한, 융통성 있는)'이 가장 적절하다.

오답풀이

① 더 이상 쓸모가 없는, 한물간
② 번역된, 번안된
③ 간결한, 축약된
⑤ 재판의, 판결의

어휘

• judge : 판사, 심판
• statute : 법규, 법령
• constitution : 헌법, 규칙, 규약
• devise : 창안[고안]하다
• refine : 개선하다, 개량하다
• a rule of conduct : 행동 강령
• have a significant impact on : 중대한 영향을 미치다
• procedure : 절차, 방법
• amend : 개정[수정]하다
• cumbersome : 다루기 힘든, 번거로운
• interpretive : 해석상의, 설명을 제공하는
• original document : 원문

해석

판사들은 지역사회의 복지에 중대한 영향을 미칠지도 모르는 행동 강령을 창안하고 개선하는 데 도움이 되고자 법규와 헌법을 판독한다. 그 지역사회는 200년 전에 살았던 사람들이 기술한 헌법에 의해 선택을 통제받는 것을 늘 달가워하는 것은 아니다. 그러나 헌법을 개정하는 과정은 매우 번거로워서 판사들은 원문을 유연하게 해석하는 과정을 이용하도록 큰 압박을 받는다.

19 ② 윗글의 요지는 좋은 것을 혼자서 경험하기 보다는 친구와 나누는 것이 배가된다는 의미이다. 즉, 본문의 내용상 친구와 Grand Canyon을 함께 보는 즐거움이 서로 다른 날에 각자 보는 즐거움을 합친 것보다 크다는 의미이다. 그러므로 빈칸에는 'is more than the sum of(합친 것 이상이다.)'가 들어가는 것이 가장 적합하다.

오답풀이

① 나눌 수 있다.
③ 합친 양과 같다.
④ 더 오래 동안 기억 속에 지속될 수 있다.
⑤ 고려할 필요가 없다.

어휘

• share A with B : A를 B와 공유하다[나누다]
• on separate days : 별도의 날에, 서로 다른 날에
• divide into : ~으로 나누다
• combined : 결합된, 합한
• take into consideration : ~을 고려[참작]하다

해석

가령, 내가 Grand Canyon에 간다. 그 광경에 너무 즐거워 친한 친구에게 "네가 여기 있었으면 정말 좋았을 텐데"라고 간단한 메시지를 적은 엽서를 보낸다. 이런 친숙한 말을 하는 의미는 무엇일까? 내가 친구와 함께 그 광경을 공유했다면 Grand Canyon을 보는 즐거움이 훨씬 더 컸을 거라는 의미이다. 내가 의미하는 것은 혼자 Grand Canyon에 있어 좋은 것보다, 친구와 함께 이 경험을 공유할 수 있다면 훨씬 더 좋다는 것이다. 바꾸어 말하면, 내 엽서는 친구들이 특별한 의미에서 Grand Canyon을 함께 보는 즐거움을 공유하는 것이 서로 다른 날에 Grand Canyon을 보는 나와 친구의 즐거움을 합친 것 이상이라고 말하고 있는 것이다.

20 ③ 빈칸의 다음 문장에서 "코요테는 항상 굶주린다. 항상 빈곤하고 불운하고 친구가 없다."고 서술하고 있으므로, 굶주림, 빈곤 등과 관련된 단어를 유추해 보면 'want(부족, 결핍, 가난, 빈곤)'와 상통한다. 그러므로 'allegory of want(빈곤의 풍자)'가 들어갈 말로 가장 적합하다.

오답풀이

① 분노의 전형
② 가학의 비유
④ 능률의 상징
⑤ 지배의 비유

어휘

• coyote : 코요테
• slim : 가냘픈, 호리호리한, 마른

- sorry-looking : 초라해[불쌍해] 보이는
- skeleton : 뼈대, 골격, 해골
- tolerably : 상당히, 어지간히
- bushy : 숱이 많은, 무성한
- sag : 축 처지다, 늘어지다
- furtive : 은밀한, 엉큼한, 음흉한
- slink : 살금살금[슬그머니] 움직이다
- mean : 천박한, 하찮은, 보잘 것 없는
- despise : 경멸하다, 멸시하다
- flea : 벼룩
- desert : 버리다, 떠나다
- in a blink of an eye : 눈 깜박할 사이에
- epitome : (본)보기, 전형
- wrath : 분노, 노여움
- analogy : 비유, 유추
- sadism : 사디즘, 가학증
- allegory : 우화, 풍자
- efficiency : 효율, 능률
- metaphor : 은유, 비유
- dominance : 우월, 지배

해석

코요테는 길고 마르고 병들고 앙상한 뼈대에, 회색 늑대 가죽으로 덮여 있고, 항상 축 늘어진 숱이 무성한 꼬리와, 음흉하고 사악한 눈, 그리고 살짝 입술을 들어 이빨을 드러낸 채 길고 날카로운 얼굴을 하고 있다. 코요테는 줄곧 살금살금 움직이는 표정을 짓는다. 코요테는 살아 숨 쉬는 <u>빈곤의 풍자</u>이다. 코요테는 항상 굶주린다. 항상 빈곤하고 불운하고 친구가 없다. 가장 하찮은 생물체도 코요테를 깔보는 데, 벼룩조차 눈 깜박할 사이에 떠나버린다.

21 ① 식품 제조사들이 호두까기에 성공했을 경우에는 온전한 호두를 '온전한 호두'라는 라벨이 붙은 병에 넣고, 그렇지 못한 경우에는 껍질로부터 호두를 분리하여 '호두 조각들'이라는 라벨을 붙인 병에 넣는 것이므로, 그들이 행한 어떤 일이란 호두까기의 결과물들을 선별하는 작업이다. 그러므로 빈칸에는 'selected their results(그들의 결과물들을 선별했다.)'가 들어가는 것이 적절하다.

오답풀이
② 특별한 종류의 호두를 재배했다.
③ 새로운 상표의 장비를 사용했다.
④ 판매용 호두와 섞었다.
⑤ 교훈을 어렵게 배웠다.

어휘
- impress : 깊은 인상을 주다, 감명[감동]을 주다

- walnut : 호두
- crack : 깨뜨리다, 부수다
- shell : 껍데기, 껍질
- intact : 온전한, 손상되지 않은
- manage to : 가까스로 ~하다, 간신히 ~하다
- manufacturer : 제조재[사], 생산업자
- stick : 집어넣다[놓다]
- breed : 사육하다, 재배하다

해석

어렸을 때 나는 식품 제조사들이 어떻게 온전한 호두를 병에 채울 수 있는지 깊은 인상을 받았다. 그들은 어떤 식으로든 호두가 손상되지 않도록 껍질을 깰 수 있다. 내가 그것을 여러 번 시도해 보았지만, 결국에 껍질과 호두가 섞이고 말았고, 대략 열 번 중 겨우 한 번만 온전한 호두를 간신히 얻었다. 그러나 나중에 비록 제조사들이 나보다 성공 확률이 더 높지만, 그들도 종종 껍질과 호두가 섞인다는 사실을 알았다. 그러나 나는 또한 그들이 그밖에 어떤 일을 한다는 것을 알았다. 즉, 그들은 <u>그들의 결과물들을 선별</u>했다. 그들이 성공했을 경우에, 온전한 호두를 '온전한 호두'라는 라벨이 붙은 병에 넣는다. 그리고 다른 경우에, 그들은 껍질로부터 호두를 분리하고 '호두 조각들'이라는 라벨을 붙인 병에 넣는다.

22 ① 빈칸의 앞 문장에서 나와 전쟁을 벌일 당신의 생존권을 기꺼이 포기하는 정도라면, 나도 당신과 전쟁을 벌일 나의 생존권을 기꺼이 포기할 것이라고 했다. 즉, 상호간에 (reciprocally) 전쟁을 포기하는 것이므로 '상호 무장해제 (mutual disarming)'에 해당된다. 그러므로 ①의 내용이 빈칸에 들어갈 말로 가장 적합하다.

오답풀이
① 이러한 상호 무장해제는 각 개인 자신의 이익을 위해서다.
② 이러한 공유된 무관심은 사회의 평화를 촉진한다.
③ 이러한 상호 권리 포기는 적대감의 조장을 의미한다.
④ 이러한 사회적 타협은 자연 법칙을 강화하는데 공헌한다.
⑤ 이러한 전쟁 발발의 규제는 약자들의 편에 정말로 이롭다.

어휘
- natural rights : 자연권, 생존권
- vital : 생명의, 생명유지에 필요한
- derive A from B : B에서 A를 얻다[끌어내다]
- surrender : 항복하다, 굴복하다
- wage : (전쟁·전투 등을) 벌이다[계속하다]
- to the extent that : ~할 정도까지, ~한 결과로
- reciprocally : 서로, 호혜적으로, 상호간에
- individually : 개별적으로, 각각 따로
- security : 보안, 안보

- mutual : 서로의, 상호간의
- disarming : 상대방을 무장해제 시키는
- self–interest : 자신의 이익, 사익, 사리사욕
- indifference : 무관심
- promote : 촉진하다, 고취하다
- reciprocal : 상호간의
- foster : 조성[조장]하다, 촉진하다
- animosity : 반감, 적대감
- compromise : 타협, 절충
- be conducive to : ~에 공헌하다, 이바지하다
- reinforce : 강화하다, 보강하다
- restraint : 규제, 통제, 제한

해석

Hobbes의 특정 어휘인 '생존권'은 우리가 이미 자연 상태에서 소유하고 있는 것이다. 즉, 우리의 생명 활동을 보호하는 어떤 일을 할 수 있는 권리이다. Hobbes는 자연 상태에서 죽음에 대한 공포로부터 첫 번째 자연법칙을 끌어낸다. 그는 첫 번째 법칙으로부터 두 번째 법칙을 끌어낸다. 즉, 상호간에 나와 전쟁을 벌일 당신의 생존권을 기꺼이 포기하는 정도라면, 나도 당신과 전쟁을 벌일 나의 생존권을 기꺼이 포기할 것이다. <u>이러한 상호 무장해제는 각 개인 자신의 이익을 위해서다.</u> 각각이 개별적으로 전쟁의 권리를 포기하는데 동의하면서 '자신에게 이로운 것'을 추구하고, 이런 이로움은 오로지 '개인 한 사람의 안전'뿐이다.

23 ③ 윗글은 문화 학습에 대해 설명하고 있는데, 마지막 문장에서 문화 학습은 학습자가 다른 사람으로부터가 아니라 다른 사람을 통해 배우려고 시도하는 학습이라고 했으므로, 학습자가 다른 사람의 활동을 직접 배우는 것에 국한되지 않고 그들이 그런 활동을 하는 방식과 관점까지도 학습하는 것이라고 볼 수 있다. 그러므로 ③의 내용이 빈칸에 들어갈 말로 적합하다.

오답풀이

① 그들은 다른 사람들을 이해하기 위해 자신의 통찰력에 의존한다.
② 그들은 전반적인 문화 융통성을 광범위하게 향상시킨다.
③ 그들은 다른 사람들이 그것을 바라보는 방식이 어떤 상황인지 보려고 시도한다.
④ 그들은 다른 사람들의 숨은 의도를 추측하는 것을 배운다.
⑤ 그들은 스스로 자율 학습에 참여하도록 권한을 부여한다.

어휘

- stimulus : 자극, 고무, 격려
- enhancement : 강화, 증대, 인상
- indispensable : 없어서는 안 될, 필수적인

- cognitive development : 인지 발달
- species : 종(種)
- qualitatively : 질적으로
- engage in : ~에 관여[참여]하다
- direct one's attention to : ~에 주의를 돌리다, 눈길을 돌리다
- extensively : 널리, 광범위하게
- enhance : 높이다, 향상시키다, 강화하다
- flexibility : 융통성, 유연성
- second–guess : 예측[추측]하다, 사후에[뒤늦게] 비판하다
- hidden agenda : 숨은 의도, 비밀 의제
- empower : 권한을 주다[부여하다]
- autonomous learning : 자율 학습

해석

자극 혹은 지역 강화의 형태로서의 사회적 학습은 많은 사회적 종들의 인지 발달에서처럼, 인간 발달에 있어 필수적인 역할을 한다. 그러나 어떤 경우에, 인간은 서로로부터 질적으로 다른 방식으로 배운다. 때때로 인간은 소위 문화 학습이라 부르는 것에 참여한다. 문화 학습에서 학습자는 그들의 관심을 다른 개인의 활동에만 두는 것이 아니라, 오히려 그들은 다른 사람들이 그것을 바라보는 방식이 어떤 상황인지 보려고 시도한다. 문화 학습은 학습자가 다른 사람으로부터가 아니라 다른 사람을 통해 배우려고 시도하는 학습이다.

24 ④ (A) However

경제학자들이 경제 발전을 측정하는 데 사용하는 가장 보편적인 도구가 국내 총생산(GDP)이라는 앞의 내용과 GDP 통계는 꽤 오해의 소지가 있을 수 있다는 뒤의 내용이 서로 상반되므로 역접의 접속사 'However(그러나)'를 사용해야 한다.

(B) Moreover

GDP 통계는 꽤 오해의 소지가 있을 수 있다는 근거로 우선 국가 간 상대적 생활비용 차이를 하나의 사례로 들었고, 다음에 국가 통화 간 환율 문제를 추가적인 근거로 설명하고 있다. 그러므로 부연 설명을 위해 'Moreover(더욱이)'가 들어가는 것이 적절하다.

어휘

- criterion : 표준, 기준, 척도
- gross domestic product (GDP) : 국내 총생산
- benchmark : 기준(점), 표준
- per capita : 1인당
- statistics : 통계, 통계학
- misleading : 호도[오도]하는, 오해의 소지가 있는
- raw figure : 원 수치, 실제 수치
- take into account : ~을 고려하다, ~을 계산에 넣다

- relative : 비교상의, 상대적인
- exchange rate : 환율, 외환 시세
- currency : 통화, 통용, 유통

해석

국가를 비교하기 위한 기본 척도의 하나가 경제 발전 수준이다. 경제학자들이 경제 발전을 측정하는 데 사용하는 가장 보편적인 도구가 국내 총생산(GDP)이다. GDP는 한 국가의 1인당 평균 소득의 기본적 기준점을 제공한다. (A) 그러나 GDP 통계는 꽤 오해의 소지가 있을 수 있다. 우선 사람들이 어떤 국가에서 다른 나라 사람들보다 훨씬 더 많이 돈을 벌수도 있지만, 그 원 수치가 그 국가에서 사는 데 필요한 상대적 비용을 고려하지는 않는다. (B) 더욱이 국가 통화 간 환율이 오르고 내릴 때, 국가들은 실제보다 더 부유하거나 더 가난해 보일 수 있다.

25　③ 윗글에 따르면 과체중일 때 건강관리를 시작하면, 진료실 뿐만 아니라 옷을 구입하는데 그리고 생명 보험을 드는데 추가로 비용이 들어간다고 설명하고 있다. 그러므로 ③의 'The Price You Pay for Extra Pounds(과체중으로 지불하는 비용)'이 윗글의 제목으로 가장 적절하다.

오답풀이

① 건강관리 비용의 증가
② 살을 빼라, 그러면 병의 위험도 낮아진다.
④ 비만인 사람들이 옷을 사는 데 더 많은 돈을 쓰는가?
⑤ 체질량 지수(BMI) : 정확한 몸무게 지표는 아니다.

어휘

- extra pounds : 과체중
- body mass index (BMI) : 체질량 지수
- annual : 매년의, 연간의
- deem : ~로 여기다, 생각하다
- obese : 비만인
- the lower end : 하단부
- add-on : 부가물, 추가물
- estimate : 평가하다, 추산[추정]하다
- aggregate : 종합하다, 총계 ~이 되다
- insurance : 보험, 보험료
- accurate : 정확한, 정밀한
- indicator : 지표, 계기[장치]

해석

과체중일 때 건강관리를 시작하면 추가로 비용이 든다. 2013년 Duke의 연구에서, 연구원들은 체질량 지수(BMI) 수치에 따라 드는 건강관리 비용을 조사했다. 저체중인 체질량 지수(BMI)가 19인 사람의 평균 연간 비용은 2,541달러였다. 과체중이라고 생각되는 체질량 지수(BMI)가 25인 사람은 2,893달러였다. 비만이라 여겨지는 체질량 지수(BMI)가 33인 사람은 3,439달러로 비용이 가장 높았다. "정상 체중의 하단부에서부터 병의 위험도는 이미 증가하기 시작한다."고 대표 연구원인 Truls Ostbye는 말한다. 추가 비용은 진료실에서만 끝나지 않는다. 2010 McKinsey 연구는 비만인 미국인들이 추가로 옷을 사는데 들어가는 비용이 총 300억 달러에 이를 것으로 추산했다. 또한 비만인 40세 남성이 생명 보험에 내는 비용이 두 배에 이를 것으로 추산했다.

26　③ 매년 자동차 경쟁 시장에서 정상에 오르기 위해 새로운 디자인과 보다 큰 모델을 출시하던 진부한 관행에서 벗어나, Volkswagen사의 크지 않고 효율적인 소형 자동차를 알리기 위한 솔직하고 재미있는 광고 기법을 소개하고 있다. 그러므로 ③의 'New Ad : Step Down From Your Ladders(새로운 광고 : 사다리에서 내려오기)'가 윗글의 제목으로 가장 적절하다.

오답풀이

① 어려운 경제 시대 : 작게 생각하라.
② 자동차 경쟁 사다리의 정상에서
④ 자동차가 사회적 지위를 나타내는가?
⑤ 국제 자동차 전쟁 : 크기의 중요성

어휘

- ladder : 사다리, 단계(조직 · 활동 분야 등에서 성공하기 위해 밟고 올라가는)
- employ : 고용하다, 이용하다, 쓰다
- perceived : 인지된, 감지된
- obsolescence : 노후화, 진부화
- roll out : (신상품을) 출시하다, 시작하다
- embarrassing : 난처한, 당혹스러운, 쑥스러운
- worn-out : 닳아 해진, 낡은, 헌
- provoke : 유발[도발]하다, 야기하다, 짜증나게 하다
- anxiety : 불안, 염려, 근심
- seemingly : 외견상으로, 겉보기에는
- out of nowhere : 어디선지 모르게, 아무 데도 없는 곳에서
- unadorned : 아무런 장식[꾸밈]이 없는
- modest : 보통의, 크지 않은, 겸손한, 수수한
- efficient : 능률적인, 효율적인
- flivver : 싸구려 소형 자동차
- contemporary : 동시대의, 당대의, 현대의
- slang : 속어, 은어
- junk : 고물, 폐물, 쓰레기
- shockingly : 깜짝 놀랄 만큼, 엄청나게
- hilarious : 아주 우스운, 재미있는

- publicly : 공공연하게, 공개적으로
- unnamed : 이름이 없는, 익명의, 무명의
- instill in : ~에게 심어주다, 주입하다
- Who cares? : 누가 상관이나 한대[알 게 뭐야?]
- represent : 대표[대신]하다, 표현하다, 나타내다
- status : 지위, 신분
- warfare : 전쟁, 전투, 투쟁

해석

자동차 사다리를 오르는 일은 힘들며, 정상을 유지하기란 더욱 힘들었다. 매년 오래된 관행에 따라 Chevrolet는 전체를 새롭게 디자인하고, 보통 더 큰 모델을 출시했다. 어제 최신식이었던 자동차는 내일은 작고 쑥스럽고 구식처럼 보였다. 상상하는 것처럼, 이 모든 것이 미국 사회 전반에 걸쳐 불안감을 야기했다. 그런데 1959년에 외견상으로 어디선지 모르게, 단순한 전면 신문 광고가 "작게 생각하라."는 헤드라인과 아무런 장식이 없는 Volkswagen사의 Beetle 자동차 이미지와 함께 실리기 시작했다. 그 광고는 자동차가 크지 않고 효율적이라는 것을 제외하고는 그 이상 말하지 않았고, 심지어 Beetle 자동차를 고물덩어리라는 당시 속어인 'flivver(싸구려 소형 자동차)'라 불렀다. 사람들은 그 광고가 깜짝 놀랄 만큼 솔직하고 재미있으며, 마케팅 담당자들이 수년 동안 그들 마음속에 품어왔던 남모르는 불안감을 공개적으로 표출했다고 생각했다. 내가 사다리 꼭대기에 올라가야만 하는가? 누가 상관하겠는가?

27 ① 윗글에 따르면 보통 어린 아이들이 특정 야채 먹기를 강하게 거부하는 데는 합당한 이유가 있는데, 그것은 혐오감이 낯설거나 해로운 물체에 대한 보호 메커니즘으로 작용하여 위험물의 섭취를 막을 뿐 아니라 사람들이 잠재적으로 전염 가능한 상황에 빠지지 않도록 해준다고 설명하고 있다. 그러므로 윗글의 주제로는 ①의 'the role of disgust in keeping people safe(사람들을 안전하게 지키는 혐오감의 역할)'이 적절하다.

오답풀이

② 적당한 영양분 섭취의 유익함
③ 위험과 전염의 차이점
④ 해로운 물질을 피하는 중요함
⑤ 유익한 위생 활동의 연습 필요성

어휘

- disgust : 혐오감, 역겨움, 질색
- be associated with : ~와 관련되다
- obdurate : 고집 센, 완고한
- refusal : 거절, 거부
- absurd : 우스꽝스러운, 터무니없는, 불합리한

- nutritious : 영양분이 많은, 영양가가 높은
- hygienic : 위생적인
- contend : 주장하다, 다투다
- protective : 보호하는, 방어하는
- mechanism : 기계 장치[기구], 방법, 메커니즘
- harmful : 해로운, 유해한
- deter : 단념시키다, 그만두게 하다
- ingestion : 섭취
- dissuade : ~를 설득[만류]하다, 권하다, 충고하다
- potentially : 가능성 있게, 잠재적으로
- contagious : 전염되는, 전염성의
- declare : 선언[단언]하다, 공표하다
- railcar : 철도 차량
- lice : (louse의 복수) 이
- wasp : 말벌
- contagion : 전염(병), 감염

해석

혐오감에 대한 정서적 반응은 보통 어린 아이들이 특정 야채 먹기를 강하게 거부하는 것과 관련이 있다. 그런 혐오감이 아이들에게 영양가 높은 음식을 먹이려고 하는 부모들에게는 터무니없는 일처럼 보이지만, 위생적인 행동에 관심이 있는 과학자들은 합당한 설명을 하고 있다. 이 이론은 사람들이 혐오감을 낯설거나 해로울 법한 물체에 대한 보호 메커니즘으로 발전시킨다고 주장했다. 최근의 연구는 혐오감이 위험물의 섭취를 막을 뿐 아니라 사람들이 잠재적으로 전염 가능한 상황에 빠지지 않도록 해준다고 말한다. 예를 들어 그 연구 대상자들은 사람들로 붐비는 철도 차량이 텅 빈 차량보다 더 혐오스러우며 이가 말벌보다 더 혐오스럽다고 단언했다.

28 ② 과학자로서 논문이 출판되었다고 성공한 것은 아니며 동료들이 그 논문을 이해하고 동기를 얻기 위해 인용할 때 비로소 성공한 것이라고 했으므로, ②의 'the importance of influencing others in scientific writing(과학 논문이 다른 사람들에게 미치는 영향의 중요성)'이 윗글의 주제에 해당된다.

오답풀이

① '더 많이 쓸수록, 더 좋다.'는 오래된 신념
③ 미지의 영역에서 연구를 계속해야 할 필요성
④ 저널 수록에 필요한 우호적인 동료들의 견해
⑤ 출판에 있어서 직업윤리와 엄격한 자질 통제

어휘

- perish : 죽다, 소멸하다, 사라지다
- dominate : 지배[군림]하다, 억제하다
- cite : 인용하다, 예로 들다
- define : 정의하다, 규정하다, 분명히 밝히다

- peer : 또래, 동년배
- enduring : 오래가는, 지속되는
- pursue : 추구하다, 추적하다
- unexplored : 탐험[탐구]되지 않은, 미지의
- favorable : 우호적인, 찬성하는
- acceptance : 수용, 수락, 동의, 승인
- ethics : 윤리학

해석

과학자로서의 성공 여부는 단순히 머릿속에 가지고 있는 아이디어 혹은 손에 주고 있는 정보의 기능뿐이 아니라 그것들을 기술하는 데 사용하는 언어의 기능에 달려 있다. 우리 모두는 '출판하거나 혹은 도태되거나'가 현실이며 전문가의 삶을 지배한다고 알고 있다. 그러나 '출판하거나 혹은 도태되거나'는 생존에 관한 것이지 성공에 관련된 것은 아니다. 과학자로서 논문이 출판되었다고 성공한 것은 아니다. 그 논문이 인용되어야 과학자로서 성공한 것이다. 당신의 일을 중요하게 만드는 것이 중요하다. 성공은 인쇄한 페이지 수에 의해 정의되는 것이 아니라 그 논문의 영향력에 의해 정의된다. 동료들이 여러분의 작품을 이해하고 그들이 직접 동기를 얻는데 사용할 때 비로소 당신은 성공한 것이다.

29 ⑤ 장수를 하기 위해 엄격한 채식주의자가 되거나 철저한 운동과 명상 등을 하지 않고 아주 작은 변화만으로도 건강한 삶을 유지할 수 있다고 설명하고 있으므로, 윗글의 요지는 ⑤의 "Achieving longevity is not as difficult as one might imagine.(장수를 하는 것은 상상하는 것만큼 어렵지는 않다.)"이다.

오답풀이

① 건강한 생활 방식으로 살아가기가 말처럼 쉽지는 않다.
② 식단의 중요한 변화는 오래 사는 데 도움이 된다.
③ 주로 앉아서 생활하는 사람들에게 운동은 중요하다.
④ 육체적 그리고 정신적 행복은 열심히 일하는 가운데 성취할 수 있다.

어휘

- vegan : 엄격한 채식주의자
- pledge : 약속, 맹세, 서약
- allegiance : 충성
- cult : 추종, 숭배, 동경, 예찬, 제례[의식]
- meditator : 묵상가, 명상가
- longevity : 장수, 오래 지속됨
- extend : 늘이다, 연장하다, 확장[확충]하다
- attainable : 이룰 수 있는, 달성할 수 있는
- miserable : 비참한, 우울한
- logging : (컴퓨터)log하기, 로그인, 접속하여 시작하기

- gym : 체육관
- counteract : 대응하다, 거스르다, 방해하다
- fidget : 꼼지락거리다, 가만히 못 있다
- excruciating : 몹시 고통스러운, 극심한
- sedentary : 주로 앉아서 하는

해석

건강한 습관으로 장기간 지속되는 혜택을 얻으려고 엄격한 채식주의자가 되거나 운동 예찬에 충성 맹세를 하거나 온종일 명상가가 될 필요는 없다. 사실 최신 과학에서 정 반대의 결과를 보여주었다. 즉, 건강한 삶을 확충하는 것은 우리들 대부분이 아주 작은 변화만으로도 이룰 수 있고, 이러한 변화는 특히 어렵다거나 우울하게 만드는 것은 아니다. 연구원들은 예를 들면 체육관에 가는 시간이 장기간 앉아 있는 부정적인 영향을 대응할 수는 없지만 몸을 조금씩 움직이는 단순한 동작만으로도 가능하다는 것을 알아냈다. 그들은 또한 얼마큼 많이 먹는 것을 줄여야 하는지 고통스러워할 필요가 없고 그것이 장수할 수 있는 가능성을 높일 수 있다는 사실을 밝혀냈다.

30 ② David가 악몽과 같았던 직장을 그만두고 새로운 시작의 가능성을 열기 시작했으므로, David의 심경은 '안도와 희망적 (relieved and hopeful)'이라고 말할 수 있다.

오답풀이

① 슬프고 불안한
③ 지루하고 무관심한
④ 긴장되고 혼란스러운
⑤ 공허하고 절망적인

어휘

- descent : 내려가다, 하강하다
- spinning : 방적, 회전, 어지러움
- nausea : 욕지기, 메스꺼움
- vanish : 사라지다, 없어지다
- nightmare : 악몽, 아주 끔직한 일
- spine : 척추, 기개, 기골, 근성
  cf. find a spine : 용기를 내다
- gloomy : 우울한, 침울한
- grin : (이를 드러내고) 방긋 웃다, 히죽거리다
- dart : 쏜살같이 달리다[움직이다], 날아가다
- direction : 쪽, 방향, 방위
- everything is under control : 만사가 순조로운
- dreary : 음울한, 황량한
- agitated : 불안해하는, 동요된
- relieved : 안도하는, 다행으로 여기는

정답 및 해설

해석

엘리베이터가 내려가기 시작했을 때, 미소가 활짝 David의 얼굴에 퍼지기 시작했다. 어지러움과 메스꺼움이 사라졌다. 가슴을 짓누르던 압박감도 사라졌다. David가 해내고 있었다. 그는 직장을 그만두고 악몽과 작별을 고했다. 그는 우울한 아침으로부터 벗어나기 위해 용기를 냈다. David는 텅 빈 엘리베이터에 서서 층 번호인 선홍색 디지털 숫자가 내려갈 때마다 활짝 웃으며 지켜보았다. 그 엘리베이터는 건물의 중간층을 통과할 때 살짝 흔들렸다. 엘리베이터가 멈추자, David는 내려서 하강하는 에스컬레이터에 쏜살같이 올라탔다. 누군가가 "어이, David, 어디 가니?"라고 불렀고 David는 마치 만사가 순조로운 듯 웃으며 그 목소리 방향으로 손을 흔들었다. 그는 밖으로 나갔고, 너무 일찍 축축하고 음울해 보였던 공기가 이제는 새로운 시작의 가능성을 열기 시작했다.

31

⑤ 파스타가 중국에서 유래했다는 학설이 Polo's Travels란 책의 유명한 구절을 잘못 오역한데서 기인했다고 했으므로, "파스타가 중국에서 유래했다는 부인할 수 없는 증거를 제시했다."는 ⑤번 문장은 글의 전체 흐름과 대치된다.

어휘

- ethnic roots : 인종적 뿌리
- debate : 논의하다, 논쟁하다
- put forward : 제안하다, 내세우다
- notably : 특히, 현저히, 뚜렷이
- far-fetched : 믿기지 않는, 설득력 없는
- enduring : 오래가는, 지속되는
- myth : 신화, 근거 없는 믿음
- misinterpretation : 오해, 오역
- sago palm : 사고 야자
- starchy food : 녹말이 많은 음식
- undeniable : 부인할 수 없는, 명백한
- originate : 비롯되다, 유래하다

해석

파스타의 인종적 뿌리는 오랫동안 논란이 되어 왔다. ① 많은 학설들이 거론되었고, 일부 학설들은 전혀 설득력이 없었다. ② 13세기 탐험가 Marco Polo의 작품을 근거로, 파스타가 중국에서 이탈리아로 왔다는 오랜 근거 없는 믿음은 Polo's Travels란 책의 유명한 구절을 잘못 오역한데서 기인했다. ③ 그 책에서 Polo는 파스타처럼 생긴 어떤 것이 열리는 나무를 언급했다. ④ 그것은 아마도 사고 야자로, 파스타와 유사한 녹말이 많은 음식을 만들지만 파스타는 아니다. ⑤ 이 나무는 아시아가 원산지이며, 파스타가 중국에서 유래했다는 부인할 수 없는 증거를 제시했다.

32

④ 서구에서는 관습, 법, 종교적 믿음을 꽤 다른 것으로 생각하지만, 비서구 문화에서 관습, 법, 종교적 믿음에 거의 구분이 없다는 것이 윗글의 요지이다. 도둑을 예로 들어, 세계의 대부분이 도둑을 범죄자로 보지만, 공동체 생활을 하고 물건들을 공유하고 있는 작은 마을에서 도둑이란 단어는 거의 의미가 없을 수도 있다고 했다. 그런데, ④번 문장에서 "강력한 처벌의 역할을 하고 범죄를 강력히 제지하는 역할을 한다."고 했으므로 앞 문장의 내용과 대치된다.

어휘

- custom : 관습, 풍습, 습관
- contrast : 차이, 대조, 대비
- sin : 죄, 죄악
- non-Western : 비서양의, 비서구의
- separation : 분리, 구분
- separate from : ~에서 분리하다[떼어 놓다]
- socially : 사회적으로, 사교상
- acceptable : 용인되는, 받아들여지는
- criminal : 범인, 범죄자
- considerable : 상당한, 많은
- communal living : 공동체[집단] 생활
- disapproval : 반감, 못마땅함, 불만
- serve as : ~의 역할을 하다
- punishment : 벌, 처벌, 형벌
- deterrent : 제지하는 것, 억제력
- impolite : 무례한, 버릇없는

해석

정의란 개념에 있어서 또 다른 차이점은 법이 무엇인가에 대한 사회의 다양한 견해에 있다. 서구에서, 사람들은 '법'과 '관습'을 꽤 다른 것으로 생각한다. 또한 '죄' (종교적 법을 어기는 것)와 '범죄' (정부의 법을 어기는 것) 사이에도 큰 차이가 있다. ① 그러나 많은 비서구 문화에서 관습, 법, 그리고 종교적 믿음에는 거의 구분이 없다. 다른 문화에서 이 세 가지는 서로 잘 구분될 수도 있지만, 그러나 여전히 서구의 것들과는 매우 다르다. ② 이런 이유들로 어떤 행동은 한 국가에서 범죄로 간주될 수 있지만 다른 국가에서는 사회적으로 용인될 수도 있다. ③ 예를 들어, 세계의 대부분이 도둑을 범죄자로 보지만, 공동체 생활을 하고 물건들을 공유하고 있는 작은 마을에서 도둑이란 단어는 거의 의미가 없을 수도 있다. ④ 작은 마을에서는 모든 사람이 어떤 의미에서 판사가 된다. 그러한 사회에서 사람들의 행동에 대한 사회적 반감은 강력한 처벌의 역할을 하고 범죄를 강력히 제지하는 역할도 한다. ⑤ 묻지 않고 어떤 물건을 가져간 사람은 그저 무례한 사람으로 여길 뿐이다.

33 ④ 카멜레온이 자동으로 주변 환경과 어울리기 위해 자신의 색깔을 바꾸는 것처럼, 사람들도 또한 주위 사람들과 어울리기 위해 자동으로 자신의 행동을 조절한다고 해야 글의 흐름이 자연스러우므로, 주어진 문장은 ④에 들어가는 것이 가장 적절하다.

어휘

- adjust : 조정[조절]하다, 적응하다
- blend with : ~와 섞다, ~와 어울리다
- interact with : ~와 상호 작용을 하다, ~와 교감[교류]하다
- mimic : 모방하다, 흉내를 내다
- unconsciously : 무의식적으로, 무심코
- mimicry : 모방, 흉내
- speculate : 추측하다, 짐작하다
- social glue : 사회적 유대감[결속력]
- identical : 동일한, 똑같은

해석

> 사람들도 또한 주위 사람들과 어울리기 위해 자동으로 자신의 행동을 조절한다.

당신이 다른 사람과 교류할 때, 어떤 식으로든 그들을 모방하고 있다는 사실을 스스로 깨달을 것이다. (①) 예를 들어, 당신은 무의식적으로 친구의 말 패턴과 억양을 따라한다. (②) 사회 심리학자들은 이런 형태의 모방을 카멜레온 효과라고 이름 붙였다. (③) 카멜레온은 자동으로 주변 환경과 어울리기 위해 자신의 색깔을 바꾼다. (④) 이런 형태의 모방 기능은 '사회적 유대감'의 한 종류로 추측된다. (⑤) 동일한 행동을 취함으로써, 사람들은 스스로를 자신의 주변에 있는 다른 사람들과 더욱 비슷하게 만든다.

34 ③ 윗글에 따르면 나이키 퍼터를 사용하고 있다고 생각한 사람들은 실제로 공을 홀에 넣기 위해 평균적으로 더 적은 퍼팅을 했고, 수학 시험을 치르는 동안 3M 귀마개를 착용하고 있다고 생각한 참가자들은 정답을 더 많이 맞혔다고 서술되어 있다. 그러므로 윗글은 "참가자들이 더 (B) 유명한(prominent) 상표를 사용하고 있다고 믿었을 때 시험 참가자들의 수행능력이 평균적으로 더 (A) 향상되었다(enhanced)."고 한 문장으로 요약할 수 있다.

오답풀이

	(A)	(B)
①	향상되었다	포괄적인
②	향상되었다	육상의
④	감소되었다	인기 있는
⑤	감소되었다	평범한

어휘

- placebo effect : 플라시보 효과(가짜 약으로 치료하는 심리 효과)
- participant : 참가자, 참여자
- identical : 동일한, 똑같은
- putter : (골프) 퍼터
- earplug : 귀마개
- putt : (골프) 퍼팅하다
- sink a ball : (골프) 공을 홀에 넣다
- initial : 처음의, 초기의
- subtle : 미묘한, 감지하기 힘든
- enhance : 높이다, 향상시키다
- generic : 포괄적인, 통칭[총칭]의
- athletic : 탄탄한, 육상의
- prominent : 중요한, 유명한
- diminish : 줄어들다, 약해지다

해석

특정 상표의 제품이 특히 효과적일 것이라는 생각은 일종의 플라시보 효과를 낼 수도 있다고 연구원들이 밝혔다. 일련의 연구에서, 참가자들은 골프와 수학 능력 시험을 위해 거의 동일한 도구를 지급받았다. 유일한 차이점은 절반의 퍼터는 나이키 상표가 붙었고, 반면에 시험 응시자들에게 주어진 귀마개 세트의 절반은 3M에서 만들어졌다고 말해주었다. 나이키 퍼터를 사용하고 있다고 생각한 사람들은 실제로 공을 홀에 넣기 위해 평균적으로 더 적은 퍼팅을 했고, 수학 시험을 치르는 동안 3M 귀마개를 착용하고 있다고 생각한 참가자들은 정답을 더 많이 맞혔다. 처음에는 자신의 능력에 자신감이 바닥이었던 사람들도 약간의 업그레이드를 통해 큰 자신감을 얻은 것으로 밝혀졌다.

> 연구에 따르면, 참가자들이 더 (B) 유명한 상표를 사용하고 있다고 믿었을 때 시험 참가자들의 수행능력이 평균적으로 더 (A) 향상되었다.

35 ⑤ 주어진 글의 다양한 입맛에 대한 예로 [C]에서 매운 맛을 사례로 들어 설명하고 있다. [C]에서 음식에 대한 선호도는 생애 초기에 경험한 맛의 차이로 결정된다고 했고 [B]에서 그 선호도는 자궁 내에서 형성된다고 설명하고 있다. [B]에서 사람들마다 미뢰의 숫자에 현저한 차이를 보인다고 했고 [A]에서 미뢰의 밀도 차이는 유전되어 나타난다고 설명하고 있다. 그러므로 주어진 글 다음에 이어질 글의 순서는 전체적인 글의 흐름상 [C] – [B] – [A] 순으로 이어진다.

- taste preference : 맛 선호도, 입맛
- taste bud : (혀의) 미뢰[맛봉오리]
- supertaster : 미각이 뛰어난 사람
- variation : 변화, 변형, 차이
- density : 밀도, 농도
- genetic : 유전의, 유전학의
- flavor : 맛, 풍미
- amniotic fluid : 양수
- in utero : 자궁 내에
- spicy food : 양념 맛이 강한, 매운
- shudder : 몸을 떨다, 몸서리치다
- hot pepper : 고춧가루

해석

가족이나 친구들과 함께 식사를 하다보면, 아마 사람들이 매우 다른 입맛을 가지고 있다는 사실을 알게 될 것이다.

[C] 예를 들면 일부 사람들은 매운 맛을 좋아하고, 반면에 다른 사람들은 고춧가루만 생각해도 몸서리를 친다. 일부 선호도는 생애 초기에 사람들이 경험한 맛의 차이로 설명된다.

[B] 사실 엄마가 먹는 음식은 양수의 맛을 변화시켜서, 일부 음식에 대한 선호도는 자궁 내에서 형성된다. 그러나 사람들 또한 그들이 가지고 있는 미뢰의 숫자에서 현저한 차이를 보인다.

[A] 평균적인 수보다 상당히 많은 미뢰를 가진 사람들의 집합을 슈퍼테스터(미각이 뛰어난 사람들)라고 부른다. 각 사람들의 혀에 있는 미뢰의 밀도 차이는 유전되어 나타난다. 여성들은 남성들보다 훨씬 더 슈퍼테스터일 것이다.

[36~37]

어휘

- conversion : 전환, 전향, 개조
- depression : 불경기, 불황
- vent : (감정·분통을) 터뜨리다, 발산하다
- greedy : 탐욕스러운, 욕심 많은
- undermine : 약화시키다, 해치다
- thwart : 좌절시키다, 꺾다
- lofty : 고귀한, 숭고한
- contend : 주장하다, 다투다
- pecuniary : 금전의, 금전상의
- parochial : 좁은, 편협한, 지역적인

- transform into ~로 변형시키다
- internal : 내부의, 내적인
- bickering : 말다툼, 언쟁, 논쟁
- splinter : 쪼개지다, 분열[분리]되다, 갈라지다
- faction : 파벌, 파당
- meteoric : 일약 ~한
- Reich : (독일) 제국, 영지, 국가
- fanatical : 광신적인, 열광적인
- obsession : 강박 상태, 집착
- efficiency : 효율, 능률
- second thought : 재고, 숙고
- technocrat : 테크노크라트, 기술관료(기술자 출신 관리자)
- dictatorship : 독재 정부[국가]
- setback : 역행, 퇴보
- abruptly : 갑자기, 불쑥, 뜻밖에
- techno-utopian : 기술-유토피아적
- constant : 끊임없는, 거듭되는
- reminder : 상기시키는[생각나게 하는] 것
- awesome : 무시무시한, 가공할
- technocracy : 테크노크라시, 기술관료제(과학 기술 분야 전문가들이 많은 권력을 행사하는 정치 및 사회 체제)
- technocratic : 기술관료제의
- downfall : 몰락, 파멸
- inevitable : 불가피한, 필연적인
- belligerent : 공격적인, 적대적인
- imbalance : 불균형, 불안정

해석

1929년에 대공황이 닥쳤을 때조차도 새로운 공학으로의 대전환의 가치가 매우 효과적이어서, 미국인들은 계속해서 기술적 전망을 옹호했다. (①) 그들은 대신 국가의 새로운 영웅들인 공학자들의 숭고한 목적과 목표를 약화시키고 좌절시키는 탐욕스러운 사업가들에 대한 분노와 두려움을 터뜨렸다. (②) 소수의 미국인들은 경제학자이자 사회학자인 Thorstein Veblen의 초창기 비판에 동의했다. 그는 1921년에 국가 경제를 고귀한 기준을 금전과 편협한 관심 우위에 둔 전문 공학자들에게만 맡김으로써 경제를 살리고 국가를 새로운 Eden 동산으로 바꾸자고 주장했다. (③) 그 지도자들 사이의 내부적 논쟁은 파당끼리 싸우는 분열의 움직임으로 이어졌다. (④) 그때 또한 Hitler가 일약 권력으로 떠오르고 제3제국의 기술적 효용성에 열광적으로 집착하는 것은 많은 사회 사상가들이 미국 내에서 기술적 독재 정부에 대한 테크노크라트(기술관료)들의 요구를 재고하도록 했다. (⑤) 기술 중심 세상에 대한 시각은 1945년에 미국의 비행기가 일본 도시들에 원자 폭탄을 투하했을 때 훨씬 더 비판적인 퇴보를 겪었다. 즉, 전 세계는

갑자기 기술–유토피아적 전망의 어두운 측면을 보게 된 것이다. 전후 세대는 현대 기술의 가공할 힘이 미래를 창조할 뿐만 아니라 파괴할 수도 있음을 끊임없이 상기하며 살아가야 하는 첫 세대가 되었다.

36

> 그러나 기술관료제의 성공은 오래가지 못했다.

③ 기술관료제(technocracy)란 과학 기술 분야의 전문가들이 많은 권력을 행사하는 정치 및 사회 체제를 말하는데, ③의 앞 문장에서는 기술관료제가 경제를 살리고 새로운 세상을 열거라는 전망을 내놓지만, ③의 뒤 문장에서는 지도자들 사이의 파당과 분열로 이어졌다는 내용이 오므로 "기술관료제의 성공은 오래가지 못했다."는 내용이 글의 흐름상 ③에 들어가야 적절하다.

37

① 윗글의 마지막 문장에서 전후 세대는 현대 기술의 가공할 힘이 미래를 창조할 뿐만 아니라 파괴할 수도 있음을 끊임없이 상기하며 살아가야 한다고 했으므로, 기술관료제의 양면성에 대해 설명하고 있다. 그러므로 ①의 'the technocratic vision and its downfall(기술관료제의 전망과 몰락)'이 윗글의 주제로 타당하다.

오답풀이

② 민주주의와 기술의 짧은 밀월
③ 기술 중심 세상에 대한 시각의 필연적 도래
④ 더 나은 사회를 위한 기술관료들의 공격적 접근
⑤ 기술관료제의 긍정적 측면과 부정적 측면의 불균형

[38~39]

어휘

• take over from : ~로부터 인계받다
• victim : 피해자, 희생자
• aggression : 공격, 침략
• aggressor : 공격자, 가해자
• evolve : 발달하다, 진화하다
• alleviate : 완화하다, 경감하다
• revenge : 복수, 보복, 설욕
• retribution : 응징, 징벌
• retaliation : 보복, 앙갚음
• bloodthirsty : 피에 굶주린, 잔인한
• connotation : 함축, 암시
• reduce : 줄이다, 축소하다
• likelihood : 그럴듯함, 가능성, 공산
• overreaction : 과잉 반응, 지나친 감정표현
• engender (감정·상황을) 낳다, 불러일으키다
• feud : 불화, 반목
• composition : (채권자와 채무자 사이의) 화해, 화의, 보상금
• blood money : 피 묻은 돈, (살해된 사람의 유족에게 주는) 보상금
• in compensation for : ~의 보상으로
• discharge : 갚다, 면하다, 변제하다
• injurer : 가해자
• liability : 책임, 부담, 의무
• transfer : 이동, 이전, 이체
• violence : 폭력, 폭행
• inflict : 해를 끼치다, 가하다
• net : (돈의 액수에 대한) 순, 실, 최종적인
• provoke : 유발[도발]하다, 야기하다, 짜증나게 하다
• institution : 제도, 관습
• bilateral : 쌍방의, 쌍무적인
• kinship : 친족, 친척[혈족] 관계
• reckon : 생각하다, 인정하다, 추정[추산]하다
• credibility : 신뢰성, 진실성
• deterrent : 제지하는 것, 억제력
• disputant : 논쟁자, 토론자, 논객
• kin : 친족, 친척
• dispute : 분쟁, 분규, 논란, 논쟁
• pity : 동정, 연민
• empathy : 감정이입, 공감
• savagery : 야만성, 흉포성

해석

국가나 사회 조직이 공격의 피해자와 그들의 가족으로부터 가해자를 붙잡아 벌을 주는 책임을 인계받기도 전에 보복 관행의 몇몇 문제를 완화시키는 관습은 진화했다. 이 중 응징의 원칙은 눈에는 눈과 같이 잘못에 대한 정확한 보복이다. 잔인하다기 보다는 오히려, 그 단어의 현대적 함축이며, 응징은 불화를 야기할 것 같은 과잉행동(내 눈에 네 목숨)의 가능성을 줄인다. 또 다른 (A) 온건한 원칙은 '보상금'(피 묻은 돈)인데, 그것으로 가해자의 책임을 면하며 피해자 또는 피해자의 가족이 피해에 대한 보상으로 돈을 받으라고 요구받거나 적어도 권고 받는다. 돈 또는 상품의 이전은 폭력 행위보다 대체적으로 사회에 비용이 덜 들며, 게다가 폭력 행위는 단순히 한 사람이 다른 사람에게 돈을 주는 것보다 사회적 순손실을 끼치고 더한 폭력을 유발할 수도 있다. 또 다른 (B) 온건한 관습은 쌍방의 친족 관계이다. 아이슬란드인들은 아버지와 어머니(많은 사회가 오직 아버지를 통해서만 그리고 일부 사회는 오직 어머니를 통해서만 그것을 인정한다.) 둘 다를 통해 친족 관계를 인정한다. 이것은 가족을 강화시킴으로써 공격을 제지하는 것

으로 보복에 대한 신뢰성을 높일 뿐만 아니라 논쟁자가 논쟁의 양 당사자 모두와 친족이 될 가능성을 높인다. Iliad에서는 연민과 공감이 보복의 야만성을 제한할 가능성이 훨씬 더 많음을 암시했다.

38 ④ 윗글은 글의 서두에서 언급한 것처럼 보복의 관행을 완화시키는 관습에 대해 설명하고 있다. 첫 번째 응징의 원칙에 비해 두 번째의 보상금과 세 번째의 쌍방의 친족 관계는 보복이나 응징에 대한 정도가 점점 약화되고 있는 원칙 또는 관습이므로, 빈칸 (A)와 (B)에 들어갈 말로는 'moderating(온건한)'이 가장 적절하다.

오답풀이

① 수정하는
② 처벌하는
③ 모순되는
⑤ 사로잡는

39 ② 응징의 원칙은 눈에는 눈과 같이 잘못에 대한 정확한 보복으로, 불화를 야기할 것 같은 과잉행동의 가능성을 줄인다고 했으므로, '눈에는 눈' 원칙은 피해자의 과잉대응 가능성을 줄였다는 ②의 설명은 윗글의 내용과 일치한다.

오답풀이

① 국가가 가해자를 처벌할 책임을 맡기 전 보복은 폭력보다는 보상금이나 이를 완화시키는 관습에 의해 이루어졌다.
③ 피해자에 대한 물질적인 보상은 공동체가 아니라 가해자가 부담했다.
④ 가족을 강화시킴으로써 공격을 제지하는 것으로 보복에 대한 신뢰성을 높인다고 했으므로, 폭력에 대한 책임을 질 필요가 없는 것은 아니다.
⑤ 연민과 공감이 보복의 야만성을 제한할 가능성이 훨씬 더 많으므로, 보복의 가능성을 줄이는 데 도움이 된다.

[40~42]

어휘

• sole : 혼자의, 단독의
• cyclist : 사이클 타는 사람
• steadfastly : 확고하게, 변함없이, 부단히
• ridicule : 비웃다, 조롱[조소]하다
• eloquent defense : 능숙한 변호[변론]
• bourgeois : 중산층의, 물질만능주의적인, 부르주아적인
• in the first place : 우선, 첫째로, 맨 처음에
• be engaged in : ~으로 바쁘다, ~에 종사하고 있다

• daredevil : 저돌적인[무모한] 사람
• in terms of : ~면에서, ~에 관하여
• reckless : 무모한, 신중하지 못한
• extreme example : 극단적인 예
• egoist : 이기주의자, 자기중심주의자
• swerve : 방향을 바꾸다[틀다]
• involve : 수반[포함]하다, 관련[연루]시키다
• trauma : 부상, (정신적) 외상, 트라우마
• minister to : ~에 도움이 되다
• medic : 의대생, 의사
• EMT : 전문 응급 구조사
• subsidize : 보조금[장려금]을 지급하다
• victim : 피해자, 희생자
• stuff : 채워 넣다, 쑤셔 넣다
• brain tissue : 뇌 조직
• crack : 갈라지다, 금이 가다
• skull : 두개골, 머리
• insurance rate : 보험료, 보험요율
• psyche : 마음, 정신, 심령
• recipe : 조리법, 요리법, 비결, 방안
• risk taker : 모험을 좋아하는 사람, 위험을 무릅쓰는 사람
• at the expense of : ~의 비용으로, ~의 희생으로
• controversial : 논란이 많은, 논쟁을 좋아하는
• regulation : 규정, 규제, 통제
• violator : 위반자, 위배자

해석

[A] 미국의 많은 주(州)에서 오토바이를 타는 동안 개인이 헬멧을 쓰는 것이 법이다. 이런 법들은 유일한 목적이 오토바이를 타는 사람들이 부상당하는 것을 보호하기 위한 것뿐이라는 이유로 종종 부딪친다.

[B] 대학에 다닐 때 헬멧 쓰기를 부단히 거부하며 오토바이를 타는 친구가 있었다. 그는 종종 이와 같이 다소 능숙한 변론을 하는 어리석음 때문에 나머지 친구들로부터 비웃음을 샀다. "봐, 나는 이런 부르주아적 생활에 싫증이 났어. 나는 모험을 하려고 나왔고, 이것이 내가 오토바이를 타는 첫 번째 이유야. 나는 위험해지기를 원해. 스릴은 위험한 거야. 위험이 클수록 스릴은 더 커지지."

[D] 헬멧 없이 오토바이를 타겠다는 내 친구의 결정은 오직 자신에게만 영향을 미칠까? 길에서 돌멩이나 다른 물체가 갑자기 날아들어 그가 다른 곳으로 방향을 바꿀 수도 있다. 심지어 본인 자신이 직접 부상을 당하고, 헬멧을 썼으면 피할 수 있었던 머리 외상도 수반될 수 있다. 그때 내 친구는 혼자 내버려두지 않고 구급차의 운전자, 의사, 그리고 전문 응급 구조사의 도움을 받기를 기대할 것이다.

소중한 시간과 돈이 그의 스릴을 쫓는데 보조로 쓰일 것이다. 의사들은 그의 갈라진 두개골 내부의 뇌 조직을 원상복구 하느라 바빠서 제시간에 다른 피해자를 받을 수 없을지도 모른다. 병원 공간과 재원 또한 세금으로 충당되며, 의사들이 요청되고, 의료보험과 자동차 보험 요율 모두가 우리에게 인상된다.

[C] 그 에피소드로부터 헬멧을 쓰지 않은 오토바이 운전자는 결국 연관된 다른 행동으로 분주할 것으로 보인다. 대중이 염려하는 것은 그 오토바이 운전자에게 무슨 일이 일어났는가가 아니다. 무모한 사람의 행동으로 인해 나머지 사람이 떠안을 비용을 걱정한다. 모든 사람의 생활방식이 그가 공공 자원에 부여하는 부담 또는 세금 면에서 동일하지는 않다. 내 무모한 친구는 그냥 자기를 혼자 내버려둘 뿐만 아니라, 그의 선택을 옹호할 것을 대중에게 요구하는 이기주의자의 극단적인 사례처럼 보인다.

40 ② [A] 논지 제시: 오토바이를 탈 때 반드시 헬멧을 써야 하는 법에 대한 반감

↓

[B] 사례 예시 : 오토바이를 탈 때 헬멧을 쓰는 것을 거부하는 친구(사례 예시)

↓

[D] 주장 전개 : 헬멧을 쓰지 않은 친구가 사고를 당할 경우 본인과 주위에 미치는 영향

↓

[C] 결론 도출 : 무모한 오토바이 운전자에 대한 에피소드를 통해 얻을 수 있는 결론

41 ④ 헬멧을 쓰지 않고 오토바이를 운전하는 무모한 친구의 사례를 예로 들어, 그 친구가 사고를 당할 경우 구급차의 운전자, 의사, 그리고 전문 응급 구조사의 지원과 세금을 비롯해 의료보험과 자동차 보험 요율의 인상 등 다른 사람이 떠안을 사회적 비용에 대해 설명하고 있다. 그러므로 ④의 'personal freedom at the expense of others(타인의 희생으로 누리는 개인의 자유)'가 윗글의 주제로 가장 적절하다.

오답풀이

① 헬멧을 쓰지 않은 오토바이 운전자의 정신 상태
② 사고 없는 사회를 위한 방안
③ 모험을 좋아하는 사람과 좋아하지 않는 사람의 생활방식
⑤ 교통법규 위반자들에 대한 논란 많은 규제

42 ② (a), (c), (d), (e)는 모두 헬멧을 쓰지 않고 오토바이를 운전하는 무모한 친구를 가리키지만, (b)의 'he'는 앞의 'everyone'을 지칭한다.

[43~45]

어휘

- handkerchief : 손수건, 화장지
- vanish : 사라지다, 없어지다
- shuffle : (카드를) 섞다, 이리저리 바꾸다
- a deck of cards : 카드 한 벌[질]
- alter : 바꾸다, 변경하다
- prestigious : 명망 있는[높은], 일류의
- illusion : 착각, 환상, 환각
- encounter : 우연히 만나다, 마주치다
- significant : 중요한, 의미심장한
- career direction : 진로결정, 직업선택
- crucial : 중대한, 결정적인
- impact : 영향, 충격, 충돌
- untold : 말로 다 할 수 없는, 아무에게도 들려주지 않은
- influential : 영향력이 있는, 유력한
- serendipity : 우연한 것[일], 뜻밖의 재미[기쁨]
- serendipitous : 우연히 일어나는, 뜻밖의 재미있는
- ubiquitous : 어디에나 있는, 아주 흔한
- junior reporter : 수습기자
- diligence : 근면, 성실
- pay off : 성공하다, 성과를 올리다
- anecdote : 일화, 에피소드
- prestige : 위신, 명망
- preconceive : 미리 생각하다, 예상하다

해석

나는 항상 마술에 흥미가 있었다. 10살쯤 되었을 때, 나는 손수건을 사라지게 하고 카드의 순서를 바꾸지 않고 완전히 섞을 수 있었다. 10대 초반에는 런던에 있는 세계적으로 유명한 마술 협회에 가입했다. 20대 초반까지 나는 일류 쇼에서 공연을 하기 위해 여러 번 미국에 초청받았다.

이 매혹적인 속임수와 환상의 세계에 대한 나의 애정은 우연한 기회에 시작되었다. 8살이 되었을 때 나는 체스 역사에 관한 학교 프로젝트를 완성해야 했다. 성실한 어린 학생이었던 나는 그 주제에 맞는 책을 찾으러 지역 도서관을 방문하기로 결심했다. 나는 서가를 잘못 찾았고 마술에 관한 책 몇 권을 우연히 보게 되었다. 나는 호기심이 생겼고, 마술사들이 불가능한 것을 해내는 비밀에 관한 모든 것을 읽기 시작했다. 만일 내가 올바른 서가를 찾아 체스 책들을 찾았다면 무슨 일이 일어났을지 모른다.

많은 사람들이 종종 낯선 사람과의 계획되지 않은 우연한 만남이 어떻게 직업 선택에 중대한 변화를 초래했는지 보고했다. 우리들 각자가 중대하고 계획되지 않은 사건들이 주요 직업에 어떻게 영향을 미쳤는지 그리고 수많은 사소한 계획되지

않은 사건들이 최소한도의 작은 영향을 미쳤는지에 관해 이야기할 수 있다. 영향력이 큰 계획되지 않은 사건들은 <u>드물지 않다</u>. 즉, 그 사건들은 매일 일어난다. 우연한 일은 우연히 일어나는 것이 아니다. 우연한 일은 어디에나 있다.

Joseph Pulitzer를 예로 들어 보자. 그는 헝가리에서 태어났다. 젊었을 때 Pulitzer는 허약한 건강과 극히 나쁜 시력으로 고생했다. 17살이 되었을 때, 그는 더 나은 삶을 위해 미국에 왔다. 하지만 그는 그곳에서 직업을 구할 수 없었다. Pulitzer는 지역 도서관에서 체스를 두며 많은 시간을 보냈다. 그러던 중 그는 우연히 지역 신문사의 편집장을 만났다. 이런 예상치 못한 만남으로 Pulitzer는 수습기자로 일하게 되었다. 그는 신문사에서 꽤 성공을 거두었고, 편집장이 되고, 마침내 당대에 유명한 두 신문사의 소유주가 되었다.

43 ② 윗글은 필자가 어릴 적 우연히 도서관에서 섭한 마술 관련 책들을 보고 세계적인 마술사가 된 것과 Joseph Pulitzer가 젊은 시절 우연히 만난 지역 신문 편집장에 의해 당대의 유명한 편집장이 된 것처럼, 뜻밖에 찾아오는 우연한 기회들이 후에 직업을 결정할 만큼 큰 기회를 가져온다고 설명하고 있다. 그러므로 ②의 'Chances Are It's a Great Chance(기회들이 모여 큰 기회를 만든다.)'가 윗글의 제목으로 가장 적절하다.

오답풀이

① 성실함은 항상 성공의 대가가 온다.

③ Joseph Pulitzer : 알려지지 않은 일화

④ 명성과 직업 선택

⑤ 오래 기억되는 마법의 순간

44 ③ 빈칸의 다음 문장에서 사건들은 매일 일어나며, 우연한 일은 우연히 일어나는 것이 아니라 어디에나 있다고 했으므로, 빈칸에는 '흔한 일이다.'라는 의미인 ③의 'are not uncommon(드물지 않다.)'가 들어가는 것이 적절하다.

오답풀이

① 예상된다.

② 환영받지 못한다.

④ 미래를 예측할 수 있다.

⑤ 영향력을 상실할 수 있다.

45 ④ Joseph Pulitzer가 17살 때 미국에서 직업을 구할 수가 없어 지역 도서관에서 체스를 두며 많은 시간을 보내던 중 우연히 지역 신문사의 편집장을 만나 수습기자로 일하게 되었다는 내용은 있지만, 프로 체스 기사가 되었다는 내용은 서술되어 있지 않다.

2016학년도 기출문제 정답 및 해설

제2교시 영어영역

01 ①	02 ①	03 ⑤	04 ②	05 ④	06 ④
07 ④	08 ⑤	09 ①	10 ③	11 ④	12 ④
13 ④	14 ①	15 ③	16 ⑤	17 ⑤	18 ⑤
19 ①	20 ⑤	21 ①	22 ②	23 ②	24 ⑤
25 ⑤	26 ②	27 ⑤	28 ③	29 ③	30 ②
31 ③	32 ③	33 ②	34 ①	35 ④	36 ③
37 ③	38 ②	39 ①	40 ②	41 ②	42 ③
43 ④	44 ④	45 ④			

01 ① 'ephemeral'은 '수명이 짧은', '단명하는'의 뜻으로 내용상 가장 비슷한 단어는 'fleeting(순간간의, 잠깐 동안의)'이다.

오답풀이

② residual 남은, 잔여[잔류]의
③ perpetual 끊임없이 계속되는, 영구적인
④ legendary 전설적인, 아주 유명한
⑤ credulous 잘 믿는, 잘 속는

해석

그 영화 스타의 명성이 단명할 줄 누가 짐작이나 했겠는가?

02 ① 'cajole'은 '꼬드기다', '회유하다'라는 뜻으로 의미상, 'coax(구슬리다, 달래다)'와 유사하다.

오답풀이

② bully 괴롭히다
③ slander 중상모략하다, 비방하다
④ provoke 도발[유발]하다, 화나게[짜증나게] 하다
⑤ hypnotize 최면을 걸다, 혼을 빼놓다

어휘

• cajole A into B : A를 구슬려서 B하게 하다
• to no avail : 보람 없이, 헛되이

해석

Karen은 그의 친구가 쇼핑몰로 데려다 준다고 꼬드겼지만, 소용이 없었다.

03 ⑤ 'fastidious'는 '세심한', '꼼꼼한'의 뜻으로, 같은 의미의 단어는 'meticulous'이다.

오답풀이

① perilous : 아주 위험한
② insidious : 서서히[은밀히] 퍼지는
③ insolvent : 파산한
④ vindictive : 앙심을 품은, 보복을 하려는

어휘

• premises : 부지, 구내
• spotless : 티끌 하나 없는
• to a fault : 지나칠 정도로

해석

그녀는 구내를 흠 하나 없이 유지하는 데 지나칠 정도로 매우 꼼꼼했다.

04 ② 'quandary'는 '진퇴양난', '곤경'이라는 뜻으로, 'dilemma(딜레마, 진퇴양난)'와 문맥상 상통한다.

오답풀이

① bonds : 유대, 끈, 속박, 채권
③ failures : 실패
④ ecstasies : 황홀감, 황홀경
⑤ irritations : 짜증, 성가심

어휘

• work through : 통과시키다, 경험하다, 해결하다
• built-in : 붙박이의, 내장된
• therapist : 치료사

해석

꿈은 그날의 심적 곤경을 해결하는 데 도움을 준다. 그것은 붙박이 치료사를 둔 것과 마찬가지이다.

05 ④ 'discreetly'는 '사려 깊게', '신중하게'라는 뜻으로 'cautiously(조심스럽게, 신중하게)'와 같은 의미이다.

오답풀이

① rashly : 성급하게, 무모하게
② mildly : 약간, 가볍게

③ enviously : 부러움으로, 질투심을 가지고

⑤ impartially : 편견 없이, 공평하게

해석

그는 나를 Clare와 같은 지위로 승진시킬 예정이라고 그녀가 질투하지 않도록 내게 <u>신중하게</u> 말해주었다.

06 ④ It(가주어)~that(진주어) 구문으로, 가주어 It에 대하여 ④의 'what' 대신 진주어 역할을 하는 'that'을 사용해야 한다.

어휘

- coastal : 해안의, 연안의
- tropical : 열대의, 열대 지방의
- diarrhea : 설사
- the small hours : 한밤중, 오밤중
- parenting : 육아

해석

나는 한때 Papua New Guinea 해안가 마을에서 살았다. 그곳의 아이들은 자기 부모들과 함께 살지 않고 그들이 원하는 대로 이집 저집 옮겨 다녔다. 조리용 불을 살피거나 아이들을 안고 다니는 열 살짜리 아이들이 목격되곤 했다. 열 네 살쯤에 그들은 자신감과 자부심을 가지고 어른들이 하는 일을 했다. 그 마을에서 가장 새롭고도 흥미로웠던 것은 12명쯤 되는 아이들이 내 베란다에서 잠을 잔다는 것이었다. 오밤중에 열대성 설사병에 걸렸을 때, 나는 융단처럼 쌓인 작은 갈색 물체들을 뚫고 지나가야만 했다. 온 마을이 육아의 노동과 즐거움을 함께 나누었기 때문에, 나는 이곳이 부모가 되기에 쉬운 곳이라는 생각이 들었다. 사실, 당시의 모든 어른이 부모였다.

07 ④의 'was'의 주어는 앞의 'Those fears'이고 그 형태가 복수이므로 복수 동사 형태인 'were'가 되어야 한다. 'Those fears'는 두 개의 동사 'fueled'와 'were'를 'and'로 연결한 중문을 이끈다.

어휘

- plunge : 거꾸러지다, 급락하다
- plunge into : ~에 처넣다, ~에 빠뜨리다
- poverty : 가난, 빈곤, 부복
- peril : 위험
- strip of : ~을 빼앗다
- midlife : 중년, 중년기
- regain : 되찾다, 회복하다
- mind-set : 마음가짐, 사고방식
- fuel : 연료를 공급하다, 부채질하다
- in par : 부분적으로, 어느 정도
- athlete : 운동 선수

해석

부유한 집에서 태어났으나 십대 때 가난으로 급락한 나는, 성공을 얻는 비결보다 그것을 잃는 위험성에 대해 더 잘 알고 자랐다. 비록 부모님은 중년에 모든 것을 빼앗기고 난 후 회복했지만, 그들은 결코 풍요로운 마음가짐을 되찾지 못했다. 그리고 나는 부모님의 성공보다는 공포에 더 완벽히 몰입했다. 이러한 공포는 경제적으로 성공하려는 내 욕망에 불을 지폈고, 성공에 도달하는 방법을 사람들에게 가르치면서 어느 정도의 돈을 별도로 했다. 나는 수천 명의 기업가들과 프로 선수들에게 소중한 성공 원칙들을 활용하여 그들의 목표를 이루는 데 영감을 불어넣는 동기부여 연설가가 되었다.

08 ⑤ 글의 문맥상 '저주에 걸릴 것이라는 믿음'은 '의도적으로 꾸며지는 것'이므로 수동태 문장이 되어야 한다. 그러므로 'may have deliberately cultivated'는 'may have been deliberately cultivated'로 고쳐져야 한다.

어휘

- gem : 보석, 보배
- healing : 치유, 치료
- intrigue : 모의, 음모
- prospector : 탐사자, 탐광자
- gemstone : 보석의 원석
- deliberately : 고의로, 의도적으로
- curb : 억제하다, 제한하다
- asset : 자산, 재산

해석

보석과 관련된 수많은 신화와 전설들이 있다. 저주받은 돌에 관한 이야기도 있고, 특별한 치유력이 있는 돌에 관한 이야기나 또는 착용한 사람을 보호하거나 행운을 가져다주는 돌에 관한 이야기도 있다. 가장 큰 것으로 유명한 다이아몬드에는 수 세기에 걸쳐 전해내려 오는 전설이 있으며, 지금은 대다수가 사라졌지만 음모와 살인에 관한 이야기들로 에워싸여 있다. 어떤 광산들은 저주받은 것으로 여겨진다. 아마도 그런 소문은 반갑지 않은 탐사자들로부터 광산을 지키려는 광산 소유자들에 의해 퍼졌을 것이다. 예를 들면 모든 보석이 군주의 소유였던 미얀마에서, 광산에서 돌을 가져가는 자들이 저주에 걸릴 것이라는 믿음이 귀중한 국유 재산의 분실을 막기 위해 의도적으로 꾸며졌을 것이다.

09 ① (A) 여성의 긴급 전화가 유선이었다면 그녀의 위치를 순식간에 정확히 찾아낼(pinpoint) 수 있었을 것이다. 그러나 휴대용 기기로 전화를 걸었기 때문에 여성의 위치를 찾는 데 시간이 걸렸다.

   (B) 긴급 전화를 한 여성의 위치를 찾는데 20분 이상이 소

요된 원인은 경찰이 무선통신 사업자가 제공하는 부정
확한(imprecise) 정보를 통해 그녀의 위치를 파악할 수
밖에 없기 때문이다.

(C) 신호 세기와 그 신호가 여러 기지국에 도달하는 데 걸
리는 시간을 비교하는 방법은 삼각측량법(triangulation)
에 해당한다.

어휘

• landline : 유선 전화, 일반 전화
• pinpoint : 정확히 찾아내다
• in a matter of seconds : 순식간에
• wireless carrier : 무선통신 사업자
• imprecise : 부정확한, 모호한
• triangulation : 삼각 측량
• circulation : 순환, 유통
• cell tower : 기지국
• approximate : 근사치를 내다[계산하다], 비슷하다[가깝다]
• radius : 반경, 반지름

해석

작년 여름, 캘리포니아에서 26세의 여성이 911에 긴급 신고 전
화를 걸었다. 그녀의 긴급 전화가 유선이었다면, 첫 응답자가
그녀의 위치를 순식간에 정확히 찾아낼 수 있었을 것이다. 그
러나 현재의 911 시스템은 1960년대에 설계된 이후로 큰 변화
가 없었기 때문에, 경찰은 무선통신 사업자가 제공하는 부정
확한 정보를 통해 그녀의 위치를 파악할 수밖에 없었다. 긴급
전화가 휴대용 기기로 이루어질 때, 통신사는 삼각측량법 –
신호 세기와 그 신호가 여러 기지국에 도달하는 데 걸리는 시
간을 비교하는 것 – 을 사용하여 전화의 위치를 대략적으로
파악한다. 이 기술로 여성의 위치를 반경 한 블록 내로 잡았
고, 그녀를 찾기까지 20분 이상의 시간이 소요되었다.

10 ③ 그리스인들이 예술이나 문학에서 성취한 것은 모두에게 친
숙하지만 수학, 과학, 철학 등 순전히 지적인 영역에서 성
취한 것은 훨씬 더 비범한(extraordinary) 것이었다.

어휘

• purely : 순전히, 오직
• realm : 영역[범위], 왕국
• mere : 단순한, 순전한
• annal : 기록
• speculate : 추측하다, 짐작하다
• fetter : 속박, 구속
• inherit : 상속받다, 물려받다
• orthodoxy : 통설, 정설

해석

모든 역사를 통해 그리스 문명의 갑작스러운 등장을 설명하
기란 그리 놀랍고 어려운 일이 아니다. 문명이라는 것이 이집
트와 메소포타미아에서 수천 년 동안 이미 존재해 왔고, 그 뒤
이웃 국가들로 퍼져나갔다. 그러나 특정 요소들은 그리스인들
이 제공하기 전까지는 충분치 못했다. 그들이 예술과 문학에
서 성취한 것은 모두에게 친숙하지만, 순전히 지적인 영역에
서 성취한 것은 훨씬 더 비범한 것이었다. 그리스인들은 수학,
과학, 철학을 창안했다. 그들은 단순한 기록이 아닌 역사를 처
음으로 서술했다. 그들은 세상의 본질과 삶의 목적을 이전의
통설에 구속됨이 없이 자유롭게 상상했다.

11 ④ 19세기 초부터 사용된 가스등은 도시의 공공장소를 고작
희미하게 비출 정도였지만, 보다 밝은 빛을 내는 전깃불의
등장으로 전국의 도로와 공공건물에 설치된 가스등은 쇠퇴
되었다(declined).

어휘

• dispel : 떨쳐 버리다, 없애다
• gloom : 우울, 침울, 어둠
• illuminating gas : 등화용 가스
• candlepower : 촉광(광도 단위)
• dimly : 어둑하게, 희미하게
• arc lamp : 아크등
• incandescent bulb : 백열전구, 백열등
• motto : 모토, 좌우명

해석

일반 시민들을 위해 밤에 도시의 어둠을 쫓아낸 전깃불은 시
대가 변했다는 가장 극적인 증거를 보여준다. 가스등 – 석탄
으로부터 추출된 등화용 가스 – 은 19세기 초부터 사용되었지
만, 12 촉광 램프는 도시의 공공장소를 고작 희미하게 비출 정
도였다. 전기의 첫 상업적 용도는 더 나은 도시 조명을 위해서
였다. Charles F. Brush의 전기 아크등은 1878년 필라델피아
Wanamaker 백화점에 설치되었는데, 밝은 빛을 내었고 곧 전
국의 도로와 공공건물에 설치된 가스등을 쇠퇴시켰다. 그 이
후로 미국의 가정에도 전깃불이 들어왔는데, 이는 1879년에
Thomas Edison의 실용적인 백열전구 발명 덕분이었다. "빛이
있으라!"라는 Edison의 구호는 현대 도시의 체험을 사실로 보
여주고 있다.

12 ④ 평균적으로 키스는 8천만 마리의 박테리아를 생성하는
데(generated), 이러한 다른 사람의 박테리아에 노출되
는 것이 실제로는 면역력을 강화하는 데 도움을 준다고
한다.

어휘

• probiotic : 생균제의, 바이오유 제품의

• strain : 종족, 계통, 품종

• germ : 세균, 미생물

• extinguish : 끄다, 없애다

• hygienic : 위생적인

• exposure : 노출, 폭로

• immunity : 면역력, 면제

해석

키스를 하는 동안 사랑 외에 어떤 것들이 전달될까? 네덜란드 연구진들은 키스가 21쌍 커플의 구강 박테리아에 어떻게 영향을 미치는지 추적했다. 그들은 각 커플 중 한 사람에게 세균의 확산을 추적하기 위해 특정 박테리아 종류가 포함된 생균제 유구르트를 섭취하게 했다. 그러고는 각 파트너에게 10초 동안 키스를 하도록 했다. 평균적으로 키스는 8천만 마리의 박테리아를 생성한다. 비록 이것이 그리 위생적이지 못하게 들릴 수 있으나, 전문가들은 다른 사람의 박테리아에 노출되는 것이 실제로는 면역력을 강화하는 데 도움을 준다고 말한다.

13 ④ ①·②·③·⑤는 모두 하늘을 나는 비행 자동차를 말하며, ④의 'one moving in two vectors(두 벡터로 움직이는 자동차)'는 도로 위를 달리는 일반 자동차를 말한다.

어휘

• make sense : 뜻을 이루다, 이치에 맞다

• mate : 짝짓기를 하다, 교미시키다

• give birth to : 낳다, 출산하다

• tweet : 트위터로 메시지를 전달하다

• airborne : 비행 중인, 하늘에 떠 있는

• pro and con : 찬반양론, 장단점

• vector : 벡터, 진로

• junk : 쓸모없는 물건, 고물, 쓰레기

해석

비행 자동차 – 첫 실용 모델이 1947년에 등장 –를 만드는 것이 그리 어려운 일은 아니다. 진정한 도전은 제대로 된 비행 자동차를 만드는 것이다. Tesla사와 SpaceX사의 CEO인 Elon Musk는 왜 두 회사를 합병해서 로켓 자동차를 만들지 않는지 지속적인 질문을 받았다. 그는 "비행 자동차의 장점 : 3차원적인 빠른 여행. 단점 : 차가 머리 위로 떨어질 위험성이 두 벡터로 움직이는 차보다 훨씬 큼"을 포함해 최근 일련의 트위터 메시지로 답했다. 그리고 유명한 발명가인 Peter Thiel은 "고물이 아닌 진짜 비행 자동차를 원한다."고 주위에 말하곤 했다.

14 ① 두 번째 문장의 "a renowned animal scientist born with autism, Temple Grandin"을 통해 Temple Grandin이 자폐증을 가지고 태어난 유명한 동물 과학자임을 알 수 있다.

오답풀이

② 저명한 신경과 의사에 의해 알려지게 되었다.

③ 자폐아들에게 특별한 영감의 원천이 되었다.

④ 소의 스트레스를 줄이는 울타리를 개발했다.

⑤ Grandin 버거의 윤리와 연민에 감사하게 되었다.

어휘

• neurologist : 신경학자, 신경과 전문의

• renowned : 유명한, 명성 있는

• autism : 자폐증

• utter : 말하다, 발언하다

• splash : 철벅 떨어지다, 첨벙거리다

• autistic : 자폐증의, 자폐성의

• patty : 패티(고기·생선 등을 다져 동글납작하게 빚은 것)

• appreciate : 인정하다, 감사하다

• ethics : 윤리학, 도덕

• compassion : 연민, 동정심

해석

신경과 의사, 소, 패스트푸드 음식점이 가지고 있는 공통점은 무엇일까? 그들 모두는 자폐증을 가지고 태어난 유명한 동물 과학자인 Temple Grandin이라는 한 여성에게 큰 신세를 지고 있다는 것이다. 비록 그녀는 네 번째 생일이 될 때까지 한 마디 말도 하지 못했지만, 저명한 신경과 의사인 Oliver Sacks 덕택에 1995년에 대중의 인식이라는 무대 위에 모습을 드러냈다. 그러나 많은 정신장애와 마찬가지로 자폐증의 폭은 넓었고, Temple은 막다른 끝에 있었다. 이런 막다른 끝의 삶은 자폐아들에게 특별한 영감의 원천이 되었다. 그녀는 또 다른 포유류, 소에게 또한 희망의 원천이었다. 동물에 대한 그녀의 독특한 마음의 창을 통해 소의 스트레스를 줄이고 삶의 질을 개선한 울타리를 개발했다. 비록 패스트푸드 산업에 계속해서 소고기 패티를 사용하긴 하지만, Grandin 버거의 윤리와 연민에 감사하게 되었다.

15 ③ "It took them just two seconds to match the colors of the sea fans, or gorgonians, they swam past."라는 문장을 통해 쥐치가 뛰어난 위장능력을 가지고 있어서, 부채꼴 산호의 색깔로 바꾸는 데 2초 밖에 걸리지 않음을 알 수 있다.

오답풀이

① 천적을 피하는 교묘한 기술이 있다.

② 눈에 안 띄게 하는 능력을 진화시켰다.

④ 보호색을 바꾸어 가짜 윤곽을 만든다.

⑤ 몸에 어두운 세로 줄무늬를 만든다.

어휘

• slender : 날씬한, 호리호리한

• filefish : 쥐치

• predator : 포식자, 천적

• evolve : 진화하다, 발달하다

• camouflage : 위장하다, 감추다

• sea fan : 부채꼴 산호

• gorgonian : 부채꼴 산호

• perceive : 인지하다, 감지하다

• coloration : 천연색, 보호색

• longitudinal : 세로의, 길이의, 종적인

해석

보이다가도, 보이지 않는다. 날씬한 쥐치는 천적을 피하는 교묘한 기술을 가지고 있다. 그것은 거의 눈에 안 띄게 하는 능력을 진화시켰다. Brown 대학의 Justine Allen은 쥐치들을 Caribbean 해에서 보았을 때 얼마나 빨리 위장하는지 놀라지 않을 수 없었다. 쥐치들이 헤엄치며 지나간 부채꼴 산호의 색깔로 맞추는 데 겨우 2초 밖에 걸리지 않았다. 그런 작용은 어떻게 이루어지는가? 어떤 사물의 형태를 보기 위해서는 그 사물의 윤곽을 인지해야 하며, 그 윤곽은 배경과 물체를 분리하는 표시가 된다. Allen은 쥐치가 "가짜 윤곽"을 만들기 위해 보호색을 바꾼다는 사실을 알아냈다. 예를 들면, 쥐치는 진짜 윤곽처럼 보이도록 몸에 어두운 세로 줄무늬를 만들어낼 수 있다. 눈이 가짜 윤곽을 봄으로써 그 물고기의 진짜 윤곽을 놓치는 것이다.

16 ⑤ 마지막 문장의 "The homeowners lost the suit,~"에서 주택소유자들이 소송에서 패했다는 사실을 알 수 있으며, 그로 인해 보험 업계는 많은 신용을 잃었고 사람들은 보상범위가 서류상으로 보이는 것보다 훨씬 작다고 생각하게 되었다.

어휘

• ambiguous : 애매모호한

• insurance : 보험

• contract : 계약, 약정

• wrought : 초래하다, 일으키다

• storm surge : 폭풍 해일

• infuriate : 극도로 화나게 하다, 격노하다

• sue : 고소하다, 소송을 제기하다

• insurance carrier : 보험업자, 보험사

• property : 재산, 소유물, 부동산

• suit : 소송

• coverage : 보도, 범위

해석

보험계약에서 실망으로 이어지는 혼동과 오해의 근원은 복잡하고 모호한 말들에 있다. 미시시피 연안의 허리케인 Katrina에 의해 초래된 수십억 달러의 피해 중 상당수가 Katrina의 거대한 폭풍 해일이 수천 채의 집과 사무실을 파괴하고 피해를 입혔을 때 발생했다. 주택소유자들은 물이 아닌 바람에 의한 피해만 보상한다는 정책을 알았을 때 몹시 화가 났고, 보험사를 고소하기 위해 주 정부와 힘을 합쳤다. 그들은 보험이 수해를 보상하지 않는다고 해도 Katrina의 폭풍이 그들의 재산상 피해를 입힌 물벼락을 몰고 왔기 때문에 보험금을 지급해야만 한다고 주장했다. 주택소유자들은 소송에서 패했지만, 보험업계는 많은 신용을 잃었고 사람들은 보상범위가 서류상으로 보이는 것보다 훨씬 작다고 생각하게 되었다.

17 ⑤ 마지막 문장의 "Her record-setting race would have earned third place at this year's NCAA championships~"에서 Candace Hill이 NCAA 챔피언십 경기에 참가한 것이 아니라, 그녀가 세운 기록이 올해 NCAA 챔피언십 경기 3위에 해당되는 기록이라는 의미임을 알 수 있다.

어휘

• benchmark : 기준, 수준

• invitational : 초청경기

• scorching : 태워버릴 듯한, 맹렬한

• smash : 박살내다, 때려 부수다

• tie for 10th : 공동 10위를 하다

해석

11초는 100미터 경주에서 성인 여성과 소녀를 구분하는 기준이 된다. 지난 토요일 시애틀에서 열린 Brooks PR 초청경기에서 16세의 Candace Hill은 10.98초의 강력한 우승으로 엘리트 그룹에 속하게 되었고, 11초의 벽을 깬 최초의 미국 여고생이 되었으며, 미국 유소년 기록과 세계 청소년 기록을 갈아치웠다. 지난 달 Georgia 주에 있는 Rockdale Country 고등학교 2학년을 마친 Candace은 다섯 차례나 국내 챔피언이었고, 이미 100미터와 200미터 경주에서 Georgia 주 기록을 보유하고 있다. 그녀가 세운 기록은 올해 NCAA 챔피언십 경기에서 3위에 해당되며, 이번 시즌 세계에서 공동 10위에 해당하는 기록이다.

18 ⑤ 사람들은 동물에게 사랑과 감사를 표하고 동물 학대를 금하는 법을 제정하기도 하지만, 동시에 수십억의 동물들이 매년 식용, 의복, 연구 그리고 다른 목적으로 죽거나 학대당한다. 그러므로 사람과 동물과의 관계는 모순(contradictions)투성이라고 할 수 있다.

오답풀이

① gratitude(감사)

② hostility(적대감)

③ protectiveness(보호)

④ responsibilities(책임감)

어휘

• fraught with : ~투성이의

• appreciation : 감사, 공감

• enact : 제정하다, 상연하다

• cruelty : 잔인함, 학대

• pet-keeping : 애완동물 키우기

• engage with : ~와 맞물리게 하다

• unspoiled : 훼손되지 않은

• exploit : 이용하다, 착취하다

• massive : 거대한, 엄청난

해석

사람과 동물과의 관계는 <u>모순투성이</u>이다. 그들은 동물에게 사랑과 감사를 표하고 동물 학대를 금하는 법을 제정했다. 미국은 애완동물 키우기가 좋은 사회인데, 개, 고양이, 앵무새, 햄스터 그리고 다른 애완동물들을 다 합치면 사람보다 더 많으며 애완동물 관리 산업이 한 해 600억 달러에 달한다. 수백만의 미국인들은 야생 동물과 어떤 식으로든 관련되어 있고, 그들의 가장 행복한 순간은 훼손되지 않은 환경에서 보내는 것이다. 그럼에도 불구하고 동시에 그들은 동물을 대량으로 이용하며, 수십억의 동물들이 매년 식용, 의복, 연구 그리고 다른 목적으로 죽거나 학대당한다.

19 ① 빈칸의 다음 문장에서 "지구상에서 17억 명 이상의 사람들이 인터넷을 통해 남들로부터 인정을 구하고 공유하기 위해 SNS를 활용한다"고 했으므로, SNS는 남들로부터 인정받기를 추구하는(in pursuit of recognition from others) 곳이다.

오답풀이

② to extend their domain of friendship(우정의 범위를 넓히기 위해)

③ despite massive criticism by experts(전문가들에 의한 엄청난 비난에도 불구하고)

④ prompting misgivings among the public(대중들에게 불안감을 촉발하는)

⑤ beyond the limits imposed by authorities(당국의 통제 범위를 넘어서)

어휘

• preoccupy : 사로잡다, 집착하다

• conform : 따르다, 순응하다

• preoccupation : 선입견, 집착

• evident : 명백한, 분명한

• celebrity : 유명인사, 명성

• validation : 확인, 비준

• performing-arts : 공연 예술

• anonymous : 익명의

• obsession : 강박, 집착

• a casual acquaintance : 조금 아는 사람, 안면이 있는 사람

• in pursuit of : ~을 쫓아서, ~을 추구하여

• recognition : 인식, 인정, 승인

• domain : 영역, 범위

• prompt : 촉발하다, 유도하다

• misgivings : 불안, 걱정, 염려

• authorities : 정부 당국, 관계자

해석

우리는 너무나 사회적 동물이라서 남들이 우리를 어떻게 생각하는지에 대해 몹시 집착한다. 순응하라는 사회적 압력은 집단으로부터 평가받는 것과 관련이 있는데, 결국 대부분의 성공이 남들이 어떻게 생각하느냐에 따라 정해지기 때문이다. 이러한 선입견은 현대의 유명 인사 문화와 특히 일반 개인들이 상당한 시간과 노력을 들여 <u>남들로부터 인정받기를 추구하는</u> 곳인 SNS의 성장을 통해 너무나 명백하게 드러난다. 지구상에서 17억 명 이상의 사람들이 인터넷을 통해 남들로부터 인정을 구하고 공유하기 위해 SNS를 활용한다. 공연 예술 학교에 관한 성공한 뮤지컬 시리즈 배우인 Rachel Berry가 "요즘은 무명이 가난보다 최악이다"라고 말했을 때, 그녀는 단순히 명성에 대한 집착과 많은 사람들 - 주로 모르는 사이이든 조금 아는 사이이든 -로부터 사랑받고 싶은 욕망을 외친 것뿐이다.

20 ⑤ 모차르트의 음악적 천재성은 누군가 한 번도 들어본 적이 없는 독창성으로 인해 모든 아름다움을 흡수할 수 없다고 했고, 그런 풍부한 아름다움(abundance of beauty)이 지나친 완벽함에서 오는 모차르트의 유일한 결점이라고 했다.

오답풀이

① plethora of faith(과도한 믿음)

② desolation of spirit(고독한 영혼)

③ command of words(명령어)

④ redundancy of melodies(중복되는 멜로디)

어휘

• originality : 독창성

• accompaniment : 반주, 반찬

• novel : 새로운, 신기한, 참신한

- incessantly : 끊임없이, 계속해서
- notion : 개념, 관념, 생각
- admiration : 감탄, 존경
- swallow up : 집어삼키다, 빨아들이다
- strain : 안간힘을 쓰다, 세게 잡아당기다
- all one's force : 온 힘을 다해
- obscure : 잘 알려져 있지 않은, 무명의, 애매모호한
- plethora : 과다, 과잉
- desolation : 외로움, 황량함
- redundancy : 불필요한 중복[반복], 정리 해고

[해석]

모차르트의 음악적 천재성을 가장 충실하게 묘사하기 위해 예술에 대한 깊은 지식과 아름다운 멜로디를 만드는 행복한 재능을 결합하여 이들을 최고의 독창성과 연결해 보자. 그의 작품 어디에서도 누군가 전에 한 번은 들어본 적이 있다는 생각을 찾을 수 없다. 심지어 반주조차도 항상 새롭다. 이를테면, 하나의 생각이 또 다른 생각으로 계속해서 이어지고, 쉴 새 없이 가장 최근의 감탄이 이전의 감탄을 계속 집어삼키며, 아무리 온 힘을 다해도 마음에 표현되는 모든 아름다움을 흡수할 수 없다. 만일 모차르트에게서 찾을 수 있는 어떤 결점이 있다면, 그것은 오로지 이것뿐이다. 그런 풍부한 아름다움이 영혼을 지치게 하고 전체적인 효과가 그로인해 모호해진다는 것이다. 그러나 유일한 결점이 그의 지나친 완벽함에 있다는 것은 예술가로서는 정말 행복한 것이다.

21 ① 한 장의 사진은 천 마디 말보다 가치가 있다고 했고, 그것을 구현하는 것이 현미경, 망원경, 고속 카메라 그리고 X선 관 같은 기계들이며, 그런 기계가 만든 새로운 형태의 증거는 바로 시각적 증거(visual evidence)이다.

[오답풀이]

② verbal testimony(구두 증거)
③ legal terminology(법률 용어)
④ linguistic eloquence(언어적 웅변)
⑤ subjective expression(주관적 표현)

[어휘]

- rhetoric : 미사여구, 수사법[학]
- trial : 재판, 공판, 시험
- common law : 관습법
- doom : 불행한 운명을 맞게 하다
- dominance : 우월, 우세
- testimony : 증거, 증언
- alert : 기민한, 경계하는
- purport : 주장하다, 칭하다
- inaccessible : 도달할 수 없는, 접근하기 어려운

- emblem : 상징
- objectivity : 객관성
- watchword : 좌우명, 표어
- verbal : 언어의, 구두의
- terminology : 전문 용어
- eloquence : 웅변, 화술

[해석]

한 장의 사진은 천 마디 말보다 가치가 있지만, 수세기 동안 법적인 영역을 지배해 온 것은 언어였다. 언어 예술인 수사학은 항상 변호사들의 트레이드마크였으며, 재판 특히 관습법에서의 재판은 언어 논쟁으로 여겼다. 아쉽게도 모든 영광은 지나게 마련이며, 19세기 후반에 우세한 설득 방식이 새롭게 선보였는데, 언어를 열등한 의사소통 방식으로 바꾸어 놓을 법한 기계로 만든 새로운 형태의 증거들에 의해 주도되었다. 항상 기민하고 결코 연관성이 없는 현미경, 망원경, 고속 카메라 그리고 X선 관 같은 기계들은 인간과 달리 접근하기 어려운 증거들을 보다 충분히, 더 잘, 더 진실 되게 전달할 수 있다고 본다. 이런 새로운 형태의 기계적 객관성의 상징은 바로 시각적 증거였다. "자연이 스스로 말하게 나둬라"가 표어가 되었고, 자연의 언어는 사진과 기계적으로 형성된 곡선의 언어처럼 보였다.

22 ② 노래 가사가 더 단순하고 반복적일수록 최고 순위에 올라갈 기회가 더 많다고 했으므로, 메시지가 이해하기 쉬울수록 사람들이 더 긍정적으로 반응한다(the more positively people will react to it)는 내용이 와야 알맞다. 그러한 이론은 광고나 코미디에서도 마찬가지로 적용된다.

[오답풀이]

① the more effort the brain has to exert(뇌가 더욱 분발하도록 노력한다)
③ the higher the likelihood of tuning out the message(가능성이 더 높아지도록 메시지를 보낸다)
④ the less the chances of people singing after the song (사람들이 그 노래를 따라 부를 기회가 더 없다)
⑤ the less likely people will decode the hidden message (사람들은 숨은 메시지를 해독하려 하지 않을 것 같다)

[어휘]

- repetition : 반복, 되풀이
- lyrics : 가사, 노랫말
- fluency : 유창성, 능숙함
- strategy : 전략, 계획
- saturate : 흠뻑 적시다, 포화시키다
- punch line : 급소를 찌르는 말, 들을 만한 대목
- loop : 고리 모양으로 만들다, 구부리다

• exert : 행사하다, 노력하다

• likelihood : 가능성

• decode : 해독하다

해석

소비 심리학 저널은 1958년부터 2012년까지 빌보드 핫 100곡 중에서 1위 곡과 과거에 히트하지 못한 90위 곡을 비교하여 반복의 힘을 조사했다. 조사자들은 노래 가사가 더 단순하고 반복적일수록 최고 순위에 올라갈 기회가 더 많다는 사실을 관찰했다. 그런 노래들은 덜 반복적인 노래들보다 차트에서 순위가 빠르게 올라갔다. 이런 발견은 메시지가 이해하기 쉬울수록 사람들이 더 긍정적으로 반응한다는 유창성 처리 이론을 뒷받침 한다. 그 비밀이 단지 음악가들에게만 해당되는 것은 아니다. 광고 방송에 몰입하도록 슬로건을 통한 광고에도 비슷한 전략이 활용되며, 심지어 코미디에도 활용된다. 스탠드업 코미디에서는 세트 전체에 똑같은 웃음 문구를 두르기도 한다.

23 ② 종교가 지녔던 자연법칙에 대한 설명적 역할이 현대에서는 과학에 의해 설명되고 있음을 천문학자, 기상학자, 동물 행동학자, 진화 생물학자 등의 예를 들어 설명하고 있다. 따라서 빈칸에는 종교의 역할이 "점차 과학에 의해 잠식되고 있다(has increasingly become usurped by science)"라는 내용이 알맞다.

오답풀이

① provides the basis for scientific theories(과학적 이론의 근거를 제시하다)

③ has risen to give the best account of nature(자연에 관해 최선을 다해 설명하다)

④ evokes controversy on the adequacy of science(과학적 타당성에 관해 논란을 일으키다)

⑤ is reinforced by creationists and evolutionists alike(창조론자와 진화론자에 의해 똑같이 보강되다)

어휘

• explanatory : 설명적인, 이유를 밝히는

• subsequent : 그 다음의, 차후의

• snap : 딱하고 부러뜨리다, 딱딱거리다

• liana : 리아나(열대산 칡의 일종)

• ironwood tree : 경질 수목

• adequately : 충분히, 적절히

• astronomer : 천문학자

• meteorologist : 기상학자

• ethology : 동물 행동학, 인성학

• evolutionary : 진화의, 점진적인

• biologist : 생물학자

• interpret : 해석하다, 설명하다

• usurp : 빼앗다, 강탈하다

• evoke : 불러일으키다, 환기시키다

• controversy : 논란, 논쟁

• adequacy : 적절, 타당성

• reinforce : 강화하다, 보강하다

• creationist : 창조론자, 천지창조

• evolutionist : 진화론자

해석

현대 서구 사회에서 본래 종교가 가졌던 설명적 역할이 점차 과학에 의해 잠식되고 있다. 우리가 알고 있는 우주의 기원은 이제 빅뱅과 차후의 물리학 법칙에 따른 작용에 의한다. 현대 언어의 다양성은 더 이상 바벨탑이나 뉴기니의 경질 수목을 붙들고 있던 리아나 칡의 부러짐과 같은 기원 신화로 설명되지 않는다. 대신 언어가 변화는 역사적 과정을 관찰하면 충분히 설명된다. 일출과 일몰 그리고 썰물과 밀물에 대한 설명은 이제 천문학자의 몫이 되었으며, 바람과 비에 대한 설명은 기상학자의 몫이 되었다. 새들의 노래는 동물 행동학으로 설명되며, 모든 식물과 인류를 포함한 동물의 종의 기원은 진화 생물학자가 해석할 몫이 되었다.

24 ⑤ (A) 마야인들에게 담배는 종교 생활에 매우 중요한 역할을 했는데, 그것은 질병을 예방하고 치료하는 중요한 요소였으며 어떤 지역에서는 신격화 되었다. 그러므로 마야인의 시각에서 기쁨을 제공하는 담배의 특성은 다른 기능들에 비해 부수적인(subordinate) 것처럼 보인다.

(B) 스페인 사람들이 통합한 식민지 원주민들의 문화적 요소들을 스페인식으로 세속화(secularization)하였을 때 마야인들에게 종교 생활에 중요한 역할을 하고 신격화 되었던 담배가 스페인 사람들에게는 단지 개인에게 즐거움을 제공하는 상품일 뿐이며, 마찬가지로 식민지 원주민들에게 신성한 생명의 양식인 옥수수와 카카오도 정복자인 스페인 사람들에게는 공물과 상업교역을 위한 물품에 지나지 않았다.

어휘

• for that matter : 그 문제라면, 그 점에 대해서

• illustrate : 삽화를 쓰다, 분명히 보여주다, 실증하다

• prevention : 예방, 방지

• deify : 신격화하다, 신으로 받들다

• commodity : 상품, 물품, 원자재

• ritualistic : 의례적인, 절차상의

• shed : 없애다, 버리다, 흘리다

• transaction : 거래, 매매

• degradation : 비하, 수모

- be in line with : ~와 일치하다
- maize : 옥수수
- staff of life : 생명의 양식
- relevant : 관련 있는, 적절한
- authorization : 허가, 인가
- enlightenment : 계몽, 깨우침
- identical : 동일한, 똑같은
- subordinate : 종속된, 부수적인
- inquisition : 심문, 취조
- secularization : 세속화

해석

담배의 용도는 그것이 스페인이나 또는 그 점에 있어서 모든 서양 문화의 일부가 되었을 때, 마야인의 시각에서 거의 종교적 요소였던 담배에 무슨 일이 있었는지 분명히 보여준다. 마야들 사이에서 담배는 종교 생활에 매우 중요한 역할을 했다. 그것은 질병을 예방하고 치료하는 중요한 요소였고, 어떤 지역에서는 신격화 되었다. 마야인의 시각에서 기쁨을 제공하는 담배의 특성은 다른 기능들에 비해 <u>부수적인</u> 것처럼 보인다. 그러나 담배가 스페인 사람들에게 넘어갔을 때 그것은 단지 개인에게 즐거움을 제공하는 상품일 뿐이었다. 마야의 모든 의식과 공동체 관계는 사라졌다. 이런 과정은 스페인 사람들이 통합한 식민지 원주민들의 문화적 요소들을 스페인식으로 세속화하는 것과 일치했다. 옥수수는 더 이상 사랑받는 신성한 생명의 양식이 아니다. 그것은 정복자에게는 공물과 상업교역을 위한 물품이 되었다. 카카오도 그와 똑같은 수모를 겪었다.

25 ⑤ 위 글은 최초의 로빈 후드가 대중문화에서 알고 있던 멋진 영웅이 아닌 부자들로부터 훔친 돈을 지키고 가끔 가난한 사람들을 도왔던 자작농이었으나, 17세기 이후 유명해지면서 점차 가난한 사람들의 권리를 대변하는 Sherwood 숲의 영웅적 범법자가 되었다고 설명하고 있다. 따라서 '로빈 후드 캐릭터의 변화(Transformations in the Robin Hood Character)'가 위 글의 제목으로 알맞다.

오답풀이

① Robin Hood as a Robber(도둑 로빈 후드)
② Origins of Medieval Yeomen(중세 자작농의 유래)
③ Earlier Struggles of Robin Hood(초창기 로빈 후드의 투쟁)
④ Ideal Society in Sherwood Forest(Sherwood 숲속의 이상 사회)

어휘

- ballad : 발라드(시나 노래), 연가
- portray : 그리다, 묘사하다
- dashing : 늠름한, 근사한

- yeoman : 자작농, 소지주
- rectify : 바로잡다
- outlaw : 범법자, 도망자

해석

최초의 로빈 후드 연가는 1450년에 인쇄되었으며, 대중문화에서 알고 있던 멋진 영웅으로 묘사되지는 않았다. 그는 자작농이었으며, 때로는 거칠고 잔인했다. 그 전설은 부자들로부터 훔친 돈을 지키고 가끔 가난한 사람들을 도왔던 강도에 더 비중을 두고 있다. 그는 숲속에서 이상 사회를 건설하기를 원치 않았다. 로빈 후드와 그의 부하들은 주로 사회적 불평등을 바로잡고 잘 살려고 했다. 로빈 후드는 17세기까지 매우 유명해졌고 사람들은 그의 이름을 따서 배나 장소에 붙였다. 19세기까지 많은 이야기와 노래가 로빈 후드 전설에 큰 변화를 가져왔다. 그의 자작농 태생은 사라졌고, 그는 점차 가난한 사람들의 권리를 대변하는 Sherwood 숲의 영웅적 범법자가 되었다.

26 ② 위 글은 교류하는 관계에 따라 몸이 어떻게 반응하는지 설명하고 있는데, 가족이나 유쾌한 친구들과 있을 때는 혈압이 떨어졌지만, 고압적인 부모나 변덕스러운 연인 그리고 경쟁관계에 있는 친구와 있을 때는 혈압이 상승했다고 말하고 있다. 그러므로 '불편한 관계 : 몸은 거짓말하지 않는다(Uneasy Relationships: Your Body Doesn't Lie)'가 위 글의 제목으로 타당하다.

오답풀이

① High Blood Pressure: The Silent Assassin(고혈압 : 침묵의 암살자)
③ Don't Be Bossed Around by Your Biorhythm(생체리듬에 좌우되지 마라)
④ Can Health Monitoring Devices Save Your Life? (건강 진단 장비로 여러분의 생명을 구할 수 있습니까?)
⑤ How Can You Deal with Uncomfortable Interactions? (당신은 불편한 관계에 어떻게 대처합니까?)

어휘

- soothing : 달래는, 누그러뜨리는, 진정하는
- ambivalent : 반대 감정이 존재하는, 양면적인
- overbearing : 고압적인, 남을 지배하는
- volatile : 변덕스러운, 불안한
- mercurial : 변덕스러운, 활달한
- loom : 어렴풋이 나타나다, 흐릿하게 보이다
- archetype : 전형, 원형
- assassin : 암살자
- boss : ~를 쥐고 흔든다, 좌지우지하다

해석

한 연구에서 백 명의 남녀가 그들이 누군가와 교류할 때마다 혈압을 측정하는 장치를 착용했다. 그들이 가족이나 유쾌한 친구들과 있을 때는 혈압이 떨어졌다. 이러한 교류는 즐겁고 마음을 진정시켰다. 그들이 골치 아픈 누군가와 있을 때는 혈압이 상승했다. 그러나 가장 큰 상승은 반대 감정이 존재하는 사람들, 즉 고압적인 부모나 변덕스러운 연인 그리고 경쟁관계에 있는 친구와 있을 때 나타났다. 변덕스러운 상사가 전형적이라고 볼 수 있지만, 이런 역학 관계는 모든 관계에서 작동한다.

27 ⑤ 시간을 초월한 바흐, 베토벤, 비틀즈, Venda의 노래와 문화적으로 다른 일본의 고토 음악, 인도의 시타르 음악, 초피족의 실로폰 음악 등에서 우리가 전율을 느끼는 것은 모든 인간의 정신에 공통적으로 존재하는 요소, 즉 음악적 보편성이 있기 때문이다. 그러므로 위 글의 주제는 '시간과 문화를 초월한 음악의 보편성(the universality of music that transcends time and culture)'이라고 볼 수 있다.

오답풀이

① the potential of music to enrich culture(문화를 풍요롭게 하는 음악의 잠재력)

② the gradual divergence of music from culture(문화로부터 음악의 점진적 분화)

③ the ability of music to nourish the human psyche(인간의 정신을 키우는 음악 능력)

④ the advantages of cross-cultural transmission of music (여러 문화 간 음악 전파의 장점)

어휘

• sitar : 시타르(기타 비슷한 인도의 악기)
• Chopi : (모잠비크) 초피족
• cross-cultural : 여러 문화가 섞인[혼재된]
• psyche : 마음, 정신
• divergence : 분기, 일탈, 차이, 확산
• nourish : 영양분을 공급하다, 키우다
• transmission : 전파, 전달
• transcend : 초월하다

해석

바흐와 베토벤과 동시대에 살았던 사람들을 흥분시켰던 그 음악은 비록 우리가 그들의 문화를 공유하지는 않지만 아직도 흥분된다. 불행히도 지금은 해체되었지만 초기 비틀즈의 노래는 아직도 우리를 들뜨게 한다. 비슷하게, 수백 년 전에 작곡된 Venda 노래도 여전히 나를 흥분시킨다. 우리 중 많은 사람들이 일본의 고토 음악, 인도의 시타르 음악, 초피족의 실로

폰 음악 등에 전율을 느낀다. 우리가 연주자와 똑같이 정확하게 음악을 받아들인다고 말할 수는 없지만, 우리 자신들의 경험에 비추어 여러 문화 간 소통 가능성이 있음을 보여준다. 나는 이러한 이유를 비록 표층구조에는 나타나지 않지만, 음악의 심층구조에는 인간 정신에 공통된 요소들이 존재한다는 사실에서 찾을 수 있다고 확신한다.

28 ③ 우리의 능력과 결과에 부합되지 않는 롤 모델을 선택하는 것은 영감의 대상이 아니라 좌절과 패배의 근원이 되므로, 네가 이룰 수 있고 이루고 싶은 것을 해낸 사람을 롤 모델로 선택하는 것이 중요하다. 그러므로 위 글의 주제는 '도달 가능한 롤 모델 선택의 중요성(the importance of selecting a reachable role model)'이라고 할 수 있다.

오답풀이

① the success stories of a realistic role model(실제 롤 모델의 성공 이야기)

② the source of frustration in emulating a role model(롤 모델을 모방하는 데 있어 좌절의 근원)

④ the necessity for having an inspiring person around(주위에 영감을 주는 사람을 소유할 필요성)

⑤ the positive effects of imitating a person of high status (높은 지위에 있는 사람을 모방하여 얻는 긍정적인 효과)

어휘

• quote : 인용문
• measure up : ~을 측정하다[재다], 부합하다
• frustration : 좌절, 불만
• tremendous : 엄청난, 굉장한
• emulate : 모방하다, 따라하다

해석

우리는 종종 영감을 주는 사람들과 놀라운 성공에 대한 이야기를 듣는다. 일부는 그들의 사진을 벽에 붙이거나 그들의 유명한 인용문을 클립으로 고정해 둔다. 그러나 영감을 주는 사람이 우리가 결코 하지 않거나 할 수 없는 일을 했다면 그게 무슨 소용이 있겠는가? 상당수의 사람들에게 롤 모델의 선택은 비교를 요청하며, 만일 우리의 능력과 결과에 부합되지 않는다면 그 롤 모델은 영감의 대상이 아니라 좌절과 패배의 근원이 된다. 네가 이룰 수 있고 이루고 싶은 것을 해낸 사람을 롤 모델로 선택하라. 큰 성공을 거둔 경험이 있지만 그 경험이 너와 별로 관련이 없는 유명한 운동선수나 지도자 또는 역사적 위인들보다 네가 존경하는 동료나 가족을 활용하는 것이 더 큰 가치가 있다.

29 ③ 회색곰의 경우 어미를 모델로 삼아 새끼가 배운 것은 삶과 죽음의 문제이고, 사람의 경우 사소한 일에 부정을 일삼는

것이 아이들에게 그런 행동을 가르치게 되므로 자식은 부모를 보고 배운다고 볼 수 있다. 그러므로 "좋은 부모란 모범이 되는 것에서 시작되고 끝난다(Good parenting begins and ends with setting a good example.)"를 위 글의 요지로 볼 수 있다.

오답풀이

① Parents are spending more time reading books on wildlife.(부모들은 야생동물에 관한 책을 읽는 데 많은 시간을 할애한다.)

② Mindful consumption lies at the center of being good parents.(의식 있는 소비는 좋은 부모가 되기 위한 핵심이다.)

④ Teaching good behavior to children outweighs earning money.(아이들에게 훌륭한 행동을 가르치는 것은 돈을 버는 것보다 중요하다.)

⑤ Children's behavior is subconsciously mirrored by their parents.(아이들의 행동은 부모들에 의해 잠재적으로 반영된다.)

어휘

• grizzly bear : 회색곰
• cub : 새끼
• rat race : 극심한 생존 경쟁[무한 경쟁]
• mindlessly : 의식 없이, 함부로
• moderation : 적당함. 온건, 절제
• cheat : 속이다, 부정행위를 하다
• mindful : 염두에 두는[의식하는]
• outweigh : ~보다 크다[대단하다]
• subconsciously : 잠재의식적으로

해석

최근에 나는 위험에 처한 브리티시 컬럼비아 해안의 회색곰에 대해 읽고 있었다. 작가는 어떻게 새끼가 먹이를 구해 잡아먹는 어미의 기술을 예리하게 관찰하는 지 역설했다. 어미를 모델로 삼아 새끼가 배운 것은 삶과 죽음의 문제였다. 그런 지식이 없다면 새끼는 아마도 살아남을 수 없을 것이다. 그와 똑같은 원칙이 우리에게도 적용된다. 극심한 생존 경쟁에서 살아갈 때 우리 아이들이 그러지 않으리라고 어떻게 장담할 수 있겠는가? 아무런 생각 없이 취하고 소비할 때, 우리 아이들이 어떻게 절제와 관계의 의미를 알겠는가? 내가 계산대에서 받은 거스름돈을 돌려주지 않거나 주은 돈의 주인을 찾아주지 않고 슬쩍하는 등 사소한 일에 부정을 일삼는다면 나는 아이들에게 그런 행동을 가르치고 있는 것이다.

30 ② Dave가 갑작스러운 폭발로 침대에서 내동댕이쳐지고 깜짝 놀라 깨어보니 배의 엔진이 멈추고 전등도 켜지지 않는

등 Dave의 심경은 매우 '혼란스럽고 불안한(confused and nervous)' 상태라고 볼 수 있다.

오답풀이

① distracted and angry(심란하고 화가 난)
③ overjoyed and proud(매우 기쁘고 자랑스러운)
④ indifferent and bored(따분하고 지루한)
⑤ irritated and stimulated(짜증나고 흥분한)

어휘

• hurl : 던지다, 욕설을 퍼붓다
• mingle : 섞다, 어울리다
• startle : 깜짝 놀라게 하다
• absent-mindedly : 멍하니, 우두커니
• throb : 고동, 진동
• abruptly : 갑자기, 불쑥
• cease : 그만두다, 멈추다
• trembling : 떨리는, 전율하는
• distracted : 산만한, 심란한
• irritated : 짜증난, 성가신

해석

Dave는 그것이 어떻게 일어났는지 전혀 알 수 없었다. 그는 단지 침대에서 내동댕이쳐지고 깜짝 놀라 깨어보니 굉장한 폭발이 있었다는 것 밖에는 모른다. 잠시 동안 그는 자기 방 데크 위에 멍하니 누워 있었고, 정신을 차리려고 애썼다. 그는 배에 탑승한 후 그 주 동안 너무나 익숙해진 엔진의 진동이 갑자기 멈췄다는 사실을 깨달았다. 어떻게 된 거지? 그는 일어나 전등 스위치로 가서 떨리는 손으로 켰다. 아무 반응도 없었고, 그는 다시 시도했다. 전등은 켜지지 않았다.

31 ③ 위 글은 암 발병률을 높이고, 토양과 하천 그리고 지하수를 오염시키며, 생태계의 생산성과 안정성을 악화시키는 등 산업화된 농업의 문제점에 대해 서술하고 있다. 그러므로 ③의 "신 기술을 기회로 여긴 회사와 정부가 산업화된 농업의 발 빠른 확산을 조성했다"는 내용은 위 글의 서술 방향과 어울리지 않는다.

어휘

• on the face of it : 겉으로 보기에, 표면적으로
• ramify : 가지를 내다. 분기[분파]하다
• decade : 10년
• a host of : 다수의, 많은
• foster : 조성하다, 발전시키다
• fertilizer : 비료
• pesticide : 살충제, 농약
• contamination : 오염, 타락

429

- groundwater : 지하수
- monoculture : 단일 재배, 단일 민족[문화]
- biodiversity : 생물의 다양성
- undermine : 악화시키다
- ecosystem : 생태계

해석

겉으로 보기에 산업화된 농업은 변치 않는 세계 기아 문제를 풀 최고의 해결책이 될 것 같았다. ① 그러나 작가이자 농부인 Wendell Berry씨가 관찰한 결과, 소위 그런 해결책들도 새로운 문제들을 분파했다. ② 그리고 지난 수십 년 동안 산업화된 농업이 사람과 지구의 건강에 영향을 미치는 많은 문제를 발생시켰다는 사실이 점차 명확해졌다. ③ 그래서 신 기술을 기회로 여긴 회사와 정부가 산업화된 농업의 발 빠른 확산을 조성했다. ④ 예를 들어 비료와 농약의 사용은 암 발병률을 높이고, 토양과 하천 그리고 지하수를 오염시켰다. ⑤ 단일 재배 농업은 생물 다양성의 손실로 이어져, 생태계의 생산성과 안정성을 악화시켰다.

32 ③ 위 글은 건강에 좋은 음식을 집집마다 배달해주는 서비스에 대해 서술하고 있으므로, ③의 "로컬 푸드에서 오는 이런 영양 결핍은 주로 앉아서 지내는 생활방식에 의해서만 악화된다."는 내용은 위 글의 문맥과 어울리지 않는다.

어휘

- artfully : 교묘하게, 인위적으로
- slow-simmered : 천천히 끓인
- bone broth : 사골 국물
- obsess : 사로잡다, 강박관념을 갖다
- virtuously : 정숙하게, 고결하게
- trim : 다듬기, 장식, 테두리
- crucial : 중대한, 결정적인
- fortify : 요새화하다, 기운[용기]을 북돋다
- a square meal : 충분한[제대로 된] 식사
- sedentary : 주로 앉아서 하는, 한 곳에 머물러 사는
- wholesome : 건강에 좋은, 유익한
- cleanse : 세척, 청결
- shape up : 되어 가다, 전개되다

해석

세련된 밥사발과 오래 끓인 사골 국물까지, 그 메시지는 분명하다. 미와 건강 세트가 영양과 함께 집중 관심이 되고 있다. ① 오늘날 품위 있게 식사하는 것은 그저 장식을 위한 수단이 아니라, 점차 건강하고 바쁜 생활을 위해 몸의 기운을 북돋아 주는 중요한 발판이다. ② 그러나 멀티태스킹 시대에 이메일과 함께 하는 점심은 누구든 제대로 된 식사 외에 너무나 자주 많은 것을 접시 위에 남긴다. ③ 로컬 푸드에서 오는 이런

영양 결핍은 주로 앉아서 지내는 생활방식에 의해서만 악화된다. ④ 전국 각지에서 걸려오는 주문 전화에 응하는 것은 사업 수완이 좋은 젊은 요리사들과 기술력 있는 개척자들이며, 이들은 건강에 좋은 식사와 집집마다 배달해 주는 편리함을 결합하고 있다. ⑤ 작년에 깨끗한 주스가 대세였다면, 올해는 디자이너 식사 배달의 해가 되어 가고 있다.

33 ② 글의 흐름으로 보아 주어진 예시 문장이 ②의 'The advice~'의 내용에 해당되므로, 그곳에 삽입되는 것이 가장 적절하다.

어휘

- clap : 박수를 치다, ~의 등[어깨]를 탁 치다
- decade : 10년
- empathetic : 공감적인

해석

한때 그는 내 등을 탁 치며 말했다. "아들아, 오늘밤 여기 있는 모든 사람과 이야기를 나누고 그들이 문을 열고 들어올 때보다 나갈 때 더 기분이 좋은 지 확인해라."

내 딸 중 하나가 최근에 결혼했고, 나는 모든 연령대의 200명의 사람들과 그 날 저녁을 축하하는 데 보냈다. (①) 그들은 3살 난 손녀부터 2차 세계대전에 참전하고 50년 동안 법률 사무와 회계 실무를 성공적으로 수행한 85세의 삼촌까지 연령대가 다양했다. (②) 그 충고는 정신적으로 예민해진다는 것이 무슨 의미인지 생각하게 했다. (③) 비록 학습 능력과 기억 능력이 성인이 되어 점차 떨어진다 해도, 중요한 정보와 경험을 이해하는 기술은 향상된다는 증거가 늘고 있다. (④) 이것은 지혜로 알려진 것이며, 과학자들이 막 연구하기 시작했다. (⑤) 지혜의 대표적인 요소로는 정상적인 판단력, 정신적 통찰력, 길고 다양한 인생 경험, 감정 통제, 공감적 이해, 그리고 물론 지식 등이 포함된다.

34 ① 위 글의 내용은 미국인들의 평균 기대 수명이 높아지고 암으로 인한 사망률도 떨어지고 있지만, 각종 조사에서 사람들이 이전보다 건강을 더 염려하고 있음을 설명하고 있다. 그러므로 위 글의 내용을 한 문장으로 나타내면 다음과 같다. "미국인들은 전보다 건강해지고(healthier) 있음에도 불구하고, 건강에 대해 무척이나 염려(anxiety)하는 것처럼 보인다."

어휘

- expectancy : 기대, 예상
- fretful : 조바심 내는, 안달하는
- apocalypse : 종말, 파멸, 대재앙

- provocative : 도발적인, 화를 돋우는
- tapestry : 태피스트리(여러 가지 색실로 그림을 짜 넣는 직물)
- trendy : 최신 유행의

해석

평균 기대 수명은 수십 년 동안 꾸준히 높아지고 있고, 흡연과 햇볕 노출로 인한 암을 제외하고 암으로 인한 사망률도 떨어지거나 안정적으로 유지되고 있다. 그러나 설문조사에서는 사람들이 이전보다 건강을 더 염려하고 있음이 거듭 드러나고 있다. Bruce Ames는 "사람들이 어디에서나 종말만을 보고 있는 것 같습니다"라고 말했는데, 그는 천연 농약이 사람이 제조한 것보다 적어도 만 배는 흔하다는 사실을 처음 지적한 사람이다. "물론 심각한 위험도 존재합니다. 그러나 모두가 조금은 진정하고 즐겁게 지내야 합니다." 가끔은 그것이 어려워 보인다. 과도한 콜레스테롤, 불충분한 비타민 A 그리고 운동이 부족한 사람에게 일어날 수 있는 것에 관한 자극적인 경고들은 미국인들 생활의 일부가 되었다. 어떤 사람들에게 암은 모든 음식에 숨어 있는 것처럼 보인다.

> 미국인들은 전보다 건강해지고 있음에도 불구하고, 건강에 대해 무척이나 염려하는 것처럼 보인다.

35 ④ 글의 서두에서 사람들이 여행자가 아닌 관광객이 되고 싶어 한다고 했는데, 그런 관광객의 속성에 대해 (C)에서 설명하고 있고, 다음으로 (A)에서 진정한 여행자가 되려면 어떻게 해야 하는지 설명하고 있다. 마지막 문장인 (B)에서는 진정한 여행자가 됨으로써 깨닫게 되는 것들을 서술하고 있다. 따라서 글의 흐름상 (C) – (A) – (B)의 순으로 글의 순서를 연결하는 것이 가장 적절하다.

어휘

- flit : 돌아다니다, 휙 지나가다
- give oneself over to : ~에 빠지다[몰두하다]
- take out of : ~을 공제하다 ~에서 꺼내다
- universe : (특정한 유형의) 경험 세계
- fabric : 직물, 천, 구조
- recreate : 되살리다, 재현하다

해석

많은 사람들이 여행자가 되기를 원치 않는다. 그들은 스스로는 절대 떠나지 않고 다른 사람의 삶의 이면을 스쳐 지나가는 관광객이 되고 싶어 한다.
(A) 그러나 진정한 여행자가 되려면 여행의 순간에 빠져야 하며 네 경험 세계의 중심에서 벗어나야 한다. 스스로 찾은 장소와 사람들의 삶을 전부 믿어야 한다.
(B) 그들의 일상생활의 일부가 되어라. 이 세상에서 삶의 가

능성은 무한하다는 것을 깨달을 것이며, 다른 언어와 문화 밑에서 우리 모두 사랑하고 사랑받으며 슬픔보다 기쁨의 삶을 소유하려는 같은 꿈을 공유하고 있음을 깨달을 것이다.
(C) 그들은 어디를 가든지 자신의 세계를 함께 데려가려고 하거나, 그들이 떠난 세계를 재현하려고 한다. 그들은 자신의 이해에 대한 안전을 위태롭게 하고 싶지 않으며, 그들의 경험이 얼마나 작고 제한적인지 보려 하지 않는다.

[36~37]

어휘

- colleague : 동료
- grab : 와락 붙잡다[움켜잡다]
- carnivore : 육식 동물
- pack : 꾸러미, 무리, 떼
- egalitarian : 평등주의의
- dictatorial : 독재의, 군림하는
- discover : 발견하다, 찾다
- dominant : 우세한, 지배적인
- flash : 비치다, 번쩍이다
- growl : 으르렁거리다
- subordinate : 종속된, 하위의, 후순위의
- obedient : 순종적인, 복종하는
- feat : 위업, 솜씨, 재주
- baffle : 완전히 당황하게 만들다, 도저히 이해할 수 없다
- bafflement : 방해, 좌절, 당혹
- ancestry : 가계, 혈통, 조상
- Canis familiaris : 개, 갯과

해석

2008년부터 Zsofia Viranyi와 오스트리아 늑대 연구 센터의 동료들은 개는 개이며 늑대는 늑대인 이유를 알아내기 위해 개와 늑대를 길렀다. "테이블 위에 고기 한 덩어리를 올려놓고 개에게 '안 돼'라고 말하면, 그것을 먹지 않을 것입니다."라고 Viranyi가 말했다. "그러나 늑대들은 무시합니다. 늑대들은 한번 쳐다보고는 고기를 덥석 물 것입니다." 그리고 이런 일이 일어났을 때, 그녀는 어떻게 늑대가 (A) 길들여진 개가 되었는지 궁금했다. "함께 살면서 그런 행동을 하는 육식 동물을 키울 수는 없습니다."고 그녀는 말한다. "여러분은 '안 돼!'라는 말을 따르는 개와 같은 동물을 원합니다."
당연한 것으로 이해되지만 개들은 늑대들처럼 평등주의적이지 않고 독재적인 (B) 그들의 무리 구조와 관련이 없다는 것을 그 센터의 연구원들이 발견했다. Viranyi는 늑대들이 함께 먹이를 먹는다는 점에 주목했다. 비록 우두머리 늑대가 서열

이 낮은 늑대에게 치아를 드러내고 으르렁거릴지라도, (C) 서열이 낮은 늑대들은 멀리 떨어지지 않는다. 그러나 개의 무리는 그렇지 않다. "서열이 낮은 개들은 우두머리 개들과 동시에 먹이를 먹지 않습니다."라고 그녀는 말했다. "개들은 그러려고 하지도 않습니다." 그들의 연구에 따르면 개들이 사람에게 협조하는 것을 기대하기 보다는 단순히 무엇을 할지 일러주는 게 낫다고 한다.

어떻게 독립적이고 평등주의적인 늑대가 (D) 순종적이고 명령을 기다리는 애완동물이 되었고 고대의 사람들이 이런 위업을 달성하기 위해 어떤 역할을 했는지 Viranyi는 도저히 이해할 수 없었다. 그녀는 당혹스러웠지만 혼자가 아니었다. 연구원들은 양에서 소, 닭, 기니피그까지 거의 모든 가축화된 종들의 시간, 장소, 조상 등을 성공적으로 알아냈지만, 그들은 (E) 최고의 친구인 개에 관한 궁금증들을 계속해서 토론할 것이다.

36 ③ (A), (B), (D), (E)는 모두 개를 가리키지만, (C)는 서열이 낮은 늑대를 가리킨다.

37 ③ 본문의 내용에 따르면 "우두머리 늑대가 서열이 낮은 늑대에게 치아를 드러내고 으르렁거릴지라도, 서열이 낮은 늑대들은 멀리 떨어지지 않는다"고 하였으므로, ③의 내용은 타당하지 않다.

[38~39]

어휘

- costly : 많은 돈[비용]이 드는, 값비싼
- commuter : 통근자
- incentive : 장려, 우대
- optimal : 최적의, 최상의
- appliance : (가정용) 기기, 가전제품
- equate : 동일시하다
- reap : 거두다, 수확하다
- manipulate : 조종하다, 다루다
- commuting distance : 통근거리
- negate : 무효화하다, 부인하다
- underestimate : 저평가하다, 과소평가하다

해석

왜 사람들은 모든 활용 가능한 정보를 동원하여 그들의 예상을 미래 가능한 최선의 예측에 맞추려고 할까? 가장 간단한 설명은 그렇게 하지 않으면 많은 비용이 들기 때문이다. 통근자인 Joe가 차로 출근하는 시간을 가능한 정확하게 예측하려는 데에는 강한 동기가 있다. 그가 운전 시간을 짧게 예측하면 회사에 자주 지각을 하게 되고 해고될 위험에 처할 것이다. 그

가 운전시간을 길게 예측하면 평균적으로 회사에 너무 일찍 도착할 것이고, 불필요하게 수면과 여가시간을 포기해야 할 것이다. 정확한 예상은 가치가 있으며, 활용가능한 모든 정보를 이용함으로써 최적의 예측을 하려는 사람들에게 강한 동기가 된다.

그와 똑같은 원칙이 사업에도 적용된다. 가전제품 제조업자가 이율 변동이 제품판매에 중요하다는 사실을 알고 있다고 가정해 보자. 회사가 이율을 잘못 예측한다면 제품을 너무 많이 생산하거나 또는 너무 적게 생산해서 이익이 감소될 것이다. 이율을 예측하기 위해 모든 활용 가능한 정보를 획득하고 가능한 최선의 미래 이율 변동을 예측하기 위해 그 정보를 이용하는 것은 회사에 강한 동기가 된다. 예상에 맞추어 최적의 예측을 하려는 동기는 특히 금융 시장에서 강하다. 이런 시장에서 미래를 더 잘 예측하는 사람들이 부자가 된다.

38 ② 위 글은 최적의 예측을 통해 비용을 줄이고 부를 얻을 수 있다는 내용이므로 ②의 '최적의 예측으로 보상 받기(Reap the Rewards of Optimal Predictions)'가 위 글의 제목으로 알맞다. 출근시간의 예측, 이율변동의 예측 또는 금융시장에서의 예측 등 그 예를 통해 미래 예상 가능한 예측의 이점들을 설명하고 있다

오답풀이

① Set Your Goals As High As Possible(가능한 목표를 높게 세워라)

③ Maximize Profit by Manipulating Interest Rates(이율을 관리하여 이윤 극대화하기)

④ The Gap Between Theory and Practice in Business(사업에 있어 이론과 실제의 차이)

⑤ How Does Commuting Distance Affect Productivity? (통근거리는 생산성에 어떻게 영향을 미치는가?)

39 ① 마지막 문장에 사용된 '예상에 맞추어(equating expectations)'와 같은 의미이므로 ①의 'match'가 문맥상 가장 적절하다. '예상에 맞추어 최적의 예측을 하는 것'이 이 글의 핵심 키워드이다.

[40~42]

어휘

- collective : 집단의, 공동체의
- curl : 곱슬곱슬하다, 돌돌 감기다
- pulley : 도르래
- exhaustion : 탈진, 고갈, 기진맥진
- in groups of two : 2인 1조로

- moderately : 중간 정도로, 적당히, 알맞게
- underlying : 근본적인, 밑에 있는
- instrumental : 중요한
- in a timely fashion : 적절한 시간[시기]에
- loaf : 빈둥거리다, 얼쩡거리다
- tug-of-war : 줄다리기
- plummet : 곤두박질치다, 급락하다
- boost : 신장시키다, 북돋우다
- conversely : 정반대로, 역으로

해석

동기 이득은 그룹의 구성원들이 협력 작업을 수행할 때 노력이 증가되는 환경을 말한다. 능력이 부족한 구성원들을 더 열심히 일하게 만드는 동기 이득은 Köhler 효과라고 한다. 어떤 연구에서 운동선수들에게 지칠 때까지 도르래에 달린 막대를 돌돌 감게 했다. 그들은 처음에는 이것을 혼자 했다가 그 다음에는 2인 1조로 진행했다. 동기 이득은 운동선수들 각 쌍이 적절하게 다른 능력이 있을 때 발생했다. (A) 반대로 동기 이득은 운동선수들이 동등하거나 또는 매우 다른 능력이 있을 때는 나타나지 않았다. 동기 이득에 책임이 있는 사람은 그룹의 약자였다. Köhler 효과에 근거를 둔 심리 메커니즘은 사회적 비교(특히 어떤 사람이 자기 팀원이 더 능력이 있다고 생각했을 때)이며 누군가의 노력이 그 그룹에 반드시 필요하다는 느낌이다. 그룹의 구성원들은 개인적으로 가치가 있다고 여기는 결과를 얻는 데 있어 그들의 노력이 중요하다고 기대될 때 협력 작업에 기꺼이 노력한다. 특히 팀의 최약자는 모든 사람이 적절한 시기에 성과에 대한 피드백을 제공할 때 더 열심히 일하는 것 같다.

좀 더 보편적으로 그룹에서 관찰되는 것은 사회적 태만이라 알려진 동기 손실이다. 프랑스 농업 기술자인 Max Ringelmann은 말, 황소, 기계 그리고 사람들에 의해 공급되는 농장 노동의 상대적 효율성에 관심이 있었다. 특히 그는 줄다리기와 같이 짐을 수평으로 당기는 상대적 능력에 호기심이 있었다. 그의 실험 중 하나에서, 14명의 남자들이 짐을 당겼고, 그들이 생성한 힘의 양이 측정되었다. 각 사람들이 개별적으로 당길 수 있는 힘도 또한 측정되었다. 줄을 당기는 팀의 크기가 커질수록 평균적으로 한 사람이 당기는 힘은 꾸준히 감소했다. 한 사람이 줄을 당길 때 낸 힘은 평균 63킬로그램이었다. (B) 그러나 3인 1조에서 한 사람당 힘은 53킬로그램으로 떨어졌으며, 8인 1조에서는 겨우 31킬로그램으로 급락했다. 즉, 혼자 일한 사람들이 낸 힘의 절반으로 떨어진 셈이다. 이는 팀워크의 기본적인 원리를 보여주는데, 그룹의 구성원들은 대개 혼자서 일할 때만큼 열심히 일하지 않는다.

40 ② 위 글의 전반부는 동기 이득(motivation gains)에 대해서, 후반부는 동기 손실(motivation losses)에 대해서 설명하고 있는데 이들 모두는 팀워크에서 각 개인들이 어떤 경우에 노력하게 되고 어떤 경우에 태만하게 되는지를 보여주고 있다. 그러므로 위 글의 제목으로 ②의 "팀워크에서 동기부여의 효과(Motivational Effects in Teamwork)"가 적절하다.

오답풀이
① 줄다리기의 메커니즘
③ 일의 효율성을 측정하는 방법
④ 개인적인 업무에 동기부여 고취시키기
⑤ Ringelmann 효과에 근거한 심리학

41 ② 본문에서 동기 이득은 운동선수들 각 쌍이 적절하게 다른 능력이 있을 때 발생하며, 운동선수들이 동등하거나 또는 매우 다른 능력이 있을 때는 나타나지 않는다고 했다. 그러므로 ②의 "동기 이득은 같은 능력을 소유한 사람들이 함께 일할 때 발생한다.(Motivation gains are likely to happen when working with people of the same ability.)"는 문항은 위 글의 내용과 일치하지 않는다.

42 ③ (A) 앞 문장(동기 이득은 적절하게 다른 능력이 있을 때 발생한다)과 뒷 문장(동기이득은 동등하거나 또는 매우 다른 능력이 있을 때는 나타나지 않았다)이 서로 대조되는 내용이므로 'Conversely(반대로)'가 적절하다.
(B) 앞과 뒤의 문장이 한 사람이 줄을 당길 때와 반대로 여러 명이 줄이 당길 때 한 사람당 사용하는 힘이 떨어지는 것을 설명하고 있으므로, 역접의 접속사 'However(그러나)'가 적절하다.

[43~45]

어휘

- intentionally : 고의로, 일부러
- rhinovirus : 리노바이러스, 코감기 바이러스
- develop symptoms : 증세[징후]를 보이다
- panoply of : 많은
- nary : ~가 아닌, 하나도 ~없는
- sniffle : 훌쩍거림
- quarantine : 격리하다
- reinfect : 재감염시키다
- nasal : 코의, 비음의
- secretion : 분비, 분비물, 숨김, 은닉
- mucus : 점액
- antibody : 항체
- come down with a cold : 감기에 걸리다

433

- numerical value : 수치, 절댓값
- ongoing : 계속 진행되는
- susceptibility : 민감, 감수성
- socialize : 사귀다, 교제하다
- counterintuitive : 반직관적인, 직관에 어긋나는
- vibrant : 활기찬, 생기 넘치는
- cortisol : 코티솔
- antibiotic : 항생제, 항생물질
- metabolism : 신진대사
- methodology : 방법론

해석

Carnegie Mellon 대학의 심리학자인 Sheldon Cohen은 일부러 수백 명의 사람들을 감기에 걸리게 했다. 조심스럽게 통제된 상태에서, 그는 조직적으로 자원자들을 흔히 감기를 유발하는 리노바이러스에 노출시킨다. 그 바이러스에 노출된 사람들 중 약 삼분의 일만이 완전히 감기 증세를 보였고, 반면에 나머지 사람들은 훌쩍거리는 일 하나 없이 떠났다.

첫째 날에 Cohen의 실험 자원자들은 다른 곳에서 감기에 걸리지 않았다는 것을 확실히 하기 위해 노출에 앞서 24시간 동안 격리되었다. 다음 5일 동안 그 자원자들은 누군가를 재감염시키지 않도록 서로 3피트 이상 떨어져 다른 자원자들과 함께 특수 유닛에 수용되었다. 그 5일 동안 그들의 코에서 나온 분비물을 특정 리노바이러스의 존재뿐만 아니라 감기의 기술적 지표(점액의 총 무게와 같은)를 위해 검사했고, 그들의 혈액 샘플들을 항체를 위해 검사했다.

알다시피 부족한 비타민 C, 흡연 그리고 부족한 수면 모두 감염의 가능성을 높인다. 스트레스가 심한 관계도 이 목록에 추가될 수 있을까? Cohen의 대답은 분명했다. Cohen은 다른 사람이 건강을 유지하는 동안 어떤 사람을 감기에 걸리도록 하는 그 요인들에 정확한 수치를 부여했다. 껄끄러운 관계를 비타민 C 결핍 그리고 수면 부족과 동일 범주에 두면, 계속해서 개인적 갈등이 있는 사람들은 다른 사람보다 감기에 걸릴 확률이 2.5배 높다. 한 달 또는 그 이상 지속되는 갈등은 감염률을 높이지만, 가끔의 언쟁은 건강에 위험하지는 않다. 계속되는 언쟁은 건강에 나쁘며, 스스로를 고립시키는 것은 더욱 나쁘다. 사교적 접촉이 풍부한 사람들에 비해 최소한의 친밀한 관계만 유지하는 사람들이 감기에 걸릴 확률이 4.2배 더 높다.

사교적일수록 감기에 덜 민감하게 된다. 이런 생각은 직관에 반하는 것처럼 보인다. 접촉하는 사람들이 많을수록 감기 바이러스에 노출될 확률이 높아지는 것이 아닌가? 물론이다. 하지만 활발한 사회적 접촉은 좋은 기분을 북돋고 부정적인 기분을 제한하여, 코티솔을 억제하고 면역 기능을 강화시킨다. 관계 자체는 감기 바이러스 노출 위험으로부터 우리를 보호해 주는 것처럼 보인다.

43 ④ 제시된 지문에 따르면 감기에 대한 일반적인 상식과 달리 많은 사람들과 접촉하는 것이 감기 바이러스에 노출될 확률이 높아지는 것처럼 보이지만, 실제로는 빈번한 사회적 접촉은 우리 몸에 코티솔을 억제하여 면역기능을 강화시킴으로써 감기 바이러스 노출 위험으로부터 우리를 보호해 준다는 실험 결과가 나왔다. 그러므로 ④의 '보통의 감기 실험과 다른 드문 결과(Uncommon Findings from the Common Cold Experiment)'를 위 글의 제목으로 보는 것이 적절하다.

오답풀이

① 체내 항생 신진대사의 본질
② 리노바이러스 노출 : 최고의 정교한 방법
③ 더욱 빈번한 사회적 교류, 더욱 심한 감기
⑤ 사이버 공간에서 발견된 새로운 건강 위험

44 ④ 본문에서 사교적 접촉이 풍부한 사람들에 비해 최소한의 친밀한 관계만 유지하는 사람들이 감기에 걸릴 확률이 4.2배 더 높다고 했으므로, 활발한 사회적 접촉은 우리 몸의 면역 기능을 강화시켜 감기 바이러스 노출 위험으로부터 '우리를 보호해 준다(protect us from)'는 표현이 문맥상 적절하다.

오답풀이

① be modified by(변경되다)
② push them to(내몰다)
③ be weakened by(약화되다)
⑤ gradually increase(점차 증가하다)

45 ④ 두 번째 문단에서 특정 리노바이러스의 존재뿐만 아니라 감기의 기술적 지표(점액의 총 무게와 같은)를 위해 코에서 나온 분비물을 검사했다(their nasal secretions are tested)고 서술하고 있다.

오답풀이

① 첫날 피험자를 감기 바이러스에 노출시킨다. → 첫째 날에 Cohen의 실험 자원자들은 다른 곳에서 감기에 걸리지 않았다는 것을 확실히 하기 위해 노출에 앞서 24시간 동안 격리되었다.
② 총 5일 동안 진행된다. → 첫째 날 24시간 동안 격리시키고 다음 5일 동안 코에서 나온 분비물과 혈액 샘플을 검사했으므로, Cohen의 실험은 최소 5일 이상 진행되었다.
③ 피험자간 신체적 접촉을 허용한다. → 다른 사람들을 재감염시키지 않도록 서로 3피트 이상 떨어져 수용되었다.
⑤ 혈액 샘플 검사는 생략한다. → 항체를 위해 혈액 샘플을 검사했다.

Chance is always powerful.

Let your hook be always cast;

in the pool where you least expect it, there will be a fish.

우연은 항상 강력하다.

항상 낚싯 바늘을 던져두라.

전혀 기대하지 않은 곳에 물고기가 있을 것이다.

– 오비디우스(Ovid) –

Life is like riding a bicycle.
To keep your balance
you must keep moving.
인생은 자전거를 타는 것과 같다.
균형을 잡으려면 움직여야 한다.

– 알버트 아인슈타인(Albert Einstein) –